With this incisive and sympathetic study of Napoleon during the last tragic years of his life, Octave Aubry has achieved a popular as well as critical success in France. First serialized in the *Revue des Deux Mondes*, it has already established the author as the greatest living French authority on Napoleon. Drawing his material from French and English sources, much of it from unedited documents, the author has created a remarkable picture of the great military genius who, when he was the most unhappy, was the most human. With an almost uncanny precision, Octave Aubry has reconstructed the atmosphere of the tremendous drama which unrolled itself more than a century ago on that stern cliff in the Atlantic Ocean. This extraordinary subject, which had previously been treated both by the English who supported Hudson Lowe, the chronicler, and by the French who denied him, has been ignored for more than thirty years. The French writer Gourgaud left St. Helena in 1818. And from the time of his departure until now there has been nothing but English testimony. M. Aubry believed it possible to recapture the truth with objectivity and good faith. Not a Bonapartiste, he has made use of the documents placed at his disposal with the utmost impartiality. A poet no less than a historian, he has painted one of the most vivid portraits of Napoleon to be found in contemporary literature. The translation by Arthur Livingston, editor and translator of Pareto's *The Mind and Society*, is superb, retaining as it does the full flavor of M. Aubry's dramatic style. *32 illustrations.*

NAPOLEON AT ST. HELENA
From the Painting by Delaroche

# ST. HELENA

BY

## OCTAVE AUBRY

AUTHORIZED TRANSLATION
BY
ARTHUR LIVINGSTON

WITH 43 ILLUSTRATIONS
IN DOUBLETONE

PHILADELPHIA
J. B. LIPPINCOTT COMPANY
LONDON
1936

# PREFACE

Travel always involves a twinge at the heart. It enriches one's life, but it adds loss to loss. For three months I lost my friends in France and now that I have them back again, here I am losing others no less dear to me. Friends of St. Helena, you proffered me your friendship like a bouquet of flowers at the very moment of my arrival, for you knew that my time was short and that the messengers of the sea do not wait. To you, now, my first thoughts are owing because in a land still reeking with the death sweat of a hero you showed me how much sweetness there can be in the roving life and how much nobility in the goodwill of strangers.

On a pilgrimage which I undertook not with enthusiasm but out of a sense of honesty towards myself, and which has repaid me beyond all my deserts, I saw so many things, I experienced so many emotions, that today my mind is in a whirl. As regards St. Helena I have not a single idea that is not coloured by sentiment. I am glad of that, but worried. Forgive me! The passing days, the passing months are sifting things out for me. I am counting on the secret influence of my native land to set me on my feet again with my thoughts in better order.

I left France in early spring to find you already deep in autumn. The voyage revealed to me the smallness of the world and the relativeness of the seasons. It also made me aware of the barrenness of the sea so that after weeks with nothing but waves in front of one a breaking shoal comes to look like a homeland inviting with wide-opened arms.

There is no port of call on the line that carries the message of Europe once a month to the lost isle. A stop for a bare two hours at Las Palmas—golden city fanned by banana trees! Then one night somewhere between a black sky and a black sea, two faraway lights—Ascension! I rose and looked out of my porthole. A barefooted sailor who was hauling a rope along the deck past my window saw me and remarked:

"Day after tomorrow, St. Helena!"

. . . . . . .

It appeared at dawn, the famed, the mysterious isle—a dark spot to the south-east. We were still thirty miles or so away, but in good

5

weather a pair of sharp eyes can pick it up at seventy. An hour passed —in what impatience! Little by little the spot straightened up, as it were, grew very tall till it stood on the empty sea like a gigantic pedestal. A bank of clouds formed a heavy ceiling above it. Another hour—for we had the trade-wind against us—and the ship dropped anchor. We were only a few cable-lengths from the prison of the Emperor!

At such close quarters one gets a terrible impression. A colossal wall of basalt, without a tree, without a bush, standing upright on the sea that breaks foaming against it. At the water's edge in a cove, a straggling yellow village cringes, looking as if it were afraid of being crushed by the cliffs. A deserted wharf. A few boats, rowed by men with brown hands and dark faces, coming out to us. As they haul alongside we can hear voices speaking in a very soft English.

Now here I am at Longwood. To reach it I have followed zigzag mountain paths over a rough, variegated, wonderful country. Everything is either chasm or precipice on St. Helena. The volcano that formed this rock at the beginning of the world made a great fuss before it died out, blistering and tearing the island's hide in all directions. But the valley-floors are green pastures, and I saw velvety slopes with deep-flowing brooks so bordered with wake-robin and blue irises that the sky was never reflected in them.

Napoleon's residence is a country house suitable at the most for a retired country lawyer. The contrast between the glory he achieved and the end he came to within those squatty grey-topped walls stifles one. That he should have lived, suffered, died here on this mildewed isle, battered for six years by the relentless wind, guarded by the sea so jealously that he found it peering at him whichever way he turned —what a sublime mockery! His curve, declining into poverty again, is more perfect that way. Napoleon is complete only at St. Helena. Had he retired, as he thought of doing just after Waterloo, into the opulent silence of America, he would have been lost like a river emptying into a waste of sand. At St. Helena he concentrated, deepened, refined, humanized, perfected himself. His real coronation—as he said—was his suffering. As a man he is to be pitied. As a hero he can only be congratulated.

. . . . . . .

So then I have lived in the place where the Emperor made his final halt! I have walked on the paths of lava gravel that his feet trod. I have breathed the air he breathed. I have seen his ghost—his ghost, I say—rising behind those plain doors in those shabby rooms, lifting the field glasses of Austerlitz to the spyhole bored in the wall to study the tents in the distant camp at Deadwood. I have heard him speak, re-telling his story to those—alas so few in number—who stood faithful to the end. And as the shadows of evening fall, I have listened, as he listened, to the inexorable song of the cricket that rises to the young stars. So perhaps I have managed to recover—I say it ever so humbly—some vestige of his soul, and I believe that if any throb of life, any persuasiveness of truth, shall ever be found in the portrait I shall draw of Napoleon, St. Helena will have given me that tremor, inspired me with that truth.

So, then, farewell! I shall never again return to this rock that weighs so heavily upon our memories and where I found the peaceful life of an English county that went to sleep a hundred years ago. Nothing surely is more melancholy for those of us who are not too detached than to realize that the wind is to erase our footprints on a land that is close to our hearts and that we shall never renew them again. But it is better so. One must never risk spoiling the pictures that are graven on the soul. When in this all too brief life we have felt a genuine heart-throb, we should stop, close our eyes, and trust for its recapture to our dreams.

Farewell, home of the Emperor, farewell, lonely grave! Pale cliffs that sprang from the depths of the South Atlantic to serve as a throne for majesty—fade from my sight forever behind the rolling waves that toss the waters from pole to pole with the changing seasons! St. Helena is too unique a place. It is enough for a man once in his life to have come into so intimate a touch with the superhuman! . . .

In writing this book I might have confined myself to retracing the outstanding episodes in Napoleon's captivity. The reader would doubtless have been grateful to me for sparing him prolixities and a monotony for which I fear he may here reproach me. But that is exactly what Frédéric Masson and Lord Rosebery, whose works are fundamental, had done before me. In attacking this vast subject—for vast it truly is—my idea could not be merely to repeat those two writers or to make an adroit amalgamation of them. The time had come, I felt, to re-raise and re-examine the whole question of St.

Helena, both in the large and in the detail, studying it with new eyes and with a deep and whole-hearted regard for truth.

Many stories have gone the rounds as to the "little isle," its climate, the life the Emperor and his companions led there, and the attitude of their jailors. We have had the French point of view and the British point of view, both with axes to grind and both incomplete. A thorough review of the case, made in an independent spirit, seemed to me both possible and necessary at this time, for the day for Napoleonic histories governed by theses or by altogether respectable pre-judgments has passed.

The chief claim of this study to originality will therefore be to have presented the tedious and sad unrolling of Napoleon's life at St. Helena as it appears not only from known sources, but also from unpublished documents that lie in the French National Archives, among the Masson papers in the *Bibliothèque Thiers*, in the English collection in the *Bibliothèque Nationale*, in the local archives of Jamestown, in the Record Office in London, and, more particularly, in the assemblage, in great part unexplored, of reports, notes, orders, letters, accounts, bulletins emanating from Sir Hudson Lowe, from his general staff, from the physicians, officers and orderlies of Longwood—a collection that fills ninety folio volumes among the "Additional Manuscripts" in the British Museum.

Such texts, which I have weighed one against the other with the utmost care, throw sufficient light on the Emperor's captivity to dissipate what has been called "the mystery of St. Helena." For that reason alone I shall doubtless hear many criticisms of my work both from England and France. Peoples do not like to have the legends they have been taught to cherish tampered with. However my main concern in this work could not be just to please.

I have tried to establish the state of mind of the English Government in 1815. I have cleared them of the reproach of seeking to bring about Napoleon's death on a horrible and unhealthy rock. On the other hand I charge them with other serious and inexcusable shortcomings. I have sought to make clear what St. Helena really was, to trace the character of the Governor, to show the irritating rôle that was played by the two households—the Emperor's and the people about Lowe. Finally on Napoleon's last moments and on the consequences in Europe of his confinement and death, I have brought together a number of facts that have hitherto lain either scattered or else unknown. I acquit Gourgaud of accusations that have far over-reached the truth. On the other hand I have tried to portray such people as Las Cases, the Bertrands, the Montholons in their true light —with all their faults but also with the considerations that help to attenuate them. I have not drawn Napoleon as an ideal figure. I have aimed at resurrecting a man who was great but profoundly complex and variable in the day of his misfortune, frequently harsh, sometimes unjust, but purified and magnified as he drew closer and closer to death.

I have worked almost exclusively on original documents. The quotations therefore that accompany this narrative, though too numerous to suit my own taste, will supply proof of the rigorous exactness of my references. For the benefit of those who may hereafter essay a subject which I do not pretend to have exhausted, I may add a few words as to the relative value of the papers to be consulted.

No end of caution has to be exercised in studying the copious testimony that has come down to our day. None of it is altogether negligible, but almost all of it is prejudiced. Statements have to be checked one on the other and a choice made between two, three, sometimes ten accounts of the same episode, always keeping clearly in mind the special aims and interests of the witness. That is why, in appraising a given piece of evidence, the letters that O'Meara wrote to his friend Finlaison are to be preferred to his *Voice from St. Helena,* the correspondence of Count de Montholon to his *Récits de la Captivité,* Hudson Lowe's notes on conversations with Napoleon or Bertrand, which he jotted down on the day they occurred, to the reports he made to Lord Bathurst in the course of the days that followed. The more remote the incident is in time the greater its distortion in the statements made regarding it. Hence the great value of the daily bulletins of the orderlies at Longwood, who reported to the Governor every evening on what they had seen and heard among the prisoners.

Among French sources, or rather sources in French, by far the most important are Gourgaud's diary (*Journal*), a marvel of brutal frankness particularly if read in its original text (for the well-known edition has been extensively expurgated), and the *Mémorial* of Las Cases, flattering and calculated, but in which the drapery of rhetoric is frequently pierced by an echo of Napoleon's own voice. Next in importance come the badly written but picturesque *Souvenirs* of the mameluke Aly, and the despatches of Count Balmain, the Russian commissioner, who was the only one telling the truth between 1816 and 1820. Less essential, though still of some worth, are the reports of the Austrian commissioner, Stürmer, and his French colleague, the absurd Montchenu. Montholon's letters to his wife, finally, are of vivid interest for the last years of the Captivity, though, having to pass under English censorship, they contain necessary falsehoods. Mme. de Montholon's *Souvenirs* serve to establish a number of interesting details. The *Narratives* (*Récits*) of Montholon, however, can be used only with the most extreme mistrust. They were written twenty years after the fact, in the prison at Ham, and are arbitrary and false. As to the *Mémoires* of Antommarchi, they can be regarded only as a tissue of impostures in which practically everything has to be discarded.

Two documents still await publication—at an early date it is to be hoped: the memoirs of Bertrand and Marchand. In spite of persistent efforts I have been unable to see the Bertrand record, which is being jealously withheld from public view. The cast and the spirit of what he says are, however, well known. The book was written long after Bertrand's return to France and by a disillusioned, embittered man who was in the main giving vent to his rancour. On that account the document would seem to be of minor importance. Marchand's manuscript memoirs were known to Frédéric Masson and used by him. I found a faithful copy of them among his papers. They have a far greater value. They supply a cross-check and control of other sources. Unfortunately their too uniform tone of respectfulness robs them of many a naïve or piquant detail.

First and foremost among English sources stand the papers of Hudson Lowe. Their massive bulk has long discouraged careful examination, but they still constitute the basic nourishment for any history of the Captivity. Lowe kept a record of everything, from his difficulties with Napoleon or the Commissioners down to office tittle-tattle and invitations to dinner. Life at St. Helena between 1816 and 1821 is stored up in his papers day by day, in infinite detail and—making due allowances for the Governor's temperament—with a fidelity to fact that can be matched only by Gourgaud's. It is incomprehensible that French writers, and chief among them Frédéric Masson, should have failed to discern the predominating interest of Lowe's record and halted at Forsyth's uninspired abstract of it, instead of

themselves exploiting such a prodigious treasure. Unlike its prede-
cessors therefore the present work takes Lowe's record as its pivot.
I doubt that this choice will be criticized in view of the new light
that will be thrown on life at Longwood by the *Minutes* of Reade
and Gorrequer, the espionage notes written by O'Meara to the Governor, O'Meara's even more significant letters to Finlaison and the
reports of the orderlies, Poppleton, Blakeney, Nicholls, Lutyens,
Crockat, Croads and Jackson, to mention only the main witnesses.

However secondary they may seem as compared with the Lowe
Papers, published British sources still hold a place of great importance. Well known are the memoirs of Maitland, Bunbury, Howe, ✗
Lyttleton, Cockburn, Mrs. Abell, Lady Malcolm, Warden, Hall,
Ellis and Henry. When checked and corrected on his *Diary* and his
messages to Finlaison, O'Meara's *Voice from St. Helena* is in my
opinion of far greater value than has hitherto been decided. In many
respects it can be balanced against Las Cases's *Mémorial*. As a man
O'Meara was despicable, but as an observer he knew how to use his
eyes and how to tell what he saw. It is easy to understand the great
success of his book when it appeared. Not so comprehensible is the
discredit into which it has since been allowed to fall and from which
it is time, I believe, to resurrect it.

And a final word of thanks may be permitted me to the many
people in France, London or St. Helena who have taken an interest
in my researches and have steered or helped them on their way: Lord
Tyrrell, Sir Spencer Davis, Messrs. Ellis and Kitching, Mrs. Bovell,
the late Mrs. Aubrey Le Blond, Messrs. Deacon and Jackson, the
Rev. Dr. Walcott, Mr. and Mrs. A. D. Pardee, Mr. and Mrs.
Meggs, M. and Mme. Georges Colin, Messrs. Gabriel Hanotaux,
Ernest d'Hauterive, Jean Hanoteau, Robert Chantemesse, Albert-
Émil Sorel, J. Arnna and Mlle. Chauffier. To them one and all I owe
it, if I have been able to complete this task. The present study cer-
tainly leaves some gaps unfilled and may even contain a few errors.
These I trust will be forgiven in the light of the painstaking effort at
impartiality which has accompanied my volume throughout.

# CONTENTS

# ILLUSTRATIONS

# BOOK ONE

## NAPOLEON'S CAPTIVITY

# PART ONE

## *FROM WATERLOO TO ST. HELENA*

### I

### *THE ABDICATION*

ALL WAS LOST. HIS OLD GUARD, SURROUNDED BY PRUSSIAN OR ENGLISH troops, was being cut to pieces to the cry of "Long live the Emperor," which was still loud enough to rise above the roar of the cannon. It had been his wish to die with them, there, under a rain of lead, in the centre of the last square, bending double over his horse, his body racked by ghastly bladder pains, his face yellow, perspiring, terrible to look upon. And not a bullet touched him! Lines of men were mowed down about him—he was left in the saddle. His mind dulled by pain and suffering, he could not grasp this disobedience on the part of Death. His lips trembled. Tears glistened on his cheeks. Then, at last, they dragged him to the rear. One of his generals, Soult [1] perhaps, said to him:

"No, sire, the enemy is too happy already!"

He rode off at a walk through the long summer twilight.

Reloading their guns the grenadiers shouted:

"We shall die! But you—save yourself!"

Past him already the disorganized army was flowing like a river. He followed it the long night through over sodden roads towards the Dyle bridge, then on to Genappe, Quatre Bras, Charleroi. He was so tired that had not Gourgaud held him up he would have fallen from his horse. Now and again, shaking off his dejection, he would try to halt a few cavalrymen in order to organize a nucleus of resistance. But the flood was too strong. Those were not soldiers anymore. They were just human beings paralyzed by fright and exhaustion.

[1] Gourgaud, *Campagne de 1815*, p. 108; H. Houssaye, *Waterloo*, p. 423.

At five in the morning he rode through Charleroi and crossed the Sambre. He drew rein in a meadow. Someone had lighted a fire. Slowly he paced around it, his head bowed, his arms folded across his breast. Near by stood his aides-de-camp and members of his staff— Bertrand, Druout, Flahaut, Labédoyère, Gourgaud. They watched him in mortal silence.

Fugitives were still rushing past, but in less crowded masses— carabiniers, lancers, now and then an infantryman. Napoleon went out to meet them once more and tried to rally them. They only fled the faster. The Emperor went back to his officers, sat down on a stone, took a bit of food.

Then he mounted his horse again and started for Philippeville. He was there two hours later, very tired. Maret and Chaboulon rode up. To the latter he dictated two letters for his brother Joseph. One was to be read to the ministers. It was so worded as to minimize the disaster. The other, confidential, was frank. It announced his return to Paris.[2]

That was a mistake. He should have halted at Philippeville and gathered the remnants of his army. After a few days of panic thousands of men, knowing that the Emperor was holding on at the frontier, would have rallied to his standard. He could have reinforced them with Grouchy's corps which had turned up again. Surrounded by his soldiers he would have had more freedom of manoeuvring than in Paris, a centre of intrigues which he could not now be sure of controlling. But his old terror of politicians blinded him. He remembered the vote of deposition by a rump Senate with which Talleyrand had stabbed him in the back in 1814 just as he was about to fall upon the Allies. This time too, if he stayed too far away, Fouché and his friends would combine with the Royalists and overthrow him. He must return to the capital to overawe them. He must appear before the Assembly. His presence would force the Members to concentrate on the defence of the country. Seconded by Davoust, by Carnot, he would scrape the provinces clean, get three hundred thousand men together and, repeating the tactic of the Campaign in France,

[2] Fleury de Chaboulon, *Mémoires*, Vol. II, pp. 200-02, says that the Emperor did not arrive at this decision till he got to Laon and then on the advice of his staff. Gourgaud, Montholon and Las Cases, however, are unanimous in declaring that Napoleon decided to return to Paris immediately after the defeat and of his own accord.

wear the enemy armies down one by one and finally drive them out of the land.[3]

That was what he was hoping for. But it was a hope without wings, a disillusioned faith resting on crumbling foundations. Ever since his return from Elba, triumphal though that had been, he had ceased to believe in his star. His wife and his son had failed him. He sensed around him a France that was too tired, deadly tired. Vainly had he striven to rouse her, force her to take up the burden again. He knew that he was poorly seconded, imperfectly obeyed. Treason was sneaking all about him, ready to draw the snare taut. He had set out for Waterloo in the state of mind of the gambler who throws his dice and waits, motionless, for the result. He had lost. Well—he would try to begin the game again. But he expected to lose everything.

He got into a barouche, alone. Maret and Bertrand, his aides-de-camp, followed in two other carriages. As far as Laon he slept. At halts for new horses a few cheers would rouse him now and then. He would wave his hand, then let his head fall again upon his chest. He was at the extreme end of his strength. The tremendous strain of those three months of sleepless nights, sustained by a sheer miracle of will up to Waterloo, now suddenly came down upon him with crushing force. He looked worn out, withered, years older.

At Vaux-sous-Laon, whither he arrived on the evening of June 20th, he alighted in the courtyard of the post and began pacing back and forth over the straw-littered ground. A timid crowd gazed at him through the door that had been left open.

"Job on his dunghill!" someone whispered.[4]

The Emperor received the prefect, a few magistrates, a number of officers of the National Guard. He issued orders for the provisioning of Laon, where, he thought, his new army might mobilize. Jerome and Ney had followed him at some distance. He received them, then dictated a comuniqué on the battles of Ligny and Mont Saint-Jean to be published in the *Moniteur*. He set out again for Paris after dark. He gave instructions to drive around the walls so as to enter by the Roule Barrier. It was eight o'clock. The shops were still closed. Slipping unnoticed along the Rue du Faubourg Saint Honoré, the barouche drew up in front of the Élysée.

[3] Chaboulon, *Ibid.*, Vol. II, p. 195.
[4] G. Lenôtre, *Napoléon*, p. 231.

Since the 17th of April Napoleon had not felt in a mood to stay at the Tuileries.

. . . . . .

Caulaincourt was waiting for him in the doorway. The General ran to meet him and helped him to alight.

Wearily the Emperor dragged himself up the steps.

"Well, Caulaincourt, there we are! Something splendid! How will the nation take this setback?"

Reaching his study he flung himself on a sofa.

"Why, the thing was won! The army had done miracles. Then, at the end of the day, a panic seizes them! I can't understand it! Ney went in like a lunatic. He slaughtered all my cavalry! I'm all in. I must have two hours' rest before I shall be fit for anything." [5]

He had been tortured with a distended bladder ever since the action at Ligny. He put a hand to his chest:

"I am smothering—here. Have them get me a bath ready."

Recovering his composure he remarked to Caulaincourt that he intended to state the situation before the two Houses, ask for their support and be off again at once.

The Duke de Vicenza replied that the Members seemed hostile—Fouché, Lafayette, Lanjuinais, Manuel, had been busy since the night before when the first rumours of defeat began circulating in Paris. The Liberals were raising their voices. The Royalists were thrilling with joy.

"I am sorry to see you in Paris, sire," Caulaincourt concluded. "It would have been better not to leave the army. That is where your strength lies."

"But I have no army left! I have nothing but fugitives! I might be able to find a few men. But how arm them? I have no guns now."

But almost in the same breath he corrected himself:

"I'll find men and guns. There's a remedy for everything. You judge the Members too harshly. Most of them are all right. I have only Lafayette and a few others against me. I am in their way. They would like to work for themselves. I shan't let them!"

He had been in his bath a few moments, chatting with Joseph and Regnault de Saint-Jean d'Angély, when Davoust, the Minister of War, arrived at the Élysée. At sight of him Napoleon lifted his arms

---

[5] Caulaincourt, *Mémoires* (Hanoteau ed.), I, p. 196; Villemain, *Souvenirs contemporains*, II, p. 257.

out of the water and let them fall again with a great splash. Davoust's uniform was drenched.

"So then, Davoust! So then!" he cried.

He gave a brief account of the battle, venting his irritations, complaining of Ney again. Davoust interrupted him:

"He has put his own neck in a halter for your sake."

"What is going to come of it all?" asked the Emperor.[6]

"Nothing is really lost," replied Davoust, "but we must take energetic steps."

He suggested the immediate dissolution of the Assembly. He was right, that soldier! With "the lawyers" scattered the Emperor would again be master. But Napoleon refused. He had become, he said, a constitutional monarch. He did not want to seem to be browbeating France.

He dressed and then ate breakfast in company with his brothers—Joseph, downcast, Lucien enthusiastic, as in the Brumaire days.[7] Both emphasized the danger of appealing to the Members. Napoleon listened, gazing at them out of large staring eyes, and made no answer.

Before the meeting of the Council he further received Cambacérès, Peyrusse, Rovigo and Lavalette: "The moment he caught sight of me," writes the last,[8] "he came up to me with an epileptic laugh that frightened me. 'Oh, my God!' he cried, rolling his eyes upwards. But that was just a flash. He recovered his self-control almost at once and asked me what was going on in the Assembly."

Shortly after ten o'clock he went with them to the Council Hall. In the gallery, between two rows of anxious faces, amid generals and dignitaries who had hastened to the Élysée at word of his return, he failed to distinguish two chamberlains in red coats: Las Cases, a sometime émigré, and Montholon, a young general, but recently in disfavour with him.

The ministers had been summoned by Joseph. They were all present. They had been waiting in fact for a long time, conversing in low tones: Cambacérès, as pompous as ever; Carnot and Maret sad, deeply moved, sincere; D'Angély and Decrès sniffing the direction of the wind; Fouché with his white face set, foreseeing and welcoming the

[6] Davoust, *Souvenirs manuscrits;* Houssaye, *1815,* p. 15.

[7] [Year VIII, 18-19 Brumaire (Nov. 9-10, 1799), when Napoleon overthrew the Directory and became First Consul].

[8] *Mémoires et souvenirs,* p. 364.

catastrophe which, he thought, would mean power for him. Under his feigned deference Fouché was the chief adversary, as Napoleon was well aware. The Minister of Police had been discounting defeat from the beginning of the Hundred Days. In May he said to Pasquier:

"The Emperor will win one or two battles. He will lose the third. Then it will be our turn." [9]

Though he was risking his own head Fouché was not afraid. During all the days that followed he was to act secretly but boldly, stampeding the Liberals with the threat of a military dictatorship and discouraging Napoleon's friends by picturing him as condemned beyond recall by the Allies, by Parliament, and by the country.[10]

The Emperor took his seat and opened the meeting. He ordered Maret to read his comuniqué on the action at Mont Saint-Jean. Then he said:

"Our misfortunes are great. I have come to remedy them. If the nation rises, the enemy will be crushed. If, instead of taking energetic steps, we waste time arguing, all is lost. To save the country I must have a temporary dictatorship. I could, of course, seize it, but it would be wise and more national for the Assembly to confer it on me."

The ministers sat silent. Most of them lowered their eyes,[11] that the Emperor might not read their thoughts. Napoleon called on them one after the other. Carnot spoke like a patriot, in the tone of a man of the Revolution. He was for calling France to arms and repulsing the invasion with the means and in the spirit of the Year II. Caulaincourt was alarmed at such language. He maintained gently that the Emperor should try to come to an agreement with the Members. Maret and Cambacérès seconded him. Fouché, calm as ever, objected to dissolution—he had too great an interest in having the Assembly in session. Fearing that the proposal of dissolution, which would have been the end of him, might be carried, Fouché hurried pencilled notes from the Council Hall itself to his henchmen in the Assembly—Manuel, Jay, Dupin, to warn them and fend off the danger.

D'Angély, one of Napoleon's oldest friends, who, however, was being worked upon by Fouché, was the first to propose a regency. The Members, he thought, would accept one.

[9] Pasquier, *Mémoires*, Vol. III, p. 195.
[10] Rovigo, *Mémoires*, Vol. VIII, p. 142; Thibaudeau, Vol. X, p. 394; Boulay de la Meurthe, p. 280; Pontécoulant, Vol. III, 378.
[11] Chaboulon, Vol. II, p. 211.

Napoleon's lips narrowed to a thin line.

"Speak plainly!" he said. "What they want is my abdication?"

"I fear so, sire."

And he added, astounded at his own boldness—but Waterloo justified anything:

"It might well be that should Your Majesty decide not to offer your abdication the Assembly would make so bold as to ask for it."

Lucien drew himself up:

"If the Assembly will not stand by the Emperor, he will get along without its assistance. Let him declare martial law throughout France and call all patriots to her defence!"

Napoleon then took the floor with his old assurance:

"The presence of the enemy on French soil will, I trust, bring the Members to a sense of their duty. I do not fear them. Whatever they do I shall always be the idol of the people and the army. I would have only to say the word and they would all be knocked on the head." [12]

In a resurgence of genius he drew a lucid picture of the danger the country was in, of its last resources, of the chances it still had to win. The army was assembling at Laon. Grouchy, untouched, was marching on Givet. The arsenals had reserves. Vincennes and La Fère could provide five hundred pieces. Napoleon guaranteed that by rapid mobilization of the reserves he could have a hundred and thirty thousand men in line within a fortnight—more than the Anglo-Prussians, so sorely taxed at Waterloo, could meet him with. The Russians and the Austrians were far away. Before they could come up, their Allies would be vanquished. Paris sat fortified and guarded. A hundred and sixty thousand men coming up from the last conscription with guns on their shoulders would fall into line beside their elder comrades.

His imagination rode rough-shod over obstacles, magnified numbers, stifled doubts. The magnetism of his voice, low at first then gradually rising till it filled the room, once more exerted its spell upon those old acquaintances, many of whom were weary, several of whom had betrayed him, and all of whom were thinking of themselves. But for fifteen years they had seen him so much the master of events that they could readily believe that he was about to work a new miracle. At the end he said with a pathos that gave them a shudder:

[12] Chaboulon, Vol. II, p. 214; Villemain, Vol. II, p. 267.

"I would have understood had they turned me back when I landed at Cannes. Today I am bound up with the nation. To sacrifice me would be to hold out its hands for chains."

Then almost all of them felt ready to follow that amazing man who had lost, it was true, but who, tomorrow, alone against all Europe, might again find himself the conqueror.[18]

Under the·spur of the master they went on to actual business. Davoust would be Commandant in Paris and the city would be placed under martial law. Clauzel would be Minister of War. The government would be transferred to Tours. The Federal Guard would be armed and combined with the National Guard. The Emperor would inform the Assembly of all that. How should he dress in appearing before them? In full ceremonial attire, or in his field uniform still splashed with mud? Preferences were for the uniform.

But just then the door opened and a message from the Assembly was handed to Napoleon. There was a sudden silence. He read it aloud:

"The Assembly declares itself in permanent session. Any attempt to dissolve it is a crime of high treason. Any person who shall be guilty of such an attempt will be a traitor to his country and immediately tried as such."

Check to the Emperor! The Liberals had not wasted any time!

"I should have disbanded those fellows before I left," he said bitterly. "This is the end. They will be the ruin of France."

His brief illusion shattered, he relapsed into his hesitancy again. The minds around him lost their bearings. Davoust began to talk of legality. Napoleon dismissed the meeting with a phrase that brought a gleam of blissfulness to Fouché's face:

"I see that Regnault was not deceiving me. I shall abdicate if necessary."

Leave the city? It was too late. Napoleon saw himself at the mercy of propertied Jacobins, of disguised aristocrats who hated him and were afraid of losing the titles, land grants and salaries which he had bestowed on them, if he clung to power. However, he decided to wait before making up his mind. He was still hoping against hope.

He sent D'Angély to the Members and Carnot to the Peers to an-

[18] "To tell the truth," said the Duke of Otranto that evening to M. de Saint-Cricq, a Royalist, "that devil of a fellow gave me a fright this morning. Listening to him I thought we were going to begin all over again. Fortunately we are not going to begin all over again" (Villemain, Vol. II, p. 266).

nounce that he was "busying himself with those measures of public safety that circumstances might demand." The dragging afternoon shook his self-confidence still more while the Assembly plucked up greater and greater boldness. Aroused by Fouché and Lafayette it suddenly voted to call upon the ministers to appear before it. Claiming that the Emperor had threatened them the Members summoned the National Guard to their aid. Napoleon passed those hours in the gardens of the Élysée discussing the situation with Caulaincourt, Maret, Savary, Lucien. The Brumaire "President," who had been shouldered out of the blessings of the Empire, was the only one in the general collapse to try to rouse Napoleon to the energy of the old days. He implored him to make a clean sweep of the Members.

"It is not a matter of a *coup d'état,* but of a constitutional decree. You have the right to do it." [14]

"The Assembly will resist," Napoleon replied. "We shall have to use force. And as for that, where is the force? There are no soldiers, even in Paris. At the very least Davoust would have to rush a few troops in from the reserve depots of the Somme. He has been ordered to. We are obliged to wait."

"You are deliberating when you should be acting. The Members are acting—they are!"

"What can they do? They are a lot of talkers."

"Public opinion is with them. They will vote deposition."

"Deposition! They will not dare!"

"They will dare anything."

"Let's see Davoust!"

Napoleon went in-doors. Lucien did not follow him. In his exasperation the Emperor's brother dared exclaim out loud in the presence of two members of the Council:

"He is hesitating—he is temporizing. The smoke of Mont Saint-Jean has gone to his head. He is a ruined man."

.      .      .      .      .      .      .      .      .

Benjamin Constant arrived at the Élysée shortly after six o'clock. He had been summoned by the Emperor. Napoleon took him for a walk under the trees and about the lawn. Finally, speaking in a casual tone, he stated his dilemma. Should he yield to the Assembly or hold out against it?

[14] Lucien, *Mémoires,* Vol. III, p. 347; Villemain, Vol. II, p. 279.

"It is not a question of myself at this moment. It is a question of France. They want me to abdicate. Have they calculated the inevitable consequences of that abdication? If I abdicate today you will be without an army inside of forty-eight hours."

Benjamin Constant made no reply. Napoleon continued:

"I am not being deposed in the cause of liberty, but on account of Waterloo, of fear—a fear of which your enemies will take full advantage." [15]

Just then Napoleon and Constant turned into a path which lay in full view of the crowds that packed the length of the Avenue Marigny. Only a low wall lay between the street and the garden. Wild shouts caused them to halt:

"Long live the Emperor! Down with the Assembly! Death to traitors!"

Napoleon smiled. His face seemed to grow young again. He waved his hand. Thunderous hurrahs acclaimed him. He seized Constant by the arm.

"You see?" he said. "Those are not men on whom I have heaped honours and riches. What do they owe me? I found them poor. I leave them poor. But they are enlightened by *the instinct of necessity*. The voice of the country speaks through their lips and, if I choose, if I so permit, the rebellious Assembly will have ceased to exist one hour from now."

He broke off, glanced at the crowds and added:

"A man's life is not worth that much. I did not come back from Elba to drown Paris in blood." [16]

Savary joined them. He had just come from the House of Peers. There they were preparing, under face-saving forms, to desert Napoleon. The latter commented:

"Since those hotheads feel so sure of doing better we must take them at their word." [17]

Benjamin Constant departed. As Napoleon was about to quit the garden he saw Queen Hortense advancing towards him. She had

[15] Constant, *Mémoires sur les Cent Jours*, 137 ff.

[16] Constant, *Ibid.*, p. 139. During those last days Napoleon had finance and business against him. Businessmen were anxious to be rid of him in order to get back to their private affairs. On receipt of the news of Waterloo on June 21 quotations on government debt bonds rose from 53 to 55. On the announcement of the abdication they went as high as 59.6.

[17] Rovigo, *Mémoires*, Vol. VIII, p. 144.

called that morning but at a time when he could not receive her. He assumed a tone of sharpness to hide his emotion:

"What have they gone and told you now!"

"That you have been unlucky, sire."

He made no answer and started towards his study. Hortense followed.[18] He sat down at his desk and began to open letters, but without reading them. He seemed to have forgotten Hortense. A servant came to announce dinner. Only then did he remember her presence:

"You have dined, I suppose? Won't you keep me company?"

In the Silver Salon the curtains were drawn. She sat beside him while he ate. They exchanged a few insignificant remarks. Hortense had nothing definite in mind. She felt that the Emperor was lost and had only an agonized pity for him. They went from table to the large drawing-room. Lucien was just coming in. He had pleaded in vain with the Members to rally behind Napoleon, but probably, after so many years of silence, he had failed to recapture his eloquence of former days. In any case the Assembly had said its say. The Allies had proclaimed that Napoleon was the sole obstacle to peace. Let him disappear and France would be saved. If he refused to abdicate the Assembly would vote his deposition.

Lucien protested against a betrayal dictated by the foe. To separate the nation from its leader was tantamount to surrender. Lafayette shouted at that point:

"You accuse us of failing in our duty towards Napoleon? On the torrid sands of Egypt as well as in the ice-clad fields of Russia three million Frenchmen have perished to satisfy the pride and the greed for power of one man. That is enough! We have but one duty now —to save the country." [19]

A little later the Assembly's committees and the Ministers convened at the Tuileries with Cambacérès in the chair. There they voted to negotiate directly with the Allies. That was usurping a prerogative of the Emperor. Lucien gave assurance that the Emperor was ready to make any sacrifice that the safety of France might require.

After an idle debate that lasted till break of day those pale and weary heads adjourned. As he left the hall Fouché said to Thibaudeau:

"We must make an end of this today."

18 Hortense, *Mémoires*, Vol. III, pp. 19-20.
19 *Moniteur*, June 22, 1815.

To save his own life Fouché had to strip Napoleon of power. On several occasions he had felt the latter's eyes glued upon him in a glance that spelled regret at not having ordered him shot.[20]

Napoleon did not sleep. On arising he received Caulaincourt, Lavalette, Savary. They urged him to yield. Cambacérès and Joseph also thought he should abandon the throne. He had gone beyond his strength and seemed ready to agree to almost anything.

The Assembly however had met again—a stormy session. General de Solignac suggested sending a delegation to the Élysée to press for the Emperor's acceptance. No one uttered a protest—not a word of loyalty, not a word of regret. Sebastiani, a Corsican, who had been showered with favours by his master, was one of the most bitter against him. They voted to grant the Emperor but one hour of grace, and that merely "out of deference to the head of the State." [21] Solignac and a few other men came to serve notice on Napoleon. He received them and replied that he was about to address a message to the Members. D'Angély by now was just a mouthpiece for Fouché. He insisted and dared even to speak of outlawing. The Emperor reared.

"If that is the way matters stand," he said, "I shall not abdicate. The Assembly is packed with Jacobins, self-seekers who want positions and disorder. I ought to have thrown them all out by the collar. But there is still time." [22]

He paced rapidly up and down, his face glowering. D'Angély spoke in noble terms of public danger, of self-sacrifice for one's country. Joseph and Caulaincourt implored. Nervous, at the end of his strength, he gave in:

"Very well! Let it be as they wish. The future will tell whether they have served France best in this way."

He called the ministers together in the Council Chamber to announce his decision. To Fouché, who sat wetting his thin lips with his tongue, he flung ironically:

"Now write and tell those gentlemen not to worry. They are going to have their way."

Fouché took a piece of paper from the table and dashed off a few lines to Manuel. Napoleon turned to Lucien:

"Sit down! Write!

[20] L. Madelin, *J. Fouché la veille et le lendemain de Waterloo.*
[21] *Moniteur*, June 23; Chaboulon, Vol. II, p. 228; Thibaudeau, Vol. X, pp. 403-04.
[22] Chaboulon, Vol. II, p. 227.

" 'DECLARATION TO THE FRENCH PEOPLE:

" 'In opening war to support national independence I counted on a union of all efforts and all wills.' "

Lucien, near-sighted, bent low over his paper. Napoleon dictated, his back to the window. Around him, in a suffocating heat, craning their necks, holding their breath, crowded most of the men whom he had made his associates in good fortune. His slow measured voice made its way into their innermost souls. A few of them were weeping—the most deeply affected was Carnot. The turn-coats themselves admired the dignity that had followed on so much indecision. From out of doors through the open windows came far-away shouts:

"Long live the Emperor!"

He resumed:

" 'Circumstances seem to me to have changed. I offer myself in sacrifice to the hatred of the enemies of France. May they prove sincere in their declaration that they aim at my person only. Do you unite one and all for the public good and in order to remain an independent nation.' "

So far he had not mentioned his son. Could he hand on a crown that was being snatched from his head? Would those cowards respect the rights of a child? [23]

Carnot and Lucien called his attention to the fact that if he were to eliminate the Bourbons he could abdicate only in favor of Napoleon II. He shrugged his shoulders:

"Ah, yes, the Bourbons! But they at least will not be under the Austrian ferule!"

Was it not a futile gesture to designate as his successor the beautiful child whom he had loved so fondly and whom he still loved in spite of absence and silence—the child whom he had hoped to rescue when he made his escape from Elba?

"Our enemies are there," he said, "and the Bourbons are behind them. We must either repulse the former or put up with the latter. As for me, my fate is of no concern to anybody. I know adversity."

He yielded, however, indifferently. He added a sentence to the message he had dictated:

" 'My political life is over and I proclaim my son, under title of Napoleon II, Emperor of the French.' "

Fleury de Chaboulon made the copies of the text that Lucien had

[23] Lucien Bonaparte, *La vérité sur les Cent Jours*, pp. 108-09.

taken down. On one of them he dropped a tear. As he stepped up to sign the document, Napoleon noticed the mark. He thanked Chaboulon with a glance and said to him in a low voice: "They want it that way!" [24]

The ministers waited till he had signed the decree in duplicate, then most of them withdrew in order to deliver the document to Parliament. Napoleon was left alone, unable to fix his mind on anything. His sacrifice was accomplished. He had no violent attack of nerves during these hours such as he had had the year before at Fontainebleau. By now he had been thoroughly steeped in fatalism. The people about him, even familiar objects, had become stranger to him.

Neither Fouché nor Lafayette dreamed of bothering with the Council of Regents provided for in the act of abdication. The provisional government was to be handed over to a commission of five Members, three appointed by the Assembly, two by the Peers. Fouché was to worm his way into the presidency in such a way as to find himself master of the State.

.        .        .        .        .        .        .

Napoleon remained at the Élysée. He realized clearly, as he said later on, that his career was at an end. Nevertheless a sort of instinct induced him to cling to that palace. It was sustained doubtless by the acclamations of the crowds. Unemployed labourers, uniformed Federals bearing tricoloured flags and green branches, soldiers home from the rout, retired officers, students, street urchins of Paris, rebelled at the thought of a new invasion that would restore Louis XVIII to the throne. They still saw Napoleon as the defender of liberty. They trooped in throngs to the Élysée, filling the air with threats against the Royalists, begging the Emperor to lead them against the enemy.

With nothing to do Napoleon wandered from one room to another, lifted a curtain to peer outside, went back to his table. With the help of Ménéval and Chaboulon he began classifying his papers, burning many of them. He chatted with his brothers or his mother and received Hortense, who was now spending all her days at the Élysée. She kept urging him to get to safety while there was still time—to choose his refuge.

"Think of no one but yourself! Do not lose a moment!"

With a common sense quite unbetrayed by her romantic eyes, she pressed:

[24] Chaboulon, Vol. II, p. 230.

"If America is to be your choice, make haste and get to a seaport before the English learn of what is going on. If it is to be Austria, make your terms at once. Perhaps the sovereign there will remember that you are his son-in-law. As for the English it would be giving them too much glory—they would shut you up in the Tower of London. The Emperor of Russia is the only one you can trust. He was once your personal friend. He is loyal and generous. Write to him—he will appreciate it." [25]

So spake Hortense, with beating heart, beside herself at the approach of danger. The advice was excellent. Alexander would probably have not resisted such an appeal. Napoleon, however, nourished an abiding grudge against the Czar. Seated before his fireplace, he replied:

"And you—what do you intend to do? Will you go to your country place near Geneva?"

Hortense could not repress a flash of anger. Would he always treat her like a child?

"Oh!" she cried. "Don't worry about me, sire! Think of yourself. The worst of the choices I have suggested is better than doing nothing, as I see you doing now."

He did not answer. An incorrigible dreamer of dreams, he may have been caressing a vision that prevented him from hearing such farsighted counsel: the mob forcing the gates of the Luxembourg and the Palais Bourbon, driving out the renegades and restoring power to him in an outburst that would terrify Europe and bring her to terms. The Revolution, mother of the Empire, would reappear at its last hour to restore it to youth and save it!

And, in fact, the demonstrations continued unceasingly. To no purpose did the patrols of the National Guard disperse the marching groups—they re-formed again the moment the soldiers turned their backs.[26] A committee of Federals made their way into the very courtyard of the Élysée. Napoleon saluted them from a window.

"Arms!" they cried. "Give us arms! We will defend our Emperor!"

"You shall have arms," replied the Emperor. "But you must use them against the enemy."

Soon afterwards, while walking in the garden, he saw a young officer who had scaled the wall emerge from a clump of shrubs and

[25] Hortense, *Mémoires*, Vol. III, p. 23.
[26] *Bulletin de Réal*, June 24 (Archives, AF, IV, 1934).

fall on his knees before him. The young man implored Napoleon in the name of his comrades to return to the army. The Emperor tweeked his ear and said simply:

"Come, my boy, go back to your post." [27]

Fouché could not be sure of anything so long as Napoleon remained in Paris. He was eager to get him away—not too far away, however, for in his hands Napoleon might serve, according to the needs of the moment, as a hostage or a scarecrow.

On June 24th an obscure deputy, Duchesne by name, demanded in the Assembly that "the ex-Emperor be invited, in the name of the country, to quit the capital where his presence could serve only as a pretext for trouble and a cause of public danger." At the same time Napoleon's intimates were warned that his life was in danger at the Élysée where he was now guarded by a handful of grenadiers. These measures failing of effect Fouché sent Davoust to the Emperor with a request that he leave.

During those three days the Marshal had changed. He was henceforward to belong to the Duke of Otranto. The sight of him roused Napoleon from his lethargy. He railed against the peers, the Members, the new Directory.[28] But he finished by saying with a shrug of his shoulders:

"They want me to go away? That will be no harder for me to bear than the rest." [29]

At the point he had reached—one sacrifice more or less! He was ready to yield, but was not being fooled either by threats or pretences.

"Fouché," he said, "tricks everybody. In the end he will be tricked and caught in his own trap. He is making fools of the Members. The Allies are making a fool of him. Through him you will have Louis XVIII back again."

Davoust withdrew. The two great soldiers, kin through glory, separated without a friendly word. A nod from the Emperor, a salute from his comrade-at-arms! Twenty years of trust gone to naught in a moment!

That evening Napoleon said to Hortense:

[27] *Bulletin de Paris*, p. 274.
[28] The members of the provisional government were Fouché, Caulaincourt, Carnot, Grenier and Quinette.
[29] Davoust, *Mémoires manuscrits;* H. Houssaye, *1815*, Vol. II, p. 102.

"Malmaison belongs to you. I should like very much to go there and you would be giving me great pleasure if you would stay there with me. I shall leave tomorrow."

Then he added, as a memory of Josephine crossed his mind:

"I do not care to occupy the Empress's apartment."

Carnot came to see him early the next morning. Of all the men who had surrounded him in his downfall that old Jacobin, whom he had so long treated unfairly, was the only one to utter a word of devotion or loyalty to him. Napoleon asked his advice regarding his final refuge.

"Do not go to England," urged Carnot. "You have aroused too much hatred there. Do not hesitate to cross to America. From there you can still cause your enemies to tremble. If France is destined to fall under a Bourbon yoke again, your presence in a free country will strengthen national opinion." [30]

Napoleon accompanied him as far as the steps. As Carnot was about to go down, his eyes brimming with tears, he bowed his head on the Emperor's shoulder. Napoleon, deeply moved, embraced him. Shortly afterwards he sent an official request to the Governing Commission for two frigates and passports for America. [31]

He had set his departure for noon. The crowds got wind that something was going on and filled the Rue du Faubourg Saint Honoré an hour in advance, shouting: "Long live the Emperor! Do not desert us!"

Napoleon was afraid he might not be able to control either his own feelings or the mob. He sent his coach out into the streets carrying Montholon, Las Cases, and his aide-de-camp, Gourgaud, the last chamberlains to remain with him. He himself entered an ordinary carriage, belonging to Grand Marshal Bertrand, at the postern opening on the Champs Élysées.

He drove along the avenue under a burning sun, passing close to the Arc de Triomphe, the foundations of which were just rising above the ground. At half-past one the gates of Malmaison closed behind him.

Four days only had passed since his return from Waterloo. He was never to enter Paris again alive.

. . . . . . . . .

[30] *Mémoires sur Carnot*, Vol. II, pp. 528-29.
[31] Montholon, *Récits de la Captivité de l'Empereur Napoléon*, Vol. I, p. 124.

Hortense welcomed the Emperor as he stepped out of his carriage. She had set Malmaison in order during the forenoon—it had been unoccupied since the death of Josephine and the gravelled walks were growing green. Napoleon's company was installed on the first floor. Hortense had reserved the wing formerly occupied by her mother for herself. She kept discreetly to her own rooms. The Emperor did not see her again all that day.[32]

He received Laffitte almost at once, and handed to him a sum of money and some securities, which the banker promised to keep on deposit. Eight hundred thousand francs in bank notes passed from hand to hand at that time.[33] Three millions in gold were removed that same night by Peyrusse from the cellars of the Tuileries and sent by wagon to Laffitte's bank. Finally came the Emperor's great collection of medals. Napoleon had perfect confidence in Laffitte who had warned him of Fouché's intrigues with Metternich.[34]

Some time after the King's re-entry, Baron Louis, Minister of Finance to Louis XVIII, ordered Laffitte to declare under oath "whether or no he held any funds belonging to Napoleon." Laffitte hurried to the Tuileries and obtained an audience with the King. "Sire," he said, "on the 19th of March, a few hours before Napoleon's entry into Paris, I received from Your Majesty a deposit of seven millions, which indiscretions on the part of your courtiers had brought to Napoleon's knowledge. But Napoleon himself took pains to reassure me, stipulating that I should send the money to England and so prove that I was worthy of the confidence which the King had reposed in me."

Louis XVIII then said to the banker: "I knew all that, monsieur. Louis has made a mistake. Do not worry. Do with the money that was entrusted to you at the Élysée as you did with mine."

Napoleon seemed less down-hearted than at the Élysée:

"I do not know what is in store for me. I am in good health and I still have fifteen years ahead. I sleep and I wake up when I wish. I can ride for four hours at a stretch and work ten hours a day. Moreover I am not very expensive to feed. I could live very well on a louis anywhere. We shall see." [35]

He said that he would leave as soon as he had received his passports. That evening General Beker arrived. He had been appointed

---

[32] Hortense, *Mémoires*, Vol. III, p. 27.    [34] Gourgaud, Vol. II, p. 325.
[33] Laffitte, *Mémoires*, p. 74.    [35] Laffitte, *Mémoires*, p. 78.

by Davoust as commandant of a body-guard—three hundred grenadiers and chasseurs, barracked at Rueil. His task was less to protect
Napoleon than to keep an eye on him.

Beker was not, as has been charged, a malcontent embittered against
the Emperor for the latter's refusal to promote him. Count de Mons,
with an income of thirty thousand francs, he was a grand officer of
the Legion of Honour and a Member of the Assembly. Napoleon had
arranged a marriage for him with Desaix's sister. He was an Alsatian,
simple, stern. He had rarely seen the Emperor. He seems to have
undertaken this mission much against his will. But the Minister of
War had commanded—he obeyed.

He was shown into the library at Malmaison, a room that had always served as Napoleon's study. He introduced himself and presented his credentials from Davoust.

The Emperor, scenting the jailor, said harshly:

"Monsieur, I should have been informed officially of an act which
I choose to regard as a matter of form and not as a measure of surveillance to which it was useless to subject me." [36]

"Sire," Beker stammered, "I am an old soldier, and so far my one
concern has been to obey your voice. I have accepted the command
of the Emperor's guard only to provide for his safety."

Napoleon sounded his man with a glance.

"Do not worry, General," he said. "I am delighted to have you
with me. Had I been given the choice, my preference would have
designated you. I know your loyalty."

He opened the glass door and drew him out into the park:

"Well, what are they doing—what are they saying, in Paris?"

They conversed till long after dark, under the stars. Napoleon
asked Beker to urge the government to place two frigates at his
disposal:

"Let them give them to me and I will leave at once for Rochefort."

His idea, as he had said to Savary, was not to flee, but to withdraw
with honour.[37]

The next day he walked about the gardens in an entrancing summer sunshine. That spot had witnessed his rise to power. There he
had been young, beloved, happy. Each step he took raised ghosts

[36] Beker, *Relation de ma mission près de Napoléon*, p. 21.
[37] Rovigo, Vol. VIII, pp. 172 ff.

of the past. On that meadow he had played at prisoner's base (goal-tag) with his friends. Along those sandy roads he had walked of an evening with Talleyrand or with Fouché, so laying the foundations of a grandeur greater than France had ever known. Today, Talley-rand, Fouché . . . !

He did not like such great solitude. He sent for Hortense. When she had come, he addressed her, but then, without waiting for her reply, he said, lowering his voice:

"Poor Josephine! I cannot get used to living here without her. I always seem to see her coming out of a path and picking one of these roses she loved so well." [38]

Had she been there, he must have thought, the woman who had been so closely associated with his early years, his real wife, his true love, he might not have felt so alone. Hortense wept.

"For that matter," he added, "she would have been very unhappy now. We never disagreed except on one subject. That was her debts. I did scold a good deal about them. She was a woman in the full meaning of the term—changeable, vivacious, and with the best heart in the world. Have another portrait of her made for me. I should like it to be a medallion."

Hortense promised.

Madame Mère arrived with Joseph and Jerome. The talk turned at once to his getting away. Fouché had requested safe-conducts of Wellington, so apprising England of Napoleon's intentions and putting her in a position to prevent the execution of them.[39] Disagreeing with his colleagues, Caulaincourt and Carnot, Fouché was inclined to hand the Emperor over to the English if they should demand him. He ruled that the frigates could not leave the roadstead at Rochefort before the issuance of the safe-conducts.[40] Napoleon saw through the ruse. He had asked to go to the United States. He was being urged to go to Rochefort, far from the people and far from the army, and await the verdict of the Allies there. From that moment he refused to leave Malmaison.

"I prefer," he said to Beker, "to receive my arrest here."

Mention was made of the enemy's advance, which might endanger his life. He replied:

[38] Hortense, *Mémoires*, Vol. III, p. 27.
[39] Bignon to Wellington, June 25, 1814 (Archives, *Affaires étrangères*, 1802).
[40] Fouché to Decrès, June 27 (Archives, *Marine*, BB 3, 426).

"What have I to fear? I have abdicated. It is for France to protect me."

He saw the danger however, for he said to Hortense:

"As far as I am concerned I have nothing to fear here. But you, my daughter, go—leave me!"

She refused to do anything of the sort and he doubtless knew that she never would.

However, Fouché and his accomplices, an ever-growing legion, were still fearful of some resort of despair that might bring Napoleon back at the head of an army. Davoust ordered Beker to request the Emperor to leave at once, and, if he could not make up his mind to do so, to take every measure "to prevent His Majesty from leaving the grounds at Malmaison."

Their fears were fanned by the crowds of callers during the first two days—habitués of the Tuileries, Peers, still loyal Members, writers, men of science, no end of army officers. Some of them came just to snatch a few francs in subsidy from the Emperor. Generals Chartran and Piré dared to make a disgusting scene, and the Emperor was obliged to give them twelve thousand francs.[41] Soon, with the approach of the Allies and the quasi-certainty of a restoration of Louis XVIII, a desert formed about him. No more dignitaries, no more men of prominence! Several members of the family appeared, however, a number of personal friends, or else people too lost to the favour of the King to hope for forgiveness. Numbers of army officers also kept coming in from the battlefields to assure the Emperor of the army's devotion. Napoleon had them received by the Grand Marshal.

. . . . . . . .

On the 27th, it seems, before luncheon, a young lad between nine and ten years old, tall, alert, handsome, of fine carriage, was brought before Napoleon.[42] He was in his private garden at the time. He sent for Hortense.

"Look at this child," he said to her, aside. "Whom does he resemble?"

"He is your son, sire. He is the picture of the King of Rome!"

"You think so? Then it must be so. I did not think I had a soft heart. The sight of him has stirred me."

41 Chaboulon, Vol. II, p. 278.
42 Queen Hortense recounts the scene, *Mémoires*, Vol. II, p. 32. She does not specify the day. But the visit could not have taken place either on the 26th or on the 28th. The context of the story fits the 27th.

It was "little Léon," the son of Éléonore Denuelle, reader to Caroline.[43] The Emperor was having him educated in a boarding-school in Paris. His guardian, Baron de Mauvières, father-in-law to Méneval, had brought him.

Hortense said that she would take charge of him herself were it not for the malicious gossip of those who had already accused her of being too friendly with Napoleon.

"Yes," said the Emperor, "you are right. I should have been glad to know that he was with you. But people would not fail to say that he was your son. When I get to America, I shall send for him."

Hortense adds [44] that she went up to the child, who was as lovely as an angel, and asked him whether he were satisfied with his school and what he did to amuse himself. "He told me that for some time he and his comrades had been playing soldier and that they had formed two parties, one called the Bonapartists and the other the Bourbonites. I asked to which party he belonged: 'The King's,' he said, and when I asked the reason why, he answered: 'Because I love the King and do not like the Emperor.' I probed his reasons for not liking the Emperor. 'I have no reason,' he insisted, 'except that I belong to the King's party.' "

On the morning of the 28th, Napoleon sent his aide-de-camp, Flahaut, to the Tuileries to inform the Governing Commission officially of his resolve: the two frigates were to set sail as soon as he should board them—otherwise he would not budge from Malmaison. Davoust was present. Without giving Fouché time to reply he shouted at Flahaut:

"*Your Bonaparte* does not intend to go at all, but he will have to rid us of himself. His presence embarrasses us—it is halting the progress of our negotiations. Tell him for me that he has to go. If he does not leave at once, I shall have him arrested—I shall arrest him myself!" [45]

Flahaut was young and hot-headed. He replied that he refused to deliver such a message, which surprised him as coming from a "man who a week before had been grovelling at Napoleon's knees." And he flung his resignation in Davoust's face:

[43] He was born in Paris, December 13, 1806. Napoleon had had some doubts as to his paternity. The child was truly his son. Known as "Count Léon" he was to lead a stormy life and die at Pontoise, April 15, 1881.
[44] *Mémoires*, Vol. III, p. 34.
[45] Chaboulon, Vol. II, p. 275; Villemain, Vol. II, p. 425.

"I could not continue service under your orders without dishonouring my epaulettes!"

Back again at Malmaison Flahaut could not dissimulate. He repeated Davoust's exact words to the Emperor.

"Let him come!" cried Napoleon. "I am ready, if he wishes, to hold out my throat to him."

Was he sincere? People about him did not think so. They were convinced that in the end, under too many insults, his genius would rear its head again, that the Emperor would seize his sword and tear up his abdication.

And yet Napoleon was making preparations for departure. He conferred with his treasurer, Peyrusse, and his notary, Noel, on the sale of a block of stock, the proceeds of which, 180,000 francs, would probably suffice for the journey.

He bade farewell to the two women who, doubtless, had loved him best, with the greatest trust and silence: Countess Walewska and Mme. Duchâtel. Pale, dignified, the latter controlled herself. The Polish woman, who had little Alexander with her, could not restrain her tears. "I felt sorry for her," says Queen Hortense,[46] "and urged her to lunch with me alone so that others might not see her in her evident grief." Mme. Pellapra, a beautiful woman from Lyons, by whom Napoleon had had a daughter (little Émilie, who was later to become the Princess de Chimay), also came to Malmaison. She had warned the Emperor through Marchand that Fouché was dickering with Vitrolles, in other words, with Louis XVIII. Napoleon loved her and thought highly of her. He was to speak of her at St. Helena. Shortly before Waterloo he sent her a bracelet.[47]

Talma and Corvisart arrived. When the latter had gone, the Emperor handed Marchand, his valet, "a tiny phial filled with a reddish liquid."

"See that I have that with me," he told him, "either in my coat, or in some part of my clothing, but in such a way that I can get at it quickly."[48]

He had resolved not to fall into the enemy's hands alive.

In spite of the anguish of the moment he still looked towards the

[46] *Mémoires*, Vol. III, p. 35.
[47] At present it belongs to Princess G. Bibesco (*Mémoires d'Émilie de Pellapra, publiés par la princesse Bibesco*, 1921).
[48] Bourguignon, *Les adieux de Malmaison*, p. 42.

future. When he was alone, he read a copy of Humboldt's *Voyages* that he had found in the library, rarely laying it down. From it he got the idea of a new career, not as a soldier, but as a scholar.

"What I need," he remarked to Monge, "is a companion who will give me an idea, at the start and rapidly, of the present state of the sciences. After that we shall travel from Canada to Cape Horn and, on such a long long journey, study all the physical phenomena of the globe."

So he saw in that a nobler end than Diocletian had chosen for himself in cultivating his lettuce at Salone, or Washington, who ended his days as a country gentleman. Even at the bottom of the ladder he had to have an aim to fire his imagination. Nothing less than greatness stirred him.

Monge was seventy years old but offered to follow him. Napoleon thanked him for his devotion but did not accept.[49]

The Prussians were drawing nearer. Cannonading was audible in the direction of Gonesse. Every now and then, as the noise grew louder, Napoleon would toss his book aside and go to the table on which he had spread out a map. It was stuck with pins with red or blue heads, showing the positions of the enemy. Delessert, a young officer of the National Guard, came to warn him that Malmaison was threatened.[50]

Napoleon looked at his map.

"Ah! Ah!" he cried, laughing, "I have let them turn my flank!"

He sent Gourgaud and Montholon into the park to reconnoitre. Gourgaud, a tall young fellow, imaginative and high-strung, seemed to be beside himself.

"If," he said, "I were to see the Emperor about to fall into the hands of the Prussians, I would shoot him."[51]

The day was drawing to a glorious end. Hortense was strolling about the park with Mme. Bertrand, the Grand Marshal's wife. Mme. Bertrand was half English and kept repeating that if the Emperor "were to take refuge in England he would be marvellously received there."

[49] Arago, *Éloge de Gaspard Monge, Mémoires de l'Académie des Sciences*, Vol. XXIV, pp. 131-33. Monge then suggested to his young colleague, François Arago, that he go with Napoleon. Arago declined.

[50] Gabriel Delessert, years later, became prefect of police under Louis-Philippe. He was twentynine years old, at Malmaison.

[51] Hortense, *Mémoires*, Vol. II, p. 43.

They sat down on a bench. Napoleon joined them. They sat for a moment in silence, enjoying the clear air, the lengthening shadows, the mottled dusting of sunlight.

"How beautiful Malmaison is!" exclaimed the Emperor. "Wouldn't it be wonderful, Hortense, to be able to stay here?"

She made a barely audible reply, not trusting her voice.

He left them and went to the library to talk with the Duke of Bassano. Hugues Maret was a man of no great brilliancy, but level-headed. He had been associated for many years with Napoleon's life and at just those moments probably was the person to whom the Emperor opened his thoughts most freely. Bessières and Duroc were dead. Rovigo was far too much of a fool. Others, such as Chaboulon or Flahaut, were too young or else subalterns.[52] In those conversations Maret gave advice that was not wide of the mark if one consider the traditional respect of the English for the law:

"Let the Emperor take flight, make the seacoast, fling himself into a boat with a few friends, land in England and immediately present himself to the nearest magistrate declaring that he has come to place himself under the protection of British law. No one would dare do violence to his liberty."

For a brief instant Napoleon weighed the notion, discarding it in favour of the crossing to the United States. But the thought that some day, if he were forced to do so, he might appeal to English honour, drifted about from that moment in his mind.

.    .    .    .    .    .    .    .

On orders from Davoust General Beker burned the bridge at Chatou, and dismantled the bridge at Bezons. It was high time. A few hours later Napoleon might have been captured by a Prussian detachment. Fouché feared just such a catastrophe. Blücher had announced that he would have Napoleon shot at the head of his columns.[53] Fouché would then have been ruined in the eyes of the French.

The Peers were already accusing the Governing Commission of

---

[52] Chaboulon had, moreover, for family reasons, refused to go with the Emperor.
[53] Blücher to his wife (Compiègne, June 27th): "It is possible and highly probable that Bonaparte will be handed over to me and Lord Wellington. I could not do better than to have him shot. It would be rendering a service to humanity" (*Blücher in Briefen*, p. 154). Two days later, June 29th, he was to send his brother-in-law, Major von Colomb, with the 8th regiment of Hussars and two battalions of infantry to take Malmaison by surprise and kidnap the Emperor (*Ibid.*, p. 156).

leaving the Emperor without means of defense and exposed to surprises. They delegated two of their number to bring pressure upon the Commission finally to hurry arrangements for Napoleon's escape.[54]

Fouché would perhaps not have yielded to that formal demand had he not received word from Bonnefoux, naval prefect at Rochefort, that the English fleet stationed off that harbour had come in so close to the coast that it hardly seemed possible for the frigates to get to sea. After that the president of the provisional government hesitated no longer—Napoleon was not to escape! Late at night he sent the naval minister, Decrès, bolstered by Boulay de la Meurthe, to inform the Emperor that "there was no further obstacle to his departure and that the interests of the State as well as his own required that he should set out without delay."[55]

Napoleon was awakened at dawn and received them in his dressing-gown. He replied that he would leave Malmaison in the course of the day.[56]

．　　．　　．　　．　　．　　．　　．　　．

He called Joseph, Bassano, Lavalette and Flahaut into private conference and announced his departure to them. Then he asked for the news of the night. Lavalette, as superintendent of transports, was the best informed. He reported that Grouchy and Vandamme were marching into Paris with the remnants of Waterloo. The Prussians were at Stains and Bourget. The English had not yet appeared.

Just then cheers and hurrahs were heard from the direction of the Rueil road. They came from a detachment of regulars that was on its way to occupy Saint-Germain. The soldiers were cheering the Emperor as they passed Malmaison.

No one spoke in the room. The Emperor seemed to be thinking. He went to the table, changed a few pins on the map, then straightened up, his eyes shining, and exclaimed:

"France must not be conquered by a handful of Prussians! I can still stop the enemy and give the government time to negotiate with the Powers. After that I shall get away to the United States and live out my days there."

He ran up the small staircase that led to his bedroom and came down again a moment later dressed in uniform as a colonel of the

[54] Thibaudeau, Vol. X, p. 443.
[55] Commission to Decrès, June 28th (Archives, *Marine*, BB 3, 426).
[56] Decrès to the Peers, *Moniteur*, June 30th.

Chasseurs of the Guard, boots on, a sword at his belt, his hat under his arm. He was ten years younger.

"General," he said to Beker, "the enemy will be at the gates of Paris tomorrow. All is lost, as you can see. Well, let them give command of the army back to me, not as Emperor, but as a general. I will crush the foreigner in front of Paris. Go—deliver this request of mine to the Governing Commission! Make it plain that I am not dreaming of any resumption of power. I promise, on my word as a soldier, as a citizen, as a Frenchman, that I will leave for America the day I shall have beaten the enemy!" [57]

The hope that shone in Napoleon's face cheered them all. If a miracle were possible he was the man to work it! Beker forgot his status as a jailor and went off like the accommodating soul he was, hoping with all his heart that he might succeed in his mission.

Madame Mère, Cardinal Fesch and Hortense had come in. Hortense asked the Emperor if forces would be equally matched.

"No," he said, "but what can't one do with Frenchmen?" [58]

He ordered his horses saddled and everything made ready for his return to the army.

.          .          .          .          .          .

Beker arrived at the Tuileries towards noon. The Commission was in session there. He was received with scant courtesy and his message with even less.

"Is *he* making fun of us?" cried Fouché with an oath. "Even if we could accept his proposal, do we not know how he would keep his promises?"

Fouché's colleagues held their peace. They had ceased to count—Fouché was everything. He did not even consult them. Carnot alone, to hide his distress, rose from his chair and walked to the back of the room. But he dared not interfere. Nor did Caulaincourt.

His feelings hurt, Beker then expressed a wish to decline the doubtful honour of escorting the Emperor to Rochefort.

"Do you think, General," Fouché retorted sharply, "that any of us are sleeping on beds of roses here? However advantageous His Majesty's offers may be we can make no change in the terms of the decision which you have been commissioned to execute."

[57] Beker, pp. 53, 55; Montholon, Vol. I, p. 48; Gourgaud, Vol. II, p. 559; Villemain, Vol. II, p. 420.
[58] Hortense, *Mémoires*, Vol. II, p. 35.

And he ordered him to return to Malmaison immediately.

Beker made his way through a crowd of functionaries and officers who were at no pains to hide their eagerness to be rid of Napoleon.

When he reported his failure, Napoleon said:

"They will be sorry for having refused my offer. Give orders for my departure. As soon as they have been carried out, you will come and let me know."

More bitter to him even than the misconstruction of his intentions, genuine as they were, was the desertion of Carnot and Caulaincourt. What? They too? He had felt so sure of them! But they had foresworn him! As between Fouché and their Emperor they had chosen Fouché!

He might have leapt upon a horse and made the outposts. With a nod he could have had Beker arrested. But his flare of energy had died down. Since he was being prevented from doing anything, he bowed his head. Once more his spirit had lapsed into a terrible lassitude.

He bade good-bye to Joseph, to Cardinal Fesch, to Talma, the friend of his lean days as a youth, who still stood loyal.[59] Day after day, during this sad period, Talma had appeared at Malmaison in the full-dress uniform of the National Guard.[60] Only Madame Mère was now left. She came in, the last of his family, to embrace Napoleon. He stood motionless in the centre of the library. Great tears trickled down the mother's cheeks. They exchanged a few words which those present did not hear. Then she held out her hand:

"Good-bye, my son."

"Good-bye, mother."

They clasped each other in a long embrace. Finally Napoleon tore himself away. Madame bowed to him and went out, with a firm step, her heart torn, but a Roman to the end.[61]

He went up to his room, took off his uniform, put on blue breeches,

[59] Lucien had started for Boulogne expecting to make the crossing from that place to London. He was to change his mind, however, and switch to Dieppe, whence, again, he veered back to Lyons. On June 26th the Emperor had an order for 250,000 francs sent to him. The order was cashed by the Treasury. Two further millions in fuel assignments went astray. Jerome had received 100,000 francs in cash at the Élysée on the 24th. On the 26th Fouché requested him to leave Paris. He did so on the 27th and took refuge at Sainte-Pésenne, near Nirot. He returned to Paris on August 14th.

[60] Larrey, *Madame Mère*, Vol. II, p. 118.

[61] She set out for Italy at once, accompanied by Fesch. She arrived in Rome August 15th and took up residence in Palazzo Falconieri.

riding boots, a maroon-coloured coat and a town hat. Then he made his way through a maze of rooms he knew so well towards Josephine's bedchamber. She had died in that room, the woman through whom he had known the most feverish love, the woman whose loss he had mourned even in the thrills of his second marriage. She had understood him too late, but she had drawn her last breath with his name on her lips!

He remained for a long time behind closed doors in that room where perchance a trace of the fragrance of West Indian isles still floated. Nothing had been changed—the sky-blue ceiling, the red-panelled hangings, the splendid bed made like a ship borne by two swans. All that was missing was a slender form!

Hortense implored the Emperor to take with him her diamond necklace which she had sewn into a black silk belt. He hesitated, then finally accepted, giving her in remembrance what perhaps was his dearest treasure—Josephine's wedding-ring. He had never ceased to wear it.[62] The officers of the little troop that had formed his bodyguard were then announced. One of them ventured to speak, and stammered:

"We see clearly that we shall not be so happy as to die in your service." [63]

A few minutes before five, Beker came in to announce that all was in readiness for the departure. Bertrand had seen to the preparations himself and delayed everything by his passion for detail. With Fouché's permission, for that matter, Bertrand had loaded a number of army vans with quantities of silverware, tableware, linen and clothing. Planat wrote: [64] "Bertrand and his wife insist on being at Court wherever they go. They clutter up the Emperor's wagon train with loads of useless people and effects." In fact nearly a hundred persons planned to follow Napoleon. For his part Marchand had taken several pieces of furniture from the Élysée, notably the silver washbasin cut by Brunier, a little bust of the King of Rome, and several portraits of Josephine and Marie-Louise.

[62] In spite of Hortense's protests, he insisted on giving her in exchange for the necklace a check for 200,000 francs, dated three months ahead. Of this check we shall speak later. He had already given her two assignments of fuel obligations amounting respectively to 828,000 and 668,000 francs. These were never honoured (Masson, *Napoléon et sa famille*, Vol. XII, p. 85).

[63] Réal, *Report*, June 29 (Archives, AF IV, p. 934).

[64] Vol. I, p. 268.

The safe-conduct issued by the Governing Commission specified that Napoleon should travel in a post-chaise alone with Beker. He was to pass as the latter's secretary. The Emperor appeared hurt at not being consulted on such a matter, whereupon it was decided to choose a closed four-seated carriage free of any armorial bearings. A postilion was to precede them to clear the road of any suspicious characters. Without a word Napoleon picked up his hat. Followed by Hortense and the few loyal friends remaining, he went out into the vestibule that was still adorned with the statues and paintings that had been brought back from the wars in Italy. He would allow none of those who were to stay behind to pass the outer doorway. With Beker, Savary, and Bertrand he walked towards the iron gate on the south side of the park that opened upon the Celle Saint-Cloud road.[65] There a large yellow coach drawn by four horses was waiting. Napoleon gazed back once more upon the pointed roofs of Malmaison that showed above the treetops, then with a sudden motion flung himself inside. His three companions climbed in after him. Aly, the mameluke, mounted the driver's box.[66] The horses started off through the woods forthwith at a rapid trot taking the direction of Rambouillet. Napoleon's company and baggage left soon afterwards. Hortense returned at once to Paris.

That same evening, General Exelmans entered Vincennes with two divisions, in advance of the bulk of the Army of the North which had been after a fashion reorganized. He told Daumesnil that he was going on to Malmaison at once and place the Emperor, by main force if necessary, at the head of his troops. Daumesnil informed him that the Emperor was on his way to Rochefort. A few hours' time—and how different history might have been!

---

[65] Druout and Lavalette refused to follow him. Napoleon was eager to take Labédoyère. They looked for him in vain. He stayed behind, to face a firing-squad!

[66] Louis-Étienne Saint-Denis had first been a stable-boy. He became the Emperor's second mameluke under the name of Aly.

# II

## *LAST DAYS IN FRANCE*

THE FIRST HOURS OF THE JOURNEY PASSED IN A PROFOUND SILENCE. Napoleon seemed to be absorbed in his thoughts. His companions were worried. They feared the Royalists might have prepared some ambush or other. But twelve leagues were traversed without any cause for alarm. They were at Rambouillet at nightfall. The Emperor expressed a wish to spend the night at the castle. That halt was not on the programme and Beker thought that Napoleon's insistence on it rested on a last hope for a change in fortunes.

Yes, he may indeed still have been hoping—he was a man of such capacities for living! His companions, for their part, could never grant that all was lost. "We still hoped," says Beker,[1] "that less distressing news might come to open up prospects of a less cruel outcome."

After supper the Emperor retired to his bedchamber with Bertrand. Shortly he had an attack of pain. Aly undressed him. The wife of Hébert,[2] the keeper at Rambouillet, made him a cup of tea. His companions, including Gourgaud, who had just arrived, slept in chairs in the salon nearby. He felt better in the morning and took some broth. It was eleven o'clock before he made up his mind to set out again, but no couriers arrived.[3]

He got into the carriage again and gave the order to drive on along the road to Tours. They made good time. At Châteaudun the mistress of the gate approached the carriage door to ask if it were true that something had happened to the Emperor. As she looked the travellers over she recognized the palest among them. She did not wait for an answer but ran sobbing away.

In the course of the afternoon, in traversing a straggling village,

---

[1] *Relation*, p. 69.

[2] Hébert had been his valet in Egypt. He was utterly devoted to the Emperor.

[3] Beker, *Relation*, p. 69. Aly says: "The Emperor, having recovered, left about six o'clock in the morning." Beker, however, was generally scrupulous and accurate in his *Relation*. We follow him. Before leaving Rambouillet the Emperor ordered Bertrand and Marchand to choose some books and maps from the castle library. They were sent on to Rochefort later, with Fouché's permission.

they passed some fruit venders' carts. Napoleon sent Aly to buy some cherries. As the villagers seemed interested in the party, the Emperor drew back into his corner and sat with a hand to his cheek. He seemed to enjoy the cherries, as did his companions. From his box Aly could see the pits flying out of the carriage doors.

They dined in a tavern at Châteaurenault. They were served in a high-ceilinged diningroom. "When the Emperor had finished his meal and rested a little, he issued from the diningroom with his companions to get into the carriage again. They were obliged to pass through the tavern kitchen which was full of people. On the Emperor's appearance the spectators drew aside to let him pass and as soon as he was seated in his carriage they burst into cheers: 'Long live the Emperor!' " [4]

They drove straight through Tours on the road to Poitiers. On the farther outskirts of the town Napoleon sent Savary back to look for M. de Miramon, who was prefect there. That gentleman came in all haste. He had been chamberlain at the Tuileries. The Emperor took him arm in arm and walked up and down with him on the roadside. [5]

The heat was unbearable. The sun blistered the white roads and in the parched fields not a blade of grass was stirring. The travellers welcomed oncoming night with relief. They had had no relaxation since leaving Rambouillet save as horses were changed or now and then on a hill, which they climbed on foot.

Napoleon supped at the posthouse at Poitiers. There he asked Beker to despatch a messenger to Bonnefoux, at Rochefort, ordering him to drive out and meet him.

The carriage reached Niort on the evening of July 1. Napoleon decided to sleep at a tavern—"At the Sign of the Gold Ball"—on the outskirts of the town. He was again having difficulty in passing his urine and was often in a doze from which he could be roused only with difficulty. From time to time he would take a pinch of snuff from a box that Beker held out to him. The snuffbox had an ivory lid, that was decorated with a medallion-profile of the Empress, delicately carved. "Once he took the box in his hands, examined it for a moment and then handed it back without a word." [6]

[4] Aly, p. 123.
[5] Rovigo, Vol. VIII, p. 193.
[6] Beker, p. 80. Lavalette and Ménéval had informed him on his return from Elba of Marie-Louise's relations with Neipperg.

Savary went to inform Busche, prefect at Deux-Sèvres, of the Emperor's arrival and appointed an audience for the following morning. When Busche appeared Napoleon was standing at a casement window "interestedly watching a number of riders who were giving their horses their morning rub." One of them looked up and spied the Emperor. His name passed from mouth to mouth. Within an hour the whole town knew that he was among them. Busche insisted on taking the Emperor to the prefecture, gave him a room there and otherwise showered him with solicitous attentions. The crowd gathered under his windows in ever-increasing numbers, cheering and hurrahing. Napoleon, however, refused to appear on the balcony.

He breakfasted alone in his bedroom. Then he received Kérangal, an officer from Rochefort, who came to deliver a letter from Bonnefoux. The naval prefect alleged illness as an excuse for not answering the Emperor's summons. He reported that the English squadron had been blockading the coast for two days. On Napoleon's order Beker immediately sent a message to Fouché asking "permission to communicate with the commander of the fleet, . . . in view of the fact that extraordinary circumstances render this step indispensable both for the personal safety of His Majesty and to spare France the sorrow and shame of seeing him seized in his last asylum and handed over unconditionally to his enemies." [7] Just as he was finishing his copy of the despatch Busche came in and announced that artillery exchanges were developing to the north of Paris. The Emperor immediately dictated an additional paragraph to the General: "We hope that the capital will hold out and that the enemy will give you time to see the outcome of the negotiations your ambassadors have initiated and to reinforce the army that is covering Paris. If, in these circumstances, the English fleet prevents the frigates from leaving port, you are free to consider the Emperor at your disposal as a general actuated solely by a desire to be useful to his country."

Again an offer of his sword to France! Nothing is harder to kill than a hope!

Joseph had planned to embark at Bordeaux, and had also got as far as Niort. General Lallemand, further, and the Countess Bertrand with her children, arrived. Lallemand was a warm and partisan soul. He advised the Emperor to yield to the wishes of the Second Hussars and join the Army of the Loire. Lamarque in the Vendée and Clauzel

[7] Beker to the Provisional Government, Niort, July 2, 1815.

at Bordeaux were ready to declare for him. For a moment Napoleon seemed shaken. The crowd outside was still cheering. However, he resisted the temptation. No, no civil war! He sent Gourgaud ahead to see whether, in spite of everything, the frigates could not gain the open sea by way of the Maumusson Passage, and set his departure for the next afternoon at four.

The whole town, virtually, had gathered in the central square. He walked down the stone steps of the prefecture amid a storm of cheering: "Stay with us! Don't leave us!" A company of hussars had been drawn up in line to hold back the crowd. They presented arms. Napoleon gravely saluted.

.        .        .        .        .        .        .        .

He had not desired an escort, but the company of horse rode off beside his coach with drawn swords. The Emperor dismissed them at the first halt, ordering a gold piece to be handed to each soldier.

The coach bore him along towards Saintonge—a Normandy-on-the-Ocean where the vineyards storm the hillsides in serried rows—then on to Aunis, under a sky of soft mother-of-pearl, along roads bordered with larches and young elms.

Rochefort! He got out at the Navy Building. Bonnefoux still thought it useless to try to run the blockade, though the *Saale* and the *Méduse*, the frigates that had been made ready, were the fastest sailers of the fleet. The frigates were new, well gunned and well manned. The crews were made up of old sailors who had been released in 1814 from English prison-barges. Captain Maitland, who was in charge of the blockade of the roadsteads at Rochefort and Aix, had only the *Bellerophon*, an old slow-sailing craft, the sloop-of-war *Slaney* (which did not arrive till July 11) and the brig *Myrmidon*. For all of Bonnefoux's claims at least one of the French frigates could have got through.[8]

Napoleon called a council of war, with Admiral Martin in the chair. A magnificent sailor, risen from the ranks, the Admiral had hastened to offer his services the moment he learned of the Emperor's arrival.

---

[8] Just a year later, July 2, 1816, the *Méduse*, under the command of the incompetent Duroy de Chaumareix, a some-time émigré, went aground on the Arguin Shoals, a hundred and fifty miles off Cape Verde, while on her way to take possession of Sénégal, which was restored to France under the treaties of 1815. One hundred and forty-nine survivors took refuge on an improvised raft. Fifteen were still alive after twelve days without food or water on the tropical ocean. Their terrible experience is well known, being none other than the subject of the celebrated painting by Géricault, *The Raft of the Méduse.*

The council sided with Bonnefoux, being largely under his influence. Thereupon Martin suggested shifting to Royan and embarking in the harbour of Verdon on the *Bayadère,* a sloop-of-war commanded by Lieutenant-Commander Baudin.

"I know Baudin," he said. "He is the one man capable of landing the Emperor safe and sound in America." [9]

Napoleon accepted, and Bonnefoux despatched a messenger to inform Baudin. The latter agreed without a moment's hesitation. He wrote not without nobility: "The Emperor can rely on me. My father died of joy at the news that General Bonaparte had safely returned from Egypt. I should die of grief to see the Emperor leave France if I thought that by staying there he could still be of any service to her. But he can leave France only if he is to go and live in honour in a free country, and not to die as a prisoner of his enemies."

It was the Emperor who shrank. To go away with Baudin seemed to him an extreme resort. Was it worthy of him? The people of Rochefort too had welcomed him with enthusiasm.[10] Would not the return of the Bourbons in the baggage wagons of the foreigner cause a revulsion in national feeling? Might not his star have one final beam of glory to cast? He sparred for time—and in truth won plenty of it. The sixth of July and the seventh passed without a decision. Bonnefoux was in a cold sweat from anxiety, and so was Beker. The Emperor's intimates toyed with romantic schemes, such as embarking on a Danish schooner, the *Magdaline,* commanded by a Frenchman, Besson, who was son-in-law to her Danish owner. They would load her with hogsheads of brandy and, in case of a search, Napoleon could hide in one of them! The Emperor listened phlegmatically and made no comment. Meantime, in order not to miss any chance, Bertrand had Las Cases draw up and sign a contract with Besson in Bonnefoux's presence.

On the evening of the seventh General Beker received a despatch from Paris in answer to his letter from Niort. It was signed by all five members of the Commission. Furious at Napoleon's delays, the Commissioners formally ordered Beker to put him aboard ship.

[9] Beker, *Relation*, pp. 86-7.
[10] "Bonaparte was received at Rochefort like a god" (General Maleyssie to the Comte d'Artois, July 11, 1815, Archives, *Guerre*). His government had carried out enormous public works in the town, giving it a modern sanitation and greatly beautifying it. He was extremely popular there.

"You are," they had the insolence to write, "to use any means of force that may be required, omitting none of the respect owing to him." Respect, as regards forms, but first and foremost, constraint! At the same time the Minister of War informed Beker that he "was ordering the generals in command at La Rochelle and Rochefort to lend him armed assistance and otherwise second him with all the means at their disposal in such measures as he should deem suitable for carrying out the orders of the Government" (July 4, 1815). Nothing could be clearer. If Napoleon resisted, Beker was to take him by the collar! Fouché had dictated the ultimatum, and he added more insolently still: "As regards the services he offers, our duty towards France and our undertakings with foreign powers do not permit us to accept them, and you are not to mention them to us again." [11]

So what they demanded was that Napoleon should embark on a frigate and keep to the harbour, far from any help from France, gazing at the English sails, till Fouché should be able to strike with the enemy or with the Bourbons the bargain he considered most advantageous!

Beker showed his orders, but he laid particular stress on the fact that once Louis XVIII were installed in the Tuileries Napoleon would no longer be safe anywhere on land. As soon as the Governing Commission lapsed he would risk arrest at any moment.

Poor Beker! On that dubious errand he managed to keep up appearances as an honest man. Napoleon understood that.

"But, General," he said to him, smiling, "whatever happens, you would be incapable of handing me over!"

"Your Majesty knows, in fact, that I am ready to give my life to cover your escape. But no sacrifice of myself would save you. The very people who are crowding under your windows every evening would tomorrow be cheering in another sense if the scene happened to change."

"Well," said Napoleon, "order boats for the Isle of Aix!"

There he would be close at hand to the frigates and in a position to board them if the winds, which for days past had been contrary, finally favoured a dash for the open.

He left Rochefort as quietly as possible and reached Fouras. The sea was covered with whitecaps. Napoleon was carried out to the

---

[11] La Commission du Gouvernement au général Beker, Paris, July 4, 1815.

GENERAL GOURGAUD
From a Contemporary Drawing

LAS CASES
From a Portrait of 1817

small boat by a sailor.[12] Crowds thronged the shore—fishermen, retired sailors, former soldiers, peasants who had come in from their
farms. Many wept. Others cheered and waved their caps. Napoleon
looked at them and waved his hand. The boat had difficulty in getting off. The sea was so rough that after more than an hour of it,
finding himself within reach of the *Saale*, that lay at anchor in the
Enet Channel along with the *Méduse*, Napoleon gave orders to
board her.

He was received by Commander Philibert with sovereign honours,
the crew lining the yards and the officers drawn up with unsheathed
swords. No salute was fired in order not to alarm the English vessels. Napoleon chatted with Philibert. He was an officer of merit,
but a Bourbonist through and through. In his Royalist zeal he had
filled all glass windows aboard his ship with panes bearing the fleur-
de-lis.[13] Stunned that his frigate should have been chosen for Napoleon, he had made all the preparations required, but his ill-will
was obvious. The captain of the *Méduse* had been placed under
Philibert's orders. His name was Ponée. He had won all his promotions under fire and was devoted to the Emperor.

. . . . . . . .

Napoleon was settled as comfortably as possible in the Staff
Council room which had been divided in two by a canvas. He took
the larger space for himself and left the other to Beker. Overhearing
the General grumbling at a shortage of linen, Napoleon sent him
some of his own. He must have slept restlessly that night, for at four
o'clock he sent for Gourgaud to ask him which way the wind was
blowing. It had gone down. The sea was calm. Napoleon was anxious
to reach the Isle of Aix, the black outlines of which, ringed here and
there with a ribbon of sand, were plainly visible through his field-
glass. A longboat from the *Saale* took him over in company with
Gourgaud and Las Cases. Beker had not been invited. He rushed
into a boat to catch up with them. The landing was made in English
Cove (*Anse des Anglais*). All the inhabitants of the island were on
the beach, and as he walked towards the village they followed him,
shouting: "To the Army of the Loire!"

Escorted by a number of artillery officers and engineers from the
island corps, Napoleon visited the fortifications and the seawalls that

[12] Silvestre, *Malmaison, Rochefort, Sainte-Hélène*, p. 107.
[13] Aly, p. 128.

he had himself ordered built for the island's defence. He conversed familiarly with the company, discussing the disposition of the batteries with an openness of mind quite unusual in him. He reviewed the 14th Marines who were drawn up in battle array, commanded drill in person and then returned to the longboat escorted by the whole garrison. On board the *Saale* again he found Bonnefoux waiting with two despatches from Decrès. Whether he were to sail on a cutter—if a light boat had more chance of eluding the enemy's blockade, or decided to board a vessel of the English fleet, was a matter of indifference to the provisional government, but under no condition was he to set foot again in France! Whatever might happen the commander of the vessel detailed to transport Napoleon was not to put him ashore at any point on French territory, under pain of high treason.[14]

Napoleon conferred with Beker and Bertrand. At their urgent suggestion he resolved to send Las Cases and Savary under a flag of truce to board the *Bellerophon,* the larger of the two ships that were guarding the thoroughfare. They would deliver a letter from Bertrand enquiring whether the safe-conducts requested of London for the crossing to the United States had arrived. At the same time they would engage the staff in conversation and sound out the attitude of the English government. Las Cases knew English, but he would feign ignorance of it in order to tempt the officers of the *Bellerophon* to speak more freely in his presence.

. . . . . . .

Captain Maitland, a thin, dry, sallow-complexioned man with rumpled hair and large deep-set eyes, received the embassy courteously on board the *Bellerophon.*[15]

He knew nothing, he assured them, of recent events, save that Napoleon had been defeated at Waterloo. He had received no orders regarding the Emperor.

In that he was lying. His chief, Rear-Admiral Hotham, who was

[14] *Arrêté du gouvernement provisoire* (enclosed with Decrès' despatches, Paris, July 6, 1815).

[15] Frederick Lewis Maitland was a Scotchman, born in 1777 of a seagoing family. He had fought at Ushant while still a mere boy and had been chosen by the British Admiralty to blockade that section of coast because of his perfect knowledge of the waters off Rochefort. He had commanded the *Esmeralda* in those same waters in 1809 when the French fleet was attacked by the English and destroyed with fireships. The *Bellerophon* was a ship of 74 guns. She had fought in '98 at Aboukir and also at Trafalgar.

cruising off the south coast of Brittany in Quiberon Bay, had informed him of the abdication:

"I acquaint you . . . that Government received, on the night of the 30th, an application from the rulers of France, for a passport and safe conduct for Buonaparte to America, which has been answered in the negative, and therefore [Government] directs an increase of vigilance to intercept him. . . . The information is very likely to be correct . . . that he has taken the road to Rochefort." [16] At the end of the same despatch, Hotham added: "I depend on your using the best means that can be adopted to intercept the fugitive, on whose captivity the repose of Europe appears to depend. If he should be taken, he is to be brought to me in this bay, as I have orders for his disposal."

These instructions were explicit and Maitland's one concern was to carry them out. Why expect chivalry of this subordinate who was trained to strict obedience of orders? Maitland spoke deceitfully, but why not? Was that not war? And was Bonaparte a man to be spared? He had turned Europe upside down. The Allies had declared him a public enemy and a disturber of the peace of the world. He had to be seized and put once and for all out of the way of doing harm. "The best means," the orders had read. Maitland would find it, and the means that fitted the moment was falsehood! It was necessary, he could say, for Napoleon might still escape him. However Bonnefoux might feel, Maitland was not so sure he could prevent the escape of the French frigates. From that point on the game he should play was clear: He should coddle the hopes of Napoleon's envoys, and meantime ask his chief for reinforcements!

Las Cases was a novice in such matters, and Savary was half a dunce to begin with. They let themselves be trapped by Maitland's affability. He assured them that he would forward Bertrand's letter to the Admiral. He invited them to luncheon. They were still at table when the sloop *Falmouth* drew near and signalled that she had news for the *Bellerophon*. Maitland read the despatches without batting an eyelash. They were from Admiral Hotham: "Quiberon Bay, July 8, 1815: You are directed to . . . make the strictest search of any vessel you may fall in with; and if you should be so fortunate as to intercept him, you are to transfer him and his family to the ship

[16] Dated from the *Superb*, Quiberon Bay, July 7, 1815 (Maitland, *Narrative*, pp. 17-18).

you command, and there keeping him in careful custody, return to the nearest port in England . . . with all possible expedition, and on your arrival you are not to permit any communication whatever with the shore . . . and you will be held responsible for keeping the whole transaction a profound secret." [17]

After luncheon the two Frenchmen were left alone with Maitland and Captain Knight, commander of the *Falmouth*. They resumed their conversation. They declared that Napoleon still disposed of formidable support in the country and that the prolongation of the war depended on him. It was therefore to the interest of England to allow him to depart freely for America.

Maitland assured them that he would report their views to his Admiral and let them know the reply the moment he received one. He actually sat down to write in the presence of his two visitors.

"But is that not to entail some delay?" they asked.

"I cannot help that," said Maitland.

Then Napoleon's envoys (Las Cases seems to have been the spokesman) put three questions to which Maitland made definite replies: [18]

"The Emperor does not contemplate a secret departure, but if the wind should turn favourable before your reply is received, and he should take advantage of it and put to sea with the frigates, what would you do?"

"If the Emperor sails out with the frigates, I shall attack them and take them if I can. In that case the Emperor will be a prisoner of war."

"If, instead of sailing out with the frigates, he were to leave on a French merchant vessel, what would you do?"

"We are at war. I would take the vessel. The Emperor would again be a prisoner of war."

"And if, instead of all that, he were to sail on a neutral vessel— an American ship for instance?"

"I should detain it and apply for instructions to my Admiral."

That was enough to crush any hope of escaping that the two emissaries might have entertained. But Maitland continued talking as he sat writing out his despatches, and in such a way as to engender other false hopes:

"The Emperor is right in asking for passports, in order to avoid

[17] Maitland, *Narrative*, pp. 25-26.
[18] Rovigo, Vol. VIII, p. 221; Las Cases, Vol. I, p. 41; Maitland, p. 32.

any unpleasantness. However, I do not think that our government will let him go to America."

"Where would they suggest that he go?"

"I have no idea, but I am almost certain of what I am saying." And Maitland added, offhand, as an afterthought: "Why should he not ask asylum in England? In that way he would be settling all difficulties." [19]

Las Cases replied that the Emperor had not dwelt on that thought because he feared the effects of a resentment born of so long a war. He thought he could find a more congenial climate in America, with greater comfort and greater freedom.

"It is a mistake," replied Maitland, "to think of the climate in England as so unpleasant and damp. In some counties it is as mild as in France—in Kent for instance. As for the amenities of social life they are incomparably superior in England to anything the Emperor could find in America."

Savary and Las Cases made no answer. They were tempted. Maitland might not be wrong—he seemed sincere at any rate. Exile to England, so near at hand to France, an exile moreover which they expected to share, was less frightening to them than exile to America. Napoleon himself had often thought of it. [20]

"As for any resentments he might fear," Maitland continued, "residence in England would be the best way to extinguish them. Living in the bosom of the nation he would be placed under the protection of its laws."

Las Cases declared that he would report the suggestion to Napoleon.

"In case the Emperor should accept the idea of going to England—and I shall do everything in my power to make it tempting to him—can he count on transport on board your ship?"

As to that Maitland would have to consult the Admiral, but if the Emperor were to ask passage on his ship before a reply was received he would begin by welcoming him.

[19] Maitland, p. 36; Rovigo, Vol. VIII, p. 229.
[20] As early as 1814, while still at Fontainebleau, Napoleon had thought of settling in England. Letter to Caulaincourt, April 11: "I wish that in your conversations with the Minister of Foreign Affairs for England you would sound him and find out whether the English government would see any objection to offering me refuge in England under the guaranties enjoyed by every English citizen and with full and absolute freedom" (Caulaincourt, *Mémoires*, Vol. III, p. 305). Castlereagh, scenting a trap, evaded the question (*Ibid.*, Vol. III, p. 342 and see Appendix, p. 450).

The Frenchmen took their leave and were rowed back to the *Saale*. The *Bellerophon* followed in the wake of their dinghy with all sails set. She dropped anchor in the Basque Roads. Las Cases had spoken of a sailing on a merchant vessel. Maitland did not wish to leave anything to chance!

. . . . . . .

While Napoleon was receiving the report of his envoys, the crews of the two frigates waxed indignant at seeing the Englishman move in so close. Was the Emperor going to be taken like a hare in a sling? Captain Ponée of the *Méduse* asked Montholon to submit a heroic plan of action to the Emperor: [21]

"Tonight, the *Méduse*, sailing ahead of the *Saale*, will surprise the *Bellerophon* in the dark. I shall engage her close aboard, keep alongside her and prevent her from moving. I can hold on for two hours. After that my ship will be in bad condition. But meantime the *Saale* will have gotten out, taking advantage of the offshore breeze that rises every evening. What does the rest of the fleet amount to? A wretched sloop [the *Slaney*] and a cutter [the *Myrmidon*]! That is not going to stop the *Saale*, a first class frigate!"

So the *Méduse* would sacrifice herself to save the Emperor! A bold plan but by no means a mad one—it had chances of succeeding! Napoleon was deeply touched, yet he felt he had no right to send so many brave men to their death. Moreover, and perhaps on the advice of Beker, perhaps again on orders from Bonnefoux, Philibert seemed, after weighing the matter, to have refused to incur a risk which would have brought him glory but also spelled ruin for him in his career. According to the log of the *Saale*, Philibert seems to have at first prepared to fight: "July 10, 9.15 A.M. General quarters, clearing for action." However, the rôle that Philibert played is far from convincing. He had the effrontery to say to Bertrand later in the day that "out of regard for the Emperor he would not consider Ponée's suggesting such a plan as an act of insubordination, but would permit no further talk of it." [22]

That same day newspapers of July 5th were received on board. They reported the capitulation of Paris. Napoleon lost the calm he had forced upon himself, flung the papers violently to the table, and locked himself into his cabin.

[21] Montholon, Vol. I, p. 78; Beker, p. 108.
[22] Montholon, Vol. I, p. 79.

He was again in pain—and in those wretched quarters! As at Waterloo his bladder was causing him unbearable agony. Beker was separated from him by a mere curtain and could often hear him stifling a groan. Pain, physical pain, was clouding his judgment and paralysing his resourcefulness! His strange apathy during those days, which were being wasted while the vise was bringing its jaws closer and closer together upon him, finds its deep-lying reason in that. At least he made up his mind to leave the *Saale*, where he no longer felt secure, for the island of Aix. But meantime he sent General Lallemand down to the Gironde to see whether Captain Baudin of the *Bayadère* were still ready to give him passage.

On the morning of the 12th, with Gourgaud, Bertrand and Beker, he landed on the Isle of Aix. At that moment a heavy cannonading was heard. It was the *Bellerophon* firing with all her batteries in honour of the entrance of the Allies into Paris.

Napoleon went to lodge in a grey house which he himself had ordered built in 1808 for the resident commander.[23] He took a bedroom on the second floor where the windows overlooked the Basque Roads. It was furnished with a walnut bedstead with white curtains, a few mahogany chairs, a three-legged stand covered in green basan. A modest refuge, echoing the constant whistling of the wind and the lapping of the water! There he was to spend his last days in France.

Since he had given up the idea of the frigates, why should he not trust himself to a light vessel that could slip along the shore at night? A number of young officers of the 14th Marines, with Lieutenant Genty at their head, came and put the question to Bertrand.[24] They offered to man two luggers—longboats decked in and with masts—and, with the Emperor and a limited number of his suite, make a try for the high seas. There they would hail the first merchantman they met and, if she could not be bought, she could be forced to change her course and head for the United States.

Oh, the burning enthusiasm, the blind devotion of youth! Deeply touched, Napoleon threw back his head. Through the open window in a cloudless summer's night he could see the harbour stretching out like a burnished shield and reflecting the moon-beams. He rested

[23] Later on the house was bought by Baron Gourgaud and turned into a valuable museum which he eventually presented to the State.
[24] Their names were Doret, Pelletier, Salis and Châteauneuf. Doret was to go to St. Helena with the French mission in 1840.

his weight on his elbow and wondered which way the wind was blowing. Would it fill the sails of flight? He paced up and down in the room, where his shadow trembled in the candlelight, stopping every now and then in front of the narrow mirror in which his fat, yellowed face seemed to bury itself.

The Emperor did not like to disappoint Genty and the young man's comrades. He ordered that the luggers be purchased and armed and his effects put aboard. A part of his company would board them, while he, with Bertrand, Savary, Lallemand and Marchand, would embark on Besson's Danish schooner. The women would remain in France.

The moment the ladies learned of this wise plan a great shout went up. Mme. de Montholon declared that, willy-nilly, she would board the lugger with her husband. Mme. Bertrand stormed, averring that, if she were left behind, she would die.

In the course of that troubled day, July 13, Joseph came to the Isle of Aix. He had chartered an American vessel which was waiting for him below Bordeaux in the estuary of the Gironde. He urged his brother to sail with him. Lallemand meantime came back with a proposal from Royan. The commander of the *Bayadère* was entirely at the service of the Emperor! Better still, Mr. Lee, consul of the United States at Bordeaux, was holding at Napoleon's orders the *Pike*, an American vessel that was about to sail for New York, and was so fast that no warship could overtake her. That was the best means to safety that had so far been offered.

Why did Napoleon fail to take advantage of any of these opportunities? Was it the total eclipse of initiative from which he was suffering? That has been said, though it is not a sufficient answer. Was an unconscious force prompting him to reject all such projects, one after the other, that, in the end, he might find himself forced to adopt the idea that was taking form in his own mind: to ask asylum of the English? Perhaps! But more than anything else he refused because of an obstacle that could not be surmounted: the opposition of General Beker and of the naval prefect, Bonnefoux. If they were to allow Napoleon to return to the mainland in order to reach Royan, they would be making themselves guilty of high treason towards the government in Paris. Beker's *Relation* pictures the dangers that Napoleon would have run in a country that was covered with white flags. He mentioned them to the Emperor, but ın the forefront, as was natural, he placed his orders. Napoleon submitted. He was in one of those attacks of depression where he simply drifted with the tide. He cut Joseph's importunings short, embraced again and again a brother he had loved so well, who had cost him so dearly, and whom he was never to see again—yes, let him get away! Under a new sky, with the millions and the valuables he was carrying away from France, Joseph at least could be happy.

Still left was the flight with Besson and the luggers. Beker not only made no objection to that, but even approved. The opposition came from the Emperor's own company and the moment preparations were begun. There were bitter jealousies and acrimonious disputes. Mme. de Montholon disguised herself as a hussar and climbed aboard one of the tenders. Learning that Napoleon could not take him on board the schooner, Gourgaud went to his poor little bedroom and lectured him as man to man. The Emperor, he said, would have done better to choose England. That would be the nobler alternative. He was not the man to play the adventurer. As he was not making a complete sacrifice, History would blame him one day for abdicating in a moment of cowardice.

Napoleon did not take offence at such language from an aide-de-camp. He argued with him. He too thought he would be well treated in England. But to think of living among one's worst enemies! In the United States, he would at least be free.[25]

"If the Emperor is made prisoner," Gourgaud replied, "he may be maltreated."

"One can always kill oneself."

"No," returned Gourgaud. "Your Majesty cannot do that. At Mont Saint-Jean there was still time. Today it has ceased to be possible. The gambler kills himself. The great man faces adversity."

Napoleon broke him off. The evening before he had thought of rowing out to the English fleet and crying on his arrival:

"Like Themistocles, I refuse to participate in the dismembering of my country. I come to ask asylum of you."

But he could not make up his mind to do that.

Just then a fledgling bird flew in by the open window. In the distance, on a water glazed with rose by the twilight, the *Bellerophon* was lying under full sail.

"It means good luck!" cried Gourgaud, running after the bird

[25] Gourgaud, Vol. I, p. 36.

that was beating its body against the walls. He finally caught it.

"There is enough unhappiness in the world!" said Napoleon. "Set it free!"

Gourgaud obeyed. The sparrow flitted hither and thither about the room.

"Let's watch for omens," suggested the Emperor.

The bird found the window at last and flew away—to the right!

"Sire!" cried Gourgaud. "He went towards the English!" [26]

The Emperor dismissed him—Gourgaud was to go with him! After the evening meal—a sad one—Napoleon's personal effects were loaded aboard the schooner. The rest of the baggage was to go in one of the luggers. Philibert and Ponée had not been taken into the plan. They thought, along with their crews, that the Emperor was going to give himself up to the English.

The preparations were now complete—Besson sent word to that effect. Beker knocked on Napoleon's door, for the Emperor had locked himself into his bedroom.

"Sire, all is ready. The captain is waiting."

Napoleon did not answer. Beker withdrew. On deck in the dark the officers fumed. It was nearly midnight. Further delay might ruin everything. Bertrand in his turn ran up to see the Emperor. As he entered Napoleon said:

"There is always some danger in trusting to one's enemies, but it is better to risk reliance on their sense of honour than be in their hands as a prisoner by law. Tell them that I have decided not to go aboard and that I shall spend the night here." [27]

This time his mind was made up. He had abandoned the idea of flight. Gourgaud's last words undoubtedly had struck him and so had the moans and groans of the women that he could hear through his door. It took a long time, but his decision was now made. He was to hold to it.

.        .        .        .        .        .        .

Napoleon bore no hatred towards England. He had always appreciated English courage, admired English tenacity. At the time of his rupture of the Peace of Amiens, he remarked to Markoff, the Russian minister: "It is with regret, nay with horror, that I turn to war, . . . for, speaking as a European rather than as a Frenchman,

[26] Gourgaud, Vol. I, p. 37.
[27] Marchand Papers, Thiers Library, Masson Material, Carton 22; Beker, p. 117.

I should be just as pained as you if I were to wake up some fine morning and learn that England had ceased to exist." [28] On leaving for Elba he had said to Sir Neil Campbell:

"I have made war on you with all available means, but I have a high respect for your nation. I am convinced that there is more generosity in your government than in any other." [29]

That generosity he had recognized in the treatment accorded to Theodore, to Paoli, and more recently to Lucien. Would it be withheld from him? He thought that he was personally popular, if not with the Tories, at least with the Whigs who, he believed, were still thinking in terms of Fox. He knew, finally, how proud the English were of their tradition of hospitality. He would appeal to that tradition—he would entrust himself of his own accord to the country that for fifteen years had waged an inexorable war upon him and finally encompassed his destruction. A noble act, he thought, worthy of his name and his destiny! It was incredible that England should fail to respond to such a manifestation of trust by a treatment that would do honour to herself and honour to him.

The news, first imparted by Bertrand, was joyously passed along from person to person. Those who had been invited to leave, those who had been told to stay behind, came out of their moods.

At dawn Las Cases and Lallemand boarded the *Bellerophon* for a parley.

"The Emperor," said Las Cases, "is so anxious to forestall any fresh shedding of blood that he will travel to America on a French or British vessel at the choice of the English Cabinet." [30]

"I have no authority," Maitland declared, "to agree to any arrangement of that sort, nor do I believe my government would consent to it, but I think I may venture to receive him into this ship and convey him to England. . . . I cannot enter into any promise as to the reception he may meet with."

Maitland was trying to lure Napoleon, and he sensed, through Las Cases' verbiage, that the decision was imminent. That Maitland was passionately eager to make the capture of Napoleon cannot be questioned. He was to say bluntly to the commander of the *Swiftsure*: "I've got him!" He was above all else a soldier carrying out orders

[28] Madelin, *Vers l'Empire*, p. 354.
[29] Campbell, p. 150.
[30] Maitland, *Narrative*, p. 43; Las Cases, Vol. I, pp. 44, 45.

without worrying as to any further consequences the orders might have. He gave Las Cases to understand, without binding himself by any pledge, that English magnanimity would make the reception more than honourable. At that moment perhaps he may actually have thought so. When Lallemand asked whether the people who were attending the Emperor were in any danger of being handed back to France (in which case Lallemand and Savary would have gone straight to a firing squad), Maitland rejected the idea as "insulting." [31]

Las Cases then said:

"Under those conditions, I imagine you will be seeing the Emperor on board the *Bellerophon*."

The two envoys returned to the Isle of Aix. Napoleon consulted with his companions. Savary, Bertrand, Gourgaud and Las Cases were for surrendering to the English. Montholon still clung to the *Bayadère*, Lallemand to the Danish schooner. The Emperor shook his head. Lallemand then proposed a landing on the mainland with the regiment of Marines and a return to the army. It would be a triumphal march for the Emperor. He could threaten Paris and, if he did not regain power, he could at least dictate terms.[32]

"No," the Emperor concluded. "If it were a question of conquering an empire or of saving one, I might risk another return from Elba. But all I want is quiet. I refuse to have another gun fired on account of me."

He dismissed them—let them stand ready! Since making his scene Gourgaud seemed to have become the favourite. Alone with him, Napoleon drew up the tentative draft of a letter to the Prince Regent of England, dated the evening before, July 12:

"YOUR ROYAL HIGHNESS:

"In view of the factions that divide my country and of the enmity of the greatest powers in Europe I have brought my political career to a close and I am going like Themistocles to seat myself on the hearthstone of the British people. I put myself under the protection of English law and request that protection of Your Royal Highness, as of the most powerful, the most trustworthy, and the most generous, of my enemies.

"Isle of Aix, July 12, 1815.

NAPOLEON." [33]

---

[31] *Narrative*, p. 46; Las Cases, Vol. I, p. 45.

[32] Montholon, Vol. I, p. 86; Mme. de Montholon, p. 42; Rovigo, Vol. VIII, p. 236.

[33] The original text presents some difficulties which are commonly surmounted by appropriate corrections: "*en but*" (in view of) to "*en butte*" (being the target of), *je vais* (I am going) to *je viens* (I am coming), *sur le foyer* (on the hearth) to *au foyer* (at the hearth). As regards "hearth" Napoleon had first written: "ashes,"

On reading those heroic lines Gourgaud broke down and wept. Napoleon told him that he had chosen him to go and deliver the letter to the Regent. He then dictated to him a memorandum of instructions—Gourgaud was to communicate it that very evening to Captain Maitland:

"Gourgaud, my aide-de-camp, will board some vessel of the English fleet with Count de Las Cases. He will sail on the ship which the commander of that fleet will send either to the Admiral or to London. . . . He will seek an audience with the Prince Regent and deliver my letter to him. If there are no objections to issuing passports for the United States of America, that is what I want; but I do not care for passports to any colony. America failing, I prefer England to any other country. I will assume the name of Colonel Muiron or Duroc. If I am to go to England, I desire to be lodged in a country house ten or twelve leagues from London, where I trust to arrive as *incognito* as possible. A fairly large house will be necessary in order to accommodate all my people. If the ministry should be inclined to place a commissioner in my company, Gourgaud will see to it that no suggestion of servitude is implied thereby." [34]

A tacit renunciation of America! Napoleon was resigning himself to living in England. He asked only decent treatment there. He pledged himself to live in seclusion. Between his first projects and this new attitude a progressive and far-reaching disillusionment lies!

Delighted with his mission, Gourgaud took Las Cases with him and hastened aboard the *Bellerophon*. Maitland expressed his admiration for the letter to the Prince, showed it to his officers, and ordered Commander Sartorious of the *Slaney* to transport Gourgaud to England.

There was a second deception in that. Maitland gave Gourgaud to understand that he was to be taken directly to London, but at the same time he was ordering Sartorious to make for the nearest English port, hold Gourgaud on board, and forward Napoleon's letter by his next in command. [35]

Maitland had cabins set in order for the reception of the Emperor

but then replaced the word *cendre* with *foyer*. His original, which was extremely neat, is quite legible. He gave it "to Gourgaud, General of artillery" at St. Helena in 1818, autographing it with his signature.

[34] Rovigo, Vol. VIII, p. 231.

[35] Maitland to the Secretary of the Admiralty from Basques Roads, July 14, 1815 (*Narrative*, p. 57).

and his suite. That evening he had the fright of his life. The English had numerous spies in their pay along the coast. A boat came in from La Rochelle and reported that Napoleon had escaped by way of the Breton Gut. He ran to Las Cases in the greatest excitement:

"Count Las Cases, you have been tricking me! While I am negotiating with you and let one of my boats go, I am told that Napoleon has just escaped. That puts me in a difficult position with my government."

His face betrayed such threatening anger that Las Cases caught the real situation in a flash. He hoped that the report was true. However, he made the best of it and asked:

"What time does your informer say that the Emperor passed La Rochelle?"

"At ten o'clock this forenoon."

"Then do not worry!" said Las Cases, disappointed. "I was with him this evening on the Isle of Aix, at half-past five." [36]

.    .    .    .    .    .    .

It was high time for the Emperor to make up his mind. Louis XVIII had re-entered Paris on July 8. On the 13th, Baron Richard, a sometime regicide, who had just been appointed prefect of the Lower Charente on nomination by Fouché, brought Bonnefoux orders from the new Minister of the Navy, Jaucourt. The naval prefect was to hold Napoleon on board the *Saale* and prevent him from communicating with the English. The idea now was to hand him over to the English as a prisoner of war. [37]

Despite his usual caution Bonnefoux acted as a man of honour. He wrote to Philibert to warn him of the Emperor's danger. Then, to give technical obedience to the King's orders, he had himself rowed out to the *Saale* late at night, though he knew very well that Napoleon was no longer on board that vessel. He then hurried to Rochefort where he assured Richard, and wrote to the Minister, that he had been unable to fulfill his mission, "Buonaparte being already

[36] Las Cases, Vol. I, p. 49.

[37] Archives, *Marine*, BB 3, p. 426: "Paris, July 13, 1815. The commander of the English squadron blockading the roads at Rochefort is authorized to request the commander of the frigate on which Napoleon is quartered to deliver the latter to him without delay. I therefore order you to deliver Napoleon Buonaparte to the English Commander as soon as his request is received. Should you be so criminal or so misled as to resist the orders herewith, you would be considered as in overt mutiny and held responsible for the blood that would then flow and for the destruction of your vessel."

on the way to the *Bellerophon*." In that manner he forestalled an outrage which neither the army nor the people would have forgiven the Restoration.

Did Napoleon sleep that night—his last night on French soil? Lying under the white curtains in that wretched bed, did his breath keep rhythm with the rote of the sea that rang incessantly in his ears? Did he lie sounding past memories or dreaming of his unknown future as the clocks struck the dragging hours?

In any event his sleep was brief. He rose towards midnight and had Marchand help him dress. He again donned a uniform that he had not worn since the last day at Malmaison: the green coat of a colonel of the Chasseurs of the Guard, a sword at his belt, the small hat on his head.

The stars of the summer's night were paling as he left the house. Day was breaking. Those who were to accompany him followed silently behind. A few fishermen from the village, rudely awakened by the commotion, appeared at their doorways, stood there in silence with heavy hearts and saluted in succession as the company passed. Half-past three! The little quay lapped by a calm sea! The tender! A few words murmured in a low voice! The Emperor gazed back at the isle and made a gesture with his hand as if to wave a farewell. The oars rose, then dipped noiselessly into the sea. The sun was just peering over the coastline when the boat drew alongside a little brig, the *Épervier* (The Hawk) which was at a mooring under one of the forts. It was to carry Napoleon to the English! He boarded it with resolute tread. He spoke to some of the men and bit nervously at his lips now and then.

The captain of the brig was Jourdan de la Passardière. Lieutenant Borgnis-Desbordes had been sent from the *Saale* by Philibert to tell Jourdan to hurry. The Emperor was in danger of being arrested at any moment! "Not on the *Épervier*, as long as I am alive!" Jourdan retorted.[38] Jourdan gave the order to weigh anchor. General Beker then stepped up to Napoleon:

"Sire, does Your Majesty wish me to accompany you aboard the *Bellerophon*, in compliance with my instructions from the government?"

"No, General. They would be sure to say that you had handed

[38] Beker, p. 126.

me over to the English. I am boarding their ship of my own volition.
I refuse to allow such a charge to rest on France."

Beker struggled to maintain his calm, but could not.

Napoleon said to him sadly:

"Embrace me, General! I thank you for all the trouble you have
been to. I am sorry I did not know you sooner. I should have
attached you to my staff. Good-bye."

Beker managed to murmur: "Good-bye, sire. May you be happier than we shall be!" [39]

He went down into the tender.

Napoleon remained on deck. Mme. de Montholon sat down beside
him. He did not speak to her for some time. He was aloof, thoughtful. Finally, passing a hand over the sleeve of his coat, he asked:

"Is this green or blue?"

He had always had difficulty in distinguishing colours, but perhaps he may have said that just to seem less impolite. In surprise
Mme. de Montholon replied:

"Green, sire."

He asked for some coffee. It was served to him on the head of a
windlass in a silver cup.[40]

Several times he got up on an ammunition box and, lifting the
field-glass of Austerlitz to his eyes, scanned the whole circle of the
horizon. The tricolour was still floating over Oleron and La Rochelle.
The white flag had not yet ventured to unfurl on the West Coast.

The *Bellerophon* could be seen far offshore with her sails slack,
for the wind was light, the sea flat and shining. The brig was making
but little progress. The sun was getting high in the cloudless sky.
Soon a longboat was sighted, rowing towards the *Épervier*. It came
from Maitland. The Captain's haste is significant. The *Superb*, a
vessel bearing the flag of Admiral Hotham, had appeared in the

[39] *Relation*, p. 127. All the same, on his return to Paris Beker did not forget to ask
for the Grand Cross of the Legion of Honour as a reward for his services as Napoleon's jailor. He was given nothing at first, but in 1819 he was created a Peer of
France, and in 1825 he received the Grand Cordon of St. Louis. Bonnefoux and
Jourdan de la Passardière were removed from their commands. The officers who
had tried to help the Emperor to escape on the luggers were dismissed from the
service. Ponée and Baudin were allowed to resign. Those acts of retaliation prove
the resentment of Louis XVIII's ministers who had planned to get Napoleon physi-
cally into their power. Philibert alone did not lose his command, a significant fact,
when judgment has to be passed on his conduct at Rochefort. He received the
rosette of the Legion of Honour in 1821 and a promotion to the captaincy in 1822.

[40] Silvestre, *Op. cit.*, p. 151; Mme. de Montholon, p. 46.

offing. Maitland hastily despatched the longboat in his eagerness to get Napoleon aboard his ship before the Admiral arrived, that he might have a clear claim to the honour and the reward for capturing the Emperor.[41]

The longboat drew alongside. The executive officer of the *Bellerophon* came on board. He greeted the Emperor in English.

Napoleon looked around. Bertrand and Mme. de Montholon turned deathly pale. The officer lowered his eyes. There was not a sound on the whole deck—a pin-drop could have been heard.

Napoleon broke the anguished tension. He asked the two ladies if they felt inclined to enter the longboat. They nodded.

"Very well! Let us be off!"

The English officer offered his arm to Countess Bertrand. The Emperor's companions followed. The officers and crew of the *Épervier* gathered around Napoleon. He addressed a brief word of thanks to them. Then he went down into the boat.

As soon as he was seated the boat shoved away from the brig. The French sailors, leaning far out over the rail, broke into a long and mighty cheer: "Hurrah for the Emperor! Long live the Emperor!" Napoleon bent over, dipped a hand in the sea, gathered a little water in his palm and sprinkled it on the hull of the *Épervier*. He repeated the gesture three times. A rite of farewell? A funeral aspersion in the classical manner? It may have been nothing more than the instinctive gesture of a soul adrift and headed for the unknown.[42]

Maitland stood watching the boat as it advanced towards his ship. At first he was unable to distinguish the Emperor. He passed his glass about among his officers. Finally they recognized him. They were all a-tremble with excitement. The prey was there, drawing nearer with every dip of the oars!

It was six o'clock when the longboat came alongside. Maitland did not deign to go to the bottom of the ladder to receive Napoleon. Bertrand went up on deck.

"The Emperor is in the boat," he said to the captain.

Maitland appeared not to understand. He waited on the quarter-deck with his staff grouped about him.

Napoleon came up the steps in his turn, panting a little. He passed

[41] *Narrative*, p. 68.
[42] Silvestre, *Op. cit.*, p. 154.

in front of a line of sailors, but they did not present arms. Maitland was to excuse himself for this discourtesy by saying that it was not customary aboard English warships to pay honours before the flag was hoisted. That took place at eight o'clock in the morning.[43]

Napoleon advanced slowly towards the group of British officers. Las Cases came to meet him and called Maitland's name. Napoleon raised his hat and said in a loud distinct tone:

"Commander, I have come to place myself under the protection of your prince and your laws."

Maitland saluted, addressing him as "sir." [44] He led him to the large room on the bridge. The Emperor looked about:

"What a fine room!"

"Such as it is, sir, it is at your service while you remain on board the ship I command." [45]

The Emperor asked to be introduced to the officers, then he visited the whole ship, escorted by Maitland.

At nine o'clock breakfast was announced. Napoleon sat at the commander's table, eating little—the dishes were cold and he was accustomed to having things hot.[46]

The breeze had freshened offshore and the *Superb* gathered speed. She dropped anchor at half-past ten. Maitland took leave of Napoleon and hurried aboard to report to his Admiral.

"Tell him, I beg of you, that I wish to see him."

Hotham came in the afternoon and called on the Emperor. Napoleon showed him his field library and chatted about service in the navy, asking a number of questions to which the Admiral replied in a deferential tone.[47]

---

[43] *Narrative*, p. 69.

[44] No offence was intended. In fact, in imitation of Admiral Hotham, Maitland was soon to begin using the forms *Sire* and *Your Majesty*.

[45] *Narrative*, p. 71. The captain's ante-room served as Napoleon's diningroom. An aide-de-camp slept there every night. Marchand slept in the same room as Napoleon, and Aly just outside, blocking the doorway. Maitland moved to lodgings in the gunroom and was very uncomfortable (Home, p. 165).

[46] That same day Maitland made arrangements for the Emperor to be served according to his regular habits. "From today on," he said, "we shall live *à la française*" (*Narrative*, p. 80).

[47] The Emperor's baggage had been transferred from the *Épervier* to the *Bellerophon*. Several boxes however were forgotten. They were stored at the Navy Building at Rochefort where finally their contents were divided among the employés. Napoleon's coronation cloak happened to be in one of them. It was cut up along the seams and hidden. Remnants of it have kept turning up at public auctions ever since.

Dinner was served at five o'clock, with the Emperor's own plate and by his own people. Napoleon entered the diningroom first and seated himself at the middle of the table, inviting Sir Henry Hotham to take a seat at his right. Countess Bertrand was at his left.

After coffee he rose and led his guests into the large room, where the conversation was friendly and intimate in tone. He retired early after having accepted an invitation to breakfast, the next day, Sunday, on the flagship.

   .     .     .     .     .     .     .

On leaving his room to board the *Superb* the Emperor found a line of soldiers drawn up to do him honour. He stopped, then reviewed them and inspected their arms. With Maitland serving as interpreter, he ordered them to fix bayonets. Finding the movement awkwardly executed he seized a musket and showed, amid general surprise, how the thing was done in the French army.[48]

His entire suite, women and children included, were to go with him. As he was getting into the boat he noted that Las Cases had appeared in naval uniform, as a commander.[49]

"What, Las Cases?" he cried, jesting. "You, a soldier? I have never seen you in uniform!"

"Excuse me, sire! I was a commander in the navy before the Revolution. I have concluded that a uniform gets one more consideration outside one's country. I have gone back to mine."

On the *Superb* the band was playing. A tent, with a large English flag for a ceiling, had been pitched over a considerable section of the deck, and a table set beneath it. Removing his cap, Admiral Hotham greeted Napoleon with the greatest courtesy and deference. He expressed the hope that the Emperor would remain on his vessel. Not wishing to mortify Maitland Napoleon declined the invitation, returning to the *Bellerophon* at noon.[50]

Shortly afterwards the veteran of Aboukir, her old planks groaning under a load of fresh paint, entered the Gut of Antioch on a

[48] G. Home, p. 167; Las Cases, Vol. I, p. 53.
[49] Montholon, Vol. I, p. 92.
[50] Maitland's account settles any question as to the rivalry that immediately arose between himself and the Admiral (*Narrative*, p. 82). Maitland refused to give up his prisoner to Sir Henry and the latter had to be resigned. He simply ordered Maitland to proceed to Torquay. Napoleon made a mistake in not accepting the Admiral's offer. He would have been treated with more consideration on the *Superb* and doubtless Sir Henry Hotham, who had many friends in the Admiralty, would have been a much greater obstacle to deportation plans than his subordinate.

beat to windward. She was followed by the *Myrmidon* on which the less important members of Napoleon's suite had been accommodated.[51] There was so little wind that by sunset the *Bellerophon* had not yet reached open water. Napoleon was seated on deck to starboard and watched the low, grey coast of France grow dim through a drapery of golden mist.

[51] During the forenoon French cutter, *No. 21*, had gone out to the English vessels laden with sheep, vegetables and fruits, that Commander Philibert was sending for the Emperor's voyage.

# III

## "ON BOARD H.M.S. 'BELLEROPHON,' AT SEA"

SAVARY WAS ATTACHED TO NAPOLEON BY MEMORIES OF THE DUC d'Enghien. Bertrand he had known since Egypt and Mme. Bertrand was a distant relative of Josephine. Apart from those three the people about Napoleon at the time of his departure from France had been brought together more or less by chance and were virtually strangers to him. Most of those who started for England in his company had been drawn to him by interests, fears, vague hopes of fortune—and devotion, too, for their motives were compounded of numberless alloys. It was among the subalterns, the humbler folk in particular, that the loyalty shone with the least impurity.

Eldest of all, in fact three years older than Napoleon himself, was Count de Las Cases, a Frenchman of noble birth and ancient lineage.[1] He had been a navy man, then an émigré. Escaping the massacre at Quiberon, he took refuge in London where he published, under the name of Le Sage, an historical atlas that was many times re-printed. Back in France again he rallied to Napoleon's standard in 1806, solicited a post and the cross, but got nothing more than a title as a Baron of the Empire, whereas he was already a Marquis of the Monarchy in his own right. In 1809 he had been named Imperial Chamberlain (a sinecure) and a year later Master of Petitions (Assessor). He was sent on several missions abroad. In 1814 he became a count. The Restoration made him a Councillor of State and—as he was to claim—a captain in the navy. On the Emperor's return from Elba Las Cases rejoined his household and the aftermath of Waterloo found him acting as chamberlain at the Élysée, along with one other similar official, Montholon. He followed to Malmaison and begged Napoleon "not to abandon him in his new fortunes." The Emperor was astonished. He had scarcely noticed this tiny weasel-faced individual with a wrinkled forehead, greying hair and sideburns, and unctuous manners, who was displaying such reckless loyalty at a

[1] Emmanuel-Auguste-Dieudonne-Marius-Joseph, Marquis de Las Cases, born in 1766, in the Château Las Cases in Languedoc.

75

time when so many old friends were either betraying him or keeping out of sight.

"Do you realize whither this may lead for you?" the Emperor asked.

"I have not thought of that," replied Las Cases.[2]

Napoleon seemed to consent and Las Cases began immediate preparations for his departure. He provided himself with funds, hurried off to get his son, Emmanuel, a boy of fifteen, who was at boarding-school. His wife approved of all that. She hoped to join him with her other children when the Emperor finally settled in a new residence.

Las Cases was a man of culture—thoughtful, resourceful, patient. He had travelled, known poverty, met all sorts of people in many different societies. He admired Napoleon and thought that a greater man than he never opened his eyes to the light of this world. He was ready to sacrifice everything for him.

Was he altogether disinterested, one may wonder? No! There is almost always some ulterior motive. Las Cases aimed at linking his name so indissolubly to the hero's tragedy that the two would be forever inseparable. To be the Emperor's historian, the man to collect his thoughts and his phrases and keep the diary of his life—that much glory would repay Las Cases for everything! He was first and foremost a man of letters. He saw himself as the Homer of this new Iliad. That that was his outlook is obvious from the very first. It alone explains his attitude towards Napoleon and his later conduct.

Las Cases was a well-bred man of exquisite manners. Now that adversity should call for tact was all well enough, but the man's exaggerated attentiveness to the Emperor was that of a fawning courtier. His comrades became annoyed. They made fun of his platitudes—they called him "Rapture." They were more annoyed still at the preference the great man was showing him. Ever since they had been aboard the *Bellerophon*, "Rapture" had made himself indispensable to Napoleon at every moment, now giving him the positions on the chart, now reporting conversations with Maitland and with the latter's staff, now acting as his amanuensis. Worst of all, he listened to the chief with all the ears he had. Napoleon had always loved to talk about himself, explain himself, expound his motives. For years past the responsibilities of an empire had held

[2] Las Cases, Vol. I, p. 19.

his tongue in leash; but now that he was at leisure—at a most galling leisure—he had to have someone to confide in. No one was half so good as Las Cases for such a purpose. The adroit question here, the suggestive remark there—Las Cases was a genius at keeping the ball a-rolling!

As a result Napoleon was soon treating this newcomer as an old friend. Is it true that the Emperor fell asleep one day, stretched out full length on deck with his head on Las Cases's knees, as a famous engraving pictures him? The point cannot be decided. We do know that he had long conversations with Las Cases in the privacy of his cabin, that he reviewed with him the considerations that had brought him on board the *Bellerophon*, and dictated a statement of them to him. In the end he authorized him to decorate his captain's uniform with the cross of the Legion of Honour. Where the soul so mean as to say that this doughty sea-dog who went around in the garb of a naval officer had somehow lost touch with the ground-swell so that he paled in visage and vanished from deck the moment the ship began to heel? As a matter of fact, it was a rough passage. The *Bellerophon* pitched and rolled. All the French passengers were sick. The Emperor was the one to stand it best of all.[3]

.    .    .    .    .    .    .

Born July 1, 1783, Charles-Tristan de Montholon was thirty-two years old. A sleek, pleasant face, dark hair, soft eyes, a strong nose over a child's mouth. The high embroidered collar of his uniform won him credit for a force of character that he was far from possessing. His intelligence might have seemed quite ordinary, but he was not lacking in wit in the French manner. He was capable of assiduity and graciousness. His manners were perfect. More extravagant than grasping, always short of cash, ambitious, frivolous, full of schemes, he had the courtier's instinct of a man of the old régime to which, for all of his aberrations, he was still attached by many many ties. His father, who died young, had been First Master of the Hunt to the King's brother. Two of his ancestors had been Chancellors of France. Towards the end of the year 1792, still therefore a lad of nineteen, while sailing on the *Junon* with his step-father, Sémonville, ambassador to Turkey, he had had shore-leave at the port of Ajaccio. There he had lodged in Mme. Bonaparte's house and was treated by her, according to his own story, as one of the

[3] Mme. de Montholon, p. 52.

family. Napoleon, then a lieutenant on furlough, gave him, he alleges, lessons in mathematics and Lucien lessons in Latin.[4] At any rate, not long after that he met Louis and Jerome at school and also Eugene de Beauharnais.[5] Thus placed on the fringes of the Consular Court, he pushed himself forward, served under Championnet, under Augereau, under Macdonald (who became his brother-in-law). Appointed adjutant to Berthier he was promoted to a colonelcy. That was fast going for a youth of twenty-six who had never figured in any striking action.

He left the service for reasons of health. The strain of military life was too much for that handsome young man. Late in 1809 Josephine made him her chamberlain. Shortly, however, the influence of the tireless Sémonville steered him towards diplomacy and he became minister plenipotentiary to the court of Marie-Louise's uncle at Würzburg. Just then an act of folly ruined his career. He became involved in a clandestine marriage with his mistress, Albine-Hélène de Vassal, a woman of fashion who had been too much talked about.[6] From the depths of Russia Napoleon hurled a dismissal at him. Such severity probably overshot the mark of fairness, for the Emperor had frequently shown more indulgence. However, he forced Montholon to "burrow in" in the provinces. Montholon was deeply in debt and found himself in sore straits. A great dearth of generals for the army in 1813 prompted an offer that he should return to his first career. He refused, alleging his wounds and an illness as a pretext. He was willing to accept a sedentary post—command of the Department of the Loire, which, in fact, he took over in March, 1814. In that capacity he raised a corps of national guardsmen and iron workers and conducted a guerilla campaign against the Austrians down to the abdication of the Emperor.

Equal to any occasion Sémonville promptly wormed himself into the good graces of the Bourbons and had Montholon appointed a brigadier general by Louis XVIII. However, he was not given any

[4] Montholon, Vol. I, p. 222.
[5] Mme. de Montholon, p. 13: "Jerome and Louis, as well as Eugene de Beauharnais, were put to school to M. Lemoine, where Charles de Montholon was already a pupil. The young men always kept the school-boy habit of 'thouing' each other."
[6] She had married the Genevan banker, Daniel Roger, a Baron of the Empire, from whom she had one son, the future Count Roger du Nord, an intimate of the Thiers. She divorced Roger, May 26, 1812. Her marriage with Montholon took place at Draveil, the second of July following, under irregular circumstances.

COUNT MONTHOLON
From a Contemporary Engraving

command.[7] We find him again retiring to the country where his wife had a second child.[8] On the return from Elba, he waited for Napoleon in the Forest of Fontainebleau and followed him to Paris. Montholon played no prominent rôle during the Hundred Days. After Waterloo, he dogged the Emperor's footsteps—from devotion, if one will, but more especially from necessity. He realized that he was compromised beyond recall with the King and he had not a penny to his name. He was young, moreover, and not averse to adventure. Nor was his wife, for that matter. He schemed as she directed and saw only through her eyes.

Mme. de Montholon was several years older than her husband. She may once have been pretty. She was so no longer. Her fresh complexion had faded, but she had kept a slender figure, two charming blue eyes and beautiful chestnut-brown hair. A born coquette, tactful, adroit, she had a precious fund of gaiety and endless patience. She never lost her temper, receiving compliments and rebuffs with the same equanimous smile. Determined to cut a figure in the world she must have realized that it would be easier for her to play a prominent part at the court of a dethroned Napoleon than at a real court where her past might embarrass her. She must have been thinking of money too. All Europe, as well as the intimates about Napoleon, supposed that he had amassed a vast treasure which he had carefully hidden away in one place or another under the care of trustworthy agents. Furthermore was not such a man likely at any moment to come to the top again? He had returned from Elba. Why not from some other place? France would be slow in settling down. If Napoleon ever rose to power again, the companions of his bad days could hope for everything. What had the Montholons to lose?

If there was calculation on their part—and it would be naïve to doubt it—the calculation was neither foolhardy nor tactless.

· · · · · · ·

Gaspard Gourgaud was of the same age as Montholon. He had an open, half-swaggering manner, frank, sensitive eyes. He was the

[7] He was under a cloud, accused of having unlawfully taken from the cash-box of the paymaster general of the Loire a sum of 5,970 francs "to be credited against the pay of the troops he commanded" (Masson: *Napoléon à Sainte-Hélène*, p. 118).

[8] Charles François Frédéric, born November 28, 1814. At the time of the departure for Rochefort, this child was left to the care of a friend. His older brother, Charles François Napoléon Tristan, the Montholons took with them. Tristan was born towards the end of 1812. The precise date is unknown.

son of a violinist in the King's choir and nephew to the actor Dugazon. His mother was one of the "trouble-makers" in the service of the Duc de Berry. Graduated at eighteen from the *École Polytechnique,* he rose rapidly in the artillery. After the campaigns in Spain and Austria in 1811 he became orderly to the Emperor. He fought in Russia, was the first to enter the Kremlin, and discovered a mine that the Russians had left there. That made him a Baron of the Empire. Ambitious, greedy for titles and promotions, he was always "on the make," working his fingers to the bone in the swirl of events in which Napoleon's fortunes crumbled. Becoming first equerry, he at last had an adequate salary and grant, but even more to the purpose, direct access to the chief. He was wounded several times and in January, 1814, at the night affair at Brienne, he saved the Emperor's life by killing a Cossack who was rushing upon him.[9] There he was a colonel, and a Commander in the Legion of Honour! In the general stampede that took place after the First Abdication, he ran to the Bourbons, crept under the wing of the Duc de Berry, and through him managed to save his commission. He was one of the first to get to the Tuileries when Napoleon reappeared and by strenuous pulling of wires obtained his pardon. He accompanied the Emperor to Belgium and on the eve of the Abdication got himself appointed brigadier-general and aide-de-camp to the Emperor, Davoust lending himself to that promotion *in extremis.*

Why do we find Gourgaud at Rochefort and at Aix?

He was devoted, passionately devoted, to the Emperor. But neither did he see any other loophole for himself. He believed his career in France ruined, and his very head, according to him, was in danger, for he exaggerated in his own eyes everything that concerned him. He was honesty itself, but restless, impatient, proud, jealous, hotheaded, ill-poised. In spite of ten years of war-making, he was still a child, knowing neither life nor men. For the rest, he had solid qualities—a keen eye, a glib pen. He could draw, and he knew German and Spanish. Among those who followed the Emperor, he had the greatest native intelligence.

. . . . . . .

General Bertrand was forty-two years old in 1815. He had succeeded Duroc as Grand Marshal of the Palace in 1813. He had the

---

[9] Napoleon was to deny this. However there seems to be no doubt about the incident.

face of a middle-aged woman who had for some unexplainable reason taken to side-burns. He was fairly tall—five feet eleven—but bald, skinny, timid. His manner made him seem more insignificant than he really was. Planat de la Faye said of him: [10] "He is a man incapable of any greatness. He is absent-minded and undecided to the last degree."

More of an engineer than a soldier, as an officer diligent but without vision, he had been nevertheless noted, promoted, established, by Napoleon who had found in him, from the days in Egypt, an honest man who could be relied on always to do his duty.

He had arranged for him to marry a protegée of Josephine's—Fanny Dillon, daughter of General Theobald Dillon who had been killed under the Terror during a mutiny at Lille. Irish by name and having lived for a long time in England she was English in tastes, in feeling, and in manner of thinking. Fanny accepted the marriage to the unprepossessing general provided for her—just a plain Count of the Empire moreover—through sheer lack of anything better. She had really been hoping for an Italian or German prince.

"What, sire," she had made bold to chant at the Emperor.

> "*Bertrand, Bertrand,*
> *Singe du pape en son vivant.*"

[Lafontaine's monkey, *Fables*, IX, 4, was named Bertrand.]

"That will do, Fanny!" scolded Napoleon, angry at the disdainful refusal. And with the aid of Josephine, and also a generous dowry, the nuptials had soon been celebrated at Saint-Leu, in Hortense's palace.[11]

Fanny was thirty years old in 1815, overly tall for her thin frame—in fact as tall as her husband, blonde, with a small head, and black sparkling eyes, the effect of which was somewhat spoiled by a large nose. Capricious, impulsive, snobbishly vain over her title and her family connections, she had immediately overawed her husband. He, for his part, was infatuated with her, gave in to her in everything, to the point even of taking an occasional cuff. When by rare chance he ventured to cross her whims she would break into loud cries. She adored pleasures, society, pretty gowns, free spending. During the last years of the Empire she had cut a big figure in Illyria whither

[10] Vol. I, p. 248.
[11] The dowry totaled: 200,000 francs to Bertrand and the domain of La Jonchère; 200,000 francs to Fanny in cash, 50,000 in diamonds, and a trousseau worth 30,000.

Bertrand had been sent as governor. After the first Abdication they had gone to Elba, he immediately, she at her leisure, and in half a pet. There she had deported herself like a spoiled child. The Emperor put up with her. She dreamed only of Paris. With all that she was honest and she was loyal. She followed Napoleon and her husband without complaining too much. She had thrown her whole soul—and in such a wretched circle of councillors her influence had counted—into persuading the Emperor to ask hospitality of England. She had harped on the sportsmanlike spirit of the English and never doubted their good faith. The fact was, she already saw herself settled in the country near London with her children, receiving relatives and friends from among the English gentry and spending gay week-ends at their manor-houses.[12]

The Emperor's escort was made up in addition of a dozen or more army men—Generals Savary and Lallemand, Majors Planat de la Faye, Résigny, Schultz, and a queer Pole—Piontkowski, three lieutenants, a page (Sainte-Catherine), and a physician (Maingault). Finally came a very large retinue of servants, sixty souls at least, who were lodged more or less haphazard in nooks and corners about the *Bellerophon* and the *Myrmidon*.

.        .        .        .        .        .        .

Napoleon systematized his life on board from the very first day. He breakfasted alone and spent the forenoon in his room. Towards one o'clock he had himself dressed and came on deck, where he walked and talked with the captain, with Dr. O'Meara, a jovial young Irishman, with Las Cases, or his French generals. When he appeared all hats were removed. No one approached him save hat in hand. Often he would sit on a gun-carriage that Maitland had had set in a shady spot on deck and hold a book which, however, he did not read.

The ship made slow progress in view of the heavy swell and light variable winds. Admiral Hotham, besides, had ordered Maitland to be in no hurry in order to give the British government time to decide on Napoleon's fate. The *Bellerophon* did not pass Ushant till the 23rd.

It was scarcely daylight and a mist hung over the sea. To the

[12] Such were the illusions among the French that one of the Emperor's suite asked Maitland during the voyage whether he thought the Prince Regent would confer the Order of the Garter on him (Maitland, *Narrative*, p. 180).

astonishment of the watch the Emperor came out of his room and walked astern. He asked the officer on duty, Midshipman Home, whether the coast that could be glimpsed through clear spots in the haze were Ushant.[13] He took a glass and looked at it. Bertrand and some English officers stood behind him, motionless. Did he have a presentiment that he would never see French soil again? He stood watching the land for several hours. When the coast finally disappeared he turned from the rail, his hand covering his face, and almost fell into the arms of Bertrand, who supported him to his cabin.[14]

Once in the Channel the ship had better wind. At every other moment now new sails were appearing. By evening the white cliffs of England were in sight. The next day, the 24th, at eight o'clock, the *Bellerophon* dropped anchor in Tor Bay.

There they found strict orders. No one was to go ashore. Soon Gourgaud came up armed with the letter to the Prince Regent which he had not been permitted to take to London.[15] He had provided himself with English newspapers that were eagerly discussing the place where Napoleon should be held captive—the Tower, Dumbarton Castle, Fort St. George in Scotland, or even the island of St. Helena, in the remote Atlantic. At Tor Bay, Las Cases received a letter from Lady Clavering, a woman of French extraction who had been a friend of his in days when she was still a milliner. The letter indicated the probability of that last suggestion.[16]

As Wellington himself has admitted [17] the idea of an internment at St. Helena was of ancient date. The conspirators of 1800 who had tried to kidnap the First Consul had planned in their day to deport him thither; and the name of St. Helena had already been mentioned at the Congress of Vienna which was alarmed at seeing Napoleon so close to Italy.[18] Paris, it seems, after Waterloo, first thought of a confinement somewhere in Europe. Metternich wrote to Marie-Louise, July 18, 1815: "According to an arrangement that has been agreed upon between the Powers, he will be established as a prisoner in Fort

[13] Home, p. 271. Home offered his arm to the Emperor so that the latter would not slip on the freshly washed deck.
[14] Home, p. 173; Maitland, p. 109.
[15] He had given a copy of it to Sartorius, who sent it on to the government.
[16] Montholon, Vol. I, p. 102.
[17] Stanhope, *Conversations with the Duke of Wellington*, p. 105.
[18] Bausset, *Mémoires*, Vol. III, p. 56: "The suggestion most generally repeated at Vienna was that Napoleon should be sent to St. Helena." Talleyrand, on October 13, had proposed one of the Azores (*Correspondance inédites*, p. 171).

St. George, in Scotland, and placed under the surveillance of Austrian, Russian, French and Prussian Commissioners. He will enjoy excellent treatment there and all the liberty compatible with the most complete certainty that he will not escape." [19]

But England had other views. If Napoleon were caught and Louis XVIII could not muster the courage to have him tried as a traitor, she was ready to appoint herself his jailor in the name of the Allies. She advocated a deportation far abroad on July 15: "The best place," Liverpool wrote to Castlereagh, "would be one far removed from Europe. The Cape of Good Hope or St. Helena would seem to serve the purpose best."

St. Helena! Did the name arouse any earlier echoes in Napoleon's mind? There is little likelihood of such a thing. Yet, in 1788, at Auxonne, at a time when he was poor and a schoolboy, in making some notes in a copybook on English possessions about the world, he had written: "St. Helena, a small island." After those four words in which he was unconsciously noting the goal of his career, he had left, perhaps because interrupted, a blank page!

St. Helena! After Maitland's assurances Napoleon could not believe such treachery possible. He could see Tor Bay covered with boats from which enthusiastic English admirers kept cheering him. The sudden shift of feeling from hatred to infatuation worried the British Cabinet. For that matter they had foreseen as much. Therefore, as early as the 20th of July, Lord Liverpool, the Premier, came out for an internment south of the Equator. He was agitated, furthermore, by another fear, that Napoleon might obtain from some judge or other a writ of *habeas corpus* that would guarantee his freedom on English soil until such time as he should appear before a tribunal.

Liverpool wrote to Castlereagh, July 20, 1816: "We are all decidedly of opinion that it would not answer to confine him in this country. Very nice legal questions might arise upon the subject, which would be particularly embarrassing. But, independent of these considerations, you know enough of the feelings of people in this country not to doubt he would become an object of curiosity immediately, and possibly of compassion, in the course of a few months; and the circumstance of his being here, or indeed anywhere in Europe, would contribute to keep up a certain degree of ferment in France."

[19] Octave Aubry, *La trahison de Marie-Louise*, p. 40.

The rest of the letter condenses into a few lines all the reasons that determined the choice of St. Helena by the English Cabinet. "Since I wrote to you last, Lord Melville and myself have conversed with Mr. Barrow on the subject, and he decidedly recommends St. Helena as the place in the world the best calculated for the confinement of such a person. There is a very fine citadel there, in which he might reside. The situation is particularly healthy. There is only one place in the circuit of the island where ships can anchor, and we have the power of excluding neutral vessels altogether, if we should think it necessary. At such a distance and in such a place all intrigue would be impossible; and being withdrawn so far from the European world, he would very soon be forgotten." [20]

To be on the safe side the Cabinet ordered the *Bellerophon* transferred to the naval station at Plymouth, pending negotiations with the Allies to secure their consent to Napoleon's deportation. The ministry had so little doubt of the docility of the Allies that on the 25th Lord Bathurst, Minister of War and the Colonies, conferred with the directors of the East India Company which owned St. Helena, so that the island might be placed under full control of the Crown for the period of Napoleon's detention.

At Plymouth armed cutters were stationed as sentries around the *Bellerophon* and two frigates, the *Liffay* and the *Eurotas*, were moored near by. The Emperor and his friends saw a bad omen in all these precautions. One by one their illusions faded. Maitland went ashore and came back very glum.[21] His silence was more disquieting than anything he said. The next day, the 27th, he had all the officers who were not attached to the Emperor's personal service transferred to the *Liffay*. Finally Keith, the Lord High Admiral of the British Navy, appeared.[22] Napoleon had asked to see him the moment he arrived in Plymouth. The Admiral apologized for the two days' delay—he had not yet received orders from London.[23] A handsome old man of great distinction, he was grateful to Napoleon for the care he had personally bestowed on his nephew, Captain Elphinstone,

[20] Castlereagh, *Letters and Despatches*, Vol. X, p. 434.
[21] Montholon, Vol. I, p. 104.
[22] George Elphinstone, Lord Keith, 1746-1823, had had a brilliant career. He had seized Capetown and Minorca and in 1800 had forced Massena to capitulate at Genoa. He had been Lord High Admiral since 1812. He was one of the most popular men in the United Kingdom.
[23] Maitland, p. 134.

who had been wounded at Waterloo. He would have liked nothing better than to be of service to him. He had written to Maitland the moment the *Bellerophon* arrived at Tor Bay: "I should be happy to know of anything that might be agreeable to him, and I should speedily meet his wishes." [24] However, he kept within the limits of formality and his visit was brief. Not long afterwards a number of ships carrying wounded French soldiers who had been taken prisoner at Waterloo entered the harbour. Their presence was kept secret from the Emperor.[25]

Savary, by means unknown, had got in touch with the great English jurist, Sir Samuel Romilly, who sent him a note as to the sort of warrant that could be served on the Admiral in order to oblige him to allow Napoleon to go ashore. His advice was followed. Lord Keith was pursued for an entire day about the fleet by a process-server bearing the warrant.[26] That was why Lord Keith ordered Maitland to "keep off all boats whatsoever" and Maitland obeyed strictly. His own wife came out in a rowboat, but was not allowed to board the *Bellerophon*. Catching sight of her from the deck, Napoleon found her "pretty," and sent her several bottles of French wine, which the Customs pitilessly confiscated.

Long days of anxiety! That broad roadstead was open to the sea and the *Bellerophon* rolled on the incoming swells and strained at her moorings. As at Tor Bay the water was covered with boats of every description, that were loaded and overloaded with curiosity seekers and admirers who tried by every conceivable means to approach the *Bellerophon*.[27] The guarding cutters made their rounds regardless of accidents. At night they even fired on imprudent sightseers. Napoleon complained to Maitland in that regard: "It worries me and grieves me," he said. "I should be obliged if you could put a stop to it." The practice was ordered discontinued forthwith.[28] Standing up in the boats one could see men with red carnations in their buttonholes, gaily dressed women and even children, who cheered and waved their handkerchiefs whenever the silhouette of "Boney," lean-

24 Rovigo, Vol. VIII, p. 244.
25 Mme. de Montholon, p. 52.
26 Rovigo, Vol. VIII, p. 251.
27 Boats rented for as high as sixty pounds. "They were so numerous," says Rovigo (Vol. VII, p. 245), "that they gradually crowded the police cutters against the sides of the *Bellerophon*."
28 *Narrative*, p. 129.

ing on the arm of a general, stood out against the sky, with his conspicuous paunch and a frock-coat that was too tight, so that it spread
its tails. "He reminded one," wrote one such spectator, "of a fat
pigeon." "The sailors of the *Bellerophon*," says Norwood Young,[29]
"exposed a blackboard on which Napoleon's occupation at the time
was written in chalk: 'At breakfast,' 'In the cabin,' 'Dictating to his
officers,' 'At dinner,' 'Coming on deck.' " He seldom appeared before
five o'clock, remaining until then either closeted in his bedroom or
walking back and forth across the poop behind the stern portholes.
He read a great deal. Sometimes he would snatch a nap, stretching out
full length on a sofa. He seemed indifferent to everything.

The newspapers provided by Maitland confirmed the report that
the place of detention chosen for Napoleon would be St. Helena.
His companions lost their heads like wild birds caught in a cage. Some
of them forgot themselves completely. Montholon overheard from a
privy a conversation between Mme. Bertrand and Maitland in the
latter's cabin. She told him (the incident is reported by Gourgaud)
that the Emperor was expecting to be deported. "Since he was a
monster of selfishness who would see wife and children perish without a twinge of emotion," she implored the captain to so arrange that
the list of persons who were to accompany Napoleon should be
drawn up by the Admiralty itself and that it should not include her
husband. Montholon, Gourgaud and Lallemand were outraged at this
attitude and protested to Maitland. Sensing that she had been discovered, Mme. Bertrand had an attack of hysterics after dinner.[30]

. . . . . . . .

At eleven o'clock on the 31st, Lord Keith and Sir Henry Bunbury,
Under-Secretary of State, boarded the *Bellerophon* and were led to
the Emperor's apartment. He received them standing, in the presence
of Bertrand. Giving him for the first time the title of "General" and
not that of "Emperor" [England having never "recognized" the Em-
pire], they informed him of the decision of the Ministry.[31]

[29] Vol. I, p. 55.
[30] Gourgaud, July 29, 1816, Thiers Library, Carton 18. Unpublished.
[31] The final protocol was not to be signed by the Allies until August 2 at Paris.
It gave England a free hand, and there was not even a discussion.
"Article 1. Napoleon Buonaparte is considered by the Powers who have signed
the Treaty of the 25th of March last, as their prisoner. Article 2. His custody is
especially entrusted to the British government. Article 3. The Imperial Courts of
Austria and of Russia, and the Royal Court of Prussia, are to appoint Commissioners
to proceed to and abide at the place which the Government of his Britannic Majesty

Not even a notification addressed to Napoleon! Just a routine letter from Viscount Melville, First Lord of the Admiralty, to Lord Keith, which Sir Henry read aloud in a French translation that was scribbled on a piece of paper:

"As it may be convenient to General Buonaparte that he should be apprized, without further delay, of the intentions of the British Government respecting him, your lordship is at liberty to communicate to him the information contained in this letter.

"It would be inconsistent with our duty to this country and to his Majesty's Allies, if we were to leave to General Buonaparte the means or opportunity of again disturbing the peace of Europe, and renewing all the calamities of war: it is therefore unavoidable that he should be restrained in his personal liberty to whatever extent may be necessary to secure our first and paramount object.

"The island of St. Helena has been selected for his future residence. The climate is healthy, and its local situation will admit of his being treated with more indulgence than would be compatible with adequate security elsewhere."

Napoleon listened to this "information" without interrupting and without moving a muscle of his face. Bunbury wrote, July 3, 1815: "The general expression of his physiognomy was earnest, almost melancholy, but he did not allow any trace of ill-temper or violent passion to manifest itself."

Himself calm and collected, Bunbury continued:

"Of the persons who have been brought to England with General Buonaparte, he will be allowed to select (with the exception of Generals Savary and L'Allemand) three officers, who, together with his surgeon, will be permitted to accompany him to St. Helena. Twelve domestics, including the servants of the officers, will also be allowed. It must be distinctly understood that all those individuals will be liable to restraint during their attendance upon him and their residence at St. Helena, and they will not be permitted to withdraw from thence without the sanction of the British government.

"Rear Admiral Sir George Cockburn, who is appointed to the chief command at the Cape of Good Hope and the adjacent seas, will con-

shall have assigned for the residence of Napoleon Buonaparte, and who, without being responsible for his custody, will assure themselves of his presence. Article 4. His Most Christian Majesty is to be invited . . . to send in like manner a French Commissioner."

vey General Buonaparte and his attendants to St. Helena. . . ."[32]

He was silent. Then Napoleon's voice rose:

"From the time when, of my own accord, I was received on the *Bellerophon*, I have been under the protection of the laws of your country. The government is violating the sacred right of hospitality in respect to me. I appeal from their decision to British honour."

Lord Keith, embarrassed, almost ashamed, requested Napoleon to formulate his protest in writing. He would transmit it to the Regent's ministers.

He saluted and walked out of the cabin. Meeting Mme. de Montholon and Mme. Bertrand in the ante-room he announced to them, in bad French, the deportation to St. Helena. They raged, indignant. He tried to calm them, then finding that a hopeless task, returned with Sir Henry to his boat.

Napoleon called for his principal officers. Crowded together in his room, they listened to a reading of the decree. The fact that Lallemand and Savary were barred seemed to indicate the scaffold for them. They stormed vehemently. The Emperor declared that he would not consent to be transported to St. Helena.

"That," he said, "would be to die in an ignoble manner."

"Yes, sire," exclaimed Gourgaud, "ignoble indeed! Better let ourselves be killed defending ourselves. Better blow up the magazine!"

A few other voices rose with his.

Napoleon dismissed them all except Bertrand.

Lallemand and Savary hurried off to write to Lord Keith and the Ministry to appeal to the promise they said Maitland had made to them that they would find an inviolable asylum under the English flag. Cornered by them Maitland gave them his confirmation without reflecting that what was valid for them was also valid for the Emperor.[33]

Napoleon had doubtless made up his mind to show a soul superior to misfortune. But for a brief instant that resolve wavered. After all he was a man, and it was as a man that he complained to the person in whose hands he had placed himself in the hope of generous treatment.

[32] Castlereagh, *Letters and Despatches*, Vol. X, pp. 444-45.
[33] Rovigo, Vol. VIII, p. 270. Maitland did take up the matter with Lord Melville and Sir Henry Bunbury and the step had its effect. Savary and Lallemand were deported to Malta with other officers not authorized to follow Napoleon. They were freed in April, 1816.

"St. Helena!" he said to Maitland. "The very idea fills me with horror. To be relegated for life to an island within the tropics, at a vast distance from any continent, cut off from all communication with the world and from all that it holds that is dear to my heart! That is worse than the iron cage of Tamberlaine! I should rather be handed over to the Bourbons!"

After alluding to the insult they had offered him in addressing him as "General," he added:

"Exile me there! It would have been better to sign my death-warrant at once. It is impossible that a man of my temperament and my habits should have long to live in such a climate." [34]

Nevertheless he appeared on deck at the accustomed hour. Going below to his cabin again he sent for Marchand.

When Marchand entered, the red silk curtains were drawn over the ports, allowing only a gleam of reddish light to enter the cabin. Napoleon undressed and lay down. Then he asked the young man to read Plutarch's *Life of Cato* to him—it was lying on the table. Marchand obeyed, terror-stricken. As the sentences passed his lips, he kept wondering what the Emperor was doing behind his curtains. He knew that Napoleon always carried poison on his person. Was he going to kill himself to escape such ignominious treatment? The young man's anguish was so real for a moment that he halted.

"Read on!" ordered the voice behind the curtains.

Marchand read on. He read for half an hour, ending with the death of Cato. When he had finished, Napoleon rose quietly and slipped on his bathrobe.[35]

He was the only one to maintain such calm. Everything was fear, anger, confusion about him. Las Cases could legitimately consider himself in large part responsible for the Emperor's boarding the *Bellerophon*. He seemed to be in utter despair. Mme. Bertrand was vociferating and cursing the Regent's ministers now in French, now in English. Lallemand, Montholon and Gourgaud tried to bully Maitland, and through him Keith, with the idea that Napoleon might kill himself.

"You can count on it!" they assured him. "The Emperor will never go to St. Helena—he will kill himself first. He is a man of determination and he will do whatever he says."

[34] Maitland, *Narrative*, pp. 144-45.
[35] Marchand, Thiers Library, Carton 22. Unpublished.

"Has he ever said that he would kill himself?" asked the Commander, unruffled.

"No, but he has said that he would not go to St. Helena. It means the same thing."

And they added—in vague threat:

"If he should consent to go there are three of us here who have resolved to prevent him." [36]

Everyone was so excited at the time that Maitland understood that the three generals were threatening to assassinate Napoleon if he should give in. He replied that "England had plenty of rope." His listeners did not seem to understand him.

After these explosions a certain amount of good sense returned. What was this St. Helena after all? And the Frenchmen began poring over all the maps they could find. To their questioning the sailors replied that it was a paradise. Las Cases, a geographer, had seen flattering descriptions of it. He did not give them the lie. The mountains were covered with beautiful trees. The valleys were rich in all sorts of vegetables and fruits that flourished from an abundant watering. Live stock, game, and fowl abounded. The sea was full of fish. No wild beasts or reptiles! The only annoying animals were rats. In a word, a delightful place to live in!

But in Napoleon's circle of intimates there were several who felt no desire to make its acquaintance. The physician, Maingault, declined without a blush. Bertrand had been shaken by his wife who wanted to live in England. He beat about the bush. Napoleon said to him: "I want to take you with me not for my sake, but for yours. If you leave me now you will lose the prestige you won at Elba." [37] At bottom the Emperor thought that Bertrand, the only Grand Officer of the Crown to accompany him to Plymouth, would be indispensable to him in his exile in helping him to keep up appearances as a sovereign. Mme. Bertrand had secretly written to the ministers to beg them to prevent her husband from following Bonaparte, assuring them that he was doing so only out of a sense of honour and to his great regret. Her excuse was that she had lost a child at Elba and feared for the health of the children she had left. Tossing all shame aside, she forced Napoleon's door in the late afternoon, and, stammering, almost threatening, her brilliant eyes swimming in

[36] Maitland, p. 154.
[37] Mme. de Montholon, p. 60.

tears, she implored him not to take Bertrand with him. The Emperor was dictating some note or other to Las Cases at the time. He listened to her in astonishment, then replied dryly that if the Grand Marshal chose to share his exile he was free to do as he pleased. The fury then rushed to her own cabin and, after more hysterics in the presence of Bertrand and Mme. de Montholon, tried to throw herself into the sea through an open porthole. Bertrand seized her around the waist and held her. Savary was watching the scene from on deck and cried out to the Grand Marshal, laughing:

"Let her go, man! Let her go!"

He detested Mme. Bertrand. Too outspoken in her chatter, she had once said that Savary had "fastened a lantern to d'Enghien's chest." The Duke of Rovigo had never forgiven her.[38]

Bertrand was too loyal an officer to follow his wife's advice. Despite her violence, it was the Countess who yielded. The Grand Marshal promised to remain away from Europe for a year only.[39] In the days following, Mme. Bertrand again made several scenes and in public. She went so far as to say to her husband that "it was easy to see that he was not a gentleman." That Captain Maitland should have reported these trifles to Napoleon speaks for itself.[40]

The Emperor could still say, even to the plain-spoken Gourgaud, that he would not go to St. Helena. Actually he was almost resigned to it. A born realist, he was already acting and planning, mentally debating the best choice of officers to take with him. Las Cases was translating the newspapers to him. He interrupted to ask what their occupations might be "in that lost spot."

"Sire," replied Las Cases gaily, "we shall live on the past. Do we not enjoy the lives of Caesar and Alexander? We shall have better than that: You will re-read yourself!"

[38] Mme. de Montholon, p. 63.

[39] Mme. Bertrand wrote to her cousin, Lord Dillon: "We shall spend a year at St. Helena. After that I shall come back to England with my husband and my three children." Retranslated.

[40] Gourgaud, Vol. I, p. 47. In his *Narrative*, pp. 157-59, Maitland states that having gone to enquire for Mme. Bertrand's health after her attempt at suicide and finding her in bed, he ventured on some reproach. The excited woman immediately sat up in bed, shouting: "I am in despair. I don't know what I am doing any more. I cannot persuade my husband to stay here." She then loosed a flood of insults against Napoleon: "So long as he gets what he wants he does not care what becomes of others. He gave Bertrand lucrative and distinguished posts, but the expenses they entailed prevented us from saving anything. He never offered him any land or anything that could improve our fortunes permanently." And she dared to add: "We owe him nothing."

"Of course!" answered Napoleon. "We shall write our memoirs! Yes, we shall have to work. Work moreover is a scythe to Time. After all, one must fulfil one's destiny—that is my great principle! Let mine be accomplished!" [41]

He had assumed, Las Cases relates, "a carefree, even a gay air. The mere idea that he would not be entirely idle gave him comfort."

On August 4th Maitland received orders to leave harbour and cruise off Start Point till the *Northumberland*, which was being fitted out in all haste at Portsmouth, should arrive to carry Napoleon to St. Helena. The *Bellerophon* had seemed too old a vessel and too slow a sailer for that purpose. Lord Liverpool and his colleagues were more and more worried by the increasing crowds at Plymouth. "Boney," so long a bugaboo, was becoming a lion! Officers and sailors on the *Bellerophon* were already taking his part openly. A little longer and he would have all England for him from the lowest commoner to the Prince Regent. Such was the opinion of Lord Keith. "Damn the fellow!" he said, "if he had obtained an interview with His Royal Highness, in half an hour they would have been the best friends in England." [42] On August 3, Liverpool wrote to Castlereagh: "Buonaparte is giving us great trouble at Plymouth. We have been obliged to order the ship by telegraph to cruise at sea until the *Northumberland* can come round."

Maitland set sail in very rough weather. All his passengers fell sick. The *Tonnant* and the *Eurotas* served as escorts for the *Bellerophon*.

During the day of the 5th, Napoleon sent Keith the immortal page, the echo of which was to sound all over Europe in successive waves and touch many hearts that had of yore been hostile or indifferent! [43]

"I protest solemnly, here, before heaven and men, against the violence that is being done me, against the violation of my most sacred rights, in disposing by force of my person and of my liberty. I am not the prisoner, but the guest, of England. . . . If the government, in ordering the captain of the *Bellerophon* to receive me, as well as my suite, desired only to set a trap, it has forfeited its honour and sullied its flag. . . .

"I appeal to history. History will say that an enemy who waged war

[41] Las Cases, Vol. I, pp. 83-4.
[42] Maitland, p. 211.
[43] Las Cases, Vol. I, p. 86, claims to have been the author of the document. He seems however to have made only a tentative draught which Napoleon corrected and then dictated to him. The Emperor's style is apparent in it in several places, to say nothing of the "immense" heading, which stirred Chateaubriand so deeply: "On Board the *Bellerophon*, at Sea."

for twenty years against the English people came of his own free will, in his misfortune, to seek asylum under her laws. What more striking proof could he give of his esteem and his trust? But what reply was made in England to such magnanimity? There was a pretence of extending a hospitable hand to that enemy, and when he had yielded himself up in good faith, he was sacrificed.

"NAPOLEON.<br/>
"On Board the Bellerophon, at Sea."

Napoleon had no hopes that this appeal, which still, after more than a century, has such an earnest ring, would intimidate Liverpool and his acolytes. He received an official reply two days later. On August 7th, Keith sent him the following letter: [44]

His Majesty's Ship Tonnant<br/>
7th August 1815

"SIR,

I have received by the Count of Las Cases the letter which you have done me the honour to address to me, and I beg to assure you that I lost no time in forwarding to my government the Protest you refer to.

The order for your removal from the *Bellerophon* is imperative and as an officer I am bound to obey it. I have Captain Maitland's letters before me, by which it appears that nothing like a promise or what could possibly be construed into a promise was made on his part, but on the contrary a simple offer of good treatment and being carried to England, and I am happy in thinking both these objects have been fulfilled with all possible kindness and attention.

The orders respecting your Property are addressed to Rear Admiral Sir George Cockburn, and as they appear reasonable and are only calculated to prevent an improper use of an excessive sum, I am sure they will be executed with all possible delicacy.

Of the laws, I am not able to judge. My habits are of a different nature. . . . It is true that I have said in the interviews that I have had the honour to hold with you that it was a painful duty to communicate anything of a disagreeable nature to anyone; and I hope you will do me the justice to believe it true, but still I am to perform the duties of my situation.

I have the honour to be, Sir, your most obedient humble servant,

KEITH, *Admiral*."

The men who were then in power in England were too mediocre to understand that in the great hours of history the only policy that is wise, far-sighted, irreproachable, skilful, is a policy of generosity. That they had very good reasons for making it impossible for Napoleon to attempt another return to the offensive, no man of good

---

[44] Thiers Library, Masson material, Carton 2. Retranslated.

faith would deny. Twice he had threatened England with an invasion which, had he set foot on the cliffs of Dover, she could not have withstood. The London triumvirate, Liverpool, Castlereagh and Bathurst, did not forget that. Much less could they forget that the war that Pitt had begun and that Wellington had ended had pushed their country to the brink of ruin. Had Waterloo resulted in a French victory, England, at the end of her resources, would have been bankrupt and seen herself driven back to the wall into a ruinous peace. They intended therefore to make an end of the terrible Corsican. He had come back from the island of Elba. He would have come back from America. He would never come back from St. Helena, a lost island beyond the Equator, two months distant on a sailing ship, and which, being masters of the sea, they would be able to guard.

The English oligarchs of 1815—to make certain of the point one has only to re-read the novels of Disraeli—had neither far-sightedness nor lofty courage. They had only vanity, jealousy, hatred, a brutal selfishness. Shall we again accuse them of treachery as it was long the fashion to do? No! The British government had promised nothing to Napoleon. If Maitland went too far in his conversations with Las Cases, and later with the Emperor himself, he had no authority to pledge his chiefs, and the French were by no means unaware of that. All the same, before their people, before the world, the members of the Liverpool Cabinet will always remain guilty of transforming the refuge which a heroic confidence asked of them into a prison.

England may well have issued from the terrible struggle bruised, impoverished, bloodless, licking her wounds. But she issued from it mistress of a Europe that obeyed her orders and bowed to her money. She should have sheltered Napoleon and bound him with a tie that nothing could have broken, the tie of a reception worthy of him and worthy of her, that would have balmed misfortune and paid tribute to glory. A group of faltering politicians forced upon her at that time a false-face which so great a people did not deserve to wear.[45]

One can further grant that those Englishmen who were thinking in terms of a narrow patriotism had a right to send Napoleon to a safe distance. But in that case they should have treated him as a sovereign

[45] No one has been more severe on the English ministers of that time than Lord Rosebery, whose book, *Napoleon, the Last Phase*, is an admirable example of impartiality and penetration. He writes, p. 65: "Fortunately, though no thanks to our ministers, we are spared the memory of their having handed over Napoleon to the French government to be shot like Ney."

even at St. Helena. To have seen in him nothing but a mere convict—that was their great sin, a sin which the most honest of their countrymen were laying to their charge even at the time the Emperor received his sentence, and which, after these many years, weighing all necessities and causes, a calm, unprejudiced History cannot pardon them.

In his protest Napoleon reached over the head of the English Cabinet which he had come to despise and from which he had ceased to expect anything. He was addressing Europe, the world which he was eager to move, the future from which he expected everything. As for himself, he was ready to suffer the penalty for his too great power, for having stamped rough-shod on the mole-hills of the Kings.

.        .        .        .        .        .        .        .

At Start Point the sea was rougher still—the Emperor succumbed to it. All those days he remained locked up in his apartment, appearing neither for luncheon nor for dinner. The little he ate was prepared by Marchand. However, as he was taking a moment's walk with Las Cases in the gallery of the ship, he handed Hortense's necklace to him. The chamberlain was to wear it from then on under his vest.[46]

About nine o'clock on Sunday morning, a large ship was sighted to leeward. As she drew nearer it was identified as the *Northumberland*. She was accompanied by two frigates laden with troops. The three vessels dropped anchor near the *Bellerophon*. Shortly afterwards Admiral Keith came aboard to introduce Admiral Cockburn, the officer commissioned to conduct the Emperor to St. Helena.

Second son of a baronet, born in 1772, Cockburn had been at sea since he was fourteen. He had fought under Nelson. He had burned an American fleet and taken Washington in 1813. He was an old seadog, somewhat gruff, haughty, stiff. He had none of the amiability of Keith. Napoleon repeated his dignified complaint in Cockburn's presence. Cockburn's only reply was to serve him with an extract of the instructions he had received from Lord Bathurst anent the Emperor's transfer to the *Northumberland*. The luggage of "General Bonaparte" and his officers was to be rigidly inspected, and all money, jewelry, valuables and weapons handed over to Cockburn.

Napoleon had sent to Keith the list of persons who were to accompany him. It had been written out by Bertrand. Among those named were Bertrand, Montholon, Planat de la Faye (whom the Emperor

46 Las Cases, Vol. I, p. 38.

liked and knew to be thoroughly loyal) and finally Las Cases. So Gourgaud had been left out! He went to the Emperor's cabin and made such a violent and tearful scene that Napoleon replaced Planat's name with his. The English objected to Las Cases. They had viewed him with suspicion ever since he had gone from the Isle of Aix to call on Maitland and had feigned ignorance of English in order to spy on their talk. The orders of the ministry, moreover, reduced the suite to three officers. Under pressure from Bertrand, Lord Keith consented to consider Las Cases a civilian, and further permitted his young son Emmanuel to remain with him in Napoleon's retinue.

The defection of Maingault caused some embarrassment. To replace him by a French physician was not to be thought of. The surgeon of the *Bellerophon*, Barry O'Meara, did not know much French, but he spoke Italian fluently, and Napoleon had enjoyed talking with him in that language. O'Meara volunteered and on the Emperor's request the Admiral agreed, not to attach him to Napoleon's service, but to "permit him to accompany General Bonaparte to St. Helena in the exercise of his medical profession." He would remain a British officer, in the Admiralty's pay, and under the Admiralty's orders. Napoleon acquiesced. He thought that that was just one detail more. Actually O'Meara set out for St. Helena under instructions from a friend of his, one Finlaison, custodian of records at the Admiralty, who had ordered him, on behalf of Lord Melville, to spy upon Napoleon.[47]

Before the inspection of the baggage Bertrand divided among the French the bulk of the gold that had been brought from Paris—about 250,000 francs—and they hid it in their belts. They further secreted a number of diamonds and certain sums in letters of credit and tender-paper. The Grand Marshal was thus enabled to declare that the Emperor's treasure consisted of but 4,000 napoleons. 1,500 were left him that he might pay his servants. The rest was taken.[48]

[47] Even on the *Bellerophon*, unbeknown to anybody, O'Meara was keeping in touch with Finlaison and writing letters that were replete with tendencious information about Napoleon and his entourage. O'Meara was to continue that during his whole stay at St. Helena. The letters he wrote are preserved in the British Museum (Lowe Papers, B.M. 20-146). They constitute one of the sources which have to be consulted if one is to understand the inside story of the Captivity. They have to be checked and controlled, for they are replete with vulgarities and lies.

[48] Las Cases, Vol. I, p. 99; Maitland, pp. 199-202. Marchand kept the 1,500 louis. The 50,000 francs that were seized were later to be handed over to Sir Hudson Lowe in London and Lowe was to carry them to St. Helena in order to apply them to the needs of the Emperor.

The humiliating inspection was carried out under Cockburn's eye by his secretary, Glover, and an agent from the Customs. Marchand was the only Frenchman present. It was rapid enough but it was extended even to the Emperor's clothing and linen. The effects of his companions were looked at casually as a matter of form.

The French officers were disarmed in spite of their protests. Napoleon was the one exception. Las Cases prided himself on having persuaded Lord Keith not to stoop to that indignity.[49] It seems more probable, as Savary relates, that Bertrand protested with an emotion that touched the old gentleman's heart. When Cockburn, more strict, objected, the Admiral reminded him that "since an officer's sword is always returned to him when he surrenders on the battlefield, there was all the more reason to do so in the case of General Buonaparte." [50]

Before quitting the *Bellerophon* the Emperor bade farewell to those who were to be left behind. They gathered together in the ante-room of the Emperor's apartment and filed before him in order of Court precedence. The majority were weeping. They kissed his hands. Savary flung himself on his knees, sobbing. The Emperor lifted him up and embraced him. He also embraced Lallemand. He refused to take back the gold-filled belt which had been entrusted to Savary. He made Lallemand a present of the cargo that had been left on the Danish vessel at the Isle of Aix.[51] Having taken leave of Maitland and his officers [52] he walked with a firm tread towards the boat that was to carry him to the *Northumberland*. For the last time, and though Maitland had already been censured in this regard by the Ministry, he was paid royal honours. The drums rolled, the guard presented arms, the whole crew was mustered, bareheaded, on the main deck and on the forecastle. Two or three times Napoleon spoke and smiled.

[49] Las Cases, Vol. I, p. 97.

[50] Rovigo, Vol. VIII, p. 263. Montholon never loses an opportunity to dramatize. He invents (Vol. I, p. 113) a fine scene in which Keith and Cockburn board the *Bellerophon* to disarm the Emperor. Lord Keith says to the latter in a voice hoarse with emotion: "England asks you for your sword." The Emperor, with a convulsive gesture, clasps his hand over the hilt. The old Admiral is crushed, his tall figure droops, his head whitened by the years falls on his chest. . . . The Emperor keeps his sword.

[51] It was worth about 30,000 francs (Gourgaud, Vol. I, p. 50). Savary and Lallemand boarded the *Northumberland* with Maitland in the afternoon. Napoleon took his last leave of them at that time. Maitland left the ship with them, and that same evening the *Bellerophon* along with the *Tonnant* headed back towards Plymouth.

[52] Montholon had offered Maitland a snuff-box on behalf of the Emperor. The commander refused "finding his situation too delicate to receive a present." Two of his officers accepted braces of pistols (Mme. de Montholon, p. 71; Home, p. 186).

Lord Keith had come to fetch him and was walking behind him. He seemed surprised at the grief of the French officers.

"You will observe, Milord," Las Cases said to him, "that the ones who are weeping are the ones who are to be left behind." [53]

The Emperor went down into the boat, followed by Mme. Bertrand and Mme. de Montholon, the two generals, Las Cases, and finally Lord Keith. For a time he remained standing, then, as the water widened between the boat and the *Bellerophon*, he seated himself beside the Admiral. He was outwardly calm. A few cable lengths away the *Northumberland* towered on high with a great cloud of yellowing sails that billowed and slapped noisily in the wind. The sky was overcast, the wind cold. The sailors raised and lowered their oars in perfect rhythm. Everyone watched from the *Bellerophon*. Napoleon did not raise his eyes. [54]

It was two o'clock when they drew alongside.

[53] Las Cases, Vol. I, p. 97.
[54] Mme. de Montholon, p. 73.

# IV

## THE "NORTHUMBERLAND"

NAPOLEON HAD BEEN TREATED AS AN EMPEROR UP TO THE MOMENT of his leaving the *Bellerophon*. On the *Northumberland* he was a "State prisoner." He was accorded only the "courtesies due a retired English general." Admiral Cockburn knew what orders were, and executed them unflinchingly—polite forms on a background of mistrust and coldness. Napoleon was at first shocked by the change, by the pointed care with which he was addressed as "Excellency," by the haste the officers showed in putting their hats on in his presence. Eventually he adapted himself.

"Let them call me what they wish," he said to Las Cases.[1] "They cannot prevent me from being I."

Immediately on his arrival the Admiral led him to the saloon and introduced the commander of the vessel, Captain Ross, his chief officers, Colonel Bingham,[2] then a number of gentlemen who had, for reasons unknown, been admitted aboard to witness the embarcation. Napoleon talked at length with two of them, both Members of Parliament, Lord Lowther and Mr. Lyttleton.

"You have sullied your flag and English honour by imprisoning me as you are doing," he repeated to Lyttleton.

"No undertaking has been violated with you, and the interests of the nation require that you be placed beyond any danger of returning to France."

"Perhaps then what you are doing may be prudent, but it is not generous. You are acting like a small aristocratic power and not like a great and free State! I came to settle on your soil. I intended to live as a plain citizen."

Lyttleton, embarrassed, answered that Napoleon still had many

[1] Las Cases, Vol. I, p. 102.
[2] Sir George Rideout Bingham (1776-1833) commanded the 53rd Infantry which was being sent to reinforce the garrison at St. Helena. On the island he was to be given general command of troops. He had served with distinction in the war with Spain. From the outset Napoleon took a liking to him.

partisans in France and that, sooner or later, if he lived so close at hand, he would answer their call.

"No, no!" replied Napoleon emphatically. "My career is ended!" [3]

Just as they were about to weigh anchor there was a collision between a patrol cutter and a boat carrying a woman and her child with a servant. They had come out at great risk to catch another glimpse of the Emperor. The boat sank almost instantaneously. Lifeboats were lowered. The mother and child were rescued, but their companion was not seen again. The accident had a depressing effect on the spirits of Napoleon's companions. A bad sign!

Meantime the anchor was being lifted. The noise of the windlass drowned out all voices. The French repaired to their quarters. They were not so comfortably lodged as on the *Bellerophon*. The *Northumberland* was a large ship but she had been equipped in such haste, and was so heavily laden, and there were so many people on board,[4] that Captain Ross [5] was to struggle vainly during the entire voyage to bring some semblance of order into the chaos and create a little elbowroom. There had not been time even to repaint the vessel at Plymouth. That was to be done during the trip—one more inconvenience for the passengers.

The poop astern of the mizzen-mast on the upper deck had been divided into several rooms: first a large room running the whole width of the vessel—the diningroom. Beyond it towards the stern opened a narrower saloon situated between two cabins about 18 feet square. The port cabin was occupied by the Emperor, the one to starboard by Cockburn. Napoleon mentioned taking the small saloon for his study. The Admiral begged Bertrand to explain that the after-cabin

[3] Lyttleton: *A Few Notes on the Arrival of N. B. on board the "Northumberland,"* London, 1836. A far cry from the story Montholon gives, Vol. I, p. 123. A hitherto unpublished letter of Cockburn's to his sister Polly, dated August 9, 1815, confirms Lyttleton's description of Napoleon's demeanour: "He was violent on first coming on board about the unjust way in which our government had treated him, but finding that kind of conversation not well received by me, he has dropped it and if I am not very much mistaken I have already got this unresty gentleman into the right tune for preventing his giving me or any other person further trouble. . . . I have endeavoured to impress on his mind and on the mind of his attendants that so long as he recollects he is my Prisoner, I shall not forget that he is my guest which will insure to him every attention and civility I can consistently pay him." (Thiers Library, Carton 21.)

[4] 1,080 souls, including two companies and the staff of the 53rd Infantry, on their way to garrison St. Helena.

[5] Charles Bayne Hodgson Ross (1778-1849), brother-in-law to Cockburn, had helped the latter in the capture of Washington in 1813.

must be considered as common to all, and that the sleeping-cabin . . . could alone be considered as exclusively his.[6] The Bertrands were packed into an even smaller cabin: the Grand Marshal, his wife, a maid and four children—three little Bertrands and a child of the maid's. This cabin belonged to Ross. He gave it up to accommodate the Bertrands. Mme. Bertrand slept on one of the Emperor's two camp beds which he had lent her.[7] The Montholons had received a cabin belonging to Cockburn's secretary, Glover. A heavy cannon occupied the middle of the room and was a good deal of a nuisance. Gourgaud and the two Las Cases had stifling holes. Whenever he could, Gourgaud slept in the saloon or on deck.

None of the French had foreseen such a voyage and they were short of everything—even linen, for they had been refused permission to make purchases in Plymouth as they had requested.

A hanging bed had been slung in Napoleon's cabin to lessen the rolling of the ship. He did not use it. He preferred his iron campaign cot with the curtains of green taffeta and mattresses of floss silk. Marchand slept on the floor on a number of blankets, as Roustan, Napoleon's Georgian mameluke, had done in his time. He had hung up a few pictures on the wooden panelling. The Emperor's servants shared a gunroom. "They assembled there," says Aly (p. 138), "at each meal to eat the biscuit and salt meat that was provided for them."

The Emperor was accustomed to roughing it. The lack of comforts did not annoy him to any great extent. His only concern was to safeguard his dignity, his title. That title had been proclaimed by a Pope and it had been spread on hundreds of historic European parchments for ten years past. Since it was being denied him, since they persisted in treating him as an insubordinate general, he had made up his mind to enforce his sovereign status by his mere demeanour. They were hoping in vain to demote him to the name of Bonaparte. For all, on all occasions and to his dying day, he was to be "the Emperor Napoleon."

The first evenings he put up with the slowness of service at dinner. But on the fourth day (August 10th),[8] he rose from table before the

---

[6] Cockburn, *Diary*, p. 17. The Admiral added that Napoleon "received this intimation with submission and good humour."

[7] Warden, *Letters Written on Board* H.M.S. *"Northumberland" and at St. Helena*, p. 30.

[8] Las Cases, Vol. I, p. 126, and Montholon, Vol. I, p. 124, place this scene on the first evening, August 7th. They are corrected by the *Diary* of Admiral Cockburn

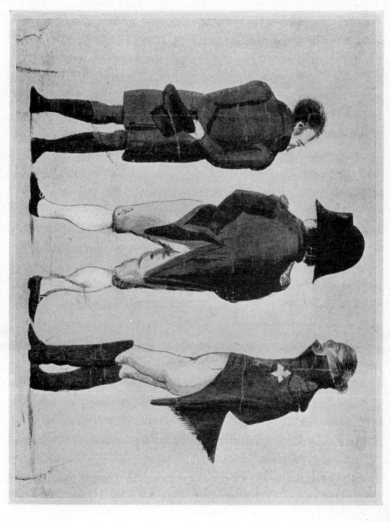

NAPOLEON BETWEEN LAS CASES AND BERTRAND

From a Water-colour by Denzil Ibbetson, Commissary

end of the meal and, followed by Bertrand and Las Cases, went for a walk on the deck. The Admiral was hurt,[9] all the more since he thought he had done wonders in finesse by speaking and ordering others to speak only French. Besides he had gone to great pains to offer his guest all the dishes that might please him. In his pique he permitted himself to say to his English companions at table:

"I suppose the General has not read Lord Chesterfield?"

Scarlet with rage, Mme. Bertrand retorted promptly:

"Do not forget, Admiral, that you are dealing with a man who has been the master of the world, and that kings have intrigued for the honour of being invited to his table."

Cockburn recovered his composure.

"My word, that's true!" he admitted.

Prejudiced as he was against Napoleon this English sailor tried to be just and, if he was somewhat stiff, he was not the man to humiliate misfortune. After that incident he shortened the meals, which had bored the Emperor by their dragging length, and ordered coffee for him while the others were still at the roast. Then when Napoleon left the table, he rose and remained standing until his guest had left the room.[10] Says Aly (p. 187): "The table was square. In the middle, facing the saloon, sat the Emperor and the Admiral. The latter was at His Majesty's right, Mme. Bertrand at his left. Mme. de Montholon sat on the Admiral's left. Present also at dinner, which began at five o'clock, were Captain Ross, Colonel Bingham, Mr. Glover, Dr. O'Meara, Dr. Warden, surgeon on the *Northumberland*, and the chaplain, Mr. Rennell. Each day, an officer of the 53rd, a naval officer, and a midshipman, were specially invited." "The food," writes Mme. de Montholon (p. 77), "was good and plentiful."

Napoleon had boarded the *Northumberland* on the 7th. The vessel was still cruising off Plymouth on the 8th, waiting for the squadron to assemble. The sea was rough. On the 9th all the ships except the *Weymouth* had come up, so the fleet set sail, passing out into the Channel in fairly good weather before a Northwest wind.[11] The *Northumberland*, a "74," bore the Admiral's flag. In her wake, fre-

which seeks no effects and states facts exactly. Napoleon did not dine at table on the 8th, the 11th and the 12th, when he was suffering from seasickness.

[9] "It is clear," he wrote (*Diary*, p. 11), "he is still inclined to act the sovereign occasionally, but I cannot allow it."

[10] Las Cases, Vol. I, p. 126.

[11] Cockburn, *Diary*, p. 21.

quently scattered by contrary winds, came the frigate *Havannah*, Captain Hamilton, the transports *Ceylon* and *Bucephalus* carrying the 53rd Infantry, the brigs *Zenobia, Zephyr, Redpole, Icarus*, and *Ferret,* and two freight ships with provisions.[12] The *Peruvian* had been sent to Guernsey to load up with wines of France. She was to overtake the fleet at Madeira.

At the beginning of the voyage, while the squadron was in the Channel heading for the Atlantic, the weather continued stormy and the sea rough. Napoleon was incommoded by it, as were the majority of his party. During the forenoon he would keep to his cabin in his dressing gown, receive O'Meara and send for one of his officers, preferably Las Cases, to learn the news on board, the day's run, and whether there were sails in sight. Then he would sit down in the one chair there was and read.

Towards three o'clock he would dress and then go into the saloon where he played chess with Gourgaud, Bertrand or Montholon until the Admiral came to announce dinner.[13] According to Bingham and Glover, he ate with good appetite, rarely touching vegetables and often using his fingers in preference to a fork. He drank a goblet of Bordeaux wine lightly watered. He led the conversation at table. When he addressed one of the officers, such as Ross who did not know French, Las Cases served as interpreter. Most often he conversed with the Admiral in a rather low voice, preferably on naval topics, though he sometimes mentioned his own campaigns. But being chiefly interested in things of the present, he compared the English navy with the navy of France, described the efforts he had made to build up the latter and his projects for coast defence. He recalled his idea of building a great navy. The Treaty of Paris, he declared, had destroyed his work.

"If it is true that Louis XVIII has recognized that he owes his crown to the Prince Regent, the latter may say with as much truth: 'I owe the empire of the sea to the Count d'Artois, who, at the instigation of Talleyrand, needlessly signed away the finest squadron France had ever had.'"

At times he confined himself to asking questions as to the route the vessel was following, the peoples of Africa, the Chinese and East Indian trade.

[12] Lowe Papers, 20-114.
[13] Cockburn, p. 23.

After dinner he walked on deck until dusk, in company with Las Cases and the Grand Marshal, if the latter had not gone below to his wife, who was susceptible to any rolling. At such times he felt free to go back to the early days of his life, family memories, first successes. He also talked of Waterloo.

"Oh! If I could do it over again!" he murmured.

Almost every evening the Admiral would come to meet him and the Emperor would finish his promenade with him. Sometimes, desirous of being alone, he would go and sit on one of the last guns to port next to the gangway, and remain there motionless, gazing at the horizon, in a revery that no one dared to interrupt. The gun, always the same one, was polished with great care by the sailors. The midshipmen called it "the Emperor's gun." When night fell, he would go into the saloon and suggest a game of cards. As a rule [14] he played with Cockburn, Ross, Bingham, Bertrand, Las Cases and Gourgaud. To them must be added the two women, of whom Gourgaud does not speak, and Glover, the Admiral's secretary. Glover sustained fairly large losses and Gourgaud, more fortunate, lent him money. He also lent to Mme. Bertrand and Montholon. On Sunday, out of respect for English customs, there was no playing.

Vingt-et-un was the Emperor's favourite game—the one that had been most in vogue at Malmaison under the Consulate. He risked a gold piece on each cut, letting his winnings accumulate until he lost, curious to test his luck. In that way he regularly lost ten or twelve napoleons. Once, however, he won sixteen hundred francs from the Admiral and stopped there, Cockburn clearly showing that he was not eager to continue. The rest of the game proved that had Napoleon continued his tactic, with partners capable of playing at such stakes, he would have won sixty thousand louis. When someone exclaimed at the length of that run of luck, an English officer pointed out that that was the eve of August 15th, the Emperor's birthday.[15]

He was forty-six years old! Such a life, and only forty-six! The next morning he received in his cabin. One by one the French came in to extend their best wishes. At first he was surprised. On the previous birthday he had been at Elba, and there the anniversary had still been celebrated with pomp. This time he had only a few com-

[14] According to Gourgaud, August 1-15.
[15] Las Cases, Vol. I, p. 127.

panions left to remember it and drink his health in the evening as
he rose to go out on deck. The English, for that matter, courteously
joined in the toast.

By now the sea was calmer. Some ships were sighted, but Cockburn avoided communicating with them. Wild stories ran about. It
occurred to someone to imagine that four French vessels had put
to sea to rescue Napoleon.

The *Northumberland* edged slowly along. She took the swells
rather heavily and came up out of the troughs leaving a deep wake
behind her. The Emperor often sat and followed with his eyes those
blue streaks with fringes of foam—wounds of the deep that closed
but gradually so that the eye could never see them healed. He would
watch the stern lift against the horizon and then fall again at an unexpected angle, an angle that took the geometrician in him by surprise. Aerial noises in the ship's rigging, sonorous as a violin, detona-
tions of the breeze in the sails, whistlings along the length of the
salt-powdered ropes, the childlike wails of seagulls, the solitude of
water and cloud—all such novelties doubtless gave him pleasure.

There were no incidents on board, except a row started by Bernard, the Grand Marshal's valet. Bertrand had him put in irons. A
number of English sailors were flogged and the Emperor protested
to Cockburn. The crew was inclined to be mutinous. Back in Portsmouth they had refused to get up anchor and twenty of the more
vociferous had been put ashore. During the voyage the sailors sometimes beat the midshipmen and used lewd language to them.[16]

Mme. Bertrand and Mme. de Montholon were gradually getting
used to the ship's motion and were to be seen on deck more frequently. They were dressing their best and already showing signs of
jealousy. Mme. de Montholon was flirting with the Admiral and
even with the Emperor, meantime redoubling her attentions to her
husband. The Bertrand children were ever romping about the decks
between the legs of the sailors, who became very fond of them—two
boys, Napoleon and Henri, and a girl, Hortense, all three healthy,
lively children. The "gang" was reinforced by a little four-year-old
mulatto from America, by the little Tristan de Montholon—when
he could escape from his mother—and finally by Tom Pipes, a handsome Newfoundland dog belonging to the Admiral. True soldier's

[16] *Letter of a Young Officer* of the 82nd Infantry, unnamed, who had been temporarily assigned to the *Northumberland, Cornhill Magazine*, March, 1933.

children, they played at war, drilled, climbed upon the guns, and made the deck shake as they charged at a gallop, shouting lustily, the dog racing after them.[17] Napoleon often watched them at their play.

One day as Bertrand was talking with his master on the quarter-deck, little Hortense ran to the Emperor, pulled him by the hand and prattled away at him volubly. Her father tried to silence her—unsuccessfully. Napoleon gave the little girl a kiss and listened to her long and complicated story.[18]

As he walked about the deck the Emperor questioned the officers and men about the battles they had fought in and he astonished them by his knowledge of naval matters. He would take for his interpreter now a midshipman, now O'Meara, now a Jerseyman, or perhaps an Italian from the Ionian isles, or from Malta. One day he had a long talk with the quartermaster, who could never aspire to epaulettes but was nevertheless responsible for the navigation of the vessel. Napoleon liked the man's frank, open countenance. As he left him he said:

"Come and dine with me tomorrow."

The poor man was greatly embarrassed. His first thought was that the Emperor had made a mistake. Then it was explained to him that Napoleon was in the habit of doing honour to merit without regard to rank.

"But," objected the quartermaster, "the Admiral and the Captain will not want me to sit at their table."

"Well," replied the Emperor, "if they don't like it, so much the worse for them. You will dine with me in my cabin."

A few moments later Sir George Cockburn joined the Emperor, who informed him of the invitation. Shocked perhaps, the Admiral met the situation and answered that "anyone who was invited by the General to his table was by that very fact exempted from the rules." He sent for the quartermaster and told him that he would be welcome at dinner the next day. The man was in fact treated with the greatest affability, and from that moment the prestige of the Emperor rose to the zenith among the sailors of the *Northumberland* and the soldiers of the 53rd.

Cockburn was worried. To break off communication between

[17] Warden, p. 17.
[18] Warden, p. 75.

Napoleon and the crew, and—who could say?—perhaps a mutiny in favour of his passenger, he stationed a sentry at his door.

The midshipmen, many of whom were still mere boys, could talk of nothing but Napoleon. They watched with one accord that he might not be disturbed on his walks or in his reveries by their work in running the ship, and they appointed themselves a police force to safeguard his well-being aboard. They followed him with shining eyes whenever he passed. They were thoughtful and courteous in their demeanour towards the members of the Emperor's suite. The little Bertrand children adopted the younger midshipmen as playmates. Cockburn and Ross secretly deplored such laxness in discipline, but they dared not be too sharp in their reprimands. They were overreached.

Not only that. Their own attitude towards Napoleon had been greatly modified. Cockburn confesses as much, unconsciously, in his *Diary*. The Emperor's dignified and patient attitude, his charm of manner, even the tone of his voice, gradually dissolved prejudice, vanquished hatred. All who came to be associated with him eventually bowed before his genius, pitied his misfortune and grew attached to him for the simple, human charm that the hero manifested.

The Admiral was soon to say to Gourgaud: [19] "General Bonaparte did well in surrendering to us, for after all it may be that some day an English fleet will go to St. Helena to bring him back to France." No, Cockburn was no longer the gruff jailor of the early days, the man who saluted and then made haste to clap his hat on his head again to keep Napoleon "from having too high an opinion of his own importance." If, as sometimes happened, during their evening promenades on deck Napoleon's thin-soled shoes would slip on the polished flooring, the Admiral would offer him an arm, and his face would beam whenever Napoleon talked to him as to a friend. Night after night Cockburn noted down his captive's words. His brother-in-law, Captain Ross, racked his brain even harder to devise ways to make the voyage easier for the Emperor. Sir George Bingham and the officers of the 53rd were ever obliging and deferential. The change in attitude was general. Though Napoleon had been greeted at Plymouth and Tor Bay with overt manifestations of sympathy, English opinion was, on the whole, still hostile to him. The English saw in the Emperor a sort of ogre or demon. That conception had

[19] Gourgaud, Vol. I, p. 55, August 26th.

been reflected on board the *Northumberland* in the early days, and been shared by everybody from the Admiral down to the humblest cabin-boy. The ship's small library contained a number of anti-Napoleonic volumes. Before the ship reached the Canaries they had disappeared.

On August 23rd, the *Northumberland* sighted Madeira. A hot wind was blowing from Africa powdering everything with a fine dust. The heat was stifling. The English squadron lay to off Funchal. Napoleon was pensive at dinner. The nearness of a land to which access was denied him brought his situation more clearly home to him. Leaving table he went up on deck and gazed at the mountainous island and the houses piled up under the palms "like flowerpots in tiers." [20]

The night was stormy and the ships were almost driven ashore. A frigate and a brig became separated from the fleet. The *Northumberland* broke two topmasts during a tack. In the morning the wind was still blowing a gale and Wilch, the English consul at Funchal, managed to get aboard with the greatest difficulty.

During a lull in the storm the ship took on cattle, sheep, poultry, supplies of vegetables and fruit, and a stock of Malvasia wine. "That wine," writes Mme. de Montholon (p. 80), "was perfect. As it was not served every day on the journey, we pretended that the Admiral gave it to us only when we were very well-behaved." The water on board the *Northumberland* had staled and the supply also had to be renewed. Contrary to his usual habit, Napoleon appeared early in the morning, did his reading on deck and showed keen interest in the comings and goings of the lighters.

By noon the fleet had more or less re-assembled and sail was set for St. Helena. Another cruel day of heat followed, then the breeze freshened and Napoleon, who had seemed depressed and had scarcely eaten, returned to better spirits. The *Northumberland* was making good time with all sails set. As they plunged deeper into the south night came on much more suddenly. The twilight talks on deck were shortened. In his conversation with Cockburn, the Emperor had expressed an interest in the Canaries. The Admiral therefore laid a course through the middle of the archipelago, between Gomera and Palma. Unluckily a thick fog covered the sea. Not one of the pas-

[20] Montholon, Vol. I, p. 132; Cockburn, pp. 68-70.

sengers could distinguish the peak of Teneriffe, which is visible at a hundred and fifty miles in clear weather.[21]

During the night of August 31st, a half-breed from Guadeloupe, who had been sentenced to be flogged for a breach of discipline, jumped overboard. A search was made for him by torchlight but without avail. The whole crew was in commotion. In the midst of the uproar a young midshipman stopped Las Cases, who was on his way to Napoleon's cabin:

"Oh, sir, don't alarm him! Just tell him it's nothing of any importance—just a man overboard!"

They crossed the tropic of Cancer amid schools of flying fish. A heavy swell was running and Napoleon was again indisposed. He came to dinner, however, but retired early after a hand at whist. He had given up vingt-et-un. The stakes were running too high.

They had counted on a halt at the Cape Verde Islands to take on water, but as the wind was still favourable Cockburn decided to profit by it in order to gain more southing. Uppermost in the minds of the English ever since Napoleon boarded the *Bellerophon* had been a fear of meeting French vessels that might make a try for a rescue. That thought had been—and was still to be—the cause of many mistaken precautions. Just here it dissuaded the Admiral from taking the usual route to the West on which, off Brazil, one picked up a steady wind that blew straight to St. Helena. He half drifted along the African coast as far as the middle of the Gulf of Guinea. Time began to drag for the French. Even those with the most endurance, Bertrand, for instance, became irritable. Napoleon tried to pass the time by learning English with Las Cases. For two or three days he put up with the lessons, then he rebelled and gave them up. Las Cases was not sorry. He much preferred to keep the Emperor talking about himself and eagerly jotted down in his diary a record of Napoleon's monologues in which, delighted to find a listener so ill-informed about the Revolution, the Emperor retraced all its phases for the benefit of his former émigré. Las Cases wrote breathlessly. Napoleon asked to see a few pages and was not ill-pleased with the result. But the diary, he thought, lacked exactness. Las Cases reddened with pleasure and suggested that he hold the pen while the Emperor related the story of his campaigns in Italy. Napoleon hesitated at first,

[21] Cockburn, p. 74. That is a fairly rare experience, however. At 80 miles, that is to say, 130 kilometres, the peak is plainly visible, hanging as if suspended in the sky.

then agreed—the days were so monotonous! On September 9th he sent word to Las Cases to come to his cabin. Pacing back and forth from one side of the tiny room to the other, his hands behind his back, he began his first dictation—on the siege of Toulon.

Shortly a great storm broke. The ocean was white, the wind howled in the rigging, monstrous waves rose as if to attack the vessel, breaking aboard, and keeping the deck awash. It rained in torrents. The ship between decks was like a steaming boiler. The Emperor remained for the most part in bed in his cabin. The forced inactivity was more than he could bear. As he looked back over his life he could find only one period of such fatuous idleness—the days when he was heading for Egypt on board the *Orient*. He thought the two voyages had their points of similarity in other respects. The one had begun the upward curve of his fortunes, this one was ending the downward half. To amuse himself on the *Orient*, the young General had organized the "Egyptian Institute." On the vessel that was carrying him to life imprisonment he had nothing to do but dictate his memoirs! But he could not dictate all the time, nor work out silly mathematical problems with Gourgaud.[22] Dropping his pencil, he would plunge into the past and draw sparkling jewels from it. He spoke of comrades in the wars, mourning Lannes, who had been killed at Eisling, singing the praises of Desaix whom he found "the best general he had ever known."

"Clauzel," he said, "and Gerard promised much. Bernadotte has no head—he is a true Gascon. He will not stay where he is. His turn to go will come too."

It was as though, in such nearness to Africa, Egypt haunted him. He defended himself before the Admiral for having had the plague victims at Jaffa poisoned. On evacuating that town, he said, he had asked the physicians whether it would not be better to hasten the death of the desperately sick by opium, rather than leave them to the headsmen of Djezzar Pascha. Desgenettes refused and asked the General to hold the town for two days more. Bonaparte agreed. By the time he left Jaffa all the patients in question had succumbed.[23]

Leaping from one subject to another, he spoke of Tilsit, of Queen Louise, his beautiful enemy, of the rose he had offered and of the

---

[22] "We subtracted square and cube roots and solved equations of the second and third degrees" (Gourgaud, Vol. I, p. 59).

[23] Cockburn, pp. 82-85; Las Cases, Vol. I, pp. 250 ff.

refusal of Magdeburg, and of the flirtatious tête-à-tête he had arranged for Alexander with the Queen of Prussia by keeping the King
at home all day waiting for the announcement of his official visit.

That seemed to have tired him of exploring his memory. He did not
join the French in the saloon, but withdrew to his cabin, where he
was to lie on his little camp cot, rocked by the waves, his eyes open.

Heat, rain, winds that blew the sails to pieces, leaving them hanging in shreds! The sun appeared over the edge of the water and rose
in a pale sky, so hot that the boards of the deck burned one's feet.
And then it sank in a red mist over America where, had Napoleon
made up his mind in time, he would at that moment have been free.
A voice floats down from the yards—some poor sailor of Ireland or
Malta, perched at ninety feet and mending a piece of gear to the
tune of a song of his homeland! Lanterns are lighted. A bell strikes
for dinner. The passengers gather in the saloon. The ladies compare
their gowns. The Admiral bows to his prisoner. . . .

There were a few clear nights when the phosphorescent sea was
nothing but a field of fire, the hull of the *Northumberland* opening
a wake of jewels behind her. The stars rose and fell according to
the movement of the vessel. Napoleon, half leaning against his cannon,
looked at them. They were all strange. His own star had never shone
in that sky! Each day new constellations rose from the sea. The
familiar dusting of heavenly bodies to which his child's eyes had been
accustomed had left the dome of the night. The Bears, the Lyre, the
Swan, Cassiopea—stars that shone on his glory, stars of France, of
Europe—would he ever see them again? Shining in all its splendour
before him now was the Southern Cross—so blue. . . . Napoleon
probably preferred cloudy nights, when there were no stars! . . .

. . . . . . . .

Lying ill in her cabin, Mme. Bertrand took by mistake a mouthful
of balsam of Saturn—lead acetate, a common home remedy for cuts
and bruises in those days. She was seriously ill for a short time—they
bled her twice. Napoleon told Gourgaud that if she were to die it
would be no great loss.[24] He was still vengeful because of her conduct
at Torquay. Perhaps, too, her enemies on board may have been de-
faming her. Mme. de Montholon was making herself very agreeable.
She was never depressed, or at least gave no signs of being. She

[24] Gourgaud, Vol. I, p. 59.

dressed her very best, and especially after the candles were brought on, made the most of the remains of her beauty.

On September 23rd, the date of the equinox, by a curious coincidence, the *Northumberland* crossed the Equator at noon, on a zero longitude with a zero declination. That day the French attended the traditional saturnalia of the "Great Beard." [25] Two sailors impersonating Neptune and Amphitrite sat on a perch over a tub at the foot of the mainmast, surrounded by musicians and men in their underdrawers, who were tattooed and painted like savages. At either side stood two giants, one holding a razor, the other a pot of tar. They were to shave anybody who had never before crossed the Line. The poor victim was then pitched headlong into a longboat filled with water.

That at least was the programme for the cabin-boys and the soldiers of the 53rd. Those who tried to escape were pursued over the whole ship, dripping from the pails of water that were dashed on them from the cross-trees. Officers had a right to ransom themselves, which reduced their initiation to a dowsing with water. Captain Ross "himself received a pail of water in his face in the most perfect good humour." [26] All the French were subjected to the common law, except the ladies. They sat on an improvised platform in the shade and were greatly amused. The Bertrand and Montholon children each paid a ransom of a gold piece. A number of sailors shouted for "General Bonaparte." Cockburn replied laughing that he "had already crossed the line." In fact the Emperor kept to his cabin. Gourgaud came and described the fun to him. He ordered a hundred napoleons given to the crew. Bertrand, who was less lavish by instinct, found that sum extravagant, and that was the opinion of Cockburn who feared any increase of the Emperor's popularity on the boat. He refused to allow a gift of more than five gold pieces. "The officers highest in rank," he said, "pay only half a guinea in ransom." Piqued, doubtless, at the lesson, Napoleon did not send anything.

He continued his work with Las Cases. He sent for him about eleven o'clock in the morning and Las Cases read the text he had written the night before. The Emperor made corrections and then continued the dictation until the time came to dress for dinner. Un-

[25] Aly, p. 141; Cockburn, p. 94; Warden, p. 72; Gourgaud, Vol. I, p. 61.
[26] Warden, p. 73.

comfortably seated, his hands cramped with overwork, Las Cases wrote as fast as the Emperor talked, unconscious of his torture. The moment Napoleon began to dress, he ran to his cabin and with the help of his son tried to reconstruct the sentences he had taken down in an improvised short-hand. This distraction amused the Emperor more and more. He always welcomed his biographer gaily, chaffing him a little:

"Lo, *the sage* Las Cases, illustrious memorialist, the Sully of St. Helena!" [27]

He was fully aware of the huge interest that Las Cases, as a man of letters, had in following his career.

"No one," he said, "will ever be able to discuss the great events of our day or write about my person without referring to your work." [28]

The little chamberlain licked his lips and wrote on. From the Emperor's mouth the words came faster and faster. "Expressions, places, dates, nothing stopped him. He dictated as if inspired." [29] And the pile of sheets grew higher and higher until Napoleon stopped pacing back and forth in his wooden prison and said: "Until tomorrow."

.     .     .     .     .     .     .

Cockburn did not find the winds he was seeking along the coast of Africa. Off the Congo the *Northumberland* went into a flat calm. Taking advantage of morning and evening breezes the ship succeeded only in wearing about, returning to the same spot on a dead sea that stretched away to infinity. Bottles thrown overboard near the ship remained there for long hours as in a pond. Twenty days passed like that. The only excitement was now a jumping fish, now a school of porpoises playing about the bow, or now and then one of those huge seagulls that soar from ocean to ocean with wings so motionless that they seem to be borne along by the sky itself.

The crew as well as the troops on board began to grumble against the Admiral. The French kept complaining. Napoleon alone remained impassive. But he was anxious over the tedium of his companions and to keep Gourgaud, a mammoth in distress, amused, he undertook to

---

[27] Las Cases, it will be remembered, had published an atlas under the name of Le Sage. Sully was the great minister of Henry IV.
[28] Las Cases, Vol. I, p. 238.
[29] *Ibid.*, Vol. I, p. 290.

dictate another book to him. Bertrand and Montholon saw in such work only an irksome task and evaded it.[30]

Cockburn sent the *Peruvian* to look for fruits and game on the Congo coast. Awaiting her return the crew amused themselves fishing for sharks that abounded there on the shallow banks. They caught several. Marchand told Napoleon what was going on and he came on deck to watch the death struggle of one of them. The huge selachian knocked four or five sailors down in his writhing. Getting too close the Emperor almost had his legs broken by a blow from the fish's tail and was obliged to go back to his cabin to change his stockings, which were spattered with blood. The monster was cut up by the sailors and the meat used to give body to their ordinary fare. Napoleon asked to have a taste of it with his dinner, but he pushed back his plate, finding the flesh uneatable.

Suddenly, and without anything to foretell the change, a breeze rose. The *Northumberland* and her companion ships began to move. The masts groaned menacingly and the yellowed sails billowed till they were as hard as wood. Once more the Emperor could see waves of deep cobalt moving along the vessel's side. The ship was heading straight for St. Helena now. The impatience of the French was no whit diminished by this change for the better. They harassed the Admiral and Captain Ross with questions as to the probable date of their arrival. Napoleon himself waited expectantly each day for the lookout perched on the highest cross-tree to give the cry of "Land!" He was in good health, but lack of exercise had thickened him about the waist. In his narrative (p. 79), which is otherwise not seldom deficient in tact, Cockburn gives the Emperor a good reference by saying that he showed himself by far less impatient about the weather and the wind and less fault-finding than any of his companions.

The days from the 9th to the 13th of October dragged unbearably. Finally on Saturday, the 14th, while they were at dinner, the cry from the lookout came: "Land!" Everyone ran on deck. Napoleon himself went forward to the bow. He thought he could distinguish a greyish mass outlined on the horizon like a block of granite. Towards the centre was a peak.

"Diana's Peak!" explained Cockburn. But it was already dark. The

[30] "We avoided work as far as we could," says Montholon naïvely (Vol. I, p. 144). "We were absorbed by family concerns. Women and children need so much looking after on a ship at sea."

Emperor went back into the saloon. At nine o'clock the *Northumberland* lay to for the night.[31]

The next day Napoleon dressed very early. When he arrived on deck the island lay before him—an immense wall jutting out of the sea, an uninterrupted succession of cliffs of brown lava, from twelve to eighteen hundred feet high, striped in spots by bands of reddish clay. Not a tree, not a blade of grass, was visible anywhere for leagues. The waves dashed foaming against that terrifying rock topped by a ceiling of clouds that seemed to be hooked to the mountain peaks in the interior. Not a beach, not even a bit of shore wide enough to rest the foot on! That gigantic mass of volcanic slag that plunged vertically into the ocean seemed to be the most impregnable of fortresses. The ship drew nearer. A fault appeared in the unbroken wall, and in it were houses with red roofs, a square church tower, a sort of castle. A number of palm trees finally ranged themselves in line behind a little wharf. To either hand were two cliffs of black basalt which bristled at various heights with tiers of guns. Behind all that one sensed a tortured, gloomy waste.

The Emperor dropped his field-glass. The French, a few feet away, stood stupefied. Was that the happy isle that only yesterday was being promised them? They thought they were gazing into a gateway to Hell. Without a word Napoleon went back to his cabin, sent for Las Cases, and worked as usual. Not till later, as the ship entered the port and was dropping anchor, did he say to Gourgaud:

"It is not a pretty place to live in. I would have done better to stay in Egypt." [32]

It was noon. The Admiral and Sir George Bingham went ashore. The Admiral came back shortly afterwards, accompanied by the Governor of St. Helena "on behalf of the Very Honourable and Powerful East India Company," Colonel Mark Wilks.[33] He was a handsome man with a fine face framed by grey curls. They presented him to the Emperor in the saloon.

Napoleon received him with a majestic air. With an eager deference that flattered the French, Wilks replied to their questions con-

---

[31] Mme. de Montholon, p. 90; Warden, p. 79.

[32] Gourgaud, Vol. I, p. 66.

[33] He was about to lose his post, the island having passed under the direct administration of the Crown. The Governor for the King was to be Sir Hudson Lowe. Colonel Wilks, born in 1760, had had a distinguished career in India. Extremely well educated, he wrote a *History of Southern India*.

THE ARRIVAL OF THE *NORTHUMBERLAND* AT ST. HELENA

From an Old Engraving

cerning the island, its climate, and the different races that peopled it.

At dinner, to raise their spirits, Cockburn vaunted the charms of the little capital, Jamestown, and its environs. Nevertheless he denied Gourgaud permission to go ashore. He wanted to choose a residence for his prisoner first. He also wanted to get the soldiers who had come with the fleet ashore that they might complete all necessary provisions for the security of Napoleon and his suite. The next day, in fact, he left the vessel at dawn and rode over the whole island accompanied by Wilks. He did not return until evening. He had found, he said, on the plateau of Longwood, and in a beautiful situation, a pleasant residence that could be made even more attractive. Awaiting the appropriate alterations the French could lodge in the straggling village. Napoleon asked for details. The Admiral readily furnished them. But the French were filled with foreboding. The evening was gloomy as was the long day that followed, the French watching the ship about them empty little by little of soldiers and baggage, while it pulled and strained, groaning on its anchors, in the face of those forbidding rocks. Bertrand alone was taken ashore to examine the lodging where the Emperor was to reside. Gourgaud stormed because he was not authorized to send his servant ashore likewise. He appealed to the Emperor, who shrugged his shoulders:

"After this trick that the Admiral has played on you," said Gourgaud, "you must be beginning to believe what I told you about the English. They have no generosity. As Paoli said: 'Sono mercanti' (shopkeepers)."

After the last dinner aboard Napoleon got into a boat with Cockburn and Bertrand. Las Cases, Montholon and the women followed them in another tender.[34] That was on the 17th of October.[35] The voyage had lasted seventy-one days. On the shore before them a few lights were twinkling. The sky was overcast, the air in a dead calm. The only sound was the dip of oars in a flat sea.

[34] Gourgaud, Vol. I, p. 69.,

[35] Not on the 16th of October as Las Cases (Vol. I, p. 303) and Aly (Vol. I, p. 142) write. On the *Record Book* for 1815 in the Archives of the Castle of Jamestown, which were opened to me in the most obliging fashion by the present Governor of St. Helena, Sir Spencer Davis, I found the following entry: "October 17. Sunday, the 15th, H.M.S. *Northumberland* arrived from England bearing the flag of Rear Admiral Sir George Cockburn and having on board General Napoleon Buonaparte and certain individuals as State prisoners." (Unpublished. Retranslated.)

THE SEA-STAIRS ASCENDED BY NAPOLEON WHEN HE LANDED AT ST. HELENA

# PART TWO

## "ST. HELENA, A LITTLE ISLAND . . ."

# I

## AT "THE BRIARS"

THE EMPEROR HAD WANTED TO DISEMBARK AFTER NIGHTFALL IN ORDER not to be seen. But the inhabitants were all there nevertheless, in lines to right and to left, and carrying lanterns. It was under their shining eyes and to the murmur of their voices that he was conducted by Cockburn to a sort of inn at the head of the single street in Jamestown, facing a public garden that the India Company had planted. It was known as the Porteous House. It was clean, bare, plainly furnished. Napoleon settled himself in a bedroom on the second floor. His domestics had brought the usual things. He went to bed almost at once.

He slept badly. Curious people gathered in crowds under his windows. He could hear them talking. At dawn he rose. Cockburn came early in order to take him to Longwood that he might inspect the place. The Emperor delaying a little, Cockburn grew impatient. Napoleon knew it and said:

"The Admiral is a boorish fellow." [1]

Cockburn had certainly shown a lack of consideration in lodging Napoleon in a furnished room in a boarding house when he might just as easily have offered him an apartment in the Castle at Jamestown where he himself had been installed.

Napoleon went downstairs and mounted. The horse that Cockburn had brought for him was a fine Arab, black. Attended by the Admiral, Bertrand and Aly, he rode along the street. Houses, all with verandahs, lined it on either side. The verandahs were decorated with

[1] Gourgaud, Vol. I, p. 70.

flowers and plants, and from almost every house came the cries of parrokeets. It all had an oldish flavour of Portuguese India. Women, yellow and brown like pottery, with big expressionless eyes, clusters of children clad in colored rags, sat on the disjointed steps, their hands on their knees, and watched him pass. He was led into a road that climbed the cliff to the left. It turned almost at once into a mountain trail separated from the chasm below by a parapet of dry stones. On the other side the road was bordered by giant aloes and cactuses which, under their embroidery of purple fruit, looked like monstrous coils of cobras.

A bitter, tormented nature! St. Helena is the débris of a volcano, one of the most powerful that ever erupted from the seas in the early ages of the planet. Precipices, crests, piles of brown and purplish-blue rocks that ages of rain, wind and sun have managed only to roughen, are just refuse from the immense submerged crater that lies to the south of the island, off Sandy Bay.

Discovered May 21, 1502, the birthday of the mother of Constantine the Great, by Juan de Nova Castella, a Portuguese navigator, St. Helena was occupied first by the Dutch and then by the East India Company (1661). The island, the most isolated of all the Atlantic—2,000 miles from Brazil, 1,700 miles from the nearest African coast, is 10 miles long and 11 wide, with an area equal to that of the island of Jersey. Though so near to the Equator (16° south) the island, by reason of its elevation above the sea (from 1,500 to 4,000 feet) enjoys a temperate climate—never less than 48°, never more than 80°. Summer begins on the 22nd of December, winter on the 21st of June. The days are eleven hours long in winter, thirteen in summer. Rains and fogs abound especially in winter with fairly frequent thunder storms. But the island, a veritable ship at anchor, is at all seasons under the influence of the sea and it often rains there in summer too.

The flora is very varied. Fodders and vegetables yield almost continuous harvests. Around the Diana Range some sixty species peculiar to the island are to be found. The autochthonous fauna is limited mostly to insects.

The island was uninhabited at the time of its discovery. In 1815 the population numbered 3,395 whites (including soldiers), 1,218 black slaves, 489 Chinese, 116 Hindus and Malays.[2] It must have

---

[2] Record Book, St. Helena, 1815.

PLANTATION HOUSE, THE RESIDENCE OF THE GOVERNOR

PORTEOUS HOUSE, JAMESTOWN
Where Napoleon Slept His First Night in St. Helena

grown appreciably after Napoleon's arrival, reaching 7,998 souls in 1820. After the death of Napoleon, the island reverted to the Company which ceded it permanently to England, April 21, 1834. Up to the opening of the Suez Canal, many vessels on the way to the Indies or the Far East called there and it was often spoken of as the "Ocean Roadhouse." As many as fifty vessels have been known to anchor at one time in the little harbour of Jamestown. After 1870 calls at St. Helena fell off. Today scarcely thirty ships a year stop there for a few hours.

As the French climbed higher they saw a change in the landscape. At certain turns in the road, the eye fell on something like the Maures Hills near Toulon, something like Corsica. There were no more palm trees, no more bananas—Jamestown had them all in its snug crevice. The chalky slopes were covered with pines, olive trees, small green oaks, and a sort of African willow with tough leaves. Nothing tropical in truth! Napoleon might have believed himself on a bit of Europe that some caprice of the ocean had swept away beyond the Equator in days when the world was still young.

As he rode on beyond the crest, he had a vast, chalky hollow on his left, which the natives called the "Devil's Punchbowl." Behind the riders, overlooking grassy valleys, rose the wooded Diana Range, draped in cloud and fog. At a spot called Hutt's Gate, he turned and took a trail, winding along the top of a sort of isthmus, between two valleys a thousand feet deep. It led directly to Longwood.

Finally, a little over five English miles from Jamestown (nine kilometres), they arrived at two stone pillars flanked by small white lodges. There a broad drive led some six hundred feet to the house that Cockburn had chosen to become the residence of Napoleon. It was visible from afar, on a barren, slightly rolling plateau, on which a few wind-twisted trees were growing. It was a sort of small farm composed of badly matched buildings in different styles, pinkish-yellow, roofed in slate. On the East stretched a pale forest of gum trees—thin affairs, fifteen or twenty feet tall, giving practically no shade (the flowers are strangely similar to asters). In front of the house on a yellowed lawn grazed a flock of gaunt-looking sheep with broad tails.

This prospect later on was to grow very disheartening to Napoleon. His first impression at that time was favourable. After those miles of rough road, along hair-raising precipices, this spacious platform had something restful about it. The sun was bright, the air soft. The Admiral informed the Emperor that Longwood, the summer residence of the Lieutenant-Governor, Colonel Skelton, was cool and salubrious and that, after the necessary alterations, the French would be quite comfortable there and masters of their own movements. He did not say—doubtless he did not as yet know—that the densest fogs gathered on that part of the island and that the trade-wind blows there for months at a time.[3]

To tell the truth there was little choice. There were few real houses on the island. The principal buildings, then as now, were Rosemary Hall, the residence of Colonel Smith, Mount Pleasant, belonging to William Doveton, The Briars, to Mr. Balcombe, Orange Grove, to Miss Mason. None of these would have been large enough to accommodate Napoleon without substantial additions. Most of the structures were bungalows and cottages. There could be no thought of the Castle at Jamestown. That was a spacious old building, but without gardens, stifling hot from the spring months on, and situated too near the harbour not to suggest worries about escapes. Plantation House, the Governor's residence, lay in a sheltered spot, surrounded by a large park. It offered several handsome apartments with broad views over the sea. It was difficult to guard, however, and in lending the island to the Crown the East India Company had stipulated that that building should continue to be used by the Governor. The English Cabinet had no intention of evicting him in order to do a favour to their prisoner. Their main concern was to get Napoleon into a place from which flight would be impossible. That that place was barren, without vegetation, subject to sudden changes in weather, and often short of water, was a small matter to them. Unapproachable from the coast, surrounded by perpendicular escarpments, in direct view of the camp at Deadwood, where Bingham was already pitching his tents, Napoleon and his friends would not be able to take a step or move a finger without the Governor's being immediately apprised by signals.

.        .        .        .        .        .        .

As he dismounted the Emperor was welcomed respectfully and with good grace by Colonel and Mrs. Skelton. He took a walk with

[3] This is not the dampest spot on St. Helena. The driest is Jamestown. After that comes Longwood where the medium rainfall is about 25 inches per year. At Plantation House it rises to 35 and at Oakbank to 45 inches.

LONGWOOD, ST. HELENA, IN THE TIME OF NAPOLEON

From an Old Drawing

them, then entered the drawingroom where a luncheon was served. Mrs. Skelton, a tall, withered blonde, spoke French. Napoleon enjoyed his chat with her.[4] He visited the house. Five rooms, small, with fairly numerous closets and other accessories! He took a few more turns about the garden, then asked for his horse. On the ride back towards Jamestown, the Admiral enumerated the improvements that had occurred to him for enlarging Longwood—on reflection, he had come to consider the place rather shabby. The Emperor found the unshaded plateau a dreary prospect, but at least he could take a ride or a drive without running the risk of falling over a precipice. And there he could be alone at last, and get some relief from the people to whom so many days of life on board ship had tied him. He was not afraid of the loneliness. He would have his memories, his work, a chance to walk, and what he liked best of all, a stretch of free sky.

They were about a mile from the valley at Jamestown when, to his left and not far off the road, he noticed a building of the Hindu type, raised by a story and surrounded by flourishing gardens that were planted on a succession of slopes and terraces. A drive of banyan fig trees led in to it. Huge laurel trees, palms, mangoes, bananas, pome-granates, lemons, formed a green and moving frame on all sides. Behind, dropping from a rock, which it had cut heartshaped, was a little waterfall clouded with spray. European flowers—white roses, geraniums—and tropical magnolias, camelias, African snow-drops, were growing all about in clumps and thickets. Shut in by hills of lava, sheltered from the sea by a rounded hillock, that cosy nook, in contrast to the very European Longwood, exhibited an exotic charm that delighted Napoleon. To obtain a closer view of it he turned into the drive of banyans.[5]

The estate, known as The Briars, belonged to William Balcombe, purveyor and financial agent of the East India Company.[6] In fact he

4 Aly, p. 145.
5 Aly, p. 146; Las Cases, Vol. I, p. 135.
6 Even today in the abandoned gardens at The Briars, one notes masses of wild roses with large pale pink flowers. When the Balcombes left The Briars it was occu-pied by Admiral Plampin, then by his successor, Admiral Lambert. Later on the East India Company bought the place back and replaced the gardens with a useless plantation of mulberry trees. The Eastern Telegraph Company owns the property today. It has installed its offices there and lodges its employés in a large brick build-ing that ruins the valley. The pavilion occupied by the Emperor has been provided with enlarged annexes and covered with a roof that quite disfigures it. The Balcombe bungalow is in ruins. White ants have gained a hold in it and before long it will fall to pieces entirely.

had just been commissioned by Colonel Wilks to assemble all the supplies that would be necessary for the maintenance of the French during their stay on the island. Balcombe had been at St. Helena since 1807, superintending public sales on behalf of the East India Company. He had formed a partnership with William Fowler and Joseph Cole for provisioning ships that touched at Jamestown. He was both a commission merchant and a banker. Gossip made him a natural son of the Prince Regent. Sent off to St. Helena, he was filling his pockets to the best of his ability only to empty them as soon as possible afterwards. A fat, light-haired man, he liked to live well and he was clever and obliging. At just that moment he was in bed with an attack of gout. His wife and four children—two girls and two boys—received Napoleon. Catching sight of a pretty pavilion where, on warm days, the Balcombes served tea and even gave small balls, he asked whether he might not be allowed to settle there while Longwood was being put in order. Built on a knoll, the structure had only one room, twenty by fifteen, with two doors and six windows. It was, however, very attractively decorated in the Adams style (what is left of it today shows very ornate detail). A loft upstairs was divided into two attics.

Las Cases called it "a sort of dance hall." [7] That was an exaggeration. Wellington had lodged there on his way back from India in 1806. That fact enabled him to write to Sir Pulteney Malcolm, who had just replaced Cockburn at St. Helena, a mocking remark that his taste for facetiousness cannot excuse: "Tell Boney that I find his apartments at the Élysée-Bourbon very comfortable and that I hope he likes mine at the Balcombes'!"

The Emperor wanted nothing so much as to avoid curious eyes at Jamestown. The Balcombes offered him their house. Napoleon declined, not wishing, he declared, that his presence should occasion any change whatever in their habits. [8] Cockburn had thought of settling in the pavilion himself. He gave up the idea. Napoleon remained at The Briars then and there, and sent Bertrand back to town. Two hours later he was at home. His little bed, his washbasin, his dressingcase, a few articles lent by the Balcombes, furnished his room. Las Cases was there at his orders. He had come alone. Napoleon said to him: "I don't want to separate you from your son.

[7] Las Cases, Vol. I, p. 306.
[8] Mme. de Montholon, p. 96; Aly, p. 146.

"THE BRIARS," WHERE NAPOLEON RESIDED BEFORE GOING TO LONGWOOD
From an Old Drawing

"THE BRIARS." ENTRANCE TO THE PAVILION

Send for Emmanuel." They took the two attics in the loft. Cipriani and Marchand found a little open arbour with a roof in the garden. They busied themselves about dinner there, and it was served to the Emperor in front of his door.

The rest of the French were obliged to remain in town, but they could come to The Briars every day. Napoleon was dissatisfied with the Grand Marshal for having allowed the English to lodge him so wretchedly at the Porteous House. The Montholons and Gourgaud did not conceal their disappointment at an arrangement which separated them from close contact with the Emperor. They were jealous of Las Cases and wearied Napoleon with their complaints every time they came to The Briars. Their first impression of St. Helena had not, however, been too disastrous. Gourgaud wrote to Mme. Caffarelli on October 21: "We are in the little town of Jamestown, the only one on the island—and shall remain here several days more. It lies between two arid mountains of terrifying aspect, but it is fairly well built. The majority of the houses are surrounded by trees and shrubs that have come from the four quarters of the world. Inside they are neat and well kept. All the inhabitants keep boarders, lodging and feeding people who are on their way from India to Europe and who stop off at this island for a few days' rest. It is famous for its good water, for its salubrious air, and its mild climate. The white women are fairly pretty. They speak English, dress like the English, and have English ways, but there are so many rocks on this island that I fear I may also find a few in the hearts of these beauties."

The Admiral had appointed an artillery officer, Captain Greatly, and two sergeants to guard his prisoner.[9] The Emperor, in anger, refused to receive Cockburn and walked up and down with Mme. Bertrand before his eyes.

Distracted by such a picturesque setting, amused by the Balcombes' style of living, he was not bored in that cosy valley, which was cultivated by coloured men and reminded him, he said, of *Paul et Virginie*.

In the morning he went down into the garden while his room was being swept, breakfasted under a shady arbour of vines, then worked with Las Cases. Then he explored the rocky maze of terraces till

---

[9] Captain Poppleton of the 53rd replaced Greatly immediately. The two sergeants were withdrawn after a few days. The officer on guard was regularly referred to as "the orderly officer."

dinner time. The gardens produced all the fruits and vegetables of Europe and Africa, and in such abundance that the Balcombes sold their surplus every year to an amount of 600 pounds sterling.

Almost always he would meet the Balcombe girls there, Jane and Betsy. Afraid of him at first, they soon became fast friends with him. They wore short skirts, white pantalets tied at the ankles, bodices with collars and bonnets. Jane was sixteen. She was dark, calm, somewhat dull. Her sister, two years younger, was a pretty little tomboy with blonde curls that were always escaping from their ribbons, eyes of piercing blue and a tiny pink mouth that delivered itself of endless impertinences which everybody excused because she had so much charm. In that climate she had developed precociously in body, less so in mind. She talked like a child when she already had the throat and breast of a woman. She treated the Emperor like an old uncle, clung to his arms, gathered fruit and flowers for him, asked him the strangest questions in fairly good French and laughed in his face. Las Cases did not like Betsy. He was shocked by her manners. But Napoleon lent himself to her games. "It's as though I were at a masked ball," he would say.[10]

Deep down in him there was a surviving remnant of childish gaiety that came to the surface in sudden bursts. His own childhood had been too serious and he had had no real youth. He liked to tease, and sometimes lent himself to incredible pranks. The little Legge girl, daughter of friends of the Balcombes, came to The Briars during those first days. She was terribly afraid of "General Buonaparte." Rogue that she was Betsy told Napoleon, and he forthwith appeared, his hair ruffled, shaking his head, and making fierce grimaces. The child was so frightened that Mrs. Balcombe had to carry her out of the room. Napoleon wanted to pass for just such a monster to all the English. He tried to frighten Betsy the same way too, but she made fun of him.[11]

A spoiled child, Betsy pushed the Emperor's elbow while he was making a wax imprint of a medal and some burning wax fell on his fingers. He did not seem angry. Cockburn was sometimes accompanied on his trip to The Briars by Tom Pipes who had amused the little Bertrands so much on board the *Northumberland*. Out of breath from his run behind the horses, the Newfoundland often jumped into

10 Las Cases, Vol. I, p. 311.
11 Mrs. Abell, p. 31.

JAMESTOWN, ST. HELENA, LOOKING NORTH

a round fountain of water that had been made near the grape-arbour. One day when Napoleon was sitting there, Betsy called the dog and made him go in for a bath. When he came out, he shook himself, as she had foreseen, against the Emperor, and his stockings, vest and coat were splashed. Betsy would steal the Emperor's papers, and then go shouting about that at last she had his secrets, but if he consented to chase her she would hand them back to him very politely. Accustomed to that free, rustic life and knowing nothing of the world the two girls were astonished at the ceremony that preceded Napoleon's repasts. Cipriani, the maître d'hôtel, would approach, make a very low bow and declaim:

"His Majesty's dinner is served."

Then he would back away, while the Emperor followed, towards the table set in the arbour, or else under a tent which the Admiral had had pitched near the pavilion.

A few days after his arrival Napoleon invited his young friends. He twitted them on their taste for roast beef and plum-pudding. Whereupon Betsy retorted that the French ate frogs. She ran home and came back producing a caricature that showed a sad skinnybones with his mouth open and a frog on his tongue. Underneath was printed: "A Frenchman's dinner." The Emperor tweaked Betsy's ear, the way he used to do with his grenadiers.[12]

Betsy did not get on well with Emmanuel de Las Cases, a boy about her own age, who could not endure her tomfooleries. Napoleon teased them, saying that he was going to marry them to each other some day. The Emperor once ordered the young boy to kiss Betsy and he held the little girl's arms while the boy grazed her cheek with his lips. Betsy pranced and kicked with rage, then the moment Napoleon let her go, rushed at Emmanuel and slapped his face. But she was not satisfied. Soon afterward as the Emperor and Las Cases were walking Indian file down a steep path, she thought up a new deviltry. Napoleon was walking in front. After him came Las Cases, then Emmanuel, then Jane, and last of all Betsy. Suddenly she flung herself with all her weight against Jane, who lurched with outstretched hands against Emmanuel, who seized his father, who collided with the Emperor, who almost lost his balance. Beside himself Las Cases seized Betsy by the shoulders and flung her against the parapet. She was hurt and wept angrily:

[12] Mrs. Abell, p. 35.

"*Monsieur*, he has hurt me!"

"Wait," said the Emperor. "Don't cry! I'll hold him while you punish him."

She took full advantage of the opportunity, giving Las Cases several resonant slaps in the face. The chamberlain at last cried for mercy and Napoleon let him go, advising him however to avoid further punishment. Betsy rushed after him to give him some more. Clapping his hands Napoleon cheered their race around the lawn. It was a long time before Las Cases forgave Betsy.

Assured of making a pretty penny with the French, Balcombe was extremely solicitous towards the Emperor and the latter responded in a friendly spirit. Mrs. Balcombe was a Puritanic creature who always talked earnestly. She bore not a little resemblance to Josephine, as Napoleon remarked on the very first day. Alarmed at Betsy's bad manners, the parents would lecture her severely. She would then appear for a time on her most ladylike behaviour, only to relapse the next moment into her tomboyish rollicks.

.     .     .     .     .     .     .     .

One evening Napoleon crossed the limits of The Briars with the little girls and Gourgaud. He began to walk through a meadow where some cows were browsing. One of them charged him, horns lowered. The Emperor leapt over a low wall and was safe, but meantime Gourgaud had valiantly bared his sword and flung himself on the cow, crying:

"This is the second time I have saved the Emperor's life!"

Napoleon laughed heartily and gibed at Gourgaud all the evening long.

He was in the habit of ending his day with the Balcombes when they had no callers, a fact that Las Cases would make sure of by peering in at a window.

They played whist in a sort of rustic intimacy that the Emperor rather enjoyed. However, he was obliged to confine himself for several days to the pavilion with a cold which he attributed to the sudden fall of night after the sunset. He was subject to bronchial infections and sore throat, and coughed violently in such attacks. Mrs. Balcombe volunteered her services as nurse, offering him brews that she sweetened with honey from her hives. But the Emperor thanked her and clung to his liquorice, which he deemed a sovereign

WILLIAM BALCOMBE, OWNER OF "THE BRIARS"
From a Contemporary Drawing

remedy, whatever Dr. O'Meara, who visited him each morning, might say.

Left alone during this attack with Las Cases and Emmanuel, he decided, as he said, to make an inventory of his wealth. Marchand got out his chest of snuff boxes. There were a fairly large number of them, some painted with miniatures of the Imperial family, others enriched with cameos or ancient medals, others still bearing his own portrait framed with diamonds. There were also three snuff boxes of Louis XVIII which the King, on fleeing to Ghent on the 20th of March, had left on a table in the Tuileries. They had no value.

Napoleon then sent for one of his campaign cases. He examined it, then offered it to Las Cases, saying:

"I have had it a long time. I used it the morning of Austerlitz. It will go to Emmanuel. By the time he is eighty years old, these things will be great curiosities. He will show it and say, 'The Emperor Napoleon gave it to my father at St. Helena.'"

Emmanuel was a sensitive lad. He did not quite succeed in restraining his tears.[13]

.        .        .        .        .        .        .

Among the two or three dozen slaves that Balcombe employed was an old Malay called Toby. In his youth he had been kidnapped and carried off on a sampan by a crew of English sailors and sold at St. Helena. He had never left the island since. With Las Cases acting as interpreter, Napoleon questioned the poor fellow. He pitied his sad lot and every time he met him about the gardens he would nod to him in a friendly way. The old man would lift his straw hat, rest his weight on his spade and look after him, grinning all over his wrinkled, yellow face.[14] Napoleon had a gold piece sent to him. Toby called him "the good gentleman" and was delighted to bring him fruit and flowers at the pavilion. It occurred to the Emperor to buy him and give him back his freedom. He mentioned the matter to Balcombe who became interested. The Admiral however raised objections and nothing came of it, to Napoleon's great regret.[15]

[13] Las Cases, Vol. I, p. 323.

[14] Las Cases, Vol. I, p. 463; Mrs. Abell, p. 57.

[15] Sir Hudson Lowe settled the matter some months later, forbidding the emancipation of any Malays. He feared that Napoleon would make too many friends among the coloured people by such an act (Montholon, Vol. I, p. 258). Slaves were sometimes harshly treated on St. Helena. Slavery was abolished there by Lowe himself in 1818.

The English were amazed at the benevolence which the Emperor showed towards humble people, as contrasted with the tone he often adopted towards people of quality, even if they were his friends. One day, as he was returning home along the road from Jamestown, whither he sometimes rode to look at the harbour and the vessels, he met Mrs. Balcombe in company with a young Scotchwoman— Mrs. Stuart. All three went back together, chatting, towards The Briars. At a turn in the path they met some slaves carrying heavy boxes on their shoulders. Mrs. Balcombe, good soul that she was, ordered them to stand aside. Napoleon stopped her:

"Respect for the boxes, Madame!"

And he stood aside himself.

Mrs. Stuart could not suppress a murmur:

"Goodness! How different he is from what they told me he was!"

.     .     .     .     .     .     .     .

Now and then Napoleon would take Betsy's young brothers on his knees and let them play with his crosses, as he had done of yore with the King of Rome. The elder, Alexander, one day found a pack of cards stamped with the usual likeness of the Grand Mogul. The child held it out to Napoleon, saying:

"Look, Boney—that's you!"

The Emperor did not understand. Betsy explained that "Boney" was the nickname the English had given him. Las Cases said that Boney meant "bony."

"But I am not 'bony,' " said Napoleon, laughing, and he exhibited his hands, small and fat, and his dimpled fingers as tapering as a woman's. Betsy was amazed that they could hold a sword. Napoleon ordered a splendid sabre taken out of its box. The sheath was of shell, studded with gold bees. Betsy took the beautiful weapon in her hands. Napoleon sometimes helped her with her French compositions. He had informed Balcombe that morning that Betsy refused to work, so that in setting out for the town the purveyor had threatened to punish his daughter if the exercise was not done in time for dinner. Here was a chance to get even with Boney now! Betsy drew the blade from its sheath and began to swing it about over Napoleon's head. He backed and backed till the wall prevented him from retreating further. Then the little minx shouted at him to say his prayers, for his time had come. Jane hurried in and implored her sister in vain. Betsy kept the Emperor at his distance until at last her arm dropped from sheer weariness. Las Cases who witnessed the scene dared not intervene. When she had lowered the sabre, Napoleon contented himself with pulling her nose.

The anecdotes about the life of the Emperor at The Briars that have been left by the writers of memoirs and especially by Betsy are too numerous not to compel a choice. Here is one however that it would be a pity to omit since it depicts colourfully the relations of Napoleon with his hosts. Betsy's boldness increased under the indulgence of the Emperor. One day she showed him a mechanical toy that had come from London. It was a sort of jumping-jack that represented him and made him climb a ladder, each rung of which bore the name of a conquered country. When he arrived at the top, a spring clicked and flung him headlong upon a little platform inscribed with the words: "St. Helena." Napoleon did not get angry, but Mrs. Balcombe was mortified and locked her daughter up in a cellar where she was left all alone in company with Mr. Balcombe's wine bottles and the rats. Poor Betsy was left to spend the whole night there, paralyzed with fear. She could hear the rats jumping about here and there and, imagining that they were going to eat her alive, she seized a bottle of wine and hurled it at them. The rats were quiet for a moment and then began again. Betsy threw bottle after bottle so that in the morning, when the slave went to carry her her breakfast, he found her sitting behind a pile of broken glass and half drunk from the exhalations of the wine which formed a veritable pond on the cellar floor.

The Emperor was highly amused at this nocturnal battle with the rats. He told Betsy that he had once seen a big one jump out of his own hat when he took it up to put it on.

The evening after the sabre episode he showed the Balcombe children some pictures. They were drawings of his son that he had brought with him. In some the baby was shown reclining, now on a bed of flags, now in a helmet of Mars. In one he was kneeling before a crucifix with the motto: "I pray God for my father and for France." In still others he could be seen riding one of the pet lambs that Caroline of Naples had sent him, or again at his mother's side on a background of clouds and roses. The Emperor seemed happy to hear the cries of delight with which the young English children admired "his little king."

They went down to the house for whist. The cards stuck badly.

Las Cases was ordered to shuffle them carefully. Meantime the Emperor talked to the girls about Admiral Cockburn's ball. He had interceded with Balcombe that Betsy, in spite of her age, might be allowed to go to this her first evening affair away from home.[16] The two girls had just been invited and Napoleon now asked Betsy what kind of a gown she was to wear. She ran upstairs to fetch her dress, the first evening gown she had ever owned and of which she was immensely proud. She spread it out before him. He admired it. Finally they started to play. They had never played for stakes before, but that evening the Emperor said:

"Miss Betsy, I am betting a napoleon."

A pagoda (a Hindu coin then current at St. Helena and valued at about ten francs) was all that Betsy owned in the world. She bet it.

In order to tease Betsy, Napoleon showed his cards to Jane. Betsy threatened to stop playing. He continued, however, and a little later, to hide his cheating, mixed up the cards. Betsy shook his arm and accused him of cheating. He replied, laughing almost to tears, that Betsy was the one who was cheating and that she had lost her pagoda. She protested loudly, but he suddenly rose, picked up the dress that was lying on an armchair, fled to the pavilion and locked himself in. Betsy ran in pursuit and finding his door locked, begged him to open. She was afraid he would tear her dress and the little tissue paper roses that were fastened on it. He was inexorable. In the end she went back home and cried herself to sleep. The next day she hoped to get her dress back, but she was not allowed to approach Napoleon all day long. Every time she appeared, Marchand or Aly would answer that the Emperor could not be disturbed. She was in despair. Not until the carriage arrived to take her and her mother and sister to town, did he reappear. With the dress over his arm he ran to the carriage in which they were seated and said:

"Here is your dress, Miss Betsy. Be a good girl now and have a good time at the ball. Don't forget to dance with Gourgaud."

She made a face. She did not like Gourgaud. She thought him ugly, and she was angry that he saw in her only a child. Napoleon walked beside the carriage to the end of the road that led from The Briars to the highway. There he stopped and asked who owned the house that they could see at the end of the gorge. Followed at a distance by the orderly officer, he went down with Las Cases and

[16] Mrs. Abell, p. 48.

came back, having been cordially received at Maldivia House by Major Hodgson who lent him horses for the return trip.[17]

Napoleon had also been invited to the Admiral's ball. He felt that he could not properly accept, but ordered all of his companions to go. It would be a diversion. Moreover, it was just as well not to hurt the Admiral's feelings. That was on November 14th.[18] The invitation had been addressed to "General Buonaparte." Once before the Admiral had invited Napoleon to dine at the Castle and the Emperor had politely refused. Another ball was given on December 2 at Plantation House, this time by Governor Wilks. Gourgaud had been complaining of the lack of consideration with which, according to him, the French were treated. He so angered the Emperor that he forbade any one of them to be present. Mme. Bertrand and Mme. de Montholon were terribly disappointed.

The island had passed under martial law. Two warships rode at anchor in the bay and two brigs cruised up and down offshore incessantly. On October 17th Colonel Wilks issued a proclamation forbidding the inhabitants to go about without the password after nine o'clock in the evening. All the fishing boats were to be in dock by sunset. No foreign vessel was to be admitted or allowed to communicate with the island. Any suspicious vessel would be fired on.[19]

Napoleon raged at the Admiral and told his companions that in their letters to Europe they must complain of the treatment which was being inflicted on him and on them. Finally, at the instance of Las Cases, he ordered Bertrand to address an official protest to Cockburn. The Grand Marshal refused. Such recriminations, he declared, were beneath the Emperor's dignity. Napoleon appeared to yield, but on several occasions returned to the subject. Finally the storm broke. The Emperor told Bertrand he was "nothing but an idiot." The Grand Marshal lost his temper:

"Your Majesty is very wrong not to listen to my advice."

So the timid Bertrand had raised his voice! The Emperor looked at him and murmured:

[17] Hodgson was a huge fellow, six feet tall and extremely impressive. Napoleon called him Hercules. He was "town major" at Jamestown and was uniformly courteous to the French. He spent the greater part of his life at St. Helena, attended the Emperor's funeral and later his exhumation. His wife was the daughter of William Doveton, of whom more later. Admiral Sir F. D. Sturdee, conqueror of the Germans in the naval battle off the Falklands in 1914, was a grandson of Major Hodgson.

[18] Gourgaud, Vol. I, p. 85.

[19] Jamestown Archives, 1815.

"You would not have said that to me at the Tuileries. Everything I did then was right."

That was more oil on the fire. Napoleon added:

"For that matter, the *Weymouth* will soon be bringing to each one of you permission to leave." [20]

Gourgaud protested.

"Those who have followed the Emperor," he said, "will never leave him, no matter how bad his lot may become, unless he himself dismisses them."

Left alone shortly afterwards Napoleon and the Grand Marshal patched up their differences. Gourgaud and Bertrand dined at The Briars. As they were about to return to Jamestown, the Emperor invited Gourgaud to come and stay with him:

"You are young. We shall talk of our love affairs—of women. They would have been the charm of my life if I had had time for them. My hours were so short—I had so many things to do. If I were ever to ascend the throne again, I would consecrate two hours a day to conversation with women. Mme. Duchatel, Mme. de Rovigo, Mme. de Montesquiou—they taught me many things that had it not been for them I should never have known." [21]

Yielding at last Bertrand sent Cockburn a protest somewhat more moderate than Las Cases had suggested. The Admiral made a rude reply:

"You oblige me officially to explain to you that I have no cognizance of any Emperor being actually upon this island, or of any person possessing such dignity having (as stated by you) come hither with you in the *Northumberland*." [22]

Napoleon flew into a rage:

"That man is insulting me. And I am very sure Bertrand did not write him what I dictated!"

Sir George Bingham paid a call on him with Major Fehrzen and he did not hide his resentment.

"The Admiral," he said, "is a regular shark."

.    .    .    .    .    .    .    .

To tell the truth, during those first weeks at The Briars, Napoleon had not been unhappy. He breathed like a man who had fallen from

[20] Gourgaud, Vol. I, p. 81; Montholon, Vol. I, p. 173.
[21] Gourgaud, Vol. I, p. 81.
[22] Cockburn to Bertrand, November 6, 1815 (Norwood Young, Vol. I, p. 121).

a height and was astounded at finding himself alive. He kept up courage in his companions, who were bored to extremities by life in Jamestown. Gourgaud complained of everyone and everything. Bertrand and Montholon were spying on each other, waging a tacit war for control of the Emperor's household—the ordering, the purchasing, the bookkeeping. Little by little Montholon was getting the better of Bertrand whose only weapons were peevishness and silence. They were eating badly. The food was of poor quality. It came from Brazil or the Cape, often tainted or spoiled by the heat. The mouldy flour they received made a detestable bread. The cattle suffered from the long sea voyage and several months in the pastures of the island would have been required to get them back into condition. Only the fish, the game and the vegetables were good. But the French were accustomed to the fastidious cuisine in France and they found nothing to their liking.

The worst situated without doubt were the women. They were left all to themselves at the Porteous lodging house. Immediately after luncheon the men set out for The Briars and did not come back until night. While waiting for them, Mme. Bertrand and Mme. de Montholon could sit at their windows looking down into the garden of the East India Company through the slats of their Chinese blinds. They took care of their children, read, mended their clothes. The heat was unbearable in that straggling village smothered by the surrounding cliffs. Mme. de Montholon did not stand it very well (she had just become pregnant), but she made less fuss about it than Mme. Bertrand, who was always in a rage and always quarrelling. Towards evening they would go out into the street for a visit to the one shop. It was kept by a Jew, Solomon, and was so run down in stock that they could not find even a paper of pins there.

Mme. Bertrand and Mme. de Montholon could not get on together—they were too different in temperament, training, and ways. They quarrelled bitterly, calling each other names that finally eventuated in the unprintable word.[23] Then they would make up for a day or two. They made some acquaintances among the island people— Mrs. Porteous, their hostess, her daughter, and a pretty friend of the latter, a Miss Knipe, whom all the island called Rosebud on account of her rosy cheeks. "A farmer's daughter," says Mme. de Montholon, "she was tall, blonde, with a beautiful figure. With her Polish sort

[23] Gourgaud, Nov. 3, 1815 (Thiers Library).

of face, she had points of resemblance with Mme. Waleswka and on that account she caught Napoleon's attention for a brief moment."

They became friendly with the Skeltons, the Wilkses, the Dovetons. Mme. Bertrand gave a handle to gossip by the interest she took in the handsome Captain Hamilton of the *Havannah*. She sometimes went to dinner on board his ship, taking Gourgaud with her, for she felt sorry for the poor boy in his loneliness.

These ladies had all gone to Cockburn's ball on the 14th with great enthusiasm. All the notables of the colony, military as well as civil, were present in the two rooms of the castle that opened through large bay windows upon the sea. "From all points of the island," Mme. de Montholon relates, "came pretty girls in white skirts and pink waists." The two Frenchwomen had put on their best and in that simple society they shone with splendour. Mme. de Montholon wore a brooch of emeralds surrounded with diamonds that "made a marvellous effect." She and Mme. Bertrand danced a great deal and, cut off as they had so long been from all pleasures of society, had a really good time.

Gourgaud wore a glum face throughout the evening. He did not want to dance with Betsy Balcombe, decked out in her famous gown, but found himself obliged to do so. The Governor's daughter, Miss Wilks, aristocratic, gracious, made a great impression on him. As for the charming Rosebud! For a moment he thought of love, for he had a tender heart and suffered from his enforced celibacy. But he was badly placed at supper. His one consolation was to see that Las Cases was no better treated than he.

The next day Napoleon made them tell him about the party. Said Gourgaud:

"Had Your Majesty gone to that ball, as M. de Montholon advised, all the fool inhabitants on the island would have been slapping Your Majesty on the back."

"I think I did well in not going, but if I had been there rest assured that they would have centred around me, just as in a big party in Paris." [24]

It took strength of soul indeed to speak that way in that camp of bohemians. However, the spirit of the group improved as a result. Each Sunday the French and O'Meara gathered at The Briars and dined formally.

[24] Gourgaud, November 21, 1815 (Thiers Library, Carton 18). Unpublished.

Some days later, November 28th, Colonel Bingham gave a luncheon followed by a dance. Las Cases took Mme. Bertrand in a carriage drawn by six oxen. Going on to Longwood, the French visited their future dwelling and were scandalized at its shabbiness, whereas Cockburn insisted that this residence "was as good as St. Cloud." Doubtless he had never seen St. Cloud.[25]

On November 29, Gourgaud went to The Briars to live. He was provided with a little tent pitched alongside the big one. Napoleon showed his emotion in his presence over news that La Bédoyère had been executed and Marshal Brune assassinated. Montholon, coming in from Jamestown, reported that all France was rising, "that an army of 150,000 men had gathered, that there were calls for the Emperor from all sides and that England, frightened, was putting her army and navy on a war footing."

Lies, but they strengthened hearts! Napoleon was the first to give rein to his imagination:

"How cruel to be a prisoner just at this moment! Who is there to head such a movement? Eugene? No, he lacks character. Soult? He is a good quartermaster, nothing more! I am the only one who could succeed! Clauzel? Yes, perhaps Clauzel! He is a man of resource, of vigour. He is the only one I fear."

"Well, sire," said Las Cases, "if he succeeds it will be a very good thing for Your Majesty."

"Do you think he would be such a fool as to yield his place to me? The last comers are always right. The past is forgotten for the present."

Bertrand suggested—to avoid difficulties with the English authorities—taking a new title, the Comte de Lyon. He cited the example of Louis XVIII, who became Comte de Lille. Napoleon seemed tempted. Gourgaud said that such a disguise would be ridiculous—the counts of Lyons were all sacristans.

The idea was given up. They were to return to it later on however.[26]

.     .     .     .     .     .     .     .

Early in December, the Admiral came and announced that the alterations at Longwood had been completed and that Napoleon

[25] Las Cases, Vol. I, pp. 455-56; Gourgaud, Vol. I, p. 91.
[26] Gourgaud, Vol. I, p. 98.

might move in at any time he chose.[27] Cockburn wanted Napoleon
to leave The Briars and settle at Longwood at the earliest possible
moment. His thought probably was that only then would his prisoner be safe. Communications with ships and with Europe were too
easy at the Balcombes'. "To please the Admiral," says Gourgaud,
"Montholon did his best to influence His Majesty to the change."[28]

The Emperor asked nothing better. He was weary of The Briars
now. After a long period of fine weather it was raining every day.
They were better sheltered in that dale than on the upper plateaus,
but the trade-wind carried Gourgaud's tent away nevertheless. Besides, as Napoleon said, those black mountains that overhung the
gorge shutting out all view, "imprisoned him a second time." He
hurried Gourgaud and Bertrand as scouts to Longwood. They came
back saying that the rooms still smelt of paint. The Emperor detested
that odour, yet he was so impatient that he decided to move over
the day after the next.

On December 10 he dined in the garden with Balcombe and received Cockburn who had come to do him the honours at his new
residence. Betsy was inconsolable at seeing him go.

"You must not cry, Miss Betsy," said Napoleon. "You will come
and see me at Longwood."

His hostess was ill at the time and kept to her room. He went to
see her and, taking a seat on her bed, thanked her for her kindnesses.
In taking his leave of her, he left a gold snuff box for Balcombe and
gave Betsy a bonbonnière. The girl fled holding a handkerchief to
her eyes.[29]

He had put off his uniform as a Chasseur of the Guard a fortnight
earlier ("November 28," says Marchand)—he was never again to
wear it alive.[30] He now put on a green coat with tails, with the cordon
of the Legion of Honour barely showing. On his head he wore the
little cocked hat.

He set out with Cockburn and his own officers—all except Gourgaud, who had gone on ahead. He rode a South African pony, young,
lively. The women, children and luggage followed at some distance
in wagons drawn by great humped oxen with white horns—the sort
that were used to do the ploughing on the island. Many people sta-

[27] Las Cases, Vol. II, p. 25.
[28] Thiers Library. Unpublished.
[29] Mrs. Abell, p. 91.
[30] The statement to the contrary, made by Las Cases, Vol. II, p. 36, is false.

tioned themselves along the road to see Napoleon pass. A number of English officers joined the cavalcade.

They reached the guardhouse about four o'clock. The soldiers came out and presented arms. The Emperor's horse was frightened as the drums beat a general roulade and pranced and backed several times as though he were unwilling to cross the boundary—a bad sign! Napoleon gave him the spur and forced him into the drive.

Cockburn leapt from the saddle in front of the steps and helped Napoleon to dismount. He led the way into the house and showed him the rooms one after the other. The Emperor seemed more satisfied than the Admiral had hoped for. Cockburn's sailors and Bingham's soldiers had worked well. They had changed "that collection of shanties" into a residence which, at first sight, appeared quite passable. Cockburn departed greatly relieved.[31]

The moment he had turned on his heels the Emperor asked for his bath. The tub that had been set up in a tiny room behind his bedchamber was a primitive affair—a long, oaken trough lined with lead. It looked like a coffin.[32] Napoleon had not had a genuine bath since leaving Malmaison and comfort in that respect was one of his necessaries. He saw the tub with utter delight, and stayed in it more than an hour, chatting with Las Cases, suggesting to him, among other things, that he should come and use the tub in his turn the next day. The little man objecting, he returned:

"My dear fellow, here we are in prison and must help one another. I could not occupy this contrivance all day long, and a good bath would do you as much good as me."[33]

He did not dress again but went to bed. He was tired. He had taken a walk that morning while his things were being moved, and the horseback ride over the bad road had shaken him up. During those five months of obligatory inactivity he had grown stout and Marchand had been obliged to let out his belts. He dined in his bedroom and retired early and, under the faithful guard of his nightlamp, slept soundly for the first time in weeks.

[31] Gourgaud, Vol. I, p. 101.
[32] It was a product of the craftsmanship of the ship carpenters on the *Northumberland*. It was later turned into a garden pool. The Admiral had ordered a real bath tub sent on from Capetown. It arrived some months later.
[33] Las Cases, Vol. II, p. 40.

# II

## *LONGWOOD*

A CENTURY EARLIER, LONGWOOD AND DEADWOOD HAD BEEN PARTS OF a plantation called The Great Wood. The first mention of it in the Archives of Jamestown is dated August 11, 1678. Little by little this woods, ill-protected, was destroyed by men and animals. In 1723 a new plantation of gum trees was laid out on a stretch of about 600 acres and girded by a wall of dry stones. The tract was about four miles (a little less than six kilometres) in circumference.[1]

Longwood House had been built in 1753. Originally it consisted of a barn and a cow-shed. In 1787 Lieutenant-Governor Robson had converted the barn into a suite of four rooms and used it as a country residence. He had added another room to it, at right angles, in the middle of the building, and beyond that he built privies and quarters for his slaves. None of the sections had cellars or basements. It was just a summer house. To enlarge Napoleon's apartment, the Admiral had built an addition to the drawingroom in pine, to serve either as an ante-room or as a billiard room. It was reached by a narrow flight of steps five lifts high and a glassed-in verandah. The billiardroom was fairly large.[2] It was lighted by five sash windows, two looking towards the Barn, a gloomy mountain that turned a giant human profile towards Africa, and three facing the Diana Range, the drive, and the sharp outline of High Knoll—a fortress to the south-west of Jamestown, overlooking the greater part of the island and a stretch of the sea. The walls were painted light green and bordered with the interlocking squares of the Greek key in black. There were two sofas, several chairs, a number of tables, a piano and, to either side of the door, a globe of the world and a

---

[1] The wall in question was made the first limit for the prisoners at Longwood. In 1817 it was to supply the stones for the new dwelling provided for Napoleon (New House). The greater part of it is still standing.

[2] 26 × 19 feet. The exact dimensions, taken with the kind assistance of M. Georges Colin, curator of the French domain of Longwood, were: 8 metres × 5.70 × 3.70. This room is commonly referred to by Sir Hudson Lowe as the "entrance room." After the arrival of the furniture from England it became the "billiardroom."

THE DRAWINGROOM, LONGWOOD

celestial globe—gifts of Colonel Wilks.[3] From there one passed into the drawingroom, covered with Chinese wall-paper with yellow designs, and lighted by two windows to the west.[4] The furniture had been gathered about the island haphazard and cheaply.[5] It was altogether wretched—a flowered carpet almost worn out, several armchairs, some low chairs in black horsehair, folding tables, a card table. On the mantelpiece stood a mirror. The curtains were of plain muslin.

Back of that came the diningroom.[6] It was studded lower—nine feet, and very dark. The only bit of daylight came from the high glass window in a door that led into the garden. The walls were painted blue.[7] This room had been furnished with a maroon carpet, ten chairs, a large table and a sideboard. A screen hid the door going into the study and to the kitchen. On the left was a cold and bare room without a fireplace.[8] The Emperor gave it to the Montholons as a temporary lodging.

On the other side of the diningroom were the two little rooms [9] which formed Napoleon's private apartment and which he called his "interior." Of these two rooms the Emperor used the first as his study, the second as his bedroom. Both received light through narrow windows opening on the lawn to the north-east. Being in the southern hemisphere that was the sunny side of the house. They were both hung in yellow nankeen, bordered with a red-flowered paper. The bedroom alone had a fireplace. The uprights and the

[3] These two globes, mounted on black wooden feet, were recognized by the author in the Castle of Jamestown where they had finally ended, no one realizing their origin. The *Souvenirs* of Aly give a precise description of them and they are mentioned in the inventory drawn up by the upholsterer Darling after the Emperor's death, which I found in the Jamestown Archives. Those two documents enabled me to identify them with certainty. They were in good condition and, since the opening of the Napoleon Museum (May 5, 1934), they have been back in their former place at Longwood.

[4] This room was 24 × 14 × 12 feet.

[5] Six hundred francs' worth, said Napoleon. Cockburn wrote on this subject to the secretary of the Admiralty, Wilson Croker: "I have succeeded in procuring all the indispensable articles at the lowest prices" (Public Record Office, St. Helena, Vol. VII, p. 247). In 1816 other furniture was to arrive from London.

[6] 22 × 15 × 9.

[7] As when Skelton lived there. Cockburn had not considered it necessary to repaint them. In 1819 this room was to be re-covered with a red paper with gilt flowers. On the same date the drawingroom was to be papered straw-colour with blue stars.

[8] 20 × 14 × 10.

[9] Study: 15 × 14½ × 10; bedroom: 14 × 14 × 10. The study was commonly designated by the English at Longwood as the "sittingroom."

mantelpiece were wooden and painted grey. A much-worn carpet
that had previously been used by an army officer at St. Helena hid
the floor.[10] It had been equipped with an easy-chair, straight chairs
caned with beechwood and painted green, a chest of drawers and an
old sofa covered with cotton cloth.

Marchand began the very first day to transform that "hole" with
his reverent taste. In front of the mirror on the mantelpiece he set
two silver candlesticks, a silver cup lined with gold, an incense
burner. To either side he hung the dearest, the supreme, mementos
of the Captive: a picture of the King of Rome, miniatures of
Madame Mère and Josephine, and—one of the last pieces of booty
from Napoleon's wars—the alarm-clock of the great Frederick, which
he had "picked up" at Potsdam.[11] Napoleon liked symmetry. To
balance things he pinned to the wall-paper on the other side the
watch that he had used during the second campaign in Italy. The
chain was made of a slender wisp of Marie-Louise's hair. To the right
of the mantelpiece Marchand placed the silver washbasin that he
had brought from the Élysée, to the left the Emperor's gold
dressing case. The camp bed, with the curtains that had been drawn
over so many dreams, stood along the inner wall. At the foot was
a protecting screen on which a portrait of Marie-Louise, her son in
her arms, was hung. The second camp bed was placed in the study.
Napoleon often went from one to the other during the night. He
had slept in the first on the eve of Austerlitz and the second had
fought the campaign in France.

Behind the bedroom came the bathroom and a corridor with a bed
for the valet on duty, Marchand or Aly as the case might be.[12] A
passageway led from there to the kitchen which was set up in a
little one-storied house. Las Cases had his room there. His son slept
in the garret, which he reached by a ladder. These buildings were
separated from the privies by an inside courtyard that had entrances

[10] There had never been at any time a cow-barn there, as Montholon claims
(Vol. I, p. 196). The former cow-shed had been the building that was being transformed at that very moment into a house for the Montholon family. Nor did the
floors in the bedroom and the Emperor's study rest directly on the ground, as
Montholon again says. Under them was an air-space of a foot and a half that diminished as it ran towards the south, so that the diningroom and the library were
flush with the ground.

[11] Aly, p. 222.

[12] When Marchand was not on duty he slept just over the Emperor's chamber in
a sheathed room with an arched window that had a fine prospect over the landscape from Diana's Peak to the sea.

NAPOLEON'S BED-CHAMBER, LONGWOOD

NAPOLEON'S STUDY, LONGWOOD

leading out towards the gum tree forest. It was often muddy. Beyond, near the wall of dry stones that bordered the estate along Sinner's Valley, stood the stables.

The Montholon family, as well as Gourgaud, O'Meara and the orderly officer (Poppleton), were to be lodged in an addition that was being built at right angles to the wall of the kitchen. When the French arrived the carpenters were just putting on the roofing of tarred felt. Meantime the Montholons camped in the Emperor's part of the house. The others slept in tents that were set up in the garden.

Mme. Bertrand refused to live with so many people in such close quarters.[13] She wanted to follow her usual mode of life and appear only when it suited her. Nagged on the subject by his wife,[14] the Grand Marshal finally asked the Emperor's permission to use a cottage that he had noticed on the Longwood road at the turn of Hutt's Gate, a mile and a half away.[15] The separation would be a matter of only a few months since the Admiral had consented to build a separate house for Bertrand, a stone's throw from Napoleon's windows.

The Emperor took this arrangement in bad part.

"Do as you please," he said. "Montholon will live with me."

He was never to forget that sign of independence. That was obvious when Napoleon, who was so particular in such matters, came to organize his household. The Grand Marshal should normally have been the man to take charge. The Emperor gave the post to Montholon.[16] From that time on Bertrand was no more than a sort of secretary-general, in charge more particularly of relations with the English. Gourgaud received the superintendence of the stables,[17] Las Cases got the administration of stores, but he was primarily concerned with remaining the Emperor's pen and portfolio.

[13] What with masters and servants, Longwood was to shelter fifty-one persons in 1816.

[14] Napoleon had at first offered Bertrand the room he gave to the Montholons and which was later to be used as the library (Montholon, Vol. I, p. 192).

[15] The house is still standing. It has become the rectory of the little St. Matthew's church. It overlooks the Vale of the Geranium.

[16] Las Cases, Vol. II, p. 49.

[17] Gourgaud, Vol. I, p. 101. Napoleon was to have six riding and four cart horses. All but two were furnished by the English government. The two were *Fringant* and *Vizir*, who came from the Imperial stables. They had gone aboard the *Épervier* on the night of July 14-15. Most of the horses came in from the Cape on December 23rd on the *Doris* (Jamestown Archives, 1815).

He did not take his other functions as commissary seriously and allowed Montholon to get them away from him.

Bertrand's feelings had not been spared in all this readjusting. Napoleon ordered Gourgaud to smooth matters out. "The Emperor," says Gourgaud,[18] "sent me to Bertrand to explain that, though Montholon has charge of the table and I of the stables, he is still Grand Marshal—under the Constitution that post is permanent. In spite of anything I could say Bertrand was very piqued that he should have been informed of the changes made in the household through a subordinate."

Bertrand sulked for a long time. To pacify him Napoleon went to Hutt's Gate on December 15th and invited both Bertrand and Mme. Bertrand to dinner. They evaded on some pretext or other and did not appear. On the 18th they came for Sunday dinner. But the Emperor was much put out with them and dined alone in his room. They sat at table with the Montholons, the Las Cases and Gourgaud and, says the latter, "went away in a rage."

· · · · · · · · ·

At Plymouth Napoleon had been allowed to take twelve servants with him, not counting Bernard Heymann (a Belgian) who was in the service of the Bertrands, with his wife as an extra, and a chambermaid, Josephine Brulé, who had likewise been allowed Mme. de Montholon over and above the specified number.

The majority of these servants were, and were to remain, servants. But some few of them, because of their intelligence or their courage, were to play a rôle in the Emperor's life far superior to their rank.

In the former group are to be counted the official chef, Pierron, a clever pastry-cook and confectioner who had also been at Elba; the two Archambault brothers, at first footmen, but now coachmen, and who drove with amazing skill; Rousseau, in charge of the silver polishing; Lepage, a mediocre cook whom Joseph had handed over at Rochefort (a man who had come without enthusiasm and whose temperament kept him friendless); an Elban, Gentilini, who had been kept in his post as footman; and finally, the former cavalryman, Noverraz, a tall, powerful Swiss, obtuse of wit but of a loyalty tried and proved.

Those who were to play an important part were, first of all and

18 Vol. I, p. 102.

HUTT'S GATE, ST. HELENA

on a plane by themselves, the valet Marchand and the steward, Cipriano Franceschi, commonly known as Cipriani.

Louis Marchand was twenty-four years old. His mother, "the good Chanchan," nurse to the King of Rome, had followed the latter to Vienna in 1814. Marchand had been a mere page when Constant and Roustan turned traitor at Fontainebleau. Marchand was picked by the Grand Marshal at that time for the post as first valet. He had gone through Elba and the Hundred Days, and Napoleon liked him, gradually taking him into his confidence. The young man was worthy of it. Tall, dark, with a handsome, earnest face, excellent health, irreproachable manners, Marchand was more cultivated than a man of his station generally is. He wrote, could draw very well, and was a good bookkeeper. He bore the Emperor a tender and wholly disinterested respect. For Napoleon he was to be the most devoted of servants and, in the Emperor's last days, the most understanding of friends.

Cipriani was a Corsican who had known Napoleon's family from childhood.[19] Under the Empire he had acted as a secret agent and spy for Saliceti at Naples—a dark period in his career. He went on to Elba and was chief butler at the Tuileries during the Hundred Days. A good deal of a clown, with a nasal voice, lively, bold, he had, though a revolutionary at heart, attached himself to the Emperor, especially since the latter's reverses, as to a leader of his clan. At Longwood he was to be Napoleon's informer—his intelligence bureau.

On a lower plane comes the little chasseur, Natale Santini, who had fought at the front from Austerlitz to the campaign in France and had gone on to Elba as usher in the ante-room. Though he scarcely knew what to do with the man, Napoleon had chosen him for St. Helena because he was a Corsican.

On a plane with Santini stands the sometime Saint-Denis, generally known as "the mameluke Aly." At Longwood he was to fill with equal zest the post of second valet, copyist, bookkeeper, archivist and librarian. He was sound at heart and a hard worker. He was another Marchand, only more self-effacing.

According to the order of service established at Longwood, the

[19] During the St. Helena period, Cipriani's wife, Adelaide Chamant, lived in Rome. Their son was with Fesch as a servant, their daughter with Madame Mère as a maid. They had amassed a small fortune which they banked at Genoa (Masson, *Napoléon à Sainte-Hélène*, p. 163).

valet on duty in the daytime stood in the passageway that led to the bathroom. Two footmen stood in the passage leading from the diningroom to the kitchen. A butler was on duty in the drawingroom. Cipriani and Pierron wore green coats bordered with silver, white vests, black silk knee-breeches, white silk stockings and buckled shoes. Marchand and Aly had that same livery but with gilt trimmings. The other domestics, including the English soldiers lent by the Admiral, wore the livery in green and gold.

.      .      .      .      .      .      .

During those first days Napoleon went about with his officers to reconnoitre his domain. He rode the length of the four mile wall, visited the Company farm that lay on the western side of the plateau of Longwood, and went down into Mulberry Gut, a ravine occupied by the gardens and vineyards of a farmer named Breame. Once he was halted by a too-zealous sentry who had exceeded his orders. Bingham came in all haste to offer his apologies.

The limits fixed by Cockburn for the Emperor's rides, unaccompanied by any English orderly, were extremely narrow: a space of a scant dozen miles in circumference, embracing the plateau of Longwood-Deadwood, the road from Longwood to Hutt's Gate and the road to Orange Grove and Sinner's Valley. These limits had been suggested by Colonel Wilks.[20] The Admiral had adopted them with some enlargement. In short, not counting the park at Longwood, Napoleon was free to take three rides of approximately seven miles, always the same, with the camp of the 53rd Infantry, the Grand Marshal's house and Miss Mason's cottage as bounds. Beyond them the Emperor had to be accompanied by an English officer, though he could go all over the island if he chose under guard. Cockburn had at first (December 16) allowed Dr. O'Meara as well as Poppleton to act as escort. He revoked that permission on the 18th.

At the gate of Longwood, around the wall, and on the three roads open to Napoleon, pickets of soldiers were posted. At nine o'clock in the evening a number of sentries entered the garden and surrounded the house. From that hour on no one was allowed to enter without the password, no one could go out except under guard.

The Emperor's slightest movements were noted. A signal station at Longwood itself kept the authorities at Plantation House and

[20] Lowe Papers, 20-114.

Jamestown informed of them at once.[21] Other sentries posted on the main heights of the island kept a lookout over land and sea. Carrying his caution farther still, Cockburn took over Ascension Island, some 1,200 miles from St. Helena, where the British Cabinet foresaw that a rescue expedition might be organized. The island was occupied by the *Peruvian* and the *Zenobia* on October 22, 1815. Less than a year later (August 2, 1816) and for the same reason, the English flag was raised on Tristan d'Acunha, a tiny isle lost in the South Atlantic.

Napoleon had at first been scornful of those precautions. Awkward mistakes on the part of subalterns were soon to make him conscious of them. The people about him, and especially Las Cases and Gourgaud, railed against them as indignities. Finally the Emperor lost his temper. On December 21, he ordered Montholon to write the Admiral an over-stiff note demanding that the limits be enlarged, that any inhabitant of the island or any officer of the 53rd be allowed full liberty to come to Longwood, that permission be granted O'Meara to accompany the French on their rides, that permanent authorization be issued to members of his household to go to Jamestown under escort of an officer or an orderly, according to their rank. Finally he requested some other residence than Longwood "which was unhealthy and uncomfortable in summer and would be intolerable in winter." [22]

Cockburn was not to leave the protest unanswered. The next day he sent a brutal reply to Montholon:

"The very uncalled-for intemperance and indecency of the language which you have permitted yourself to use to me respecting my Government, I should not perhaps, Sir, condescend to notice, did I not think it right to inform you that I shall not in future con-

---

[21] The principal signals were as follows (Lowe Papers, 20-114):

"1. All is well with respect to General Bonaparte and family.

2. Is unwell.

3. Requests permission to . . .

4. Is not properly attended beyond the cordon of sentries.

5. Is out, but within the cordon of sentries.

6. Has been out longer than usual and is supposed to have passed the sentries not properly attended.

7. Missing (In this case a blue flag was to be raised and all the troops and the fleet warned. That signal was never used).

8. Is returned home.

9. Is in want of . . ."

[22] Lowe Papers, 20-114.

sider it necessary to answer any letters which I may receive couched
in a similar strain of unfounded invective." My instructions, the
Admiral added, "breathe throughout the same moderation and justice
which have hitherto characterized the whole conduct of my Government and which will, I have no doubt, obtain the admiration of
future ages. . . ." [23]

Repenting, perhaps, of his harsh language, he visited Longwood
two days later with the captain of the *Doris* and two ladies who
had arrived from India. Napoleon replied dryly that he was not receiving anyone and that they should leave him alone. The Admiral
invited Montholon, his wife and Gourgaud to dinner. They refused
on the Emperor's order.

. . . . . . .

At The Briars Napoleon had lived in the simplest fashion. At
Longwood he issued from a system of makeshifts and set out to
create a mode of life that would keep his sovereign status at all times
before the eyes of the English and of the world in general that was
spying on him. He insisted on a strict observance of etiquette in the
rustic mansion and led a veritable court life as though he were still
in his palaces in France. It was a fiction of grandeur that he imposed
less out of vanity than out of pride, a consciousness of what he had
been in a recent past and of what he still represented for the future.
He stiffened even towards his companions, tacitly reminding them
at every moment that he had sat on a throne, becoming more and
more insistent on forms. It was as though he feared that a daily
routine of exile, a sad community of hardship, might weaken too
quickly in them the perception that he was still the Emperor.

Towards dawn—about six o'clock in that latitude—he rang for his
valet, who entered and opened the shutters. Napoleon rose from his
camp bed, put on a pair of trousers of white velveteen, a knitted
dressing gown and red leather slippers. Humming a tune of his childhood—always off key, he sipped a cup of black coffee, then shaved
himself. Then came his toilet, fastidious, painstaking. He had his
chest and back rubbed vigorously with eau de Cologne—lavender
water when the cologne was not available. Then he dressed—a green
hunting coat with tails and chased silver buttons, a black tie, vest
and trousers of white dimity, gold-buckled shoes that gave way to
boots when he went out.

[23] Lowe Papers, 20-114; Norwood Young, Vol. I, pp. 183-84.

THE VERANDAH, LONGWOOD

If the weather was rainy or foggy the ride would be postponed till afternoon and Napoleon would spend his forenoons reading and dictating. But when the weather was satisfactory he went riding every morning, generally with Las Cases and Gourgaud.[24] They took a gallop on the plateau of Deadwood or followed the highroad as far as Alarm House, returning by way of Miss Mason's cottage, perched on its hill, Woody Ridge and Sinner's Valley.

On the floor of that valley they came across a cabin and, standing in the doorway, a child of fifteen or sixteen—Mary Ann, daughter of a farmer, Robinson. The girl dropped a curtsey. Napoleon raised his hat, smiled and questioned her, using Las Cases as interpreter. Ever prone to christen people he called her the Nymph. That part of Sinner's Valley was thereafter to be known to the French as the Valley of the Nymph. They returned there often, though the slope was very rugged, the floor boggy, and in spite of the fact that that first day the Emperor almost fell into the mud. It was Las Cases who first spied Mary Ann Robinson and called the Emperor's attention to her. Returning exhausted from the dangerous ride, Napoleon said, laughing: "That's what one gets for trying to play the young gallant with a pretty face. My dear Las Cases, if I had broken my neck, it would have been your fault. Why the devil did you want me to see your nymph? Had she been pretty at least!"[25] However, he liked to see this girl from the fields running to meet him, flowers in hand, whenever his company approached. A naïve face, rosy cheeks, large brown eyes, Mary Ann Robinson was charming without being shy.[26]

Gourgaud pretended to think that Napoleon had designs on the girl. The Emperor held, to the contrary, that she was thinking of Gourgaud:

"She pays more attention to you than to me because you are not married. Poor girls think only of marriage!"[27]

Returning home Napoleon got into his bath and lingered there for some time. He thought that prolonged and excessively hot baths, to

[24] Accounts of the way the Emperor spent his time at Longwood vary considerably. Masson and Frémeaux follow Las Cases, Montholon and Gourgaud. The differences that appear in this narrative arise from the fact that I have taken into account a number of English sources and notably the daily reports of the orderly officer.

[25] Montholon, Vol. I, p. 199.

[26] The author found an attractive picture of her at Jamestown.

[27] Gourgaud, Vol. I, p. 115.

which he had become accustomed in France, alleviated his bladder trouble. Physicians, however, without exception had warned him against abusing them as they tended to be weakening. "However, on everything touching his health and the sort of treatment that was good for him, he had his own ideas, and nothing could shake them." [28]

After his bath, Napoleon received his physician, O'Meara, gossiped with him in Italian and got the news of the town and the talk about camp. Underneath his vulgarity the Irishman was not lacking in humour, amusing the Emperor as Benjamin Constant had amused him of yore. Bertrand came in and, in case of a summons, Gourgaud and Montholon. Las Cases was almost always present. The Emperor lunched on a stand in his bedroom, as a rule alone, unless the weather was unusually fine, when he would sometimes move to a tent that had been set up in the garden not far from the verandah. Then he would invite one or another of his officers to share his meal, sometimes all four—a sign that he was in a good humour.

The luncheon was, for that age, of the simplest—two dishes only. Eggs, roast chicken, a breast of lamb breaded and grilled, chops, cold mutton, beans or lentils in a salad—those were Napoleon's favourite dishes. He seldom took more than one dish after his soup, which he wanted "boiling." He drank a glass of watered bordeaux, the English not supplying him with the chambertin to which he was accustomed. At the end of the meal came a cup of coffee. It was all a matter of ten, fifteen minutes. He ate hastily with an air of distraction, yet he never complained of indigestion. The food left much to be desired, as we have seen. Indifferent as he was to such things Napoleon would scarcely have noticed it, had his companions not raised their voices every day in complaint. At first luncheon was served to them in common, but as their uncongeniality increased and their relations outside of the Emperor's presence became too strained, each of them was served in his own room.

Napoleon took a turn about the garden, then went back to the ante-room, which he found the driest and best lighted of all. It was very hot there when the sun beat on the pine partitions. In damp weather it was impossible to keep a fire going, for the chimney drew badly. There he could pace the floor according to his habit, his hands crossed under his coat-tails, while he dictated comments and notes on strategy and tactics—links in his future memoirs—to one of his

[28] Mme. de Montholon, p. 139.

THE DRIVE, LONGWOOD

NAPOLEON'S TERRESTRIAL SPHERE
The White Speck Shows St. Helena

officers. He used them by turns, distributing subjects about: Bertrand for Egypt; Las Cases for the first campaign in Italy; Gourgaud for Waterloo; Montholon for various subjects. In addition the Emperor dictated to Marchand an abstract of Caesar's wars. Most of the copying was entrusted to Aly who wrote a beautiful hand. Speaking rapidly, in a voice that rose as he grew animated, he paced back and forth from the door of the drawingroom to the verandah door, flanked by the two globes. As he passed, we may assume that his hand would stray out and give them a whirl. Many a time too he must have examined the terrestrial globe to find, in the enormous waste of the blue Atlantic, that infinitesimal dot to which the hatred and the fear of the world was confining him. On the globe, in fact, many fingernail prints can still be seen about St. Helena. His hand would caress continents and seas that had resounded with his name. His finger could trace the stages in his rise to power—Corsica, Italy, Egypt, the wars with Austria and Prussia; and the stages of his decline—Spain, Russia, the campaign of 1814. He probably turned his eyes away from the spot that represented France, at the time so reduced in size. In the Mediterranean he could see the island where he had once before been a captive but still a prince. Sometimes he would break off and, moving over to one of the windows, gaze with his pocketglass through the little opening in the shutters. The slats were always half-closed, for the Emperor did not wish to be watched by the English officer.

In the afternoon visitors came. Visits were very frequent during those first two years—Mr. Arnold Chaplin has compiled a list of over a hundred.[29] The Wilkses, the Skeltons, the Binghams, the Balcombes were received as friends. The Emperor enjoyed his chats with Wilks, who had long been accredited to the courts of Hindu princes and knew Asia well. He had met Tippoo Sahib, with whom Bonaparte had thought of striking an alliance while in Egypt. Tippoo Sahib's power had been broken by that same Wellesley who later, under the name of Wellington, was to break another power at Waterloo! Mrs. Wilks was generous, obliging, the best of company, and so was her daughter Laura, whom poor Gourgaud dreamt of marrying. Lady Bingham, diminutive, "neither ugly nor pretty, neither witty nor foolish," [30] nevertheless found favour for her air

[29] In his conscientious work, *A St. Helena's Who's Who.*
[30] Stürmer to Metternich, January 10, 1817.

of breeding and her fashionable gowns. Mrs. Balcombe sometimes came with her daughters. But Betsy no longer dared take liberties with "Boney" as in the days at The Briars. She saw him now surrounded by a formality, a magnificence, that held her at arm's length. Napoleon delighted to hear the purveyor insist that the English were indignant at his deportation, that there was talk in London of a change in ministry. He used to say of Balcombe:

"He is good for me—he always brings me good news!"

To Longwood also came army and naval officers and Englishmen of note on their way to China or India or going home, who begged the honour of being presented to Napoleon.

On such occasions a regular ceremonial was followed. Armed with a written permit from the Governor, the visitors first appeared before the Grand Marshal who handed them an audience note. They were then welcomed in the ante-room by Montholon or Gourgaud in uniform. The footman Santini or the cavalryman Noverraz, in their best livery, announced the newcomer to the Emperor, who received them, standing, in the drawingroom, his hat under his arm. Napoleon had received his visitors standing ever since Cockburn one day took a seat in his presence without being invited to. When he grew too tired he would rest a hand on the back of a chair or against the wall. Las Cases stood near by to act as interpreter, for Napoleon still knew only a few words of English.

Nearly every day, about four o'clock, he ordered the carriage and invited one or two ladies—Mme. de Montholon, a visitor, or Mme. Bertrand, when she was there—to go for a drive with him in the open barouche, an old seagoing contraption of Wilks which the Governor, for lack of a better, had sent to Longwood. Bertrand and Las Cases took their places on the seat opposite. Montholon and Gourgaud followed on horseback. The wagon was drawn by six horses, which in time were reduced to four. Driven by the two Archambaults and galloping at full speed, they made the round of the park which, when all was said and done, was just a run-down gum plantation in which a few paths had been cut.[31] The pace was so swift that it took only a quarter of an hour to cover the whole plateau and the carriage bounced so hard on its high springs that the

[31] Under orders from the Admiral. Napoleon's park later became a pasture and is now a fairly good golf course, with too much wind, perhaps.

ladies could scarcely get their breath.[32] The round completed, they did it over again. Sometimes they would leave the park and drive as far as the camp. On other days, when for one reason or another Bertrand would not be present, the barouche would go up the drive, pass the guard and fly swiftly towards Hutt's Gate. Those were the moments when Mme. de Montholon was really afraid, for the road ran along the Punch Bowl, on the edge of a precipice that had no parapet. A moment's distraction on the driver's part and the carriage would have rolled a thousand feet below. However, the Emperor liked speed and the danger probably excited him.

Sometimes they took a walk instead of a drive, the ladies wearing plaited skirts, leg-o'-mutton sleeves, large hats and capes of lace or embroidery. Napoleon would walk slowly, chatting with one or the other of them. They rarely left the garden or the little woods. On some days such walks would last for hours by dint of going over and over the same path. Mme. de Montholon writes (p. 141): "If one grew too tired, one tried to get out of sight by slipping down a cross path. But no matter how clever you managed to be the Emperor always caught you, though he might be absorbed in his conversation. Even when he was quite a distance ahead, he always noticed when someone disappeared and never failed to say: 'There's Madame de Montholon (or some other of us) trying to get away.'"

But the sun vanished into the sea between High Knoll and the slopes of Flagstaff without a twilight. The gun on Alarm Hill shook the air.[33] They returned to the house and for a moment each one was free again. Sitting on his sofa the Emperor would read French or English newspapers three months old, or books that had been brought from France, or still others lent by the Governor or Cockburn. He read rapidly, turning pages with his thumb, then throwing the book or paper on the carpet. When he left the room, the floor was littered with pamphlets and newspapers. In the beginning Napoleon had Las Cases translate the English newspapers to him. Later on he was able to skim them himself. On such occasions Aly stood at his elbow and looked up the words he did not know in a dictionary.[34]

[32] Mme. de Montholon, p. 139.
[33] The big gun still sits near Alarm House. It was fired every evening at sunset and every morning at sunrise. High Knoll fired at noon.
[34] Aly, p. 179.

Dinner was set at first for eight o'clock.[35] Later it was put ahead to seven. Finally the Emperor's preference settled on nine. Mealtimes varied greatly during the Captivity. Napoleon changed them in a sort of sad whimsicalness, as if to escape the weight of habit and shorten the time which was so long, so long!

The Longwood pantry had to supply not only the Emperor's table that usually accommodated Las Cases and his son, M. and Mme. de Montholon and Gourgaud, but several other tables as well. The Bertrands had their own kitchen, but received certain dishes already prepared. The English orderly officer and O'Meara had a separate table at which Piontkowski joined them later on. Finally there were two tables for the principal and subordinate servants. To complete the establishment the English sailors or soldiers lent by the Admiral or Sir George Bingham took their meals at Deadwood.

Just before dinner, the Emperor would go to the drawingroom where he would find his officers in full dress and Mme. Bertrand and Mme. de Montholon in décolleté, their arms bare and their hair dressed for the evening. Napoleon would lift his hat in greeting and invite the ladies to be seated. The men, however, remained standing. "At times," writes Mme. de Montholon (p. 144), "they would almost faint from weariness. General Gourgaud used to lean against the door. I saw him turn pale on some occasions as he watched the chess game."

As his opponent at chess the Emperor took each of his generals in turn. He played badly, by sudden inspirations, always attacking and always exposing his pieces. Though his adversaries were not first-rate players, and, further, were inclined to spare him (all except Gourgaud), he often lost. He was unfair at games. "Sometimes," says Mme. de Montholon (p. 144), "he would insist on 'touch-move.' But that rule was only for his opponent. He always had some good excuse to explain why his touch did not count, and if anyone noted a breach of the rule on his part he would laugh."

Cipriani would finally throw open the diningroom door and announce dinner. The Emperor passed into the adjoining room, followed by the ladies and the officers in file, according to rank of service or title—precedence was a subject of never-ending quarrels among them. Napoleon would seat himself in the centre of the table, his back to the fireplace, with Mme. de Montholon on his right and

[35] Las Cases, Vol. II, p. 65.

NAPOLEON'S "INTERIOR," LONGWOOD

THE DININGROOM, LONGWOOD

Las Cases on his left. Young Emmanuel, Gourgaud and Montholon sat opposite. This arrangement was changed when the Bertrands came to dinner—that was on Sunday—or when the Emperor chose to honour some visitor, as he often did in the early months of the Captivity.[36] Napoleon was served by Aly and Noverraz who stood behind his chair. Gentilini and sailors from the *Northumberland*, transformed into butlers, served the other guests. The room was brilliantly lighted. Dishes, plates, and service were of silver.[37] At dessert the beautiful Sèvres service, known as "General Quarters," was used, filled out with knives, forks and spoons of silver lined with gold. The dishes were more numerous than at luncheon: soup, a meat, two entrées, a roast, two side-dishes, sweets. Even when the French were alone four courses were served. When there were strangers, one or two dishes were added. The occasion still had a touch of the imperial about it. One forgot the place, the distance, the narrow walls, the shabby furniture. The lights, the gold and silver, the precious crockery, the graceful, silent service, formed a sort of French islet about Napoleon. The English did not look upon it with favour. Bingham was to write to his wife after a dinner at Longwood:

"It was a most superb dinner which lasted only forty minutes, at the end of which we retired into the drawingroom to play cards. . . . The dinner was stupid enough. The people who live with Bonaparte spoke out of a whisper, and he was so much engaged in eating that he hardly said a word to anyone. He had so filled the room with wax candles that it was as hot as an oven." [38]

They went into the drawingroom for coffee. It was served by Pierron in admirable Sèvres cups painted with Egyptian scenes. The men were then given permission to be seated. Rarely they played cards. The game most often chosen was *reversis* (give-away). Napoleon played recklessly,[39] "trying almost every time to '*make reversis*'—to

[36] Guests at his table at one time or another were Sir George Cockburn, Sir George Bingham, Colonel and Mrs. Skelton, Major and Mrs. Hodgson, Major Fehrzen, Captain and Mrs. Younghusband, Captains Ross of the *Northumberland* and Devon of the *Icarus* and Surgeon Warden. The Emperor kept Balcombe for lunch on several occasions and also his daughters. The last of the English to be received at dinner were the Skeltons, April 11, 1816. They left for Europe a month later.

[37] A considerable supply of tableware had been brought from France. 130 pounds of it were to be broken up in 1816 and cashed. Even then 96 sets of knives, forks and spoons remained, 34 platters and 134 plates, to say nothing of other table utensils.

[38] *Cornhill Magazine*, January, 1901, p. 34.

[39] Las Cases, Vol. II, p. 66.

take all the tricks. That is a very difficult thing to do, but he succeeded quite often." [40]

Occasionally, at the Emperor's request, Mme. de Montholon would
sing at the piano. She did not have much of a voice, but she possessed
a fair repertory of light and gay Italian songs. Napoleon listened to
them with pleasure. As he sat there with closed eyes might he sometimes have thought of the concerts at the Tuileries where, under
gleaming chandeliers, before an audience of princes and ladies in
dazzling gowns, his violins played cantatas of Paër or Cimarosa?

More often, when the French were alone, the evening was spent
in reading. The Emperor would choose a tragedy by Corneille or
Voltaire, a novel—*Don Quixote, Faublas, Manon Lescaut,* sometimes
Homer, the Bible, Ossian—and begin to read aloud. He read verse
in the manner of Talma, but in general in a monotone, with no
regard for metres. "He had no ear for rhythm," writes Mme. de
Montholon (p. 150). "He would often add one or two syllables to
a line, not realizing what he was doing. With the book before his
eyes he would change a word and adhere to the change regularly.
So in declaiming *Cinna* he invariably said: 'Sylla, let us be friends,
Sylla!'" During such readings the ladies would stifle their yawns.
Let him notice one and out of spite he would hand the volume to
the culprit, begging her to continue. He himself would then promptly
fall asleep. Only when Napoleon, an inveterate talker—indeed, to tell
the full truth, a great chatterbox—related some episode of his amazing career did the evenings become lively. Then not a single head
felt drowsy. They would sit up all night listening to him. On one
occasion (January 9, 1817) the Emperor's monologue lasted until
three in the morning. Then suddenly tired, or perhaps because
another thought had crossed his mind, he would break off, make a
little bow to the ladies and dismiss them all.

He would go back to his "interior" where Marchand was waiting
for him, and undress in a rush. "He was no sooner in his bedroom,"
writes Aly (p. 167), "than he flung his hat on the floor, threw off
his coat and rid himself of the cordon and of his vest, collar, cravat
and braces. In a flash they all lay scattered helter-skelter about the
floor." He would then tie a madras handkerchief around his head,

---

[40] [*Reversis,* a kind of give-away, was played with a trump, the object being to
take as few tricks as possible. One could avoid "cut-throating" by trying to take all
the tricks.]

lie down and, in the light of his bedside chandelier, which had three candles, take up a book again. Sometimes he would read for long hours, lulled by the strident chirp of the cricket, the roar of the trade-wind, or the drip-drop of the rain on the slate roof. As soon as he nodded, Marchand would steal on tiptoe to remove the candles and light the night lamp. The Emperor's breathing was on the whole regular, but sometimes a catch would come in it. Then Napoleon would open his eyes, turn over, cough, sigh, get up, go and sit near his fire and try to write, or else change to the other bed. For years and years Sleep had come at his command. Since Waterloo he had lost his prestige with Morpheus as well.

．　　　　．　　　　．　　　　．　　　　．　　　　．　　　　．

On December 29th an unexpected guest arrived at St. Helena: Piontkowski, the officer of the Polish lancers, who had made his way into the Emperor's suite and accompanied him from Malmaison to Tor Bay but had not succeeded in getting aboard the *Northumberland*. No one knew him except Bertrand, who had seen him at Elba. He was viewed as a suspicious character by everyone. How had he managed to persuade the English to transport him thither? The French could not make him out. At first Napoleon was unwilling to see him, but on reflection he thought the man might be bringing a message from Europe and, on Bertrand's advice, consented to an audience. Piontkowski had the impudence to appear in the uniform of a staff officer, to which he had no more right than to the rank of captain which he had assumed. He delivered himself of innumerable inventions about the state of mind in France, flattered the Emperor with an ostentatious display of devotion and was allowed to stay at Longwood. The first day he dined at Napoleon's table, then for a time was served alone, and finally ended with O'Meara and Poppleton. He was given a vague sort of post in connection with the stables. He was to remain at St. Helena for eight months, useless, ostracized, regarded with disfavour by French and English alike.

Both sides took him for a spy. Actually he was a mere adventurer. He had lived up to that time, and was to live thereafter, on his impostures. He flitted across St. Helena like a dubious ghost. Soon aware of the fatuousness of his boasting, the Emperor paid no further attention to him down to the moment of his departure.

．　　　　．　　　　．　　　　．　　　　．　　　　．　　　　．

On January 1, 1816, at ten o'clock, Napoleon found his friends gathered in the drawingroom to present their New Year's wishes. He caressed the children and gave small presents to all. Going down into the garden he told his companions that they must try to live together as one family without quarrelling:

"You are no more than a handful at the end of the world. Your consolation must at least be your loving one another." [41]

His hunting-guns were brought to him on behalf of the Admiral who had so far withheld them. The Emperor handed them to Aly who, already the librarian, now became the armourer.

The weather was hot. Napoleon took a drive in the coach, then a ride on horseback down into the valley. In the evening he was gay and talked about his love affairs as a lieutenant.

It was now mid-summer, though at St. Helena the seasons are not sharply marked. There are no changes in the landscape. Always the same trees! Save for some red tops on the oaks in autumn, they never grow yellow and are never bare. This everlasting green wearies the eye. A change of season is a new hope. It was denied to Napoleon.

The sky is hardly less capricious, hardly less variable. The sea is blue. A harsh sun scorches brown lines in the plush of the meadows and in the gardens brings out all the reds of the hibiscuses, the geraniums, the bougainvilleas, and of those poinsettias that bear dazzling diadems at the ends of flat leaves. Javanese sparrows in innumerable flocks chirp on the gum trees, on the pines in the grove, on the oak under which the Emperor often sat. A moment later the riot of colour is gone. A heavy blanket of cloud is lowered over the island; the mountains, now tawny and black, now striped with green, have disappeared. An opaque cotton-wool settles on everything. One cannot see six feet away. Then a puff of air, a stirring of the trade-wind, which is never more than half asleep, and the mists fade away, the light floods everything again. A second later it is gone once more and a fine, steady rain begins, that will last perhaps for a quarter of an hour, or perhaps for a week.

Now that they were settled at Longwood and the distraction of novelty had worn off, those men and women who had been accustomed to the finest mansions and castles in France began to suffer from the inconvenience of the location and the wretchedness of their accommodations. Fifty souls huddled together in one place; a

[41] Las Cases, Vol. II, p. 118; Gourgaud, Vol. I, p. 112.

house clattering with the comings and goings of workmen who were busy putting up additions and who would not leave Longwood for almost a year; rats that came out in swarms from under the floor, terrifying the women and children! [42] The extreme dampness was forever taking the press out of coats, hoop-skirts and flounces, so that they had to be constantly ironed. The chimneys smoked. The kitchens were too near the living quarters so that they smelled. The servants complained and were dissatisfied with everything. Flies and mosquitoes were so numerous that not even screens on the windows or nets over the beds could keep them out. Add to all that the close, insufferably petty surveillance of the English! Not to be able to overstep the narrow boundaries that had been set without the escort of a redcoat, to run into sentinels at every turn and be stopped with crossed bayonets, to have incessantly before one's eyes the drilling of guards and the manoeuvres of a camp that has been established for the express purpose of guarding one—those were petty annoyances that in the long run became a torture.

The English were always on the alert and a number of imprudences and roguish pranks on the part of the Emperor lent ground to their fears. One afternoon he sent word to Poppleton that he wished to take a ride half way to Sandy Bay. Since that meant crossing the boundary lines, the captain was obliged to accompany him. Napoleon started off ahead, followed by Bertrand and Gourgaud. Poppleton trotted along about a hundred yards behind. They rode down into the Valley of the Nymph and climbed up again to Miss Mason's. Napoleon stopped at several cottages, each time showering gold pieces on the slaves. As he crossed a ravine he noticed that Poppleton had ridden up a little closer.

"Don't let him come so near!" he cried to Bertrand.

[42] Rats have always been and still are one of the plagues of the island. During the Captivity they supplied ample subject matter for caricaturists in London and Paris—Napoleon commanding an army of rats, Napoleon chased by rats, Napoleon attended by a court of rats, and so on. At Longwood they were caught in traps that were opened in the morning in the little courtyard. There two dogs fell on them and strangled them as they came out.

Those dogs were never allowed indoors. Only a big hunting dog was admitted to the Emperor's presence, being a gift of Miss Mason. His name was Sambo and he came of a Chinese pedigree. His coat was whitish, spotted with brown, and his ears cut in Chinese fashion. Gourgaud, or the officer on duty, often took him hunting. Bertrand carried him back to France in 1821 and allowed him to end his days in honourable retirement at Chateauroux. He may still be seen there, stuffed, in the Grand Marshal's mansion, which has been converted into a museum.

And Bertrand, turning haughtily to the officer:

"Why, Captain, do you think we are trying to escape? You are almost on our heels. His Majesty wishes you to keep farther off."

Poppleton obeyed. At a turn in the trail Napoleon gave his horse the spur:

"Come on, Gourgaud, let's gallop!"

And followed by the two generals he dashed, breakneck, down a road. Poppleton's horse balked and he was soon lost to view. The Frenchmen arrived panting at Rock Rose Cottage, greeted the mistress, Mrs. Pritchard, and strolled about the garden. Napoleon admired the view overlooking the two valleys and the sea—one of the most beautiful on the island, then gave the order to return. They rode back to Longwood by Woody Ridge. The Emperor was delighted with his lark. He counted on repeating it. He would go and make lunch with "the natives," he told Gourgaud.

"A horse will bring the luncheon with a silver service. That will make an impression. All I shall want from them will be water, and from time to time I shall invite them to eat with us." [43]

Meantime, beside himself with alarm, Poppleton was hastening to the Admiral, who was dining with Bingham at The Briars.

"Sir," he exclaimed, "I have lost the Emperor!"

"The Emperor!" cried Cockburn, and he glared at the unlucky man. Then when Poppleton had told his story, he commanded him calmly to return to Longwood where he would undoubtedly find "General Buonaparte."

Bingham, however, appeared to be nervous. Cockburn reassured him:

"It's nothing. There is no danger. But this should be a lesson."

From that day, in fact, Poppleton received orders to follow Napoleon more closely. The surveillance got on the Emperor's nerves. Though the rides quieted him, gave him an appetite, helped to shorten the long, tedious days, he refused to go outside the boundaries, and limited the scope of his rides rather than have the Englishman forever at his heels.

That relationship of exile to guardian—no matter what the form—could not fail to be a delicate matter. There is no doubt that Cockburn, though rather brusque, frequently showed real thoughtfulness. On January 3, 1816, learning by signal that Napoleon wished to go

[43] Gourgaud, Vol. I, p. 118.

to Sandy Bay, he hastened to Longwood to escort him in person. The Emperor met him coming towards him on the road from the stables, hat in hand. Cockburn offered to accompany him. Napoleon invited him to breakfast, went off on the ride and returned well pleased. "His Majesty assures me," Gourgaud noted the following day, "that in his ride yesterday with the Admiral, he quite won the latter." [44] William Doveton had entertained the party at Mount Pleasant.

But those relations were made even more uncomfortable by differences in nationality, by the inability of two races to understand each other. The English held the Frenchmen of Longwood in the contempt that they have always cherished for Continentals. They found them frivolous, garrulous, mendacious, fussy, quarrelsome. They were amazed at the respect and courtesy they used towards the "defeated" general. Mme. Bertrand—"poor Mme. Bertrand"— was the only one they liked. But that was because she was almost one of them by birth, and entirely so by tastes and instinct. The Frenchmen around Napoleon, on the other hand, had to struggle with the strange customs, the English ideas, into which life had plunged them. In their eyes the British were rude, haughty, pedantic, absurd. Added to the misfortunes that had embittered them, exile stirred in them an excessive national pride that separation from home always arouses in human beings. They shut themselves in, refused to open their eyes and rebelled against everything that was not and could not be French.

They managed to pass the time with more or less success, according to the day. The Las Cases were absorbed in the dictations, of which they were to make the *Mémorial*. Bertrand read and busied himself with his children. The Montholons pressed their courtship of the Emperor. The husband ruling over the expenditures, the wife tried to rule in the salon. Gourgaud played the despot in the stables, rode as often as he could to tire himself out, went hunting and brought down partridges and pigeons which he offered to Mme. Bertrand. He also went to the camp games at Deadwood (December 26, 1815).[45]

For that matter, save for the Emperor, who felt unable to accept

[44] Gourgaud, Vol. I, pp. 114-15.
[45] "I have just been to the Christmas celebrations at the camp," he writes (Vol. I, p. 107). "The soldiers ran after a pig with a greased tail, the tail being the only part they were allowed to catch it by. There were also foot and bag races."

any invitations, the French had a thousand opportunities to go out. They were invited to all the houses of the colony. Life was lavish there and hospitality sumptuous. Enriched by the forced stops of ships to or from the Far East, the island was prosperous. People kept open house. Every steamer call was the pretext for great banquets, receptions, teas, open air picnics. Gourgaud often went, either alone or with O'Meara or one of the Las Cases, to Plantation House.[46] On January 3rd, Colonel Wilks sent his carriage for Mme. Bertrand and Las Cases—they dared not borrow the Emperor's, since he did not offer it. There were thirty guests at that dinner.

Gourgaud would take long walks with Laura Wilks in the park. Mrs. Skelton, as a friend, preached morality. He could not expect to marry the governor's daughter—she was soon going away with her father. General Hudson Lowe had been appointed to replace Wilks, and was expected by one of the next boats.

Napoleon tried to console his aide-de-camp:

"I will arrange a better marriage than that for you in France."

The Emperor's companions went to town very frequently, and Poppleton was obliged to seem willing to escort them. He had been hurt by his misadventure and was not always willing. What the town was everybody can imagine! But for the exiles at Longwood it meant a few stores where they could buy little articles. It meant the street and the wharf where they could meet people. It meant the harbour filled with boats and, a little farther off, at anchor under the cliffs, great ships with flags flapping in the wind and speaking to those hermits of spacious seas which they would someday cross again. In town moreover they heard the news. Every ship that came in from Europe brought rumours that reshaped the imagination and kindled hopes. The Allies were no longer agreeing! It was said that Fouché had been executed! The King of Rome was about to be called back! The slightest incident aroused great hopes. On February 5, 1816, a whaling boat, having failed to reply to the hail of one of the brigs that kept strict guard over the waters near the island, was pursued, and fifteen shots were fired. Longwood was in the greatest excitement. Might it not be a friendly fleet come to rescue the Emperor? The day passed in feverish expectations. On the next they learned that it was all a misunderstanding, and Napoleon said:

[46] Gourgaud, Vol. I, pp. 114, 118-19, 124.

"We are just big children. I should be setting you an example in good behaviour, and I am as bad as any of you." [47]

Newspapers arriving off and on were passed from hand to hand and read and discussed feverishly. They told of Murat's execution, of Ney's trial. Against Murat the Emperor still cherished a grudge: "He must have been insane to land in Calabria with fifty Corsicans!"

But at a remark of Gourgaud, he softened. Again he saw the admirable cavalry officer who became King of Naples.

"It's horrible. The men who ordered his death are monsters."

"Dinner was gloomy that night," writes Gourgaud.[48] "Some English newspapers had come in. Sad, preoccupied, His Majesty toyed mechanically with some gaming counters while the paper was being read aloud. He was evidently in low spirits."

As for Ney, the Emperor's feelings followed the same curve. On hearing Ney's testimony on the stand, his comment was harsh:

"Stupid answers! His character never did match his courage!" [49]

He was thinking of the Marshal's promise to take him back to Louis XVIII "in an iron cage." Then a justifying thought:

"One must not forget that Ney saved sixty thousand Frenchmen during the retreat from Russia."

When he learned of Ney's terrible end he exclaimed:

"The death of Ney is a crime. His blood was sacred to France. Louis XVIII and his émigrés have taken revenge on him for their own cowardice." [50]

So they were gone—Murat and Ney, incomparable soldiers! What assurance could there be that the Empire was not wholly of the past? Those great names which had been associated with his days in power suddenly brought the mediocrity of his present entourage more vividly home to him. About him now he had nothing but errand-boys!

. . . . . . . .

However, in the routine of daily life at Longwood hours of relaxation, even of gaiety, followed. Complaints about the food ceased for a time, bickerings and rivalries were stilled for a few days. The Emperor was in a good humour again. The climate and the location when viewed with an unprejudiced eye seemed less frightful. "This

[47] Montholon, Vol. I, p. 216.    [49] Gourgaud, Vol. I, p. 141.
[48] Vol. I, p. 134.    [50] Montholon, Vol. I, p. 227.

mild and monotonous temperature," Las Cases wrote, "is perhaps more tedious than unhealthy." [51] "As places of exile go," said Napoleon, "St. Helena may perhaps be the best after all. In some high latitude we should have had much more to suffer from the cold, and we would have expired miserably in the burning heat of any other island in the tropics.[52]

And the English were not always hateful. After cursing Poppleton for many months, the Emperor came to understand that he was only doing his duty, and he invited him to his table. Napoleon enjoyed watching the work on the farm, and while the men were ploughing he would even take the plough in hand himself and draw a furrow in the red clay. He would go and sit for long hours at Miss Mason's. She was an old maid with mannish ways, brusque and kind-hearted, who was to be seen on all the roads on the island riding on an ox— for that matter she was a consummate horsewoman.[53]

During these good days Napoleon was more just towards the Admiral.

"We shall miss Cockburn," he said. "He is a man of honour. His manners hurt, but when all is said and done, he is a fine old soldier." [54]

The Emperor was more than pleased with his good physical condition. He felt as strong as he had ever been. He was himself surprised to note how little the great events through which he had passed had told on him.[55] "His conversation showed that he did not doubt an eventual return to Europe and a re-entry into France. There the future would the more bounteously repay them—him and his companions—in proportion as they had the more courageously endured those momentary trials.

[51] Las Cases, Vol. II, p. 43.
[52] *Ibid.*, Vol. II, p. 265.
[53] Her memory is still alive in St. Helena. Her house overlooking the Valley of the Nymph was surrounded by charming terraced gardens. A huge hemlock (Cape yew) under which Napoleon sat a number of times is still standing and can be seen at long distances.
[54] Montholon, Vol. I, p. 225.
[55] Las Cases, Vol. II, p. 285 (February 11, 1816).

# III

## *SIR HUDSON LOWE*

THE NEW GOVERNOR, SIR HUDSON LOWE, ARRIVED BEFORE JAMESTOWN on the *Phaeton* on the evening of April 14, 1816. The French had been awaiting his coming with impatience. An article in the *Morning Chronicle,* which Cockburn had sent to Longwood, criticized the severity of the measures that were being used against Napoleon. Longwood saw in that a sign of a change for the better. The French conceived a most favourable picture of Lowe's character and his person. Speaking several languages, a good soldier, used to frequenting high commands and hobnobbing with princes, he would be more deferential than Cockburn and would doubtless not refuse to treat Napoleon as a sovereign.[1] That afternoon Bingham came to Longwood and informed the Emperor that the vessel bearing the Governor and his suite was in sight. The Emperor dressed in his presence, called for his carriage, and so ordered his drive as to see the frigate drop anchor in the harbour.[2]

The next day Poppleton sent word that Sir Hudson Lowe would make his official call at Longwood on the 16th at nine o'clock in the morning.

That the Governor should himself have fixed the moment for his audience displeased Napoleon. Therefore, when, accompanied by Cockburn, Sir George Bingham (who had just been made a general) and his general staff, Lowe dismounted in front of the little flight of steps at Longwood, in a storm of rain and wind, Aly replied that the Emperor was indisposed and had not yet risen. Actually Napoleon was peering out from behind a shutter in his bedroom. Disconcerted, Lowe resigned himself to going to Bertrand's house at Hutt's Gate and asking when "General Buonaparte" would care to receive him. The Grand Marshal named the following day at two o'clock.

Lowe came back a second time with the Admiral and his officers. Bertrand welcomed them in the ante-room and went to get orders

[1] Las Cases to Lowe, December 19, 1816.
[2] Montholon, Vol. I, p. 240.

from the Emperor. The Emperor kept them waiting.[3] Noverraz was in charge of the introductions. He stood in front of the drawingroom door. Bertrand opened it and told him to show the Governor in. The valet obeyed, but when Cockburn tried to follow, Noverraz, in too literal obedience to his orders, barred the way and closed the door. Cockburn sat down again and, thinking that he would be called, waited in the ante-room with Las Cases, Montholon, Gourgaud and the English officers.

As he entered the drawingroom, Lowe bowed to the Emperor who was standing in front of the fireplace. Since Napoleon remained silent, he spoke first:

"I have come, *monsieur*, to pay my respects to you."

"You speak French, *monsieur*, I see. But you also speak Italian. Did you not command a regiment of Corsicans?"

Lowe bowed.

"We shall therefore speak Italian."

A few exchanges followed—on Abercromby's Egyptian expedition in which Lowe had participated. Then came some personal questions. Was he not married? As the Governor replied that Lady Lowe had come with him to St. Helena, Napoleon heaved a sigh.[4]

"Oh! You have your wife! You are very lucky."

"How many years have you been in the service?" he continued.

"Twenty-eight."

"Then I am an older soldier than you. I can count almost forty."

"History, however," said Lowe, awkwardly, "will speak of our services in very different ways."

Napoleon smiled and made no reply. Lowe then asked permission to present his officers.[5] Bertrand called them in. The Emperor addressed a few courteous remarks to them, then bowed to indicate that the audience was at an end.

The English withdrew. Cockburn was enraged at not having been received. He protested to the Governor. They seemed to hesitate a second, then went their way.

The affront to the Admiral had not been premeditated. Napoleon

[3] For this entire scene, Las Cases, Vol. I, p. 448; Gourgaud, Vol. VIII, p. 159; O'Meara to Finlaison, April 22; Lowe to Bathurst, April 21 (Lowe Papers, 20-115).
[4] Lowe Papers, 20-115.
[5] Sir Thomas Reade, his chief of staff, Major Gorrequer, his aide-de-camp, Lieut. Colonel Lyster, Inspector of Drills, Emmett, Major in the Engineers, Lieutenants Wortham and Jackson, and Dr. Baxter, Superintendent of Hospitals at St. Helena.

SIR HUDSON LOWE
From a Pencil Sketch by Wyrill

was not aware of his presence. Bertrand's absent-mindedness had been aggravated by a slow-thinking footman. But at that moment the Emperor was angry at Cockburn. He was delighted when informed of it. He rubbed his hands gleefully, and laughed aloud, "with," says Las Cases, "the delight of a child who has just caught his tutor napping."

"Oh, my dear Noverraz!" he exclaimed. "So for once in your life you showed some intelligence!"

Then, warming to the theme, he added that the Admiral had not lost anything by his absence, for he would have rebuked him in the presence of the newcomers for his lack of generosity.[6] Then he added:

"I would not give this day for a million!"

However, as time went on, he thought better of it. The insult had been glaring and was, taken all in all, undeserved. Cockburn had his faults, but on many occasions nothing but praise could have been said of him. He therefore sent Montholon to present his apologies. The Admiral replied coldly.

The Cockburn incident was unfortunate in every way. It set many of the English on the island against Longwood, though they blamed Napoleon less than his companions, whom they accused of an "ugly" attitude.

Napoleon had not received a bad impression of Hudson Lowe. He said to O'Meara:

"I believe the new Governor is a man of very few words, but he appears a polite man. However, it is only from a man's conduct for some time that you can judge him." [7]

Born July 28, 1769, Sir Hudson Lowe was of the same age as Napoleon. He was short, slender, freckled, red-haired. The thinness of his face was accentuated by his features: a spacious forehead, prominent cheekbones, a long nose drooping over a thin mouth, a pointed chin. His eyes, oblique and greenish, were deep-set under heavy brows. His military stiffness—for he held himself very straight—hid a deal of timidity. His gait and his gestures were quick and jerky.

His career had been without brilliancy. Son of an army surgeon, ensign at eighteen, he had taken part in all the operations conducted against France in the Mediterranean during the Revolution and

[6] Las Cases, Vol. VIII, p. 70.
[7] O'Meara to Finlaison, April 22, 1816.

under the Empire. He was studious and full of ambition. While still very young he had learned Spanish, French and Italian in his leisure moments. He was in Corsica during the English occupation, garrisoned at Ajaccio, going on from there to Elba and thence to Minorca, where he organized a troop of Corsican refugees under the name of the Corsican Rangers and led them in Egypt. He is found again in Portugal, at Naples, in Sicily. At Capri he became chief of an espionage service. By 1812 he had attained the rank of Colonel. After a mission to Scandinavia and Russia in 1813 he fought at Bautzen, and there caught sight of Napoleon for the first time. Attached to the Prussian army he followed Blücher to Leipzig and during the Campaign in France. It was he who carried the news of Napoleon's abdication to London. He was knighted at that time and promoted to the rank of major-general. Wellington disliked him because of his inability to make up his mind and sent him to Genoa just before Waterloo. Suggested by Lord Bathurst, on the recommendation of Sir Henry Bunbury, for the government of St. Helena, he was at first surprised. That post would cut him off perhaps from more desirable opportunities, but he was to have the rank of lieutenant-general locally, and he would receive a salary of 12,000 pounds.[8] Without a family and penniless, Lowe accepted, but nevertheless lingered nearly six months in London where he married a widow, Mrs. Johnson, who was burdened with two daughters and brought no fortune, but did have connections with a fashionable society that Lowe admired from afar and which up to that time had not known him.

Hudson Lowe was not lacking in good qualities. He was a devoted patriot, a good administrator, honest, simple, even austere, in his tastes. He was not without a certain natural kindliness, though he was commonplace in ideas and manners of feeling. Unstable, excitable, already suspicious by temperament, the career he had had with spying and policing in the Mediterranean had inclined him to an extreme distrust that went beyond the bounds of common sense and prompted him to idiotic fears and rages.

He had a passion for official routine, piled up reports, letters and notes, and treasured the most insignificant scrap of paper on which

[8] About $200,000 today, taking account of monetary depreciation. In addition Sir Hudson Lowe received his pay as a lieutenant-general—2,000 pounds. At St. Helena he had his lodging, heat, light, service and provisions at the expense of the government.

a word had been written. A stickler for forms, literal-minded to excess, tactless, and angry with himself for being so, his humble education frequently trapped him into breaking the rules of good manners. He had neither delicacy nor perception. His fellow countrymen have damned him with a harsh phrase: He was not a gentleman.[9] Hudson Lowe did not think or act as a gentleman, as a man, that is, who held honour higher than interest or duty. Historians like Sir Archibald Alison have judged Hudson Lowe in the most objective language: [10] His nomination to St. Helena "was an unhappy selection. His manner was rigid and unaccommodating, and his temper of mind . . . was little calculated to alleviate the distress which the Emperor endured during his detention." And here is Wellington as recorded by Stanhope: [11] "The Duke, in answer to my inquiries, said that he thought the treatment of Napoleon at St. Helena gave no substantial ground of complaint, but that Sir H. Lowe was a very bad choice. He was a man wanting in education and judgement." And again, December 21, 1835: "I told the Duke that I supposed the Duke had scarcely known Sir Hudson personally. 'Yes, I did, I knew him very well. He was a stupid man.' 'I conceive,' said I, 'that he had a bad irritable temper, and in that point was ill-qualified for his post.' 'He was not an ill-natured man. But he knew nothing at all of the world, and like all men who know nothing of the world, he was suspicious and jealous.' "

The instructions Lowe had received from Lord Bathurst on September 18, 1815, were, by and large, the instructions that Cockburn had been applying. General Buonaparte was to be treated as a prisoner of war and "accorded every indulgence which may be compatible with the entire security of his person, that he should not by any means escape, or hold communication with any person whatever excepting through your agency" (Forsyth, Vol. I, p. 487). But the regulations had been aggravated in spirit by a number of considerations.

On April 11, 1816, just as Lowe was arriving at St. Helena, an act was voted by Parliament, decreeing the death penalty for any English subject "who shall rescue, or attempt to rescue, the said Napoleon Buonaparte, or shall knowingly and wilfully aid or assist" in his escape from the island or from his confines within the island (Forsyth,

[9] Lord Rosebery, p. 66.
[10] *History of Europe*, Vol. XIV, p. 195.
[11] *Conversations*: October 31, 1835.

Vol. I, p. 450). That was the attitude in England, and it was reflected in the oral interpretations of the instructions which Bathurst supplied to Lowe *viva voce*.

Bathurst stressed the responsibility that weighed on Lowe and frightened him by citing the precedent of Sir Neil Campbell whom Napoleon had so prettily tricked at Elba. Desirous of reducing expenses at Longwood by detaching as many companions as he could from the Emperor, he handed Lowe the text of a declaration that all the French were to sign, failing of which they should be sent back to Europe. In the interviews he had with Lowe before the latter's departure, Bathurst had been at no pains to hide his contempt for Napoleon. His idea was that the rascal "Boney" should end his days on the little isle at as little expense and with as little talk as possible. Lowe liked neither the French nor France, but he had seen Napoleon in action on the battlefield and he did not have such a low opinion of him. Bathurst's words had a powerful effect on him and inclined him to severities towards his prisoner which perhaps would never have occurred to him of his own accord. He was on his knees before power. A word from a superior was law to him.

He lost no time in executing the orders that had been transmitted to him. Even before being received by Napoleon, he served notice of them on Bertrand.

The Emperor said to Gourgaud:

"Well, have you heard the great news? You'll have to go to the Cape or else promise to share my destiny in perpetuity."

The whole household was thrown into consternation. Gourgaud raged: "So they want to rob us of the hope of ever seeing our families again!" The women wept. Mme. Bertrand could not sleep. Napoleon himself passed a bad night. He saw the reluctance of his companions to take the oath that was demanded of them. Even the most submissive of them hesitated. Was the British government going to succeed, then, in isolating him? Hudson Lowe had sent a model draught of the oath, and the Emperor was mentioned in it—by his companions, his servants!—as "General Buonaparte." Las Cases, Montholon, Gourgaud, rejected that formula in vehement language. Under nagging from his wife, Bertrand refused to sign anything, preferring rather to leave. Two days passed in comings and goings between Jamestown and Longwood. They dickered with Lowe, con-

ferred with the Admiral.[12] In the end, before the Governor's ultimatum, they were obliged to yield. They all handed in their declarations. The Grand Marshal was the last to obey under threat of being
shipped off in a week's time on the *Phaeton*.[13]

The French had signed texts approved by Napoleon. Lowe had the
bad taste to go to Longwood, have them brought before him one by
one and asked whether they had given their oath of their own accord.
They all declared that they had.

Apparently he had shut his eyes to the rejection of his formula,
but on transmitting the declarations to Bathurst, he suggested that
the majority of Napoleon's officers should be banished from St.
Helena. "The insolent presumptuous manner with which they manifest their opinions on all occasions, both verbally and in writing, respecting the measures which the British Government has thought fit
to adopt respecting Bonaparte himself, . . . might afford a sufficient
pretext." [14]

During this same time Longwood was mourning the departure of
English friends who had manifested the greatest consideration for
Napoleon. Before sailing Colonel Wilks and the charming Laura
came to take leave of the Emperor, and he paid the young girl many
compliments. The evening before, Bertrand had gone to Wilks and
asked him whether he would consent to transmit a sealed communication from the Emperor to his government. The Colonel asked to
be excused, saying that he could not intrude on Sir Hudson Lowe's
prerogatives, and he reported the unusual proposition to his successor.

Napoleon talked for more than two hours with the former Governor in the drawingroom and in the presence of Miss Wilks, Mrs.
Younghusband,[15] Las Cases and Gourgaud. He talked of India, of his
struggle with England, of the peace he had always desired and which
the Pitt faction had managed to make impossible. Fox was the only
man who had understood him.

[12] The latter told Montholon that "they ran no risk in signing the paper, for
within two or three years Napoleon would not be at St. Helena" (Gourgaud, Vol. I,
p. 161).

[13] He did not make up his mind till April 24th. The Emperor knew him through
and through and had never had a moment's doubt. "You can be sure," he said to
Montholon, "that he will talk and talk about going away, but when the time comes
to leave me, he will not have the courage."

[14] Lowe Papers, 20-115; Forsyth, Vol. I, pp. 156-57.

[15] Mrs. Younghusband, wife of a captain in the 53rd, was a great-granddaughter
of Cromwell. She had accompanied the Wilkses on their visit. She had a malicious
tongue and was a born trouble-maker.

"England and France," he said, "have held in their hands the fate of the world, the fate especially of European civilization. How much harm we have done each other! How much good we might have done!"

He had rarely shown more animation and eloquence. He insisted on his respect for the British nation. He had given a striking proof of it in going on board the *Bellerophon*. He reproached Wilks, without bitterness, for not consenting to serve as his courier to the Prince Regent:

"There is no man in France who would refuse to transmit a sealed letter from a prisoner to his sovereign."

"Nor in England perhaps," replied Wilks, "when no special orders have been given!"

They separated good friends.[16]

The next day Napoleon received Captain Hamilton, commander of the *Havannah*, the frigate on which the Wilkses were sailing. The Frenchmen considered him a friend. He too refused to carry a letter to London. The Emperor received him in the garden and charged him to tell the Prince Regent that he wanted either freedom or the gallows.[17]

Hamilton went away "much affected."

Two days later the people at Longwood heard the guns saluting the departure of the *Havannah*.

"Farewell, Laura!" sighed Gourgaud.

.     .     .     .     .     .     .

Hudson Lowe had been struck by the reports of Wilks and Hamilton. So Buonaparte was trying to go over his head and correspond with London! The affair of the declarations had already enlightened him on the state of mind of the Frenchmen. His disappointment was extreme. Arriving on the island still under the thrill of his new promotion, he had been received at Longwood in a cavalier style by people who, he thought, were not his equals. His vanity was wounded. General Buonaparte's pretensions to being treated as a monarch seemed to him insufferable. He thought of "General Buonaparte" as a man "almost his equal," though he still considered that

[16] Wilks left an account of his double interview with Bertrand and the Emperor. It was published in the *Monthly Review* for January, 1901. It is very different from the accounts of Montholon and Las Cases, who again "embroider" scandalously at this point.
[17] Gourgaud, Vol. I, p. 164.

his own career in the army had been more regular. He began to realize the difficulties of a mission in which at first blush he had perceived nothing but advantages and prospects. The haughty attitude of the prisoners, the insolence which the affront to Cockburn showed them capable of, gave grounds for thinking that Napoleon and his people would never grow resigned to their captivity. That man, alone in his wretched house with a handful of loyal souls, frightened the Governor.

Lowe was afraid, though he had at his disposal three regiments of infantry, five companies of artillery, a force of militia, a naval squadron that was at all times cruising around the island! He was afraid with hundreds of guns bristling on the hills, with miles of trenches! [18] The fear was absurd, but it was never to cease influencing him, and it was intensified by little incidents which his mania distorted. If in a short time it was to make him odious to the French, it was also to turn his own life into a hell.

Taking his orders literally he began by restricting the liberties of the inhabitants of Longwood. He forbade the merchants in Jamestown to give the French credit. No communication, however insignificant it might appear, was to be received by them nor forwarded to them under penalty of most severe punishments.[19] The officers of the 53rd and their wives who called on Mme. Bertrand at Hutt's Gate were informed that their visits were not viewed with pleasure. The guard took the names of those who still ventured to go there and asked them for detailed accounts of the conversations they held. The number of sentinels at Longwood was increased. No one was any longer to be admitted without a permit from the Governor, whereas up to that time a word signed by Bertrand had been sufficient.

However—for he was an unbalanced mind and his conduct always showed contradictions that laid him open to suspicions of duplicity— Lowe seemed disposed to maintain conciliatory relations with the captives. He went to see Las Cases and Montholon, found them lodged "in bivouacs rather than in quarters" and said he was going to remedy that. He had brought from fifteen hundred to two thousand volumes in French with him which he would put at their service

[18] On July 10, 1816, the garrison at St. Helena consisted of 493 commissioned and non-commissioned officers and 2,291 soldiers. That made a total of 2,784 men. There were more than 600 cannon. The fleet comprised three frigates, two armed vessels and six brigs (Jamestown Archives, 1816).

[19] Jamestown Archives, Orders, May 21, 1816.

as soon as they were unpacked. Meantime he was sending a complete series of the war bulletins of the Grand Army and a collection of documents that had been published on the expedition to Egypt.

Las Cases went to Plantation House and called on Lady Lowe. He found her "pretty, amiable, somewhat of an actress." [20] She was a tall woman of about thirty-five who dressed expensively, wore very low-cut gowns, and painted a little too much. Beautiful eyes, brown hair, a pretty neck! Full of animation, she twitted her husband whom she had come to know in three months of married life and even went so far as to say that Reade, his chief of staff, "was the real Governor."

Reade, in fact, exercised a profound influence on Hudson Lowe. Still quite young—thirty-three—he had made the rank of lieutenant-colonel and won his knighthood. For what services? Not military altogether. He had taken part in the campaigns in Egypt and Spain, but had particularly distinguished himself on some diplomatic and espionage missions in the long struggle of the English with Murat. Lowe took him to Genoa as his chief of staff and since then had not been separated from him.

His clean-shaven face, fat, smiling, was not displeasing at first sight. For a time the Emperor thought him agreeable. He was to change his opinion before long. The gentle manners covered a tireless malevolence. In Napoleon's presence he maintained a deferential attitude, but with all his strength and on every occasion he kept urging the Governor to take stricter and stricter measures. He reproached him for his "easiness," reminded him of Bathurst's orders, encouraged him in spying tactics and ever aroused his mistrust the moment he saw it dying down. The Russian Commissioner, Balmain, was to say of him later on in a letter to Nesselrode, July 15, 1818: "Reade is the Governor's intimate friend and councillor, and his sole confidant. On that account he has nothing to do with anyone at Longwood. He knows a little Italian, but he has no education and is not an agreeable or intelligent man, nor a person one would care to meet. He is a John Bull in the raw. Napoleon scorns to see him or talk with him. The English are afraid of him."

Major Gorrequer, aide-de-camp to the Governor and his secretary, failed to counterbalance Reade's influence, though his feelings, it seems, were more moderate. The man was shrewd, ironical, cautious.

[20] Las Cases, Vol. III, p. 106.

He had piercing black eyes, the hooked beak of an eagle, a small mocking mouth. He saw through his chief to perfection. His taste for work, his perfect memory, his rapid style, his knowledge of French, made him indispensable. All Lowe's reports to Bathurst were based on his minutes. However, he was not trying to play a personal rôle. He effaced himself, content to follow day by day the developments in a situation that was soon to become unendurable through mistakes on the part of all the principal actors.

On April 30th Hudson Lowe went to Longwood. Napoleon had caught cold. The Governor sent in his name by Montholon, who showed him into the bedroom.

The Emperor was lying on his sofa in dressing gown and slippers. A two days' growth of beard intensified his haggard look. A number of books were scattered about on the floor around him. He raised himself a little as Lowe entered and waved him to a chair near the couch.[21] The Governor inquired after his health and offered the services of Dr. Baxter.

"I do not want any doctors," the Emperor replied.

Lowe complained of the delay of the *Adamant* which was bringing a number of essential articles for Longwood. Napoleon replied briefly. He seemed to be in a heavy depression. He declaimed energetically against the agreement of August 2nd whereby the Allied sovereigns declared him their prisoner. The Emperor had known of the existence of the accord, but had only just scanned its exact text.

"What does that mean? They have no authority to do any such thing either in law or in fact. It takes courage to kill a man, but it is cowardice to imprison him here and let him die. This island is too small for me. I am in the habit of riding ten, fifteen, twenty leagues a day on horseback. The climate is not like ours. It is not our sun, nor does it have our seasons. Everything breathes a mortal boredom here! The location is disagreeable, unhealthy. There is no water. This part of the island is a desert. It has chased all its inhabitants away."[22]

Lowe replied that he would spare no trouble or expense to make Napoleon's residence more comfortable.

"Let them send me a coffin! Two bullets in the head—that's what I need. What difference does it make to me whether I sleep on a mattress of velvet or one of haircloth? I am a soldier and accustomed to

---

[21] Lowe to Bathurst, Lowe Papers, 20-115.
[22] Las Cases, Vol. III, p. 146.

everything. But they put me ashore here like a convict. Proclamations forbid the inhabitants to speak to me!"

The boundary lines were too narrowly drawn. If they refused to enlarge them, he would ask nothing more. Hudson Lowe assured him that his government had prescribed them and he let fall the words:

"That's what happens when they issue orders so far away regarding a person they do not know!"

The Emperor reproached Lowe for the questioning to which he had subjected his generals. The Governor laid the blame for that on Bertrand.

"Well," said Napoleon, "that's all over and past."

The interview had been correct as to forms, but on no point had Lowe yielded. The Emperor began to think that they would get less from this man than from the Admiral.[23]

"What a sinister face that Governor has!" he said to Las Cases. "Leave that man alone a second and you wouldn't dare to drink your coffee afterwards! My dear fellow, they may have sent me worse than a jailor."

. . . . . . .

A foggy period caused the Emperor's cold to develop into bronchitis. He coughed and spat up so loudly that he could be heard all over the house.[24] He took hot potions, ate very sparingly, went from his bed to his sofa, read, and saw no one but O'Meara and Las Cases. In spite of all his efforts Poppleton was unable to catch even a glimpse of him through the window. He sent word to the Governor. Lowe took Reade and went to Hutt's Gate and made a veritable scene with Bertrand.[25] He demanded that Poppleton be allowed to perform his duties. Was General Buonaparte ill? He doubted it. M. and Mme. de Montholon spoke of his vomitings, but Marchand assured them that Napoleon had spent the night writing. Bertrand replied coldly that he would report to the Emperor. There were cavillings about details in which Lowe's anxiety is plain to be seen. It would have been appeased for a time had Napoleon agreed to see Dr. Baxter, at least in consultation with O'Meara. But the Emperor

[23] This interview has been related in detail both by Las Cases, Vol. III, pp. 141-48, and by Hudson Lowe himself (Lowe Papers, 20-115). The two accounts check and complete each other. Gourgaud makes a bare reference to it. Montholon places it mistakenly on the 9th of May.

[24] Aly, p. 169.

[25] May 4th (Gourgaud, Vol. I, p. 172).

ST. HELENA IN MIST

HIGH KNOLL FORT, ST. HELENA

would not consent to place himself in that way at the Governor's mercy.

"One would have to be crazy," he kept repeating, "to accept a doctor from one's enemy."

He asked O'Meara whether he considered himself a prison doctor appointed by the Governor or a private physician replacing Maingault. In the first case Napoleon would dispense with his services, since such a doctor would be obliged to report to Lowe on the Emperor's state of health, his mode of life, his conversations. He could not tolerate a spy near him. In the opposite case, he would continue to allow O'Meara to attend him.

The Irishman was anxious to keep his post, so he swore to the Emperor that he considered himself His Majesty's personal physician and that he would be discretion itself. He pledged himself not to repeat any conversation to Lowe unless it related to some plan of escape. In such a case, as an officer and a British subject, he could not make himself an accomplice by maintaining silence. Napoleon agreed to that reservation and offered O'Meara a salary of 240 pounds to be added to his official salary of 365. O'Meara refused, but he was soon (August 6th) to make use of the offer to address a request to Lowe for an increase in pay. His demand was accepted and that brought his official salary to 520 pounds.

O'Meara's attitude had all the earmarks of a sense of honour. It increased Napoleon's confidence in him. Actually O'Meara was a despicable soul. Three times a traitor under the false-face of an honest man, he was to continue keeping the Governor informed as to the way things were going at Longwood. He was to write scandalous and sometimes obscene letters about the women of the household to Finlaison, that the latter might bandy them about in London. Finally he retailed to the French everything he heard in Jamestown and at Plantation House that might hurt their feelings and embitter them against the Governor, St. Helena and the English.

Lowe's absence of tact led him to commit a blunder that was keenly resented at Longwood. Lady Loudon-Moira, wife of the Governor of India, stopped over at St. Helena on her way back to England. Lowe hit upon the idea of inviting "General Bonaparte" to Plantation House "to meet the Countess." Lowe's letter, addressed to Bertrand, was worded as follows: "Should the arrangements of Gen-

eral Bonaparte admit it, Sir Hudson and Lady Lowe would feel grati-
fied in the honour of his company to meet the Countess at dinner on
Monday next at six o'clock. They request Count Bertrand would have
the goodness to make known this invitation to him, and forward to
them his reply." [26]

Bertrand and Gourgaud were petrified at the impropriety. Las
Cases burned red with indignation. Napoleon burst into a laugh:
"It is too idiotic! No answer!"

Too idiotic, it was, in truth, and all the more so, since Lowe had
not acted with unpleasant intent.

Lowe was so little aware of the elements involved that on August
4th, following, he asked Bertrand whether Napoleon "would care to
come to his house on the birthday of the Prince Regent." [27]

Out of courtesy towards Lady Loudon, Napoleon intended to send
Bertrand the next day to call on her, and a few days later he actually
said to her aide-de-camp, who had called on him:

"Please assure Lady Loudon that had she been within the boundaries of Longwood, I should have paid my respects in person."

And he sent her a box of candy for her children.

•     •     •     •     •     •     •

The *Adamant* arrived from England on May 6, bringing the long-
announced furniture for Longwood and materials for the construction of a new house for Napoleon. The old buildings had seemed
insufficient from the beginning. The Liberal newspapers had grown
excited about it and reproached Liverpool's Cabinet for its stinginess.
The latter replied that "Buonaparte being still at sea, in September,
1815, plans had been drawn up for building him a comfortable, in
fact, a luxurious place of residence." [28] The historians have talked a
good deal about a wooden palace, though no question of any such
thing ever came up. Lowe went to Longwood, May 16, 1816,[29] to
consult Napoleon's wishes, and he intended that step as a mark of
consideration. But nothing could have been less to the Emperor's
liking than the notion of a permanent establishment. He preferred

26 Lowe Papers, 20-115; Forsyth, Vol. I, p. 168.
27 Gourgaud, Vol. I, p. 233.
28 Lowe Papers, 20-114. Retranslated.
29 Not on May 17 as Forsyth (Vol. I, p. 217) mistakenly says. Las Cases, Gourgaud, Montholon, O'Meara are definite on the point. For that interview, as for the
one preceding, the basic sources are Las Cases, Vol. III, p. 341, and the Lowe Papers,
20-115.

the temporary arrangement he had. That left him at least the illusion that he would escape from exile some day.

It was three o'clock. Napoleon dressed quickly and received the Governor in the drawingroom. He did not ask him to sit down. His demeanour overawed Lowe who stood there twisting his hat in his hands. He said that he was at the General's service, either to have a new building erected or—which would take less time—to use the materials that had been sent on from England to improve the present residence by adding two or three rooms to it. The Emperor listened without saying a word. Then a wave of anger rushed over him. Without replying to the questions that Lowe had put to him, he let loose a torrent of reproaches:

"Did you come here to be my executioner? How are you treating me? It was an insult to invite me to dinner and to call me General Buonaparte. I am not General Buonaparte. I am the Emperor Napoleon." [30]

He was the Emperor, that was true, and his misery lent him a pathetic grandeur. But Lowe could not see it. He had no feeling for a misfortune so great. Before him stood a man who had been the master of Europe and who was now an outlaw, but he could not excuse such outbursts, such paroxysms, that a more noble soul would have understood and forgiven.

"Sir," he replied, haughtily. "I have not come here to be taught a lesson."

"Not that you do not need one."

"Sir, I have come to treat of an affair which concerns you more than it does me. If you are not disposed to speak about it, I will retire."

"I had no intention to insult you, but how have you treated me? It is not worthy of a soldier."

"I am a soldier after the fashion of my country—I do my duty towards it. If you think you have any cause to complain, you have only to write. I will transmit your representation to England."

"What will be the use? It will not be attended to there any more than it is here."

"I will have it published in all the papers of the Continent if you wish it."

"I am told that you have offered to give me some of your officers

[30] Lowe Papers, 20-115.

in place of Captain Poppleton to escort me around the island. It is not the colour of their coats that bothers me. When soldiers have received their baptism of fire they are all alike in my eyes. But I cannot admit that I am your prisoner. I am in your hands only because of a most horrible abuse of confidence."

He then asked a question about the new house. Was it to be built on the site he preferred or on one chosen by the Governor?

Lowe replied that the matter would have to be decided between them.

"You had better speak to the Grand Marshal about it and settle it with him."

"I prefer, sir, addressing you upon it."

The tone of the interview had improved. But as Napoleon walked from the mantelpiece to the window, Lowe's impassiveness again enraged him. He advanced upon the Governor:

"Shall I tell you the truth? I expect anything from you. I believe that you have received orders to kill me."

He looked at him fixedly. Meeting his gaze Lowe answered:

"You remarked, sir, at the last interview I had with you that you had misunderstood the character of the English people, and you have equally misunderstood that of the English soldier."

They both stood silent for a second. Lowe finally said:

"Sir—"

Napoleon turned.

"I should like to present to you an officer of my staff, Lieutenant-Colonel Wynyard, whom I have brought with me." [31]

"I do not care to receive him at present," the Emperor replied. "There can be no social intercourse between jailors and prisoners."

Lowe bowed and withdrew, very red in the face. He went to Bertrand's to complain of Napoleon's attitude:

"General Bonaparte is not satisfied with having created for himself an imaginary France, an imaginary Spain, an imaginary Poland, as Abbé de Pradt says. He also wants to create an imaginary St. Helena."

Meantime the Emperor was saying to Las Cases:

"Well, it was a bad moment. I lost my temper, my dear fellow. I

[31] Lieutenant-Colonel Wynyard had come in on the *Adamant*. Lowe had put him in charge of alterations at Longwood. He was to superintend the construction of New House.

received Lowe with my hurricane face. We glared like two rams about to gore each other. I must have been terribly excited for I felt a twitch in my left calf. That is a great sign with me. I had not felt it for a long time."

He went for a drive in his coach. He had regained his composure, but later on, in his bath, he referred to the scene again and remarked to Las Cases:

"My dear fellow, they are going to kill me here—that is certain."

He was soon to admit, however, that he had been too hard on Lowe. On May 31, after dinner, he said to Las Cases:

"I treated him very badly, I know, but I have a right to a little bad temper. I should be ashamed of it in any other situation. Had it been at the Tuileries I should consider myself in all conscience bound to offer an apology." [32]

.     .     .     .     .     .     .

Springtime in Europe brought autumn to St. Helena. The fogs drifted along the ground or at the caprice of the winds, rising and falling on the horizon like the curtain in a theatre. It rained more. The clay of the roads turned to a slime upon which a person dared to venture only on horseback.

The life of the exiles dragged along, one day like the other. Work with the Emperor, walks on the roads, endless conversations, petty bickerings! They measured their heights against the door-jamb. They bowled. The little Balcombe girls came for luncheon and Betsy made a face behind Mme. de Montholon's back when that lady scolded her. Mr. Balcombe gave a ball at The Briars. Las Cases came back from it enchanted, and Gourgaud in bad humour.

The Skeltons called to say good-bye. The Emperor offered Mrs. Skelton a cup from his Sèvres service in remembrance. [33] Emmanuel fell ill. Dr. Warden came from the *Northumberland* to examine him. Napoleon talked to him for two hours, then invited him for a drive in the carriage with the Bertrands. He tried to talk English with the horses galloping at full speed and teased Mme. Bertrand, who had

---

[32] Las Cases, Vol. III, pp. 430-31.

[33] Mrs. Skelton secretly undertook to deliver a letter from Las Cases to Cardinal Fesch, and on setting foot in Europe sent news of Napoleon to Rome, the first his family had received of him. The attitude of the Skeltons towards the Emperor is all the more remarkable since the latter's arrival in St. Helena cost the Lieutenant-governor his post, and he returned to England only to find himself in a difficult situation.

been indisposed for some days, and who he thought needed cheering up. He put an arm around her waist and said to Warden: "This is my mistress!" [34]

Mme. Bertrand tried to draw away, while the Grand Marshal burst into a laugh. Napoleon asked whether he had made a mistake and when they explained to him what "mistress" meant in English he exclaimed:

"Oh, no, no! I say my friend, my love. No—no love—my friend, my friend!"

Between January and April, 1816, Napoleon had tried again to learn English with Las Cases. He made little progress. His pronunciation showed that he was speaking a tongue altogether strange to him. Las Cases nevertheless complimented him highly. He heaped lavish praise on a short letter that the Emperor wrote to him—the sole example of any English correspondence by Napoleon:

"Count Las Cases. Since sixt wek y learn the english and y do not any progress. Sixt week do fourty and two day. If might have learn fivty word for day, i could know it two thousands and hundred. It is (Italian, *c'è*) in the dictionary more of (Italian, *di*) foorty thousand; for knows it (*perciò si sa*) on hundred and twenty week which do more two years. After this you shall agree that the study one tongue (*lo studiare una lingua*) is a great labour who it must do (*bisogna fare*) into the young aged (*nella giovine età*).[35]

"Longwood, this morning, the seven march, thursday, one thousand eight hundred sixteen after nativity the yors Jesus-Christ.

Count Las Cases, Chambellan of the S.M., Longwood; into his polac(?); very press." [36]

Not long afterwards the Emperor gave up the lessons for good. His companions urged him to take up riding again, but going

---

[34] Warden, p. 205.

[35] [This letter, which could only have been intended humorously, is obtained by translating from Italian, taking the first English rendering the dictionary supplies: e.g., *fare*, "do," for "make," *di*, "of" for "than," etc. *Into his polac*, barring a misreading, may mean, "Into his palace." The letter, as *thought* by Napoleon, may have run something as follows: *Da sei settimane imparo l'inglese e non faccio nessun progresso* [A gallicism]. *Sei settimane fanno quarantadue giorni. Se avessi potuto imparare cinquanta parole per giorno, la potrei sapere* [The Emperor not venturing on the compound tense] *in due mila cento. C'è* [A gallicism] *nel dizionario più di quaranta mila. Per ciò si sa in cento venti settimane, che fanno più di due anni. Dopo ciò converrete che lo studiare una lingua è un gran lavoro che bisogna fare nella giovine età.* A. L.].

[36] Lowe Papers, 20-117.

round and round about himself, as he said, bored him. He felt as if he were in a riding-school and was sick to death of it.

In the end they dragged him out. He rode with Las Cases and Gourgaud to the outskirts of Flagstaff, returning by way of the camp at Deadwood.[37] The soldiers ran out of their barracks and drew up at attention saluting him. Napoleon was delighted, but not so the Governor. When he learned of the proceeding, he forbade a repetition of such homage in the future under pain of the cat.[38]

Montholon had taken into his service a Persian domestic whom the Skeltons were leaving behind. In a pique because his permission to engage him had not been asked Lowe had the man collared and forbade him to return to Longwood. Montholon and his wife delivered themselves of a flood of abuse against the Governor in O'Meara's presence, and O'Meara thereupon sent a poisonous report of the incident to Plantation House.[39]

The Bertrands went to Jamestown to call on Lady Bingham. Lowe met them and remarked insolently:

"You people don't seem to understand your situation very clearly. You think you are still at the Tuileries. You think you can grumble the way Napoleon does. Monsieur de Montholon has just written that the wine sent by my government was of the sort drunk by the lowest class of people in France. You think my government is like yours!"

Bertrand reported the tirade to the Emperor who sent for Montholon.

"What does this stupid complaint mean?"

And he shrugged his shoulders helplessly. Oh, how petty everything about him was!

The buildings designed for Montholon, Gourgaud and O'Meara were finally nearing completion. The house where the Bertrands were to live, a hundred and twenty yards from the Emperor, had reached the roofing stage. Since the Countess found the house too small, the Governor added a square wooden verandah that was all windows on three sides to fill out an attractive drawingroom.

The new furniture was being arranged. A billiard table was set up in the ante-room. Napoleon did not know how to play—he stopped at pushing the balls about with his hand as he passed. But he found

[37] Montholon, Vol. I, p. 289.
[38] Gourgaud, Vol. I, p. 186; Lowe Papers, 20-115.
[39] Lowe Papers, 20-115.

the green cloth convenient for spreading out his maps and plans. The
room became a sort of topographical study, though serving at the
same time as an ante-room or reception parlour. The drawingroom
got a carpet, a chandelier, a marble-topped console, some curtains,
two sofas, six armchairs and six black wooden chairs ornamented with
gilded bronze and covered in green velours. A new table and several
chairs came for the diningroom. A desk and a mahogany stand went
into the Emperor's bedroom. Marchand received a large wardrobe
to hold his master's linen and clothes. The arrival of three bookcases
with curtains and brass trellis-work doors prompted Napoleon to
decide that the library should be the room formerly occupied by the
Montholons. The old furniture that so became useless was divided
among the Emperor's companions.

The brig *Mosquito* from England brought letters on May 29, 1816.[40]
Napoleon received one from his mother, the first apparently that had
come from any of his relatives.

"I am very old," Mme. Letizia wrote by the hand of Fesch, "to
make a journey of two thousand leagues, and I shall probably die on
the way. But no matter—I shall die near you." The Emperor appeared
greatly touched. He reread the letter, heaved a sigh and tore it up.
He began looking through the *Journal des Débats*—Lowe had sent a
collection up to March 5th. Then after a moment, he laid down the
paper and said to Las Cases:

"It was from poor Madame. She is well and wants to come and
join me."

Join him—no! He would never consent to having anyone of his
family, even were it his mother, see him in his abasement.

The Honourable John Elphinstone, brother to the officer of the
same name who had been wounded at Waterloo, sent him from Canton
a very handsome game of chess, a box of gaming counters stamped
with the Imperial crown and two ivory baskets. Napoleon received
those presents with delight, but the three guns that had been sent
him from England he returned to Plantation House. The only good
hunting on St. Helena lay outside the boundary lines. At Longwood
the only things one could shoot at would have been rats.

.    .    .    .    .    .    .

On June 17th the frigate *Newcastle* anchored at Jamestown. On
board she had Rear Admiral Sir Pulteney Malcolm, who had been

[40] Las Cases, Vol. III, p. 418.

appointed to replace Cockburn at the Cape, and two of the three
commissioners of the Allied Powers—Count Balmain, representing
Czar Alexander, and the Marquis de Montchenu, representing Louis
XVIII. On the 18th the *Orontes* landed Baron Stürmer, the Austrian
Commissioner. The Court of Prussia had refrained from naming a
representative.

These arrivals excited intense interest at Longwood. Napoleon's
imagination was always running away with him. He thought the
representative of Emperor Francis might bring news of Marie-Louise
and his son, and that the Russian Commissioner would have a message for him from the Czar, his friend at Tilsit and Erfurt, with
whom he could forthwith begin a correspondence. When Alexander
learned how Napoleon was being treated at St. Helena, would his
generosity not incline him to bring pressure upon the Allies to end
the Captivity? As for the envoy from France, a Royalist with service
stripes, however ill-intentioned he might be, he would nevertheless
be a Frenchman. At such a distance from home political rivalries
ought to lose some of their violence. Napoleon would find a way to
tame him! He had charmed more refractory men than that, men
who had had personal motives of enmity against him! So henceforward there would be a little diplomatic corps accredited to him. That
would reflect some distinction on Longwood, and the prestige of the
Emperor would be enhanced. His people, for their part, rejoiced at
the thought of the new distractions which this addition to St. Helena
society would bring them. Mme. Bertrand and Mme. de Montholon
might find a friend in Mme. Stürmer. They would no longer be
condemned to seeing only English people.

O'Meara went to town to see how things were going. On his return
to Longwood he told the Emperor that he had seen the Commissioner
from France.[41]

"What sort of a man is he?"

"An old émigré, the Marquis de Montchenu. I was standing with
a group of officers. He came up to me and said: 'For the love of
Heaven, if any of you speak French, tell me. I have come to end my
days in the midst of these rocks and I don't know a word of the
language.' "

"A chatterbox and a fool!" laughed Napoleon. "What idiocy to
send commissioners here where there is nothing to do and no responsi-

41 O'Meara, Vol. I, p. 62.

bility! They will spend all their time running up and down these roads. The Prussian government has shown more sense and saved its money."

Nevertheless he sent Gourgaud off to try to meet Montchenu and see whether he was really the absurd creature that people said he was.

Gourgaud's report was encouraging. At the Porteous House where the Commissioners were staying, he had met the Marquis and his aide-de-camp. Though Montchenu had given himself airs, the two gentlemen were nevertheless extremely courteous. Napoleon warned Gourgaud not to trust them.

"Monsieur de Montchenu looks down on you because you are of the people. You are a commoner."

To which Gourgaud replied, not without wit, that he was "the same sort of a gentleman that the Emperor was, and that that was enough for him." [42]

Monsieur de Montchenu could bow and say little nothings with all the airs of a genuine red-heels, but at fifty-nine he was nothing but a superannuated courtier, a piece of driftwood from the Emigration. Short, fat, rubicund, with fairly handsome features, he wore his hair in the old style, powdered and in a long queue. He came from an ancient family but owed his title of marquis strictly to his own liberality. Napoleon may have seen him at Valence when he was second Colonel at the Cavalry Cadets' Academy. In 1792 he emigrated and lived for eight years in Westphalia, returning to France under the Consulate to live obscurely at Lyons. In speaking of the Emperor he was wont to say: "When that man falls, I shall beg the King to make me his jailor." He would have gone over to Bonaparte perhaps had he found the way, but where, under the Empire, could such an idiot have been used? On the Restoration he hastened to Paris, asked for gratifications, titles and a cross, as the price of his enforced loyalty. He obtained nothing at all at first. He turned up at Vienna where he put in a claim before the Congress—a matter of hay and fodder dating from the Seven Years' War. He was laughed at but somehow managed to worm his way into Talleyrand's circle. Talleyrand saw through that empty bottle at a glance. When it came to choosing a commissioner for St. Helena he remembered Montchenu and, as a sort of practical joke, appointed him. Montchenu tried at once to draw all possible profit from the windfall. He failed to get

[42] Gourgaud, Vol. I, pp. 207-08.

the red cordon, but was given an honorarium of 30,000 francs, the rank of brigadier-general with a salary of 10,000 francs to be added to his Commissioner's fee, and finally, for a secretary, a young Guard officer of twenty-five, Jean-Claude de Gors, who adopted the *de* and the title of aide-de-camp the more worthily to serve under such a noble master. Gors received a salary of only 6,000 francs, because it was thought in Paris that Montchenu, with whom he was living, would defray all his expenses. That was a mistaken guess by a wide margin.

Travelling with them on the *Newcastle* Count Alexandre de Balmain had evinced little taste for their society. Balmain was a distinguished gentleman, amiable, cultivated, speaking easily and elegantly and with wit and good sense. His family was of ancient Scotch origin and was connected with the Ramsays of Balmain. An army officer in his younger days, Balmain had early veered to diplomacy, serving as Embassy secretary at Naples, Vienna and London. In 1813 he went back to the army and fought the campaign in Germany. He had been attached to Wellington's staff at Waterloo. Czar Alexander was delighted with his mind and entrusted several missions to him. He had not sought the post at St. Helena, but accepted it willingly enough and without much thought as to the material environment he would find there. The distance did not frighten him. Was he not certain by the very character of his task of remaining under the eye and in the thoughts of his sovereign? That for him was the essential thing.[43]

The Austrian Commissioner, Baron Barthelmy Stürmer, was twenty-nine years old. He began his career as secretary to Schwartzenberg at the Congress of Chatillon. In Paris he fell in love with a fat little French girl, very pretty, daughter to a clerk in the War Office named Boutet. She was eighteen years old at the time of her arrival in St. Helena. Las Cases had known her as a young girl: "A clerk in the War Office, a very good man so far as I know," he told the Emperor, "came to my house to give my son lessons in Latin and in handwriting. He had a daughter whom he hoped to place as a governess and asked us to recommend her if the opportunity arose. Mme.

[43] He had set out with a slender salary of 1,200 pounds sterling which he was almost immediately obliged to increase to 2,000. Later on he received 1,600 pounds to pay arrears on debts that he was obliged to contract during the early part of his stay at St. Helena.

de Las Cases sent for the girl. She was charming and most attractive in appearance." As a baroness and wife to a diplomat, Madame Stürmer tried to forget the humbleness of her early estate. But she did not forget France and she secretly admired Napoleon. However she took care not to recognize either Las Cases or Emmanuel. But going to The Briars one day to visit the bungalow where the Emperor had formerly lived, she could not restrain her tears. She spoke of the King of Rome with tender pity.

Loyal as her husband was to Metternich he was lacking neither in intelligence nor in judgment. He was a mild, polished gentleman, well educated, though a trifle dull in appearance. He was always much concerned with his career and strongly Austrian in everything. Stürmer came with the same salary as Balmain—1,200 pounds. It was never increased. The household he was to establish at Rosemary Hall was to cost him on the average 4,000 pounds. He was to be half ruined.

The moment the Commissioners arrived, Hudson Lowe gave them a dinner at Plantation House. His idea was to remain on good terms with them without doing anything to make their mission effective. The English government did not relish this surveillance on the part of the other Powers. Liverpool wrote to Castlereagh; July 21, 1815: [45]

"We are very much disinclined to the appointment of Commissaries on the part of the other Powers: such an arrangement might be unobjectionable for a few months, but when several persons of this description got together in a place in which they had nothing to do, they would very soon be tired; they would be very likely to quarrel amongst themselves; and the existence of any disputes amongst them might seriously embarrass the safe custody of the prisoner."

And in a confidential letter to Lowe, written April 15, 1816, Bathurst cautioned him to avoid any possible "cabal" of the persons attached to Buonaparte's household with the Commissioners, "who will have too little to do where they are going, not to be tempted to do a little mischief." [46]

Lowe for his part expected nothing except annoyances and complications from them. Like Bathurst he feared that the Commissioners would end by getting on too well with the French. But since the Cabinet had not been able to prevent their being sent, the policy

[45] Castlereagh, *Letters and Despatches*, Vol. X, pp. 434-35.
[46] Lowe Papers, 20-115; N. Young, *Op. cit.*, Vol. I, p. 262.

had to be to limit their activity as far as possible, and if possible, to prevent them in indirect ways from having any contact with Napoleon.

The instructions which the Commissioners bore and which they communicated to the Governor did not agree. Montchenu and Stürmer had orders from their courts to "make sure with their own eyes of Bonaparte's existence." Each time they did so "a certified report was to be drawn up and forwarded to Paris and Vienna."

Balmain's orders were somewhat broader. The Czar had put them into his hands in person. "Your rôle is to be purely passive. You will observe everything and report everything. In your relations with Bonaparte, you will act with the reserve and tact that such a delicate situation requires and with the personal consideration that is due to him. You will neither avoid nor seek occasions for meeting him, conforming strictly in that regard to the rules that the Governor shall have laid down." [47]

The Czar had underlined the words: *the personal consideration that is due to him.* When he learned of that, Napoleon conceived extravagant hopes from it.

Montchenu sought to be taken to Longwood on the very day of his arrival.

"I cannot let the *Northumberland* sail," he said, "without transmitting to my Court a report that will establish the existence of Buonaparte. That is of the greatest importance to France." [48]

Lowe remarked that it was not such a simple matter to see Bonaparte. The irate marquis replied that one had only to go to his residence with a company of grenadiers.

Lowe persuaded him to abandon that fine plan for the time being. But the next morning Montchenu appealed to his colleagues: "Gentlemen, I count on you if I am compelled to use force."

Stürmer and Balmain decried such impulsiveness and, in the face of their opposition and the Governor's, he was obliged, willy-nilly, to resign himself to waiting.

He was to have a very long wait. For one thing the despatching of the Commissioners was based on the Allied agreement of August 2, 1815. The Commissioners were to serve it on the Governor along with their instructions. Now neither Montchenu, Stürmer nor Bal-

[47] Nesselrode to Balmain. Paris, September 18-30, 1815.
[48] Stürmer to Metternich. September 2, 1816.

main had taken the precaution to bring copies of that basic document
with them. Cursing their clumsiness they rummaged around for three
weeks and finally found, in Stürmer's luggage, a page of an old number of the *Débats* in which the agreement had been published. They
at once had copies made from it.

.          .          .          .          .          .          .

Lowe came to Longwood on the 20th of June to introduce the
new Admiral, Sir Pulteney Malcolm, to Napoleon. Cockburn had left
for England on the *Northumberland* the evening before. He did
not pay a farewell call on the Emperor, contenting himself with a
visit to Bertrand. When the *Northumberland* sailed, twelve sailors
who had been put at Napoleon's disposal were replaced by soldiers
from the 53rd.

Napoleon received Admiral Malcolm with the best grace, in order
to nettle the Governor. With Lowe himself he was courteous. He
talked navy with the Admiral and invited him to come back and
see him, bringing Lady Malcolm. He knew that she was an Elphinstone and a niece of Lord Keith, of whom, in spite of Plymouth, he
retained a good impression.

The Admiral went away enchanted and Napoleon, for his part,
found him much to his liking.

"There is a man with an agreeable, open, intelligent and sincere
face," he said to O'Meara. "A fine specimen of an Englishman! Really
he is as pleasant to look at as a pretty woman. He says what he thinks
frankly and courageously and is not afraid to look at you in the
eye." [49]

That was a thrust at Lowe who often turned his eyes away in
embarrassment.

Five days later the Admiral reappeared at Longwood with his wife.
Lodged at Plantation House, they rode on horseback as far as Hutt's
Gate where they found the Emperor's carriage which he had sent
to meet them. Lady Malcolm got in with Mme. Bertrand, Bertrand
and Malcolm escorting them on horseback. According to their usual
custom the Archambaults drove the horses at a gallop. Lady Malcolm
took fright, but Mme. Bertrand reassured her. She was extremely
anxious to win the good graces of the newcomer, who had connections through family ties with all the English aristocracy. She talked
to her of her loneliness, her unhappiness.

[49] O'Meara, Vol. I, p. 63.

REAR-ADMIRAL SIR PULTENEY MALCOLM
From an Engraving by W. Ward

Arriving at Longwood they were introduced into the drawingroom. Napoleon seated Lady Malcolm near him on the sofa and invited the others to take chairs. The conversation was general but lively. Napoleon spoke of Lord Keith and asked for news of Europe. The Admiral said that armaments were going to be reduced and the income tax suppressed. Lady Malcolm, at a question from Napoleon, confessed that she found St. Helena charming—it reminded her of Scotland, her own country, she said. Then he spoke of Ossian, the poet of his youth:

"I am the one who made him fashionable. I have even been accused of having my head filled with Ossian's clouds!"

If the Admiral had conquered Napoleon by his handsome, soldierly bearing, Lady Malcolm proved just as delightful to him on very different grounds. She was small, round-shouldered, frankly ugly.[50] Powdered and painted she had no taste in dress and wore a display of colours that made her look like "an aging macaw." Mme. de Montholon described her as "a dried peachstone—one of those ugly grotesques they paint on fans in China." But she was lively, amusing, full of wit, kind-hearted, a noble human sympathy transpiring through everything she said. She looked at Napoleon with all her eyes, finding him strangely simple in his worn coat set off by the star of the Legion. What struck her in particular was his kindliness.[51] Was he not the man who had saved her brother at Waterloo? She was filled with gratitude and respect for him.

From that day the Malcolms were to be treated as favourites at Longwood. Napoleon was to have intimate conversations with the Admiral. He would receive him in his bedroom without dressing. On July 4th, for instance, he had a long conversation with him.[52] They talked of Trafalgar, of Napoleon's plans for invading England, of Waterloo. Malcolm's fleet had brought the English troops in America to reinforce Wellington. The Admiral—as well, for that matter, as Wellington himself—had thought the battle lost. He had hastened to Brussels to prepare for re-embarkation when Blücher's army had suddenly come up on the British left and made their victory certain.

Napoleon would walk with Lady Malcolm in his garden, teasing

[50] Stürmer to Metternich, January 10, 1817.
[51] Lady Malcolm, Diary, p. 23.
[52] Lady Malcolm, Diary, p. 25; Gourgaud, Vol. I, p. 214.

her in order to call forth her repartees. Those two loyal English people were never to do anything against the authority of the Governor, but they did try to soften Lowe's harshness and make the Captivity less burdensome, and to bring the people on the island to understand the exiles' state of mind. They were to be the best and most attentive friends that Napoleon met during those sorrowful years among foreigners.

.       .       .       .       .       .       .

As they were leaving at the time of Malcolm's first visit the Emperor had had Bertrand ask Lowe "whether the Commissioners were bearers of letters from their sovereigns and what the special purpose of their mission might be." The Governor replied that they had no letters, and requested Bertrand to ask his master just when and how it would be agreeable to him to receive them.

The Emperor fell from the clouds. So Europe had sent him not ambassadors but turnkeys! No news from Marie-Louise and his son— not a line from Alexander! The sovereigns refused to see in him anything but a prisoner. Was he therefore to submit by receiving the Commissioners officially? Should he resign himself to hearing "General Buonaparte" from them? For eleven months he had been struggling to protect his title, which might never serve him again but would at least be a heritage for his son! But to shut his doors to them would be to cut off every tie with Europe and thereby remain more than ever at the mercy of the English. He hesitated for three weeks. His advisors held differing views. The Montholons, Gourgaud and Mme. Bertrand were eager to profit by the social advantages and the European atmosphere that the Commissioners brought. Bertrand and Las Cases were for maintaining an uncompromising attitude of protest. Lowe used Admiral Malcolm to sound Napoleon out.[53] The Emperor voiced his indecision. He would be glad to see the Commissioners as individuals. He disliked giving them an audience in their official capacities.

"What could I say to the Austrian Commissioner who comes here without a word from my father-in-law to tell me that my son—his grandson—is alive? A man who implored me to marry his daughter and to whom I have twice restored his states! And what language should I use to this Russian whose Emperor was at my feet and who

[53] Lowe Papers, 20-115.

called me his best friend? I have letters of his that prove it. I shall show them some day. I am less embarrassed with the Frenchman. Louis owes me nothing." [54]

.        .        .        .        .        .        .

While Rosemary Hall, a pretty dwelling not far from Plantation House, was being made ready to receive the Stürmers (Balmain was to settle with them there), the three Commissioners lived at the Porteous House. Occasional chats with English officers and the comings and goings in the street of Jamestown were their sole distractions there, and they were rotting with tedium. Montchenu sent home to his friends in France a veritable circular in which he deplored the uncouthness of the island:

"It is a hideous place. You see nothing but mountains, without vegetation, from a thousand to three thousand feet high. One small town of some sixty houses and not a blessed village—just a few scattered huts that they dignify with the name of country houses and of which about ten are livable! Some very pretty roads that have been cut out of the rock are always bordered with terrifying precipices. There is not a path one can travel on! That, my dear fellow, is your friend's abode. You can get absolutely nothing here and everything is exorbitantly high." [55]

Stürmer, more moderate, also had his complaints for Metternich: "I have learned to know the countless difficulties one meets here in every direction and in the most insignificant matters. The geographical position of the island makes communications slow and painful. Bonaparte and everything and everybody connected with him are kept in complete isolation. Then there is the difficult temperament of the man on whom everything depends here [Lowe]. Those are so many obstacles—and they are frequently insurmountable—with which we have to contend. The beauty of the climate is the sole compensation we hoped to have for so many annoyances, but it does not deserve half the praise that is bestowed on it." [56]

And Balmain: "St. Helena is the saddest, the most inaccessible place in the world and the most easy to attack—the most unsociable, the

---

[54] July 25. Lady Malcolm, *Diary*, p. 41; Stürmer to Metternich, September 2, 1816.
[55] Montchenu to Dinens, superintendent of posts at Angoulême, July 25, 1816. In part unpublished. The author gained access to it through the kindness of M. Jean Texcier.
[56] Stürmer to Metternich, September 2, 1816, January 10, 1817.

poorest, the most expensive, and especially the best suited to the purpose to which it is now being put." [57]

If the Commissioners were marooned—for how long they could not say—upon such a rock, they at least wanted to fulfil their mission. They requested the Governor in writing "to procure them the earliest possible opportunity for seeing Napoleon Buonaparte." [58]

Lowe transmitted this request to Bertrand, without pressing it, however. Attached to his letter was a copy of the agreement of August 2 which he expected would fortify Napoleon in his resolve not to see the Commissioners on an official basis.

As to their reception "as individuals," he flattered himself that he could dissuade them from consenting to such a thing. That would leave him alone with his prisoner face to face and free to guard him as his anxiety should dictate quite apart from any comment by curious or ill-willed foreigners, and beyond the possibility also of any appeal through them to the sense of justice or the tardy generosity of Europe.

A month was to pass without a reply being sent to the Governor. Not till August 23, after the last interview that Napoleon was to have with Lowe, did Montholon address him with a protest of a general character in which the Emperor refused to recognize the official status of the European envoys.

.     .     .     .     .     .     .     .     .

At that moment one notes a sort of relaxing on Napoleon's part. The arrival of six boxes of books with the *Newcastle* (June 22) [59] had given him keen delight. He was so impatient to see them opened that he took a hammer and chisel and worked at the cases himself. During the weeks that followed he busied himself in classifying the volumes in the bookcases, and since these were not sufficient, on pine-board shelves that were set up and painted green. Aly began to make a catalogue, working on a white wooden table that had been spread with Baron d'Albe's huge map of Italy.

Seven other boxes arrived on the 24th and 25th of June. They were the books Bertrand had asked for in a letter that he had sent to London from Madeira. The English Cabinet sent in a bill of 36,000 francs for them. The sum was never paid, because, in spite of the Grand Marshal's repeated requests, he was never supplied with the invoice. These volumes formed the nucleus of the library at St. Helena to-

[57] Balmain to Nesselrode, June 29, 1816.          [59] Gourgaud, Vol. I, p. 208.
[58] July 21, 1816, Lowe Papers, 20-115.

gether with 588 volumes, stamped with the Imperial arms, which came from the library at the Trianon, and some thirty or so that had been borrowed from Malmaison. Other shipments were made by Lord Bathurst and, in particular, by Lord and Lady Holland. At the end of the Captivity the library comprised 3,370 volumes. Aly had all he could do to keep the library in good order. The Emperor was an exacting reader. Bertrand wanted novels, Las Cases and Gourgaud histories or military treatises. The Montholons borrowed and never returned: "I am the despair of Aly," Montholon was to write to his wife, August 11, 1819. "He insists that I have more than a hundred volumes out, and that I have never returned one. That is true, but I pay no attention to him." That placed the poor librarian in the most embarrassing situations, for Napoleon knew his books well, and when he asked for one and it was not available, Aly was treated to a scene.[60]

Among the books the Emperor found the complete collection of the *Moniteur*. That was indispensable for the writing of his memoirs, which of late, for lack of data, he had been neglecting. He fell upon it and refused to put it down again. No more rides—the weather was frightful! At dinner the sole subject of conversation was books, and he would spend whole nights running through tome after tome and dictating notes to Marchand. He told Las Cases that "he enjoyed all that as much as a novel."

Another joy fell to Napoleon's lot at this same time. Philip Welle, a young botanist employed at the gardens of Schönbrunn, had come to St. Helena with the Austrian Commissioner. Before his departure from Vienna, his chief, Boos, had handed him an unsealed package containing a curl of blonde hair with a scrap of paper on which Mme. Marchand, nurse to the King of Rome, had written in the latter's behalf:

"Here enclosed you will find some of my hair. If you have any way of having your portrait painted, send me your portrait. Your mother, Marchand."

A harmless trick devised by a poor woman to transmit to the exile far beyond the seas a memento of his lost child! The silken hair was so fine! Marchand would never mistake it! He would know that it had belonged not to his mother, but to the little king!

Marchand was informed by a certain Richard Prince that Welle

[60] Cahuet, p. 201.

had a message for him.[61] He went down from Longwood accompanied by a soldier, who waited for him in front of the Porteous House. Welle handed him the package and orally gave him news of his mother, and also of the Imperial heir whom he had often glimpsed in the park at Schönbrunn, pretty, graceful, the picture of health. He also gave Marchand a letter and a silk handkerchief which Mme. Gourgaud had entrusted to him in Paris for her son.

Marchand hurried back to Longwood. The Emperor took the lock of hair and caressed it lovingly. A French servant had had a pity on him that neither his father-in-law nor his wife had shown! He locked the memento in his dresser, putting it with a lock of Josephine's that Hortense had sent to him at Elba.

All that put the Emperor in a more conciliatory frame of mind and he showed the change in a reply he sent through Montholon to Lowe (July 8, 1816). Lowe had first written to Bertrand, but Bertrand had not answered him. He then wrote to Montholon on July 6th.[62] The Governor insisted on knowing whether Napoleon wished to live in an enlarged Longwood or preferred a new building elsewhere.

"This letter," Napoleon dictated, "is written in the intent of being amiable. It contrasts with the ignoble vexations that are being daily devised for my benefit. That does not accord with the conversation I have had with Sir Lowe [May 16th] and to which he refers in his letter. Of that conversation I have only a very painful remembrance. . . . This island is very bad for my health. It is the dampest country on earth. . . . My residence on it is being studiously rendered more unhealthy and frightful."

Montholon regretted afterwards that the Emperor had not been established in Plantation House. Adding wings to Longwood would simply be enlarging a shanty. They asked only for the more urgent repairs. The roofs of tarred paper let the rain into the apartments of Las Cases and Gourgaud. The Governor ordered the necessary repairs at once.

But he spoiled those better relations by repeated breaches of tact. He started a personal quarrel with Bertrand for a mere trifle. Learning

[61] Shortly after, Richard Prince was banished from the island by order of the Governor and for that cause alone.
[62] Lowe Papers, 20-116.

from Gourgaud that Montchenu had seen her sick mother in Paris,
Mme. Bertrand invited him to come to Hutt's Gate to give news of
her.[63] Her letter was entrusted to Porteous who handed it to the
Governor. Lowe returned it to Bertrand with a scolding, reminding
him that all communications directed to Longwood or coming from
there must pass through his hands, unsealed. Bertrand replied in his
most vigorous tone.[64] Longwood would not submit to his visa. As for
the Emperor he refused to receive any more letters with seals broken.
If any came for him Lowe "was at liberty to burn them." Before
making this reply Bertrand had consulted the Emperor, who remarked
to Gourgaud, after reading it: [65] "I have just dictated a good reply
to him."

The Governor, however, stuck to his orders. If Bonaparte's companions did not care to defer to them, they had only to leave St.
Helena. The bridges between the Grand Marshal and the Governor
were burned.

Another incident came to irritate Napoleon. Two richly bound
volumes of the works of J. C. Hobhouse, *Letters Written by an Englishman Resident in Paris under the Reign of Napoleon*, had been sent
by their author "to the Emperor"—*imperatori Napoleoni*, the Latin
words being struck in gold on the flat side of the cover. Napoleon
now learned that they had been confiscated by the Governor, who
did not dream that *imperator* might mean "general" as well as "emperor." That the present should have come from an Englishman
seemed to him treasonable. It was never to be delivered. Napoleon
said to O'Meara in a rage:

"That convict did not want me to get the book because he thought
I might be pleased to see that all men are not like him, and that some
of his countrymen hold me in high esteem. I did not think that a man
could be so low or so vile!" [66]

It is only fair to add, however, that in a note addressed to Sir Hudson Lowe, Hobhouse had authorized the Governor, in case he found

[63] Montchenu had also brought letters to St. Helena from Mme. Dillon to her
daughter, from Mme. de Las Cases to her husband, and other missives for Montholon.
They had been delivered as soon as he arrived by way of the Governor's office
(Gourgaud, Vol. I, p. 208; Montholon. Vol. I, p. 313).
[64] Bertrand to Lowe, July 3, 1816.
[65] Gourgaud, Vol. I, p. 213.
[66] O'Meara, Vol. I, p. 82.

the delivery of the gift "incorrect," to place the volumes in his own library. Lowe elected to keep them.[67]

Lowe called on the Emperor on July 16 to make final arrangements for improvements at Longwood.[68] That day Napoleon had a toothache.[69] During luncheon, which he had ordered served under the garden tent with Las Cases, Montholon, Gourgaud and the doctor, he had railed against Lowe, who had told Las Cases that when he had any shoes to mend he should send them to him. That was to prevent Longwood from establishing any direct contact with the shoemaker in Jamestown. After that, as it happened, Gourgaud started a quarrel with Las Cases and the Emperor said some harsh things to Gourgaud and Montholon. Lowe appeared at Longwood about two o'clock in that stormy atmosphere.[70] He saw at once from the Emperor's attitude that the interview would be difficult. Napoleon did not utter a word for the first ten minutes. Lowe, embarrassed, beat about the bush. Suddenly the Emperor turned on him:

"You pay us compliments in your letters and at the same time you stick pins in our backs. There is no way of dealing with you. You are a lieutenant-general. You should not carry out your orders like a sergeant. Think of your reputation. It will suffer from the manner in which you are treating us."

Lowe defended himself. Napoleon's entourage, he said, took delight in spoiling their relations—they "poisoned everything." He had not come to St. Helena to make a reputation but to do his duty. He had not asked for the post. When he returned to the matter of building, the Emperor shrugged his shoulders:

"A new house? It would take six years to build it! In two years there will be a change of ministry in England or perhaps a new government in France. I shall not be here."

The conversation lasted two hours, both of them standing. Lowe

[67] Hobhouse, a friend of Byron, was a Member of the Liberal Opposition in the House of Commons. The Latin dedication to the volumes may be translated in complete form as follows:
"To the Emperor Napoleon who has borne adversity with equanimity, the English writer J. C. Hobhouse offers these volumes in which he has retraced recent events that have occurred in unhappy France during the effort of a hero escaped from exile to restore to her her freedom."
[68] Lowe's notes place this interview on July 17th, but Gourgaud, O'Meara, Las Cases, Montholon, give the date definitely as the 16th.
[69] O'Meara, Vol. I, p. 74.
[70] Gourgaud, Vol. I, p. 219.

LONGWOOD. PRESENT-DAY VIEW

concluded by saying that he would report to London. Napoleon nodded. Lowe bowed and took his leave.[71]

Faithful to his word—for that petty individual was not dishonest—he sent Bathurst an accurate report on the interview. On several occasions in talks with O'Meara, Napoleon had indicated, as his preference for a new site, either The Briars, or the neighbourhood of Rosemary Hall. The Briars was too near town, Lowe thought. To his superior therefore he recommended choosing Rosemary for Napoleon's future residence.

On July 24th Napoleon had a very pretty tent set up in the Longwood garden to replace Cockburn's, which the wind and rain had torn to shreds. The next day he received Malcolm, who brought the collection of the *Journal des Débats* down to May 13. It had just arrived by the *Griffon* with letters from Madame Mère, Pauline and Lucien. The Admiral talked of events in France—the dissolution of the Chambers, the insurrection at Grenoble, General Bertrand's condemnation to death by a military commission. Finally Napoleon said of the Governor:

"He has not the character of an Englishman—he is a Prussian soldier. He is tricky and he writes well. He must be sending in some clever reports to his government. I dislike his ways to such an extent that if he were to come and tell me that a frigate was ready to take me back to France, he would not give me the slightest pleasure."

Malcolm thought Lowe was narrow-minded. Nevertheless he defended his countryman. The Governor's intentions were kindly, even if he sinned in manner. Napoleon agreed, but the manner was the important thing with him. What he could not stand in Lowe was his affectation of treating him as an equal, with just that nuance of deference that he considered owing to Napoleon's seniority in rank.

"We cannot get along," he said. "Call it childishness if you wish, but that is the way it is."

Why didn't they let him ride anywhere he chose on the island without Poppleton's following him? It was absurd to be afraid of an escape:

[71] Lowe to Bathurst, July 27, 1816; Gourgaud, Vol. I, p. 220; Las Cases, Vol. V, p. 27; O'Meara, Vol. I, p. 76. Lowe further wrote to Sir Henry Bunbury, July 29: "He abused me, but with much less asperity than before. His conversation abounded with repetitions. I involuntarily fell back during one or two pauses towards the door, when he renewed the attack, sidled himself almost between me and the door, and could not have done the thing more cunningly had he a design to prevent my escaping from him" (Forsyth, Vol. I, p. 233).

"Only a bird could get away from this place. Of what use are those sentinels on the hilltops? It's enough if the coast is guarded . . . Lowe is not a general. He has never commanded anything but some Corsican deserters. . . . I should rather have been shut up in the Tower of London than on this ugly island. I shall die here inside of three years." [72]

The Emperor kept Malcolm until dark. At a certain moment Napoleon asked him "whether he thought he would always have to stay at St. Helena."

"Yes," replied the Admiral, and he urged him to accommodate himself as best he could to his situation.

The Admiral returned to Longwood while they were experimenting with an ice-machine of the Leslie type that the Prince Regent had sent. The machine was defective and gave wretched results. The Emperor broke a thermometer.

"That's just like me!" he exclaimed, laughing.

And he dragged Malcolm off into the wood for a chat about naval matters.

August 15 came. Gourgaud prepared a bouquet of violets to offer to the Emperor "from the King of Rome." Napoleon entered his bedroom at eight o'clock, unexpectedly. Gourgaud delivered his little compliment after a fashion.

"Bah!" said the Emperor. "The King of Rome is thinking of me about as much as he is of you!" [73]

They got Las Cases and went out into the garden. The Montholons, then the Bertrands, appeared with their children. Congratulations, homage, best wishes! Big and little they all lunched under the tent. The day passed *en famille*. In the evening the servants had a big supper and after that a dance.

. . . . . . .

Lord Bathurst had urged Lowe in his despatches to cut down expenses at Longwood so as to keep them under 8,000 pounds a year. The Governor sparred for time. He thought himself that expenditures were excessive (they were well along towards 17,000 pounds), but he was afraid that such a violent reduction would rouse a storm from Napoleon. The minister insisting by every post, Lowe was obliged to act. He broached the matter first to Montholon who, at

[72] Lady Malcolm, *Diary*, pp. 35 ff.
[73] Gourgaud, Vol. I, p. 235.

least in words, seemed to contemplate some economies. When Montholon reported the matter to Napoleon the latter replied that "he had enough money to meet his total expense, but that he would ask for a remittance from Europe only in sealed letters."

Sealed letters! Lowe took fright. That would be a means for Napoleon to establish correspondence with Europe and—who could say? —through it to make preparations for an escape!

The days passed, the expenses continued. The Governor determined to put an end to it. On August 14th he went to Longwood and, according to Gourgaud, told Montholon that his credit was exhausted. His Majesty did not receive him, nor Bertrand either. He came back on the 16th and asked to speak to the Emperor. The Emperor referred him to Bertrand. Bertrand hid away. Lowe came back the next day and handed the Grand Marshal a bill of accounts asking that Napoleon take steps to procure funds in Europe. Bertrand replied harshly and Lowe got angry:

"Count Montholon assured me that General Bonaparte would have no objections to discussing this question with me."

That hurt Bertrand by setting Montholon against him. He was scarcely speaking to Montholon. He handed the account back to Lowe:

"Very well, give the paper to Count Montholon. As for me, Your Excellency, I desire to have as little communication with you as possible, either orally or by letter." [74]

Lowe left the room, saying:

"I can assure you, sir, that wish is quite reciprocal on my part."

He went to lodge a complaint with Napoleon. The Emperor would not receive him. He then wrote to Montholon that he would be obliged to reduce expenses at Longwood to 8,000 pounds a year unless Napoleon agreed to cover the remainder.[75] And the next day, although it was Sunday, he reappeared at Longwood, flanked by the Admiral, whom he had asked to accompany him, that he might come to a decisive understanding with Napoleon.[76]

[74] Gorrequer, *Minutes* (Lowe Papers, 20-115); Forsyth, Vol. I, p. 244.
[75] Lowe to Montholon, August 17, 1816.
[76] The interview is described by Las Cases, Vol. V, pp. 346-50, by O'Meara, Vol. I, pp. 90 ff., by Gourgaud, Vol. I, p. 237, by Montholon, Vol. I, p. 356, and finally by the two men with whom Napoleon talked: Lowe, in a report drawn up immediately after the interview, and the Admiral in Lady Malcolm's *Diary*, pp. 55 ff.

Taking advantage of a clearing in the weather, for wind and rain had raged furiously during those two days, the Emperor was pacing up and down in front of the house with Las Cases and Mme. de Montholon. As soon as he caught sight of Lowe, he turned on his heel and moved off towards the little wood. A second later he came back, Montholon having informed him that the Governor insisted on speaking with him. He received the Admiral in the usual way but did not say a word to Lowe. All three walked along the central path in the garden, Napoleon between the two Englishmen. Mme. de Montholon, Las Cases and Gourgaud remained apart. Catching the first opportunity, Lowe addressed the Emperor:

"I am sorry to have to bother you, but General Bertrand's conduct towards me obliges me to discuss the expenses of your household with you directly."

His hands behind his back, Napoleon walked along on the lava gravel without answering. Finally, avoiding a direct address of Lowe, he turned to the Admiral:

"Count Bertrand is a man who has commanded armies and *he* treats him like a corporal. *He* treats us as if we were Corsican deserters. *He* deserved what the Marshal said to him. Governments have a use for two sorts of people, for those whom they respect and for those whom they despise: *he* is one of the latter. They have given *him* the situation of an executioner."

The red blazed on the Governor's face in patches. He replied:

"I am a subject of a free country. I detest despotism. You are trying to soil me with slander because no other weapons are available against me. I can do nothing else but carry out my instructions."

"So," said the Emperor, "if they gave you orders to assassinate me, you would obey?"

"No, sir. The English do not murder."

"Your instructions are the same as those of Sir George Cockburn— he told me so; but you interpret them with fifty times more severity. You are intractable. You suspect everything and everybody. You do not know how to behave with people of honour. You have too base a soul. At least treat us as prisoners of war and not as convicts from Botany Bay!"

Beside himself, he hammered out his words, accompanying them with nervous gestures. One by one he went over his grievances again.

Lowe had deprived Bertrand of the right to issue passes for Long-wood.

Malcolm interrupted.

"That was not Lowe, but Cockburn."

"No, sir. He told you so, but it is not true. I cannot write a note unless he sees it. I cannot receive a lady without his permission. I cannot receive the officers of the 53rd. He has no delicacy. When the soldiers of the 53rd pass me they look at me with compassion and weep. He has kept a book that had been sent to me by a Member of Parliament and he has boasted of it."

"What do you mean—I boasted of it?"

"Yes, sir, you boasted of it—to the Governor of the Île de France.[77] He told me so."

The Admiral interfered again:

"Sir Hudson Lowe kept those volumes because they were dedicated to you with the title of Emperor. He was forbidden to turn them over to you."

"He has sent me letters addressed to the Emperor."

"Yes," said Lowe, "but they had been passed by the Secretary of State, and they came from relatives of yours, or from former subjects of yours, not from Englishmen."

"He has committed the indiscretion of talking in public of the content of letters that came opened to him. My old mother wrote me that she wanted to come to St. Helena to die with me. The whole island knows it."

The Admiral protested. The Governor held such letters sacred.

"I am not the one who talked about them," said Hudson Lowe. "It was undoubtedly people in your establishment who misrepresent everything to you. You are badly surrounded, sir."

Malcolm agreed with that:

"Yes, you are badly surrounded."

"In a few years Lord Castlereagh, Lord Bathurst, and you, will be buried in oblivion, or if you are known at all it will be because of the indignities you have heaped upon me. My body is in your power, but my soul is free. It is just as courageous as when I was master of

[77] Colonel Keating, Governor of the Île de France—after its abandonment to the English, in 1814, known as Île Maurice—had been received by Napoleon on July 27. In the *Illustration* of August 25, 1934, M. René Moulin published a very interesting letter of the Duke of Orleans (the future Louis-Philippe) to whom the Prince Regent had reported Napoleon's conversation with Colonel Keating.

Europe. Europe will later be the judge of the treatment that is being inflicted on me. The shame of it will rebound on the English people."

"When my government ceases to approve of my conduct, I will hand in my resignation."

"You will be doing well both by yourself and by me. You want money? I have none save what is in the hands of my friends, but I am not permitted to send letters to them. If you can no longer feed me, put me on rations. If I am hungry"—and he pointed to the tents in the camp—"I can go and sit down at the table of the officers of the 53rd, or I can even go and ask to share the mess of the soldiers. They, I am sure, will not rebuff the oldest soldier in Europe!"

He added after a second:

"It is Lord Bathurst's blind hate that has sent you here. You are not a general—you are just a staff clerk."

That thrust was too true and hurt Lowe more than the harshest insults would have done. He lost the self-control which, in all justice to him, he had so far maintained.

"You make me laugh, sir," he said.

Napoleon turned on him:

"What? I make you laugh?"

"Yes, sir. I can only pity the false judgment you have of my character and the crudeness of your manners. I wish you good day!"

His hat on his head, without bowing, he left the Emperor who stopped short in his tracks. The Admiral then said to him, bowing:

"So I too—I must wish you good day."

He could not linger without disavowing his countryman and his chief.

Napoleon asked him to carry his compliments to Lady Malcolm. The Admiral caught up with Lowe and both rode back along the road to Plantation House.

The Emperor had gone too far. His antipathy for Lowe had made him overstep all bounds. He realized it and admitted it to Las Cases and Montholon:

"That is the second time in my life I have made a mess of things with the English.[78] Their complacency is more than I can stand and

[78] He was referring to his interview with Lord Whitworth, February 18, 1803, the prelude to the rupture of the Peace of Amiens. He had buried the Ambassador under such abuse that the latter wrote to Addington: "I thought I was listening to a captain of dragoons and not to the head of one of the greatest States in Europe." Re-translated.

I say more than I should. I refuse to see the Governor any more. He makes me too angry and I forget myself."

He was never again to see him, in fact. Napoleon was to stand loyal to the rule he had thrust upon himself. Five years were to pass. On several occasions Lowe was to try, and vainly, to be re-admitted to his presence. He was not to succeed till one morning in Maytime in the presence of silent men who were weeping. That time Napoleon was not again to stab him with his eyes or with his words. Stretched out on his little camp bed, pale, he was to let his jailor approach in silence. And Lowe was to walk on tiptoe, with bared head.

# PART THREE

## *THE STRUGGLE*

### I

### RESTRICTIONS

MME. DE MONTHOLON GAVE BIRTH TO A DAUGHTER WHO RECEIVED THE
name of Napoléone. That was June 18, 1816. In the absence of a
Catholic priest, Mr. Vernon baptized the child according to the
Anglican rite.[1] Mme. de Montholon's accouchement was attended by
Dr. Livingstone, supervisor of the St. Helena hospital. It gave O'Meara
a chance to exercise his wit at the expense of a woman in exile who
was under his care. In a letter to Gorrequer, June 24, 1816, he wrote: [2]
"I don't imagine there was half as much anxiety over the birth of the
King of Rome. You would have thought it the case of a girl of fifteen,
newly married, instead of a wrinkled, middle-aged woman who has
had three husbands (all living) and eight or nine children, no one of
whom seems to have been too repressed since his arrival in this world."

Such a letter gives the measure of O'Meara!

The Emperor paid the mother a visit every day, sitting by her
bedside and talking with her for long periods. Was the child his,
as has been said?

There is nothing to support such a theory. The conception took
place in mid-September, 1815. At that time Napoleon was on the
*Northumberland*. Living quarters were so crowded that the most
discreet liaison would have been known at once. Mme. de Montholon
lived with her husband, her children, and their nurse, in a little room
where a visit from the Emperor would have appeared very unusual.
In his own cabin Napoleon was almost never alone. A quasi-impossi-
bility from the material standpoint, therefore. But there is the moral

[1] *Parish Register*, Jamestown.
[2] Lowe Papers, 20-116. Retranslated.

207

impossibility further. Saddened by his disaster Napoleon was not
thinking of women, and at that time his relations with Mme. de
Montholon were distant, not to say hostile. Gourgaud tells everything
—especially in the unexpurgated text of his *Diary*. He notes when
one person or another took medicines and reveals their intimate peculiarities. He records unblushingly the spiciest conversations at Longwood where "the talk was often very free." He would not have failed
to note a rapprochement between Mme. de Montholon and the Emperor. He did, for instance, accuse Mme. de Montholon of trying
to seduce Cockburn. On the other hand, however much of a courtier
Montholon may have been, he was in love with his wife and jealous
of her. It seems, moreover, that during the early part of the stay at
Longwood, Gourgaud made several advances to her himself and was
rebuffed.

Really, Mme. de Montholon liked admiration. She had the habit
of it and the instinct for it. She tried her best, Gourgaud was later
to note,[3] to play the love-lorn maid with His Majesty: she made eyes,
showed her ankles, pulled her dress taut around her figure, in short,
tried to be dazzling—and that was not easy. But was not that just the
manner of the coquette? Mme. de Montholon was the same with
everybody—English officers, chance visitors, Gourgaud himself, on
the gayer days. She was a *Parisienne*, a woman of the world. Gourgaud had known only life in the camps. He gave trifles an importance
they did not have and saw manoeuvres in mere effusions of a temperament. For that matter, Mme. de Montholon gave herself such airs
as to encourage malicious gossip. She once assured Gourgaud that it
had been foretold of her that she would "some day be a queen in
fact, if not in name."

Napoleon never showed her any special attentions. One evening
before dinner, on entering the drawingroom, she found him alone
with Gourgaud. The Emperor asked her to go into the billiardroom
and play something for him. However he continued talking grammar
with his aide-de-camp. The poor woman sat down at the tuneless
piano, without a light. She played *Marlborough*, did scales, reversed
the pedals, to attract the Emperor's attention. From a distance he
kept calling to her to go on and did not invite her to come back for
a long time.[4]

[3] January 4, 1817. Unpublished.
[4] Gourgaud, February 11, 1817.

He allowed Gourgaud to talk about her before him in insulting terms.

"Mme. de Montholon is not good form," said the young man.[5] "She thinks she has a throat, and pretty feet."

"Well," said the Emperor, who wanted peace. "Say something nice to her."

"She is always scratching her neck and spitting her food into her plate. The woman has no manners. I never thought that Your Majesty would like her for—that! But she does her best to make people think you do."

Napoleon himself spoke of her slightingly.

"Do you think," he said to Gourgaud, "that I don't realize all that they are up to? They are thinking of themselves more than of me. They have taken the rivalries of my [old] court to themselves. Well, I pretend not to notice. You ought to be able to get along with them. Don't imagine that I like her. I have been accustomed to living with too many charming women not to be aware of Mme. de Montholon's ridiculous aspects and her bad manners. But after all, here one would have to make one's society out of a green parrot if there were nothing else. We have no choice." [6]

On the same date he further agreed, says Gourgaud, that "the Montholon woman is here only because she is in bad odour in Paris. Her stay here will give her a coat of whitewash and a certain amount of esteem. But what do I care about her reasons? They all make company for me, and if the woman were prettier, I would take advantage of her for—that too."

He was right—there was no choice! Of the two women who had come to St. Helena to share his exile, Mme. de Montholon alone made an effort to amuse him, flatter him, keep him cheerful. She often talked to him of a probable return to France and of the certainty that his son would ascend a throne.

"Who knows?" she even said. "Your Majesty may some day found a vast empire in America!"

"Oh! I am very old!" replied Napoleon.[7]

Without seeming to she surrounded him with those little womanly attentions which are so sweet in hours of gloom, and so she became

[5] January 20, 1817. Unpublished.
[6] Gourgaud, February 12, 1817. Unpublished.
[7] Gourgaud, Vol. I, p. 522.

more and more necessary to him. At her house he took a seat in the corner of the fireplace and, while she chattered and babbled, stirred the fire. She was his favourite companion for his walks, to the rage of Mme. Bertrand and the fury of Gourgaud, who thought himself insulted the moment he was not the chosen one.

However, if Mme. de Montholon manoeuvred herself into that position of intimacy, Napoleon had no physical inclinations for her and he was angered that Gourgaud should by repeated allusions be seeking to give an impression that she was his mistress.

"It isn't so," he said to Bertrand.[8] "She is too ugly. Such talk might get into the newspapers and do harm."

He always had his pleasantry when he saw a pretty girl, but it really seems that carnal impulse troubled him hardly at all. Some years before his departure for Elba, his senses, on his own admission, had lost their edge. On one occasion Mme. de Montholon was lamenting:

"How rapidly one ages at St. Helena!"

For her it was a fact, alas! But Napoleon replied that "he could no longer think of paying court to a lady."[9]

"At forty-eight," she protested, "many men are still young!"

"Yes, but they have not been through what I have been through. Gourgaud in full dress seems older than he really is. He is still in the age of illusion. He is like Bertrand, who adores his wife and children. But I am done with all that. If I were to lose the Empress, I would not marry again."[10]

"At fifty," he had said ten days earlier, "a man cannot love again. Berthier managed to keep on loving. As for me, my heart has hardened (*j'ai le cœur bronzé*)."

When Gourgaud complained[11] of "not being able to have a woman at Longwood when everybody else had one," Napoleon replied that there was nothing to prevent him, and added:

"Bah! Women! When you don't think about them, you don't need them. Do as I do!"

Whereupon Gourgaud noted: "His Majesty is forty-eight. I am thirty-five."

In fact, if the Emperor seemed to have recovered from loving, his companions made a serious business of it. Not to mention the Mon-

---

8 Gourgaud, January 4, 1817.          10 Gourgaud, April 17, 1817.
9 Gourgaud, Vol. II, p. 25.           11 September 2, 1817. Unpublished.

tholons, who were to have two girls in eighteen months, or the Bertrands who were having one miscarriage after another—five or six before and after the birth of little Arthur—the bachelors were tormented with desires that idleness increased and perhaps the climate itself.

The island of St. Helena is still a very prolific locality. Families of ten, twelve, fifteen children are the rule there even today. However, one should not exaggerate. Masson attributed such strong sentimental tendencies to the "colonial" climate of St. Helena. "St. Helena," he wrote,[12] "is below the Equator. One notes there an exasperation of all the brute passions—of the desire to shed blood and to feast the eye on tortures. There are hatreds that under a gust of passion can only be sated by murder. There is a sort of erotic delirium that modifies all the relations of civilized human beings and makes them revert to barbarism under the lure of the female. The white man is intelligent, educated, sociable, yet one notes in him as it were an upboiling of the unreasoning violence of the black man. The sense of responsibility is weakened, conscience becomes atrophied, the moral law is superseded."

That thesis is fundamentally mistaken. The famous historian of the Bonapartes worked in his study and conceived a wholly *a priori* notion as to the climate of St. Helena. The climate there is almost European. The population is hard-working and peaceable. Misdemeanours are rare and serious crimes unknown. There is no evidence that there were any greater disorders in morals in Napoleon's day, when the island was overrun with soldiers. Several of the exiles at Longwood seem to have been very much preoccupied with sentimental questions, but that must have been due much more largely to their long privation, to their tedium, to the French desire for feminine society, than to geographical latitude.

Even the stern Las Cases yielded to Venus. According to Gourgaud,[13] Las Cases several times frequented a woman named Blake, who must have been an "inhabitant." Women were more on Gourgaud's mind than any regret for France, or more exactly, his homesickness was increased many fold by his abstinence. Secretly and on several occasions he admitted a half-breed from Jamestown into his quarters. He enticed native women to Longwood, notably on June

[12] *Autour de Sainte-Hélène, 1ere série,* p. 116.
[13] December 25, 1816.

25th and September 24th, 1816. As to the one elected on the former date, he noted: "I gave her six pounds. All the varletry of the household rose in insurrection. His Majesty told me that I was wrong and I sent her back to town." [14] After that he pursued a maid of the Bertrands—at the Emperor's own suggestion, it would seem, made out of sheer pity for his state of mind. But the Bertrands grew suspicious and whenever Gourgaud appeared, they were careful to send the mulattress out. In the end, to avoid complications with Gourgaud, Mme. Bertrand decided to dismiss her (December 16, 1817).

Between such attacks, as for instance in the case of Laura Wilks, Gourgaud was always thinking of marriage—an advantageous marriage of course. He fell in love with Miss Amelia Churchill who landed at St. Helena on the way home from India with her sister and her parents. He rode out to meet her, escorted her about, promised to have her and her sister received by Napoleon (a thing they desired more than anything else in the world), or, if that were not possible, at least to get her some autographs. He referred the matter to Napoleon who goodnaturedly agreed to play a game of chess "for the reception of the young ladies and a word in his handwriting," Gourgaud wagering in return eight turtle-doves that he was to catch out hunting. The Emperor lost, but went back on his word. Gourgaud got out of the difficulty by cutting several words in Napoleon's handwriting from a piece of paper, and taking them to Miss Churchill in Jamestown as she was sailing for Europe. The Emperor tried to console the poor boy by assuring him that within a year they would all be in England and that he would arrange a marriage for him "with some young lady from the City" who, out of sheer enthusiasm, would bring him seven or eight hundred thousand francs. Napoleon would go and call on him and try fox hunting on his lands.[15]

The others, too, got along as best they could. Marchand had taken up with Mme. de Montholon's pretty waitress, Esther Vesey, daughter to a retired sergeant living on Ladder Hill. He was to have two children by her. The second, a girl, died at an early age. The eldest, a boy named James-Octave and nicknamed Jimmy, stayed behind on the island with his mother in 1821.

Napoleon looked with a disapproving eye on that intimacy. He rebuked Marchand several times and then asked Mme. de Montholon

[14] Thiers Library. Unpublished.
[15] Gourgaud, Vol. II, p. 174.

to dismiss Esther. She did so, we may assume, since Esther Vesey ceases to figure in the "list of persons making up the household at Longwood" in April, 1817.[16] But once a week Marchand still received his mistress at Longwood where she spent the night. Whenever he went down to Jamestown he saw her at her home. She became pregnant and he wanted to marry her, but the Emperor forbade that. He had become attached to the young man and promised to arrange a marriage for him himself. Arranging marriages, as is well known, was one of Napoleon's hobbies.

Noverraz courted Josephine, Mme. de Montholon's chambermaid, though that did not prevent him, as well as Aly and the Archambaults, from ranging the negro quarter.

In a word, the people in the kitchen were always complaining about one thing or another, but, the bottles helping—and they drank dry, things were often very gay there nevertheless.

. . . . . . . . .

After his last scene with Lowe Napoleon dictated a long *Remonstrance* to Montholon, which was addressed to the Governor but was intended to reach the English ministry and, beyond them, European opinion. It was signed by Montholon and despatched, August 23, 1816, to Plantation House. Napoleon declared himself very well pleased with it. He had it re-read to him several times. Aly made copies to be sent to Europe.

The fact that the document was signed by Montholon underscored Bertrand's fall from grace. In his capacity as Grand Officer of the Crown Bertrand should have signed a paper of such importance. He may have raised objections as to the opportuneness or the form of the protest. It was read aloud on August 20 before Gourgaud and Las Cases, who approved of it after a few corrections.[17] At Jamestown it was rumoured that Napoleon "had stabbed Bertrand with a knife for refusing to sign the letter." [18]

A few days later (August 28th), the Emperor committed a tactical error. He wrote, again through Montholon, that he did not care to receive officers, visiting foreigners, or inhabitants of the island any longer, if it was necessary for them to have a pass from the Governor. Lowe leapt at the opportunity. Nothing could better facilitate his task than complete isolation on the part of the French. He

---

[16] Lowe Papers, 20-118.                    [18] *Ibid.*, Vol. I, p. 241.
[17] Gourgaud, Vol. I, p. 238.

acknowledged the request in a letter to Montholon.[19] Napoleon saw his mistake at once. He tried to remedy it by sending for Poppleton and assuring him "that he considered the English officers honest men and good soldiers, and that he would always receive them with pleasure." Poppleton reported the conversation to Lowe who commented: "He [Bonaparte] has placed a restraint upon himself by the letter you brought me from Count Montholon, and now wishes to release himself from it by means that are indirect. Be mindful of what is said and done." [20] However, Lowe made haste to inform Malcolm and Bingham that they were to issue no further permits for Longwood. In that wretched warfare of pin-pricks he had scored a point.[21] When Bertrand got to Longwood (he took possession of his house there October 20th) the question was to lose its interest. Being himself situated inside the grounds of Longwood, the Grand Marshal could no longer issue permits for entry there.

The British Cabinet was still afraid of an escape. Such fears were maintained by fantastic, and sometimes anonymous, delations which came in from all directions to give warning of pretended plots, financed now by Joseph Bonaparte, now by former Imperial dignitaries. The ex-King of Spain was by that time in retirement in the United States and was thinking much more of arranging a pleasant and sumptuous life for himself there than of seeking new adventures, even were Fortune incidentally to bestow on him the crown of Mexico. As for the high servants of the Empire, if they could not get back into the good graces of the Bourbons, they were concerned at least to remain forgotten. Not one of them ever sent the briefest message, the least remembrance, to the Emperor.

But fear never reasons. Bathurst and his acolytes, Bunbury and Goulburn, addressed letter after letter to Lowe, urging him to keep eyes and ears open and pointing out that a relief expedition was being organized in Brazil, that a native farmer had already been bribed by the French at St. Helena, that an American named Carpenter was outfitting a fast sailer in the Hudson to deliver the captives.[22]

[19] August 29th. Lowe Papers, 20-115.
[20] Lowe Papers, 20-115.
[21] Lowe Papers, 20-116.
[22] Sir Henry Bunbury to Lowe, May 4, 1816; Lord Bathurst to Lowe, July 25, 1816; Sir Charles Stuart (British Ambassador in Paris) to Lord Castlereagh, July 8, 1816 (Copy forwarded to Lowe) (Lowe Papers, 20-116).

GRAND MARSHAL BERTRAND'S HOUSE

BERTRAND'S HOUSE WITH THE HOLE IN THE SHUTTER FOR
NAPOLEON'S FIELD GLASS

See Page 319

If the people in London were anxious, much more so must have been Lowe, on whose shoulders the actual responsibility rested. He was literally unable to sleep. He kept receiving directly letters from cranks or practical jokers that revealed imaginary plans for an escape. A born collector of archives Lowe carefully preserved them all. He must have given little credence to them, but they served to justify him in his fears.[23] Let Napoleon, by one ruse or another, succeed in escaping, and the Governor was lost, his career ending in a disgraceful failure. Now he wanted to succeed in his mission. It was an honour to him, he thought, in the eyes of England and Europe, and he held to that opinion down to the end. On March 5, 1821, he was to write to Lady Holland: "I hold myself much more flattered in being the guardian of his person at St. Helena than I should be to be his Minister at the Court of the Tuileries." [24] At no moment did it ever dawn upon Lowe that his status as a jailor might be an odious one.

He clung to his post not only in view of the future that it might bring in its train, but also because of the sumptuous existence that it allowed him at the moment. At St. Helena he was a little sovereign, vested with virtually absolute power, and provided with a delightful residence and a magnificent salary. Had he given the matter a moment's thought he would have seen that the escape of Napoleon, which was at all times so terribly on his mind, was materially impracticable. The captive might conceivably slip through the cordons of the guard at night and make the shores of Prosperous Bay. But that was a long road, steep, precipitous, perilous. A man of nearly fifty, over weight, inexperienced in travelling over quagmires and rocks, and with poor eyes—for Napoleon, it is too often forgotten, was nearsighted—would undoubtedly lose his life or be seriously injured in such a terrible country.

Napoleon had realized that from the very outset. At one time or another now Las Cases, now Montholon, now Gourgaud, would put suggestions forward. Every time the Emperor discouraged them. Gourgaud was to write: [25] "Montholon says that H. M. will never get away from here, that he has grown 'soft.' He might compromise any number of people, but at the garden gate he would say that he

[23] Lowe Papers, 20-204.
[24] Lowe Papers, 20-132; Young, Vol. II, p. 350.
[25] October 4, 1817. Unpublished.

was too tired and did not want to be the target for a gunshot." Admitting that by an unheard-of stroke of good fortune he should reach the sea, how could the ship that would be waiting for him offshore elude the incessant patrol of the English brigs? It was ridiculous to think of an escape by force of arms. That would have required a fleet and an army, and they would have needed months to reach Longwood.

For the rest, even if the impossible were realized, even if Napoleon by some miracle should get away from the island, where could he go? He could think only of America. Now he had long since given up the plans that he had sketched of yore at Malmaison. The democratic customs of the United States were not to his liking. He was not sure of a good reception there. He was afraid, moreover, of "risking his glory." For himself, and for the future of his son, it was better to stay on St. Helena until some great event should open Europe to him again. If nothing of that sort occurred, it was better to die on that faraway rock. Nowhere else would he ever find a pedestal so lofty.

. . . . . . . .

On the 17th of June, Bathurst gave a set of general directions to Lowe, who had informed him of his difficulties in a letter of May 26th (Forsyth, Vol. I, p. 299):

"There is a wide distinction between the conduct which you ought to hold towards General Buonaparte and towards those who have chosen to follow his fortunes by accompanying him to St. Helena. It would be a want of generosity not to make allowance for the intemperate language into which the former may at times be betrayed. The height from whence he has been precipitated, and all the circumstances which have attended his fall, are sufficient to overset a mind much less irritable than his. . . . With respect to his followers, they stand in a very different situation: they cannot be too frequently reminded that their continuance in the island is an act of indulgence on the part of the British Government; and you will inform them that you have received strict instructions to remove them from the person of General Buonaparte, and to transport them out of the island, if they shall not conduct themselves with that respect which your situation demands, and with that strict attention to your regulations which is the indispensable condition on which their residence in the island is permitted."

Meanwhile, by the *Eurydice*, Bathurst was sending still stricter orders. The orderly officer was thereafter and by any means required to verify the presence of Napoleon at Longwood twice a day. That the Emperor's expenses and his resources for action might be reduced, four at least of his attendants should be put aboard ship for Europe.[26] Those who were to remain should be forced to sign the uniform pledge of submission that they had replaced by declarations "insolent" in tone. If they refused, Lowe should expel them from the island.

Bathurst was counting on a refusal. Lowe's military secretary, Gorrequer, came to sound out Bertrand first. He told the Grand Marshal that according to the latest instructions that had been received from London, the Governor could overlook his former declaration and authorize him and his family to leave for the Cape, in view of Mme. Bertrand's condition. Bertrand declined the offer. He owed everything to the Emperor. He refused to desert him. Gorrequer insisted: Bertrand had fulfilled his undertaking to remain a year at St. Helena. He could now honourably depart. The Grand Marshal held his ground. Gorrequer then appealed to Mme. Bertrand. The poor woman was sorely tempted, but she declined, perhaps through fear of the effects of seasickness on her condition. She was also afraid that once at the Cape she would not be permitted to return to England.[27]

That same day Lowe appeared at Longwood. Refusing to see him, Napoleon said to O'Meara:

"Let him talk to Bertrand or send me Colonel Reade. I will receive Reade and listen to him without anger, if his mission is unpleasant, because he will only be carrying out his orders."[28]

Lowe insisted and in vain. Then he had the fatuous notion—for all that he was professing conciliatory intentions—of demanding an apology from Bertrand and even from Napoleon.

Bertrand, Lowe said, owed him an apology for "the language and conduct to which he [Lowe] was exposed on the occasion of his last interview . . . and he conceived the same expressions of concern were also due him for the manner in which he was received and spoken to by General Buonaparte himself when he went to complain

[26] Despatches of Bathurst, June 26, July 3, 17, 25, 1816; of Goulburn, July 20 (Lowe Papers, 20-116).
[27] October 1, 1816, Lowe Papers, 20-142.
[28] O'Meara to Finlaison, October 10, 1816 (Lowe Papers, 20-216).

of Count Bertrand's conduct." With that granted, he, like a good fellow, would "not have the slightest hesitation to express his own concern at anything in his manner or expression which may have been thought unpleasant." [29]

So Lowe wanted an apology from the Emperor! Caesar was to apologize to the former colonel of the Corsican Rangers! Napoleon smiled disdainfully. The Governor then sent Reade to him. Napoleon received him in the garden (October 4th) [30] and Las Cases translated a summary of Lord Bathurst's despatches. The Emperor asked whether the four persons who had to be sent away were his officers. Reade was either unable or unwilling to reply. Napoleon looked at Las Cases and said in Italian:

"Before long they will take all the others away and then one of these fine mornings they will murder me."

Pacing nervously up and down in the garden path he twice murmured:

"What a rage for persecution! But the more they persecute me, the better it will be as regards the world."

Las Cases thought a threat of a general exodus would induce Lowe to yield. But supposing he did not yield? On October 3, the Governor sent Bertrand the formula that was to be signed by all the French. It was worded as follows:

"I, the undersigned, do hereby declare that it is my desire to remain on the island of St. Helena and to participate in the restrictions imposed upon Napoleon Buonaparte personally." [31]

Once again the French substituted the expression "the Emperor Napoleon" for the words "Napoleon Buonaparte." Lowe refused to accept the change. In that he was only obeying Bathurst, but one feels that in executing his instructions he was not sorry to be avenging his own sense of hurt.

The Emperor forbade them to sign. Sir Hudson came to Longwood and established himself in the house where the Bertrands were to settle a few days later. He ordered Napoleon's officers to appear one by one before him. Bertrand, in great agitation, tried in vain to reason with him. Las Cases lost himself in "the labyrinth of his sentences." Montholon played the diplomat. All three refused to sign a

[29] Lowe Papers, 20-116; Forsyth, Vol. I, pp. 316-17.
[30] Reade has left a report of the interview, Lowe Papers, 20-116.
[31] Lowe Papers, 20-116; Forsyth, Vol. I, p. 323.

declaration that by implication recognized the deposition of the Emperor. Gourgaud naïvely remarked that "he would sign without attaching any importance to the absence of a title," but that he had "to obey the order he had received." [32]

The Governor's ultimatum reached the Emperor that evening after dinner. Those who refused to obey must prepare to leave for the Cape at once, the only exceptions to the measure being the Grand Marshal and his wife (in view of Mme. Bertrand's condition), Cipriani, Marchand, Pierron the cook, and one other domestic. [33] Napoleon was reading *Don Quixote* aloud at the time. He tried to preserve his composure and go on with his reading. But in a moment he laid the book down:

"One cannot laugh at trifles in such circumstances." [34]

There was general consternation. Usually so courageous, Mme. de Montholon broke down and wept. The painful silence was suddenly terminated by Gourgaud's voice:

"I am going to sign!"

He would rather yield, he said, than abandon the Emperor. He moved towards the door. Montholon did the same. Napoleon looked at them and did not call them back. His pride had bent. He knew very well that he could not live there without them.

The three Frenchmen returned the papers to Poppleton and at midnight the anguish was at an end. The next day Bertrand sent in his declaration in his turn. All the servants signed except Santini.

O'Meara profited by the opportunity to describe to Finlaison in his usual mocking and treacherous style the scene in which Montholon, Las Cases and Gourgaud came into Captain Poppleton's bedroom late at night, "with crest-fallen countenances, streaming eyes, and the declarations signed in their hands, imploring of him to send them at that unreasonable hour of the night to the Governor." [35] No such haste was necessary. O'Meara invented those details to make fun of the French. Poppleton's report of October 15th supplies a simple and accurate note: "Between eleven and twelve o'clock on the night of the 15th of October, General Montholon, General Gourgaud and Count de Las Cases came to my room, with four sheets of paper

[32] Gourgaud, Vol. I, pp. 247 ff.
[33] Lowe Papers, 20-116. Unpublished.
[34] Gourgaud, Vol. I, p. 250; Montholon, Vol. I, p. 420.
[35] December 23, 1816, Lowe Papers, 20-116; Forsyth, Vol. I, pp. 328-29.

which they told me were the declarations required of them (three of
them were signed by the above named officers and the other by all
the domestics except one—Santini), requesting of me to forward
them to the Governor. I was addressed by Count Las Cases, who
said they were determined if possible not to quit Bonaparte; that they
had signed these papers out of regard to him; that it was an act of
their own, and not by the direction of Bonaparte; that he was un-
acquainted with it." [36]

Having triumphed on this head, Lowe passed on to the others. He
designated Piontkowski and three servants, Santini, Rousseau and
Archambault, as the ones to leave the island. One should note that
Lowe might easily have deprived Napoleon of one or more of his
principal officers without fear of being disavowed by his ministry.
He acted on that point therefore with moderation. He designated
people whom Napoleon could most easily get on without.

The departure of Piontkowski could neither have annoyed nor
pained Napoleon. Whatever the Pole may later have asserted, the
Emperor did not entrust any messages for Europe to him—he held
him in too little esteem. He did grant him as an act of pity the rank
*ad honorem* of squadron-commander with a year's pay. The three
servants received recommendations attesting their services, two years'
wages and a pension for life amounting to a third of their wages.
These payments were to be made by the Emperor's family, in particular by Prince Eugene, who held 800,000 francs on deposit. The
second groom, in other words the younger of the two Archambaults,
and Rousseau, the custodian of the silver, had announced an intention of going to the United States. They were given messages of
greeting for Joseph.

The usher, Natale Santini, received a veritable mission. Santini had
no clearly defined position at Longwood. Clever and a jack-at-all
trades he was useful in many small ways. He cut the Emperor's hair
and put new linings in his hats. He made him a coat out of an old
grey ulster, and then again some flannel vests and a pair of slippers.
But his more special function was to go poaching on the plateau at
Longwood, shooting wild pigs or goats on the Company's lands. His
victims figured as embellishments on the menu at Longwood. That
Corsican with close-cropped hair would have let himself be hacked
to pieces for his master. He had a fiery hatred for Lowe. A patient
hunter, he was always beating about the neighbourhood of Long-

36 Lowe Papers, 20-116; 20-208.

wood with his shotgun. He dreamed of finding Lowe one day in line with the sights on his weapon, and there is no doubt that he would have been the man not to miss such a chance.

Napoleon realized that. One evening at dinner he called to Santini: "What is this I hear, you brigand? You intended to kill the Governor? You wretch! Let such ideas get into your head again and you will see what I do to you!"

Then turning to his officers:

"That rascal was about to get us into a pretty mess!"

Napoleon himself ordered Santini not to sign the declaration, that the Governor might designate him as one of those to leave. Since they had not so far succeeded in getting the *Remonstrance* of August 23 to Europe, Santini would deliver it there.

It was written out in very fine handwriting on a piece of white satin cut from one of Mme. de Montholon's dresses. Santini sewed it into the lining of his coat, and to make doubly sure, though hardly able to read, he learned the long text by heart in two days, and recited it without a mistake to Napoleon, who said to him in Italian, tweaking his ear:

"With that idiot's face you have, I really think you will succeed." [37]

The Emperor's instructions were simple.

"If you manage to get to London you will have it printed. You will find good people in England. There are many there who do not share the prejudices of their government concerning me. Go and see them and they will help you." [38]

The four deportees left St. Helena October 19th on the *David*, which was to take them to the Cape. Napoleon received Archambault and Rousseau before they left. He decided not to see Piontkowski.[39] The four men were rigorously searched. The English were specially suspicious of Piontkowski, who was compelled to strip naked.[40] At the Cape they were to be detained for a month at the fortress, and were not to arrive in Portsmouth till the 12th of February.

Beginning with October 10, the limits within which Napoleon could move about without the attendance of an English officer had been reduced from twelve to eight miles. So his tether was shortened by a third without any real reason and with a sudden brutality.

[37] Santini, p. 43.
[38] *Ibid.*, p. 42.
[39] Gourgaud, Vol. I, p. 254.
[40] O'Meara, Vol. II, p. 161.

More than that he was thenceforward forbidden to enter any house or speak to any person he might meet when not in the presence of an English officer. Lowe had thought of that as a way of avoiding the danger of a possible encounter between Napoleon and the Commissioners. The prohibition soon came to seem exaggerated even to him, and he suppressed it, December 26, 1816.[41]

Letters were all to be handed to Poppleton. They were opened and sealed again with great care at Plantation House. In a fragment of his original manuscript Las Cases writes: "Letters that were actually read showed no sign of it. Precautions were perfect. The moment anyone was put on the surveillance list, his coat of arms and his seal were engraved at the office (the Governor's) and so well that after his letters had been read they reached their destinations intact without any suspicious sign." [42]

Hitherto sentinels had not appeared before nine o'clock in the evening. They were now posted around the garden at Longwood at sunset, and they surrounded the house itself from nine o'clock till daybreak. During the daytime watch over the prisoners was kept by eighty-two men picketed around the boundaries of Longwood. Four sentries guarded the park, sixteen men the gate, and twenty-three the stables. Those numbers date from November, 1817.[43] However, they varied but slightly during the Captivity. Each evening, a quarter of an hour after the gun was fired on Alarm Signal, twenty-eight sentries surrounded the garden. At nine o'clock sixteen came in close to the house. There were forty-two besides at Longwood Gate and fourteen at the stables. To these numbers must be added twenty-four men and an officer who handled the signal station.

Napoleon pitied those soldiers who were continually harassed by picket and guard duties and by dangerous patrols along the edges of the precipices.

"Those poor devils," he said, "would be right in hating me and wishing I were dead, but they must see that the grind that is forced on them is useless and tyrannical. The mere sight of this island would convince anyone not a suspicious idiot (*coglione*) that any escape from it would be impossible." [44]

Lowe could have extended the limits at the very beginning instead

[41] O'Meara to Finlaison, December 29.
[42] Lowe Papers, 20-215.
[43] Lowe Papers, 20-225.
[44] O'Meara to Finlaison, October 10, 1816 (Lowe Papers, 20-216).

of restricting them—he was to do so later on. For all such annoyances he was personally responsible. Bathurst had merely decided that there must be limits and that they must be reasonable ones.

The money question had remained unsettled for two months, in spite of long palavers between Montholon and Gorrequer. The sum of 8,000 pounds fixed by the government seemed insufficient to Lowe himself. He undertook on his own responsibility to raise it to 12,000 while awaiting further word from Bathurst,[45] whom he apprised of his decision in a letter of September 8. Napoleon again offered unsuccessfully to defray all his expenses provided he might procure the necessary funds by sealed letters. He did not want the British Cabinet to know the amount of money he had in Europe. He was convinced they would seize it and that he would then find himself at the mercy of his enemies.

The problem of expenditures at Longwood has been the subject of angry controversy for over a century. Today we may discuss it without prejudice. All told, Napoleon had 250,000 pounds (five million francs) in Europe. The English believed him to be much wealthier. It was said in London that he had a treasure of at least several tens of millions in safekeeping. Bathurst therefore considered that he was well able to pay for a part of his maintenance.

Lowe proposed to set apart for the French household 12,000 pounds, or 300,000 gold francs—that was the amount of his own salary as Governor. It permitted him to live in luxury. That sum was, without any doubt, adequate for maintaining the French provided waste were done away with. The wastage was extreme. Montholon was a big eater and an exacting one. He wanted a lavishly garnished table. Under his direction a magnificent and quite too Imperial squandering had become the order of the day. Bertrand made a momentary effort to remedy conditions, but then seeing a coalition of the servants behind Montholon and frightened in advance at the battle he would have to fight, he drew back and fell silent. Gourgaud showed more courage. He was disgusted at the thieving that he could see on every hand and tried to open the Emperor's eyes.

"There is too much wasting," he said to him. "How can we possibly be drinking seventeen bottles of wine a day or eating ninety-eight pounds of meat and nine chickens! It is just laying ourselves open to attack."

[45] Gorrequer, *Minutes*, Lowe Papers, 20-116.

Then he added, with great good sense:
"To accept the least possible is the best policy for us in our position." [46]

Napoleon agreed with Gourgaud's criticisms. He suggested allowing each servant a fixed sum for food—eight francs for the French, three francs for the others. That would make his table thereafter much less elaborate and it could be more closely watched.

He spoke to Montholon, Gorrequer reports,[47] with much urgency and good humour of the economies that might be made by dismissing a number of English servants. He ended by ordering that six of them and one black servant, who lived on the island, should be sent away. He found the quantity of wine consumed excessive. "You must use the greatest discretion," he said, "and not uncork one bottle more than is necessary." He actually ordered that the amount of Cape wine consumed should be "cut down proportionately to the reduction in the number of servants." Those wise directions were not carried out. Montholon persuaded Napoleon to give up the idea of rationing on the ground that on that basis "the Emperor would be keeping too bourgeois an establishment." The kitchen staff fought all measures of reduction to the last ditch and in time got the regulations cancelled.

And yet the rationing idea would have been the sound solution. The pilferings in the pantry were never to diminish. Marchand alone was orderly and kept good accounts. The servants were too many in the first place for such a small household. After the departures of October, 1816, there were still twelve French domestics, assisted by eight islanders, ten soldiers and two Chinese—in all, thirty-two servants for eight masters. A fairly large number of Chinese further were employed about the gardens. Almost all the French servants had

[46] Gourgaud, Vol. I, p. 213. The amount of wine furnished, in total was, per day: 9 bottles of bordeaux, 24 of Cape wine, 6 of teneriffe, graves and constantia, 1 of madeira; per month, 14 bottles of champagne and 4 of port. The other supplies of victuals were in the same proportions: per day, 30 eggs, 6 chickens, 30 pounds of mutton, 46 of beef, 2 of ham, 2 of lard, 5 of butter, 10 of sugar, 6 of fish, 10 of fruits, 20 of vegetables, 60 of bread; 2 gallons and a half of milk, 2 pounds of coffee; per week, 8 ducks, 2 turkeys, 2 geese, 1 milk-fed pig. Such the provision made for 38 persons, five of whom were children. The orderly officer and the English soldiers who helped as servants were fed separately (Lowe Papers, 20-145). The amounts mentioned went even higher later on, so that at a time when there were twenty-eight persons at Longwood, four of whom were children, the supply of meat alone rose to ninety-six pounds per day. That did not prevent Cipriani, and after him Pierron, from buying more poultry and eggs in Jamestown.
[47] September 7, 1816, Lowe Papers, 20-116.

known the days of reckless expenditure in the Imperial palaces. They felt it beneath their dignity to stint themselves. The very disorder made up to them to some extent for their exile, for they could make money by selling supplies of food and wine to the inhabitants and to the soldiers at the camp. Little incidents betray the state of mind of the personnel at Longwood. The Colony archives preserve traces of a "bottle war" between Longwood and Plantation House. Bottles were scarce and expensive on the island, all of them being imported from Europe or the Cape. Now Lowe sent up an average of 630 bottles every fortnight and insisted that the empty ones be returned. Napoleon's servants broke them deliberately and whenever the Governor went to Longwood he was annoyed to find pieces of broken bottles scattered about the grounds. Several times he threatened to suspend all allowances of wine if the little game were continued. It lasted, however, for a good two years.

Expenditures were further increased by the fact that many provisions were delivered in poor condition. Poppleton wrote to Lowe, July 5, 1816 (Forsyth, Vol. I, p. 241): "The beef sent to Longwood yesterday was not eatable; it was returned; the mutton sent was likewise returned. I wrote a letter to the person who has contracted to serve Longwood with beef, and I made a signal to the purveyors, but no meat arrived; they purchased a number of fowls in lieu." On July 10, O'Meara wrote to Reade: "Montholon has been making great complaints today, and, I am sorry to say, with reason. He made an agreement with Cole or Fowler to try if fifty pounds of beef daily would do, with a whole sheep and nine fowls. Yesterday 100 pounds of beef came up, and only three fowls about the size of crows; today, three quarters of mutton, and five fowls of the same magnitude nearly, and no beef; and was it not for the turtle sent up by the Admiral, and a pig shot yesterday by General Gourgaud (which was rooting up the garden, and for which he paid afterwards four pounds), they would not have enough to eat." [48]

Did Balcombe, the purveyor-in-chief, abuse his monopoly? Without a doubt, and along with him his agents, who supplied Longwood in irregular quantities at top price, and according to the ups and downs of a variable stock which the unexpected requirements of ships that called at the port sometimes exhausted. As for Balcombe,

[48] Lowe Papers, 20-115.

Stürmer reports Napoleon as saying: [49] "I think Balcombe is trying to make a good thing out of me." And Stürmer adds on his own account that "the supposition did not seem altogether unfounded." Living had always been high at St. Helena as was natural in view of the ratio between its population and the unproductivity of the soil. It had become more so through the influx of the troops that had been sent to guard Napoleon.

Napoleon was not so shorn of money that he could not have made up, for some time at least, for the balance of expenditures which England refused to pay. The two hundred and fifty thousand francs in gold that had been brought from France were still untouched. But they had so far been kept hidden from the English. Suddenly to bring them out would have aroused new suspicions in Lowe. In any case the Emperor wanted to hold them in reserve "as a war treasure" in order to be prepared for any eventuality. Before he touched that reserve he would borrow from Bertrand and Las Cases, both of whom had funds in London.[50] Later on the Emperor was to use his own treasure to pay personal expenses, the allowances of his officers, and the wages of his servants. Just then he was not ready to do that— Bathurst's stinginess was supplying him with too good an opportunity for arousing the indignation and the pity of the world.

He was not to let it escape. He sent for Balcombe and informed him that he was going to have some of his silver plate sent to Balcombe's office that it might be sold. The proceeds would help to cover his expenses.

The purveyor was astounded. Napoleon then explained:

"Of what use can my plate be when there is nothing to eat on it?"

He ordered that a part (about a quarter) of his silverware—he had an over-abundant supply to tell the truth—be stripped of its eagles and hammered out—"I don't want my eagles to be put up at auction!" he said.[51] Cipriani would then turn the metal over to Balcombe in that condition and Balcombe would convert it into legal tender and deposit the proceeds to the credit of the Emperor. In pursuance of this scheme Cipriani made three different deliveries of silver: October 15, 1816, 952 ounces; November 10, 1,227 ounces; December

[49] Stürmer to Metternich, July 4, 1817.
[50] Bertrand, 12,615 pounds with Baring Brothers, Las Cases 4,000 louis (which he was to offer the Emperor on his departure).
[51] According to Santini, p. 38.

30, 2,048 ounces. It totalled in value 1,065 pounds 14 shillings, or a little more than 26,000 francs.[52]

Lowe was much annoyed at all that. What would they think in London? Would they not blame him for doing nothing to prevent Napoleon's coming to such a pass? But what could he do? When Cipriani went down to Jamestown for the third time to deliver the silver, the Governor summoned him to the Castle.

"Why do you need so much money?" he asked.

Cipriani was enjoying Lowe's anxious mood and replied simply: "To buy something to eat, Excellency."

Lowe leapt to his feet:

"What? Haven't you enough food?"

Cipriani assured him that the quantities allowed were not sufficient for the maintenance of the household and that he was obliged to buy more in addition.

"Why so much butter? Why so much game?" repeated the Governor, greatly flustered.[53]

He had informed Bathurst as soon as he learned of Napoleon's intention. Frightened in his turn by the scandal the news could not fail to cause—the ex-Emperor of the French reduced to selling his silver to keep from starving!—the minister capitulated. He not only approved Lowe's raising the allotment for Longwood from 8,000 to 12,000 pounds but authorized him to make any further expenditures that he might deem reasonable. "The papers enclosed in your despatch," he said, "appear satisfactorily to prove the present inadequacy even of the augmented allowance of £12,000, and I have therefore no difficulty in authorizing you to incur on General Buonaparte's account such additional charge as may be necessary to provide against any reduction in the expenditure of which he can reasonably complain." He yielded finally on a capital point. He agreed that Napoleon should send a sealed letter to a banker in England for the purpose of obtaining funds which he might personally need.[54]

That concession seemed too dangerous to Lowe. He did not inform Napoleon of it for over a year. The Emperor, therefore, was to resort to further financial expedients.

Irritated as Napoleon was by the restrictions, he evinced even at

[52] Lowe Papers, 20-221.
[53] O'Meara, Vol. I, p. 286.
[54] Bathurst to Lowe, November 22, 1816 (Lowe Papers, 20-118); Forsyth, Vol. II, pp. 120-21.

that time a desire to make peace. His insistence on his Imperial title was the cause of incessant difficulties. We know how attached he was to it and why. He proposed, however, a compromise, doubtless out of weariness. On October 16, 1816, he ordered O'Meara to hand Lowe a note in which he declared "that he was still disposed to assume a name that would make its way into current usage—Colonel Muiron or Baron Duroc." During his stay at The Briars he had already conveyed the same suggestion to Cockburn through Montholon. Cockburn had referred it to London but had received no reply.[55]

"What is a name?" Napoleon said to the doctor. "It doesn't matter to me. I have made enough noise in the world—more than any other man will ever make and too much perhaps. I am growing old. I want to retire." [56] And he added: "I further reiterate that when they find it convenient to release me from this cruel residence I am of a mind to remain a stranger to politics, no matter what is going on in the world."

By the device of the change in names Longwood and Plantation House might have arrived at an armistice, and social relations, at any rate, would have been made sensibly easier.

Lowe measured the importance of such a change and on the 18th informed Bathurst of Napoleon's suggestion. The next day he called on Bertrand and had a fairly amiable conversation with him. But the decision rested with London. Bathurst was greatly embarrassed and dared not reply with a categorical refusal. He wrote to Lowe on December 14, 1816: [57] "On the subject of General Buonaparte's proposition I probably shall not give you any instruction. It appears harsh to refuse it, and there may arise much embarrassment in formally acquiescing in it. You will not, therefore, encourage any renewal of the conversation." So Bathurst's plan was to reject by silence a solution that would have mitigated Napoleon's lot immeasurably. Of all the severities of the English Cabinet, that one is the hardest to excuse. Napoleon would have been no less a captive and under English control, but his confinement would have lost some of its odious implications. He would have escaped many sorts of vexations, along with his isolation and, to an extent, his tedium. The people about him would

55 O'Meara to Finlaison, December 23, 1816 (Lowe Papers, 20-216).
56 O'Meara to Lowe, October 16, 1816 (Lowe Papers, 20-117).
57 Lowe Papers, 20-117; Forsyth, Vol. II, p. 122.

have felt freer and would have found it less difficult to leave him. The Commissioners could have been received at Longwood—and that connection would have had far-reaching consequences for the future. Undoubtedly that was what Bathurst wanted above all else to prevent.

Lowe obeyed. He said nothing. The Emperor could go no farther. The painful conflict over the title was to be prolonged down to the end of the Captivity.

.         .         .         .         .         .         .

In this struggle with England, more even than with Lowe in whom he saw little more than a clumsy executive, Napoleon had gained a number of advantages. But he had made no headway as regarded his physical freedom. On that point Lowe was less than ever inclined to yield. His altercations with the Emperor and with Bertrand, and the general attitude of the French, had brought him if not to hatred— that word might be too strong—at least to a lively dislike of them all. His assistants aggravated it. Reade and Gorrequer were always pushing him towards greater severity. Most of Gorrequer's reports that are preserved as "minutes" among Lowe's papers show the Governor's military secretary frequently reverting to the idea that it was not customary for a prisoner-of-war to have such a house and such a lavish style of living. According to a memorandum of September 5, 1816,[58] Reade is alleged to have said to O'Meara on December 12th that Bonaparte was a wretched outlaw, a prisoner, and that the Governor had the right to treat him with as much severity as he considered suitable. In his letter of December 29, 1816, O'Meara wrote to Finlaison: "I must confess that I am one of those who think that a great deal of unnecessary rigour has been practised towards him, as you may yourself conceive from the nature of the restrictions, and I know that such is the opinion of every officer on the island *except Sir Hudson's personal staff*" (Forsyth, Vol. II, p. 77). But the basest rôle was played by O'Meara himself. He was a hornet that flitted back and forth between Longwood and Plantation House stinging everyone with poisoned darts.

Gourgaud and the Montholons were not inclined to go to extremes. But Bertrand was inflexible in his dislikes and stood for resisting inch by inch. Las Cases was even more bitter. According to him the Emperor should miss no opportunity, and use every means to compel Europe sooner or later to reverse its verdict. Napoleon himself did

[58] Lowe Papers, 20-142.

not think that silence was good policy. The world might forget him. It was better for him to struggle, to struggle unceasingly, now with Lowe and now with Bathurst, that public interest might be kept awake, that constant difficulties might be created for the Cabinet in London, that, in short, the English might be continually harassed. One must not underestimate, either, the state of mind of the domestics, whose complaints, demands, and general discouragement were reflected even in the Emperor's immediate environment. On December 16, 1816, Gourgaud wrote a significant sentence: "If the Governor of St. Helena were an angel they would still complain of him." [59]

So with both groups putting the worst face on everything, prisoner and jailor moved in an atmosphere of exasperation. No adjustment was possible, no attempt to understand or to palliate—at least during those years. But when one puts everything on the scales, one comes to the conclusion that for Napoleon himself a battle was better policy than renunciation. Tedium would have ended by crushing him! As long as he fought, he still had hopes of winning. Those hopes were rooted to the bottom of his soul. They would take a long time to die.

[59] Thiers Library. Unpublished.

## LAS CASES "BANISHED"

ON NOVEMBER 25, 1816, NAPOLEON WAS SEATED ON A TREE TRUNK at the turn in the path that led to the foot of the garden. He was chatting with Gourgaud, Las Cases and Montholon. He had just received Admiral Malcolm who was back from the Cape and was bringing him newspapers and a crate of fine oranges. The Admiral had gone to the Cape on September 22nd, and Lady Malcolm with him. The Emperor was in a good humour. Aly came and presented him with five of the oranges on a plate with a knife and some sugar. The Emperor gave one of the oranges to Las Cases for his son and began to cut the others into slices which he distributed among his companions or ate himself.

"I have been building fortifications with Bertrand all day long," he said. "As a result the day has seemed very short to me." [1]

He rose and took a few steps. Though it was springtime the wind was cold. The conversation turned on the Admiral, then on Piontkowski, who had tried to pass himself off at the Cape as an intimate friend of the Emperor. Finally Napoleon dismissed the two generals with a nod and went indoors with Las Cases.

He continued the conversation by fits and starts first in the billiardroom, then in the drawingroom. Suddenly he stopped in front of a window. He had spied a little troop of horse, their plumes waving in the wind. They entered the enclosure and he was able to distinguish the Governor, Bingham, Reade, Captain Blakeney, Rainsford (the new inspector of police) and two dragoons. Sheltered behind his shutter Napoleon saw Lowe and Gorrequer draw rein, while the others proceeded on towards the house. Almost immediately Gentilini came to announce that Reade was asking to see Las Cases.

"Go and see what that beast wants with you, my dear fellow," said the Emperor.

A quarter of an hour afterwards Marchand entered in the greatest excitement. Reade had just arrested Las Cases for clandestine cor-

[1] Las Cases, Vol. VII, p. 345.

respondence with the outside world. All the papers in his room had been seized by Rainsford. Napoleon ran to the window and he saw his confidant being taken away by Reade and a soldier towards Hutt's Gate. Emmanuel was following after his father, escorted by Blakeney and Rainsford. They were carrying two trunks filled with papers.

Longwood buzzed like a bee-hive that had been attacked. Napoleon called for his officers. What could Las Cases have done to lend a pretext for such a scene? A few days previous the Chamberlain had asked him for permission to write to Lucien Bonaparte and to his friend Lady Clavering, using as a go-between a young mulatto servant whom the Governor had withdrawn from Las Cases' service— one James Scott—and who was about to leave for Europe with a new employer. The Emperor replied "that that would be madness" and thought no more of it. Las Cases must have gone ahead and been reported by Scott to the Governor.

Although "that stupidity" angered him, Napoleon was eager to rescue Las Cases from his ugly situation. He ordered the Grand Marshal to repair at once to Plantation House to reclaim his Chamberlain.

"Go, don't waste any time! Poor Las Cases must be suffering cruelly!"

Bertrand did not obey. Las Cases, he thought, had got just what he deserved for playing with such intrigues. He said to Gourgaud: "Alas, I have far other worries on my mind than the predicament of Las Cases." [2]

He had been greatly distressed by a letter from Mrs. Skelton to the Governor which the latter had just shown him. It reported the death of his mother-in-law, Mrs. Dillon. His one idea was to get back to his wife from whom he was anxious to keep the news hidden.

The Montholons learned of the arrest with equanimity. Gourgaud had a kind heart. He alone seemed moved.

Dinner was set for four persons that evening. Afterwards Napoleon went to his room and undressed. O'Meara sent in his name. He was back from town and knew what had happened. He had met the Governor on the road and Lowe had said to him ironically:

"You will find your friend Las Cases in safe-keeping."

O'Meara had learned further details at Jamestown, where the arrest was the topic of every conversation. Lowe, it seemed, had been informed by the Austrian Commissioner that Las Cases had sent a

[2] Gourgaud, Vol. I, p. 277.

message through Scott to Baroness Stürmer, and the Governor had notified Las Cases on November 13th that he was to dismiss Scott. Las Cases refused to take another servant whom the Governor had chosen. Napoleon thereupon gave him Gentilini.[3] Now in fact Las Cases had written two more letters, copied them on taffetas, and slipped them into the lining of one of James Scott's vests to be carried by the mulatto to England. Scott had told the whole story to his father, John Scott, a white man. The latter was frightened at the risk his son was running and at once informed Lowe. Las Cases had committed a flagrant crime—he had broken the promise he had given! That supplied the Governor with too good a pretext for shipping him back to Europe. Meanwhile the Chamberlain had been taken with his son to Major Harrison's little cottage at Hutt's Gate and was being held there in strict custody.[4]

Napoleon was staggered! How could a man of such intelligence have trusted to a slave who could neither read nor write, who knew nobody in England, and whom the Governor, unless he were a brainless idiot (*coglione, scioccone*), would never have allowed to leave the island? It was incomprehensible! Las Cases must have taken complete leave of his wits!

The Emperor assured the doctor that he knew nothing about any such letters. They must have been for Lady Clavering or for Las Cases' banker. He was very much annoyed. Las Cases had all of Napoleon's papers and Lowe had taken them. What should he do about that?

"What assurance have I," he continued, warming to the subject, "that, when I have almost finished my story, the Governor will not come here under some pretext or other and take possession of that too? I shall have to burn everything I have written! It was a pastime for me in this dreary place and it might have been interesting to the world. But with that hangman (*boja*) one has neither security nor guarantee. There is no law he will not violate. His eyes were shining when he came here because he had found a new way to torment us. When he surrounded the house with his staff, I was reminded of so many South Sea cannibals dancing around prisoners they were about to devour." [5]

[3] Las Cases, Vol. VII, pp. 229-30; O'Meara, Vol. I, p. 207.
[4] O'Meara to Finlaison, December 29, 1816 (Lowe Papers, 20-216); Gourgaud, Vol. I, p. 278.
[5] O'Meara to Finlaison, December 29, 1816; Gourgaud, Vol. I, p. 279.

By noon the next day Bertrand had made up his mind to go to Plantation House. He had no luck. His eloquence must have failed him and, in fact, he seems to have been extremely lukewarm in his plea.[6] However, he did bring back some definite information. Lowe showed him the Las Cases letters.

The first was a *résumé* of all that had occurred since the departure from Malmaison. It was addressed to Lucien Bonaparte. During the Hundred Days, the Emperor had attached Las Cases temporarily to Lucien's service. The letter to Lucien is complacently displayed in the *Mémorial* as a reproduction of a letter that Las Cases had already sent to the same recipient in September, 1816. It therefore had no real interest, and there could have been no point in taking huge risks to get it away from St. Helena.[7]

The second letter, equally futile and imprudent, was addressed to Lady Clavering.

The Emperor still was greatly worried. Might the diary that Las Cases had been keeping not be compromising? Aly had been transscribing it. He sent for him and questioned him:

"How does it treat Admiral Cockburn?"

"So so, sire" (with a gesture that meant neither well nor badly).

"Does it say that I called him a shark?"

"Yes, sire. But it also says that Your Majesty is aware of his honesty and cannot refuse him your esteem."

"And Sir George Bingham?"

"It speaks very well of him, as also of Colonel Wilks."

"Does it mention Admiral Malcolm?"

"Yes, sire, it treats him extremely well."

"It says nothing of the Governor?"

Aly could not keep from smiling.

"It says a great deal about him, sire."

"Does it repeat what I said: 'He is a low creature,' and that his face is the meanest I have ever seen?"

"Yes, sire," said Aly, but he added that the language was often more moderate.

"Does it say that I called him 'a Sicilian bum-bailiff'?"

[6] Gorrequer, *Minutes*, November 26, 1816 (Lowe Papers, 20-117).
[7] Count Corti found the latter among the papers of Metternich, whose "black cabinet" must have been functioning perfectly (*Revue napoléonienne*, January-February, 1926).

"Yes, sire."
"Well, he is!" [8]

. . . . . . . .

Lowe had sorted out Las Cases' papers in the latter's presence. Among them were found, in addition to the voluminous diary, Napoleon's description of the campaigns in Italy with notes and documents annexed, the correspondence exchanged between Napoleon, Cockburn and Lowe, a number of projects in duplicate, and finally personal papers of Las Cases—family letters, his will, and so on. They were classified in a number of packages which young Emmanuel sealed with his father's ring. The fragments of military history and the official correspondence were sent back to Napoleon, at such intervals, however, that the Emperor was convinced that they were being returned to him only as they were copied.[9] As a matter of fact the Governor had merely skimmed through particular papers here and there.

Through Bertrand the Emperor asked for the diary on the plea that "it was kept at his express orders and was the only memorandum he had of all that had been occurring to him." [10] Bertrand manifested considerable bad humour in signing and sending the letter.[11] Las Cases had authorized Lowe to look through the diary. He also asked for it on his own behalf "as belonging to him personally." The Governor elected to hold it himself, pending decision by Lord Bathurst. Bathurst was to order him, February 7, 1817, not to let it get out of his hands under any pretext until further instructions.[12] The diary was not to be restored to Las Cases—and then through the efforts of Lord Holland—till September, 1821. Before returning it to Las Cases Lord Bathurst was further to exact the written consent of Napoleon's executors. Montholon seems to be accurate at this point. "There were," he writes, "nine hundred and twenty-five pages half margined under the triple seal of Count Las Cases, Count Bertrand and Sir Hudson Lowe." [13]

Napoleon sent Gourgaud and Montholon to the neighbourhood of Hutt's Gate to catch a glimpse of Las Cases if possible and get

[8] O'Meara, Vol. I, p. 222. "Bum-bailiff" for the untranslatable *sbirro*.
[9] O'Meara to Finlaison, December 29, 1816.
[10] Lowe to Bathurst, December 3, 1816 (Lowe Papers, 20-117).
[11] Gourgaud, Vol. I, p. 286.
[12] Lowe Papers, 20-118.
[13] Vol. I, p. 446.

news of him. Las Cases spent two days in Harrison's cottage. Then he was transferred with his son to Ross Cottage, a pleasure camp around which Balcombe had developed a poultry farm. The two Las Cases' were both in poor health, especially Emmanuel, who for several months had been suffering from violent palpitations of the heart. O'Meara and the surgeon-in-chief on the island, Dr. Baxter, were sent to him by Lowe. They feared the enlargement of a cardiac artery and its possible rupture.

"After all, what is the death of a child as compared with public policy?" Lowe is alleged to have said.[14] This cynical remark, which Las Cases got from O'Meara, was certainly never made. Lowe sent Dr. Baxter to Ross Cottage himself. The malady from which young Las Cases was suffering had nothing to do with the climate. But O'Meara expressed the opinion that "the sedentary occupations of reading and writing, in which the young gentleman was almost constantly occupied at Longwood by his father's direction, notwithstanding the highly injurious tendency of them had been frequently pointed out to him . . . must have most considerably aggravated his son's complaint." [15]

Emmanuel's complaint seems to have been more particularly of a nervous order. He looked "remarkably healthy." He was to recover completely and die in 1854, a Senator of the Second Empire.

From their little house that faced Longwood but was separated from it by a number of chasms and precipices, it was possible for the prisoners to watch the comings and goings of the Emperor's people through a field glass. "The building was small, but at least very liveable," writes Las Cases.[16] "There was some grass, and a few trees. Large numbers of chickens were raised on the place for the supply of Longwood, with a few guinea hens and other large fowl that we soon tamed." The prisoners were well treated. Hudson Lowe came almost every day to examine Las Cases' papers or to answer his letters, and regularly enquired as to their needs. He sent them their meals from Plantation House. Las Cases often invited the orderly officer to his table. "I must admit," he writes, "that from the moment the Governor held me in his hands, he treated me with the most attentive courtesy and the most refined consideration. I saw

14 Las Cases, Vol. VII, p. 381.
15 O'Meara, *Report,* December 24, 1816 (Lowe Papers, 20-117).
16 Vol. VII, p. 356.

him personally remove a sentinel, whom, as he said, it might annoy me to see, and station him behind some trees where I would not notice him."

However, he addressed an emphatic protest to Lowe, the terms of which are worth considering:

"As a result of a trap, according to all appearances, laid by my valet, I have been forcibly removed from Longwood and all my papers seized. Though I have still no idea what your plans as to my person may be, I have already brought the greatest sacrifice on myself. A few days ago you could have forced me to submit to the most abject conditions, through my fear of seeing myself separated from the Emperor Napoleon. Today you could not send me back to him. I have been sullied by being seized almost under his very eyes. I could henceforth be of no consolation to him. In his eyes, I would be merely a blemished object and a painful memory!" [17]

On December 4, Lowe came to see Las Cases with Gorrequer and protested against his charge that a trap had been laid for him. Las Cases declared with no great difficulty that since the Governor assured him that that was so, he was ready to believe him and was glad to be undeceived.[18] When he came to publish his letter in the *Mémorial*, Las Cases cancelled the phrase "according to all appearances," so reinforcing after the fact his accusation against Scott, and therefore against Lowe.

What does all that mean? How could his arrest have dishonoured Las Cases? Was he afraid that, in the event of a return to Longwood, the Emperor and his companions might rebuke him too sharply for his imprudence? Was it not rather that under all his rhetoric, he was really pursuing a definite plan that he had carefully mapped out? In breaking the Governor's rules was he not trying to provoke a scandal that would compel Lowe to banish him from St. Helena?

For several months past, the little Chamberlain, who had been so long-suffering and so enthusiastic in his submissiveness, had been faltering under the weight of his chains. He was at the end of his endurance—he was too unhappy.

Las Cases was worried about his son's health and was himself far from well, suffering from attacks of dizziness and often from abdominal pains. Worse housed than the domestics, he was detested

[17] Las Cases, Vol. VII, p. 361.
[18] Gorrequer, *Minutes*, December 4, 1816 (Lowe Papers, 20-117).

by Montholon and Gourgaud, who ragged him unmercifully as a
courtier, a "has-been" and a "civilian." An exclamation of young
Emmanuel's that Gourgaud reports is pregnant with meaning. Meeting him on the day of the arrest O'Meara asked him if it were true that
his father had given letters to James Scott. Emmanuel in tears
replied:

"What do you expect? We are living in such horrible discomfort!"

"Discomfort" here can be taken only in the sense of moral discomfort, persecution.[19]

The attitude of Montholon and of Gourgaud towards Las Cases
transpires eloquently from Gourgaud's *Journal*. On November 13,
a few days before the arrest, he noted: "If Las Cases walks in to
dinner in front of me again, I'll give him a kick." [20] And again for
December 23: "They tell me that when Balcombe gave assurances
that Las Cases was to be allowed to come back, M. de Montholon
nearly fainted with rage." [21] The very servants treated Las Cases
insolently. It is understandable that, in the end, he should have tired
of it.

Napoleon always received him with friendliness, but Las Cases no
longer enjoyed the intimacy that had made the sojourn at The Briars
so delicious to him. In particular he was no longer receiving the
supreme recompense of being Napoleon's sole historian. The others
were now having their share in the work. Las Cases saw clearly that
he must abandon the great dream for which he had given up everything—the dream of writing the authorized history of his hero's reign!
His diary as it stood would require five or six volumes when it came
to the printing. Las Cases had no doubt of its prodigious interest. He
believed that its publication, from which he would derive personal
prestige, if not a fortune (for money problems did not trouble him),
would certainly serve the cause of Napoleon in France and might
even lead to a revulsion of feeling in his favour.

If he could get back to Europe a new rôle might open before him,
a rôle well calculated to tempt a servant who was devoted, yes, but
who was also eager to make a noise in the world—to become Napoleon's ambassador, to be the trumpet of his misfortune. That is
why he had resolved to leave the island, without consulting his
master and by a ruse which no one would suspect. He was wrong,

[19] Gourgaud, Vol. I, p. 278.              [21] *Ibid.*, Vol. I, p. 339.
[20] Unpublished.

in that respect, however. O'Meara was to write to Finlaison, December 29: ". . . he gave those letters to the slave *purposely to be discovered*, in order that he might be sent off the island, not being able, after all his professions of eternal and unalterable fidelity *à l'Empereur* . . . with any decency to ask permission to go away."[22] For that matter Las Cases made an unfortunate remark at the time of his arrest. Laughing, he said to Reade, who was taking him to Hutt's Gate: "So I am arrested as a result of Scott's denunciation? I was sure the Governor sent him to me!"[23] The same note was sounded by the French. On December 12, Gourgaud said to the Emperor that Las Cases had "made no sacrifice in accompanying him. If he had come to St. Helena it was not through devotion, but to get himself talked about, to collect anecdotes and earn money."[24] Napoleon contented himself with replying: "Drouot, too, was like that. He was always running risks, but he did so for the sake of notoriety!" And on the 24th, Gourgaud wrote again: "I consider that people will not hesitate to say that he managed this whole business in such a way as to have an excuse for leaving us."[25]

For the same reasons, having succeeded in getting himself "banished," he showed himself very anxious to recover the famous diary. He even suggested that Lowe would correct anything that he found erroneous in the passages that concerned him personally.[26] He failed, but it was only a postponement. Sooner or later it would have to be returned to him. Meanwhile his pen was fertile enough to retrace the essentials of the Captivity from memory, to describe the wretched life at Longwood, the devotion and the sufferings of the French fraternally united in the cult of a great man, and to proclaim the Olympian serenity of the Emperor amid so much suffering. His letters, his appeals, his lectures would attract public attention and perhaps stir the sovereigns to remorse. In any case the world would echo with his name. At that thought his imagination took fire. He flung himself at his paper and began to write, breathlessly, mixing a brew of truths, lies, accusations, panegyrics, virtuosities, imprudences, in a sort of literary consecration in which in the end he could hardly recognize himself.

[22] Lowe Papers, 20-216.
[23] Reade, *Report* (Lowe Papers, 20-117).
[24] Vol. I, p. 316.
[25] Vol. I, p. 342.
[26] Gorrequer, *Minutes*, December 22, 1816 (Lowe Papers, 20-117).

In his excited state of mind he was to send the Governor, not to mention almost daily letters, a memorandum fifty pages long, which poor Emmanuel was obliged to copy. Sentences like the following give the general tone of it. "December 19, 1816: Our sufferings in that residence [Longwood] are such that were it possible to interrupt for a moment our devotion to the sacred duty that fills our souls and governs them, were it possible, I say, to have that moment of distraction which allows each man to be himself again, I would not be surprised if our unfortunate companions should use it to kill each other, after the example of some of the ancients, in order to free themselves of the troubles of life, and that one morning word would be brought to you that Longwood was nothing but a sepulchre and that you were standing guard over nothing but corpses."

Las Cases wrote too much and he also talked too much. In his conversations with Lowe and Gorrequer, he allowed himself to be led into judgments that later on supplied the Governor with vantage points. Caught unawares by Sir Hudson's attentiveness, he told him that everything now appeared to him under a different light: "At Longwood one looks at facts through a veil of blood." He expressed himself freely regarding the Emperor. "He must be looked upon as a sick man. Great allowances should be made for him." [27]

These meetings gave an unexpected turn to their relations. They came to discuss the way in which Lowe might reconcile his duties with a broader understanding of the Emperor's situation. Sir Hudson asked Las Cases "to draw up a memorandum suggesting the improvements that seemed to him necessary," and he promised to take it into consideration in good faith. He was, he said, "pained at the sad situation of the French at Longwood, but they were making it worse than it really was. Whenever he sought to ameliorate it, they were the ones who stood in the way." [28]

Lowe was sincere. He feared the repercussions that Las Cases' return to Europe might have and the criticisms the Ministry might make of him regarding a measure that he himself had come to judge excessive. It would only serve to attract to St. Helena an attention that it was to English interests to keep diverted. He also feared, as Gourgaud quite soundly pointed out to him [29] and as O'Meara had

[27] Gorrequer, *Minutes*, December 16, 1816 (Lowe Papers, 20-117).
[28] *Ibid.*
[29] Gourgaud, Vol. I, p. 312.

warned him in advance, a complaint on Napoleon's part to the Prince
Regent. Even in those days, when O'Meara was on good terms with
the Governor and was acting as his spy at Longwood, he took real
delight in playing on his anxieties. Lowe was afraid of "being sacrificed by his government."

Lowe had already gone to Longwood on December 4 to restore
Napoleon's papers to Bertrand. Afterwards he had a long conversa-
tion with O'Meara. He asked the doctor to explain his policy to the
French. His actions, he said, had always been wrongly interpreted.
It was not his fault if his orders were more severe than Cockburn's.
And he expressed a desire to arrive at some agreement.[30]

"Well," replied the Emperor, "if he wants to set us in order, let
him put things back on the footing they were on in the days of the
Admiral. Let him deport himself decently towards me and I will say
that I have been mistaken in the bad opinion I have held of him. But
that man is treacherous. He says that Las Cases does not want for
anything. He pays no attention to his moral needs. He considers only
the grossest physical needs."

The next day Lady Lowe came and called on Mme. Bertrand and
Mme. de Montholon in formal attire. It was her first visit. She had
been unable to come before, it seems, because she was either pregnant or in confinement.[31] Gracious, she regretted that Plantation
House was too far away for the children to be able to play together.
Mme. Bertrand bluntly remarked that Sir Hudson Lowe would give
the Emperor a great pleasure if he were to send Las Cases back.
Lady Lowe looked embarrassed and said nothing. She asked whether
she could see Napoleon and was told that he was indisposed and not
receiving.[32] Three weeks later, December 24th, she was to send Mme.
Bertrand some baby's caps and dresses.

The Emperor was surprised by the visit. Was the Governor trying
to pull the wool over their eyes—gettare la polvere negli occhi? [33]

"Anyhow," he said, "she has chosen her time badly. Her husband
sends her at a moment when he is treating Las Cases so barbarously.
Nothing could be more insulting than to add irony to injustice." [34]

The arrest of Las Cases had deeply affected the Emperor. So

[30] O'Meara to Lowe, December 7 (Lowe Papers, 20-117).
[31] O'Meara, Vol. I, pp. 246-47.
[32] Gourgaud, Vol. I, p. 291.
[33] O'Meara, Vol. I, p. 246.
[34] O'Meara, Vol. I, p. 216.

his little Chamberlain, in his blue coat, with his tall, grey beaver in his hand, and who followed him everywhere like a poodle dog, was gone! He began to realize what a place the man had filled in his habits. He made his regret too apparent to suit the tastes of those who were left behind. Bertrand grumbled. Montholon pretended that the Emperor was thinking of negotiating an exchange of Las Cases for Gourgaud and himself.

"The Emperor does not see us," cried Gourgaud, "because they have taken his Las Cases away from him. The last comers are always the favourites!" [35]

The Emperor rarely left his "interior" now. He had stopped working and was not even dressing. He refused to see the Malcolms. For that matter he was really ill: fever, headache, a nervous insomnia. O'Meara advised him to take some exercise. "If he doesn't," the doctor predicted, "he will inevitably have some alarming fit of illness, and that probably very soon."

"*Tanto meglio!*" replied the Emperor. "The sooner it will be over, and they won't torment me any more!" [36]

Thinking that he was never to see Las Cases again, he dictated an affectionate letter of farewell to him. Written out by Marchand—"with some mistakes in spelling," adds the always charitable Gourgaud [37]—it had not yet been signed by Napoleon when, on the evening of December 12, after dinner, the Emperor asked Gourgaud to go and get it and read it aloud to the Montholons. Then he asked them what they thought of it. Gourgaud replied "that the laudatory and tender style was not suitable as coming from the Emperor to a M. de Las Cases, whom he had known only eighteen months and who had never made any sacrifice for him or given any great proofs of devotion." And, his anger rising, he added that "never had His Majesty written such a letter to an old and better friend, such as Duroc or Lannes." [38]

Napoleon got up, disappointed. He was not asking for advice as to what he ought to do. He only wanted to know what effect such a letter would produce on Lowe.

Mme. de Montholon, sitting with her elbows on the table, declared that the letter was very good and that Gourgaud was mistaken.

[35] Gourgaud, Vol. I, p. 284.
[36] O'Meara to Lowe, December 16, 1816 (Lowe Papers, 20-117).
[37] Vol. I, p. 314; Las Cases, Vol. VII, pp. 431 ff.
[38] Gourgaud, Vol. I, p. 314.

Gourgaud made an insolent reply and Napoleon began walking up and down in the drawingroom. To pacify Gourgaud Montholon murmured, naïvely cynical:

"All the better that the letter should be like that! That proves that His Majesty will write us just as good ones."

The Emperor sat down, asked for a pen and, as he signed the letter, added in a spirit of contrariness a most unusual "Yours faithfully" (*Votre dévoué*). He ordered Montholon to deliver it to Poppleton.

Soon recovering his poise, he turned to Gourgaud gaily:

"Come, Gourgaud, let's have a game of chess. It will cheer you up. Why are you always stewing?"

The young man gave free vent to his rage.

"Sire, I have the great defect of being too deeply attached to Your Majesty. What I said was not dictated, as you may suppose, by jealousy. I could not be jealous of a man who has not done Your Majesty any service. I thought it my duty to tell you that that letter is not worthy of you! It implies that you are deserted here, that we are all so many zeros. I see clearly that in this world one must never tell the truth to sovereigns and that intriguers and flatterers are the ones that get on best!"

The Emperor interrupted him:

"My wish is that Las Cases should be your best friend some day!"

"Never, I despise him!"

"Now, Gourgaud, that is not generous!"

"He is a Tartuffe. Some day Your Majesty will see it."

Napoleon shrugged his shoulders and said bitterly:

"Dear me, what can you expect? He will betray me? He will speak ill of me? Well, bless us! How did Berthier, how did Marmont, act? And I loaded them with honours! I defy anybody to fool me. Men have to be scoundrels indeed to be as bad as I think they are." [39]

But Gourgaud was enraged and came back again, and Napoleon, bored, could do nothing but leave the room.

.      .      .      .      .      .      .

Lowe's fears and his desire to avoid a scandal prompted him next to a significant step.

In reply to the letters with which Las Cases kept bombarding him, he suggested that, while waiting for instructions regarding their de-

[39] Gourgaud, Vol. I, pp. 313, 316.

parture to arrive from England, the two prisoners should return to Longwood where Emmanuel could be under the daily care of O'Meara.[40] Las Cases refused. All he wanted was to be transferred to a place where a doctor would be within easy reach. He did not want to return to Longwood—he dared not, save on an express order of the Emperor.

He knew very well that Napoleon's pride would keep him from giving such an order!

What finer *exeat* could he ever have than the letter he had received from the Emperor? He feared that if he were to return to Longwood, he would not be able to get away again, and that he would be held there, like Napoleon, a prisoner for life. He implored Lowe to let him leave the island at the earliest possible moment. On the 22nd he wrote to the Governor: "I ask you therefore and shall continue to ask at every moment: Send me away from this place of suffering!" [41] He repeated to him orally: "Whatever your decision is to be, I implore you to send me away from the island as soon as possible!" [42]

When Napoleon was told that Las Cases had received permission to return to him but did not care to take advantage of it, he was incredulous, in spite of O'Meara's assurances:

"If he can, why doesn't he come back?" [43]

And he added that he "would like to see a letter from Las Cases himself, declaring that he had been authorized to return."

Lowe insisting, Las Cases finally ended by writing Bertrand, not without embarrassment, that he had rejected the offer. The Emperor shrugged his shoulders. One of his last illusions regarding men had collapsed! He said that he intended to order his three generals to leave, since then he would not need to fear that the Governor would torment them to get revenge on him,[44] and he could feel independent. All the same he seemed to dread being left more and more alone in a visible future. Seeing those mournful faces around him and those eyes that kept sizing each other up—for Montholon and Gourgaud, formerly allies against Las Cases, were already at swords' points themselves—he tried to pacify them. They were all very well off there,

[40] Gorrequer, *Minutes*, December 17, 1816 (Lowe Papers, 20-117).
[41] Las Cases, Vol. VIII, p. 36.
[42] Gorrequer, *Minutes*, conversation of the 23rd (Lowe Papers, 20-117).
[43] O'Meara to Lowe, December 21 (Lowe Papers, 20-117).
[44] O'Meara, Vol. I, p. 267; Gourgaud, Vol. I, p. 333.

he said to them. They might even consider themselves fortunate. They could ride on horseback everywhere accompanied by an officer. They had a good table. If they complained it was because they always had to complain about something. They were free to go away whenever they wished. They had covered themselves with glory in times past. They would be received everywhere, and have topics of conversation for the rest of their lives.[45] As for himself, he could not go riding even with an escort. He was not free. His every step was spied upon. And suddenly growing angry he rebuked Gourgaud for his stupid talk, his mean disposition, the quarrels he was constantly trying to pick with Montholon.

Gourgaud kept his black eyes lowered and retorted awkwardly. Then the Emperor, losing patience in his distress, struck furiously from the shoulder:

"What difference does it make to me whether you are an honest man? Go away! Your virtues are uncivilized. Las Cases was a man of character. You were jealous of him and you had the bad taste to show it. You thought that in coming here you would be my comrade—but I am nobody's comrade. You would like to be the centre here. You have caused me all my worries ever since we have been here. If I had foreseen this, I would have brought only servants. If you are so badly off, instead of picking quarrels with Montholon you can leave us!"

Gourgaud stammered, tears in his eyes. His suffering touched Napoleon:

"Come! Gourgaud! You are too out-spoken. It is not good to say everything one thinks! To live in society one has to dissemble."

Gourgaud calmed down again. It was one o'clock in the morning, and they went off to bed.[46]

. . . . . . .

Alleging Emmanuel's ill-health, Las Cases solicited the favour of being shipped directly to England, but Lowe would not consent. To gain time and allow London to get used to the idea, Las Cases should first go to the Cape! He hoped for that matter that the prospect of months at sea and a long wait would discourage Las Cases and incline him to a return to Longwood. In that he was failing to know his man.

[45] Gourgaud, Vol. I, p. 342.
[46] Gourgaud, December 25, 1816.

In reply to a demand from the Grand Marshal that Las Cases be allowed to come and take leave of the Emperor, Lowe declared that an English officer would have to be present at the interview. That was making it impossible. He wanted to prevent Napoleon from giving his confidant any message for Europe.

On the 24th Las Cases was transferred to the Castle in Jamestown. "Everything was placed at my service," he writes.[47] "They seemed to go out of their way to supply us with an abundance of everything. 'Have everything you want,' the majordomo would often say to me. 'The Honourable Company pays for everything!' The Governor came in every day." On the 29th Bertrand went to Plantation House and Lowe escorted him to the Castle. The Grand Marshal embraced Las Cases and his son.

"So, Las Cases," he said to him, "you are going away!"

Las Cases asked for news of the Emperor. He talked in a confused, excited manner. Later on when Bertrand described the interview to Napoleon the latter said: "Oh, he has lost his head. He will be sure to do something foolish. They have kept him shut up so long that they have driven him mad." [48]

The interview took place in the presence of Lowe and Gorrequer. Speaking in a low tone Bertrand implored Las Cases to give up his plan:

"Why not stay and come back to Longwood? What difficulty is there in that?"

"There is a great difficulty and a great impropriety. I have made this decision because I believe that I must act in this way."

"But if the Emperor should ask you to stay?"

"I would stay, because his wishes would be law for me."

Bertrand could only repeat what Napoleon had said to O'Meara and to himself, "that he left Las Cases strictly to his own devices, that he would be pleased to see him stay and pleased to see him go." [49] In his letter to Finlaison,[50] December 29, O'Meara adds, nevertheless, that Napoleon had ordered him to tell Las Cases (which he did with the Governor's permission) "that he thought it would be much bet-

[47] Vol. VIII, pp. 39-45.
[48] Las Cases, Vol. VIII, p. 43; Gourgaud, Vol. I, p. 355.
[49] Las Cases, Vol. VIII, p. 43; Gorrequer, *Minutes*, December 29, 1816 (Lowe Papers, 20-117).
[50] Lowe Papers, 20-216.

ter for him to return to Longwood . . . amongst friends than to go to the Cape amongst strangers."

As he was about to part from this companion whom he did not like, Bertrand none the less felt stirred. He urged him to stay on on his own account. Las Cases did not yield. He had offered the Emperor the use of four thousand louis that he had on deposit in England. Bertrand begged him to prepare thirteen letters of credit to his order. Balcombe could collect them. They would help to cover private expenses at Longwood. He would come back and get the checks the following day.

He came back in fact, accompanied by Gourgaud, whose hatred was melting into pity. With Lowe's consent Las Cases handed the letters of credit to Bertrand, taking in return a receipt from the Emperor that would enable him to be reimbursed by Prince Eugene. The existence of this document has often been denied. It was worded, however, as follows: "Received from Count de Las Cases the sum of 100,800 francs, to be repaid to him on demand. Napoleon. Longwood, this 30th of December, 1816." [51] Finally, the first moment the English officers were looking the other way, he slipped into the Grand Marshal's hand Hortense's necklace that the Emperor had entrusted to him on the *Bellerophon* and which he had not had an opportunity to restore to him at the time of his arrest at Longwood.

Lowe allowed the Frenchmen to lunch together under the surveillance of Poppleton, who knew little of their language and understood not a word when they spoke rapidly. The Governor was well aware of that. But he wanted to leave Las Cases with a good impression. "Be it kindness or calculation," Las Cases writes, "he gave me a number of private letters to acquaintances of his at the Cape, and assured me that they would be very kind to me. I did not have the courage to refuse them since they seemed offered in such good part." [52] It was probably at that moment that Bertrand handed Las Cases a beautiful diamond which he commanded him to take to little Émilie Pellapra in Napoleon's name. The stone must have been one of those that were taken to St. Helena in a sachet-bag. It reposes today in Princess Bibesco's jewel-box.

When the father and son were ready to go, the Governor escorted them in person to the Castle gate and bowed courteously to them.

[51] Lowe Papers, 20-141.
[52] Vol. VIII, p. 54.

"To do them honour" his officers accompanied them to the tender which was to take them off to the *Griffon*. By his own admission Las Cases "flung himself eagerly into the boat." As he crossed the little harbour he passed close to the *Orontes*, which had come in from the Cape and was about to sail again for Europe. On board were Piontkowski and the three domestics. They waved to him.

During the enforced stop in the harbour of Jamestown—from the 18th of December to the 3rd of January—the four men were not allowed to go ashore. The elder Archambault, however, was permitted to board the vessel in order to see his brother. Through him the Emperor sent the deportees a basket of good things to eat and Gourgaud gave him fifteen louis for Piontkowski, who was just beginning his career as a mendicant.

At three o'clock the *Griffon* weighed anchor. As night fell the recluses at Longwood stood watching it with a heavy heart as it rounded the Barn and headed towards the South, carrying the first deserters on board.

To think that Las Cases went away without a regret would be unfair to him. On the last page of the *Mémorial* he was to write:

"Ah, why did I not choose to stay? Why did I not go on with my duties there at home instead of dreaming of duties far away? I could then have prolonged my daily attentions for some time still, I could have gathered a few more details of interest, and, when the fatal moment came, I could have had my share in the common suffering. I too could have contributed to softening his last moments! I too could have helped to close his eyes!"

# III

## *LOWE IN THE SADDLE*

N EW YEAR'S DAY, 1817, WAS GLOOMY. THE EVENING BEFORE THE EM-
peror had seemed overwhelmed.[1] "I feel as if I were in a tomb," he
said to Bertrand. He sent word that he would lunch alone in his own
rooms and receive his company at four in the afternoon.

In the morning the Bertrand children and Tristan de Montholon
came to wish him a happy New Year. Gourgaud distributed to them
some toys that he had bought at Jamestown after Las Cases sailed.
The departure of the Chamberlain somehow brought the fact of exile
home to the French, and it drew them closer together. Montholon
and Bertrand said to Gourgaud:

"Come now, cheer up! No more despondency!"

Gourgaud presented Mme. Bertrand with a box of China tea on
the inside of which he had written: "May her years equal her virtues
and become more numerous than these tea leaves." They went for
a walk and met the Nymph as she was going to a ball. Then they
repaired to the Emperor's apartment.

He welcomed them goodhumouredly and gave little Hortense a
bonbonnière which Pauline had given him. He assured her that it
had cost fifty louis. Gourgaud received a lorgnette which had been
a gift from the Queen of Naples. Afterwards Napoleon sent for the
box that had come from Elphinstone and divided the shawls and silks
that it contained between the two ladies. Bertrand got a chess set,
Montholon a mosaic cross, the young Napoleon and Tristan a drum
apiece, O'Meara a gold snuff box.

The weather was so foggy that the signal mast at Deadwood was
invisible. The children played marbles in the drawingroom. They
danced and sang around the Emperor. He played a game of chess
with Bertrand.

Now that he had lost Las Cases, Napoleon found himself forced
to dictate much more to Gourgaud and Montholon. Sometimes he

---

[1] Gourgaud, Vol. I, p. 365.

even called on Mme. de Montholon. However he no longer felt the same taste for his work. Las Cases had made it easy for him. He found less enthusiasm in the others, and their indifference angered him. He still dictated on occasion for a part of the night, but afterwards he would spend several days in a sort of stupor. Meanwhile Montholon and Gourgaud awaited his orders and dared not go out for fear lest the Emperor might call them during their absence. This inactivity all but suffocated the two young men.

On January 17, Mme. Bertrand gave birth to a boy. The child was baptized by the Reverend B. J. Vernon as Arthur François Alexandre. Her pains came on during the night. Because of the regulations, they could not send for the *accoucheur*, Dr. Livingstone, until daybreak. Mme. de Montholon posted herself at the patient's bedside and, for a moment, there was danger. Napoleon was worried, but did not pay her a call until the week following, on January 26th. Mme. Bertrand was much offended by his seeming indifference.[2] As he entered her bedroom the Countess raised herself up on her two pillows, her eyes shining, and showed her child to the Emperor:

"Sire," she said, "I have the honour to present to Your Majesty the first Frenchman who has come to Longwood since our arrival without a permit from Lord Bathurst."

Napoleon smiled. He found the child lusty and handsome.

. . . . . . .

Lowe was well satisfied with the way things were going.[3] The departure of Las Cases, he thought, improved the atmosphere. Gourgaud had always been very civil towards the English. Bertrand had virtually ceased to count, since Montholon was running the household. Relations with him were promising to be easier. Lowe therefore was shortly to write to Bathurst that nothing seemed calmer than the guests at Longwood. He had ordered the sentries withdrawn on the road leading to Miss Mason's and to Woody Ridge as an encouragement to the Emperor to resume his rides. Receiving some coffee from Reunion Island, he sent a case of it to Longwood. Cipriani pretended to be afraid of poison and Montholon himself thought the "courtesy" suspicious. Napoleon remarked with good sense: "Have the case sent to the kitchen. Good coffee is a precious thing in this

[2] Gourgaud, Vol. I, p. 434.
[3] Lowe to Bathurst, January 23 (Lowe Papers, 20-118).

horrible place." [4] "In a word," Montholon concludes, "the coffee was excellent."

Having nothing for the moment to worry about Lowe turned his anxiety on the Commissioners. He had learned at last that the botanist Welle, who had come with Stürmer, had given Marchand a lock of hair from the King of Rome. The discovery excited him tremendously. He had already suspected Stürmer, wondering whether he might not be the bearer of secret instructions from the Emperor Francis to his son-in-law. Believing that Welle could have transmitted message and souvenir only with Stürmer's consent, he asked the latter to send the botanist either to the Cape or to England. Metternich's envoy refused haughtily. Balmain wrote to Nesselrode, January 6, 1817: "The Commissioner of Austria and the Governor of St. Helena are at loggerheads. For six weeks there has been a constant exchange of futile notes, letters and explanations—and all over a matter of no importance." Welle, however, who was botanizing on the island, was forbidden the plateau of Longwood and the coasts. He appeared before the Governor sitting in council and was subjected to a thorough questioning. Lowe pronounced no sentence. Welle had all but finished his work and intended to spend only a few weeks more on the island. He left on the first of March.

With Montchenu everything had gone very well at first. Camping at the Porteous House with Gors, the Marquis dined as often as he could at Plantation House. He kept borrowing money from the Governor. Dismayed at the high prices of rent, provisions, and the most insignificant articles imported from Europe, he found his salary too slender and cried poverty by every post that left for Paris. He got an advance of 800 pounds from Lowe in order to give a great banquet on Louis XVIII's birthday, but he spent only 171 pounds on the affair, Balcombe having taken charge of everything at a rate of 3 pounds per plate "including dessert and coffee, but without wine." "Wine," wrote Montchenu to his minister, "is a very expensive commodity here, and much used, for they drank thirty pounds' worth." Montchenu ascribed far-reaching political consequences to his enterprise: "The entertainment has already lowered our prisoner's prestige. The day following he sent his people to town to find out how it had gone off, and ever since he has been in a terrible humour."

Then things began to sour. Lowe had Montchenu watched and

[4] Montholon, Vol. II, p. 51.

on occasion gave the chatterbox a lecture on the virtues of holding one's tongue. Then, overstepping his prerogatives, Lowe made a pretext of the Welle incident to inform the Commissioners that, according to the act of Parliament, they were to consider themselves during their sojourn at St. Helena as amenable to English law, in case they should ever procure means of correspondence or of escape for Napoleon. Montchenu protested. He considered himself an ambassador. Lowe bluntly told him to be silent and the old parasite lowered his flag without a fight.

Of the three envoys of the Powers, Balmain was the only one to inspire Lowe with any respect, and he treated him with gloves. However he was not less mistrustful of him for all of that, and Balmain felt no sympathy whatever for a man who concealed his real thoughts, quibbled over bagatelles, had a captious manner of thinking, flew into rages without reason, and who, if he was honest at bottom, did not always seem to be.

Ill-satisfied with the Commissioners, Lowe was no less so with the Admiral. Since his return from the Cape Malcolm had again won the friendship of the French. More courageous than the Binghams, he and his wife pitied Napoleon and were eager to ameliorate his lot. Malcolm therefore tried to reconcile Lowe with Longwood.

In his talks with Napoleon, the Admiral admitted that the Emperor was being treated with too great severity. He thought he should have the whole island at his disposal. Longwood, as he saw it, was a shabby affair—Plantation House would have been far more appropriate to the former host at the Tuileries. That had been Balmain's opinion. He asked Lowe one day why he did not transfer the French to Plantation House. The Governor replied: "Because those people would ruin everything there. The maintenance of house, garden and farms costs a great deal of money. It is a magnificent establishment and the East India Company would sustain too great a loss." "Besides," he added, "I would be obliged to live at Longwood myself. Lady Lowe would not be as well off there and I will never sacrifice my wife's health to the good pleasure of Bonaparte." [5]

At the same time Malcolm protested against the conception that Napoleon had formed as to the intentions of the Liverpool Cabinet. He was not hated in London. He was feared. So long as he never went back to make trouble in Europe, they were eager to do his pleasure

[5] Notes annexed to the report of January 8, 1818. Retranslated.

and make his confinement as agreeable as possible. He defended Lowe, who was, he said, quick-tempered, but not bad at heart. He could not have acted otherwise in the Las Cases matter, or in the case of Welle.[6] He had manifested his good will moreover by attenuating the restrictions of October in several respects. He was disposed to do better still.

"Especially," said the Admiral, "there are between you misunderstandings that have arisen from false reports, from the want of a free personal communication" (Forsyth, Vol. II, p. 125).

"Perhaps it was so," replied the Emperor, well disposed. "The Governor does not understand my character: he has never seen me but when I was irritated, and when I spoke folly."

Malcolm was unbiased enough to tell the Emperor that the letters written by Bertrand and Montholon were in bad taste and that neither Lowe nor Sir George Cockburn, in his opinion, had taken sufficient notice of such improper letters (Forsyth, Vol. II, pp. 126-27). Napoleon replied that their painful situation had to be taken into account, so seeming to forget that he had dictated the letters in question himself.[7]

Confidential as the conversation had been Malcolm relayed it to Lowe and in a rather patronizing tone. The Governor took offence. He thought that the Admiral wanted to replace him—and not without reason, for as Stürmer wrote to Metternich, July 4, 1817: "I have it from good sources that he [Malcolm] has written by the *Larkins*, December 15, to offer to remain here three years more, at half the salary allotted to Sir Hudson Lowe, if they will give him the post." Longwood was eager for such a change. Under Malcolm the situation of the French would be improved. Lowe did not dare to break with the naval commander, but avoided meeting him. Balmain wrote, July 4: "For about three months Sir P. Malcolm and the Governor have been at odds. They have ceased to see each other, to invite each other to dinner, to confer together." Viewing the Admiral's mediation with disfavour, Lowe condemned it then and there to a halt.

.    .    .    .    .    .    .    .

[6] Malcolm to Lowe, March 8, 1817 (Lowe Papers, 20-118). "He then said that he was prevented from seeing the Austrian botanist before he quitted the island. 'This man,' he added, 'came from, and was going to, the place where my wife and child resided.'" A simple sentence but after these score of years it still has a ring of sadness!

[7] *Ibid.*

On March 6, 1817, O'Meara handed Napoleon, at the Governor's request, a book that had been published in London early in 1816 [8] —*Letters Written on Board the* Northumberland *and at St. Helena*. The author was Dr. Warden, surgeon on the *Northumberland*, who had hastened to put it in press on his return to England. Warden described the Emperor's voyage and the first days of his stay at St. Helena in the form of letters addressed to a woman friend. The style was pretentious but fairly picturesque. He attributed to the Emperor statements and confidences which, to tell the truth, Napoleon could never have made to him, but the gist of which had been taken from the surgeon's conversations with the Emperor's officers. The Emperor, as well for that matter as all the others among the French, found the book improper. He said to O'Meara:

"The substance of the book is true, but it contains *cento coglionerie e cento bugie* [a hundred absurdities and a hundred lies]. He puts into my mouth expressions that are unworthy of me and which are not in my style." [9]

However he could see that Warden's intentions had not been bad, and that the success of the work, which had gone into several editions, would help his cause. The pamphleteer had never completely died in him. It suddenly came to life again. He began at once to dictate letters to Bertrand in reply to the letters of Warden—and all that unbeknown to O'Meara and even to Gourgaud. "His Majesty," writes Gourgaud, on June 19th, [10] "assured me that he had made no reply to Warden's work. 'Las Cases, they say, is intending to reply from the Cape.' I thereupon pointed out to the Emperor that I had seen more than ten letters dictated by him go to the Grand Marshal in shape to be printed, and that one of them even was on the table where I was writing. The Emperor could not deny it after that."

Mme. Bertrand translated the letters into English. They would be printed in London under title of *Letters from the Cape*, and in that form pass as the work of Las Cases. What more natural than to suppose that he would be writing from his "austral quarantine" to defend the Emperor from slander and falsehoods?

Visitors were becoming rare at Longwood, the people of St. Helena knowing well that to appear on too good terms with the French

[8] Gourgaud, Vol. I, p. 523.
[9] O'Meara to Lowe, March 10, 1817.
[10] Vol. II, p. 151.

would draw the Governor's hostility. Balcombe was protected by his business and still came often. On the 12th of February, Mrs. Balcombe, Jane and Betsy went to Longwood to see little Arthur Bertrand, and at the dinner hour Napoleon sent Gourgaud for them. The Emperor chaffed Betsy on rumours that she intended to marry Reade. The young girl defended herself and later in the drawingroom played a number of her roguish tricks. As it was against the rules to cross the boundary lines at night, Gourgaud took the ladies back to the Grand Marshal's and they were there provided with beds. They were so enabled to spend two days at Longwood. Betsy played cards with Gourgaud and flirted with Fehrzen and Reade. The Emperor paid a call on her. At last Balcombe came to get his three women and they rode off on horseback, accompanied as far as Hutt's Gate by Mme. de Montholon and O'Meara, who were returning Lady Lowe's call. Napoleon had asked Mme. de Montholon to do that.[11] She was extremely well received and said that "the Governor seemed delighted when she paid attention to his child."

The autumn races at the camp at Deadwood took place on April 7. Those races gathered the notables of the island together twice a year. Lady Lowe offered to take Mme. Bertrand in the Governor's carriage, but Napoleon told Bertrand that his wife had better not become too friendly with Lady Lowe. The latter was already on the way to Longwood when Poppleton wigwagged that Mme. Bertrand would not go out. Mme. de Montholon was compelled to follow suit, in order not to take an unfair advantage. Gourgaud, on the other hand, received the Emperor's permission to attend the races—he would see the Commissioners and the opportunity should not be neglected.

Gourgaud trotted off towards Deadwood. The Governor, his wife, the three Commissioners, Baroness Stürmer, Gors, the Binghams, the Malcolms, the Balcombes, were gathered under the same tent. Gourgaud was cordially received and Balmain was introduced to him. The conversation became animated during the races. Balmain, Stürmer and his wife deplored their not having any relations with Longwood. "Time," said Stürmer, "would pass more agreeably." They teased Gourgaud on his unlucky affair with Miss Churchill, Montchenu making a broad remark. After the races, the Commissioners and Gourgaud went to tea at Mrs. Younghusband's: [12] "The Russian almost

[11] Gourgaud, Vol. I, p. 476.
[12] Gourgaud, Vol. II, p. 6.

let slip: 'The Emperor, that great man.' Montchenu used the form: 'Bonaparte' once or twice, and then twice, in Lady Lowe's hearing, 'the Emperor.' Stürmer never actually used any one of the three denominations."

On the way home the young man lingered along the road with Stürmer and Balmain. The latter remarked that the *Conqueror* was expected shortly and that he hoped it would bring new instructions to the Commissioners that would permit them to visit Longwood. The young man was delighted with his day and Napoleon almost regretted that he had not gone himself.[18]

.      .      .      .      .      .      .

No one at St. Helena had any idea at that time that the situation of the Captive had just been brought before English opinion by a public debate in the House of Lords. That had been due to the most humble of the Emperor's servants, Santini. After a forced sojourn at the Cape, the little Corsican reached London in February, 1817. He did not know a word of English, but he manoeuvred so well that at last he made his way to Sir Robert Wilson, the chivalrous colonel who had saved the life of Lavalette after his escape from prison. Santini recited to him the *Remonstrance* that the Emperor had dictated to Montholon. Always tempted by a noble cause, Wilson took fire and hurried with Santini to Lord Holland. With the help of the dubious Maceroni, a former officer in Murat's army, then a refugee in London, and probably of Piontkowski also, the three got out in French and English a pamphlet entitled: *Appeal to the English Nation Regarding the Treatment Experienced by Napoleon Buonaparte on the Island of St. Helena.* Maceroni boasted of being the sole author of the pamphlet. In reality he did nothing but hold the pen. The French version used the expression: "By the Emperor Napoleon." The pamphlet was issued by Ridgway, on March 13, 1817. The same day the *Morning Chronicle* and the majority of the opposition papers re-published the essential portions of it—in other words, Montholon's *Remonstrance.* The pamphlet ran through seven editions in ten days. On March 18, Lord Holland, one of the leaders of the Liberal Party, questioned Lord Bathurst in the upper House with a view to "rescuing the character of Parliament and the country from that stain which would attach if any harsh or ungenerous treatment had been used towards Napoleon Buonaparte."

[18] Gourgaud, Vol. II, p. 7.

What sort of a person was this Lord Holland, whose name will live because he thought that England ought not to stamp on a man who was down? A strange character, to tell the truth! One of the leaders of the English Liberal Party, Henry Richard, third Lord Holland, was a nephew of Fox, the great Whig leader. Born in 1773 he had been Lord of the Privy Seal in 1806. He was a traveller and a writer rather than an orator. He was also a distinguished lover. After a varied career in sentiment, he had married a pretty creole, Elisabeth Vassall, who had previously become Lady Webster through her marriage to Sir George Webster, M.P., the father of her five children. Standing at Holland's side she received all the prominent men of the United Kingdom at Holland House. If her past caused the ladies of the Realm to disdain her, Lady Holland's influence was no less strong. Ministries, even Tory ministries, took her into account. She was a generous soul and among the first to pity Napoleon, who had appealed to England's magnanimity only to meet vindictiveness. She had seen him, apparently, once only. That was during a riot in Paris under the Consulate. Fearing him as a good Englishwoman should, she had admired him from that day, and now that he had come upon misfortune, she warmly took his part and was eager, till such time as he should be released, to make his imprisonment, and that of the Frenchmen who had followed him, more bearable. So she began—and very soon—to send books, newspapers, knickknacks, comforts, and for the children, like a mother thinking of her own, hosts of beautiful toys. On November 8, 1816, she had sent, for example, a carrom table, a magic lantern, cards and dominos. But especially she worked on her husband, trying to persuade him to attack the Liverpool Cabinet.

In his speech Lord Holland could not raise any question as to the principle of the detention itself. He had opposed the bill which legalized it, but that bill had passed. However, in the name of English honour, he did want to make sure that the measures that had been promulgated in regard to the Captive were not inhumane, and he went on to make a complete statement of Napoleon's grievances. Bathurst answered by reading the instructions he had issued to Lowe, and he justified the restrictions by the fear of an escape. Longwood was not, he said, an unhealthy or a gloomy place. Buonaparte and his people were being treated liberally. Basely he tried to amuse his audience by listing the bottles of wine that had been supplied the prisoners, implying that all the Frenchmen in question, Napoleon included, were drunkards and that it would be a mistake to lend the slightest credence to their complaints. With Bathurst even more than with Lowe, the physical consideration came first. As Napoleon was suffering more particularly on moral grounds, the antinomy was never to be reduced.

The Peers supported Bathurst as was to be expected. But public opinion was worried. The reverberations of the debate expanded in waves. The Continental press took up the question. The world's interest had been languishing. It was now focussed on Napoleon again. The Emperor's family took courage and sent Lord Bathurst letters which the Minister promised Lord Holland to have delivered at Longwood. But, for a vulgar revenge, he sent them by way of the Cape so that they were not to reach Napoleon till they were five or six months old.

Nevertheless the campaign that Santini had begun,[14] and that Lord Holland and his Liberal friends had prosecuted, was bound to impel Bathurst, to say nothing of Lowe, to greater prudence and also to greater consideration of their prisoner. Lord Bathurst, for example, decided that boxes addressed in the handwriting of Lady Holland should be delivered without being inspected. Too many army and naval officers, too many British officials, had seen Napoleon at St. Helena. Their stories almost without exception voiced sympathy for him. Fissures opened on all sides in the secrecy in which Bathurst had tried to bury the exiles. The jailors could feel too many eyes weighing on them to hope that they could blind them all.

Napoleon learned of Santini's *Appeal* and of the debate in the House of Lords at the same moment through three newspapers that Lowe sent to Longwood on May 27th.[15] According to Gourgaud,

[14] Santini soon exhausted his resources. Shortly after the debate he made his way to the Continent and set out for Italy to give Madame Mère news of the Emperor. He did not reach that destination. Rebuffed at Brussels by Cambacérès he was denounced to the police and expelled from Bavaria by Prince Eugene. Stephanie, Grand Duchess of Baden, was the only one to take pity on him. She sent him a thousand francs. He made his way across Switzerland, but on arriving at Como he was arrested and deported again. He then lived for four years and a half at Brunn, in Moravia, on a pension of 180 francs a month. The death of Napoleon set him free. Thereafter he saw Caroline at Frohsdorf, Jerome at Trieste, and finally Mme. Letizia in Rome. Going home to Corsica, he drifted about there until Louis-Philippe made him a footman at the Ministry and then a mail-carrier. The Prince-President appointed him janitor of the Emperor's tomb. Masson accuses him—and very soundly —of trading a little too much on his memories. He died in 1862.

[15] Gourgaud, Vol. II, p. 93. On the 28th according to O'Meara, Vol. II, p. 80.

"Bertrand ran to take them to the Emperor's house without dressing."
Gourgaud did not like the pamphlet. He thought that Montholon's
*Remonstrance* would appear ridiculous. When Mme. de Montholon
had read the *Times*, she exclaimed:

"Ah, those Corsicans! They are all intriguers!"

That was not very tactful in the presence of the Emperor!

Napoleon, for his part, was very much pleased.

"Well," he exclaimed, "that Santini is doing wonders! He ought
not to have talked so much about food however. That will make
people put less trust in what he says."

He approved of Holland's motion. Bathurst's defence showed an
out and out duplicity.

"Almost all ministers are liars," he said to O'Meara. "Talleyrand
is their corporal, then come Castlereagh, Metternich and Harden-
berg."

"I am very glad," he added, "to see that the English minister finds
nothing but lies to justify his conduct towards me before the Parliament, his nation and the whole of Europe. However, the reign of
falsehood will not last forever!"

He set to work the very next day [16] on a reply to Bathurst's speech,
dictating to Montholon.

"It's going to be a fine thing," he said at dinner, "this reply to Bathurst. His Lordship is a fool, an ignoramus. He does not know what he
is talking about. He is going to see how I work him: I will *pulverize*
him! That's the advantage of a good logician over an idiot."

And he added:

"It will make a great noise in Europe. It will be better not to sign
any name. I shall just write: 'Approved—Napoleon.' " [17]

The *Remarks on Lord Bathurst's Speech* (*Observations sur le dis-
cours de Lord Bathurst*) reached Europe by a number of routes. Lowe
received them officially from Bertrand on October 7th. They were
in a sealed package addressed to Lord Liverpool. He transmitted
them, he swears, without breaking the seal. Stürmer, however, forwarded a copy of them to Metternich on October 31. O'Meara had
already sent one to Finlaison. As we shall see, Irving, Malcolm's secretary, and Captain Poppleton, each carried a copy with them when
they left the island.

[16] Gourgaud, Vol. II, p. 99.
[17] *Ibid.*, Vol. II, p. 103.

The English at St. Helena were impressed by the debate in the House of Lords. Lowe was more nervous than ever. He knew that his orders, his written statements, his slightest gestures were now to pass under the scrutiny of Parliament and public opinion. He kept therefore on the *qui-vive*, wavering between his foolish terror of a rescue and a better grounded fear of an attack from the Opposition in London which, from one post to the next, might earn him his walking-ticket.

His inclination to worry was the direct cause of a new incident, in itself trivial, but which was to be exaggerated and which Napoleon was to turn to account. The supply ship *Baring* reached St. Helena towards the end of May with a master-gunner, named Redwitch, who had received from the Biaggini brothers in London a little marble bust of the King of Rome, and a commission to sell it at the best price obtainable to Count Bertrand. The *Baring's* captain, one Lamb, reported the matter to Reade and the bust was taken to the Governor at Plantation House. Lowe sinned through indecision rather than malevolence in all this matter. Could he send this bust to Longwood without an authorization from his superior? Suppose it somehow conveyed a communication? He hesitated a long time. Reade was said to have suggested breaking up the bust or throwing it into the sea. That, however, is far from certain, but news to that effect reached Longwood [18] and Napoleon began at once to dictate a broadside of vengeful phrases to Montholon. Lowe made up his mind to mention the bust to Bertrand when he learned that Longwood already knew of its existence.[19] He went to see Bertrand on June 10th and asked him whether he should send on the wretched bust for which the Biagginis hoped to receive a hundred louis.

Bertrand replied:

"Send it all the same. It will please the Emperor."

The bust reached Bertrand the next day and Napoleon first sent Gourgaud on ahead to open the box. When Gourgaud returned he asked him:

"What decoration does it wear?"

"The eagle."

[18] O'Meara to Finlaison, August 18 (Lowe Papers, 20-146); testimony given by Captain John Lamb before Sir H. Lowe, July 24, 1817 (Lowe Papers, 20-119).

[19] Taken all in all, Lowe's attitude in the matter was creditable. "He yielded," Masson writes, "after some hesitation no doubt, to a feeling of deference and, one may even add, of pity" (*Napoléon à Sainte-Hélène*, p. 349).

"Not certainly the eagle of St. Stephen!"

"Oh, no—the eagle Your Majesty wears!"

Reassured, the Emperor then told Gourgaud to go and get it.[20]

Napoleon was enchanted with the sorry piece of work. His son, the son of whom he had heard nothing, of whom he seldom spoke in order not to stir too painful thoughts, was there before him. He identified the features, caressed the long curls, sought to recover from that marble mouth the fresh lips that had pressed against his cheek of yore. He found the child pretty "though his neck seemed to be too deep-sunken." He looked like Marie-Louise.

With the bust Lowe had sent Bertrand a letter and a memorandum from the Biagginis that clearly betrayed the imposture. Those schemers claimed that the child had been with its mother during the summer of 1816 at the baths of Livorno. There two busts had been made of him. "One had been kept by the distinguished mother of the prince who generously rewarded the artist"; the other had been sent to London and entrusted to Redwitch. Now everybody knows that the King of Rome never went to Italy. Examples of a fraud more disgusting would be hard to find.

Napoleon had no doubt that the Empress herself had sent him the bust of their child in a roundabout way. He would never have admitted, had anyone ventured to hazard the suspicion, that the Biagginis had speculated on his sentiments, that the weak and very conventional image had been made in London by a stone-cutter and decorated with the badge of the Legion of Honour only to trick him the better. His joy would have held its ground—it was too great. He placed the bust on the mantelpiece in the drawingroom with his own hands, sent for the Montholons, and showed it to the Balcombes, who went into raptures over it. He must have been proud, said Mrs. Balcombe, to be the father of such a beautiful child. And proud he was, in fact, and happy. His face beamed. "My mother often said," Mrs. Abell relates, "she never saw a countenance at the time so interestingly expressive of parental fondness." [21]

Napoleon said to O'Meara:

"Had the Governor not sent it to me, I intended to write him a complaint that would have made the hair of every Englishman stand on end. I would have said things that would have made every mother

[20] Gourgaud, Vol. II, p. 130.

[21] Recollections, p. 174.

see in him an object of execration, a monster in human form." [22]

Lowe had hinted that the bust was not worth the hundred louis they expected to get for it.

"To me it's worth a million!" exclaimed Napoleon.

Bertrand was to count out three hundred guineas to the sailor from the *Baring*. The Emperor was eager to see the man Redwitch himself. Lowe pretended to acquiesce in that desire and sent the gunner to Longwood. But Poppleton was ordered not to let him talk to anyone alone,[23] so the Emperor gave up the idea. However on his master's order, Bertrand wrote Redwitch a letter which, it was fondly hoped, would have an echo in Europe.

"I am sorry," the Grand Marshal wrote, "that you have not been able to come to see us and give us a few details that are always so interesting to a father. From the letters you have sent, it appears that the artist values his work at 100 pounds. The Emperor has commanded me to forward to you a check for 300 guineas. The balance will repay you for the loss he knows you have sustained in the sale of the other goods you brought and for the annoyances which this errand—simple though it was—has occasioned you, and for which any man of sense would have given you due consideration. Kindly present the Emperor's sincere thanks to those who entrusted you with this amiable errand. July 16, 1817."

So the fraud that Lowe had suspected succeeded perfectly. Perhaps one should not regret it. It gave the fallen Emperor a moment's illusion.

The Malcolms came to Longwood on June 19 to bid Napoleon farewell.[24] Malcolm's term as commander being at an end he was returning to England. He hoped indeed to come back and the Emperor hoped so too. He offered to show the Admiral the reply to Bathurst that he was preparing, but Malcolm refused.

He went to a table, took a cup and saucer from his Sèvres service and offered them to Lady Malcolm. She thanked him effusively. Laughing, he said that he would not make any present to the Admiral because the latter was not a man to listen to reason. "The ladies have

[22] O'Meara, Vol. II, pp. 108-13. The bust was to remain on the mantelpiece in the drawingroom till the end of the Captivity. Today it reposes, under a false ascription to Bosio, in the little museum that has been installed on the roof of the City Hall at Ajaccio. Mme. Letizia sent it to Ajaccio after the Emperor's death.

[23] Poppleton, *Report*, July 1, 1817 (Lowe Papers, 20-119).

[24] Lady Malcolm, *Diary*, pp. 148, 164.

a softer heart for us unfortunates. I have worn the Imperial crown
of France," he added, "and the iron crown of Italy. England is now
giving me a more glorious one—a crown of thorns. Oppression and
insult add to my fame. To England I shall owe the radiation of my
glory."

Then he thanked them for their attentions:

"You did not expect anything from me. I have no power any longer
to be of service to anyone. You came here out of generosity alone."

Before taking his leave Malcolm told the Emperor that Lord Amherst, the English ambassador in China, was to touch at St. Helena
on his return voyage and that he could be used as a negotiator between
Longwood and Plantation House.[25]

Napoleon made no reply. He murmured simply:

"You are so much of an Englishman there is no reasoning with
you; like all Englishmen, you think everything your countrymen do
must be right, and a foreigner must be wrong." [26]

He said good-bye to Lady Malcolm in his most affable manner.
The "makaw" had become a real friend to him. He could not see her
depart without real regret.

That same day Lieutenant-Colonel Fagan, who held a high judicial
post in India, was received by Napoleon. He addressed him as "Sire"
and "Your Majesty." The next day Reade reported it to Lowe.[27]

.    .    .    .    .    .    .

When Lord Amherst arrived, June 27, 1817, Napoleon hesitated
to receive him. He was suffering from a cold. The Ambassador had
gone with Lowe to Bertrand in order to ask for an audience. Napoleon was peeping at them through the shutters and suddenly cried
to Gourgaud:

"Quick, my glasses! There they are!"

A moment later he said:

"That ambassador has a mean face. Shall I receive him or not?
I think the Governor would be happy if I didn't." [28]

In that Napoleon was mistaken. Lowe counted on Lord Amherst's

[25] Lord Amherst (William Pitt, first Lord Amherst, 1772-1857) had failed in his
embassy in China where he had refused to submit to the humiliating protocol of
the Pekin Court. On the voyage home, his ship, the *Alcestes*, was wrecked off Java.
After many adventures the mission set sail for England again at Batavia on the
*Caesar*.

[26] O'Meara, Vol. II, p. 119.

[27] Lowe Papers, 20-118.

[28] Gourgaud, Vol. II, p. 170.

seeing the Emperor. He calculated that Amherst would be able to vouch for his good management to Bathurst and the Regent.

"I think, sire," said Gourgaud, "that if you did not receive him British pride would be hurt. Lord Amherst will go away from here with false information and angry at Your Majesty."

Napoleon consented but gave orders that he be presented with strict attention to forms. "The Emperor was ready half an hour in advance," relates Gourgaud.[29] "He went to the billiardroom with me, expressed his annoyance because Montholon was not in full dress, and scolded Noverraz for not having buckles on his shoes. He was extremely nervous."

"My greatest desire for twenty years has been to see you," said Amherst with a bow.

He spent an hour with Napoleon and introduced his staff. Amherst's secretary, Ellis, has drawn a striking portrait of the Emperor.

"Buonaparte's manner," he writes,[30] "was throughout dignified, affable, and pleasing, in person he was not by any means overgrown, and then appeared in good health. He expressed himself with great fluency and strength, the sentences short and epigrammatic. He walked backwards and forwards during his conversation, or rather harangue, to me. I was much struck with the expression of his upper lip: even when not actually speaking there was in it a tremulous motion approaching to convulsive, yet conveying the notion of his thoughts constantly pressing for utterance. Had Buonaparte been in the plenitude of his powers, his manner could not have been more dignified or more calculated to command respect."

The Emperor, for his part, inveighed against Lowe's ways and the useless limitations that were set to his liberty. He begged his visitor to inform the Regent. Amherst replied with evasive courtesy and so diplomatically that that evening Napoleon said to his companions in great satisfaction:

"Oh, I can assure you that the Governor got a very pretty lesson!"

He thought that the Ambassador was intending to delay his departure in order to force his mediation upon Lowe. As a matter of fact Amherst stated Napoleon's grievances to the Governor and the

[29] Vol. II, p. 177.
[30] Journal of the Proceedings of the Late Embassy to China.

latter refuted them point by point. Amherst set sail for England in
the persuasion that Buonaparte's allegations were "unfounded."

.     .     .     .     .     .     .     .     .

The 53rd Infantry was about to leave the island to be replaced
by a battalion of the 66th, which was arriving from India. Also to
disappear were a number of names that often recurred in conversations at Longwood—officers who, in two years' time, had become old
friends with the French: Major Fehrzen, Captains Younghusband
and Poppleton, Lieutenants Fitzgerald and Nagle. The officers of the
66th were not to have such close relations with Longwood. Two
names only were to be retained—the physicians, Burton and Henry.

Napoleon received the departing officers. Headed by Bingham
they formed a circle around him, and he went from one to the other,
asking each one his rank.

"I have been very pleased with the 53rd," he told them. "I shall
always be happy to hear of anything good that happens to them."

Then turning to Bingham:

"You must be sad to lose this regiment. They were your family,
your children. How long have you served with them?"

"Thirteen years."

"To console yourself you must give Milady a little Bingham." [31]

Bingham blushed. Napoleon saluted the officers and they left the
drawingroom.

Poppleton, the orderly officer at Longwood, belonged to the 53rd
regiment and was scheduled to leave with them. He asked to be
allowed to remain, but Lowe was opposed to it, though he did recommend him to the Ministry for promotion to the rank of major. [32] Poppleton had become suspicious to Lowe. His daily reports to be sure
were still strict and trustworthy, but Poppleton could not conceal a
sort of deferential pity for Napoleon. The French were not mistaken
in him. "He did his duty with all possible delicacy. He could have
tormented us, but he was as decent to us as anyone could be, without
being disloyal to his government." [33] Gourgaud insisted that Napoleon
should give him a present. Bertrand objected, seeing in it "a breach
of dignity." On the morning of Poppleton's departure the Emperor
sent him a gold snuff box, [34] and a lock of hair. Lowe appointed a

---

[31] Gourgaud, Vol. II, p. 204.
[32] He obtained it immediately on his return to England (Lowe Papers, 20-121).
[33] Gourgaud, Vol. II, p. 189.

Captain Blakeney of the 66th to replace him.[35] Blakeney was a short, thick-set man, a petticoat-chaser and a lover of the bottle. He was married and his wife shared his taste for liquor. With him the French at no time had any relations, though they lived under the same roof. They accused him of inspecting the soiled linen at Longwood to make sure that it contained no correspondence.

The exiles had by no means given up hope of a closer relationship with the Allied Commissioners. Balmain reported that impatience to Nesselrode: "He sends out his Frenchmen one after the other to attract us. Gourgaud comes to see me, follows me everywhere, and importunes me to satisfy his master. Bertrand is doing the same with Mme. von Stürmer. The other day he happened to be seated near her. He pretended to pick up her handkerchief in order not to be over-heard and whispered: 'Madame, in the name of Heaven, come and see the Emperor, I implore you. He is expecting you. He speaks of nothing else. He needs society. He sees nothing but Englishmen and that is very sad.' " [36]

After their introduction at the Deadwood races Gourgaud had met Balmain twice on the road between Longwood and Hutt's Gate. On April 25th they had a twenty minutes' talk "on one subject or another." Malcolm informed Balmain that Lowe was worried by the tête-à-tête and three days later Balmain tried to avoid Gourgaud. The General, however, caught up with him and greeted him, assur-ing him of his desire not to compromise him. Balmain, piqued, drew

[34] Poppleton cherished the snuff box all his life. "It was kept well filled, therefore, white snuff at one end, black snuff at the other," his grand-niece, Mrs. Callwell re-lates, "and underneath lay a piece of white paper, as it had come from the jeweller's hands. Many years afterward, when snuff-taking had ceased to be the fashion, and the box was only a curiosity, a gentleman to whom it was shown asked the reason of that piece of paper. 'To keep the fingers of the snuff-takers from scratching the box,' he was told. More inquisitive, however, than all who had gone before him, he prised up the bit of paper, and underneath lay another closely folded paper—a letter from Napoleon himself to the Count of Las Casas, sending messages to his adherents in France, and his wishes for the bringing up of the King of Rome. . . . It had lain where he had hidden it for nearly forty years. . . . Louis Napoleon reigned at the Tuileries. The Count of Las Casas' son, however, was alive, and to him the long-concealed letter, destined for his father, was sent" (Mrs. Callwell, *Old Irish Life*, p. 266).
[35] Henry Peter Blakeney (1782-1822) was the son of a Member of Parliament. He had seen service more particularly in Spain.
[36] Balmain to Nesselrode, July 8, 1816. It was during luncheon at Admiral Mal-colm's house.

rein. They chatted. The Russian Commissioner declared that he would be delighted if the *Conqueror* were to bring instructions that would at last permit him to call at Longwood. Gourgaud replied that the Emperor would be very pleased to see him:

"He has a very friendly feeling towards you. Come and see him at your convenience, informally. You will be giving us all a very great pleasure." [37]

Lowe, for his part, tried to keep the Commissioners away. He urged them to go and take a vacation at the Cape. It would be, he said, an absence of only three months. Sounded out on the point a number of times, Stürmer refused:

"Supposing Bonaparte should die during my absence?"

Lowe replied, half sarcastically:

"In that case the newspapers would not fail to report it." [38]

Lowe was not the only one to be impatient at the long stay of the Commissioners. In a conversation with Stürmer and Montchenu, Malcolm had said: "Your presence embarrasses us. If they should make me Governor, as is very possible, I would urge my government to appeal to your courts to recall you." [39]

The *Conqueror* brought the Commissioners authorization to call on Napoleon privately.[40] Balmain made haste to inform Lowe, for he was anxious to satisfy the Czar who was greedy for all the details he could gather about life at Longwood. "Having forewarned the Governor a month in advance, I found him ready to co-operate—more than that, he encouraged me." [41] However, when Balmain returned to the attack Lowe answered with a flat refusal, expressed in his strange and incoherent manner:

"The thing is impossible. I have thought it over carefully. I have no orders on the point. Suppose we write to our ministers again. Bonaparte treats me like a swine. He insults me, slanders me. He would tell you horrors, abominations. I cannot stand him. That man is too sly. He is still restless in his mind. He is always up to something, giving orders, working, starting new projects, as if he were at the Tuileries. His entourage is bad, terrible. They are nothing but in-

[37] Balmain, *Report*, July 20; Gourgaud, Vol. II, pp. 29, 38, 40.
[38] Stürmer to Metternich, July 4, 1817.
[39] Stürmer, *Report*, July 4, and Montchenu, July 7, 1817.
[40] June 29, 1817.
[41] Balmain to Nesselrode, July 20, 1817.

triguers. You ought to help me, defend me, espouse my interests."

Balmain was astonished. The safekeeping of the prisoner at Long-wood was in no danger. "He does not make a move that is not per-ceived, he does not say a word that is not heard. He rarely goes out of his house and never off the grounds. He writes to no one. He is surrounded by guards, cannon, trenches." [42] In the notes he sent to St. Petersburg the following January 8th on Montholon's *Remon-strance*, Balmain was to go farther: "The Governor's conduct is arbi-trary, capricious. People are subject to his whims, to any silly idea that flits through his head. Down to now he has not settled anything definitely. He has not given any order that he has not revoked the next day. No one knows what is allowed and what forbidden."

He openly criticized the methods that were used in guarding the French: "If I were given charge of guarding Bonaparte, the entire island except the seashore would be his property. I would not force him to undergo any direct surveillance by day. I would station all my sentry posts on the coasts. That would make a great improve-ment in his drives and rides, for he would not see any soldiers or anything else that might sadden or humiliate a prisoner. In the eve-ning I would set up a cordon of troops at a musket's range from Longwood and no one would pass without my knowledge. Any other safety measure in the interior of the island is vexatious and serves no purpose." [43] However the Russian yielded.

"I should have had to argue and fight a long time," he wrote, "and I thought it best to recede from my request."

Again meeting Gourgaud, who was so naïvely eager for company, he told him that the Governor had raised objections and that "he was obliged to bow to Lowe's decision."

"What?" exclaimed Gourgaud. "Not even a little how-do-you-do to Mme. Bertrand?"

"No, not as long as Longwood and Plantation House are at logger-heads. So long as Bonaparte's door is closed to Sir Hudson, not even a little how-do-you-do to Mme. Bertrand! Make peace with him. He is a good fellow. He is not badly disposed. He would like to be on better terms with you. You would be at his dinners, among his guests. People would come to see you once in a while and time would not seem so long."

[42] Balmain to Nesselrode, July 21, 1817.
[43] Thiers Library, Carton 19.

"Oh, monsieur," said Gourgaud, discouraged. "He made a false start at the beginning. The harm is beyond repair."

The other Commissioners decided to maintain the same reserve. Metternich ordered Stürmer to show more deference towards the Governor, and the only way to please him was to keep clear of Longwood.[44] Informed by Stürmer and Montchenu that they would not insist upon seeing Napoleon, Lowe "appeared in the highest degree satisfied and thanked them on several different occasions."

Montchenu found an excellent pretext. He could not apply to Bertrand (an obligatory measure for anyone who wished to be presented to Napoleon) because that General had been condemned to death in France for high treason. He was all the more eager to avoid hurting Lowe since he had fallen in love with his wife. In his handsome uniform that had never been soiled by the smoke of battle, his head plumed like a bird's, his face red from other people's wine, the former émigré was paying solicitous court to her. She was amused, and did not discourage him. The Marquis made fun for the whole colony by the utter absurdity and clownishness of his person, his costume, his airs, his fatuous vanity, his eagerness to avoid expense and enjoy the outlay of others. The army officers called him: "Monsieur Montezcheznous (Won't You Come In)," and to the inhabitants he was "Munchenough." No one had any respect for him. Stürmer wrote to Metternich, September 2, 1816: "He has scant means and a very poor education and he is absolutely lacking in tact. Naturally talkative and indiscreet he shocks the English sense of propriety and inspires no confidence whatever. All his acts are motivated by a boundless vanity. He has not made himself liked here and the ridiculous airs he gives himself every day have brought him into complete disrepute." And Balmain wrote to Lieven, April 3, 1818: "An ass, a nonentity, whom no one considers, who is good for nothing, whom the Governor himself openly disdains, of whom everyone makes fun." Montchenu was sordidly mean to Gors, his adjutant. Gors detested him, and rather disloyally reported his incompetence to the ministry.[45]

For that matter Montchenu played an unfortunate rôle as regards Lowe. Of the Governor's official advisers he was beyond any doubt the most spiteful towards the French. In September, 1817, for example,

[44] Stürmer to Metternich, July 26, 1817.
[45] Continually beset by his protests and demands for money, Richelieu raised Montchenu's salary to 60,000 francs (February 20, 1817). The Commissioner was not satisfied, kept asking for more and got nothing. Gors received no increase.

said to Sir Hudson: "I assure you that if I were Governor I would t let a single foreigner go to Longwood. Everyone who comes from ᴜᴇre is filled with the greatest enthusiasm and takes it back to Europe. That, I think, is of no great help." [46] And when Lowe was thinking of enlarging the boundaries he wrote to Richelieu: "I have formally urged upon him that his instructions and his responsibility do not permit him to grant such freedom." [47]

Admiral Plampin, Malcolm's successor, came to Longwood on September 5 and presented to Napoleon, on the Governor's behalf, an anonymous pamphlet that had appeared early in the year, under the title: *Manuscript Coming from St. Helena by Unknown Means.*[48] In it the Emperor was represented as discoursing on the principal events of his life. It was a bold concoction, made by a Genevan, Lullin de Chateauvieux.[49] Riddled with misstatements and fantastic improbabilities, it frequently misrepresented Napoleon's character, his thoughts and his career, making him out, for instance, as repudiating the Revolution. But there was a certain incisiveness about it, a heroic brevity that inspired conviction. The success of the *Manuscript* had been immense from the day of its publication, both in London and Paris. Talleyrand, Marmont, Fontanes, Molé, did not doubt that it was by their former master. The government of Louis XVIII ordered it seized, but could not prevent it from being copied and broadcast in an atmosphere of mystery that increased interest in it tenfold.

On looking through the pamphlet Napoleon could see in it only one more imposture. He vowed however that he would annotate it.[50] Any pretext was good for his restless activity. They talked of the *Manuscript* for days at Longwood, wondering who the author could be. Bertrand thought it had been written by Benjamin Constant or Mme. de Staël. Mme. de Montholon leaned towards Sieyès. Napoleon

---

[46] Montchenu to Richelieu, September 2, 1817.
[47] Montchenu to Richelieu, January 8, 1818.
[48] Published by Murray (in French), London, and April 12, 1817, at Brussels, by P. J. De Mat.
[49] Lullin de Chateauvieux was an economist and a man of letters, a friend of Mme. de Staël. He wrote the pamphlet for amusement and sent it, anonymously, to Murray. The authorship of the *Manuscript* has long been disputed, but M. Éd. Chapuisat, formerly editor of the *Journal de Genève,* has definitively cleared up the little mystery in a very kind communication addressed to the author of this book.
[50] Gourgaud, Vol. II, p. 291. He actually did so. His notes appear in Vol. XXXII of the *Correspondance.*

thought of Roederer. So the exiles tossed back and forth across the room names around which the whole history of their past floated, and the lost atmosphere of France. In spite of the long months, the pain and hardships of their lives, the hope of seeing France again still blazed in flashes in their hearts.

On the evening of September 25, Bertrand rushed to Gourgaud's house. Great news! The Catholics of Ireland had been set free! That was considered as a triumph for Napoleon's party. The Royalists had been massacred on Guadeloupe and Martinique. Everybody in France wanted Napoleon. Montholon had learned all that from Balcombe. The Governor had asked Balcombe to take the news to the Emperor the next day and then go on to dinner at Plantation House.

Gourgaud had his doubts. But ordinarily so taciturn, Bertrand was joyous and seemed to be sure.

The next day the Emperor sat in the billiardroom with his glass glued to the road along which the purveyor would have to appear.

"You know the news?" he said to Gourgaud. "There must be something very good if the Governor is sending Balcombe to us. A disaster in Guadeloupe may bring on a revolt in Paris. Perhaps Lowe has learned that Napoleon II has ascended the throne."

Gourgaud was never afraid of displeasing. He replied:

"Why choose a man like Balcombe? To show that amount of consideration Lowe would have to have changed a great deal."

Balcombe was late. Finally, well on towards two o'clock, he appeared. They could see him making his way towards Bertrand's house. He stayed a long time and the Emperor grew impatient. At three o'clock Bertrand entered. This time he was not running. Balcombe had merely brought an out-dated newspaper that mentioned unimportant disorders on Martinique.

Napoleon's face fell. He wanted to see Balcombe. When the Emperor had received and dismissed him, Gourgaud found him trembling with rage. "Bertrand told me later," writes Gourgaud,[51] "that he had never seen the Emperor so angry. Balcombe was quite distressed by it all." To restore his calm the Emperor "emptied the bottle" at dinner that night. It was one of his remedies. He seems to have resorted to it only two or three times at St. Helena.

"One doesn't joke with the people one is murdering. It is infamous to circulate such rumours." (He threw a leg over the corner of the

[51] Vol. II, pp. 327-28.

table.) "I urged Balcombe to tell Lowe that I have contracted scurvy and that my legs are swelling."

In his stubborn struggle in Corsican style with the Governor, was he resorting to a trick and trying by a threat of illness to force Lowe to come to terms? [52] He may have exaggerated certain symptoms, but Napoleon's health was already impaired by the second half of 1817, though he was not seriously ill as yet. The year before he had experienced a number of slight indispositions, due most often to the fogs and the wind. For that man of the South who had been used to a dry climate, the weather at St. Helena was detestable. During the winter months, from May to September, clothes, articles of leather, the woodwork, the most trivial objects were covered with mould. Weapons rusted in a few days. Before cards could be dealt they had to be dried in an oven for a moment. "Every evening," the Emperor said to O'Meara, "when I leave my little livingroom where there is a fire and go into my bedroom, I feel as if I were entering a cellar." [53] The great dampness had earned the Emperor a number of illnesses—colds, sore throats with fever, muscle and abdominal pains. To tell the truth, he had often suffered from just such indispositions during his years on the throne. He himself attached no importance to them. After a few days on chicken broth—his panacea, and of keeping warm in bed without dressing, he was cured.

Towards the end of March, his legs swelled. That symptom was not a new one either—he had had it before at Moscow.[54] But in September the trouble grew worse. On the 27th O'Meara brought the matter to Lowe's attention, adding that the Emperor's gums were soft and bled easily. He had lost his appetite.

Lowe went up to Longwood the next day flanked by Reade and Gorrequer. He again proposed that Dr. Baxter be called in consultation. Bertrand replied that the Emperor's health had deteriorated only because of the lack of exercise that resulted from the restrictions that had been laid upon him. The tent that had been set up in the garden had not withstood the rain and the sun. Lowe suggested putting up a wooden summerhouse in which Napoleon might take walks shel-

[52] That is the thesis of Messrs. Seaton and Norwood Young, following Forsyth.

[53] O'Meara, Vol. II, p. 220. The author lived for two months in the Emperor's house and had the same experience. On foggy or rainy days everything at Longwood is covered with a fine mist.

[54] Gourgaud, Vol. II, p. 344.

tered from the wind.[55] Bertrand replied two days later. He rejected the Governor's proposal as ludicrous and asked that the restrictions be lifted. "The whole question could be stated in two words: Are you or are you not trying to kill the Emperor? If you persist in your conduct you will yourself have answered in the affirmative, and unfortunately your aim will probably be achieved after a few months of agony." [56]

Was Napoleon trying to frighten Lowe and so obtain a change of residence, get back to Europe and—who could say?—be interned at Malta? "Within the next few days," writes Gourgaud, "the Emperor is going to ask for a consultation that may get us away from here, if the physicians are in good faith." [57] That he was ill is certain, but that he was somewhat exaggerating is also probable. A close reading of Gourgaud's diary for this period inclines one to think so. Napoleon had been ill since September 27. He had not dressed, complaining of his liver and the swelling in his legs. He ate very little. But on October 2, "he dined well," and during the days following virtually resumed his usual routine of living. By the 7th he seemed to be quite recovered. Montholon, curiously, does not mention any illness of the Emperor at this time. He contented himself with writing on October 12: "Today the Emperor had severe palpitations of the heart." And on the 13th: "He claims that he has taken cold, refuses to take his dinner and asks for a lentil soup." Not until October 15th does he write: "He complains a great deal of the swelling in his legs and of the pain in his liver." [58]

On October 1, in a bulletin addressed to the Governor, O'Meara uttered the dread word: *chronic hepatitis.* "This morning General Bonaparte complained of a dull pain in the right hypochondriac region, and a similar sensation in the right shoulder, neither of which were severe. Should the pain continue or increase there will be every reason to believe that he has experienced an attack of chronic hepatitis." [59] On October 5 comes another report, this time explicit: "A tumefaction is also evident to the sight and touch in the right side, but I have not yet been able to determine whether it proceeds from

[55] Gorrequer, *Minutes* (Lowe Papers, 20-120).
[56] September 20, 1817 (Lowe Papers, 20-120).
[57] Gourgaud, Vol. II, p. 344.
[58] Marchand makes the same observation (Thiers Library, Carton 21).
[59] October 1, 1817 (Lowe Papers, 20-120); N. Young, Vol. II, p. 64.

an enlargement of the liver or is external to it. . . . It is most probable that the complaint is chronic hepatitis." [60]

O'Meara did not dare attribute this liver complaint categorically to the climate, but he realized perfectly that such an ascription was possible. And Lowe did not have any doubt as to the physician's implication.

What then was the climate of St. Helena? As murderous as many have pretended? In interning Napoleon on that rock did the British hope to hasten his death there? To believe any such thing would be pure childishness. Neither the English, nor even Bathurst, ever had any such idea. The climate at St. Helena has not changed. St. Helena has today, as it had a hundred years ago, the climate of a ship at anchor, beaten incessantly by the sea and by the trade-wind. Not at all unhealthy now, it was no more unhealthy in 1815. It has been claimed that the climate has been improved by the foresting of the island, which was due in great part to Sir Hudson Lowe himself. However, the pines and poplars that were planted by Napoleon's jailor have almost all given way to the cultivation of a sort of flax, the fibre of which is used for rope and ship-rigging. St. Helena today is back again in the conditions the Emperor knew. The only change has come from a better water-supply system, the construction of which also goes back to Lowe. Dysentery, furthermore, seems to have disappeared. The abundance of fog may be depressing in the long run, but people live and grow old on St. Helena. There are, relatively speaking, more centenarians on St. Helena today than is usual elsewhere. The mortality rate was, to be sure, very high in Napoleon's day.[61] How explain such a contradiction? Quite simply, and it is strange that no one has noticed it sooner: through the inadequacy of public hygiene in those days. Conditions at St. Helena were deadly. Water was poor and scarce. It was brought from springs under Diana's Peak by poorly covered drains and it was polluted all the way by animals. The valley bottoms were swamps where mosquitoes multiplied and propagated all sorts of swamp diseases. Finally the blacks

[60] Lowe Papers, 20-120.

[61] The mortality statistics that the author collected in the Archives of Jamestown for the years 1815-21 allow of no discussion on the point. Among the troops stationed at St. Helena deaths reached 40 per 1,000, a much higher figure than any of the countries in the temperate zone show. The soldiers of course were fed chiefly on salt meats and drank too much alcohol. That must have impaired their physical tone and resistance.

CENTRAL RIDGES WITH DIANA'S PEAK, ST. HELENA

that were imported from Africa brought dysentery with them. Numbers of English soldiers who were housed in tents died of it, and almost all the Emperor's companions at one time or another had attacks. He himself suffered from it for a few days at the very beginning of his stay.

"The 66th Infantry has lost a quarter of its effectives." Gourgaud noted, August 16, 1817: "Depression reigns at Longwood as well as at the camp, where four soldiers have died of dysentery within seven days." There was also an epidemic of typhus at Deadwood. Balmain reported September 10, 1816, that sanitation conditions on the island were bad and that inflammatory fevers raged.

English scientists, among others, Professor Keith and Sir William Leishman, have advanced the opinion that Napoleon suffered from a sort of "Malta," or "undulant," fever, which results in an inflammation of the liver. This hypothesis deserves serious consideration. Goats are great carriers of Malta fever germs and they infested all the slopes of the island during the years of the Captivity. Malta fever had long been one of the most frequent causes of mortality at St. Helena.[62]

Whether resulting from Malta fever or not, whether due to poor nourishment and too much meat or to the dampness of the climate, liver complaints were common on St. Helena at that time. Montchenu wrote to the Duke de Richelieu in December, 1816: "Enlargement of the liver is the most common disease here. Count de Balmain has already caught it but he was taken in time." Balmain seems to have had only a slight attack. Montchenu always exaggerated the disagreeable aspects and the dangers of his position in order to increase his pecuniary compensation. That state of mind on his part has to be taken into account. But Stürmer wrote to Metternich, January 10, 1817: "No end of people among the English suffer from an obstruction of the liver and inflammatory diseases. Not a day goes by without a burial."

Napoleon was particularly susceptible to liver complaints. The yellowness of his complexion during the Campaign in France and during the Hundred Days, as well as his general puffiness after 1810, indicate that he was already suffering from functional disorders in the liver. That was the case with his mother. She was not a rich woman, but she had taken the cure at Vichy before the Revolution.

[62] J. C. Mellis, St. Helena, p. 308.

His brothers and sisters all, at one moment or another in their lives, showed liver symptoms. He lived almost continuously indoors in small overheated rooms. "The closeness and high temperature of his apartments is such that Mr. O'Meara some days ago was under the necessity of quitting them and getting speedily in the open air to avoid fainting," [63] Baxter wrote to Lowe, January 6, 1818. O'Meara had actually fainted once before. Napoleon picked him up himself and bathed him with *eau de Cologne* to revive him. His terrible baths, of two and three hours' duration in a steaming water in which others could not put their hands, his irregular and rapid meals in which vegetables played too small a part, could not fail to aggravate those tendencies. He was afflicted with a stubborn constipation and he had taken on weight. His deep-set eyes gleamed feverishly in a bloodless face. Dr. Baxter had talked with Napoleon privately several times. He wrote to Lowe on September 28: "From the first time I saw General Bonaparte, it occurred to me that in all probability dropsy would be the complaint from which he would soon suffer. I was led to draw this inference as well from the evident flabbiness of habit and apparent laxity of fibre, as from the very sedentary life he led." The swelling of the ankles, he added, marked "the incipient stage of dropsy" and indicated "debility and relaxation of the system generally." [64]

Perplexed, the Governor decided to modify his restrictions. O'Meara and Baxter both declared that if Napoleon were willing to resume his rides on horseback and his drives he would not be long in getting back his health. Lowe therefore gave him access to the new road over Woody Ridge, so going back almost to the old boundaries.

Lowe should not be given the credit for that. Bathurst had suggested it away back on February 7: "If it shall appear that his having the permission to go over the whole range of the enclosure, twelve miles in circumference, without the attendance of an officer would reconcile him to a freer use of exercise in the air, it may be advisable for you to consider whether, if the state of his health shall really render that indulgence necessary, you cannot make such arrangements as may enable you to consult his feelings in this particular. . . . But some allowance may reasonably be made for the caprice which ill-health, sorrow, and disappointment are apt to excite in minds under better discipline and of a happier disposition." One notes the con-

[63] Lowe Papers, 20-121; Young, Vol. II, p. 68.
[64] Lowe Papers, 20-156; Young, Vol. II, p. 65.

descending tone of the noble lord, but he was nevertheless suggesting an amelioration. Lowe waited six months before taking account of it. In this, as in several other respects, he was more severe than his orders obliged him to be.[65]

Lowe also made concessions as to the sentinels, who again were not to pass the boundaries of the garden till nine o'clock in the evening. As for visits, a list was to be drawn up of persons who were authorized to go to Longwood with Napoleon's consent. The orderly officer was to do his best to facilitate correspondence with the inhabitants of the island.[66] Lowe further ceased to insist on using the expression "General Buonaparte" and in his dealings with Longwood from then on adopted the form "Napoleon Buonaparte." He explained to Bertrand, October 6, 1817: "I shall, Sir, with great pleasure accede to your suggestion of not again using the name of *General Bonaparte,* and adopting that of *Napoleon Bonaparte.* I have been accustomed to use the former, under the impression it was of the two the most respectful, and consequently the least likely to create offence" (Forsyth, Vol. II, p. 211). Finally he offered to rent Miss Mason's house for the use of the Emperor during the summer season. It was situated on a smiling, well-shaded slope, in a charming landscape sheltered from the wind.

Thus Lowe gave in and on almost every point. But he did so ungraciously, and, as was his custom, with all the why's and wherefore's. His concessions angered Napoleon more than they quieted him. He commanded Bertrand to reply that if Lowe did not entirely suppress the restrictions of October, 1816, he would not step outside of Longwood again: "My health is suffering especially from the insults I have to submit to at every moment from the perverse individual who is ruling in this country." [67] He would have no halfway measures. He demanded that Lowe completely disavow his orders of the past year. Everything had to be brought back to what it had been in the days of Cockburn, notably in the matter of free communication with the inhabitants.

"The idea!" he exclaimed. "If Gourgaud wants a negress, does he have to ask the Governor for her? Ridiculous!" [68]

[65] Lowe Papers, 20-118.
[66] Lowe Papers, 20-120; Gourgaud, Vol. II, p. 350.
[67] Bertrand to Lowe, October 8, 1817.
[68] Gourgaud, Vol. II, p. 350; Montholon, Vol. II, p. 211.

As for the offer of Miss Mason's cottage, no reply was given.

During those months of October and November, 1817, an exchange of letters between Bertrand and Lowe ensued in a tone of increasing animosity. On November 23rd Napoleon wrote on the back of one of Lowe's letters a comment which Bertrand made haste to communicate to the Governor. It gives the tone of the discussion. "This letter, and those of July 26 and October 26 last, are full of lies. I have confined myself to my apartment for eighteen months in order to protect myself from the outrages of this officer. Today my health is shaken. It no longer allows me to read such disgusting writings. Do not forward any more of them to me.

"Whether this officer thinks himself authorized by verbal and secret instructions from his minister, as he has given to understand, or whether he is acting of his own accord, as might be argued from the care he takes to cover his tracks, I can treat him only as my murderer.

"If they had sent a man of honour to this country I would undoubtedly have suffered a few torments less, but the English would have spared themselves many a reproach from Europe and from History, which will never be misled by the rubbish heap of writings composed by this scheming person.—Napoleon." [69]

Meantime O'Meara was subjecting the Emperor to a rather strange treatment: hot sea-water baths, purgatives, mercury, massages. Napoleon was a poor patient. Spoiled by Corvisart, believing neither in medicine nor in physicians, he proved to be capricious, refractory, bad-tempered. When he did not recognize a remedy from the taste he would have nothing to do with it. In him always was a more or less conscious fear of poison.

He demanded that O'Meara send the Governor no further bulletins as to his condition, which had not previously been submitted to him and that in such bulletins he be referred to as "the Emperor." If O'Meara refused he would receive him no longer. He could not, he said, get accustomed to being insulted by his physician:

"I lost the throne for a point of honour. I shall lose my life a hundred times rather than degrade myself by consenting to be named according to the whim of my oppressors." [70]

Lowe found a way out: O'Meara should send him no more writ-

[69] Lowe Papers, 20-120. The text given by Forsyth (Vol. II, p. 288) is faulty in a number of respects.
[70] O'Meara, Vol. II, p. 306.

ten bulletins, but he would confer at frequent intervals with Baxter who would thus keep in touch with the patient's condition and each time draw up a report for the Governor. Lowe's responsibility would in that way be safeguarded. For he was suspicious of O'Meara and took no more stock in his medical knowledge than in his loyalty.

Since October, 1816, he had known that O'Meara was keeping officials in England informed, by way of Finlaison. Furious that a subaltern should be reporting all his acts to the minister and appraising them as he pleased, he had ordered O'Meara to put an end to that intrigue. The Irishman continued. When Lowe, enraged, complained to Bathurst, the latter was inclined to mark time, since Melville, the first Lord of the Admiralty, was communicating all of O'Meara letters to him.[71] Lowe had rebuked O'Meara on several occasions. O'Meara took it badly and twice handed in his resignation. The growing antipathy that he now felt for the Governor was driving him towards a definite alliance with the French. Had he also come to think that it would be to his better interests—for he loved money —henceforward to serve the Captive? He had refused an increase in salary from Napoleon, but late in September, 1817, he accepted a substantial amount and that probably helped him to go over to the French.

On the 26th Napoleon said: "The English can all be bought. I would have done better to buy Poppleton. He would have let me ride as I pleased. Do you believe that O'Meara is sincerely with us? He is hoping to make a fine thing out of us. He estimates his post at 3,000 pounds sterling." [72] And again on October 4: "The doctor was never so devoted to me till I began giving him money. Oh, I am very sure of him, that fellow."

So matters dragged along for several weeks. Napoleon was neither better nor worse. He was again going out into the garden and his legs were not so heavy, but he kept suffering from palpitations of the heart. O'Meara kept Baxter informed as to the variations in his condition, and Lowe reported to the Commissioners in his turn.

Lowe's suspiciousness was, however, becoming almost pathological. O'Meara having asked Darling, a furniture dealer, for a chamber-mug for Mme. Bertrand, Lowe became alarmed. "Isn't there some trick

[71] Goulburn to Lowe, January 23, 1818 (Lowe Papers, 20-21).
[72] Gourgaud, Vol. II, pp. 331, 346.

in that, some intrigue?" [73] On November 25, the Governor's mania for espionage brought on a scene between him and O'Meara. The Governor reminded the Irishman that he was to keep him informed as to the conversations he had with Napoleon. O'Meara flew into a rage, perhaps designedly, and declared that he would not play the *mouton* ("stool pigeon"). He forgot that for two years he had been doing nothing else. Lowe ordered him out of the room. On the 18th of December another storm broke. In Gorrequer's presence O'Meara confessed that he had given Napoleon his word not to reveal anything about their interviews, save in case there should be some question of a plot to escape. Lowe buried him in insults, calling him a man without honour and again ordered him from the room. If he did not ship O'Meara off to England at once it was because he did not dare on his own authority to deprive his prisoner of the only medical aid he would accept. But he sent word to Lord Bathurst, that the latter might rid him at the earliest possible moment of an unscrupulous enemy who, he knew, would be such to the death.

[73] Gourgaud, December 13, 1817. Unpublished.

# BOOK TWO
## THE DEATH OF THE EMPEROR

# PART FOUR

## TEDIUM

### I

## DAY AFTER DAY

REGARDLESS OF THE GOVERNOR'S EFFORTS TO EFFECT A RECONCILIATION, Napoleon did not yield. He refused to resume the horseback rides that might have restored his health. He could see that anxiety as to his condition was his most powerful weapon and from it sooner or later he expected the complete capitulation of Lowe and the Ministry. He did not care to deprive himself of it by showing that he was better. He took at the most a few turns about the paths in the garden. But the English soldiers, the gardeners, the orderly officer, were there watching him. He could not tolerate that surveillance. Eyes looking at him everywhere! He could not exchange a greeting with a passerby without Blakeney's making a note of it for his daily report. He retreated to his own apartment again. That was still the place where he felt least like a prisoner.

So also he now obliged his officers to hold aloof from the social life of the island. Longwood, however, did not lack for news. O'Meara, Balcombe, the orderly officer, the servants going for provisions, all brought in their quotas. Mere gossip, small town scandal-mongering, sometimes nonsense or malicious lies—it all reflected the local state of mind, and the echo of it amused Napoleon.

Admiral Plampin had raised a puritanic crusade against himself. Short, thick-set, full-blooded, looking like a fat sailor masquerading as an officer, he had put on board the *Conqueror*, on sailing from Portsmouth, a girl of twenty, with whom he was living at The Briars and whom he was trying to pass off as his wife. An unheard-of scandal, all the more since a number of officers belonging to his staff had shared the beauty's favours! The Admiral had thought of presenting her to Lady Lowe and her friends. They waxed indignant, while the Rev. Mr. Boys, an upright and merciless sectarian, ascended his pulpit in St. Paul's to denounce an impudent dotard who was setting such a sorry example for his officers, and, soaring on the wings of his holy horror, the pastor drew such a grotesque portrait of Plampin that the service ended in laughter and applause.[1] For several days at St. Helena there was talk of nothing but the love affair of the Admiral. It was said that Sir Hudson Lowe intended to pack the woman off to the Cape by the first boat and then to demand Plampin's recall. He did nothing of the kind. Decried, ostracized, kept at arm's length by all good people, Plampin would be only the more securely under the Governor's thumb. Lowe had such an advantage over him that if Plampin were ever to take it into his head to play the part that the Malcolms had played, he could ruin him in a trice.

They were taking Plampin so lightly that one evening Lady Lowe, just for the fun of it, and with the complicity of Reade and the commander of the frigate *Eurydice*, that was anchored in the harbour of Jamestown, started a mock naval battle. In the middle of the night the *Eurydice* burned bengal fires, other ships sent up flares, a gun or two fired blanks.[2] It was enough to arouse the whole island, send the sentry posts leaping to arms, bring all the inhabitants on a run to their windows, and finally to interrupt Plampin's frolickings at The Briars. A party of adventurers had come to free Bonaparte! The Admiral despatched his orderly on a breakneck ride to Jamestown, while he himself was getting into his clothes. By the time he arrived in sight of the village, Lady Lowe and her companions had disappeared, delighted to have created such an alarm and to have played a jolly trick on the old roisterer.

If, in spite of real qualities as an administrator, Lowe had made himself disliked by all St. Helena, his wife was the most popular person on the island. Lowe had many difficulties with the Rev. Mr. Boys, with Bingham, so easy to get on with as a rule, and with the East India Company, which for that matter, he was obliged to handle with gloves. He was not upheld by the Directors in 1819

---

[1] St. Paul's church, situated on a pretty site near Plantation House, was often called Country Church at the time of the Captivity. Today it is the cathedral. A cemetery planted with beautiful hemlocks surrounds it. Cipriani was to be buried there.

[2] November 10, 1818. Nichols, *Diary;* Lowe Papers, 20-120.

ST. PAUL'S CHURCH, ST. HELENA

when he dismissed the Company's farmer, Breame, from his employ because of an irregularity in his accounts. A sharp letter was to be sent to him from London, May 2, 1821, signed by all the members of the Company's Council. But everybody found Lady Lowe charming. "The real housewife," Stürner says of her.[3] "Fond of entertaining, and doing it with grace, she keeps open house at The Plantation where she welcomes army and naval officers, officials of the civil service, and all travellers of any note. She is the hub of insular society, always eager for horseback rides, excursions to Diana's Peak or Sandy Bay, picnics, parties, balls. That does not prevent her from being a good mother to her grown daughters, Charlotte and Suzanne, and to the babies that her second husband has given her."

To amuse her, Lowe had brought on from London four black ponies with a phaeton. She drove the outfit herself, in bright-coloured gowns, her neck tickled by the feathers of her big hats. Charlotte or Suzie were usually with her, while several officers or ladies from St. Helena followed on horseback all over the purpled roads of the island. She played at being a queen, made tumultuous entries into the humble street of Jamestown, and caused the inhabitants to stare openmouthed from the verandahs as she came sweeping in like a whirlwind. Everything on the island that was controlled by the Governor—and what did he not control—was at her feet. Even the Church! The harsh and redoubtable Boys crooked his spine before her, and when she had a headache, the Reverend Vernon silenced his bells.

In the end the Marquis de Montchenu overstepped the bounds in her regard. He sent her a missive that was a little too torrid. Some days later, on calling at Plantation House, he found the doors closed. The jack-in-the-box then dared to complain—and to the husband no less! Lowe found an excuse for his wife—she was giving her daughter a piano lesson when the Marquis called! Anyone else would have been satisfied. Not so Montchenu, who argued and strutted and preened himself in letters six pages long.[4] His first protest, delivered November 7, 1817, ran: "I shall never be convinced that eight or ten minutes

---

[3] Stürmer to Metternich, July 10, 1817. The Austrian Commissioner was one of the few people who did not succumb to Lady Lowe's charms. The Welle affair had created an irreparable breach between Plantation House and Rosemary Hall. Lady Lowe was of American descent, her father being a Delancey, of New York.

[4] That amazing correspondence is still to be found complete among the Lowe Papers in the British Museum. I give mere extracts above.

taken five or six times a year from Mlle. Suzanne's lessons can jeopardize her education." He goes on to complain of his solitude. "My whole desire is centred on playing a game of whist after dinner, as often as I can, in order to pass two or three hours, because I do not like to busy myself with serious matters on leaving table. My sole purpose is to kill time before it kills me." [5]

Lowe's reply was written in an amusingly English French:

"Monsieur le Marquis, I have never refused to receive your visits; therefore, so far as your argument concerns me it falls of itself. Neither have I ever given you any cause in a letter to tell me that you agree with me that 'Everyone is master in his own house.' What I said was: 'Every lady is mistress in her own house.' I was careful to make a distinction between my public position and my wife's. A lady can refuse to receive callers in the forenoon, at least in our country, without offence to them. Generally all that is necessary is to say that she is not at home and one never enquires beyond that. . . . You speak of a visit of eight or ten minutes. But when Lady Lowe receives, she is too polite to leave her guest before that person has taken his or her leave. . . .

"The first two notes of which you speak made no impression on me. The other was neither in the tone nor in the language customary in our country. However I have never known Lady Lowe to refuse the Marquis de Montchenu's attentions nor to be lacking in the consideration due him. . . .

"We shall understand each other better after these little explanations and our society will not have lost by them." [6]

The Marquis' discomfiture was confided to the discretion of the four winds and delighted the St. Helenans to whom he had boasted of "having known four thousand English ladies, the majority of whom had crowned his prayers." He was less fortunate in Jamestown. Trying to make up to his landlady, Mrs. Martin, a woman more than fifty years old, he was treated to a sound slap.[7] When O'Meara recounted the episode at Longwood the Emperor laughed uproariously.

But gossip in that small and secluded community was not confined to the Admiral and the Lowes. Count Balmain, it was said, had

[5] Lowe Papers, 20-203.
[6] Lowe Papers, 20-120.
[7] He had ended by leaving the Porteous House to take lodgings with Gors, across the way, at the Widow Martin's. She had given up three furnished rooms to him

asked for the hand of Miss Brooke in marriage and been refused—
Miss Brooke was a daughter of the secretary of the Council for the
East India Company. Mrs. Younghusband, the most vicious tongue
on the island, lost a defamation suit that Mrs. Nagle brought and
paid damages in the amount of 300 pounds. M. de Montholon had
kissed the hand of a sailor's wife, and the sailor, little experienced in
Continental usages, had taken offence. The commander of a ship not
belonging to the Company had staved in his casks of fresh water in
order to get permission to take on a new supply at St. Helena, where
he hoped to catch a glimpse of Napoleon. Learning of it, the Governor redoubled his precautions.

At just that moment the island was suffering from a veritable
famine. Farmers and merchants were profiting by it, but the English
officers and the three Commissioners could only complain. Montchenu
wrote to Richelieu on November 30: "The food shortage is very
serious. The Governor himself has gone two weeks without fresh
beef and in the hospitals they are making bouillon of salted meat.
For two months there has not been a pound of butter available at any
price whatever. Mutton is so scarce that we are paying 3 shillings a
pound for it." At times even necessaries were lacking at Longwood,
such as fuel for the stoves and fireplaces. The amounts allowed were
300 pounds of wood and ten sacks of coal, per day. Only five sacks
of coal were required at Plantation House. The French disliked the
damp air and had to have many more fires. Napoleon could not endure the odour of burning coal,[8] and wood was scarce on the island.
He took advantage of that situation to play a little trick on Lowe.
Says Gourgaud: [9] "The Emperor ordered Noverraz to break up a
wooden bedstead in public in order to show that the French did not
have enough wood to keep warm. The incident is causing great talk on
the island. The Governor's tyranny is pretty well done for."

There was a shortage of fruits. Blakeney was obliged to signal the
fact to Gorrequer in order to obtain an additional supply. On January
23, 1818, in midsummer, the orderly officer wrote to Gorrequer:
"General Bonaparte having taken the fancy of eating more fruit than
formerly, do you think that another supply could be allowed for this
season, the existing quantity not being sufficient for the whole

[8] Lowe Papers, 20-119.
[9] Vol. II, p. 299.

family?" [10] All that was shabby enough, and Lowe and his assistants were in those respects failing in due attentiveness.

. . . . . . . . .

Isolated by Napeoleon's will as well as by the difficulties laid in their way by the Governor, the Emperor's companions dragged on their weary lives.

Like animals bellowing in the hold of a vessel where they had been stowed, the three generals and their two wives clawed and snarled at each other. As they gazed towards Europe everything there seemed sweet, easy, delightful, and they envied Las Cases. All of them were counting the days that separated them from the time when they would be able to leave Napoleon. Montholon said to Gourgaud one day (September 19, 1817), that he "hadn't come to St. Helena to do what they were doing there. He would certainly like to have a chance to get away, but as he had got himself mixed up with the party that—God knows why!—shouted 'Long live the Emperor!', he would have to wait. He ought really to have followed the advice of the Duke of Vicenza who had tried to dissuade him from coming. 'Oh, you don't know His Majesty! You will soon be sorry you followed him. Meantime, be sure not to sell anything. His Majesty will never give you a penny.' His wife was in a perpetual fury, utterly despondent and sick." [11]

Is one to say that they did not understand the nobility of the rôle they might have been playing in the service of the greatest unfortunate in history had they but had some loftiness of spirit? Undoubtedly! But can one be resigned all the time, day in and day out? And for how many years? Who could say how long the exile might last? And they were in no way prepared for it. They had never been heroes—they did not pretend to be. They were just poor people who were waiting for a miracle to free them and meantime were shuddering at the thought of growing old on that rock, far from their families, unable to educate their children, cut off from life and the future.

Only at rare intervals now was there any relaxation in their mutual hostility. They spied on each other, eyed each other up and down, spoke only to complain of their fate or to accuse their

[10] English reports frequently refer to Napoleon's companions as "the family" (Lowe Papers, 20-121).
[11] Thiers Library. Unpublished.

neighbour. Their animosities had not escaped the English or the Commissioners. "All those Frenchmen," wrote Balmain as early as September 8, 1816, "hate each other cordially. Each of them wants to be the master's favourite and aspires to personal control of the important affairs of Longwood." Rages, threats over an attention from the Emperor, quarrels as to children, servants, gowns! The two women met, outside the Emperor's presence, only as a matter of form. They paid formal calls on each other in that desert! Mme. Bertrand, for instance, told Gourgaud that "the Montholon woman came to see her. As she started to leave after five minutes or so, Mme. Bertrand said to her: 'Oh! Of course! You have to have a pretext for coming to see me!' Thereupon Mme. de Montholon, who had not been there for a fortnight, sat down again and stayed an hour." [12]

Their relations were all in that tone. They called each other "Monsieur," and "Madame." They addressed Bertrand as "Monsieur the Grand Marshal" and he insisted that the service call him "Monseigneur."

The Montholons were taking everything for themselves—furniture, jewels, cash, allowances. They were steering the generosity of the master in the direction of their own profit. The Bertrands waxed wroth at that. Says Gourgaud: [13] "Mme. Bertrand told me that His Majesty often went secretly to call on the Montholons and that he gave them a great deal of money—more than fifty thousand francs a year." Mme. Bertrand accused Mme. de Montholon of being an arrant flirt. She claimed that Montholon was unhappy because of his wife's neglect of their children. If Gourgaud seemed to be more friendly with the Montholons for a day or two, Mme. Bertrand would accuse him of "courting Albine." Let him continue and she would not speak to him again! [14]

Had Napoleon now slipped into intimate relations with Mme. de Montholon? It is not impossible, nor is it at all probable, either. Gourgaud preferred to think so—his hatred for the Montholons was so cordial. That Napoleon should have received Mme. de Montholon while in his bath is in fact strange. "Mme. de Montholon," writes Gourgaud, November 5, 1817, "went in full court dress to call on His Majesty. He was in the bath. Montholon came out and I said to him:

[12] Gourgaud, April 26, 1817. Unpublished.
[13] January 21, 1818. Unpublished.
[14] Gourgaud, June 15, 1817. Unpublished.

'That's fine! They put you out when Madame goes in.' I stood out-side the door chatting with him for nearly an hour. Then His Majesty asked for Montholon. 'Yes—the candles!' I almost said." [15]

However the Emperor comported himself towards her as he did towards Montholon, Bertrand or Gourgaud, quite disregarding her sex. He said to her as she was beginning a new pregnancy:

"Are you trying to be like Mme. Tallien—always with a peaked belly?"

Mme. de Montholon was shocked and offended and did not answer. [16]

However lacking in chivalry the Emperor may often have shown himself, it is hardly probable that he would have made just that sally had he been Mme. de Montholon's lover, and perhaps respon-sible for her condition.

When the child came—little Josephine, born on January 26th, with a lock of hair (a sign of good luck that was not to come true) [17]— Mme. Bertrand urged Gourgaud to go and have a look at her:

"She resembles neither Montholon nor Mme. de Montholon. She has a broad, heavy chin."

"Does she look like His Majesty?" Gourgaud asked.

Mme. Bertrand replied with another question:

"Did you see how worried His Majesty was while the Montholon woman was in labour?" [18]

In short, they guessed, they suspected, they sniffed the air, they hinted—they were not sure of anything.

Gourgaud noted for December 15, 1819: "I go and call on Mme. Bertrand. She asks me whether I think that His Majesty has been intimate with Mme. de Montholon. She tells me that really she thinks that Esther—how does His Majesty manage? The nights are long! . . ."

For anyone who has visited Longwood and seen the close quarters to which the French were reduced, such uncertainty on the part of Mme. de Montholon's two bitterest enemies speaks for itself. The French witnesses of the Captivity, Las Cases, Marchand, Aly, leave nothing to suspicion, nor do the English—Lady Malcolm, Mrs. Abell,

15 Unpublished. ["To hold the candles" is an expression used of consenting cuckolds.]
16 Gourgaud, October 15, 1817. Unpublished.
17 Josephine died in Brussels in 1820.
18 Gourgaud, February 6, 1818. Unpublished.

Warden, Henry, Verling. Dr. Verling merely says [19] that "Mme. Bertrand had told him" that the little Napoléone "might very well be the Emperor's daughter." We have seen that the facts prove the contrary. Verling himself adds that Mme. Bertrand seemed to him "half hysterical" at the time. Lowe's papers, so rich in tattle and gossip, are mute. As for the Commissioners, Balmain was anxious enough to keep his Czar amused with spicy stories, but he maintains a complete silence. Stürmer, however, was to write to Metternich, March 31, 1818: "He [Napoleon] is now surrendering unreservedly to the fancy he seems suddenly to have conceived for Mme. de Montholon, and which Gourgaud has taken it upon himself to thwart and turn to ridicule. After flattering the caprices of the ex-Emperor for some time by fulfilling the noble functions of a procuress for him, Mme. de Montholon has at last managed to triumph over her rivals and exalt herself to the Imperial bed." Procuress! Really it is difficult to imagine to just what Stürmer may have been alluding. To the attentions which, according to Gourgaud, Mme. de Montholon showed Miss Knipe (Rosebud), who looked a little like Mme. Walewska, and whom the Emperor cordially welcomed at Longwood? "Mme. de Montholon," writes Gourgaud, January 7, 1818, "thinks that Rosebud is going to become His Majesty's mistress and is playing up to her in great style." But Miss Knipe came to Longwood but once—July 21, and then in her mother's company. She exchanged only a few words with the Emperor and that was in the garden. In 1820 she was to marry a man named Hamilton and leave the island. Rosebud being out of the question, was the Commissioner referring to Esther? She was Marchand's mistress and had a son by him. Gossip in the kitchen, it is true, attributed the paternity of Esther's child to the Emperor, but on wholly fantastic grounds. It really seems that Stürmer must have dashed off his caustic remarks (which Montchenu was to copy) in a wholly irresponsible spirit.

Montchenu questioned Gourgaud, on the eve of the latter's departure, about private life at Longwood. To the question: "How did Mme. de Montholon succeed in winning him?" Gourgaud replied: "By playing the blue stocking. She knows French history fairly well and keeps forever repeating to the Emperor that eighty Parisians a day ought to be guillotined to punish them for having betrayed him,

[19] *Diary*, October 3, 1818. Retranslated.

that France deserves to be twenty times more unhappy than she is, and so on. He likes to listen to talk like that." [20]

Gourgaud could not have been more full of rancour against Longwood. Had he had more spicy information to retail, he would have done so. And if Montchenu had caught wind of anything worth telling, he would not have failed to regale his Court with it. On that tiny island of the hundred echoes where the slightest gossip was the object of detailed reports to Plantation House, any intrigue on Napoleon's part could not have remained secret. It would have left its traces somewhere in the enormous mass of documents that the Captivity has bequeathed to us.

Quite to the contrary, at St. Helena and notably among the army officers at the camp, who were well placed to know what was going on at the nearby Longwood, Napoleon had an established reputation for continence. Dr. Henry, the surgeon of the 66th, lived at St. Helena from July 5, 1817, until after Napoleon's death, and he attended the autopsy. He wrote the following significant lines, *as an addendum* to the notes he sent, September 12, 1823, to Sir Hudson Lowe, for use as testimony in the suit which the former Governor had brought against O'Meara: "The whole genital system of the deceased seemed to show a physical basis for the absence of sexual desire and the continence which *are known* to have been characteristic of him." [21]

In such matters it is a delicate question to deny or affirm. Our opinion is that Napoleon certainly did not have any relations with Mme. de Montholon during the first two years of the Captivity. That he "formed a habit" with her later on, as Frédéric Masson asserts, is, we believe, very doubtful.

.     .     .     .     .     .     .

An immense, a subtly penetrating tedium engulfed Longwood from the firing of the cannon at sunrise to the gun that at sunset brought the sentries in close about the garden. Gourgaud's *Journal* is admirable for the veracity of its picturing of common everyday truths. It repeats on almost every page: "Boredom, sadness, bad humour. His Majesty is gloomy. Suffocating dullness; melancholy." Here is one week among countless others: "Tuesday, 25. Dull, dull! Wednesday, 26, *Idem*. Thursday, 27, *Idem*." For that matter the

---

[20] Montchenu to Richelieu, March 18, 1818.
[21] Lowe Papers, 20-214. Retranslated.

foreign Commissioners had nothing whatever to do and found things almost as dreary. Stürmer confided to Lowe naïvely: "I certainly wish Bonaparte would die. That would make my happiness, for then my mission at St. Helena would be over." To which Lowe replied that he, for his part, would be very sorry to have General Bonaparte die while he was in charge.[22]

It was the dulness of uniform hours, of a petty environment, of limited interests, of an unstable climate, of a wind that never went down, of faces that were always the same, of no news or bad news, of necessaries that were lacking or else worn out, of living in a foreign country under perpetual suspicion, of never feeling sure of others even among the French, of tasks set by the Emperor, of meals where one could neither eat nor talk at one's ease, of everlasting chess games where His Majesty had to win regardless of his poor play, of evenings of four to which the absence of the Bertrands almost always reduced them. Vainly did Mme. de Montholon keep at the piano in an effort to liven things up. Napoleon would shuffle the cards mechanically or say a few words to Montholon, whom Gourgaud, surveying him with fixed eyes, would have liked to kill.

"Does your little girl still cry?" Napoleon would ask the Countess.

And Mme. de Montholon would affect a winsome smile, "talking of her child like a good mother, though she took no care of it at all." [23]

"And you, Monsieur Gourgaud—you had a walk?"

"No, sire."

"Why not?"

"Because the road as far as Alarm House bores me, and because one is constantly watched by Mr. Harrison and three sergeants."

Napoleon would sigh and pick up the first book at hand—a Molière, open to the École des femmes, quote several risqué words that Mme. de Montholon might find them shocking.

Whereupon Gourgaud would remark that "as one's morals grow corrupt, one becomes more particular as to words."

The thrust would find its mark. The Countess, playing the prude, was always declaring "that Molière was of the worst tone."

[22] Lowe Papers, 20-145. Unpublished.
[23] Gourgaud, Vol. I, p. 420.

Everyone would begin to nod. At last the little clock would strike. Ten o'clock! The Emperor would rise:

"Let us go to bed."

Another evening gone! One more miserable victory over Time—until the next day, for it was only ten o'clock!

. . . . . . .

For those few Frenchmen who made up his last court and adorned his misfortune, Napoleon was the sole pivot—he was at once their reason for being and their torture. His temper had become more unstable. He was quick-tempered and irritable, and he had been trained by fifteen years of supremacy not to consider his words. He made remarks which, if one were to take them literally, would have made him out a monster of selfishness and insensitiveness. Napoleon's rages, which gossip exaggerated, gave him the reputation on the island of being a despot. Balmain wrote, September 8, 1816: "He lets coarse language fly at every moment and treats the French like slaves." Were it the custom of staff-headquarters, or a need of Imperial rule—in exile at any rate, it could seem only an abuse of good nature—he would waken his valet if he could not sleep at night and send for Montholon or Gourgaud. "The Emperor," writes Gourgaud,[24] "sent for me at four o'clock—Montholon being worn ragged—and dictated to me his reply to Bathurst, to the restrictions, and so on. He worked and chatted with me until eight o'clock." Half asleep, unwashed, uncombed, hastily dressed, the young man would come running, his teeth chattering from the cold. Lying in bed, or, if he had put on his dressing gown, making his squatty shadow move back and forth in the light of the covered candles, the Emperor would dictate notes that would serve, or not serve, for a new protest against the English ministry or against Lowe, for a pamphlet destined for Europe, for a tenth, but not final, version of his "Battle of Waterloo." Montholon would write for hours at a time, dying of sleep, his mind wandering, not understanding a word.

In the end Napoleon would look at the poor fellow whose eyes were falling shut:

"That's enough, Montholon. You are asleep on your feet. Have them send for Gourgaud."

Of course he might have waited for daylight when days were so hard to kill. However, Marchand assures us that he seldom disturbed

24 Vol. II, p. 133.

the two generals during the night after 1817. "He sometimes said to them in the morning: 'I did a lot of work last night—and what did you do, Mr. Lazybones?' " [25] But every thought of his had to be satisfied and without delay. Let an idea come into his mind and he would see nothing but policy, his fame, the future of his dynasty.

He looked inhuman, but alas, only because he was a man—that great man—and the most fickle of all men, and the most complex, the most instinctive, and for that reason the most difficult to place! From his boyhood he had held men in contempt, and the events of 1814 and 1815 had not served to change his opinion. Cruel words escaped him readily—Montholon was nothing but a "jackanape," Bertrand "an idiot," a "bumpkin from the backwoods of Berry." [26]

Montholon would vanish at such times. The Grand Marshal never dared reply. His lack of character as well as his reverence for the Emperor had reduced him to nothing but a silhouette in a worn uniform, high unpolished boots, a big military hat with ragged plumes.

The Emperor would say to Mme. Bertrand:

"Your hair is a fright. And that gown—it came from China? It is not pretty." Or again: "In an evening gown she looks like a peasant dressed up for Sunday." [27] Or again, to the two ladies, that they "looked like washerwomen."

He had been no different at the Tuileries. But at St. Helena the two Frenchwomen could find few resources for freshening their wardrobes, and such brutalities were cruel. They grew discouraged and often now were not dressing for dinner at all. [28]

Mme. Bertrand, for her part, was seeing the Emperor at very rare intervals. Napoleon said to Gourgaud, in speaking of Bertrand: "It's his wife, the ugly creole! She torments him. Do you think she would have married him if she hadn't been so wretchedly poor? She is so stupid that she does not come to see me, and yet I might give her a diamond necklace. Don't tell her that! At least let her do what she wants." [29] Mme. Bertrand would sometimes let weeks go by without calling on the Emperor. She said to Montchenu, who inserted the conversation in his despatch of January 8, 1818: "To see him I have

[25] Thiers Library. Unpublished.
[26] Gourgaud, November 24, 1817. Unpublished. Bertrand was born at Chateauroux in the province of Berry (Orléans).
[27] Gourgaud, Vol. II, pp. 407-15.
[28] Gourgaud, Vol. II, pp. 88, 203. Unpublished.
[29] Gourgaud, June 11, 1817. Unpublished.

only to cross the courtyard, yet I never do. I have dined there only once in the past three months. For some time he has been dining alone and does not see anyone."

Gourgaud was sharing her disgrace. Napoleon kept him short of money for his evenings out and inflicted punitive tasks on him. Really he was ridiculing him. An open dislike? Not yet! But the Emperor thought that if that sensitive and imaginative young man were not held firmly in hand, he would grow impertinent, upset the household and compromise the policy that the Emperor had imposed on himself towards the English.

However, as may have been noted, Napoleon enjoyed setting his officers one against the other without considering sensibilities, and systematically, it would seem, as he had done in the days of his power, believing that in that way he would be more the master, that he would know everything that was going on and that intrigues would be more difficult to manage. For one example among a hundred, he told Bertrand that Gourgaud considered him incapable of building a redoubt and accused him of having started the bridge at Vienna.[30] Casual about confidences and malicious, he assured Gourgaud that, according to reports at Longwood, little Arthur was the son of Captain Hamilton. And "His Majesty told me further that I ought to present Bertrand with a pair of horns."[31]

And yet, at other moments, Napoleon showed the persons about him delicate attentions and a considerateness which, coming from such a man, a man fallen from such a pinnacle and still tossed by the storm, could not fail to have something touching about them. He boasted of Bertrand and said of him, in the hope that his words would be repeated: "He is the best engineer in Europe," and he praised his devotion and his loyalty. He exchanged watches with the Grand Marshal with the remark: "Look, Bertrand! It was striking two, that morning at Rivoli, when I ordered Joubert to attack!"[32] He addressed unexpected compliments to the Countess. "The Emperor," writes Gourgaud,[33] "embraced Mme. Bertrand, who was very well dressed, showered her with countless endearments and insisted that she play a game of chess, though she did not know the moves.

[30] Gourgaud, November 7, 1817. Unpublished.
[31] Gourgaud, October 11, 1817. Unpublished.
[32] Marchand, *Précis des Guerres de César*, p. 19; Aly, p. 161.
[33] Vol. II, p. 388.

The Montholon woman nearly died of jealousy. We went in to dinner. His Majesty had eyes for no one but Mme. Bertrand and said: 'Now there! There's a head and pair of shoulders for a dinner-party, or a drawingroom!' Mme. de Montholon turned very red."

He smiled at Mme. de Montholon and applauded her husband's eagerness for work. And Gourgaud, whom he was always jostling— let Gourgaud fall ill and he thought of ways of amusing him. Let a play be given at the amateur theatre at Jamestown and he would send him to attend it:

"Go and see it! We have to find some amusement for you! You are as sad as a nightcap! The tragedy they are giving today is superb. It hurts me to see you so depressed." [34]

Gourgaud was worrying about his mother, whom he had left almost without resources. The Emperor had him write to Prince Eugene ordering him to pay Mme. Gourgaud an income of 12,000 francs, beginning January 1, 1817. Gourgaud was not to be grateful to the Emperor for that liberality because, on the back of the note ordering Eugene to pay the pension, the Emperor had him write a few lines asking Eugene to open a credit account of 500 pounds sterling per month with Andrews, Street and Parker, in London, on which Bertrand could draw regularly from St. Helena in order to meet additional expenses (wages, stables, clothing, etc.). Gourgaud was afraid that his mother might be compromised if the note were intercepted.

The Emperor flattered the young man, called him, "Gorgo, Gorgotto, my boy." And he lectured him:

"You have an excellent heart, resources, talents. But you are too fond of arguing—you are always trying to contradict me. When I put forward an idea, there you are quick as a flash using your logic— you really have some, you know—and your skill at looking at a question from an opposite point of view. You caused me no end of trouble in the day of Las Cases. You were jealous of everything. Do you think I care a snap for nobility? You are mistaken. I am no more noble than you are. Nor Bertrand either! Montholon has forgotten his nobility—his wife is the daughter of a banker. I have never asked you to go away, but if you cannot adapt yourself to St. Helena, it would be better if you went. Now I do not want to get angry—I

[34] Gourgaud, Vol. II, p. 285.

am speaking to you as a friend. If you do not control your imagination you will go mad."

Gourgaud was not to go mad, but his nerves became too strained under these extremes of treatment. His homesickness was going to increase, and soon he was to find himself unable to hold out.

They were not happy, that handful of French people shut in at Longwood. Napoleon was well aware of that. But they were inclined to forget that the most unhappy of all was Napoleon. A man who had moulded a universe in his hands was now confined to a wretched hovel, at the mercy of English chicanery and of petty bickerings among his companions! He felt attacked, he felt wounded, at almost every hour.

"Do you think," he said to Gourgaud, who was complaining, "that when I wake up at night and remember what I was and where I am now, I do not have my bad moments?" [35] And he said to him on another occasion (October 2, 1817): "You are dissatisfied with yourself—you! And what about me? How many humiliations I have had! How many things I have to blame myself for! You have nothing to blame yourself for." At times a great sigh would escape him: "How the time drags! What a cross! It takes famous courage to stay alive in a place like this!" [36]

Picking up the *Imperial Almanach* to verify a date, he became distracted and began to skim through its pages. France, stretching from the Tiber to the Elbe—one hundred and thirty departments, Paris and Rome for capitals! A tidal-wave of memories engulfed him.

"It was a pretty empire!" he said in a husky voice. "I had eighty-three millions of human beings to govern—more than half the population of Europe!"

One day he went up to Marchand's room. There his valet kept his coats and linen in a mahogany wardrobe. He wanted to see them, and had everything brought out and unwrapped. What? So many things still? The coat of the First Consul, the blue cloak of Marengo, a grey frock, a green one, scarves, laces! [37] His hand fell upon them. Pensive, without a word, he turned away.

Fallen among dwarfs, the giant tried at moments to stoop to their

[35] Gourgaud, Vol. I, p. 430.
[36] Gourgaud, Vol. II, pp. 340, 410, 450.
[37] E. d'Hauterive, "*Les objets de l'Empereur à Sainte-Hélène*," *Revue des Études napoléoniennes*, February, 1933.

stature, and succeeded. We see him asking to have a second helping at table, watching the road over which the Commissioners are riding, eavesdropping on the gossip in the kitchen, jesting with O'Meara, and then saying to Montholon:

"After all, we aren't as badly off as that!"

And then suddenly a word, a thought, would recall his grandeur. And his companions with a sort of chill in their bones would see Napoleon come to life again in that flabby, jaundiced man who tied a madras handkerchief about his head or wore a broad-brimmed farmer's hat.

He was keeping more than ever to his little suite of rooms. There at least he could lay down his burden. There he found silence, was alone. Born on an island, cast up on a continent to conquer it, he had doubtless been marked by destiny to live apart from men and above them. He had always been alone—among his ministers, his courtiers, his women. Today his solitude was simply more perfect. Exile had made an abyss of it, into which he could plunge without finding shore or shelter. If he indeed felt the weight of his misfortune, he was too imaginative not to understand the profit his historic figure would derive from it, and the principles he represented.

"Misfortunes," he repeated, "also have their heroism and their glory. Adversity was all that was lacking to my career. Had I died on the throne among the clouds of my omnipotence I would have remained a problem for many people. Today they will be able to judge me in my nakedness."

For that matter, after two years of confinement, though he sometimes gave way to black depression, he was still convinced that a near future would soften his fate.

"On the death of Louis XVIII great things can happen! Or suppose Lord Holland comes into power! They might transfer me to England! But what is most to be hoped for is the death of the Prince Regent. That will put the little Princess Charlotte on the throne. She will call me back!" [38]

Unfortunately, early in February, 1818, news of Charlotte's death arrived in St. Helena. Napoleon was stunned.

"Well," he said to Gourgaud, "there we have one more unexpected blow. So does Fortune frustrate!"

[38] Gourgaud, Vol. II, p. 153.

Fearing that his companions might all leave him if his exile were too long protracted, he could see no surer means of retaining them than to appeal to their interests. He made promises to all of them and they were to be valid whether he were to see Europe again or end his days on St. Helena. "His Majesty," writes Gourgaud, "assures us that if he dies, he will divide what he has between us five—the two Montholons, the two Bertrands and me." [39]

Talking with Gourgaud he argued:

"What would you do in France? By staying here you make yourself famous. And besides I shall not live long and I can make your fortune. I shall leave you four or five hundred thousand francs. With that amount you will be perfectly received anywhere."

Promises also to the Grand Marshal, both for himself and for his children! Promises further to the Montholons and, on divers occasions, substantial gifts! [40]

Like an old uncle dangling his will about, the Emperor was going to insure the futures of them all! Now just what was the most probable outcome? His intimates often discussed the question coldbloodedly among themselves, and they could not make up their minds. Napoleon kept telling them that he had only a year to live. They looked at each other. No one believed that, nor did he himself. It was just a good thing to say to the English!

"Your Majesty will bury us all!" the Grand Marshal replied.

Left alone with Gourgaud, Napoleon sighed:

"Who knows? We may live fifteen or twenty years more, perhaps."

Gourgaud was angry at him that evening. He let the despondent words rebound off the walls and made no answer. [41]

· · · · · · · · ·

If Napoleon can be criticized for harshness, not to say calculation, towards his comrades, at least he showed a great good humour and a real kindness towards the small fry—the children and the servants, and probably because he had no need to remind such people of his rank, to hold off their familiarity, or calculate attitudes and words in view of a future.

[39] Gourgaud, March 20, 1817. Unpublished. He had already said the same thing on January 20th. He was to repeat it on June 19th.
[40] July 28, 1818, Napoleon was to give them 3,000 pounds sterling in one lump.
[41] Gourgaud, Vol. II, pp. 450-51.

Children he had always loved. Even before he had a son, he caressed his nephews, teased them, laughed at their rages and their gaieties. With the birth of the King of Rome that instinct sent out deep roots in him. Undoubtedly he could not see two innocent eyes or a little round face, or feel a light and quivering body press against his knees, without a tender memory coming into his mind. At Longwood the children were growing up in carelessness and disorder, reared mostly by servants. Mme. Bertrand was spoiling hers beyond repair. Her husband gave them a few lessons, but most often they ran free, living out of doors. Mme. Bertrand was grieving one day over her children's lack of schooling. Gourgaud offered "to give lessons" to the largest. "I would gladly give them one or two hours," he noted.[42] Just why the offer came to nothing is not clear. Little Tristan de Montholon was just one more vagabond among them. Those four children (Napoléone Montholon and Arthur Bertrand were still babes in arms) were the only gleams of brightness, the only gaiety, at Longwood.

The Emperor had Pierron make them cakes and sweets. He invited Hortense and Tristan to drive with him and would have the horses gallop about the park, with the young Napoleon clinging on at the carriage door. When Hortense wanted to learn to ride, Mme. Noverraz cut a riding-habit for her. On August 17, 1818, the Emperor gave Hortense a necklace of imitation pearls and two dresses that were bought in Jamestown.[43] He explained the fable of the Wolf and the Lamb to Tristan, who got mixed up in retelling the story to him. The child confessed to him that he had studied as little as possible, whereupon the Emperor urged strenuous application:

"Don't you eat every day?"

"Yes, sire."

"Well, you must work every day! One must not eat if one does not work."

"In that case I shall work every day."

"There you have the influence of that little belly," said Napoleon, tapping Tristan on that part of his body. "It's hunger—it's the little belly—that makes the world go round. Come—if you are good, we shall make you a page of Louis XVIII!"

[42] November 10, 1817. Unpublished.
[43] Verling, *Diary*.

"But I don't want that!" cried Tristan, for whom Louis XVIII was a fabulous and a wicked monster.[44]

With his servants Napoleon was kindness itself. He reprimanded them and shook them, but took an interest in them, in their needs and their families, closing his eyes to their pilferings or their escapades. "His bad humour was never of long duration," writes Aly. "If he happened to be in the wrong, it was not long before he would come to give a tweak of the ear or a slap on the back to the person on whom his wrath had fallen. Then, after a few words relating to the subject of the outbreak, he would lavish such agreeable epithets as 'my son,' 'my boy,' 'my child.' "

The Emperor lived much with his servants, much more in fact than with his officers. Marchand and Aly were constantly coming and going about his rooms. They dressed him, served him his meals, wrote at his dictation, read him the newspapers, kept his papers in order. They were not only valets, but secretaries and confidants, and infinitely devoted ones. Marchand especially offered the Emperor a touching veneration. He surrounded him with attentions, smiling, submissive, never talking about what he saw or heard, never weary or out of sorts. Napoleon saw Cipriani almost as often, talking with him in Corsican dialect. Cipriani went to town every day to make the necessary purchases. He learned all he could and reported it without colouring to the Emperor. But he also spied on the French.

The lumbering household, laxly managed by Montholon, ran more or less well, more or less badly. There were the same rivalries, the same jealousies, between the servants as between the masters; and mutual hatreds were as cordial in the kitchen as in the drawingroom. Archambault thought he was not paid enough and regretted not having gone away with his brother.[45] He drank heavily and was guilty on occasion of serious misdemeanours. For example, at the September fair of 1818, he was to be seen wearing his livery and riding one of the Emperor's horses, scraping acquaintances among the English officers in order to take part in the races. He was hooted at and finally chased off the grounds with their whips. Napoleon put Archambault under arrest for a month. The cook, Lepage, and his

[44] Las Cases, Vol. VI, p. 257.
[45] Gourgaud, Vol. II, pp. 42-99.

wife, Jeannette, kept complaining and asked to be released. Jeannette was a Belgian and her real name was Catherine Sablon. She arrived, June 13, 1816, to assist Lepage, who had hurt his thumb. The latter declared his intention of marrying her at once. O'Meara wrote:

"Cipriani, to whom he expressed himself, told him that it would be necessary first to ascertain that she had not *already* a *husband*, or perhaps, if not, a lover. 'Oh, that *last* is nothing,' said Lepage; 'I don't care how many she may have had of *them*.' Then, running, with his arm in a sling, towards her, said he, 'Madam, are you married?' 'No, Sir.' 'Then, if you please, I will marry you immediately.' She told him, however, that she could not think of it so very soon: 'at least,' said she, 'let us wait *two* or *three* days first'; which he consented to with great apparent reluctance." [46]

The Lepages were dismissed by Napoleon, May 28, 1818, when he learned that, the evening before, they had both gone to Plantation House to ask to be sent back to Europe and had accommodatingly replied to Lowe's questions as to the state of his health. The questioning took place in the presence of Gorrequer, who as usual immediately drew up a report on it.[47] Lepage seems to have had too ready connections with Plantation House. After his dismissal he was again questioned by the Governor. His testimony is interesting: "Marchand came to see me and asked me what I had been doing at Plantation House and whether I had been asked for news of Longwood. I told him that Major Gorrequer had asked me how the Emperor was and that I had told him that he was *very well*. At that Marchand began to laugh and said: 'You should not have said that. The Emperor is very angry with you.' General Montholon asked me the same question and I made the same reply. He told me: 'You made a mistake. You should have said that he was not well at all, not as well as usual.' 'The Emperor,' he added, 'is very angry because you have been to Plantation House.' "

Lowe insisted—did Lepage himself think that Napoleon was really ill? "I could not say that positively," replied the cook, "as I see him but seldom. But Marchand, the chief steward Pierron, and the other servants who are close to the Emperor, Aly and Noverraz, have told

<hr>

[46] O'Meara to Gorrequer, June 14, 1817 (Lowe Papers, 20-115); Forsyth, Vol. I, p. 185.
[47] Gorrequer, *Minutes*, May 27, 1818 (Lowe Papers, 20-122).

me that he complains a great deal about his side and that the doctor thought he had liver trouble." [48]

.        .        .        .        .        .        .

Napoleon's activity had long been prodigious. It now seemed to be clogged. Periods of work came at longer and longer intervals. Little by little irregularity made its way into his geometrically ordered life. The air was too enervating, the environment too monotonous. The unchanging prospect of Flagstaff, of the human profile of the Barn, of the camp at Deadwood, of the sea high on the horizon and hardly distinguishable from the sky! The crowing of cocks in the morning and at night the clacking of frogs—so many castanettes— or the scrambling of rats, those were the sounds that struck the ear of a man accustomed to the roar of guns and the music of army bands. He struggled to shake off that paralysis—but what effort would not prove vain? Yes, he could change the hours for meals, go over his maps and books again, once more review his snuff boxes, his medals from France, his pictures, or give another reading to the newspapers, the least stale of which were two months old! [49] Reading was still his main reliance. When books or periodicals came in

[48] Gorrequer, *Minutes*, June 6, 1818 (Lowe Papers, 20-122).

[49] Napoleon received more newspapers than Las Cases, Montholon and O'Meara seem to indicate. The last, for instance, states (Vol. II, p. 430) that "none, however, except some unconnected numbers of the 'Times' and 'Courier,' 'Observer,' etc., with a few straggling French papers of a very old date, reached Longwood during my residence there. In one instance, in March, 1817, I think, the Governor permitted me to take the 'Morning Chronicle' for some weeks, as a great favour, which was not again repeated." That is not the whole truth. The actual situation, for that period, is better described in a letter that O'Meara himself wrote to Lowe on June 20, 1817: "In reply to your inquiries to be informed of the names of such newspapers as General Bonaparte may have received, I have the honour to inform you that the following are the only ones which (to my knowledge) have ever reached him, viz.: London papers—the 'Courier,' 'Times,' 'Star,' 'Observer,' 'Bell's Weekly Messenger,' and the 'St. James's, or Englishman's Chronicle' . . . Provincial papers—the 'Hampshire Telegraph,' the 'Hampshire Courier,' and the Macclesfield paper. Of the above-mentioned papers, by far the greatest number have been the 'Times,' 'Courier,' 'Star,' and the 'Hampshire Telegraph'; of the 'Observer,' not more than three or four numbers; probably as many of the 'St. James's Chronicle' and 'Bell's Messenger'; of the 'Hampshire Courier' probably eight or nine. On one occasion I recollect that amongst a file of 'Couriers' given by Sir Thomas Reade there was one number of the 'Globe' and one or two of the 'Traveller.' These, with the usual series of papers sent by yourself, some French papers, and 'Morning Chronicle' for October, November, and part of December, also sent by yourself, form the whole of the newspapers he has received." According to Balmain, Longwood was especially wanting in French and English Opposition newspapers (Balmain to Nesselrode, January 15, 1818). In the last years of the Captivity Lowe regularly sent many more newspapers, English as well as French, to Longwood.

from England, he would not take time to dress, but would sit looking through them over and over, laying them aside only to pick them up again. His mind found a replenishment of vigour in such work. "At those times," says Aly, "he was not the same man: his carriage, his voice, his gestures—everything, showed that fire was circulating in his veins. He seemed to be commanding Europe again. That condition would last for several days, whereafter the Emperor would relapse into his habitual routine."

.        .        .        .        .        .        .

Though he had ceased working, Napoleon was still talking a great deal. The conversations of the early years, as recorded especially by Las Cases and Gourgaud, show him in a relief, a verity, a brilliancy, that no historic personage will ever attain. He talked about himself unwearyingly. It is as though he could not think without thinking aloud, and if it was revery, he always told his dreams.

Nowhere else did he ever reveal himself so completely—how could he, when he was overwhelmed with affairs of state, with cares, with worries, had to smooth out a quarrel here or check an ambition there, rushing now from Jena to Vienna, now from Madrid to Moscow? At St. Helena that burden had been laid aside and he was free to make a minute inspection of the complicated cogs and wheels of his inner mechanism. He felt of himself, questioned himself, sought almost always in good faith the reasons for the various acts in his past. He liked to go back to the Revolution and proclaim that he had come of it. He would resurrect it in graphic phrases, ingenious expressions—the death of the King, the siege of Toulon, Vendémiaire. One could sense an age that was dying in a smell of blood and gunpowder, in the smoke of conflagrations. One could see the French rushing in tatters to the assault of thrones and, laughing, overturn them in a tumult above which bursts of the *Marseillaise* rose. Then the first Campaign in Italy and his rise to the stars! He went over his battles, noting on occasion his mistakes in strategy. His errors in statesmanship he confessed without trying to excuse them. Was he not above excuses? If History were to condemn this or that of his acts, he would turn and look History in the eye: What of it?

In that ramshackle house that echoed to his waddling footstep, he never wearied of recapitulating all the enthusiasms, all the flashes of will and genius, that he had experienced. Oh! How eager he was to explain himself! How he thought of the future! There he was, just as he saw himself, a being of flesh and blood, a mottled shifting spirit with his caprices, aberrations, smallnesses, prejudices, his acrid musty Jacobinism, but with his princely glance, his sense of order, his marvellous passion for work, his energy, and the superb certainty he had that no wine was finer for intoxicating the French than glory.

Full of artifice, yet deeply stirred by elementary instincts, he was endlessly fertile in trenchant sallies. But he had his moments of relaxation and of candour as well. He contradicted himself at every turn, now lauding war, now condemning it, now vituperating the mob, now praising it, now denouncing suicide, now justifying it. He said he could get along without friends, then a moment later he talked of Duroc or Bessières with words that drew tears. He often extolled Caesar and Alexander, but he set Hannibal above them. One day he called for the fourth volume of Rollin's *Histoire Romaine*, and with a pencil figured up on the margins the number of troops that the Carthaginians had at their disposal. As he had declared, the moment before, to his incredulous audience—they never used more than 30,000 men.[50]

To be sure, as he recalled his campaigns and allotted credits to his various lieutenants, he distributed more blame than praise. Unfair to Murat and Ney, he was severe on Carnot, Jourdan, Juno, Druout, Moreau, Augereau, Bernadotte, Davoust. He admired Hoche and Desaix, "the only ones who could have gone very far." He spoke well of Kléber, Lefèbvre, Rapp, Launes and Cambronne.

On the whole, he considered, he had been badly seconded, badly understood. How he had let himself be duped! How stupid he had been! Why did he keep a Talleyrand or a Fouché, though he felt they were traitors? Oh, weakness, just weakness! Because he had known them in days when they were in positions far superior to his own, and that had impressed him! And also because he appreciated their intelligence, their talents! He could not resign himself to leaving them unemployed, when his vast State had such a crying need of brains! And then again, Talleyrand and Fouché—though he flayed them alive, hacked them to pieces—well, one could understand that men of their size should have played their own game against him. But there were all the others—nobodies, men who had acquired names

[50] The volume of Rollin that the Emperor used passed eventually to Caroline Murat, and then to Mosbourg. It now belongs to M. Gabriel Hanotaux.

and reputations only through his favour, men who stood closest to him—and they had betrayed him too!

It had been a mistake to pass thrones around among his relatives. "People have often vaunted my strength of character. Well, I was nothing but a wet hen, especially for my own people—and they knew it. Once they had swallowed the first rebuff they kept at it, and their stubbornness and persistence always won the day—I got tired of haggling. They did with me what they pleased." [51]

"Joseph? He was no soldier! He has no heart. It was a great blunder on my part to make him a king, especially in Spain. In Madrid he thought of nothing but skirts. If he goes over to the revolutionists in America, he will not have resources enough to behave well there." [52]

Lucien was just a climber, posing as a republican. He had pestered him to let him marry the Queen of Etruria early in the Consulate.

"Seeing that I did not intend to let him make that marriage, Lucien told me he would go and marry a whore. I was never afraid of him in any way. He stole a lot when he was minister and the republicans had no respect for him. And then—what an idea to go and dedicate a poem to the Pope! [53] I made a bad mistake in 1815 when I thought he could be useful to me. He did not bring me one supporter."

Louis? A dunce! Yes, he was the one, probably, for whom he had done most.

"While I was an artillery officer garrisoned at Auxonne, my mother sent my young brother, Louis, to live with me. I had nothing but my pay, and it meant a big increase in expenses for me. I wanted him to dine with me at the officers' mess and so I was obliged to go without breakfast and call a roll and a cup of coffee a meal."

He added: "I got that from Madame. She had brought us up to think that we should eat black bread at home and put the rest into appearances and position outside. Oh, a mother is a man's whole education! Madame was above revolutions!" [54]

Each time that the thought of his mother crossed his mind he would salute her with the formula: "She is a Roman—a woman of the old school!"

[51] Las Cases, Vol. VI, p. 257.
[52] Gourgaud, Vol. II, p. 307.
[53] It was a poem called *Charlemagne*. Gourgaud, Vol. II, p. 158.
[54] Mme. de Montholon, p. 146.

Of Hortense, almost nothing! He ranked Eugene fairly low—a good executive, but "square-headed." He stormed when he learned that, enormously rich as he was, Eugene had put Malmaison up for sale,[55] and he was furious too when a newspaper from the Cape announced—falsely for that matter—a remarriage of Caroline to General Macdonald.[56]

"That would be a very great disgrace. She is thirty-four, with children sixteen or seventeen. She ought not to be bothering about 'the little business' anymore! And then, why marry? I hope we shall find that the Governor at the Cape had that little item published out of meanness. Dear me—if that news is true, it will surprise me more than anything else in my whole life! Oh, the human species is very strange!"

The memory of Josephine had remained sweet to him.

"She was full of grace, going to bed and dressing. I wish an Albani could have seen her then, and drawn her. I would never have left her if she could have had a child. But dear me . . . I can say that she's the woman I loved most. She was the woman to have gone with me to Elba!" [57]

Going on naturally in that direction he leapt to Marie-Louise and evoked memories of their short and happy married life together.

"Marie-Louise was innocence itself. She liked me and always wanted to be with me. Had she been at all well advised and not had that rascal of a Montebello around her, and that Corvisart, who, I now agree, was a scoundrel, she would have come with me. But they kept telling her that her aunt had been guillotined, and circumstances were too strong for her. And then her father puts her into the hands of that rogue of a Neipperg!" [58]

He often separated his words, pronouncing them each very distinctly, meantime gesturing with his beautiful hands, of which he was not a little vain, looking at them frequently. To either side of him sat his companions, silent, lost in reverie.

"Eight thousand miles from France," writes Mme. de Montholon, "and the Emperor has been telling the story of his life! [59] I had the

[55] Aly, p. 248.
[56] Gourgaud, Vol. I, p. 281.
[57] Gourgaud, Vol. II, pp. 277-330. Mme. Bertrand broke the news of Josephine's death to Napoleon when he was at Elba. He exclaimed: "Oh, she is very lucky—now!" (Gourgaud, Vol. II, p. 385.)
[58] Gourgaud, Vol. II, p. 330.
[59] P. 148. Read, four thousand.

impression of being in the other world, listening to the *Dialogues of the Dead!*"

The windows were open, the air warm. Mosquitoes were humming around the candles that dripped over their candle-sticks in the puffs of draught.

Let him surprise on their faces a trace of incredulousness and he would be nettled—he wanted to be believed. Then again, he would laugh:

"Oh, Monsieur the Grand Marshal does not believe that!" Or else, "Milady Montholon does not believe that. So I am a liar!"

.     .     .     .     .     .     .

Of his son during those years he spoke very little, restrained probably by a sort of embarrassment. He knew that the King of Rome would not even be Prince of Parma,[60] that they were bringing him up as an archduke, and had already foisted a title on him as Duke of Reichstadt. The boy's education worried him.

"What doctrines will they bring him up in as a child?" he would murmur. "What if he turned out to be a weakling and followed the Legitimists?" Would they bring him up to feel a horror for his father?

He seemed deeply affected.

"Well, let's talk of something else," he would say forcefully. But he would not talk of anything else. He would fall silent altogether.[61]

.     .     .     .     .     .     .

Later events were those that occupied him most insistently. So of the return from Elba.[62] He had come back six months too soon—but then, there had been every reason for him to do so! He had nothing left to keep his soldiers on. His very life was threatened. All the same it would have been better to wait for the dissolution of the Conference of Vienna. Metternich and Talleyrand would not have found it so easy to throw Europe upon him. He admitted that he had been in doubt the moment he landed on the Gulf of Juan.

"A mayor in a town there noticed the slimness of my resources and said to me: 'We were beginning to be happy and peaceful—now you are going to stir everything up again.' I could not tell you how that remark affected me, nor how much it hurt me."

[60] Gourgaud, Vol. II, p. 365.
[61] Las Cases, Vol. VI, p. 328.
[62] Chiefly Gourgaud, Vol. I, pp. 373, 492, 499, 501, 506.

If the Montholons pretended that a return to France would be even better received at that time than it had been in 1815, Napoleon very sensibly rejected the flattery:

"No, no, quite apart from the attitude of the foreign powers, the army is no longer the same. To get back again I would have to have from twenty-five to thirty thousand men just to begin with and give the malcontents time to join me and work up a war." [63]

Time after time he reverted to the Battle of Waterloo. How could he have lost it? He never could quite comprehend, it would seem. He went over and over the data, taking account of everything—the fog, the rain, the weariness of his troops, to say nothing of the immense share that had to be accorded to chance, and each time he arrived at conclusions which, far from satisfying him, re-opened the wound that lay deep down in his spirit.

. . . . . . .

At St. Helena, he said, it was not the outward shabbiness that made him uncomfortable.

"If I were not a slave and this were Europe, the life I lead here would suit me very well. I like country life. It is the pleasantest of all. A sick sheep makes a topic for conversation." [64]

However, what he would really have preferred, would have been to "live in Paris on twelve francs a day, dining for thirty sous, going the rounds of the literary centers and the libraries, and finally a cheap seat at the theatre." One louis a month would pay for his room!

He broke off:

"But I would have to have a valet. I have grown too accustomed to one. I have forgotten how to dress myself alone. I would have a very good time even if I kept mostly to people of my own fortune. Yes, indeed! All men have the same gift for being happy. Surely I was not born to become what I am! Well, I would have been quite as happy as M. Bonaparte as in being the Emperor Napoleon."

"If I could disguise myself so as to be really incognito," he said further, "I would go travelling in France with three carriages with six horses each. I would go by little stages with three or four friends and three or four women, stopping anywhere I saw fit, visiting everything, talking with the farmers and their farmhands. If I ever get to England I shall go travelling there in just that way. . . . Of course

[63] Gourgaud, Vol. I, p. 501.
[64] Gourgaud, Vol. I, p. 460.

we should have to make up our minds to put up with an Englishman in the company! . . . That style of travelling is altogether in
good tone. What fun to arrive like that at Parma and surprise the
Empress at Mass!"

He was not greedy for money, or rather, if he had his economical
moments, he was most often inclined to be generous. But his sense
of order compelled him to limit, to classify, everything. Such parsi-
monious traits as he had came from that. The question of domestic
expenses was much on his mind. He went over Cipriani's accounts
personally and checked his additions. He often amused himself by
setting his listeners the problem of how one might live on various
amounts of income, beginning with a budget of 12,000 francs and
ending at 500,000. Interested in practical details he liked to appraise
objects, and especially furniture. Waiting one day for Montholon in
the drawingroom, he inventoried the furniture in it and estimated it
as a whole "at thirty napoleons, at the outside."

. . . . . . . .

One evening he asked the circle at what period of his life they
thought he had been happiest.

"On the birth of the King of Rome," replied Bertrand.

"At Your Majesty's marriage," said Gourgaud.

"As First Consul," guessed Mme. de Montholon.

"Yes," he said slowly, as if he were little by little lifting the curtain over his memory, "I was happy as First Consul, at my marriage,
at the coming of the King of Rome. But at those times I was probably not altogether on my feet. I believe it was at Tilsit. I had just
been through most trying experiences with many worries—at Eylau
among other places; and there I was, victorious, dictating terms, with
emperors and kings dancing attendance around me! Perhaps I really
enjoyed myself most after my victories in Italy. What enthusiasm!
What shouts! 'Long live the Liberator of Italy!' That at twenty-five!
From that day I foresaw all that I might become. I could already see
the world spinning under me as though I were being swept along on
the air."

Those could not have been unpleasant memories, for almost immediately he began to hum. He paced back and forth for a few moments, then turned to the subject of the women he had had—readers,
actresses, Mlle. Guillebeau, Mlle. George, Mme. Gazzani. He talked

of his affairs unblushingly, unchivalrously, like a soldier in camp.[65] He was highly amused on reading a pamphlet called *The Secret Love Affairs of Buonaparte*, which O'Meara borrowed from Lowe. Quoting that absurd work, Napoleon swore that he knew practically none of the women whom it credited him with winning. "They make me out a Hercules," he said, laughing.[66]

That man, who was supposed to be one solid block of pride, nevertheless showed veinings of humility:

"I found all the elements of the Empire ready to hand. The world was weary of disorder. They wanted to have done with it. If I had not come, someone else would have done what I did. France would have ended by conquering the world! I say it again: A man is only a man. His talents are nothing, if circumstances, public opinion, are not with him." [67]

However, after reading the diatribes of Goldsmith, he paid tribute to himself, embracing his whole life in one summary glance:

"They can whittle me down, they can suppress me and mutilate me all they want, but they will find it hard to obliterate me altogether. A French historian will be obliged to say something about the Empire, and if he has any heart he will have to give me back some credit—he will have to give me my share, and his task will be easy, for the facts speak for themselves—they are as radiant as the sun. I closed the yawning chasm of anarchy, I brought order into chaos. I stimulated all worthy emulation, I rewarded all merit. I expanded the boundaries of glory. On what can they attack me without an historian's being able to defend me? My despotism? But he will show that the dictatorship was a crying necessity. Will they accuse me of having been too fond of war? He will show that I was always attacked. Of having wanted universal monarchy? He will make it evident that that was just the fortuitous result of circumstances, that our enemies themselves forced me into it step by step."

He knew that people about him were all keeping records of his words. There had been Las Cases and Gourgaud. But Montholon, too, was keeping a diary, his wife was writing her *Souvenirs*, Marchand and Aly were taking notes, and, as he could well surmise, the English who were admitted to Longwood, from O'Meara down to little Betsy. Napoleon was sometimes peeved at realizing that he had so

[65] Gourgaud, Vol. II, p. 56.
[66] Gourgaud, Vol. I, p. 432.
[67] Gourgaud, Vol. II, p. 78.

many annalists. "You hardly dare open your mouth, anymore," he said, March 12, 1817. "Every last thing goes into some diary!" [68]

So he concocted little by little a theory for his career, bringing his acts and his ideas under a body of doctrine—which was quite arbitrary, to be sure, but had the merit of being harmonious, simple, grand—and sowing broadcast around him the elements of history, as he intended it should be written, the better to serve as a spring-board for his son. Relying on the embellishments that the imagination would be sure to add, he outlined the broad features of his legend which was a thousand times more beautiful, more sonorous, more inspiring, than his life could possibly have been. He kneaded his dreams and his regrets into a great message and addressed it to the world without distinguishing between the friends of yesterday and the enemies of the present.

Europe had managed to conquer him by force. He would get his revenge in the domain of the intelligence. He felt that on that terrain he was waging his decisive battle. The hatred of kings, the fear of peoples, would fall before the prolonged echo of his voice. He lifted himself up as the apostle of a policy of reconciliation and liberation that would one day rescue a Europe that had again fallen under the yoke of her oligarchs. He would die perhaps on that rock there, but his last breath would have given life to the scattered clay and, rejected of men, he would have brought happiness, peace and brotherly love to mankind.

.      .      .      .      .      .      .

Religion and the existence of God were among his favourite subjects. Questions of faith had always been much in his mind. He claimed to follow "the system of Spinoza," [69] but that, perhaps, was as a foil to Gourgaud's ideas. In order to shock the young man, he sometimes professed materialism:

"What makes me think there is no avenging God is to see that good people are always unhappy and rascals happy. You just watch—Talleyrand will die in his bed! There is nothing but matter. If I had ever believed in a remunerating God, I would have been afraid in battle. I know very well that death is the end of everything.[70] Where is the soul of the unconceived child? I do not remember what I was before I was born. It was as though my soul did not exist. What

[68] Gourgaud. Unpublished.          [70] *Ibid.*, Vol. II, p. 130.
[69] Gourgaud, Vol. II, p. 408.

punishment can be inflicted on me after I am dead? My body becomes a turnip, a carrot!"

Gourgaud protested:

"God gives us conscience and remorse."

"Oh, I am not afraid of remorse. . . . And then, in the army, I have seen men die while I stood talking to them. Bah! Their souls died with them!" [71]

He admitted, however, that in default of a religion moral rules were necessary, and when Gourgaud declared that morals had no basis apart from religion, Napoleon appealed to the gendarme:

"Bah! The law is what makes people good. Morals are for the educated classes. For the masses? Gallows, gallows!" [72]

He did not believe, he said, in Jesus, but saw in Christianity a man-made edifice which one could admire. All the same, he was inclined by taste rather in the direction of Mohammedanism. During his stay in Egypt he had talked with the Imans, and had felt ever since a certain leaning towards the religion of the Prophet. He made fun of Gourgaud, predicting that he would end a Trappist.

"One can never be sure of anything, sire!" the young man replied.

Mme. de Montholon remarked that the Emperor himself might turn to religion some day.

"Well," he answered, "when you begin to break up, you lose what brains you have. People never turn to religion without that." [73]

However, he was sympathetic towards Catholicism, which he declared superior to the Anglican religion. He esteemed a "good" priest:

"The Bishop of Nantes agreed with all my ideas on ecclesiastical property, but he believed in Jesus and always talked like a true believer. He was a holy man. Priests like that are useful to a country and to a family." [74]

Suddenly a wave from deep down in him, an inner impulse, would force Napoleon's lips:

"The notion that sins can be remitted is a very beautiful one. That is why religion is beautiful and will never perish. No one can say

[71] Gourgaud, April 16, 1817. Unpublished.
[72] Gourgaud, Vol. II, p. 409.
[73] Ibid., Vol. II, p. 275.
[74] Ibid., Vol. I, p. 441. In noting this remark, Gourgaud added naïvely: "Cardinal Consalvi and the Pope also believe in Jesus."

that he does not believe, or will not some day.[75] Only a madman could say that he will die without confession. There are so many things that one does not know, that one cannot express in words." [76]

．　　．　　．　　．　　．　　．　　．

Day after day life flowed on, marked by little incidents that seemed for a moment to halt it, like the barriers that are built in riverbeds. They divide and for a second arrest the waters, which whirl about undecided but then resume their course, a little more slowly and as it were regretfully, and finally are flowing along again smooth and calm.

Tristan de Montholon fell ill with dysentery, then for the second time Gourgaud and finally little Arthur. Bertrand sprained an ankle. August 15, 1817, the Emperor's birthday, was a dull occasion. Everybody expected presents, but Napoleon gave each child a double napoleon of Italian mintage, and that was all.[77] The Grand Marshal expressed the hope that the Emperor's next birthday would not find the French at Longwood. The Emperor sighed:

"Yes, we do need a little happiness, in fact!"

He had had his old hunting coat turned and was wearing it almost all the time. "The Emperor," writes Gourgaud,[78] "has been wearing his maroon coat, but since the 15th he has been displaying a green coat, the old one turned, as I hear. He asked me what I thought of it. He preferred that to a coat cut from English cloth. 'At least this one is French,' he said."

He had put away his tricolour cockade, reserving it for "great occasions."

He gave a few audiences, but by now the Emperor was coming to dislike them. After October 11, 1817, he was to receive no one except the Balcombes (on their departure in March, 1818), and, on April 2, 1819, Mr. Ricketts, a cousin of Lord Liverpool. With those exceptions his door was not to open to any Englishman again. Visits from people who merely stopped off at St. Helena and asked to see him angered him. Was he nothing but a strange beast in a menagerie? For a long time he had hoped to impress people who came ashore at St. Helena, fill them with sentiments of admiration or perhaps of sympathy. Now he had come to the conclusion that it might be

---

[75] Ibid., Vol. I, p. 474.       [77] Ibid., Vol. II, p. 244.
[76] Ibid., Vol. II, p. 43.       [78] Ibid., Vol. II, p. 256, August 21, 1817.

better to drape himself in a cloud and menace his captors with invisibility and silence.

One of his last visitors was Mary Ann Robinson, the girl whom he had called the Nymph, whom Piontkowski and Gourgaud had courted in vain, and whom he had seen four or five times in the early days, when he was still riding in Sinner's Valley. At that time she had offered him little bouquets.

The day—the 26th of July—was sunny.[79] The wind had fallen. Napoleon had taken a walk about the park with Bertrand and Gourgaud. On returning home, he saw Mary Ann Robinson and a young man in naval uniform approaching. They greeted him. The Nymph had just married the youth, a certain Edwards, captain of a merchantman. She was about to leave the island and had come to say good-bye to the Emperor.

He showed them into the drawingroom, drank to their health and to their first child. He asked the husband if he knew that his wife had had an officer of the 53rd for a beau.[80] The poor man blushed and made no answer. Napoleon asked him a number of questions pertaining to his profession. He offered candy to the Nymph. "He seemed dejected at her leaving the island. . . . On their leaving the house he stood in a studious manner until they had walked on some way, then followed them; . . . he embraced Captain Edwards, saying he could not help it, he put him so much in mind of his own brother Joseph." [81]

He also received Captain Basil Hall, who had been a member of Lord Amherst's mission to China.[82] Having severed that connection at Manila, Hall was returning home on his brig, the *Lyra*. He waited all one afternoon at Mme. Bertrand's for an audience with the Emperor, only to be refused in the end. He went away much discomfited, but then hit on the idea of telling O'Meara that he was the son of the Scotch scholar, Sir James Hall, who had been living at Brienne at the time Napoleon was a student there. The next day Blakeney signalled to Plantation House that "General Bonaparte

[79] Gourgaud, Vol. II, p. 229. And see Robinson's report to Lowe of the same date (Lowe Papers, 20-143), for Mary's father at once sent a report to the Governor on his daughter's interview. That detail shows in what a network of espionage Napoleon was caught in his every movement.
[80] Lieutenant Impett. Napoleon once told Robinson that he would give 500 pounds to his daughter if she married that officer.
[81] Robinson, *Report*. Forsyth, Vol. II, p. 466.
[82] August 11, 1817. Basil Hall, *Voyage to the Eastern Seas*, p. 318.

would receive Captain Hall at two o'clock." Hall immediately galloped to Longwood.

He found the Emperor in the drawingroom with an elbow resting on the mantelpiece. A fire was burning in the fireplace. Napoleon looked at him, took two steps in his direction, and then replied to his bow with a simple nod.

He spoke at once of Hall's father.

"I knew him when I was in military school. I remember him perfectly. He liked mathematics. He never mingled with the young students, but frequented priests and professors."

As Hall expressed his surprise at the Emperor's keen memory:

"Oh," said Napoleon, "your father was the first Englishman I had ever seen. I have remembered him all my life."

In a half mirthful tone he asked:

"Does your father ever speak of me?"

Hall replied that he had often heard him praise the encouragement the Emperor had given to science during his reign.

Napoleon smiled, and the smile seemed to light up his face. Until then Hall had seen in him only a heavy man, pale as marble, without a wrinkle. The statue now came to life. The eyes shone with a youthful light, the forehead became radiant.

Speaking to Hall of the voyage the latter had just taken, he asked him for details as to a stop he had made on the island of Loo Tchoo. Questions followed one after the other with a precision that the Captain admired. Napoleon exclaimed in astonishment when he learned that the natives of Loo Tchoo had no weapons.

"No weapons? You mean no cannon. But they have guns!"

"Not even shotguns."

"Well, then, spears, or at least bows and arrows!"

"No weapons at all, sire."

"But—" cried the Emperor, clenching a fist, "without weapons, how do they fight?"

Basil Hall assured him that as far back as their memory reached the people on Loo Tchoo had never known wars.

"No wars!" exclaimed Napoleon.

The traveller went on to tell him that they had no money and attached no value to our gold and silver coins.

"How then were you able to pay them for their cattle and the goodly supply of provisions they sent aboard for you?"

Hall replied that they had declined to accept any sort of payment. He showed the Emperor some of his drawings—landscapes, costumes of Loo Tchoo and Korea. Napoleon was much interested and questioned him on the climate, products and ways of those countries. His familiarity, his good humour, made one forget ranks. On several occasions Hall remembered himself and showed his confusion. But the Emperor urged him to continue in the same intimate tone.

"What do your friends on Loo Tchoo know of other countries?"

"Only China and Japan."

"Yes, yes, but Europe? What do they know of us?"

"They know nothing of Europe. They do not know France or England. They have never heard of Your Majesty."

Napoleon laughed. After inviting Hall to introduce two comrades who had accompanied him, he dismissed the Captain in the most gracious manner. "His health and his spirits," Hall writes,[83] "seemed excellent, though at that time in England it was thought that he was dying of grief and some disease or other. He spoke quite slowly and very distinctly, waiting patiently for replies to his questions. One could not describe the gentleness, I might even say, the kindness, of his facial expression. If he were really ill or melancholy, he must have had extraordinary self-control to manifest it so little."

On Bingham's request Napoleon also consented to receive the officers of the 66th who had come from Madras to relieve the 53rd. That was September 1, 1817. In the course of the audience Sir George, who made the presentations, inadvertently addressed Napoleon as "sire." When informed of the slip, Lowe expressed great dissatisfaction.

Passing in review in front of the semicircle of red uniforms, he spoke to Lieutenant-Colonel Nichols of the Sepoys of India and jested about the habit English officers had of sitting long over their whiskey after dinner.

"Drink? Drink, eh?" he said in English, winking an eye.

His attention was caught by the decorations that covered Colonel Dodgin's chest—the latter was a handsome soldier who had distinguished himself in the Peninsula Campaign. One medal commemorated the Battle at Vittoria where Wellington defeated Jourdan, June 21, 1813, so compelling Napoleon to evacuate Spain. As soon as he identified it, he let it drop without comment.

[83] Hall, p. 329. Retranslated.

Bonaparte S.t Helena 1.st May 1818 AD. 1818

A CARICATURE OF NAPOLEON IN 1818

The officers seemed satisfied, as Napoleon remarked to Gourgaud.[84] That evening at mess they could talk of nothing but Napoleon. They tried to remember everything he had said. They laughed at the conception the Emperor had of their taste for the bottle. *"Drink, drink, eh?"* became a *cliché* in the camp at Deadwood. However, Walter Henry, the adjutant-surgeon of the 66th, declares that the general feeling was one of disappointment: [85] "The interview had dissolved a glory. The great Napoleon had merged in an unsightly and obese individual." Henry, however, was extremely hostile to the French and to Napoleon. Of his own impressions he wrote: "His general look was more that of an obese Spanish or Portuguese Friar than the Hero of modern times."

. . . . . . .

September brought back the races again. The Emperor watched them through his glasses from one of Bertrand's windows, then he went back to his own house and sat down on the bottom lift of the verandah steps. As the races were ending he saw the three Commissioners approach the enclosure of Longwood. He told Montholon and Gourgaud to go and meet them. Bertrand and his wife went too, and all the children. Stürmer and Balmain greeted them coldly at first, then the conversation warmed, and the whole party took the road to Hutt's Gate, chatting all the while. Stürmer gave his arm to Mme. Bertrand, Gourgaud his to Mme. Stürmer. Balmain and Bertrand walked behind with Gors. Mme. de Montholon joined them, and later Montchenu. Lowe, his staff, the colony, never took their eyes off them. The Governor was furious. He dashed across the farm "like a madman," to find out whether the foreigners had entered the park or not.[86]

He had good reason to be worried. The French were making another campaign to win the Commissioners. Montholon trotted almost every day over all the roads in the hope of a meeting. He finally caught Balmain and Stürmer and had long talks with them, especially with the Russian, whom he felt was more friendly and more at his ease.

Was there an invitation? Was it accepted? In any case, one Sun-

[84] Gourgaud, Vol. II, p. 285.
[85] Henry, *Events of a Military Life,* Vol. II, p. 23. Henry was born in 1791 and died in 1860.
[86] Balmain to Nesselrode, October 1, 1817.

day, September 28, Balmain and the Stürmers came as far as the inner gate at Longwood and met the Bertrands and Montholon there. Watching from a distance Napoleon found Mme. Stürmer pretty, with a fine complexion. He ordered some flowers sent to her. Unfortunately the foreigners had already gone. That evening the Emperor said that when they came back he would have refreshments served for them. They were expected the following Sunday. Montholon contended that they had said as much. The two ladies therefore put on their best gowns, and the children were decked out in holiday attire. The Emperor had a basket of sweets made ready. Gourgaud insisted that the Commissioners would not come. Bertrand, "playing important," gave assurances that they would.

Time went by. Nobody came in sight except a few inhabitants. Vainly Napoleon kept his glasses to the road, often losing patience. Once he mistook Archambault for one of the Commissioners. But no, it was nearly five o'clock! Gourgaud was right—they would not come. The Emperor distributed the bonbons among the children and went back to his apartment. He was tired, he said.

Lowe summoned the three Commissioners to a conference at which Plampin was also present. He denounced such meetings. "They so influenced his prisoners that he could always tell from their language the next day that one of the Commissioners had seen them the day before."

The Commissioners repeated what Balmain had already said, "that Longwood was the only agreeable excursion on the island, that one met many English officers there, and that they saw nothing in their talks with the French that could endanger the proper custody of the latter."

Hudson Lowe adjourned the interview, having gained nothing. The rides continued and the meetings. Montholon first made a try at Stürmer. The Emperor, he told him, was not very well. He would like to see the Commissioner from Austria in particular.

"If he were in danger of dying and sent for you, would you come?" [87]

Stürmer made no answer, and Montholon did not press the question—the Austrian was just "a stuffed goose"! He then turned his attentions on the Russian. On November 2, he said to him directly:

"The Emperor warmly praises your conduct during the first year.

[87] Balmain to Nesselrode, October 14, 1817. Of all that Stürmer says not a word.

It was wise. You knew neither the terrain nor the people. You could do no better than temporize. But in view of all the advances he has made to you, you are now carrying reserve too far. Have you been told to avoid him, to keep away from him? Are you entirely subject to the caprices and the madness of the Governor?"

In his report to his Court, Balmain avers that he "answered not a word." But that did not prevent Montholon from continuing:

"Longwood laments your indifference, but does not hold it against you. You will always be received there with open arms, as well as Monsieur and Madame von Stürmer and Captain de Gors. As for the Marquis de Montchenu, he is barred. His conduct is disgraceful. He tells the most ridiculous tales about us and keeps the newspapers filled with them." [88]

That attempt failed too. Lowe was just then at violent war with Longwood, and came down so heavily on Balmain and Stürmer that they yielded again. They avoided the French for several months.

An earthquake occurred on the night of September 21. About ten o'clock three powerful tremors rocked the whole island, but without doing any great harm. Each shock was attended by a dull rumbling sound as of distant thunder. Napoleon was in bed. He thought at first, he said the next day to O'Meara, that the *Conqueror*, anchored in the bay, had blown up. Speaking of the incident shortly afterwards to his companions he remarked:

"I agree with Gourgaud. We should have gone down with the island. It is a pleasure to die in company."

The pleasure did not tempt Mme. de Montholon. She insisted that the Emperor was not sincere and that he would be unwilling to forego his share of such happiness as might still be in store for him.[89]

. . . . . . .

By shutting himself in at Longwood Napoleon had only succeeded in arousing the curiosity of the inhabitants, who for the most part disapproved of Lowe without saying as much.[90] They were always questioning the servants and the soldiers. The health of "the General"

[88] Balmain to Nesselrode, November 2, 1817.
[89] Gourgaud, Vol. II, p. 323.
[90] Balmain to Nesselrode, October 1, 1819. "Sir Hudson Lowe's conduct towards his prisoners is a little mad. Even the English criticize it and public opinion is against him."

was of special concern to them. Was he as ill as his intimate friends
and O'Meara pretended? Nobody in short knew anything.

One day a Miss Vincent, a young and pretty chambermaid of
Lady Lowe's, who spoke French fairly well and had become friends
with Aly, ventured as far as Longwood and succeeded in getting a
peep at the Emperor through a keyhole. When Napoleon heard of
it—from Cipriani—he manifested his displeasure.[91] Shortly afterwards
Miss Vincent left St. Helena. It was rumoured in Europe that she was
to become the mother of a child by Napoleon.

Once again talk of building a house to replace Longwood had come
up. Lowe had received *carte blanche* from Bathurst.[92] The Minister's
letter had ended with the words: "In building a new house, or in
repairing and adding to the old, you will look, first, to the security
of his person; secondly, to his comfort and accommodation; and lastly,
to expense. . . . As great delay and inconvenience has arisen from
General Bonaparte having declined to give any explicit answers to
the applications made to him on the subject of his house, you will
make it to be clearly understood that your instructions to proceed on
the building are peremptory."

This time Lowe was resolved to get somewhere. He sent Wynyard
to Bertrand to come to an agreement on the choice of a site. The
Grand Marshal declined the proposals which, for that matter, were
considerate enough.[93] Finally, to put an end to the matter after several
months of waiting, Lowe decided to build at Longwood itself, two
hundred yards from the old structures and not far from Bertrand's
house. The plateau was to be cut back quite a distance that the building might be sheltered from the wind. The foundations were finished
on October 2, 1818. By November the left wing had risen as far as
the roof. Napoleon watched the work indifferently. He seemed to be
certain that he would never live in that house.

[91] Aly, p. 153.
[92] Bathurst to Lowe, September 17, 1817 (Lowe Papers, 20-121); Forsyth, Vol. II,
p. 415.
[93] A memorandum from Lowe that Wynyard presented to Bertrand enumerates
the sites where the building might be done, with the arguments for and against each.
The expression: "*Local objections*" frequently recurs. It meant lack of security,
difficulty of proper surveillance.
"*Wm. Doveton.* Very small. Damp. Local objections.
*Briars.* Too hot. Local objections.
*Miss Mason.* No local objections.
*Leech.* No local objections. Good situation, trees—but will the family give it up?
*Rosemary.* Trees. Good situation.
*Smith. Ditto.*" (Lowe Papers, 20-143). Retranslated.

# II

## GOURGAUD DEPARTS

STOWED AWAY IN HIS ATTIC GOURGAUD WAS ON THE VERGE OF A NERV-
ous breakdown. He was a man for work or for fighting and quite
unable to adapt himself to so relaxed a manner of living. Furious at
the preference shown the Montholons, having struck in the Bertrands
a ledge of solid indifference, he was finding no support in the Emperor
either. "I see His Majesty only a quarter of an hour a day," he wrote,
"and then just to watch a game of chess, put the pieces away or snuff
out the candles." [1]

In spite of the Emperor's harsh rebukes, Gourgaud was still devoted
to him. But his hatred against Napoleon's acolytes was getting beyond
his control. That woman—mistress or not—who was forever cajoling
the Emperor to get something out of him! That husband, perhaps a
complaisant cuckold, certainly a hypocrite, who lorded it over everybody at Longwood!

Scenes followed on scenes. On certain days, forgetting everything—
who he was, to whom he was speaking, where they were—Gourgaud
would throw in the Emperor's face in outrageous language, his long
services, his wounds, his wasted youth, his ruined future.

Napoleon was not aware of his aide-de-camp's mental strain. He
was suffering deeply enough himself, from his own troubles. Gourgaud bored him, and St. Helena was not a place where one could
very long endure annoying people. Gourgaud [2] teased Napoleon by
wearing for everyday attire a pair of loose red trousers that the
Emperor detested. And when Napoleon wanted to know why, he
replied: "Because my others are worn out." That was not true, but
when it came to money, Gourgaud was never satisfied. He would ask
Bertrand for some, and Marchand would hand him a certain amount.
That humiliated him. What he really wanted was the same allowance
as Montholon, who had a family. It was not a matter of greed. It was

[1] Gourgaud, January 19, 1818. Unpublished.
[2] Gourgaud, Vol. II, p. 67.

a matter of principle. He did not choose to yield to Montholon in anything.

Napoleon knew that Gourgaud had a turbid, exacting, but genuine devotion to him. He would say to him: "You are young and form too violent attachments. One has to laugh, be good-mannered and amiable, but not go dizzy over people as over a mistress!" [3] He might have shown him more indulgence. But he too was under tension and his rage burst forth in terrible words. For one example among a hundred—on July 29, 1817, he said: "You do nothing but insult me! You are not devoted to me! If you can't be of use to me, you at least might try not to be a nuisance." And on December 18th: "You talk against others who are devoted to me. You are a mean person—you have a disposition like Mr. Lowe's!" Gourgaud began to weep. Now the Emperor abhorred tears. "Bertrand," he pressed, "says there is no living with you! If you are bored, why don't you go hunting with Archambault and Noverraz? Why don't you make friends with Marchand or Cipriani? But you hate people who are fond of me."

"Sire, I have never been proud, but I shall not choose my company from among valets." [4]

In rejoinder Napoleon made a remark so coarse that it is frankly unprintable.

Gourgaud's fall from grace became known throughout the island. On information supplied by O'Meara and Mme. Bertrand, Balmain wrote to his Court, February 27, 1818: "Bonaparte has looked on Gourgaud for some time with ill favour. That officer's nervous, moody disposition has disgusted him. His aversion for him is overt. He delights in persecuting and humiliating him and driving him to the limit."

With the master and the servant both embittered, everything came to be misinterpreted, everything became a pretext for an outbreak. The Emperor said:

"I shall be dead within a year and you can all get out (*vous vous en irez tous*)."

Gourgaud misunderstood, taking *irez* for *rirez*—"you will all be glad." He flew into a rage:

"Your Majesty treats me very harshly as a rule. What you have

[3] Gourgaud, Vol. II, p. 143.
[4] *Ibid.*, Vol. II, p. 410.

just said to us today is going too far. I trust you do not mean a word of it!"

The Emperor explained his remark, but his utter disgust was apparent from the way he shrugged his shoulders.[5]

Gourgaud had been wanting to leave St. Helena for months. He had said so explicitly long before. On May 28, 1817, he wrote: "I count on getting away at the first chance that offers." [6] On July 15th and 30th and on August 1st, he repeated the statement. Things came to a climax between September 1st and 5th. Hurt by the Emperor's attitude towards him—the Montholons were not in question just then— Gourgaud decided to call on the Governor and ask permission to leave the island. Bertrand dissuaded him with great difficulty. Nevertheless he wrote his mother that he wanted to get back to Europe. The letter had been read both by Lowe and Bathurst and the latter made it the subject of special instructions to the Governor, dated December 13, 1817. Bathurst wrote Lowe to further Gourgaud's plan in every way. He himself had informed Mme. Gourgaud that if her son were not permitted to return to France, the British government would see no objection to his settling in England. He was well disposed towards Gourgaud, who, he said, had maintained a consistently correct attitude, but Bathurst did not exempt him from the quarantine at the Cape in the event of his return to Europe.[7]

Gourgaud's mind was made up. He would go. Bertrand talked and argued, hoping to bend that stubborn head to reason, but Gourgaud only worked himself into a greater rage. The Montholons were the cause of his disgrace with the Emperor. He would challenge Montholon to a duel. He had sent such a challenge previously—shortly after Las Cases' "expulsion," but the Emperor had given him a good scolding and Gourgaud had withdrawn his provocation.[8] On November 18, 1817, the aide-de-camp informed Bertrand that he could not stand the situation in which he was placed any longer. "Bertrand answered that I had only to make myself liked, that it all depended on me." Gourgaud replied with a coarse remark, and then said: "You might as well tell me to go and make gold! Be liked, be liked! But, Monsieur the Grand Marshal, what must one do to be liked?" Bertrand finally lost patience. "He told me," Gourgaud writes, "that he

[5] Gourgaud, Vol. II, p. 439.
[6] Ibid., Vol. II, p. 92.
[7] Lowe Papers, 20-121.
[8] Gourgaud, Vol. I, p. 331.

would inform His Majesty that I wanted to go away." [9] On the 21st
Bertrand called on Gourgaud. "I asked him," writes the latter, "if
there was anything new. He told me that he had not said anything
to His Majesty since the latter had been very depressed the day
before. I told him that he had to make up his mind nevertheless, that
I certainly could not endure the insulting disdain that His Majesty
was manifesting towards me. I had lost more than His Majesty and it
wasn't for myself. . . . He had millions and I had nothing—I had
lost everything and for his sake! I was born in luxury and I found
myself in poverty. Bertrand told me dryly that he would not say such
things to His Majesty. I told him: 'Monsieur the Grand Marshal, I
am losing patience. I shall slap Montholon's face.' " [10]

Gourgaud was announcing his intention of going away to everybody haphazard, even to Balmain whom he met on January 30,
1818: [11] "He [Balmain] assured me twice over that the news in town
was my departure for Europe. Annoyed, I answered that it was true,
that I was desperately sorry to leave His Majesty, that I was obliged
to, however, by the bad treatment to which he was subjecting me
at the hands of a rogue, but that I would square my accounts with said
rogue."

Meantime he decided to ask the Emperor for his release. Napoleon
had been warned by Bertrand and tried to avoid an outburst. Such a
breach of harmony would be hailed with joy by the enemy! Though
angry underneath he showed Gourgaud a smiling face that February
evening as he sat playing chess with Bertrand. [12] Suddenly he turned
on the young man and asked him whether he were "chewing Jomini"
[the leading author of textbooks on military tactics, in the Napoleonic period]. Gourgaud made no answer.

"Why so glum? Come, cheer up!" said the Emperor.

"Your Majesty knows that I cannot cheer up."

"And why not?"

"I am too badly treated."

Napoleon's face darkened. He sent Montholon out of the room,
ostensibly "to go and see how many sentries had been posted around
the house." Then he rose and went up to Gourgaud:

[9] Thiers Library. Unpublished.
[10] Gourgaud, November 21, 1817.
[11] Gourgaud, Vol. II, p. 469.
[12] February 1, 1819. The scene is all in Gourgaud, except for such portions as
relate to Mme. de Montholon (Thiers Library. Unpublished).

"Just what is it you want?"

"I beg Your Majesty to allow me to withdraw. I cannot endure the humiliation in which you wish to keep me. I have always done my duty. I do not please Your Majesty. I do not care to be a burden to anyone. Let the Emperor permit me to go away."

So he had come that far—that Gourgaud, who back there on the *Bellerophon* had violently insisted that his name be substituted for that of Planat on the list of those who were to accompany the Emperor! With a kindly word Napoleon could still have held him, for the young man was quivering with emotion in front of him. But he did not utter it. Undoubtedly he had had enough. He was free, he declared, to treat Monsieur and Mme. de Montholon as he saw fit, and he added that Gourgaud was mistaken in believing that he had given that lady a child.

"And suppose I should be sleeping with her—what harm would there be in that?"

"None, sire! But I have never said anything to Your Majesty on that subject. I could never suppose that Your Majesty had such a depraved taste."

A reply that overstepped the bounds! Napoleon was in a great rage, but controlled himself. He said to Gourgaud that he "ought to get on with Montholon—go and see him."

"Sire, they have done me too much harm. However I was wrong in speaking of it to Your Majesty. I must have my talk with M. de Montholon."

"If you threaten Montholon," cried the Emperor, "you are a bandit, a murderer!"

"Look at my hair! I have not had it cut for several months! I shall not cut it till I have had my revenge on that rascal who is driving me to despair! Your Majesty calls me a bandit! In that you abuse my respect for you. You call me a murderer! I do not think I can be accused of that. I have killed no one! I am the one they are murdering! They are trying to worry me to death!"

"I forbid you to challenge Montholon. I shall fight for him if you even— I shall put my curse on you!"

"Sire, I cannot allow myself to be ill-treated without calling the aggressor to account. It is my natural right. I am worse off than a slave. There are laws for slaves. For me there is only the law of caprice. I have never done anything beneath me and I never shall."

The Emperor recovered his calm:

"Let's see now—if you fight, he will kill you!"

"Sire, I have always held to the principle that it is better to die with honour than to live with shame."

Again Napoleon was in a rage. He stamped back and forth in the badly lighted salon, gesturing, muttering disconnected sentences. The Grand Marshal stood leaning against the wall in consternation. He had not uttered a word. Gourgaud in uniform, his hat under his arm, held himself as stiff and straight as a post. He turned to Bertrand and implored him to bear witness that a long time previous he had begged him to speak to the Emperor. The Grand Marshal made no answer. Napoleon had a sudden flare of pettiness. He said that Gourgaud had spoken ill of Bertrand and his wife, but then, as if weary of the whole business, he changed his tone of voice and asked Gourgaud what he wanted—to be promoted over Montholon? To see him, Napoleon, more often? To dine with them every day?

Stubbornly Gourgaud replied that a murderer, a bandit, had no right to ask for anything. It was then the Emperor who yielded, yielded out of common sense, out of sorrow, perhaps from a remnant of friendship:

"I beg you to forget those terms."

Gourgaud weakened. He agreed not to challenge Montholon if the Emperor would order him in writing not to do so. The Emperor promised. Then he tried to induce Gourgaud to change his mind as regarded his plan for going away. They would hold him at the Cape, perhaps put him in prison.

"Ruin for ruin, I should rather die doing my duty."

Napoleon shrugged his shoulders:

"I am certain you will be well received! Lord Bathurst likes you."

"What do you mean?"

"Yes, you delighted him with the letters you wrote."

The allusion was to the letters that Gourgaud had written to his mother describing life at St. Helena in the rosiest terms. Bathurst had used Gourgaud's confidences to discredit the complaints from Longwood. Gourgaud wrote, for instance, January 12, 1816: [13]

"My health could not be better. . . . The climate here is very mild, the air very salubrious. We live in a perpetual springtime." He announced his return within a year—"for I could not get on longer

[13] The first letter (unpublished) I owe to the kindness of Messrs. Meggs Brothers.

without you. We are now well settled in a pretty country house. Reading, walking, riding, hunting, editing interesting memoirs, and the hope of returning to all of you, help me to pass the time as pleasantly as one can when one is eight thousand miles from those one loves most."

Two other letters were so glowingly optimistic that Lowe had copies made of them. One dating from early in 1817 said, among other things: "The fact is I am in splendid health, perfectly acclimated, and have no desire to serve again as a pretext for a discussion on dysentery."

The second was dated January 25, 1818: "I have a charming abode at present. As for our meals even a man more difficult to please than I am would be well satisfied. In a word, if I have anything to complain of, it is Longwood, but not St. Helena."

It is easy to imagine that Lowe was delighted to have such testimony to send to Europe from one of the Emperor's companions.[14]

Gourgaud caught the Emperor's thrust and replied:

"I always told Mother I was getting on well in order not to frighten her. I do not care about living. I have nothing to reproach myself for."

The Emperor gave up. Gourgaud should arrange everything with the Grand Marshal! At least they should be careful to save their faces in the eyes of the world!

"You must say that you are ill—I will have O'Meara give you a certificate to that effect. But listen to my advice—you must not complain to anyone, nor speak of me. Once in France, you will see the sort of board you have to play on."

The next day Gourgaud had not received the letter forbidding him to fight. He thereupon sent his challenge to Montholon.

"You are the cause of all my misfortunes," he wrote. "You schemed to triumph by reducing me to the harsh extremity of going away. I shall not leave until I have avenged myself for the success of your intrigues. Whatever fate may be in store for me, I shall carry away with me the esteem of all honest men." [15]

Montholon refused to accept the challenge, on Napoleon's order:

14 Lowe Papers, 20-141.
15 Gourgaud's letter, Montholon's reply and Gourgaud's rejoinder are also preserved among Lowe's papers. Gourgaud communicated them to the Governor (Lowe Papers, 20-141).

"Any duel between us would be a great scandal and one more afflic-
tion to add to the Emperor's situation." [16]

Gourgaud threatened, even promising to take a whip to Montholon. "He is crazy," Napoleon is said to have exclaimed.[17] "He
should be placed under arrest." At any rate Gourgaud got nothing.
Paying no attention to the Bertrands, he hastened his departure. In
his *Voice from St. Helena* O'Meara does not speak of the Gourgaud
episode. But on February 6th he informed Lowe that the General
intended to ask leave of him to quit St. Helena. Questioned by the
Governor as to Gourgaud's reasons, the physician said that in addition
to his falling-out with Montholon, the young man was often ill, that
he ate scarcely anything and was losing weight. "He lives miserably,"
said O'Meara. He was almost always alone, rarely saw Napoleon, and
dined with him only from time to time on Sunday when he was invited, but not by any means as often as the Montholons or the Bertrands.[18] Gourgaud went to Plantation House, saw Lowe, and in Gorrequer's presence announced his decision:

"I beg you," he told him, "to put me up at High Knoll, or any
other place of your choosing, so that I can get away from Longwood
as soon as possible. I could not live there any longer without dishonouring myself. I have been treated like a dog. I would rather die in
prison in France than live here acting the part of a chamberlain with
the total loss of my independence. He has wished me to do things
contrary to my honour, to force me, by bad treatment, to leave him.
I told the Marshal: 'I shall say nothing against the Emperor, because
that would do harm to myself, but let them not attack me.' " [19]

Lowe acted considerately towards the overwrought youth. He
warned him that in Europe he would be "regarded as a person charged
with a secret commission from Bonaparte, or he would be reproached
for having abandoned him." [20] Gourgaud replied that in order to avoid

---

[16] In his *Récits de la Captivité*, Montholon does not breathe a word about this
quarrel. He contents himself with writing for February 13th: "Gourgaud left us
today." Gourgaud's challenge, dated February 4, 1818, is to be found in the French
Archives, *Affaires Étrangères*, 1804, fo. 295, whither a copy had been sent by
Montchenu.

[17] Stürmer to Metternich, February 23, 1818.

[18] Gorrequer, *Minutes* (Lowe Papers, 20-145); Forsyth, Vol. II, p. 247.

[19] *Ibid.* (Lowe Papers, 20-143).

[20] Gourgaud, Vol. II, p. 469: "I went and saw Hudson Lowe. He received me
courteously, advised me to be patient, to arbitrate, for I was between two rocks—
one group would say boredom, the others a mission: I urged him to treat me with

suspicion he wanted to be treated severely, but that anyhow he was indifferent as to what people said. In a letter to Bathurst, February 13, 1818, Lowe notes that "Gourgaud wept as he talked."

Since Gourgaud had made up his mind Lowe did not insist. The Governor was concerned above all else to deprive Napoleon of any power of acting and he could only congratulate himself on being rid of that one of the Emperor's companions whom he considered the most capable of a bold resort and the most loyal. On the other hand, he would not have been the professional intelligence expert, not to say detective, that his career shows him to have been, had it not occurred to him that by treating Gourgaud well and humouring him in his grievances—impressionable and easily influenced as he was—he might obtain valuable information from him as to Napoleon's manner of living at Longwood, his intentions and plans. He therefore lavished attentions on Gourgaud, and ordered that a little house be made ready to receive him pending his departure, which he would try to arrange at once.

Gourgaud returned to Longwood and, without seeing anyone save the Bertrands, "packed his trunks." At the instant urging of the Grand Marshal he addressed an official letter to Lowe basing his decision on reasons of health. In that way, as Napoleon and Bertrand hoped, Gourgaud's departure would serve the cause of the prisoners instead of proving a harm. It would show that Europeans could not live long in that climate.

However Gourgaud did not allege his state of health as the sole reason for his request.

"February 8, 1818:

"Since the serious illness I went through two years ago, my health has always been more or less precarious. I have frequently suffered recurrent attacks of dysentery and liver trouble. In addition to these physical sufferings I have had moral sufferings. I have experienced great disappointments and their effects have been deadly to me, destroying the little health I had left and to such an extent that I am obliged to ask you kindly to arrange for my return to Europe where the air of my native land and the care of my family will alleviate all my troubles."

. . . . . . . . .

the greatest severity." The citation is interesting in that it shows by a comparison of two absolutely independent sources the extraordinary accuracy of Gourgaud's testimony. Forsyth, Vol. II, p. 247.

The day before his departure Napoleon sent for Gourgaud:

"Well! So you are going away!"

"Tomorrow, sire."

"You are doing right! Go to the Cape first, then on to England! In France they are building up a national army. I see you in no time commanding artillery against the English. Be sure to tell them in France that I detest all these rascals, these scoundrels."

At that moment, without a doubt, he regretted the young man's departure. Gourgaud had served him well, he said—he was a good officer. With him he had been able to talk of science, of his campaigns. But no—there was no going back! Things had gone too far! He gave Gourgaud a little slap on the back as in the good old days.

"We shall meet again in another world. Come, good-bye! Embrace me! Just see the Grand Marshal about the letter." [21]

Half in a faint, Gourgaud embraced his master, then hurried to the Bertrands to write his letter of farewell. The touching missive gives a full-length picture of Gourgaud.[22]

"Longwood, February 11.

"Sire: At the moment of leaving this place, I am conscious of a deep sense of pain. I forget everything. My mind is filled with the one thought that I am about to take leave forever of the one to whom I had consecrated my whole life. That thought crushes me. I can find consolation only in the conviction that I have always done my duty. I yield to Fate! In my unhappiness I dare to hope, sire, that you will retain some memory of my services and of my devotion, that you will even do justice to my feelings and to the motives that prompt my departure, and that finally, if I have lost your good-will, I have not lost your respect.

"Deign, sire, to accept my farewell and the prayers that I utter for your happiness. Pity my fate, and may Your Majesty, in thinking occasionally of me, say: 'That fellow at any rate, had a good heart.'"

The Grand Marshal was to hand Gourgaud the Emperor's reply the next day. It was short and stiff.

"GENERAL BARON GOURGAUD:

"Sir: I thank you for the sentiments you express in your letter of yesterday. I regret that liver trouble which is so deadly in this climate should have necessitated your departure. You are young, you have talent, you should have a long career ahead of you. I trust that it may be a happy one. Never doubt my interest in you.

"NAPOLEON."

21 Gourgaud, Vol. II, p. 470.
22 Ibid., Vol. II, p. 529 (Lowe Papers, 20-121).

At Gourgaud's request Bertrand tried to obtain a "better" letter. He did not succeed. That disappointment was reinforced by an incident provoked by a piece of clumsiness on Aly's part. Napoleon had ordered the mameluke to give the General any duplicates there might be in his library, "to amuse him during the voyage." Aly made a mistake and gave, in addition to ordinary volumes, others that were stamped with the Emperor's coat-of-arms. The Emperor thereupon sent Aly to get them back and Gourgaud, offended, returned them all.[23] Still in pain from this double hurt, the young man refused to accept 500 pounds that Bertrand wanted to pay over to him on Napoleon's behalf to cover his travelling expenses. If necessary, he said, he preferred to give lessons in mathematics.[24]

Gourgaud was lodged quite near the Governor, who gave him rent, service and table, under the respectful surveillance, to be sure, of Lieutenant Jackson. He was immediately surrounded, caressed and flattered, not only by Lowe, but by the three Commissioners. Almost every day he lunched or dined now at Plantation House, now with the Stürmers, now with Balmain, now with Montchenu, the Admiral, English officers. Lady Lowe and Baroness Stürmer sent him tidbits, books, flowers. His papers were scarcely inspected and he easily secreted his diary. Lowe authorized him to keep his sketch of a history of the Battle of Waterloo and of numerous notes that he had taken under Napoleon's dictation.

For a whole month Gourgaud lived prey to the influence of that little world of inquisitors, without news of Longwood save such as O'Meara brought him from time to time, and shunned by his own people like a mangy beast. He answered the questions that were put to him carelessly and without sufficient thought. To obtain some conception of the pressure that was brought to bear on him, one has to read the last ten pages in Gourgaud's diary that are devoted to the month he spent away from Longwood just before he sailed. Every day some one or other questioned him. The conversations were interminable. Lowe, Reade, Gorrequer, the Commissioners, Wynyard, the Reverend Vernon, Emmett, Baxter, not to mention Jackson, who never let him out of his sight, came to see him and spent hours with him, drawing him into conversation on all sorts of topics.

Gourgaud spoke bitterly, angrily, without realizing that everything

23 Gourgaud, Vol. II, p. 471; Aly, p. 154; Balmain to Nesselrode, March 16, 1818.
24 Gourgaud, Vol. II, p. 471.

he said would leave for Europe in black and white as soon as he did. He may perhaps have overcoloured his insults, exaggerated his resentments, designedly. That was the way, he might have thought, to avoid a long quarantine at the Cape, sail straight to England and be admitted there. He seems, for instance, to have been exaggerating deliberately when he gave Balmain reasons for his refusing the 500 pounds that Napoleon had offered him. "It was," he said, "too much for my needs and not enough for my honour. The Emperor gave as much as that to his groom and his valets when they were sent back home. Las Cases got 200,000 francs. I will sell my watch, but I will not stoop to baseness. As for Count Bertrand, please ask him to return the 20 pounds he owes me. I ask nothing more of him. And remind him while you are about it, that I am in a position to blackmail the Emperor, that I can reveal his secrets, that my diary of Longwood is worth 15,000 pounds in London, and that it is important not to push me too far." [25] Interesting is the reference to Gourgaud's *Journal*. It was the only one he ever made, and Balmain, who never betrayed secrets, cannot have said anything to the Governor about it.

The "indiscretions" which were jotted down by Lowe and the Commissioners have, for that matter, less importance than has been pretended. One notes among them falsehoods that can have had no other aim than to mislead the enemy. When Gourgaud said that Warden's book was written under the direction of the Emperor, when he told Stürmer and Montchenu that Napoleon and Bertrand had advised him to commit suicide in order to put an end to his worries,[26] that they had received a large sum of gold at the time the silverware was broken up,[27] his imposture is obvious. One does note imprudences that were contrary to the policy Napoleon was pursuing in an effort to obtain a change in his place of exile. He confessed that the Emperor's health was not bad,[28] that he could escape if he wanted to and go to America, but that he did not want to, preferring to be a prisoner in St. Helena rather than free in the United States; [29] that Longwood had means of corresponding secretly with Europe. Finally one encounters a number of references to the Emperor's state

[25] Balmain, *Report*, March 16, 1818.
[26] Montchenu to Richelieu, March 18, 1818.
[27] Lowe to Bathurst, March 14, 15, 1818 (Lowe Papers, 20-121).
[28] Stürmer to Metternich, February 23, 1818.
[29] Stürmer to Metternich, March 14, 1818. The report is a veritable résumé of Gourgaud's conversations. Montchenu copied it and sent it on to Paris, as if it were his own.

of mind, his occupations, and manner of living, with which no fault can be found and which are in the nature of current conversation. What did Napoleon think of the Bourbons? What was he saying about Marie-Louise and about his son? Was he writing his memoirs? Who was the author of the famous *Remonstrance* that Montholon had signed? What was Napoleon like in strictly private life? And so on. Gourgaud was a born chatterbox and he had long been deprived of an audience. He replied to all the curious garrulously.

He declared to Lowe—in the case of any other man it would have been in the direction of softening him—that Napoleon's invectives and the hostility he manifested towards the Governor "were to be attributed to tactical and not personal motives." Napoleon wanted to leave St. Helena, and to attain that goal he was obliged to complain constantly and of everything. Gourgaud also had an explanation for the Emperor's obstinate silence regarding the new house. "As long as he stayed where he was, he could flatter himself with the idea that his exile would be something temporary. The construction of another building would suggest a permanent residence." [30]

The rumour had spread at St. Helena that the dispute with Montholon was just a pretext to enable Gourgaud to get to Europe on errands in the Emperor's interest. Gourgaud himself denied the charge in Lowe's presence on several occasions and in the most emphatic terms. Balmain wrote to Nesselrode, March 4, 1818: "It is believed at St. Helena that Gourgaud has a secret mission for Bonaparte, that his quarrel with Longwood is just comedy—a clever way of deceiving the English, and that therefore they should be all the more suspicious of him. That is not my opinion at all. Gourgaud is incautious [two words erased]. He has little knowledge of men, still less of affairs. It would be impossible, without taking huge risks, to entrust him with a rôle at all difficult. He would betray himself at every moment."

Lowe had asked Stürmer: "Do you think Gourgaud is in good faith—that his quarrel with Napoleon is genuine?" Stürmer replied "that the General was too little restrained to suppose that he could be charged with any secret mission." [31]

"I give you my word of honour," Gourgaud told Lowe, "that I have never had any political aims, that I have not tried to interfere

[30] Gorrequer, *Minutes*, February, 1868 (Lowe Papers, 20-121).
[31] Stürmer to Metternich, February 23, 1818.

in public affairs. I am not entrusted with any errand whatsoever." [32]

The Governor believed him. Was he right in doing so? Was Gourgaud leaving with an errand for Napoleon as has been asserted, and as Montholon was himself to declare? Hopes, it is said, had been held out by Balmain of a "royal hospitality in Russia." [33] On arriving in Europe, Gourgaud was to appeal directly to the Czar's generosity. Montholon himself, according to the same story, sent a letter from Longwood urging him "not to overact his part":

"The Emperor, my dear Gourgaud, finds that you are overplaying your rôle. He fears that Sir Hudson Lowe will open his eyes—you know how shrewd he is. Be constantly on your guard therefore, and hasten your departure without however seeming to desire it. Your position is very difficult. Don't forget that Stürmer belongs body and soul to Metternich. Avoid talking about the King of Rome, but bring the conversation around to the Emperor's devotion to the Empress at every opportunity. Be on your guard against O'Meara. His Majesty has reason to fear that he has kept up some connection with Sir Hudson Lowe. Try to find out whether Cipriani is double-dealing. Sound out Mme. Stürmer, since you think you are in a position to do so. As for Balmain, he is with us as far as is required. Make a loud cry about the matter of the 500 pounds and write in that sense to Bertrand. Have no worry in that direction. He does not suspect your mission. I have your yesterday's report. It interested His Majesty greatly. Montchenu is an old émigré, a man of honour. Keep him talking, but that is all. Every time you go to town send a report to 53. That is absolutely the safest way. 15. 16. 18. Montholon. Longwood, February 19, 1818." [34] Montholon is likewise said

[32] Conversations of March 10th and 11th, 1818 (Lowe Papers, 20-121 and 20-143).
[33] Montholon, Vol. II, p. 246.
[34] Gourgaud, Introduction, Vol. I, p. 15. This document, which has caused the spilling of so much angry ink, has never, that I know, been produced in the original. For some unknown reason—did he consider it too bald?—Gourgaud made no use of it. He was right. The forgery is too apparent. Montholon could not have written it at St. Helena. A new presumption of forgery seems recently to have come out of the production (at a sale directed by M. J. Arnna, April 27, 1934) of three pages and a half in octavo with erasures, in a text written on paper and water-marked "Johannot" (at the time there was nothing but paper of English make at Longwood) and which really seems to be the first form, the rough draft, of the famous letter: "Above all, do not on any provocation whatever overstep the rôle that His Majesty has set for you and which seems to be the only impenetrable mask for veiling your mission to the extremely practised eyes of the infernal policy of the Cabinet of St. James." For that matter everything that Montholon urged upon Gourgaud in the letter, at the risk of destroying him, and of destroying O'Meara, Cipriani, Balmain and himself, was of no use whatever. Gourgaud was at all times

to have sent Gourgaud instructions.[35] In all that one can see only a romantic fabrication, devised much later by the fertile imagination of Montholon and designed to protect Gourgaud, with whom he had by that time become reconciled, from embarrassing criticisms. Far from making any communication, Balmain had even pretended not to understand Bertrand when the latter suggested sending a letter to Alexander.[36]

The quarrel with Montholon was not a pretence—the diaries of Gourgaud and Marchand, and the papers of Sir Hudson Lowe, attest that. The conflict was patent, bitter, and of long standing. Gorrequer wrote to Blakeney, February 7, 1818, urging him to prevent any violent scene between the two Frenchmen, using force if necessary. "If you observe any quarrel or personal encounter leading to an act of violence on the part of one or the other, you will immediately interfere and separate the adversaries, calling the orderly officer to your aid if necessary." [37] Gourgaud left St. Helena not as an ambassador but as a malcontent. The first lines of a letter that he was to write to the Emperor of Austria, October 25, 1818, is convincing on this point:

"Though the collapse of my health caused me to foresee an early death if my stay there was prolonged, that reason would never have had sufficient weight to induce me to leave had the Emperor not been turned against me as a result of manoeuvres and intrigues. I had the extreme sorrow of thinking that the one to whom I had consecrated my whole life . . . saw in me perhaps only a man embittered by

accompanied by Jackson and could not have sent reports to Longwood. The French had no spies among the English on the island. Finally, if Montholon was using a code, we do not see how he could have left the essential portions of his letter clear and have coded only the last line (15. 16. 18.), which has all appearances of a greeting. One rarely finds so brazen, but at the same time so clumsy, a forgery. If there had been a rôle or a mission Bertrand would have known of it. There was no reason for keeping him in the dark.

[35] The "instructions," whether they were those that Montholon claims the Emperor dictated to him on the night of the 10th to the 11th of February, 1818 (Montholon, Vol. II, p. 251), or those of which an insignificant fragment is given in Gourgaud's *Journal* (Annex 22), also appear in an unconvincing text. To take only the first "instruction": Balmain never asked Napoleon any questions by order of his master, and never could Napoleon have thought of clearing himself point by point and eating humble-pie for the mistakes for which Alexander is alleged to have reproached him. The whole thing, besides, is in Montholon's flat and mawkish style. Napoleon wrote in a very different sort of ink, or dictated in a very different tone of voice.

[36] Balmain, *Report*, April 10, 1818.
[37] Lowe Papers, 20-121. Retranslated.

discontent and worn out by unhappiness." Gourgaud was not the
man to play a double game even with his enemy. He would not have
covered a lie with his soldier's oath. If later on we find him working
in Europe in his master's cause, he will be doing so—and that is to his
credit—on his own initiative.[38]

He left the island March 14, without seeing anyone at Longwood
except O'Meara. Just before sailing he went as far as the guard lines
and sent Jackson in to look for the Grand Marshal, that he might
say good-bye to him. Bertrand refused on the pretext "that he did
not care to see him in the presence of an English officer." (Bertrand
had acted in the same way in the case of Las Cases.) Gourgaud did
not have a red cent and sent Jackson back to ask for some money.
To that Bertrand replied that, since Gourgaud had not accepted the
500 pounds that had been offered him,[39] he could not, in deference to

[38] We cannot go into a detailed discussion of the "Gourgaud case" just here. In
Autour de Sainte-Hélène (1re série) Masson peremptorily dismissed the notion of
a "mission," but he was too severe on Gourgaud (Masson is responsible for making him the scapegoat of the Captivity). The young General's faults are undeniable.
But he has obvious excuses. Blunt, straightforward, naïve, peevish, given to worrying, Gourgaud was a man who saw too clearly and in whom instinct spoke too
strongly. Life in the narrow confines of Longwood, poisoned by the talk and the
gossip of two women, by the hypocrisy of Montholon, and the mean antagonisms
of domestics, became an inferno to him. Though he had left Longwood in a definitely hostile frame of mind, he was to recover his balance again in Europe and on
the eve of the Conference of Aix-la-Chapelle raise an eloquent voice in Napoleon's
behalf.

[39] Gourgaud, Vol. II, p. 482; Stürmer to Metternich, March 31, 1818. Gourgaud
ended by accepting the 500 pounds from the Emperor but Balcombe had not received any orders and could not or would not supply the cash (Balmain, Report,
March 16, 1818). The funds were sent on to London through Lowe the day after
Gourgaud's departure. Gourgaud duly paid off the debt he owed the Governor and
sent him, June 20, 1818, a letter (unpublished) which clearly shows the frame of
mind in which he sailed:
"I have learned that, since I left St. Helena, it has been common talk there that
my mother has been receiving a pension from the Emperor Napoleon. The unfortunate circumstances in which I find myself along with my family would victoriously
answer those lies; but I can further assure you that what I reasonably surmised at
the time of my departure has proved to be altogether true. The letter referring to
this matter has not yet been delivered at its address. My poor mother has never
had any knowledge of this so-called pension and has not collected a cent from it.
. . . [The pension was in fact not paid till the middle of the following year by
Prince Eugene]. I cannot yet return peacefully to my country, nor do I know
when I shall be able to. But however frightful my situation may be I shall never
seek to escape from it at the cost of my honour. My enemies believed that I was
going to attack them in print and otherwise. They are again mistaken. My heart
needs a nobler sort of vengeance than that.
"Accept, General, my renewed thanks for all the courteous treatment you were
kind enough to accord me from the time of my departure from Longwood down
to my embarkation" (Lowe Papers, 20-141 and 20-204).

the Emperor, make him any loan. Gourgaud was finally obliged to borrow a hundred pounds from the Governor. He sailed on the *Camden* in company with Mr. William Doveton, the old colonist of Mount Pleasant, whom he had often met when he was riding in the grandiose half-moon amphitheatre that rises behind Sandy Bay.[40]

Gourgaud was booked directly for Plymouth. Lowe had excused him from the wait at the Cape.

. . . . . . .

Napoleon was not deeply affected by Gourgaud's departure. He spoke of the young man during the days following without any particular good-will: "I truly believe the man was in love with me—and it began to bore me. Really now, I could not take him as my mistress. He is losing his mind. He will get himself hanged or shot in France. That is the fate that awaits him." [41] The Emperor was much more distressed by the death of his majordomo, informer and confidant, Cipriani.

Cipriani was little liked at Longwood where his spying and tattle-taling spread ill-will and uneasiness. He had at first been suspected by the English, then, somehow (how, in fact?) managed to make his way into their good graces. His end came suddenly. He was serving dinner on February 23, when a severe pain in the intestines seized him. He fell to the floor, uttering terrible cries. O'Meara took charge of him—bleedings, baths, hot applications. Perceiving that the case was beyond his depth, he sent for Dr. Baxter and young Henry. They could do nothing either. On the 27th Cipriani died.[42]

During the three days of his illness Napoleon sent every few moments to have news of him. On the 25th at midnight, he called for O'Meara. Cipriani had fallen into a sort of coma.

"I think," said the Emperor, "that if I went to see my poor Cipriani,

[40] William Doveton (1753-1843) was a member of the Council of St. Helena. He was to be received in London and knighted by the King, returning to his island as "Sir William." He was a simple man. Meeting a lady on one occasion in a crowded street in London, he suggested that they postpone their conversation "till after the procession had passed." The inhabitants of St. Helena were called "Yamstocks" by the English. They had a reputation for ingenuous ignorance. A lady from the island asked one day whether London had not become very gloomy since the China fleet had sailed. [Yamstocks: yam hoes, yam diggers.]

[41] Stürmer to Metternich, March 31, 1818. Balmain and Montchenu made almost identical notes.

[42] In his *Events of a Military Life* (Vol. II, pp. 36 ff.) Henry gives many details about Cipriani's condition. He seems to have suffered from what would now be called a ruptured appendix.

my presence might act as a stimulant and give him strength to combat the disease and perhaps overcome it."

O'Meara replied that Cipriani was still conscious and that the attachment and respect he had for his master was so great that on seeing him he would make an effort to rise and the shock would be severe enough to kill him.

Napoleon regretfully submitted to this ruling. As Cipriani's condition grew desperate, his grief became very marked. In his report to Lowe on the 27th Dr. Baxter noted the Emperor's condition. "He is low-spirited and looks ill to-day, probably owing to the approaching death of his faithful servant Cipriani." [43] And Montchenu wrote to Richelieu, March 18, 1818: "It is to be hoped that Death will not halt on such a good road."

The Emperor wanted to have the grave dug at Longwood itself within the precincts of the reserve. That would enable him to attend the obsequies. The little favour was not granted—it is not known why. Cipriani was buried in the little cemetery at St. Paul's, near Plantation House. In default of a Catholic priest, Mr. Boys read the Protestant service over the coffin. Bertrand and Montholon followed the procession, accompanied by Sir Thomas Reade and a number of army officers and natives of St. Helena.

Napoleon spent the whole day at the Bertrands'. He seemed unable to sit still in one place and kept walking incessantly from one room to another.[44] In recognition of the care the assistant-surgeon had given Cipriani, the Emperor ordered O'Meara to ask Henry to accept a silver tea service. Dr. Henry was a stickler for niceties and replied that he would have to ask permission of the Governor. Napoleon thereupon preferred to abandon the idea. Henry was to bear him a grudge on that account: "A palpable attempt at a bribe," he wrote, "to enlist even so humble an individual as myself, 'l'homme d'Empereur!' " [45]

Something similar happened with the clergyman, Mr. Boys. Boys was famous for his fanatical sectarianism. Napoleon had been agreeably surprised to see him perform the burial service for a heretic with such perfect good grace.[46] He sent him a silver snuff box through

[43] Lowe Papers, 20-121; Young, Vol. II, p. 94.
[44] Stürmer to Metternich, March 14, 1818.
[45] Henry, *Events*, Vol. II, p. 39.
[46] Stürmer to Metternich, March 14, 1818.

O'Meara, with a gift of 25 pounds for the poor. The Reverend Vernon thereupon interfered, perhaps out of jealousy, and reminded his colleague that it was forbidden to receive gifts from the French. Boys sent the snuff box back to O'Meara.

In spite of the rustle of cloth about his final resting-place Cipriani was an outspoken unbeliever. "Although Voltaire was his Evangelist," says Henry, "he was no admirer of the tolerant principles of his great favourite, but declared 'war to the knife' against all Priests, all Kings— all Emperors (except his master)." O'Meara makes a similar observation [47] and Lowe wrote to Bathurst, November 3, 1816: "Cipriani came out one day from General Bonaparte's room to Dr. O'Meara, saying, in a manner indicative of great surprise, 'My master is certainly beginning to lose his head. He begins to believe in God, you may think. He said to the servant who was shutting the windows, "Why do you take from us the light which God gives us?" Oh, certainly, he loses his head. He began at Waterloo.' Then, continuing to speak of himself, Cipriani added, 'I do not believe in God, because if there were one, he would not have allowed a man who has done so much harm to live so long.' " [48]

So Napoleon's circle constantly narrowed. Balcombe had long been in ill favour with Lowe, who suspected him of lending himself to clandestine correspondence between Longwood and Europe.[49] Lowe could not tolerate the friendly relations which Napoleon maintained with the Balcombes. On January 1, 1818, the Emperor had two plates from his General Quarters service filled with candies and delivered to Betsy and Jane. Lowe ordered that they be sent back to Longwood.[50] The jovial purveyor could sense about him a hostility that might lead to anything. He judged it wiser to get a fair start and asked for a six months' leave to return to England.[51] He pleaded his wife's poor health. On March 5, Balcombe suggested that his partner, Joseph Cole, replace him as purveyor for Longwood. Suspicious of the choice Lowe appointed to the post the Commissary, Denzil Ibbetson. Ibbetson had come to St. Helena on the *Northumberland* with the 53rd. The Governor and the Council acceded to Balcombe's request for leave of absence. The purveyor visited Longwood with his two

[47] O'Meara, Vol. II, p. 423.
[48] Lowe Papers, 20-117.
[49] Lowe to Bathurst, February 24, 1818 (Lowe Papers, 20-121).
[50] Gourgaud, Vol. II, p. 455.
[51] Request of March 3, 1818 (Jamestown Archives, 1818).

daughters on March 16, to take leave of the Emperor. He had lived fatly at the expense of Longwood, without losing any of Napoleon's good favour. He had a secret understanding with him which made him the richer by a draught of 3,000 pounds on Laffitte [52]—the reward for services rendered and an advance on services to come. He undertook while in Europe to see the members of the Bonaparte family and apprise them in detail as to how the Emperor was being treated, and, finally, it would seem, to do what he could in London to have the Governor replaced.

Lowe found out about the draught on Laffitte in June, 1820. He demanded an explanation of Montholon in a conversation of the 17th. Montholon replied that the purveyor had made urgent representations to the Emperor. "He came to the billiardroom and asked him to advance that amount as a favour, since he was in dire need and almost ruined—the loan would be the saving of him. Meantime he would leave The Briars and his properties on the island as security for the sum." Betsy also came and interceded with Napoleon. O'Meara and Bertrand exerted pressure too. Napoleon finally gave in and told Bertrand to "do what he wished." [53] In a word, Balcombe abused the Emperor's generosity.[54]

It was with great sadness that Napoleon saw his little friends at The Briars depart, especially Betsy, who had enlivened the first weeks of his exile. She wept. The Emperor wiped her eyes with his own

[52] Lowe Papers, 20-133.
[53] Lowe Papers, 20-144.
[54] Among other things, Balcombe was to have books, pamphlets and newspapers which the Emperor needed sent to Longwood. Balcombe was not very scrupulous and contented himself with the despatch of a few volumes. He did not go to the Continent, had the 75,000 francs drawn on Laffitte by his associate, Holmes, and neglected to get in touch with Madame Mère and Eugene. Did he really try to return to St. Helena? That is by no means certain. In any case, by September, 1818, as we shall see, Lowe was thoroughly informed as to his collusion with Longwood and there could be no question of his return. Balcombe stayed on in London out of work for five years. In 1823, through the influence more especially of Sir Thomas Tyrwitt, he obtained an advantageous post as paymaster-treasurer of New South Wales, in Australia. He moved thither with all his family, to die in 1829, at the early age of 47. His daughter Betsy married a Mr. Abell in 1832 and had one daughter by him. Returning to London she received a call from Joseph and Louis-Napoleon. After the "Return of the Ashes," in 1843, she published her *Recollections* in the *New Century Magazine*. Her story met with success and went through three editions. Falling upon days of impoverishment, Mrs. Abell appealed to Napoleon III, who came to her rescue and gave her a vast grant of land in Algeria. She died in 1871.

handkerchief and then told her to keep it as a souvenir. He also gave her a lock of his hair.[55]

In the friendship he manifested for that impulsive and unrestrained girl evidence of a more tender sentiment has been sought.[56] Napoleon certainly never thought of Betsy in any other way than as a child. He was interested in her, was amused by her successive or simultaneous flirtations, and always was delighted to see her. When, on the other hand, he was busy or ill, he closed his door to her.[57] But if, through her departure, he was sorry to lose one of the rare elements of gaiety in that environment, he seems to have forgotten her very soon, and almost never to have mentioned her again.[58]

[55] Balmain to Nesselrode, March 27, 1818. Many years later, Mrs. Abell was to embroider this great memory and pretend that while walking with her and her sister in the garden Napoleon had pointed to the ocean, which rose high on the horizon in the interstices between the hills, and said:
"So you are to sail off towards England, leaving me to die on this wretched rock! Look at those mountains—they are the walls of my prison! You will soon be hearing of the death of the Emperor Napoleon."
Nothing could be less convincing. At that particular moment the Emperor was in fairly good health, and he could not have bidden a final farewell to the Balcombes for they, he thought, were going to return within six months.

[56] Frémeaux, *Une petite amie de Napoléon*. Frémeaux's work on St. Helena is not without merit, but contains inaccuracies in large numbers. He adopted the romantic legend about Betsy, though it rests on nothing more than one of Montchenu's yarns. In a number of his letters, Montchenu gave malicious twists to the stories about Napoleon and Betsy, and a number of newspapers in Europe echoed his words. When these papers arrived at St. Helena the Balcombe family was greatly displeased by the talk, and to even the score on her own account Betsy vowed she would chase the Marquis through the streets of Jamestown and throw wet clay on his wig. Napoleon promised her a fan, she declares, if she did so. Unfortunately Mrs. Balcombe vetoed the enterprise (Mrs. Abell, p. 105).

[57] He did this on December 23, 1818, and on October 18, 1817.

[58] The Binghams did not go back to Longwood, because the General had been refused admittance three times, Napoleon being either indisposed or in a bad humour for guests (Montchenu to Richelieu, January 8, 1818). The Binghams left the island May 30, 1819, on the *Regent*. Sir George Bingham had asked for his recall because the India Company had not confirmed him in his position as a member of the Council of St. Helena. He did not pay a farewell call on the Emperor.

# III

# *LOWE AND O'MEARA*

HUDSON LOWE COMPLAINED CONSTANTLY OF O'MEARA IN HIS DESpatches to Bathurst. The doctor was in open revolt against Lowe's orders, was now refusing to keep him informed as to the intimate life at Longwood, and seemed to have gone over definitely into Napoleon's service. Lowe drew Bathurst's attention to "the almost nullity of all restrictions upon communication or correspondence with Napoleon Bonaparte, when a person of Mr. O'Meara's turn of mind and disposition is permitted to remain near him." [1] Finally, as his pretext for obtaining O'Meara's recall, Lowe seized on the snuff box that O'Meara had handed to the Reverend Mr. Boys. Sir Thomas Reade wrote to the physician that "except in the event of anything extraordinary occurring which you might feel it your duty to report immediately in person to him, you are not to quit Longwood without permission." [2] That was putting him under arrest without giving any reason.

O'Meara was not at all disposed to take such treatment meekly. He believed that the Admiralty was behind him—and with good reason. Finlaison had written to him, January 24, 1818:

"My dear O'Meara: Your last letters up to the 14th November have all come safe and I am specially commanded by my Lord Melville to express his Lordship's approbation of your correspondence, especially of the minute attention you have paid to details, and to add his wish that you continue to be equally full, candid, and explicit in future. Sir Pulteney Malcolm, who is now beside me, begs I should express to you his particular wish that in every future discussion or report, you will as much as possible avoid bringing up his name, as he is of opinion it can do no good. He sends his compliments and wishes you well through your arduous employment, which he thinks no one could ever be found to fill so well. Believe me, . . . John Finlaison." [3]

[1] Lowe to Bathurst, December 18, 1818, January 20 and 25, 1818 (Lowe Papers, 20-120, 20-121); Young, Vol. II, p. 97.
[2] Reade to O'Meara, April 10, 1818 (Lowe Papers, 20-122); O'Meara, Vol. IV, p. 178; Forsyth, Vol. II, p. 486.
[3] Lowe Papers, 20-231; Young, Vol. II, pp. 101-02.

Breaking his arrest O'Meara went down to The Briars "to submit the matter" to Admiral Plampin, his immediate superior. Plampin refused to see him. O'Meara thereupon sent in his resignation as physician to Longwood.

The Grand Marshal immediately protested. "The Emperor," he wrote to Lowe, "has been sick for seven months with a chronic illness of the liver, which is fatal in this country, and which is due to the lack of exercise which he has been unable to take for two years on account of the abuse you are making of your powers." [4] Bertrand also sent for Gorrequer and complained violently to him, declaring "that the fact of separating O'Meara from attendance on the Emperor was proof of the scheme they had long since formed for murdering him." [5]

The Governor accepted O'Meara's resignation and informed him that he could remain at Longwood until he, Lowe, had received instructions from the Ministry as to replacing him. But Napoleon hastened to declare that his physician having no longer the independence required, he would refuse his attentions thenceforward. Expecting that O'Meara was to leave Longwood, the Emperor handed over to him at that time a check for 100,000 francs to be honoured by King Joseph or Prince Eugene.

How was Lowe going to get out of that fix? Naïvely he insisted that Napoleon should at last consent to accept Dr. Baxter. In that way Lowe would get ample information as to the actual condition of the prisoner. What idea could he have had of his adversary? The reply was a new annotation ending with this haughty phrase: "Let the Prince Regent be informed as to the conduct of my murderer, that he may punish him publicly. If he does not do so, I bequeath the disgrace of my death to the ruling house of England." [6] The note further declared: "After assailing my physician and forcing him to resign, they are now holding him under arrest at Longwood, trying to give the impression that I am using him, knowing well that I cannot see him, that I have not seen him for two weeks and that I shall never see him, as long as they do not set him at liberty, release him from the oppression he is subjected to, and restore to him his

[4] Bertrand to Lowe, April 13, 1818 (Lowe Papers, 20-122).
[5] Gorrequer, *Minutes* (Lowe Papers, 20-122).
[6] April 27, 1818. Stürmer to Metternich, May 3, 1818.

moral independence as far as the exercise of his duties is concerned." [7]
At that time, in fact, the Emperor was suffering from an undoubted
liver attack. He had two bad days, April 18 and 24. O'Meara gave
him some "blue pills" with a mercury base—a treatment in general
use in those days, but in secret, for ostensibly the doctor had ended
his services.

There was great anxiety at Plantation House, and it grew greater
still when, on May 5, a letter was received from the shrewd physician
suggesting to the Governor that, out of sheer humanity, they go back
to the original basis while awaiting a decision from London. "The
actual state of matters now is appalling, and will probably produce
very unpleasant sensations both in England and Europe. His Excellency may perhaps reflect upon the terrible responsibility which
weighs upon him if (as is possible and very probable) Napoleon
Bonaparte, deprived of assistance, was to die before the expiration of
the five or six months required to obtain an answer from England."

A magnificent piece of blackmail! On Lowe's tense mind it met
with immediate success. The idea that Napoleon might be seriously
ill and die without medical aid terrified him. He had to avoid that.
Reversing his decision of April 10, he cancelled O'Meara's arrest so
that the physician might resume his services as before (May 10, 1818).
O'Meara did so and immediately addressed to Plantation House a
report declaring that Napoleon Bonaparte was evidently suffering
from a "hepatitis in a chronic and insidious form." In spite of his mistrust of O'Meara, Lowe believed this report. On July 11 he was to
write to Bathurst: "Napoleon's illness seems to have taken a serious
turn and his surgeon not to be a little alarmed on his account." [8]

Shortly afterwards, however, Lowe got hold of himself again and
regretted having yielded. Blakeney's reports, kitchen gossip, and
Napoleon's speedy recovery, as well as his formal refusal to accept
the services of another physician, induced him to think that he had
been tricked and that a passing indisposition on the part of his Captive had been used for a scare. *From that time on he refused to place
any credence in Napoleon's being seriously ill.*

However it was in the Governor's character to harass people and

---

[7] Thiers Library, Carton 19. Unpublished. The comment, dictated by Napoleon
and written out on the margin of one of Reade's letters to Bertrand (April 25, 1818),
gave a résumé of the Emperor's complaints.

[8] Lowe to Bathurst (Lowe Papers, 20-123); Young, Vol. II, p. 102.

complicate matters. He asked Colonel Lascelles, commanding the
66th, to forbid O'Meara to get his meals at Deadwood. That was the
doctor's sole distraction in that solitude. O'Meara rebelled, protested,
and was obliged in the end to yield. Officers, such as Lascelles and
Lieutenant Reardon, who seemed too openly to take his part, were
shortly afterwards sent back to England. That was in October, 1818.
In the course of an encounter with the Bertrands, Reardon had made
the mistake of criticizing the Governor's conduct towards O'Meara.

Hudson Lowe continued to receive reports from British or foreign
sources that Napoleon's partisans had not given up their plans for
liberating him. Hyde de Neuville, French Minister at Washington,
hated the fallen Emperor as cordially as he had hated the First Consul. He spied on the comings and goings of the Bonapartist refugees
in the United States and transmitted to his English colleague, Bagot,
fantastic stories about an alleged conspiracy to proclaim Joseph
Bonaparte Emperor of Mexico. Either a fool or a liar, Neuville
added: "I have strong reasons for believing that the scheme in question is connected with other enterprises no less culpable, and notably
with the project relative to St. Helena. . . . I am still convinced
that 'the Napoleonic confederation of the United States' is nothing
but a link in a revolutionary chain that is being forged in the two
hemispheres with a view to stirring up new trouble through anarchy
and usurpation." [9] Bagot sent the references on to London without
verifying them.

In actual fact, the whole affair was a swindling operation engineered
by a number of shady characters in hopes of extracting $20,000 from
Joseph, who, for that matter, did not fall into the trap. It was sufficient however to enable Neuville to write to Richelieu that "unless
the surveillance of St. Helena is . . . unheard of in its strictness, there
is everything to fear," and to try to give the alarm to President Madi-
son, who showed him the door.

Newspapers received at St. Helena early in 1817 had previously
announced, with no basis in fact, that "King Joseph had received a
deputation of Spanish insurgents who had invited him to become
their leader." "I do not like that," Napoleon had said. "Joseph has
brains, but he does not like work, and he knows nothing about mili-

[9] September 22, 1817 (Lowe Papers, 20-119). Retranslated.

tary affairs. He is very wrong to get mixed up in such a revolution." [10]

Another plot, even more terrifying, materialized. A certain Colonel Latapie had taken refuge at Pernambuco on the coast of Brazil. That was the nearest port to St. Helena (though it was still 2,000 miles away). Latapie was said to have come to an agreement with General Brayer, one of the leaders of the Army of Independence, who was at the time in Buenos Ayres.[11] It was a very simple plan, which, if care were not taken, would have fine prospects of succeeding! The conspirators were first to foment a revolution at Pernambuco and organize a government there. With that detail out of the way, they would equip at that same port a number of swift and well-armed vessels, which would carry a fleet of steam launches. These would steal upon St. Helena at night and try to rescue the Emperor. They forgot only one thing, though it was fairly important—at that time there were no steamboats capable of operating at sea.

Longwood learned of the Latapie scheme through Balmain, who reports (January 15, 1818) that "Napoleon refused to take it seriously and said: 'It is something they have thought up in order to justify Sir Hudson Lowe's vexations.' " A letter from Count Molé to the Duc de Richelieu, dated September 22, 1817, discussed the chances of another plan originating in America: [12] "Two schooners of 300 tons carrying guns, and a vessel of 74 armed by Lord Cochrane, was to make up this expedition, which would be manned by 80 French officers and 700 men recruited in the United States. The three vessels would rendez-vous at Fernando de Noronha [coast of Brazil] and start from that point for the island of St. Helena." Obviously such a plan never existed. Can one ever imagine a Liberal peer engaging in an affair of high treason in order to succour Napoleon? To do so would be to know little about the feelings of those Englishmen who were most hostile to the Tory Cabinet. They were all strict loyalists.

Admiral Plampin sent to London in all seriousness a letter from

[10] Gourgaud, Vol. I, p. 443.

[11] General Brayer had been one of the first to rally to Napoleon in March, 1815. Made a Peer of France during the Hundred Days, he was proscribed on the return of Louis XVIII, but escaped and made his way to Buenos Ayres where he took service against Spain. During the campaign on the Rhine in 1800, he had seduced a young Bavarian girl, Philippine von Freyburg, whom he had been obliged to marry. She was a colourful creature, given to coarse and picturesque language. She was a fanatical admirer of Napoleon. A daughter of the Brayers, Mathilde, was to marry Marchand in 1823.

[12] Archives, *Affaires Étrangères*, 1804

one Captain Sharpe, commanding the *Hyacinthe*, and revealing that
a young man recently arrived from the Platte had brought designs
for a boat that could be rowed under water. The boat could carry
six men and navigate on the surface or under water for several hours
at will. The boat was made of iron and could be transported by a
vessel of 150 tons! [13]

After the attack in open day the surprise attack by night! And
now finally an escape by submarine! The gamut was complete!

These corrosive day-dreams soaked into Lowe's porous mind as
into a sponge. Balmain notes mockingly: "The activities of the Bonapartists at Pernambuco are giving Sir Hudson Lowe the keenest
alarums. He is working feverishly at the fortifications of St. Helena,
setting up signal stations and batteries in different spots and doubling
the sentries around Longwood. I always see him on horseback, surrounded by engineers, riding at breakneck speed now hither, now
thither." [14] Lowe discovered dangers, intrigues, communications, con-
nivances, everywhere. Soldiers, sailors, inhabitants, all were alike suspect. Everything terrified him—thoughts, possibilities, shadows in the
dark. Let Napoleon not be seen for two days and he would gallop
to Longwood to bury Blakeney under reproaches. Who could say
whether the prisoner were still under those wretched slate tiles,
whether he might not be hiding behind a rock somewhere in the
country, waiting for the canoe that would come to carry him over-
seas?

Bathurst, from his end, kept urging stricter and stricter watchful-
ness. A letter of April 23, 1818, arrived in St. Helena in July. It informed Lowe that a clandestine correspondence had been established
between Longwood and Bahia (Brazil) by way of the Cape. "Only
a few days since, a package of letters from Longwood was handed to
a person from London by someone arriving from Brazil." It is certain
that on a number of occasions the French did take advantage of the
good offices of captains of merchantmen.

.        .        .        .        .        .        .

Fears of an escape, and now his quarrel with O'Meara, had cost
Lowe the little balance of mind he had to begin with. At the same
time he was at war with the foreign Commissioners. After several

[13] *Revue des études napoléoniennes,* May, 1932. Communication from Mlle.
Dechaux.
[14] Balmain to Nesselrode, February 18, 1818.

months of good behaviour, Balmain, in sheer desperation for something to do, had resumed his horseback rides to Longwood with Gors,[15] and again the Russian Commissioner lured his Austrian colleague to accompany him. Late in March they chanced to meet the Montholons and the Bertrands. An insignificant conversation ensued.

The next day Stürmer had business at Plantation House. Lowe looked him over without uttering a word. Stürmer started to leave, and the Governor called him back.

"You were at Longwood yesterday!" he said to him in a cutting tone. "I know all about it!"

"That does not surprise me," the Austrian replied, trying to keep his temper. "Our interview took place on the highroad. Anyone could have seen us." [16]

Lowe did not dare show the same sharpness towards Balmain, but what would he not have dared had he known that the Russian's courtesy and amiability encouraged Longwood to a point where, early in April, Bertrand said to him, encountering him alone:

"Overwhelmed with tedium, inhumanly treated on this barren rock, abandoned by the whole world, the Emperor wants to communicate with the Emperor Alexander, his one hope. I beg of you—take charge of his letter."

And he made a movement as if to take it from his pocket.

"No," Balmain replied, "that would be impossible. It would be a breach of my duty."

"Not in the least! In it the Emperor Napoleon makes important revelations to the Emperor Alexander. It is not a matter solely of protecting a great man who is being oppressed, but of serving Russia. This document will be read with pleasure, nay, with eagerness, in Russia. They will be delighted with it. Not to send it to your Court would be to neglect its interests, to lose sight of them, or rather to sacrifice them to the English. I further point out to you that it paints a picture of you that will advance your fortunes."

"I promise to report faithfully to my Court anything you tell me.

[15] Shortly after arriving at St. Helena, Gors had gone to the Cape to buy horses for Montchenu and for himself. When he came back he fell from his saddle in such a way as to break a thigh. He was confined to his bed for long months and was left a cripple. The accident contributed not a little to embitter him against Montchenu, who had taken no interest whatever in his misfortune. Not until early in 1818 could Gors resume his exercise on horseback.

[16] Stürmer to Metternich, June 1, 1818.

But I cannot become the bearer of any letter. I have no right to do so. And if I did, I should be disavowed."

"Bah!" exclaimed Bertrand. "They will disavow you at St. Helena as a matter of form, and in Russia they will reward you. I am sure of it. Well, take time to think it over carefully." [17] That was the second time that Bertrand had offered Balmain a letter from Napoleon.[18]

On Sunday, May 3, Balmain accompanied Montchenu and Gors down to Mulberry Gut, below Longwood, and without doubt on purpose. Napoleon was watching them and resolved to risk a decisive advance. The Commissioners had been joined by the Bertrands and the Montholons, little and big. He sent down a collation, with champagne and coffee served by Pierron and his men in silver cups. The meal was a gay one and the guests did not separate until nightfall. By that time Balmain, and even Montchenu, had received formal invitations to visit Longwood.[19]

As they rode back towards Hutt's Gate the Commissioners laughed in advance at the bilious attack the incident was going to cost Lowe. But now the Governor knew nothing about Longwood, since Napoleon would not admit him and he had quarrelled with O'Meara. They therefore would have to tell on themselves and in the ways they judged best.

Balmain especially enjoyed crossing Lowe, who had just played on him a trick that he could not overlook. A Russian brig-of-war, the *Rurick*, arrived off the island. Its commander signalled a request to see Balmain. Reade told the Russian Commissioner that he would go and arrange the matter and hurried with Plampin to Jamestown. They boarded the *Conqueror* that was stationed in the bay and moved down towards the *Rurick*. They must have given her orders to be off, for the brig, after firing a salute, disappeared.

The insult was gross and Balmain resented it keenly. Lowe had acted impulsively—he had tried to prevent Balmain from communicating with countrymen of his. Did he fear that he might concert with them for a rescue of Napoleon? When the Emperor learned of the adventure he was enchanted.

"Ah! Ah!" he exclaimed. "So I am not the only one who has to

[17] Balmain, *Report*, April 10, 1818. This advance would have had no sense if, on the assurance that Balmain would consent to be helpful, Napoleon had sent Gourgaud back to Europe to plead his cause before the Czar.
[18] *Ibid.*, January 15, 1818.
[19] *Ibid.*, April 26, 1818.

swallow insults! That one is mortal and done in public, and to Russia, to a sovereign who has to be reckoned with!" [20]

Plampin tried in vain to offer excuses. Balmain did not forgive him, nor Lowe either, for a long time.

Between the Commissioners and the Governor therefore a war had begun, still cloaked, to be sure, by certain forms. But social relations had ceased—no more invitations to Plantation House, no more drives with Lady Lowe and her daughters!

Lowe soon lost all sense of measure. First it was an angry call on Balmain, to ask whether he had received Bertrand at luncheon. Then it was a long diatribe hurled at Montchenu.

"They write!" cried the Marquis. "They accuse me! But I shall write too, and my government will believe me!"

Stürmer came as usual to ask for the items of information that went into his reports to Vienna. Lowe first treated him to a mute scene by refusing to speak. Then he broke into violent language. The Austrian mentioned Napoleon's health:

"When you told me that Bonaparte had an obstruction in the liver . . ."

The Governor interrupted. Was Stürmer espousing the thesis of the French, who were insisting that the climate of St. Helena was deadly?

"I—I told you that he has an obstruction in the liver? No, Baron, I told you nothing of the kind. I mentioned *incipient* hepatitis."

"*Incipient* hepatitis means a beginning of inflammation in the liver!"

Lowe replied, weighing each word:

"I spoke to you of an *incipient* obstruction—not of an *obstruction*. The difference is very important. They must have told you that at Longwood! I can see clearly that Napoleon Bonaparte is being used as a pretext . . ."

The Commissioner of His Apostolic Majesty drew himself up to his full height:

"You are mistaken, Governor. We are not using Napoleon Bonaparte as a pretext. We each have enough discernment to be able to disentangle the truth from the things people may be interested in trying to make us believe."

"You would do better not to go to Longwood." [21]

[20] Balmain, *Report*, April 26, 1818.
[21] Stürmer to Metternich, June 1, 1818.

Gorrequer, who was working the pen, repressed a smile.

Lowe and Stürmer thereupon assailed each other openly.

"You are always in a rage," said the Austrian, "and it is your rages you have to blame if people try to avoid having an understanding with you. No one cares to listen to nonsense."

"What do you mean—nonsense! I am talking nonsense! Gorrequer, did you hear that? I am talking nonsense!"

Stürmer went away avoiding an open rupture with greatest difficulty. In reporting the scene to Metternich, Stürmer added: "We shall never succeed in arriving at satisfactory relations with the Governor. To please him one would have to stop thinking, seeing and acting save as he wishes and according to his whims. One would have to approve of all his extravagances, not notice what is going on here, confine oneself to reporting that Bonaparte is alive, never set foot in Longwood, join in persecuting anybody who quarrels with him—and the number is increasing daily—spy for him and report faithfully everything that is said, and finally allow oneself to be cross-questioned every time he sees fit and submit to the most humiliating interrogations. . . .

"I doubt whether Sir Hudson will long remain in a post that is so greatly above his capacities. Public opinion is against him. According to him the honesty of his intentions justifies all that he does. Acting on that principle he spares no one and makes himself odious to all. The English fear him and shun him, the French make fun of him, the Commissioners complain of him, and everyone agrees in saying that he is not quite sound of mind." [22]

In order to find an issue from this quarrelling, to complain and get support, the Commissioners wrote to their respective courts, and Lowe to Bathurst. The first to receive a reply was Stürmer and it was much more than a reprimand—it was a recall. Metternich was out of sorts as a result of the Welle affair. He did not want to have any difficulties with England. He found it simpler therefore to disavow his agent and send him—a manifest demotion—as Consul-general to the United States. Montchenu would add to his title as Commissioner from France the title of Commissioner from Austria.

Stürmer was dumbfounded and protested, but packed his bags all the same. Lowe could hardly contain his joy. But before leaving, the Austrian Commissioner made a very natural request of him. So

[22] *Ibid.*

long as he had been in an official capacity, the Governor had not permitted him to see Napoleon privately. Now that he was transferring his powers to Montchenu and was about to sail on the *Northumberland*, he would like to see Europe's prisoner just once as an individual. Lowe bristled up. Would not Napoleon seize on that opportunity to make his father-in-law's representative the bearer of a message? Yet how could he refuse?

His first act was of a studied awkwardness. He sent Gorrequer to negotiate for the interview with Montholon, knowing perfectly well that in doing that he was insulting Napoleon since Stürmer should have presented himself in person to Bertrand. But just then the Emperor was taken with a fresh attack, so Lowe hastened to write to Stürmer that any visit seemed impossible. Stürmer insisted. If necessary he would delay his departure for several days. The Governor then replied categorically that he could not authorize the interview. "Since he would not receive you on my introduction," Lowe wrote to Stürmer, July 10, "either as a Commissioner or as a private individual, nor as a private individual introduced by General Sir George Bingham, I cannot so far recognize the claims of Count Bertrand and Count Montholon as to consent to your presentation by any of those gentlemen." [23] Stürmer left the island without recriminations. His money was wholly gone, and he was obliged to appeal to Lowe for a loan of 300 pounds.

Longwood saw Stürmer depart with sorrow. "Napoleon is outraged that Austria should have recalled her Commissioner," Balmain wrote. "He sent word to me through Montholon that he was delighted that he still had me near him, that I exercised an indirect and absolutely essential control over his safety on this rock, that he relied on the magnanimity of our august master never to desert a prince who had come upon misfortune, that he implored him, in the name of an old friendship, to rescue him from this horrible exile and to select for him another less damaging to his health, as he could easily do, being the arbiter of Europe."

Granting that Montholon must have embroidered on it a little, the appeal to the Czar Alexander had its pathos nevertheless. The Czar had seized Napoleon's hand at Erfurt, as Talma delivered a line from Voltaire's *Oedipe:*

"The friendship of a great man is a gift of the gods!"

[23] Lowe Papers, 20-123. Retranslated.

Would he now remain deaf to his plea? Balmain could only transmit it. Undoubtedly he would have asked nothing better himself than that his master should make a propitiatory gesture. But he could hardly hope for as much. With Europe in the full tide of political and religious reaction, Alexander was at that time the least capable of all the sovereigns of Europe of succouring Napoleon—as he was soon to show. At the end of his despatch Balmain requested his Court to recall him. The case of Stürmer had given him food for thought. Sniped at by the French and denounced by the Governor, he feared that his career might be compromised.

A fresh advance from Longwood was about to confirm him in that feeling.

Montholon said to him one day: "Baron Stürmer acted badly towards Longwood. As a family Commissioner he might have played a handsome rôle there. All that was asked of him was news of Marie-Louise, and he refused to give it. He went away penniless. The Emperor was willing to lend him a hundred thousand francs or to hand over to him a number of historical memoirs that he could have sold for six or seven thousand pounds. But he evinced very little confidence in us and has thereby done himself great harm."

Balmain caught the implication. If he was willing to act as go-between between the Czar and Napoleon, he had only to name his price. He was not insulted. He smiled. Convinced that he was taking the bait, Montholon unbosomed himself more imprudently:

"It is by giving up the profit on our publications to travellers, army officers, captains of merchantmen and transports, that we get everything through to Europe and printed there. The *Observations on Lord Bathurst's Speech* went through in that way, and we now have a valuable manuscript that we would like to publish. Will you take it? We offer it to you in good faith."

Balmain replied jestingly that "if he were in possession of any of Napoleon's writings, he would send them straight to Emperor Alexander." [24]

And cutting the interview short he turned on his heel.

He informed his minister of the incident with great pains, and since the air around him was growing blustery, he thought of changing it. An opportunity presented for him to take a trip to Rio de Janeiro. Admiral Plampin offered to let him sail on a brig, which was leaving

[24] Balmain to Nesselrode, April 14, 1818.

for Brazil at the end of April and expected to be back in St. Helena by October. He sailed on April 22, delighted to be escaping for five months from that life of mistrust, quarrelling and constant worry, which the conflict between Plantation House and Longwood was providing for the European Commissioners.

. . . . . . . .

Difficulties on matters of accounting had already arisen between Gorrequer and Bertrand as a result of Balcombe's replacement by Ibbetson. Wishing to be in a position to present vouchers for everything, Lowe required that in future every expenditure be covered by a draught drawn on Ibbetson.

"Soon," said Napoleon, "I will not be able to have my shirt washed without a draught." [25]

In one of the discussions with Gorrequer, Bertrand was guilty of an imprudence of the sort for which Gourgaud has been so much criticized, and which can also be noted in Montholon's case. Perceiving that Lowe's scheme of the draughts was to avoid putting any considerable amounts of money into the hands of the French, he exclaimed:

"The Emperor has only to open his mouth to have millions! He has only to sign a scrap of paper like this and it would be worth a fortune!" [26]

Such remarks upset Lowe and prompted him to redouble his precautions.

An incident occurred to strain Lowe's relations with the French even more, and again it was due to his tactlessness.

The orderly officer Blakeney, disgusted with "performing," as O'Meara said, "duties degrading to a British officer," asked to be relieved. Several captains of the 66th were sounded out to succeed him. All refused. In desperation Lowe turned to Lieutenant-Colonel Lyster, a former regimental comrade of his, whom he had brought on to St. Helena to fill a sinecure as inspector of coasts and militia. That was a bad choice. Lyster was too much the creature and the intimate of Lowe. The Governor gave him an adjutant, Lieutenant Jackson, who had served as Gourgaud's guard.

On arriving at Longwood, Lyster began with impertinences towards Mme. de Montholon. Then he refused to take his meals with

[25] Lowe Papers, 20-153. Unpublished.
[26] Lowe Papers, 20-122.

O'Meara, as Blakeney had been doing. The offence was deliberate.[27] Napoleon resented it and, knowing that Lyster had served in Corsica, had Bertrand give Lowe a lashing in a very insulting letter of July 22, 1818. It said in part: "We have noted with surprise that Lieutenant-Colonel Lyster is the same who was in command at Ajaccio, a city in which the Emperor's parental home is located. He has reasons for considering him as a personal enemy. Mr. Lyster does not belong to the English army. He will say anything you please, having no other will, no other conscience, than yours—that is to say, those of a declared enemy. Such a man undoubtedly suits you better than a captain who has a reputation and a conscience of his own." [28] The Governor replied that he would not replace the Colonel, who had already assumed his duties. By a truly superfluous act of foolishness, or by one of those bilious impulses that robbed the man of all balance, he showed the letter to Lyster. The latter was furious and sent Bertrand a challenge in which he went so far as to call him "a vile and infamous sycophant of the illustrious Corsican." The Grand Marshal disdained to reply, and Lyster then wrote him that if he refused to give satisfaction he would receive a horse-whipping. Bertrand sent the challenge to Lowe, with a statement that he considered himself at Lowe's orders, since Lyster was nothing, he said, but Lowe's figurehead. If Lowe had had the slightest nobility of spirit, he would have punished that subaltern who had been cowardly enough to address a General and a prisoner in such terms. Out of friendship for Lyster, he quashed the matter, contenting himself with withdrawing Lyster from Longwood and re-instating Blakeney.

Mme. Bertrand for her part long held a grudge against Napoleon for having the Grand Marshal sign his name to such a letter. Verling notes, September 9, 1819, that "she was not ready to forgive the Emperor for having compromised her husband by dictating his letter to Lyster to him." *

Hudson Lowe made another and more serious mistake. He gave the officers of the garrison to understand that they were to consider themselves as on a par with Lyster in the affair and from that moment Count and Countess Bertrand were boycotted. Balmain wrote to Nesselrode, December 20, 1818: "Since Count Bertrand refused to fight a

[27] O'Meara to Finlaison, August 10, 1818.
[28] Lowe to Bathurst, July 27, 1818 (Lowe Papers, 20-123).
* Retranslated.

duel with Lieutenant-Colonel Lyster, he has become an outcast, so that no one sees him, speaks to him, salutes him. Being Russian I did not think it necessary to join the English boycott and I continue to have courteous relations with him." When the new orderly officer, Captain Nicholls, came to replace Blakeney, Bertrand was to pay him a courtesy visit. Nicholls, on order, did not return it.[29]

The Governor saw a double advantage in that petty manoeuvre. He was again narrowing the contacts of Longwood and making Bertrand's place untenable, for Bertrand, his *bête noire*, would in the end be unable to act effectively as Napoleon's representative.

At just this time O'Meara left St. Helena. The Admiralty had not been able to save him. The Under-Secretary of State, Goulburn, had had several conversations with Gourgaud since the latter's arrival in London, and he informed Lord Bathurst that Napoleon's health was better than O'Meara declared.[30] Bathurst therefore no longer hesitated to defer to Lowe's repeated complaints and allow him to send the doctor home. From then on Napoleon could be cared for by Dr. Baxter or by any other physician on the island that he might prefer.[31]

Lowe immediately struck at the Irishman whom he despised and feared at the same time. He ordered Wynyard to inform him that he was to leave his employment "immediately," without communicating with anybody at Longwood.

O'Meara went to Napoleon at once. The blow was a harsh one for the Emperor—he was a man of habits and always disliked changes in the faces about him. He had enjoyed the obsequious and amusing company of the doctor. Since Cipriani's death, he had been his sole outside agent, his one connection with the island and its inhabitants. Besides it was no light affront to deprive him of his surgeon without even consulting him—Lowe had sent Bertrand a mere notification. He could see from the episode, finally, that the matter of his health would henceforward have little weight in Lowe's decisions.

However, he received the news calmly.

"The crime will be consummated the sooner," he said. "I have lived too long for them. Your Ministry is very bold. When the Pope was in France I would rather have cut off my arm than have taken his physician from him." [32]

[29] Nicholls, *Diary* (Lowe Papers, 20-120).
[30] Goulburn to Bathurst, May 10, 1818. We shall return to this matter hereafter.
[31] Bathurst to Lowe, May 16 and 18, 1818.
[32] O'Meara, Vol. II, p. 443.

O'Meara gave him advice as to the regimen he should follow in his absence and the remedies he should use in case of a fresh attack, which was to be expected.

"When you reach Europe," the Emperor resumed, "you must go and see my brother Joseph, or send someone to him. Tell him that I want him to give you the confidential letters which the Emperors Alexander and Francis, the King of Prussia, and the other sovereigns of Europe, wrote to me and which I delivered to him at Rochefort. You must publish them to cover those sovereigns with shame and show the world the homage which those vassals paid me when they had favours to ask of me, or when they were imploring me to leave them their thrones. When I had strength and power, they intrigued for my patronage and the honour of alliance with me—they licked the dust under my feet. Now they oppress me in my old age—they take my wife and my child from me." [33]

He stopped short, overcome perhaps by memories that were too dear to him. Then he added:

"If you hear of any lies being published against me bearing on the time that you have been with me, and if you can say, 'I saw with my own eyes that that is not true,' contradict them."

He then dictated to Bertrand a letter accrediting O'Meara to his family and his friends, and handed the Irishman a little note penned with his own hand:

"If he sees my good Louise, I beg her to allow him to kiss her hand. Napoleon. This 25 July, 1818."

O'Meara took the note to Europe hidden in the sole of his slipper.[34]

Finally he gave him as personal remembrances a snuff box and a bronze statuette. He also entrusted to him a number of manuscripts to be published in Europe—notably the answer to the allegations that had been ascribed to him in the *Manuscript of St. Helena*. The pamphlet was entitled: *Reasons dictated in reply to the question: 'Is*

[33] The letters of the Sovereigns to Napoleon were not found for a long time, either in the originals or in copies. Joseph protested that he had received nothing. Maret declared that he had kept nothing. Late in 1820, however, Emperor Alexander was informed by Jomini that a certain Monnier, who was undoubtedly acting as a figurehead, was offering the letters written by the Czar for a sum of 10,000 pounds. They bargained, and Alexander regained possession of his own autographs—thirty-two letters in all, plus two letters from the Emperor Paul—for 175,000 francs. The letters of the other sovereigns were recovered by Napoleon III. Today they form part of the collection of Prince Napoleon.

[34] O'Meara, Vol. II, p. 445.

*the publication entitled the* Manuscript of St. Helena, *printed in London in 1817, the work of Napoleon or not?* " O'Meara also took with him a copy of the *Campagne de 1815.* The Emperor repeated that he did not want any of his relatives to come to St. Helena "to witness the humiliations he was undergoing."

"You will assure my good Louise, my excellent mother, and Pauline, of my affection. If you see my son, embrace him for me. Let him never forget that he was born a Frenchman. Assure Lady Holland of my esteem and my gratitude for her kindnesses."

Then he gripped the doctor's hand—a gesture rare with him—and murmured:

"Good-bye, O'Meara. We shall never see each other again. Good luck to you." [35]

As the physician came out of the Emperor's bedroom Wynyard rebuked him for having violated his arrest. O'Meara replied that he no longer recognized the Governor's authority. Wynyard then accompanied him to Jamestown where he was immediately put on board the *Griffon*, though that vessel was not to sail till the following week, August 2, 1818.

In spite of his precipitate departure, O'Meara managed to conceal his more important papers. While he was with the Emperor, Montholon, at his request, ran to the medicine closet to get O'Meara's diary, which he had hidden away there against mishap. Montholon says the diary was written in Italian, that he forwarded it to England, and that O'Meara used it, supplemented by his voluminous letters to Finlaison, to write his *Voice from St. Helena* (1822), a work of wide renown, as we shall see.

O'Meara's luggage did not go aboard in the same boat with him and he considered the delay in its arrival suspicious. Lowe had his bags examined, but dared not go farther. "I do not think," Bathurst had written, May 18, 1818, "you will be authorized in seizing his papers." O'Meara claimed that effects of his, including jewels, had been stolen and that his writing desk had been forced. Sir George Bingham held an enquiry, which came to nothing.

The next day O'Meara sent Bertrand a detailed memorandum on Napoleon's malady. He refused to allow Dr. Verling, whom Lowe had named to replace him at Longwood, to see it. He did offer how-

[35] O'Meara, Vol. II, p. 445; Montholon, Vol. II, p. 307.

ever to communicate the series of his health charts and a résumé of his treatments.[36]

Verling was assistant-surgeon to the artillery and was already known to Napoleon from having made the same voyage on the *Northumberland*. He too was an Irishman, very young, with a pleasant, prepossessing face and an approachable manner.[37] However, Napoleon could not grant the right of the English to force upon him in his own house any health officer they chose. On his order Montholon wrote to the Governor that when he came to the death rattle "he would receive no physician except O'Meara, or one who might be sent him from Europe as he had already requested."[38]

O'Meara went away with the Emperor's trust and friendship. As we well know he was not worthy of either. Down to the time when Napoleon bought him he had spied on the French and tricked them. The Governor's insults quite as much as French money had brought that low nature, compounded of vanity and greed, to become a turn-coat. But O'Meara enjoyed a fight and put a curious enthusiasm into one. Cuffed by Hudson Lowe he was to strike back with a bitter hatred, spatter him with truths, lies and insults alike, so becoming Napoleon's most active advocate during the last years of the exile and, when the hero was dead, the loudest trumpet in defence of his reputation—but, let there be no mistake about it, in his own interest, for his own profit and vengeance, and not out of generosity, the sole merit that might redeem that adventurer in the eyes of honest people, be they English or French.

.        .        .        .        .        .        .

Refusing to recognize either Verling or Baxter, the Emperor was left without medical care. Lowe's worries were redoubled. Not that he believed by this time that his prisoner's health was a fit subject for alarm. He thought that with O'Meara gone, the Emperor's illness, being a sham in the first place, would disappear of itself. What

[36] Lowe Papers, 20-123.

[37] He was a doctor of medicine which, it seems, O'Meara was not. He was to reside at Longwood and attend the Bertrands, the Montholons and the servants, until September 20, 1819, when Antommarchi came to replace him. He left St. Helena, April 25, 1820, with the respect of everybody, to become inspector-general of sanitation in the army. His diary, interesting for a number of details, is preserved in the National Archives (A. B., XIX, 92, entry No. 34). It was published—clumsily and in mutilated form—in a very limited edition in the *Sabretash Notebook*, as was that of Nicholls.

[38] In a letter from Bertrand to Fesch, April 13, 1818. Montholon to Lowe, July 26, 1818 (Lowe Papers, 20-123).

worried him now was that he had no further assurance of the Emperor's presence in his custody. Treacherous as O'Meara may have been, he would never have been party to an escape. In replacing Blakeney, Captain Nicholls of the 66th had received orders from the Governor to make certain twice a day that Napoleon was actually at Longwood.[39] The unlucky soldier found that a herculean task. The Emperor outdid himself in efforts to deceive him. Two whole days would often pass before Nicholls could get a glimpse of him. This game of hide-and-seek brought Lowe to the limits of exasperation. He was rushing over from Plantation House at every other moment to give his officer a dressing-down.

In the end he went to Montholon (October 3, 1818) and delivered an ultimatum. Was Bonaparte, he persisted, going or not going to see the orderly officer and the doctor?

Unlike Bertrand Montholon was for conciliation and eager at all costs to keep Lowe's good-will. He replied that the Emperor would never consent to "report like a prisoner," but he denied that he was deliberately keeping out of Nicholls' sight. Napoleon's aloofness was really due to his bad health. "I am very far from approving the life he leads," said Montholon, "his refusal to take exercise—to ride on horse-back—to see anyone, even the doctor—his persisting all the more when recommended to change his habits. Not to call in a doctor when one is ill is to punish oneself—it is ridiculous. All these things are childish, pure follies. He is seldom up more than two or three hours a day; he is so used to this that it has now become a necessity for him to remain long in bed. He becomes weak in body— his blood thickens—he declines every day. The habit of remaining in bed becomes an absolute necessity. Then he is in a bad humour, sulky; his temper is soured and irritable. Let the fine weather come, and I do not say that he will not then walk out in his garden as formerly." [40]

By the Lusitania, September 10, two letters for O'Meara had come to St. Helena. That was after his departure. They were more than sus-

---

[39] Nicholls was appointed orderly officer at Longwood September 5, 1818, and was to hold that position till February 9, 1820. His Diary (Lowe Papers, 20-120) bears witness to his patient and ingenious efforts to assure himself each day of the Emperor's presence. When, in order to thwart Lowe's orders, Napoleon shut himself up in his room, he succeeded 286 times in 421 days. The Governor might, it would seem, have been satisfied with such an average.

[40] Lowe Papers, 20-124.

picious, being distributed among several envelopes and addressed to various persons, among others, to Dr. Stokoe. One was from William Holmes, O'Meara's London correspondent. It was of no particular interest. The other was from Balcombe. It informed him that a change in the ministry was in the offing and that O'Meara would be supported. "No stone will be left unturned to serve our friends on the island." *

This last letter was extremely inopportune. It seemed to prove what Lowe had always feared, that Balcombe was an active agent of Longwood and had gone to England to obtain a change of Governors. Montholon vigorously ridiculed the notion that any intrigue was being engineered by the French. The Emperor had never dreamed of trying to escape. As the conversation continued Lowe complained of Napoleon's attitude towards the English. Montholon laid the blame for that on Las Cases, "who had misrepresented many facts and interpreted many incidents in an unfortunate manner."

The Governor returned to Longwood nine times between October 5 and October 24, 1818.[41] All points in controversy were threshed out anew. Montholon protested against the arbitrariness and uselessness of the rules. Lowe excused himself on his orders from London, urging that Nicholls be looked upon as a comrade rather than as a guard, protesting his own good will and calling attention to all the rides and drives that Napoleon might take, unaccompanied, in the most charming parts of the island, merely by informing Nicholls an hour and a half in advance. Montholon went in and reported the Governor's words to the Emperor. The latter replied:

"I shall go out of doors, I shall be glad to take rides—I sorely need them—and I shall begin to lead the sort of life that I led during the first nine months, but first of all I must be able to have self-confidence. I must know that there is a definite system not subject to caprices, so that I can say: 'Tomorrow I shall do what I did today.' I must be able to systematize my daily occupations and be assured that the regulations are not going to change from one day to the next—in a word that the arrangements determined on shall remain permanently fixed."

Lowe stood firm. He could be criticized for laxness as well as for severity. He could therefore make no changes in his regulations.

* Forsyth, Vol. III, p. 61.
[41] Lowe Papers, 21-210.

They were "his foundation and his law." On September 28, Bathurst had insisted explicitly on the necessity of the orderly officer's assuring himself twice a day of Napoleon's presence at Longwood. He rebuked Lowe for hesitating to carry out that measure. On the other hand he declared that if Napoleon would agree to that arrangement (how little he knew him!) Lowe might allow him to walk, ride or drive over virtually the whole island, unaccompanied.[42]

So all the talk came to nothing, nor could it have been otherwise, since neither side had any essential concession to make. Napoleon persisted in refusing to see the physicians Lowe suggested. He refused to allow himself to be seen by English officers. The Governor on his part held his ground. The struggle that had begun more than two years before was to continue with the same stakes: the Emperor's freedom and health pitted against Bathurst's vanity and Lowe's terrors.

[42] Lowe Papers, 20-124.

# IV

## EUROPE AND NAPOLEON

ABOVE ALL ELSE NAPOLEON WISHED TO AVOID BEING FORGOTTEN BY a Europe that was wholly absorbed in rebuilding itself. Even at a distance of four thousand miles it was important, he thought, for him to be ever present, in the memories and in the ideas which he impersonated, and which, as a result of the reaction undertaken by the Holy Alliance, were to blend more and more with the principles of liberty and nationality that had issued from the Revolution. Painful as they may have been, those three years had at least not betrayed his expectation. Though the eagle had fallen, its shadow still lay over Europe. Its imprint in the sky would never be obliterated again. It had soared too high, and too far abroad.

Captive in the South Atlantic, he had become just a fat, jaundiced invalid, suffering from ills that were growing worse through lack of treatment or a mistaken treatment. Around him he could see attachments wearying, loyalties crumbling, only promises of money being able to patch them up again. He was living silent and alone, a prey to petty irritations.

Yet meantime an unparalleled prestige was lifting him on high on his gibbet, so that his silhouette was dominating a world that had thought to bury him alive. Overreaching the network of meridians and tropics it was the besetting nightmare of the kings of Europe and their ministers, and of those swarms of State clerks who were scratching busily at treaties to erase his name. A sneeze at Longwood made Louis XVIII turn pale in his gouty armchair. Bathurst sat up in his bed every night in terror lest the Convict might have escaped. Metternich kept wrinkling his forehead under his powdered hair at the thought that the sea might once more cast up the man whom he had sold and jeered at. Europe's capital mistake was now apparent— to have interned Napoleon in order to make sure of peace in defiance of those unwritten laws that obligate towards the vanquished. In treating Napoleon in that manner Europe had only added to his glory. The prisoner of Longwood had a very different hold on the public imagination from what a gentleman-farmer in some English county or a planter in the New World would ever have had.

The seclusion, moreover, in which he had chosen to keep himself at Longwood was the origin of many false alarms that ran riot in Europe, their echoes reverberating against the cliffs of St. Helena to arouse the greatest astonishment there. Stürmer was able to write to his Court (July 4, 1817): "It is rumoured in France and England that M. de Montholon was hanged at the yard-arm on an English vessel on the very day when Mme. de Sémonville, his mother, was giving a ball in Paris; that Mme. Bertrand was in prison in London for having sought to foment disorder and hatch a conspiracy with money that Bonaparte had put at her disposal, and also for taking secret part in a seditious movement against the Governor; that there has been a fire at Longwood in which all of Bonaparte's papers were burned and the greatest havoc caused; that an American vessel was caught manifesting evil intent upon St. Helena; that the Commissioner of a great Power had become involved in a plan for an escape by acting as intermediary in the forwarding of written communications and clandestine correspondence; that St. Helena on that occasion had been set on fire and drowned in blood."

And the delegate from Austria commented: "Now, Your Highness, for the actual facts: M. de Montholon has not yet received his merited reward, and Mme. de Sémonville is still free to keep people dancing in her house. Mme. Bertrand continues to share her ruler's prison, and has all she can do bringing up her children and increasing their number. There happens to have been a fire at Longwood, but it was in the chimney in the ex-Emperor's drawingroom, and it resulted in nothing more serious than a few moments of fright and a broken window pane. The only disorder resulting at St. Helena was in Hudson Lowe's head, which he nearly lost when news that there had been a fire was brought to him. The appearance of the American vessel is a pure fiction devoid of any basis in fact whatever. For anyone to dare approach this island with evil intent he would need to come with at least five or six ships-of-the-line. As to the Commissioner of a great Power, and the secret and dishonourable machinations ascribed to him, one can see in that nothing but the result of conjectures made from a number of incidents, true or supposititious, that occurred at the time mentioned. Since our arrival at St. Helena absolute calm has prevailed here and the upheaval that is supposed to have taken place is the purest fancy."

In England more than anywhere else the thought of Napoleon was in the public mind. The Whig minority that claimed to represent the British tradition of fair play, and which had denounced the Liverpool Cabinet away back in the days of Plymouth, had not disarmed in spite of the check that Lord Holland had suffered. The question of the treatment that was being inflicted on Napoleon was still a subject of frequent and vigorous discussion in magazines and newspapers. The *Morning Chronicle* had come out openly against Bathurst. What was demanded was not so much that the prisoner be set at liberty as that Lowe be replaced and the forms of the Captivity mitigated. Some, however, did demand the return of Napoleon to Europe or to a less humid climate where his health would be less likely to suffer.

Opposition statesmen were not the only ones to take an interest in Napoleon. There were the poets too—one of them in particular, and the greatest of the day, the most passionate, the most sonorous— Byron. He raised magnificent cries that were not unknown, we may be sure, to the prisoner of the Kings on his black islet.[1]

In France, however, as well as in Germany and Austria, the censor forbade any newspaper to print the name of the former Emperor. Complete silence as regarded him and St. Helena! On the other hand pamphlets depicting Napoleon in grotesque guises were favoured by the police. He was playing Robinson Crusoe on his isle with negresses, tyrannizing over his few remaining companions, or being roundly brought to reason by the English, who were disgusted with his coarse talk. Caricatures in huge numbers insulted him basely: "Napoleon Surrenders but Does not Die." "The Imperial Candle-Snuffer." "Hold Him Tight!" "The Devil Take Him!" "Greetings from France!" The acme of all human foulness! And, it must be confessed, in such blind fury the French pamphleteers and cartoonists manifested the greatest wantonness of all.

Early in 1819, while the last of his hopes were being trampled into the ground, Napoleon received a supreme tribute from the greatest of his opponents. In an article in the *Conservateur*, Chateaubriand had written:

"Born on an island, destined to die on an island at the farthermost limits of three continents; cast into the midst of the sea where

[1] *Childe Harold*, Canto III; Ode to St. Helena, 1816.

Camoens placed the genius of the storms as it were in prophecy of him, Bonaparte cannot stir on his rock without our feeling a shock from it. This new Adamastor lets fall a footstep in the other hemisphere and we feel it in this one. If Napoleon were to escape from the hands of his jailors and withdraw to the United States, his glance would still reach out across the Ocean to trouble the peoples of the Old World. His mere presence on the American shore of the Atlantic would force Europe to camp under arms on the opposite shore." [2]

Worthy of him, those words of a writer who had hated him for monopolizing the age, but who admired him to the marrow of his bones and whom he himself had held in esteem! They touched him deeply. He said to Montholon:

"Chateaubriand has received the sacred fire from nature—his works give evidence of that. His style is not Racine's—it is the style of a prophet. If he were ever to reach the helm of affairs Chateaubriand might possibly go astray. So many others have met their doom there! But what is certain is that everything that is great and national must bow to his genius." [3]

"Old René" was to pay for that encomium in the *Mémoires d'Outre-Tombe*, in pages devoted to the death of Napoleon, and the noblest, one may venture, that will ever be written on that subject.

.     .     .     .     .     .     .

Publications relating to the Emperor's captivity followed one another at short intervals, wandering over the entire Continent with the police on their heels. First of all came a French translation of Warden's *Letters*.[4] It appeared at Brussels in 1817.[5] That volume had been followed by the *Manuscript of St. Helena*, Santini's *Appeal*, Montholon's *Remonstrance*, and the *Observations on Lord Bathurst's Speech*. They made a deep impression and Napoleon was encouraged. Through O'Meara, Balcombe, and still other channels he got more particularly to the publisher Ridgway, in London, a number of controversial pamphlets, notes and explanations, which served to place

[2] *Conservateur*, I, 333 (November 17, 1818).
[3] On other occasions Napoleon had spoken harshly of Chateaubriand; O'Meara, April 30, 1817 (January 28, 1818); *Mémorial*, June 1, 1816; *Lettres du Cap*, No. 9.
[4] On Bathurst's request Warden had been struck off the list of surgeons in the British navy "for having dared to defend Buonaparte." He was reinstated later on and became surgeon at the arsenals of Sheerness and Chatham. He was a frequent and welcome visitor at Holland House. He died in 1849 at the age of 72.
[5] The publisher was T. Parkin, editor of the *Philanthropist*. A few months after the Belgian publication, Gide and Sons brought out a pirated edition in Paris.

his case before the public and make the public judge of the indictment he was drawing against his conquerors from the rock piles of
his reef in the sea. Among them were his *Letters from the Cape*,[6] a
reply to Warden's book, the *Manuscript from the Isle of Elba*,[7] the
*Letters from St. Helena*,[8] and finally the small tract entitled: *Is the
Manuscript of St. Helena by Napoleon?* [9] Logical disquisitions,
varied narratives, vivid anecdotes, a clear and persuasive style with
here and there the rhetoric that was much in favour in those days,
but also pages of manly eloquence! All those pamphlets that the
trade-wind blew back to Europe showed the mark of the master and
the lion's claw.

He protested, he threatened, he argued. His instinct as a born pub-
licist drew him into endless controversies. Bertrand, like Gourgaud
before him, did not approve of them. How could the great Emperor
fly into rages at a man like Lowe, draw up briefs, wrangle about cere-
monials, bills of fare, a trifle more or less of space around his walls?
Oh, but the fact was—Napoleon was still hoping and suffering, still
keeping, at forty-nine, too much vigour to give up without a last
long struggle.

By autumn of that year, 1818, he could count as his aides and
assistants three men, different indeed in type of mind and in motive,
but all three of whom had lived in close contact with him at St.
Helena and were now in a position to bear witness for him before
Europe—Las Cases, Gourgaud, O'Meara.

After the odyssey that had tossed him from St. Helena to the Cape,
from the Cape to London, from London to Frankfort—residence in
France being forbidden him—Las Cases had set himself up as Napoleon's secret representative. All his hopes were staked on that work,
his honour also, and a loyalty on which not even his flight from Longwood could cast any doubt. To that new rôle he brought both
enthusiasm and tactlessness. Never mind that he should annoy Liver-

---

[6] *Letters from the Cape of Good Hope* "in reply to M. Warden, with extracts of
the great work in preparation under the direction of Napoleon," London, Ridgway,
1817. They made a great stir in the press—the *Times* devoted four articles to them
alone. However, they did not sell well. They were not to be translated into French
until two years later.

[7] *Manuscrit de l'île d'Elbe ou Les Bourbons en 1815*, published by Count X——.
Ridgway, 1818.

[8] *Letters from the Island of St. Helena exposing the unnecessary severity exercised
towards Napoleon.* Ridgway, 1818.

[9] *Raisons dictées en réponse à la question si l'ouvrage intitulé "Manuscrit de
Sainte-Hélène" est l'ouvrage de Napoléon ou non.* London, Philipps, 1820.

pool and Bathurst with interminable letters, and Parliament with a
defence seventeen pages long! He wrote to Metternich as well, and in
a tone of too great assurance, and worse yet to Czar Alexander on
too familiar a footing. By his torrential verbiage he ran the risk of
turning the Czar against Napoleon—and, in fact, did so.

His activity was almost as dangerous when it came to the Emperor's family. He wrote to Marie-Louise and sent her a lock of
Napoleon's hair, receiving, of course, no reply. He wrote to Madame
Mère to give her news of her son and inform her as to his health,
his needs. He wrote to Lucien, Joseph, Pauline, Louise, Jerome,
Elisa, Caroline, Hortense, trying to arouse their pity, to revive affections that distance was lulling to sleep and that personal cares and
worries had diverted. So too he was to get to Bertrand, over the
obligatory route of Goulburn, the first detailed information that
Longwood had received concerning Napoleon's near relatives. His
letters did not all reach St. Helena, but from those that the English
Cabinet allowed to pass, Napoleon learned the essential facts about
his family down to the 19th of May, 1818, when Las Cases wrote to
Longwood for the last time. Suffering from strained eyes and headaches, he gave up all consecutive work after that. The Bonaparte
family had been displeased with his excess of zeal, but were nevertheless to consult him again on a number of occasions.

His letters to Bonaparte were read by all the police in Europe and
displayed hopes that were to prove irritating to the rulers. In a flight
of enthusiasm he wrote, for instance, to Elisa, March 18, 1818: "The
Emperor is badly off on his terrible rock. There he is, assailed by the
hatred of his enemies; but for all of their efforts he shows himself
still, and will always remain, their master." With the best of intentions he intimated that he received news from St. Helena through
secret channels. He gave his word that the Emperor had money and
that his health was improving. "His liver complaint has lessened in
virulence and he has regained much of his strength," he wrote to
Dr. Cailliot, October 15, 1818. Such statements were hardly calculated to obtain Napoleon's recall to Europe, and they were to have
as disastrous effects on the measures of the Allies as did Gourgaud's
chatter.

Gourgaud had left for England armed with a letter from Montchenu to the Marquis d'Osmond, French Ambassador at London.
Arriving on May 8th he saw Goulburn, then Osmond, then the Rus-

sian Ambassador, Lieven.[10] As had been the case at St. Helena, he talked too much. Still filled with rancour against Longwood, and led on by eager questioners who wanted to hear that Napoleon was in good health and the severity of his surveillance therefore justified, he allowed himself to make the most unfortunate admissions—though not more than Las Cases had already made, and on the same points: health, secret communications, money. Osmond's letter to Richelieu gives the general tone of his talk. Gourgaud was hoping at that time to inspire sufficient confidence in the French government to win a reinstatement in the army. He was soon to be disillusioned in that regard. Meanwhile he was meeting a number of Bonapartist officers who were living in London in exile. With them he soon forgot his troubles and became rebaptized in his cult for the Emperor. He set in order the manuscript he had brought on the *Campagne de 1815* [11] and published it under his own name, though it was understood to be shielding a greater one. He sent a letter to Marie-Louise (August 25, 1818), begging her to intercede with the Allied sovereigns, who were about to meet at Aix-la-Chapelle, in order to obtain a surcease to Napoleon's torment. The letter was printed in a number of English newspapers. Gourgaud sent it to Marie-Louise, bound into a copy of the *Campagne de 1815*, in the hope that it might escape Neipperg's supervision. Did Marie-Louise open the volume? Did she read the letter? That is not known.[12]

Finally he appealed to the Czar and to the Emperor of Austria. Thenceforward boldly following the policies of Longwood, he wrote the former (October 2, 1818): "Napoleon's health is being undermined and exhausted. . . . He is being worn down with severities that have no bearing on his security. He has been placed under the guard of a man who is killing him with pin-pricks." To the second he declared: "He will soon be dead—that is certain. He hopes so himself. It is with joy that he sees the symptoms of his decline increase

[10] Goulburn to Bathurst, May 10, 1818 (Lowe Papers, 20-123); Osmond to Richelieu, May 12; Lieven to Capodistria, May 13; to Balmain, May 21. These last two letters, as, for that matter, the ones that Gourgaud was to write to the Emperors of Russia and Austria, completely destroy the theory that he had any "mission" from Napoleon.

[11] It was published almost simultaneously in Paris (by Mongie) and London (by Ridgway). Edition followed edition.

[12] The truly touching document was auctioned after her death. Today it is the property of M. Robert Chantemesse.

and multiply from day to day. He cannot sleep anymore." And he begged Francis to interfere at the Congress.[13]

Thereupon the British Cabinet applied the Alien Bill and had Gourgaud deported. He went to Hamburg and got into touch with Prince Eugene. From that time on his conduct deserves nothing but praise. He was again wholly devoted to Napoleon.[14]

The last "missionary" to arrive from St. Helena, O'Meara, no sooner reached England than he sent to his chiefs, the lords at the Admiralty, a long bill of accusation against Lowe. Overstepping the mark in his hatred, he did not hesitate to repeat to them what he had already said on his stop-over at Ascension, to naval officers and physicians such as Blackwood Hall, Malcolm and Cuppage, that, on a number of occasions since May, 1816, the Governor had given him significant hints as to "the benefit which would result to Europe from the death of Napoleon Bonaparte." [15] He declared that Lowe had tried to induce him to "rid him" of Napoleon.[16] With good reason the naval lords found the imputation slanderous. They dismissed O'Meara from the service, November 2, 1818. But the Irishman was not the man to submit. He protested in the *Morning Chronicle*. Then, the following year, and in a volume, he attacked Lowe in a fight to a finish, representing that uneasy, worried man as a torturer and a criminal, and so beginning to dishonour him in the eyes of his own country.[17] Lowe requested Bathurst to bring suit, but the minister advised him to be patient for a time.

As much concerned with his interests as with his hates, O'Meara undertook that same year a "retrieving" expedition. Prince Eugene cashed the check for the hundred thousand francs that Napoleon had given him. Madame Mère granted him an annual pension of 8,000

[13] October 25, 1818. The two letters were found in rough draft among Gourgaud's papers. Masson saw in them nothing but outlines of letters still to be written. There is, however, every reason to assume that they were sent to their addresses.

[14] Gourgaud got back to France in March, 1821, a few weeks before the Emperor's death.

[15] October 28, 1818. Forsyth, Vol. III, p. 433.

[16] Lowe Papers, 20-125. There can be no doubt that O'Meara was lying. Lowe never had such a thought. He had the greatest personal interest in keeping his prisoner alive as long as possible. And he was wholly incapable of committing a crime, even a crime of State.

[17] *An Exposition of some of the Transactions that have taken place at St. Helena, since the appointment of Sir Hudson Lowe as Governor of that Island.* London, Ridgway, 1819 (Paris, Chaumerot, July, 1819).

francs. The physician failed in his effort to reach Marie-Louise at Parma.

In the view of Napoleon, those who returned from St. Helena ought to combine their efforts with those of the Bonaparte family to obtain his internment in Malta or in England or at the very least a change of Governors. He knew that his family was impoverished, scattered, spied upon by the sovereigns, but he also knew that some of its individual members still possessed copious resources. Forgetting that certain of his relatives had already shown themselves utterly indifferent or ungrateful towards him, he was counting on his "clan" to join with one accord in an effort to rouse the pity of the nations in his favour and so exert pressure upon the kings.

In 1818, three years after the disaster, what was the exact situation—what were the feelings of Napoleon's nearest of kin?

Since finding refuge in Rome under the generous protection of Pius VII, Madame Mère had resumed her former rôle as head of the family. She had settled in the gloomy Palazzo Falconieri, leaving it in March, 1818, for Palazzo Rinuccini in Piazza Venezia. Pius VII, admirable soul, manifested a high esteem for Madame Mère and an unfailing sympathy. Often, as he drove about the Roman Campagna, his coach would meet a carriage bearing the green and gold markings of Napoleon's mother, for though she had put on mourning and was never to take it off again, she still kept the Imperial livery. With great simplicity Pius VII would get out, go to the carriage door and greet Madame Letizia, and then, walking a few steps along the road with her, he would ask:

"Have you received any news from our good Emperor?"

A woman of little knowledge but of a heart tough enough to withstand all the extremes of fortune, Madame Mère was guiding, helping, reprimanding, her children. Wealthy in her own right, she would give them money but not without considerable persuading. In that she was right, for wastrels like Lucien, Jerome and Caroline would soon have done for her savings. She intended to keep the bulk of her property for Napoleon, in case he should ever need it.

"Everything," she repeated, "belongs to the Emperor, from whom I got everything I have."

Instinctively her favourite had always been the child she knew was least happy. For a long time it had been Lucien. Now it was Napoleon. She would have gone to St. Helena had Napoleon allowed her to. Fesch, her half-brother, whom she loved too well, was look-ing after her affairs. Archbishop and Cardinal by the grace of his nephew, he had only a lukewarm friendship for him. Had Louis XVIII left him his diocese he would have asked nothing better than to go over to the Bourbons. He wrote to that monarch, July 10, 1815: "Your Majesty will not fear, I trust, that personal affections could ever prevent me from fulfilling the duties of a bishop or cause me to default in any undertaking I have assumed."

The King, through Fouché, had him given his passports for Rome. That did not prevent Fesch from sending Louis XVIII on important feast days singularly platitudinous congratulations. Despite pressure from the Royal government and Consalvi he stubbornly refused to resign the archbishopric of Lyons. Not till 1823 was it possible to appoint an apostolic procurator there.

Obliged to live in Rome and engrossed in a mystical form of devotion, the Cardinal none the less continued to amass money and collect paintings. His ascendancy over his sister, his nieces and nephews, served merely to alienate them from Napoleon. He may still have been jealous of him, or he may have been merely a fool, but certain it is that that Corsico-Swiss mule was loyal only to powers on which Fortune smiled.

The some time King of Spain, Joseph Bonaparte, had gone to the United States with his archives, his jewels and his millions. He was living in magnificent style at Philadelphia in the winter, and at Point Breeze in the summer, with a little court about him.[18] He had received news of his brother through Archambault and Rousseau, who had called on him after their dismissal from St. Helena; from his wife, Julia, who saw Las Cases; from Las Cases himself; from Bertrand, who sent Balcombe to him with a letter of introduction as a start towards establishing a regular correspondence;[19] and finally from O'Meara, who handed him a short note from the Emperor, dated July 26, 1818. Why O'Meara did not send it on to Joseph until a year later (July 31, 1819) is hard to imagine.[20]

[18] Regnault de Saint-Jean d'Angély, Arnault, Grouchy, Réal, Lakanal, were his principal intimates.

[19] March 15, 1818. Balcombe was referred to under the pseudonym of "Monsieur Bale."

[20] Joseph had sent a certain number of letters to St. Helena. We know of several of them only through Gourgaud's diary. One of the first, written in July, 1816, ar-rived March 11, 1817, another in May of the same year. A letter of February, 1818, reached Longwood through an American named Feldman. The last seems to have

Napoleon knew Joseph and asked no great effort of him—merely the publication of the letters from the sovereigns. Joseph could not find them and did not care much. He received the two servants from Longwood kindly, paid them their salaries five years in advance, sent a thousand pounds to Las Cases, another thousand to O'Meara and Stokoe each—Stokoe he was to take into his employ for a time, after 1820. That was the sum of his efforts. He was sorry for the Emperor, naturally, but he was too busy trying to keep comfortable to associate himself even at long range with the misfortunes of a brother whom, after all, in spite of incalculable—and regrettable—favours, he had neither understood nor truly loved.

Marked out by the Hundred Days as a man to be mistrusted by the Allies, Lucien managed to worm his way back into the Pope's good graces, and by that route into a position as a Roman prince both opulent and in debt, writing bad poems, turning his land upside down to unearth antiques, receiving much from his wife with whom he was still infatuated, and repaying her almost every year with a child. In the spring of 1817, he had ideas of joining Joseph in America, but Europe vetoed the project and Lucien burrowed in at Canino to continue his rural labours. When he received the letters from Las Cases he declared himself ready to leave for St. Helena with or without his family. Was he sincere? He may have been. He was a man of fiery imagination, hungry for publicity. That *beau geste* may have tempted him. Las Cases asked the English ministry in his name for permission for Lucien to undertake the journey. Bathurst declined to make a decision—it was for the Holy Alliance, he declared, to decide. He knew very well that the Holy Alliance would decide in the negative.

Jerome made a similar application at almost the same time, appealing directly to the Prince Regent and subscribing in advance, as Lucien had done, "to the measures of supervision and surety which the British government might consider necessary." His wife, the good Catherine, also wrote. The only result was a dry "Denied."

Pauline had separated from Prince Camillo Borghese by an advantageous agreement. In the charming Villa Paolina, buried in flowers, she was living a sheltered life of fashion, receiving many English guests as a matter of policy, for she had thought of winning allies for Napoleon in the enemy camp itself. Her acknowledged chevalier was

been that of May 9, 1820, which related in the main to the letters of the sovereigns. It did not reach Longwood until after the Emperor's death.

the Marquis Douglas, son of the Duke of Hamilton, an ardent Napoleonist, who had visited the Emperor at Elba. With him or with Lord Kensington she took the waters at Lucca or the baths at Livorno. Neither pleasure nor illness—for too riotous a life had undermined her health—could prevent her from thinking of her brother, hoping for his return, and being ready to sacrifice everything for him.

Louis had become a sour valetudinarian, at swords' points with the family, hating Napoleon. Elisa was thinking of her fortune [21] and of her children. She was living in great splendour at Trieste, though that did not prevent her from crying poverty. Caroline was making out a difficult existence in Austria. Hortense, a refugee at Arenenberg in Switzerland, was quarrelling with her husband. Both of those women were devoted to the Emperor but could do nothing further for him. Eugene might have done a great deal. Was he not son-in-law to the King of Bavaria and a friend of the Czar? But Eugene was transfigured. He had become a German prince. Duke of Leuchtenberg, a Royal Highness, he was enjoying an income in excess of two millions in francs. He paid the sums indicated on the draughts he received from the Emperor, but would not give anything more. Resolved to look out for the future of his own family, to protect his shekels and not to compromise himself, this good subordinate who had never shone for anything except obedience, had successfully forgotten that he was Napoleon's adopted son. Flattering deference to the King of Prussia and the Emperor of Austria, humility towards the Czar, bowings till the back ached before the Bourbons—nothing was too much for Eugene. Of all the Emperor's kin, he, with the least excuse, was the most ungrateful.

If they could not relieve the condemned man's loneliness by their presence, at least his relatives might have eased his material circumstances by their remittances. Madame Mère could have done that all by herself—she had sufficient means. But she thought the whole family ought to join in. Politics and penny-saving mixed! Las Cases had become treasurer as well as Secretary of State to the Bonapartes. He collected their quotas.[22] The amount was large enough to

[21] On her death she was to leave an income of eighty thousand dollars, not including jewels and other valuables.

[22] 65,000 francs from Madame Mère; 25,000 from Joseph; 21,000 from Eugene; 15,000 from Jerome. The others absorbed a deal of urging and ended by not giving anything.

cover drawings by Bertrand at a rate of 12,000 or 15,000 francs a month.

But by that time Eugene had received the Emperor's definite instructions from Longwood as to the disposal of the funds he held on deposit.[23] First Eugene was to reimburse Las Cases for the 100,000 francs he had lent, then to put at Napoleon's disposal the 12,000 francs a month required for his personal expenses. There was nothing left for Las Cases to do but return the contributions to the various Bonapartes, and he did so.[24] In future Madame Mère was to content herself with sending books, clothes, wine and coffee direct to St. Helena.

Were the Bonapartes to stop at these scant donations, these "stateroom remembrances"? No, indeed. Catherine, Jerome's wife, and Hortense, conceived the idea of making a collective appeal to the sovereigns. Las Cases advised against it—for fear of diminishing his own importance. He gave Madame Mère her cue and, unbeknown to her children, she copied a petition which he had forwarded to her but which was of so pompous a turn that it could never have moved anyone:

"Sires: A mother afflicted beyond all words has long hoped that the meeting of Your Majesties would restore her to happiness. It is impossible that the prolonged captivity of the Emperor Napoleon should not be a subject of discussion among you and that your greatness of soul, your power and remembrances of times past should not incline Your Majesties to interest yourselves in the delivery of a prince who has had such a share in your fortunes and even in your friendships. (August 29, 1818.)"

Louis wrote on his own account—one wonders in what terms. The others waited to sign all the same petition, and so signed nothing—and Catherine complained of that to her mother-in-law in forceful language. But Las Cases lost no opportunity to blow his own horn and himself announced to the sovereigns and to Lord Liverpool that the Emperor's condition was much worse and that he was without a physician (November 10 and 13, 1818).

Eugene, for his part, sent a weak letter to the Czar, directing the attention of that sovereign upon "the fate of a man who had been

---

[23] Bertrand to Prince Eugene, March 15, 1818.
[24] However he was to keep Madame Mère's 65,000, since he had already paid 55,000 to meet drawings by the Grand Marshal. The day after Napoleon's death Fesch was harshly to reclaim the balance.

his [Eugene's] mother's husband and his guide in his military and diplomatic career." He also lay in wait for Morgentheim as the latter was returning from the Conference and spoke a few words to him in Napoleon's behalf, but many more words in his own behalf. Acting more out of a sense of human decency than from conviction he was resigned in advance to obtaining no results.

On arriving at Aix-la-Chapelle the sovereigns had already made up their minds to keep Napoleon where he was. Had they not insulted the Pope a year before by failing to answer him when he begged for their mercy on the prisoner? On October 6, 1817, Pius VII asked his Secretary of State, Cardinal Consalvi, a bitter opponent of the Bonapartes, to intercede with the Prince Regent in favour of Napoleon. The Pope's letter was an extremely beautiful one. In it the pontiff spoke from the heart—we are far indeed from the verbiage of a Las Cases:

"We must both remember," wrote the Pope to his minister, "that next after God it is Napoleon who is chiefly responsible for the re-establishment of religion in the great kingdom of France. The pious and courageous enterprise of 1801 causes us to forgive and forget subsequent wrongs. Savona and Fontainebleau were but errors of the mind, disorders of human ambition: the Concordat was a Christianly and heroically saving act.

"It would be an unparalleled joy to our heart to have had a part in lessening Napoleon's sufferings. He cannot be a danger to anyone. We wish that he might not be a remorse to anyone."

Consalvi made the best of it and wrote to the Regent of England. The Regent did not even acknowledge receipt of the letter.

The paper war that Napoleon was indefatigably waging from his jail worried the kings, hurt them, angered them. Less than ever were they disposed to have that incorrigible storm-compeller any closer to Europe. More than any other of his crowned colleagues was Czar Alexander inclined to severity. Indifferent to the suffering of his former ally, for whom he had never felt more than an interested sympathy, he was now eager to seem cured of any weakness for Napoleon. His representatives were the ones to bring before the Congress a resolution tending, not as has been systematically repeated, to make the Emperor's captivity harsher, but to rejustify it in principle and to encourage England and her agents to keep sharp watch over him.[25]

Napoleon represented "the power of the Revolution concentrated in one individual." He was "the prisoner of Europe." England had treated him gently, liberally. His captivity would be even less painful than it was "did he not insist upon being treated like a sovereign. He rejects the facilities that are offered him for distraction. . . . He declares himself ill and refuses a visit from any physician other than the one who had become his accomplice, and who was never even able to certify that General Buonaparte was suffering from any serious or apparent indisposition of which a few days of exercise would not completely have cured him." Napoleon's other complaints concerning his residence and his mode of life were as "false as they were childish." "They are presented to curiosity and malice only as one more means of arousing the interest of his partisans."

The resolution then went on to deal with the publications for which Napoleon's emissaries were responsible. The members of the Bonaparte family were "furnishing money and maintaining through correspondence that underhanded activity which still exercises the public mind." Taking Gourgaud's "revelations" as its text the memoir declared that Napoleon was "stirring up all the quarrels with the Governor of St. Helena, with which he wearies him only the better to hide his real designs. . . . A plan for his escape had been worked out by the persons attached to his service and it might have been possible to execute it had their chief not seen fit to defer it."

So Russia demanded that Napoleon, "who had placed himself outside the law of nations," should stay there, that the precautions England had taken be approved, that all the Bonapartes be confined to the residences that had been assigned to them, that, finally, "any correspondence or transfer of money between Europe and the prisoner of St. Helena which has not been submitted to the inspection of the English authorities should be regarded as an act endangering public safety."

A week later, November 21, the Conference adopted the Russian proposals unanimously and without debate. The sovereigns declared

[25] The Czar's resolution was probably drawn up by Napoleon's arch-enemy, Pozzo di Borgo. This basic document, dated November 13, 1818, appears in Vol. 1804 of the French Archives, *Affaires Étrangères*. It was published for the first time by Hanns Schlitter, *Kaiser Franz und die Napoleoniden*, 1898.

their united will to put an end to any illusions born of the debates in England, of publications in the press, of advances made by relatives and friends of the conquered hero. A free hand was given to England and to Sir Hudson Lowe. Napoleon was not to be treated with any greater severity, but he was to remain at St. Helena, without hope in future of being released from prison or of seeing his prison changed. All his efforts for those three years had so proved vain. The chain he had tried to break had been reforged. The slab had first been placed over the opening to his tomb. Now the tomb was sealed. The Holy Alliance did not believe in his illness. It did not believe in his material and moral distress. It did not choose to believe in anything except his indomitable spirit of revenge. In the eyes of those kings, Napoleon represented Revolution, Liberty, Peoples' Rights, everything they feared and detested. How could anyone have hoped that once having him in their hands they would ever set him free?

# PART FIVE

## *NAPOLEON VANQUISHED*

### I

## *DEPARTURE OF MADAME DE MONTHOLON*

NEWS FROM THE CONFERENCE HAD NOT REACHED BELOW THE LATI-
tude of the Senegal on the road to St. Helena when, for the first time,
Napoleon's health seemed to be seriously impaired. He had not been
looking well since the month of October, as Nicholls noted on several occasions in his diary. On October 10, 1818, Nicholls saw Napoleon "at his dressingroom window with a red handkerchief round
his head. He continued there a considerable time talking to Madame
Montholon and the children. . . . His countenance appeared . . .
cadaverous." [1] However, the Emperor did not complain and was even
in a good humour.

On January 1, 1819, he kept to his room, without dressing. His
legs were more swollen than usual. On the 6th while dictating to
Montholon he fainted. On the 16th, according to Mme. de Montholon, he was ill again. However, Nicholls wrote for the 16th: "Rising early Napoleon went down into his garden and walked about,
watching the few sheep on the lawn in front of the house. He went
as far as the gate and looked at the new buildings through his
telescope. Saint-Denis [Aly] was in attendance." * For several days
Bertrand and Montholon had been urging him to send for Stokoe,
the surgeon on the *Conqueror.* Napoleon knew him. O'Meara was
a friend of Stokoe's and had intrdouced him, October 10, 1817, in
the garden at Longwood. The conversation on that occasion was conducted, as almost always with O'Meara, in Italian. It was said that
Stokoe was to marry Jane Balcombe. Napoleon mentioned the matter

[1] Lowe Papers, 20-120; Forsyth, Vol. III, p. 93 (Nicholls' *Diary*).
* Retranslated.

to Balcombe, who denied it. Stokoe had been censured by Admiral Plampin for "having procured an introduction to General Bonaparte without first asking any permission."

The Emperor had been pleasantly impressed with the man. He had even consented to let O'Meara call him in consultation on July 10th. At the time Stokoe declined the invitation for fear of incurring the Governor's wrath.[2]

During the night of January 17, between midnight and one o'clock, Napoleon was seized with a sort of apoplectic stroke and lost consciousness. Forbidden by the Emperor's express command to summon Verling, Bertrand sent Nicholls with an urgent call for Stokoe. The letter was taken first to Lowe and then to Plampin by a dragoon. It reached Stokoe shortly after five o'clock. He answered the call immediately.[3] The physician arrived at seven o'clock in the morning. The Emperor was sleeping, after taking a bath. Stokoe waited till he wakened.

As Stokoe sat talking with Montholon, the latter suggested that he become official physician to the Emperor on conditions that he had jotted down in a note, and which were in every respect similar to those that O'Meara had previously accepted.[4] The note was promptly submitted by Stokoe to Plampin and by Bertrand to Lowe. There was nothing clandestine therefore about it.

At eleven o'clock Stokoe was admitted to the Emperor's room. Napoleon's face was flushed and he complained of the old pain in his right side. Stokoe examined him and unhesitatingly diagnosed the condition as hepatitis. He made a formal declaration to that effect in a bulletin which he sat down and wrote.

Stokoe handed the bulletin to Bertrand and then hurried off to report to Plampin before returning to his ship.

"Having been called to visit Napoleon, I found him in a very weak state, complaining of considerable pain in the right side in the region of the liver, and with shooting pain in the right shoulder. . . . From the evident tendency of a determination of blood to the head, it will be highly necessary that a medical man should be near his person, in order that immediate assistance may be afforded in case of a recur-

[2] O'Meara to Gorrequer, July 10, 1818 (Lowe Papers, 20-123).
[3] Bertrand to Stokoe, Lowe Papers, 20-125. Everything that Montholon has to say on this subject, Vol. II, p. 321, is deliberately false.
[4] Lowe Papers, 20-125.

rence of the above alarming symptoms, as well as for the daily treatment of chronic hepatitis which the above symptoms indicate." [5]

That evening the Emperor had further attacks of pain and Bertrand sent for Stokoe again. That was January 17, at nine in the evening. That evening Montholon went to Plantation House with Nicholls to ask Lowe for his reply on Stokoe's establishment in residence at Longwood. The Governor seemed mistrustful and reserved decision. [6] The doctor scaled the winding paths that led to Longwood under a torrential rain and by lantern light. He arrived at half-past five in the morning and stayed with Napoleon till four-thirty in the afternoon. He left the following bulletin: "The patient passed a restless night but without any alarming symptoms. At half-past three p.m. I found him rather more debilitated than yesterday, and advised a more nourishing diet. It appears from the symptoms of chronic hepatitis (the first appearance of which he experienced about sixteen months ago) that this is the principal cause of the present derangement in his health. . . . I do not apprehend any immediate imminent danger, although it must be presumed that in a climate where the above disease is so prevalent, it will eventually shorten his life. Longwood, January 18, 1819." [7]

Losing no time Gorrequer informed Nicholls that the Admiral could not dispense with Stokoe's services on the *Conqueror*. The Governor nevertheless agreed that Napoleon might resort to his care, but with the assistance of his colleague, Verling. As Napoleon would not accept Verling, that was equivalent to a refusal of Stokoe.

Lowe did not want O'Meara's friend to become the regular physician at Longwood. He did not believe that Napoleon's illness was dangerous. In particular he would not admit that the trouble was hepatitis. Lowe was strengthened in that persuasion by his friend, Dr. Baxter, who wrote to Verling on January 16th that he did not consider his illness serious. [8] The Governor was convinced that the French had won Stokoe over to their cause and that the doctor, like O'Meara before him, was becoming involved in an intrigue designed to procure a change in the place of exile for Napoleon. Lowe's job was once more in danger.

[5] *Ibid.*; Young, Vol. II, p. 135.
[6] Gorrequer, *Minutes*, January 17 (Lowe Papers, 20-125).
[7] Lowe Papers, 20-125; Young, Vol. II, p. 137.
[8] *Ibid.*

Stokoe returned to Longwood on January 19th, on a call from Bertrand, and he went to The Briars to ask Plampin's permission. Plampin subjected him to a thorough and formal questioning. Elliot, the Admiral's secretary, kept an official record of it. Plampin rebuked Stokoe for referring to Napoleon as "the patient" rather than as "General Buonaparte." [9] The questioning took time. Stokoe did not reach Longwood till six o'clock in the evening. Not daring to call Verling, Bertrand did what he could for the Emperor himself—the patient had a fever. After rebelling for a long time, Napoleon allowed himself to be bled and purged. A fresh examination confirmed Stokoe in his opinion. The liver appeared to have hardened. Like O'Meara he ordered mercury pills, extract of columbo (African bitters), and extract of cantharides.

He made his report in due form to the Admiral who, in agreement with Lowe, was amassing reasons for ruining him. Stokoe understood that, and therefore refused to go up to Longwood a fourth time. That was on January 20th. The night before Stokoe had left Bertrand a note of which the following are the essential passages: "I have every reason to think that my visits will soon come to an end, either because my superiors will formally forbid them, or because the situation will be made so disagreeable for me that I myself shall be obliged to discontinue them. . . . In either event I beg you to urge the illustrious patient to follow the treatment that I have prescribed. Hepatitis is always dangerous at St. Helena. . . . The sluggishness of the patient's liver, his habitual condition of constipation, and the disturbance of his digestive functions, may cause a rush of blood to the brain even more violent than that of Saturday." [10]

Before leaving, Stokoe received in payment for his attentions a draught on Joseph autographed by the Emperor and worded as follows:

"I beg you to pay Dr. Stokoe a thousand pounds sterling which I owe him. In sending you this note he will give you all the details you may wish to have regarding me. Napoleon."

For Stokoe to accept this honorarium was a very serious breach of military ethics. Luckily for him the fact remained unknown for almost a century. Masson brought it to light in 1912.

Plampin ordered Stokoe to go, but the next day reprimanded him

[9] Elliot, *Minutes,* January 19, 1819 (Lowe Papers, 20-125).
[10] *Ibid.* Retranslated.

for having stayed too long. Feeling himself more and more endangered Stokoe announced that he would refuse to go to Longwood again, whereupon the commander of the *Conqueror* warned him that the Admiral was intending to bring him before a court martial. Stokoe hastily asked for leave and sailed for England, January 30th.

The same ship carried a complaint against him drawn up by Plampin. The moment he arrived in London, therefore, the unfortunate doctor received orders to return to St. Helena. Back on board the *Conqueror* again, he was at once placed under arrest preliminary to trial by a court martial. He arrived at St. Helena August 21, 1819. On his two trips he had spent 188 days at sea. Stokoe set out for St. Helena with the conviction that his conduct was looked upon with approval. Word had been received at Longwood that he was on the way back and Bertrand, unfortunately enough, had even requested, August 19, that he again be authorized to attend Napoleon, who had had, he said, a fainting spell during the night.

The indictment charged Stokoe with having "communicated with the said General or his attendants on subjects not at all connected with medical advice," with having drawn up "alarming health bulletins," with having retailed O'Meara's calumnies against the Governor, with having designated General Bonaparte by the phrase, "the patient," and finally with "having in the whole of his conduct . . . evinced a disposition to thwart the intentions and regulations of the said Rear-Admiral, and to further the views of the said French prisoners in furnishing them with false or colourable pretences for complaint."

The trial began on the 30th of August. Stokoe had left his most important papers in England. He found no one to defend him. "No one," wrote Balmain,[11] "despite his urgent pleas, was willing to be his counsel. He spoke in his own defence and with quite a bit of skill and presence of mind. He admitted acts of insubordination and allowed it to be surmised that he had perhaps been the dupe, but not the accomplice, of the enemies of Plantation House. He moved his judges and the audience to compassion and today is considered a weak man, imprudent and unfortunate. So the mountain was delivered of a mouse. Nevertheless, after a summing up lasting four days, Stokoe was retired from service, sent home to England on a wretched

11 Balmain to Nesselrode, September 2, 1819.

civil pension of 100 pounds annually, and was to plead in vain for a review of his case.[12]

Stokoe had been treated severely—all the more so since no one knew that he had received money from Napoleon. But in view of the scandal stirred up by O'Meara, Lowe, and then Plampin, and behind them the Admiralty and the Ministry, wanted to make an example that would discourage anybody who might be tempted to become an accomplice of the French. At the same time it would prevent any consulting physician from expressing a free opinion thereafter, for if he were minded to pronounce Napoleon ill with liver trouble, he would be likely to remember what had happened to Stokoe.

But the people on the island wondered—how had they managed to get him before a court-martial, while O'Meara, "a great rascal" according to Lowe, had escaped without any trial at all? Because O'Meara knew too much. Lowe was afraid of the Irishman's combative spirit and had not dared to drive him to extremes. But also times had changed. He now felt greatly strengthened by the approbation of Europe, and he struck from the shoulder.

The results of the Conference of Aix were not known in detail at St. Helena until early in March, 1819. But newspapers arriving from London in January had given an inkling as to what the decision was to be. The Emperor was all the more upset since he had received a letter from Las Cases that gave him some hope, and he had read Gourgaud's letter to Marie-Louise in the press. Balmain wrote in his *Report* of March 1, 1819: "Napoleon was convinced that the Allied sovereigns, and the Emperor of Austria in particular, would take his side against the Governor of St. Helena. He waited for the newspapers with the keenest impatience and had the articles on the Conference of Aix-la-Chapelle translated word for word. He had many disappointments, for the *Morning Chronicle*, his most active defender, hardly mentioned the Conference. The *Courier* buried him under insults and abuse, while the *Observer* of October 12 positively announced that our August Master was leaving him to his fate. All

---

[12] He had completed twenty-five years in the service. He received expressions of thanks and fairly substantial gifts from Madame Mère, Fesch, and Louis. In 1821 he accompanied young Charlotte on her trip to America to see her father, Joseph. He remained with Joseph for two years and then returned to Europe, where he married. He tried again a number of times to get back into the navy, but without success. He died in 1852 at the age of 77.

that has thrown him into anger and despondency. He has again shut himself into his study and will not see anyone. As a result we do not know what he is doing nor whether he is well or ill. No one has any news of him."

When Napoleon read the text of the Russian resolution and the final agreement at the Conference his disappointment was complete, brutal, terrible. Europe had spoken! After three years of the harshest exile, she was reasserting her vindictiveness! Against that decree there was no appeal. Gone was all hope of ever leaving St. Helena! He would drag out his remaining years there. The protocol of the Conference of Aix was communicated to him officially, May 26, 1819, Nicholls serving it on Montholon.[13]

His depression during the days that followed was extreme. He shut himself up in his room. Only Marchand was allowed to approach him and he scarcely spoke even to him. Stretched out on his old sofa, he skimmed a few papers inattentively, flooded by an infinite disgust with everything. What should he do now? Continue his written war on England, appeal to world opinion? What was the use of that? Go on with his memoirs again? He had no heart left for such work. He had come to the point where he doubted everything—France, his family, his glory. Twenty dizzy years were ending in naught. Like the conquered heroes of old there was nothing left for him but to draw his mantle over his head and die.

Die? But death does not come at a man's ordering! It will come, but meantime one has to live! And Napoleon lived. His nights, in particular, were ghastly. He would lie open-eyed in his bedroom in the flickering light of his night-lamp, dreaming waking dreams, brooding over the past. He would get up, go and press his hot forehead against the window pane and gaze at the film of sea that shimmered in the monlight to the left of Flagstaff. Alarmed, Marchand would enter the room, tiptoe to his master's side, and suggest a hot drink. Napoleon would look at him tenderly and send him back to bed. Then he would lie down again and fall into a heavy sleep. In the morning he would often say: "I dreamed of Paris," making no further explanation. Strange visions must have visited him, born of a past that had escaped its forms and was blending perhaps with premonitions of the future. He would awaken dripping with perspiration, awaken to a new day that was exactly like the day before

[13] Lowe to Bathurst, May 28 (Lowe Papers, 20-126).

and would be like the day to come—a damp, windy, uneventful day that would show him the same landscape, the same prison, the same companions, who, deep down under their outward respectfulness, were, as he well knew, longing to bring that period of self-sacrifice to an end.

Masters and servants all were eager to get away. Pierron and Aly had gone to Plantation House to ask permission to leave Longwood at the first opportunity.[14] Mme. Bertrand kept urging her husband to return to Europe for at least a year to make plans for the education of the children. The Grand Marshal was still holding out, but he was almost at the end of his resistance. The Montholons too had made up their minds. They were not admitting it as yet to the Emperor, but on January 7th the Countess had consulted Dr. Livingstone and Dr. Verling and obtained a certificate that "the bad condition of her liver and stomach required thermal treatment." [15] Montholon was to go with her. At the races in April, 1819, Gorrequer asked him whether the Countess were still thinking of leaving. "Oh, I should say so! Of course!" "And you, monsieur, you will stay here?" "No, I am thinking of going too. I do not want to be separated from my wife." [16] Napoleon's illness took a turn for the worse a week later. That had forced the Montholons to wait. But at Plantation House, as well as at Longwood, there was no doubt in anybody's mind that the certificate would soon be made use of.

The only solution would be an early death for the Emperor! But those about him did not see any immediate prospect of that, in spite of his terribly yellow complexion, his rapidly falling hair, his heavy step. They realized with terror in their eyes that he could still last for a long, long time. He sensed their thoughts. Like his enemies, like the implacable Europe that was craning its neck at St. Helena and sighing hopefully at every variation in his health, his friends were counting the days and measuring the wastage in his face. For the whole vast universe the tiny dot called Napoleon was holding up the future! However—it would not be long! As he said: "The time will come when all of them, enemies and friends alike, will be satisfied. My enemies will have nothing further to fear from a power that crushed them. My friends will find themselves freed of any obstacle

14 December 17, 1818. Nicholls, *Diary* (Lowe Papers, 20-210).
15 Lowe Papers, 20-126; Verling, *Diary*.
16 Gorrequer, *Minutes*, April 28, 1819 (Lowe Papers, 20-126).

to their future plans. The grey coat will have ceased to frighten them and they will onward march with never a glance backwards." [17]

.    .    .    .    .    .    .

Napoleon received his last caller April 2, 1819. It was Ricketts, a cousin of Lord Liverpool and a member of the Calcutta Council. Ricketts was on his way home from India. Learning that he was stopping over for a few days the Emperor told Bertrand to invite him to come up to Longwood. It was thought at Longwood that Ricketts was Lord Liverpool's brother. The letter which Bertrand sent to him shows as much:

"Longwood, March 31, 1819

"Sir: The Emperor Napoleon, having learned that Lord Liverpool's brother is on this island, wishes to see him, though he is ill and in bed. I therefore beg you, sir, to be kind enough to come to my house, Friday, the day after tomorrow, between three and six o'clock in the afternoon that I may present you. Count Bertrand."

Ricketts replied on April 1:

"I shall accept with much pleasure the invitation with which one has deigned to honour me." [18]

To that Englishman, a man so closely associated with the Prime Minister, the Emperor would bare his full wretchedness for the first time. Since Europe was crushing him, England was the only country to which he could appeal. He would appeal to Lord Liverpool's humane sentiments to obtain his transfer to another place. No more anger, no more recriminations! Just a dignified, sorrowful lament that might at last be heard by the nation that was treating him so harshly but was, nevertheless, a last hope. Lowe raised no objection and did not even insist on presenting Ricketts himself. He was probably eager to avoid any unpleasantness where a relative of the Prime Minister was concerned.

Ill, or willing to seem so, Napoleon was in his bedroom when Ricketts entered, accompanied by Bertrand. He was lying on his camp bed in his shirt with a coloured handkerchief around his head. His cheeks and chin were dark from a three or four days' growth of beard. The room was poorly lighted and only by degrees could Ricketts make out the Emperor's features in the dim candlelight.

---

[17] Aly, p. 183.
[18] Lowe Papers, 20-125. Retranslated.

Napoleon was propped up on his pillows and had passed his right arm around the iron frame of his bed. When he moved, as he did two or three times, he seemed to be in pain. The visitor thought his appearance was normal, being struck only by his stoutness. "He resembled," Ricketts wrote,[19] "the picture of him leaning on the capstan of the *Northumberland,* and a French picture with laurel round his head. His complexion did not appear to be sallower than what it is ordinarily represented to be: not particularly dark under his eyes, nor exhibiting otherwise . . . any particular marks indicative of his being afflicted with the liver or any other severe bodily complaint."

The Emperor asked him to sit down and began speaking to him in a manner which Ricketts—warned in advance by the Governor—considered abrupt. However, his sentences were rapid and well turned. At times he became animated, and even jested. Ricketts had little chance to answer. From time to time the Emperor would say: "Do you understand?"

Confidently, in detail—the interview lasted four hours—Napoleon stated his requests:

"Tell Lord Liverpool that I should like to leave this island which is fatal to persons suffering from my trouble. I have been ill a long time. St. Helena is unhealthy. There is a heavy mortality among the troops in the garrison. Let them put me somewhere else—in Europe. Your ministers can assign me a residence no matter in what county. They will never regret it—I am a soldier, I keep my word. Your government has already spent a million pounds in watching me and there is no end in sight. It is madness to squander so much money. To let me live comfortably in Europe would be sounder policy than to keep me locked up behind these walls in the tropics. Lord Liverpool probably has not the faintest idea as to how Hudson Lowe is persecuting me. The Governor has instituted a police system that reminds one of Sicily. He has taken my doctor away—O'Meara, who did not share his views. He is preventing me from having another physician though he knows that I am ill in bed.

"He has had a letter sent to Count Bertrand in which he declares that if I do not appear in person before the orderly officer, my apartment will be entered by force. Tell him that because of that measure I am living in these wretched rooms under lock and key. They shall cross this threshold only over my dead body. One can die

[19] Record Office, C. O., 247, 25; Young, Vol. II, p. 152.

only once. A bayonet thrust or some other way—what difference does it make? If they want to murder me, let them do so immediately.

"I shall not take the exercise required for my health as long as Sir Hudson Lowe remains here, for I refuse to expose myself to insults or to cause the expulsion from the island of anyone to whom I should perchance say a few words.

"The measures that are being taken to prevent my escape are useless and odious. As the height of folly they are now building me a house that will cost huge sums and which I shall never occupy. I hate its location, which is bare of trees and faces the camp. I could never put my nose against the window pane without seeing redcoats. My ears would be dinned by all the drums. I would even hear the challenges of the sentries. Could anything be more insulting to a soldier who is held prisoner?

"Let Lord Liverpool deal directly with me. If Pitt were alive he would treat me very differently. Yours is a generous nation. In the end it will grow indignant." [20]

A heartbreaking cry coming from such a man, who had been reduced to beseeching his conqueror from his wretched hovel beyond the seas!

Bertrand gave Ricketts a memorandum of the conversation to hand to the Prime Minister. It has Napoleon's very words and almost the sound of his voice:

"1. To be removed from the island because I am suffering from chronic hepatitis.

"2. That in whatever position I may be, the proper policy is to place me near a man of honour who understands the forms of politeness.

"3. To send back to me my doctor O'Meara, or give me a Frenchman, or send me an English civilian who has no military tie and is of good reputation.

"4. Not to compel me to occupy the new house, because there are no trees, because it is too near the camp, and it is in that part of the island where there are no trees; an oak is what I want.

"5. Lord Liverpool should authorize a direct, sealed correspondence with himself, which should not pass through Lord Bathurst; or with a Peer of the Realm who would act as our advocate with the

[20] *Ibid.*

Ministry, such as Lord Holland; in that way the public would be kept out of all this." [21]

The visitor seemed to be touched and promised to intercede with his cousin. But the moment he returned to Plantation House, Lowe took him in hand and declared that Napoleon's illness was strictly diplomatic. Back in London Ricketts was to speak to Liverpool in such a way as to increase the minister's mistrust. The sole result of all the high hopes the French had placed in the visit was to be an ironical letter from Bathurst to Lowe: "Nothing could have been more fortunate than Mr. Ricketts' visit at St. Helena. He has given the most satisfactory reports concerning the real state of the business, and saw through all the manoeuvres which were practised to impose upon him." [22]

From that time on Napoleon remained practically invisible to the English. Poor Nicholls could manage only by burlesque stratagems to catch a glimpse of his silhouette or of a shadow wearing a tricorne, or a sound that was recognizable as Napoleon's voice. Cut off from news of Longwood, Lowe stormed perpetually at his officer, and vainly did the latter bribe gardeners, question servants, dog Montholon about. He simply could not answer for Napoleon's presence. The business of being a jailor began to get on his nerves. On the 15th he wrote to Gorrequer: "In execution of my duty yesterday I was upon my feet upwards of *ten hours*, endeavouring to procure a sight of Napoleon Bonaparte, either in his little garden or at one of his windows, but could not succeed. . . . During the whole of this time I was exposed to the observations and remarks of not only the French servants, but also to [sic] the gardeners and other persons employed about Longwood House; . . . I have very *frequently* experienced days of this kind since I have been employed on this duty." [23]

Montholon made fun of him. He would assure him that the Emperor was in bed. A moment later Nicholls would see him in the garden, fully dressed, taking a walk with the Bertrands.[24] He would advise him to look through the drawingroom keyhole,[25] and the officer

[21] Lowe Papers, 20-204.
[22] July 13, 1819 (Lowe Papers, 20-128); Young, Vol. II, p. 154.
[23] Nicholls to Gorrequer, May 15, 1819 (Lowe Papers, 20-126); Young, Vol. II, pp. 161-62; Forsyth, Vol. III, p. 160.
[24] Nicholls, *Diary*, June 14 (Lowe Papers, 20-210).
[25] *Ibid.*, July 5.

would go away angry. "The weather at present is so very bad," he noted on July 21, "that I fear my health will be greatly injured if I am under the necessity of continuing the system of walking round Longwood House and garden in the execution of my duty." [26]

The whole household, from the Emperor behind his blinds down to the lowliest of the Chinese "boys," were amused at Nicholls' torments. He always played in bad luck. If Napoleon went out, chance would have it that Nicholls would miss him. He felt that he was being made a fool of—and in fact was a little. "I am pretty certain that he keeps some of his servants constantly employed to watch my movements, so that it's nearly impossible for me to procure a sight of him." [27] He tried to offer his resignation on one occasion. [28] Finally on September 11, he gave a cry of triumph: "I *believe* that I saw General Bonaparte today at a little before 2 o'clock p.m. The person who I took to be him was standing at one of the General's dressing-room windows and in a *white dressing gown*, but soon after I made my appearance opposite the window he let down the blinds, which prevented me from seeing his face."

Taking pity on him Bertrand would sometimes send word that Napoleon was in his bath and that he could see him by looking through the open window. In that way Nicholls caught sight of him one day immersed in water up to his neck. He thought that he "had a most ghastly appearance." Marchand was with him.

Napoleon's stubborn refusal to allow the orderly officer to approach him enraged the Governor. His prisoner, he thought, would act in just that way if he were preparing for a flight. The slightest movement on the part of the French aroused his suspicions. Since their dramatic interview in August, 1816, Lowe had himself not been able to catch a glimpse of Napoleon except on one occasion, August 4, 1819. He reported it as follows to Bathurst: "I had repaired to Longwood to give directions about some alterations he had himself desired in his garden, when I suddenly found myself quite close to him. He had his back turned to me, and he had a long stick . . . in his hand, was dressed in his usual uniform, looked as lusty as I had seen him, but walked with a gait that bore somewhat the appearance of in-

[26] *Ibid.*, July 21; Forsyth, Vol. III, pp. 169-70; Young, Vol. II, pp. 162-63.
[27] Nicholls to Reade (Lowe Papers, 20-125); Young, Vol. II, p. 163.
[28] Nicholls to Gorrequer, June 29 (Lowe Papers, 20-126).

firmity. The children of Count Bertrand were with him." Napoleon moved slowly away as soon as he spied the Governor.[29]

Now, however, Lowe thought himself the man to put a check on the Commissioners. Besides, since his return from Brazil, Balmain had made up with him. Reade wrote to Lowe of Balmain that "since his return from Rio de Janeiro, he had quite altered his opinion in regard to the French people at Longwood. He now thought them a curious set, but particularly Count Montholon whom he described as a very intriguing character." [30] Balmain had revised his opinion of O'Meara and seemed, for his part, not to take Napoleon's illness seriously. On learning the outcome of the Conference of Aix and that his own court had proposed maintaining the conditions of the Captivity, and convinced now that the Czar had lost all interest in Napoleon's fate, Balmain completely reversed his attitude. Henceforth no guest was to be so welcome at Plantation House. Having nothing else to do Balmain became more and more attentive there and soon the beautiful eyes of Charlotte Johnson, eldest daughter of Lady Lowe, had captured a heart otherwise unemployed. Balmain's reports began to take on a different tone. The change was helped along by a scolding he received from Count Lieven, the Russian Ambassador in London, who disapproved of Balmain's attitude towards Lowe and notably in regard to the O'Meara affair. Later on, in deference to his father-in-law, Balmain was even to tone down his old reports by altering their texts.[31] He ceased railing against the Governor's arbitrariness and tyranny. With true Russian adaptability he applied himself to getting along on the best possible terms with Lowe. He reported to the Czar, June 28, 1819: "I experience a genuine satisfaction in being able to announce to Your Majesty that my personal relations with the English authorities are peaceful and amicable, that I go constantly to Plantation House and am received there with open arms, that dinners, balls and receptions have increased in number since the arrival of the latest news from Europe, and that all that charms the tedium of my exile. I regret, however, to be obliged to state at the same time that, seeing nothing more of either Bertrand or Montholon, I know absolutely nothing of what is going on at Longwood." His suspicions

[29] Lowe Papers, 20-127; Forsyth, Vol. III, pp. 171-72; Young, Vol. II, p. 164.
[30] Lowe Papers, 20-125.
[31] The "attenuated" reports are the ones to which we have been referring. In their earlier forms they were even more hostile to Lowe.

once allayed, Lowe became obligingness itself and was to prove to be an easy-going and generous father-in-law to Balmain.

. . . . . . . .

With Montchenu, on the other hand, Lowe experienced a disappointment. It was not at all the fault of the old courtier. The Duke de Richelieu had sent him new instructions dated August 27, 1818, and they reached St. Helena towards the end of the year. They urged Montchenu to establish more intimate connections with Longwood: "I greatly approve of your trying to multiply relations with the people who surround Bonaparte. Since you cannot see him personally, it is the only way to find out anything about his mode of life and his physical and mental condition. It is so important to us to know what they are, it is so obvious that the great expense occasioned by your sojourn at St. Helena can have no other aim, that I cannot believe that Sir H. Lowe can have any serious objection." Richelieu added: "The spot where you are residing is for us the most important spot in the world. All our glasses must be incessantly trained on that rock. Nothing that happens there can be uninteresting to us and you must see that you are in a position to tell us what is in their minds and what they can undertake and peradventure carry out. The King will be grateful to you for anything you may do to keep him informed as to the plans and aspirations of the inhabitants of Longwood, and the surest way to keep well informed yourself is to maintain relations, as far as possible, with them. If you meet objections on the part of the English authorities, do not fail to report them to me in detail, that I may take them up with the British government and have them removed." On reading the document Balmain said with a sigh of regret: "If I only had been sent orders like that! What a dance I would have given Mr. Lowe!" [32]

The Duke was mistaken in his attitude. Lowe was enraged at seeing Montchenu visiting Montholon, inviting him to luncheon—an unheard-of novelty—and holding long conversations with him. Lowe furthermore was obliged by his minister's despatches to object energetically to any regular relations between Montchenu and the Emperor's circle. He informed Bathurst of the instructions Richelieu had sent, and received the following reply from London, dated July 7, 1819: "His Royal Highness entirely approves of your conduct in resisting the pretensions with which the French Commissioner . . .

[32] Balmain, *Report*, March 18, 1819.

endeavoured to maintain an unrestricted intercourse with the followers of General Buonaparte, as well as with the General himself. The British Government is alone responsible to Europe for the safe custody of General Buonaparte, and that responsibility must cease if any person not named by the British Government, nor acting under its authority or control, has a right to have what communications he may choose with the inhabitants of Longwood . . . you will exercise your judgment with regard to the time and manner in which they may have occasional communications with the Commissioners; or you may prohibit them altogether if, as may be in the case of Count Bertrand, their insolence should appear to be encouraged, or their falsehoods be countenanced by too frequent intercourse with the Commissioners."

The Marquis viewed Bertrand as "a dangerous fanatic," but Montholon, the perfect man of the world, with his polished duplicity, his eagerness to let it be known in Paris how respectful he was towards the re-established monarchy and how enthusiastically he would hasten to serve it as soon as he should be free, could not fail to be pleasing to that ghost from Versailles. In all fairness to Montchenu it should be noted that he refused to go to the reception that Lowe gave to celebrate the anniversary of Waterloo. His letter, dated June 17, 1819, quoted a remark of Louis XVIII: "Though the battle of Waterloo was the cause of Bonaparte's downfall, it was none the less won against Frenchmen." Montchenu added, not without wit: "The Austrian Commissioner is not in the same situation, but you know that the one and sole order he has received is never to be at odds with the Commissioner for France." [33]

Montholon had tried to bribe Balmain. Did he make a still more strenuous effort with Montchenu? Probably. In January, 1819, the latter wrote to Richelieu: "About a month ago Montholon came to town to pay off a number of merchants to whom money had been owing for some time. He came to see me and said: 'They dicker with us over a few louis! They are wrong, for with so little money how can we even pay to get a letter through? I came into town with 8,000 francs—here are the receipts. What man here would risk his life for such a paltry sum? Either we have money or we haven't. If we have, no one can keep us from passing on a scrap of paper assigning a certain sum.' Then, *looking straight at me*, he said: 'The Em-

[33] Lowe Papers, 20-126.

peror knows how to buy. A man can be useful to him and he gives *six millions.*' 'I know,' I replied, 'that he has made good use of it and without stinting.' We both laughed and then we separated. As he turned away he said to me again: 'The Emperor knows how to pay.' And he mounted his horse."

Never stopping to think whether he was misrepresenting the Emperor's thought or demeaning his character, Montholon retailed to Montchenu no end of nonsense which he passed off as his master's opinions, now on French relations with Spain, now on laws relating to elections, censorship, army ranking, religion, and so on. According to Montholon Napoleon found the suffrage bill too liberal. We know, however, how limited suffrage was at that time. He was said to have thundered against a public subscription that had been opened in favour of newspapermen who were threatened with arrest under the new law: "It is an overt insult to the authority of the King and the Assembly!" he was said to have declared. Can one see Napoleon expressing himself in such terms? "He admitted that his indifference in matters of religion had been fatal to him, and especially his antipathy towards the Catholic faith." The Catholic religion should be made as august as possible. "I was surrounded by nothing but atheists who persuaded me that I could regulate religion as easily as anything else. The Pope refused to bow to my will. I had him arrested and that act was one of the main causes of my downfall."

That is Montholon at his best!

According to Montholon, the Emperor's ideas were those of a loyal subject of Louis XVIII and even went farther. He would have favoured the seizure of Naples and Spain by the Holy Alliance and suppressed the University—one of his basic institutions. He was always talking like a deeply devout man. Of course, in all that, Montholon thought he was whitewashing himself in the eyes of the Bourbons and promoting his own return to France. But there is little excuse for a treachery that attacks the mind. Luckily Napoleon never had any suspicion of it.

· · · · · · ·

The departure of Madame de Montholon was finally decided upon. The Emperor had been unable to object to it. The Countess had just had a miscarriage. She was thin and pale and complained of her liver —only the waters of Cheltenham or Spa, said the doctors, could

restore her health.[34] She had other problems too. Her mother, Mme.
Vassal, had died and she had matters to attend to in connection with
the settlement of the estate. The two children whom she had left
behind in France required her care.

With great difficulty Napoleon succeeded in persuading her husband to abandon his intention of accompanying her. Nicholls' *Diary*
makes the following entries for April:

"April 13.—I went to see Montholon this morning because I had
been unable to obtain information concerning Napoleon Bonaparte.
Montholon told me that he [the Emperor] was in very low spirits,
particularly because of the Montholons' plan to return to Europe in
view of the health of Mme. de Montholon.

"April 14.—Montholon told me that Napoleon was very sad and
that he was very desirous that Montholon should not go. He asked
him to consider two or three days before making any decision." [35]

Montholon, Napoleon thought, should stay with him for a time,
until he could be replaced by some loyal follower who would come
on from France. Meantime Napoleon had showered him with gifts
in order to hold him: a pension of 20,000 francs to be paid by Eugene
—the certificate was handed to him on June 15; another pension of
24,000 francs to be paid by Madame Mère and a draught for 144,000
francs to be cashed by Joseph. Those two generous gifts date from
June 28. Montholon may have received other sums still. In addition
he was to continue drawing his salary of 20,000 francs a month. But
in spite of all that he still held out. The idea of remaining at St. Helena
without his wife terrified him.

In the end she herself was brought in to persuade him. Napoleon
asked that favour of her one evening, when he had invited her to
dinner alone that they might talk more freely. "During the conversation," wrote Aly (p. 156), "the Emperor sought to persuade her to
leave M. de Montholon by telling her that she could easily find a husband in Europe. She replied immediately: 'Sire, a woman can easily
find a lover, but not a husband.' " And Aly adds: "*They must have
made him pay through the nose.*"

In fact, they had too much, both present and future, at stake in
pleasing the Emperor. After all, the time would not be so long! As

---

[34] Lowe to Bathurst, May 28, 1819. Mme. de Montholon was really ill. O'Meara
had unwisely treated her with mercury for her liver (Verling, *Diary*, p. 1).

[35] Lowe Papers, 20-120. Retranslated.

soon as she arrived in France she would attend to having her husband "relieved." Once more she led him down her road.

There was nothing to it but gifts. Napoleon was obliged to promise extremely liberal testamentary remembrances. This sordid negotiation filled the months of May and June. Montholon easily arranged with Lowe to have his wife excused—as Gourgaud had been—from going to the Cape. He went to see the Governor at Plantation House on May 26. Lowe asked him to send him an official request, which was delivered on the 30th. He immediately informed Bathurst. Montholon told him that "he would not prolong his stay on the island more than six months after the departure of his wife." He added that he was already making a great sacrifice to the Emperor in delaying that long.[36]

Napoleon gradually accustomed himself to the thought of seeing the Countess depart. Nevertheless during the last days he suffered genuine grief and was at no pains to hide it. For four years Albine de Montholon had proved an attentive and solicitous friend to him, always ready, always eager, to disarm and please. Living next door to the master, what patience had she not shown! To what discomforts had she not been put with a flock of young children who must never speak, laugh, play or cry except in a hush. No noise—the Emperor was working or sleeping! Good behaviour now—the Emperor was passing that way! Light-minded, frivolous, as she was, there had been calculation in all that. But she had the domestic genius of the Frenchwoman. If there had been any ray of light in Napoleon's environment on certain unusually dull days, it had come from her. She was the last smile of the Captivity.

That Mme. de Montholon was generally liked at Longwood and even at St. Helena and that she was keenly missed, the following lines of Balmain amply bear witness:

"This morning Countess Montholon left for England. She is a woman of wit and wisdom and amiable in the highest degree. She has been a great resource for me at St. Helena, and in her departure I sustain an irreparable loss." [37]

She sailed July 2 on the *Lady Campbell*, which came from Bombay. With her were her three children, her two servants, William and Adele Goff, and a maid from St. Helena. Napoleon gave a reception

[36] Lowe Papers, 20-126.
[37] *Report*, July 1, 1819.

to the whole family the evening before. He nad previously passed a great part of the day with them. He did not go out of doors [38]—it was raining. The window panes rattled under violent gusts of wind.

The Emperor gave Mme. de Montholon a gold box painted with his portrait in an oval of diamonds. He also offered her a number of beautiful books [39] bound in red morocco and stamped with his coat-of-arms—among others the three volumes of Voltaire's plays that had caused her so many yawns during the evenings at Longwood. On the fly-page he had written with his own hand: "Albine." He thanked her with a trembling voice for the sacrifice she had made for him in coming to live for four years at Longwood and for the sacrifice which she was still making in leaving her husband behind. He asked her to remember him to his family and friends and entrusted Elphinstone's chess set to her to send to Marie-Louise as soon as she should arrive in Europe. He had already given little Napoléone a turquoise brooch that had belonged to Mme. Stürmer and which that lady had sold on leaving St. Helena.[40] Montholon, the Countess, and the children were all in tears. Napoleon embraced them one after the other. Then he walked to the door and entered his own room.

"Their tears hurt me," he said to Marchand.

Within a few minutes he went into his bathroom. He heard the garden gate open. It was Mme. de Montholon leaving for Jamestown. At that moment Albine turned for a last look at Longwood. Did she see the raised curtain and the pale face that was looking after her?

As he got into his bath Napoleon spoke to Marchand, pitying Montholon for thus being separated from his family:

"But he understands perfectly well that he cannot leave me for two years yet [Prophetic words!].[41] Oh, but you will all go back to Europe—you will all see your families again—Montholon his wife and children, you, your mother. I shall have died—alone in this solitude!"

It was evening. On being told that Mme. Bertrand was ill, he started to go to see her. But night was falling. The sentries were being changed. He went back into the house through the diningroom door, tripping on the threshold as two rats ran between his legs. He spent the evening alone with Marchand, who read the tragedy *Mahomet* aloud.

[38] Nicholls, *Diary*, July 14.
[39] Aly, p. 157.
[40] Aly, p. 156.
[41] Marchand Papers (Thiers Library. Unpublished).

Mme. de Montholon left Longwood in a carriage sent by Lady Lowe. The Governor's wife had also sent a carriage for the children. Montholon followed on horseback. They dined at the Castle with the Commissioners,[42] then Montholon returned to Longwood, late at night and in a downpour of rain. He caught bronchitis from it and a rheumatism that kept him in bed for a long time. Mme. de Montholon had expected to leave the evening following—July 2, but Lowe forbade the *Lady Campbell* to hoist anchor because Nicholls had not seen Napoleon that day and he could not make up his despatch for London certifying the presence of the prisoner. Nicholls caught a glimpse of the Emperor on the 3rd at seven o'clock. He signalled Plantation House to that effect and the ship set sail almost immediately.[43] At the last moment Montholon sent his wife a note which could not be delivered to her. Lowe read it and copied out a passage: "The Emperor shows great regret at your departure. He shed tears for you, perhaps for the first time in his life."

No, not for the first time, certainly! But if Napoleon really wept (Marchand and later letters of Montholon make no mention of any tears) it was to be for the last time.

. . . . . . .

The days that followed were probably the gloomiest that Napoleon had ever known. He spent several hours at Montholon's bedside. Sometimes he would take a short drive with Mme. Bertrand, who had recovered again. On the 5th Napoleon called on her and gave her "a beautiful muff and a box with a miniature in a circle of 32 diamonds." [44]

The Emperor kept repeating to the Grand Marshal:

"Well, Bertrand, what did I say to you a fortnight ago when you told me of your fears for your wife? I told you that she would get over it because the doctors knew what the matter was with her, while I would not recover because they do not know what the matter is with me. You seem to doubt what I say. Well, don't! I haven't long to live." [45]

Towards the middle of August he suffered a return, but much less severe, of his hepatitis. Verling, and Dr. Arnott, the surgeon of

[42] Verling, *Diary*.
[43] Nicholls, *Diary*, July 1, 2, 3, 1819.
[44] Verling, *Diary*.
[45] Marchand Papers (Thiers Library, C. 22. Unpublished).

the 20th, were sent by Lowe to offer their services. The Emperor was ready to accept either one provided the conditions formerly signed by Stokoe were agreed to. Both refused. Napoleon continued to suffer without other care than that of his servants, who followed O'Meara's old directions as best they could.

Lowe viewed that attack too as mere stage-play. However Napoleon was actually ill. He felt much weakened and even thought himself in danger. The best proof of that is that he drew up his will and for the first time. The drawing of this will was absolutely unknown to the English. Montholon, Bertrand and Marchand were the only ones to know of it. It was not therefore an act calculated to impress Lowe. By the terms of the document the Emperor bequeathed his weapons, silver-plate, books and personal property to his son, to be delivered by Bertrand, who would meantime have charge of them. He redivided the 300,000 francs in gold that he had at Longwood: 120,000 to Bertrand, 50,000 to Montholon, 50,000 to Marchand, 20,000 to Aly, Noverraz and Pierron, 10,000 to Archambault and Gentilini. His diamonds were to be divided between Mme. Bertrand and Mme. de Montholon. In addition Napoleon provided in detail for the use of the money he had in Europe, and notably the amounts on deposit with Laffitte, dividing it among his companions. According to a pencilled note that Montholon found among the Emperor's papers, he gave 750,000 francs from those funds to the Bertrands, 600,000 to the Montholons. Those figures are interesting as compared with the ones that were to appear in his last will. Napoleon requested finally that his memoirs should not be published till they had been supplemented with all the important documents that were lacking.[46]

That was the moment the Governor chose to order Nicholls to force Napoleon's door, if need be, to assure himself of the Emperor's presence at Longwood. Reade gave the following written instructions: "If . . . it should . . . occur that you do not see him before ten o'clock in the forenoon . . . you will on such occasion proceed to the hall of his apartments . . . and if he does not present to you an opportunity of seeing him, or reply in such a way as to justify a delay on your part (which can only be in case of indisposition) . . . you will proceed to his inner apartments . . . and on arriving at the

---

[46] It was this will that he sent Marchand to Bertrand's house to get, April 30, 1821, and which was at that time to be thrown into the fire.

room in which he may himself be, you will, on seeing him, make your salute and retire." [47]

The Emperor immediately ordered doors and windows barricaded, and loaded pistols and guns placed near his bedside. "He swore that he would stretch on the threshold anyone who was bold enough to cross that line." [48] Longwood was put on a war footing. Aly slept in the diningroom, Noverraz in the kitchen corridor, Marchand in the bathroom, all three armed. Nicholls demanded to be admitted to Napoleon's presence in vain. Colonel Harrison came to the rescue. Both pounded violently at the outside door, made their way into the drawingroom, and tried to force the diningroom door. They did not succeed and did not dare to go any farther.[49] In his report of August 19th, Balmain mentions an amusing detail: "On the 14th of this month the orderly officer as usual stepped up to the window of the bathroom at Longwood to get material evidence of Bonaparte's presence. Bonaparte had been in his bath for an hour. He suddenly got out and in spite and anger showed himself to Captain Nicholls *in naturalibus*."

On August 16th Bertrand addressed an energetic protest to Lowe. The Governor replied with a veritable declaration of war. He served notice in the most emphatic language of the powers he had given the orderly officer for seeing Napoleon daily. Lowe's personal malevolence during this period is proven by an entry in Nicholls' diary: [50] "The Governor asked me why I knocked so gently on the parlour door. I replied that I did not want the French to be able to say that I was making a disturbance, General Buonaparte claiming to be ill. The Governor saw no reason why I should not knock as I would do on entering the house of any plain gentleman." Lowe further ordered that if anyone in General Buonaparte's retinue placed any obstacle in the way or offered any resistance he was to be immediately removed from Longwood and headed for the Cape.[51] Montholon answered this order at the Emperor's command on the 31st.[52] On September 3, Bertrand sent the Governor a new note.[53]

One might have thought that such a situation would lead to an

[47] Lowe Papers, 20-217; Forsyth, Vol. III, p. 174.
[48] Aly, p. 231.
[49] Nicholls, *Reports*, August, 1819 (Lowe Papers, 20-127).
[50] Lowe Papers, 20-210. Retranslated.
[51] Note by Lowe, August 29, accompanied by a memorandum of Reade.
[52] Montholon, Vol. II, p. 359.
[53] Lowe Papers, 20-128.

irreparable outburst and perhaps even to bloodshed. However the atmosphere cleared almost immediately. Lowe again took fright and yielded. He dared not push Napoleon too far, dared not force him to the last resort. He therefore abandoned his efforts to compel him to receive Nicholls every day. For that matter during the early part of September Napoleon went out of doors regularly for a walk or a drive and Nicholls therefore was able to see him. That made Lowe feel more comfortable. Lowe furthermore was soon to recall Verling. The arrival of the physician that Napoleon had requested was to deprive the enforced presence of an English doctor of any further significance.

# II

## *FIRST RELIEF*

Shortly after cipriani's death, bertrand had written to fesch asking him to send to St. Helena a Catholic priest, either French or Italian, a maître d'hôtel and a cook. Taking his time the Cardinal wrote to Lord Bathurst who not only had no objection but replied that he would further authorize the departure of a physician chosen by the Bonaparte family.

A physician was ready to hand, one that had attended Napoleon for years, was wholly devoted to him and knew English as well—Foureau de Beauregard, an honest man and an excellent practitioner who furthermore urgently requested to be sent out to St. Helena.

Foureau de Beauregard had been first physician to the Emperor and had followed him through the whole campaign of 1814 and then on to Elba. Foureau being a deputy in 1815, Napoleon had ordered him to continue in his seat in the Assembly till the end of the session and then join him if he could. Foureau was unable to obtain passports, so he fled to Austria and joined Jerome, with whom he found Planat de la Faye. As soon as he learned, through Las Cases, that a physician might finally be sent to the Emperor, he immediately volunteered. "I want my place back," he wrote to O'Meara, November 19, 1818, and asked to be shown O'Meara's medical records. Fesch rejected him because Foureau wanted to take his wife with him. He also made the point that Napoleon had asked for a surgeon, not for a physician.[1]

In Foureau's place Fesch selected a young Corsican, Francesco Antommarchi, prosector to Professor Mascagni in Florence, short in knowledge but long in rhetoric, who would be satisfied with a salary of 9,000 francs. Antommarchi had been recommended to Fesch by Colonna Leca, steward to Madame Mère, who had known him in Florence. He was born at Morsiglia, Corsica, in 1789. Planat said of him to Louis Bonaparte: "He is a man of no knowledge, who has served merely as dissection assistant in the student laboratory in Florence." Sir John Webb wrote to Lord Burgesh, English minister

---

[1] Fesch to Las Cases, December 5, 1818.

405

to Tuscany: "I hear from good sources that he has more talent for intrigue than medical knowledge. . . . He has a good deal of self-assurance and so generally gives an impression of being more capable than he is."

The choice of the priest was equally deplorable. It would have been easy, as we shall soon see, to find a volunteer among the distinguished ecclesiasts who had seen service in the former Imperial Almonry. Fesch paid no attention to them and selected a Corsican priest, Antonio Buonavita, a man sixty-seven years old, who had been a missionary for twenty-six years in Mexico and then chaplain to Pauline. A good and altogether worthy soul to be sure, he was devoid of any breeding and uncouth of person. His stooping shoulders, halting speech and expressionless eyes gave him the appearance of being already in his second childhood. According to Fesch's own confession, the Cardinal-Vicar had fruitlessly called his attention to the fact that "the advanced age of the man Buonavita, further aggravated by an attack of apoplexy, did not allow one to assume that he would be of any great help to the colony at St. Helena." And Fesch naïvely wrote to Las Cases: "This priest, it is true, has suffered a stroke. At times he is unable to express himself. . . . But he is full of courage and devotion and he is accustomed to the heat of the torrid zone."

A man of wholly clannish instincts, Napoleon's uncle sent another priest along, Angelo Vignali, also a Corsican, but young and still a shepherd in spite of his cassock. Vignali however wrote French fairly well. We have a letter of his to Montholon dated Rome, December 10, 1821. It shows a legible handwriting and a very fluent style. He was said to have a smattering of medicine. Therefore, Fesch explained to Las Cases, he would be able to substitute for both Buonavita and Antommarchi. The "little caravan," as the Cardinal called it, further comprised one of Madame Mère's footmen, a certain Coursot, who was expected to act as maître d'hôtel at Longwood, and a cook, Chandellier, furnished by Pauline. In 1813 Jacques Chandellier had been page and spit-turner at the Tuileries. Twenty-one years old he was in poor health, but he was intelligent, honest, devoted. He told Pauline "that for the honour of serving the Emperor he would go to New Holland if need be." He refused a sum of money that the Marquis of Douglas offered to give him and never worried about his wages. Coursot had been a servant to Duroc. He was a good fellow but knew little about his work and could not even brew a cup of coffee.

That Fesch should have recommended such a pair of priests and such a physician to his nephew and that Madame Mère should have allowed them to go, seems hard to believe. At the time, it is true, both of them were prey to a sort of insane mysticism and more or less unbalanced. A German clairvoyant, undoubtedly acting as a spy for Metternich, had wormed her way into their confidence and intimacy. She pretended to be receiving directions straight from the Virgin, who was supposed to have revealed to her that Napoleon had escaped from his prison. The mother and the uncle were at that time convinced of it. "As a result of that information," Pauline was to write to Planat, July 15, 1821, "all the letters that Madame and the Cardinal have managed to receive for the past two years, they have looked upon as forgeries—letters with false signatures devised by the English government to make believe that the Emperor is still at St. Helena, whereas the Cardinal and Madame know of certain knowledge that His Majesty has been carried off by angels and transported to another country where he is in very good health and whence they are receiving news of him." In a letter of July 11, again to Planat, Pauline gave further distressing details: "For two years Louis and I have been doing everything possible to counteract the influence of the witch, but all to no purpose. My uncle has hidden from us the news and the letters that he has been receiving from St. Helena, *and then has told us that Napoleon's silence ought to be proof enough.*

"Mamma is a devout believer and gives a great deal of money to the woman, who is in league with her confessor, who in turn is the right-hand man of still other priests. That is all a hideous intrigue and Colonna [Leca] is at the bottom of it. He is in church from morning till evening."

Pauline added: "Madame and the Cardinal have tried to drag me into their belief, as well as my brother Louis, but they saw that we were both trying to find ways to cure them of their blindness and that we always ended by ridiculing their credulousness. I will say nothing of the scenes, the quarrels and the resulting coldness to which their conduct has naturally led among us." [2]

Early in October, 1818, Madame mysteriously informed her daugh-

[2] This letter from Pauline shows that Louis, hitherto indifferent or hostile, had recently changed in his feelings towards Napoleon.

ter-in-law, Catherine, that Napoleon was on his way to Malta. Catherine said bluntly that the report was not true, but that did not bother Fesch. "I do not know," he wrote to Las Cases, December 5, "what means God will employ to deliver the Emperor from his captivity, but I am none the less convinced that that will be happening before long now."

So the incredible finds its explanation. Fesch was sending a number of figureheads to St. Helena at the least possible expense, knowing well that when they got there they would find no Emperor. On February 28, 1819, he was to write again to Las Cases: "The little caravan has left Rome at a time when we ourselves believe they will not get to St. Helena, because there is someone who assures us that three or four days before the 10th of January the Emperor received permission to leave St. Helena and that the English are taking him somewhere else. What shall I say? Everything in his life is miraculous and I am greatly inclined to believe in this miracle."

And still again to Las Cases on July 31: "Though the newspapers and the English continue to insinuate that he is still at St. Helena, we have reason to believe that he is no longer there, and though we know neither the place where he is nor the time when he shall become visible to us, we have sufficient proofs to persist in our belief. . . . There is no doubt that the jailor at St. Helena is compelling Count Bertrand to write to you as though Napoleon were still in his chains. . . ."

The mania was not to be dissipated, as we shall see, till the return of Buonavita, bearing a letter from Montholon to Pauline and dated March 17, 1821. By the time Madame Mère's eyes were opened her son had been dead for two months.

The "little caravan" was in no haste. It took two months to get from Rome to London. As soon as he was in England Antommarchi sought to promote a career in society and kowtowed on all hands to English physicians and newspapermen. He saw O'Meara and Stokoe and discussed Napoleon's condition with them. Antommarchi pretended to believe that the Emperor's illness was purely diplomatic. Was Bathurst afraid that Buonavita and his acolytes might turn conspirators in a plot to free Napoleon? One might think so, for he did not allow them to sail until July 9, after a wait of three months in London.

They arrived at Jamestown on September 20th and were splendidly welcomed by Lowe, who had them to dinner at Plantation House along with Reade and Gorrequer. They then went up to Longwood and presented themselves to Bertrand. Napoleon was annoyed that they had allowed themselves to be entertained by the Governor and refused to see them that evening.[3] He did consent to talk with the two servants, Coursot and Chandellier, questioning them for an hour about his family. Coursot reported that Madame was sad and resigned and that she never sat down to table without saying: "If only I could send this dinner to my son!" Napoleon seemed satisfied with them. He told Marchand to allow them a wage of 2,500 francs and to have Pierron train them in their duties. Cardinal Fesch had neglected to furnish his emissaries with credentials of any sort. The Emperor therefore ordered Bertrand and Montholon to question each of the newcomers. The Grand Marshal, ever a stickler for forms, obliged them all to write out their separate "records" or biographies.

The two priests and the physician were amazed at this mistrustful reception. The next day Napoleon received them one after the other while still in bed. He surveyed with pitying eye the aged and broken Buonavita, who approached his bedside and knelt to kiss his hand. He bade him be seated, asked his age, enquired after his health, then about Madame Mère, vaunting her fortitude and strength of spirit. He told Vignali, a short, stocky, dark-complexioned individual, that from then on he wanted Mass celebrated every Sunday at Longwood. Verling saw Vignali and describes him bluntly as a savage.[4] Montholon pictured him to his wife (October 31) as "a Corsican mountaineer whose savage and brutish exterior has not been modified by any trace of breeding."

Last of all came Antommarchi. Napoleon questioned him about his native town, his family and his studies. He was not dissatisfied with the answers he received though he considered the man "young and presumptuous." He bade him look after Father Buonavita, who, he said, "seemed to have come to St. Helena only to get himself buried there." On the whole he was painfully disappointed with the "little caravan." This, then, after four years, was the only help he could get from his family! Like all the others they too were deserting him!

Antommarchi was given the room formerly occupied by O'Meara,

[3] Verling, *Diary*, September 20, 1819.
[4] Verling, *Diary*, September 20, 1819.

Buonavita that of Gourgaud, Vignali the one occupied by the orderly officer who moved to vacant quarters in the Montholon house. The three Corsicans were to share a common table. Each had a Chinese servant to wait on him.

If the Emperor was disappointed in the new arrivals, the disillusionment of Bertrand and Montholon was bitter indeed. "I am impatiently waiting," Montholon had written to his wife away back on July 31, "for the arrival of the three priests or physicians, who, the newspapers say, are coming. If they prove to be all they should be, I shall leave the accursed soil of Longwood." Faced now with the fact, Montholon hastened to beg his wife to find a substitute for him in Europe, and all the more since Antommarchi had refused to help him in the work with which Napoleon was still burdening him: dictations, copying, and other drudgery.[5] Though Mme. Bertrand was again pregnant, she and her husband were talking openly of leaving the island in March.

However, distractions were now so rare at Longwood that Napoleon took an interest in the opening of the boxes that had been entrusted to the newcomers. A portrait of the King of Rome wearing a little white satin coat chained his attention. "It was an oil painting," writes Aly (p. 214), "in a gilt frame, a foot and a half high and about a foot wide." Napoleon had it hung between the two windows in the drawingroom. On his desk he set a green leather case that held a medallion of the child—a present from Jerome. "He often opened it," says Aly, "and gazed on the features of his son." A miniature of Madame Mère was hung over the mantelpiece in the study. Pauline sent some handsome toilet articles, Lady Holland games and albums. Two boxes were filled with newspapers and books, these last poorly chosen. "Half of them were nothing but second-hand books that the priests had bought." "The Cardinal," Napoleon said to Marchand, "could easily have spent a few thousand francs and sent me something worth reading." In Antommarchi's luggage the Emperor found some orange-blossom water. He was very fond of that perfume and had not had any for some time. Finally one trunk contained sacerdotal vestments and all the articles required for setting up a chapel. These had been paid for by Fesch. "The chasubles were magnificent," says Aly, "the albs very beautiful. The chalice and the paten were of silver lined with gold, as well as the baptismal font and

[5] Montholon to Mme. de Montholon, October 31, 1819.

the altar-cruets. There was a silver ciborium and a little silver crucifix
on an ebony cross." [6]

On the first Sunday following the arrival of the Corsicans, Napoleon attended Mass in the drawingroom, where a table served as the
altar. Then he decided that the diningroom, which was now being used
but rarely, would be more suitable. The whole household turned to
to make it ready for this new career. A Chinese wall-paper with a red
background and golden flowers was pasted on the walls. The mahogany sideboard was raised on two steps and transformed into an altar.
Pierron fashioned a pasteboard tabernacle to sit on it, surmounted
by the silver crucifix. To either side, on a lace cloth, stood a six-
branched candlestick and a China vase filled with the loveliest flowers
in the garden. A head of Jesus was hung over the altar—a gift from
Bertrand. White satin hangings fringed with gold lace and marked
in the corners with an embroidered N under a crown were draped
about the altar. Since gold tassels were lacking Montholon gave up
one of his old uniforms which supplied all that were needed. Josephine
did the sewing required for these decorations.[7] A green velvet carpet
was stretched in front of the altar as far back as the Emperor's fold-
stool. The doors were hidden by two large screens that Noverraz
had made with the help of a Chinaman. Towards the front of the
room stood the Emperor's armchair, then a little farther back, chairs
for Mme. Bertrand, the Grand Marshal and Montholon. The domestics were expected to stand on either side near the screens.

Everything was completed within the week. It was a great occasion
for the exiles when, the following Sunday, the Emperor entered the
candle-lighted chapel followed by the two generals.[8] Father Buonavita advanced to greet him and offer him holy water, as his Grand
Almoner had done of yore; and then, mounting the altar, the priest
began to say Mass assisted by Vignali in his surplice and by Napoleon
Bertrand, who could not contain his delight with the robe he wore as
an altar-boy.

The Emperor himself seemed pleased. Shortly afterwards he said:
"I hope the Holy Father will not find fault with us now that we
have become Christians again. If he could see our chapel he would

[6] Most of these articles are preserved today in the private museum of Prince
Napoleon.

[7] Aly gives the whole picture in minute detail (pp. 216-19).

[8] October 5, 1819, according to an unpublished note of Montholon's (Thiers Library, carton 20).

shower us with indulgences." And he added: "If any one of you has a conscience overburdened with sins, Buonavita is there to take charge of them and give you absolution." "Mass over," writes Aly (p. 219), "and the Emperor having withdrawn to the garden or the drawing-room, the chapel was a diningroom again in less than a quarter of an hour, with everything back in its proper place."

From that time on Mass was said every Sunday and in that form. When Napoleon was indisposed he remained in bed. "The door of his room was thrown open and the screens rolled back so that the priest's words could reach his ears." [9] Shortly afterwards Aly reports: "The Emperor permitted Father Vignali to say Mass every Sunday at the Grand Marshal's house so that Mme. Bertrand would not feel obliged to go to Longwood when the weather was bad." In reality, Mme. Bertrand was ill from another miscarriage and was not anxious to leave her house.

Napoleon's ideas regarding faith had little by little changed. He seemed to be reverting to sentiments of his childhood. Mechanically, often, he would make signs of the cross in the Italian fashion, as his mother had taught him. He was thinking no doubt that if not for himself he at least owed it to his fame and to the future of his son to become re-attached in his solitude to the religion that he had established in France—and the Pope was protecting his family. Perhaps at first it was the sovereign in him that wanted to hear Mass. Gradually the man himself came to find in it a relaxation for an over-burdened heart. Certain rites nevertheless roused the pupil of Jean-Jacques in him. He rebuked the zeal of Buonavita and Vignali when, one day, they went up to the servants' corridor and said a prayer in front of each door. "That ceremony," says Aly, "might have been all right in Italy or in Corsica, but at St. Helena among not very religious Frenchmen, it was turned into a jest by those who had rooms along the corridor." Aly also relates (p. 230) an incident which goes to show that, in spite of his respect for religion, the Emperor was impatient with observances that were at all exaggerated. On Holy Thursday, 1820, he was ill. He therefore stayed in bed and heard Mass from his chamber. When it was over the intervening door was closed. Then the two priests, as was the custom in churches, began the service of the Watch at the Sepulchre. They were to spend the night that way, reading or meditating. Vignali had been praying for

[9] Aly, p. 219.

about an hour when Napoleon, hearing his voice, frowned and called to Marchand:

"Haven't they finished yet?"

"No, sire."

"Well, tell them to get through with it!"

Marchand informed the Abbé and he obeyed.

Shortly after their arrival Buonavita and Vignali performed marriage ceremonies for Noverraz and Josephine, former chambermaid to Mme. de Montholon, whom the Emperor had kept as linen maid; for Archambault and Mary, nursery maid in the Grand Marshal's household, and finally for Aly and Mary Hall, governess to Hortense Bertrand. The first two of those marriages had already been celebrated in July and August with the Anglican rite.[10] The Emperor had readily consented to Noverraz's marriage, which had been consecrated on July 12 by the Reverend Vernon in Montholon's parlour. He likewise approved of Aly's plan, on condition that his wife keep her position with Mme. Bertrand. On the other hand he opposed Archambault's match and threatened to send him away. The coachman, however, did just as he pleased and Napoleon shut his eyes. In vain Marchand implored Napoleon to allow him to regularize his relation with Esther Vesey. But he was more deferential than Archambault, and finally yielded.[11]

The Emperor's new cook, Jacques Chandellier, replaced at the ovens two Chinese who had been giving fairly poor service under Pierron's direction ever since the departure of Lepage. The ingenious Pierron had invented a stove that gave out less smoke in the narrow room where the air often became thick enough to make one ill, and an oven of the English type for pastry cooking. Chandellier roused the Emperor's appetite for a time with many well-prepared dishes. But he soon fell ill. Young as he was, he was threatened with "serous apoplexy," and a successor had to be considered.[12]

The building of the new house was slowly proceeding. Lowe had

10 *Parish Register,* Jamestown, 1819.
11 Montholon to Mme. de Montholon, July 7, August 3 and 11, 1819.
12 On April 20, 1820, Montholon was to ask his wife to send on two chefs, if possible men who had already served in the Imperial household. Towards the end of 1820 Mme. de Montholon discovered two such: one named Chandellier, a cousin of Jacques, and the other named Peyrusset. They were shunted off to the Cape, however, and were never to get to St. Helena, the Emperor's death having occurred before their departure thence. Through force of circumstances, therefore, Jacques Chandellier remained Napoleon's chef to the end.

appointed Major Emmett, chief of engineers at St. Helena, to oversee the work.[13] After Mme. de Montholon's departure the work had been pushed more energetically. "Everybody who could be used in construction work in any way," writes Aly (p. 228), "had been requisitioned—soldiers, labourers, Chinese, slaves, each according to his abilities. Every day the road from town to Longwood was lined with men and wagons, transporting hewn stone, timber, iron, lead and other materials." One Sunday when the carpenters were not at work, the Emperor visited the building with Marchand. He criticized a number of interior arrangements, but could not help finding the rooms large, airy and comfortable. Sheltered from the trade-wind, the main façade fronted on the plateau of Deadwood. It was flanked by two wings. The apartment designed for Napoleon comprised a large gallery, a diningroom, a library, a bedroom, a dressingroom, a bath. An adjoining room was reserved for the valet on duty. Montholon was to have the left wing and he would be almost as well lodged. The windows and doors were wide and high, the decoration expensive. The mantelpieces were finished in gilded bronzes. The outside walls had niches for statues. In comparison with Napoleon's old quarters New House was a palace.[14]

Nevertheless the Emperor seemed less inclined than ever to leave Old Longwood. Lowe wrote to Bathurst, November 27, 1819: [15]

"The circumstance of General Bonaparte having walked to the new house might lead to the supposition that he intends to occupy it when completed; but in proportion as he sees an evident endeavour to hasten its completion, he seems inclined to make improvements and alterations in his present residence. This desire on his part has proved in several instances extremely inconvenient, because it tends to take the workmen from the new building . . . I endeavour . . . to meet his desires in such a way as to avoid complaint, without suffering them . . . to interrupt the progress of the principal work." Convinced now that he would never leave St. Helena again, Napoleon began to take an interest in improving his "interior" and in arranging the garden.

[13] Emmett did not like the Governor and speaks unpleasantly of him in the extracts from his diary that were published in the Century Magazine in 1912.

[14] The building with its furnishings was to cost all in all a little more than 32,000 pounds. It should not be forgotten, of course, that construction, like everything else, was expensive at St. Helena. The following measurements for Napoleon's apartment will give an idea of the scale on which the house was built: reception-room, 38 ft. × 22; diningroom, 26 × 22; library, 28 × 25. The studding was 14 ft. generally.

[15] Lowe Papers, 20-128; Forsyth, Vol. III, p. 198.

With an instinctive human reversal he was becoming attached to his gloomy refuge and trying to decorate it and make it more attractive. The servants, too, were settling down. For four years they had camped, as it were, in their garret-rooms, making no effort to improve them. Towards the middle of 1819 they began to work at them busily. The Emperor climbed the break-neck ladder that led to the attic and visited each bedroom. In Noverraz's room he came upon an engraving that he did not like. It pictured the opening of Waterloo Bridge in London. "The 'Waterloo' made him frown," says Aly (p. 188). The attractive way in which the chapel had turned out gave him the idea of changing the hangings in his bedroom and study. The nankeen on the walls was falling in shreds from the damp. With the help of the Chinese servants, Marchand and Aly re-covered the ceilings and walls with white paper, hung the bedroom in striped mousseline and the study in percale, put up new curtains large and small, and laid new carpets. The furniture was mended and polished. The camp beds were curtained again in green taffetas and the tops of the legs and the tips of the backs were decorated with the silver eagles that had been saved from the covers of the silver serving-dishes at the time the silver had been broken up. The Emperor moved into the drawing-room while this work was in progress. He insisted that everything be done by people of his own household. He disliked asking the Governor for anything and admitting anybody who was English into the intimate parts of his quarters. When all was in readiness he entered his bedroom: two cones of Houbigant were burning in a perfume pan and the frames of the pictures above the mantelpiece gleamed from a fresh polish. Napoleon looked at everything with childish delight and boasted to Montholon of the talents of the servants:

"It isn't a bedroom—it's a coquette's boudoir."

Shortly afterwards the whole apartment was re-papered. At that period the Emperor was sleeping by preference in the little room opening off the diningroom. For some time, during the hot weather, he slept in the billiardroom, on a brass bed that had been bought by Mme. de Montholon long before. One leg was broken, however, and the Emperor thought he was more comfortable in his own camp beds. He therefore gave it back to Montholon. He had given the billiard table to the servants, having caught them playing on it one day when he had gone out for a drive. It was moved to a canvas-roofed addition that was built of boards, with a door leading into the corridor behind the building occupied by Napoleon.[16]

But it was the gardens that occupied most of Napoleon's thoughts and gave him greatest amusement. Soldiers supplied by Lowe had already built an earthen mound to the eastward to cut off the wind. It had been sodded with grass. On the 27th Montholon drew plans for enlarging the gardens.[17] Marchand writes: "Napoleon saw in this enterprise a means of amusement for himself and the colony, but he also saw that it offered the further advantage of pushing the cordon of sentries that were posted every night at nine o'clock farther from the house." On August 3, 1819, Montholon wrote to his wife that for some days past they had been busy "enlarging the little garden."

Antommarchi encouraged the Emperor in all that. Gardening, he declared, was the best possible exercise to take the place of the horseback rides that had been discontinued. Pierron went to Jamestown to buy wheelbarrows, picks and shovels for the members of the household. The Emperor had his own rake and his own spade. Every morning at daybreak, as soon as the sentries had evacuated the garden, he sent the valet on duty to get everybody out of bed by ringing a large bell that had been hung on the outside wall of the house.[18] All the domestics—French, English, Chinese (at that moment eleven Chinese were employed at Longwood) [19]—Antommarchi, the two priests, and even the maids, had to report for work.

In a nankeen coat and trousers to match, like the farmers on the island, wearing a broad-brimmed straw hat on his head and red morocco slippers, Napoleon went in person to toss a clod of earth against Aly's shutters.

"Aly, Aly!" he cried. "You're asleep!" Or else:

"Aly, ho! Allah! It's daylight!"

And he hummed the old song:

*You'll sleep more at ease, she said,*
*When you're home in your own little bed . . .*

Aly would put his head out of the window.

"Come along, lazybones! Don't you see the sun?"

[16] Aly, p. 189.
[17] Nicholls, *Diary*, July 19 and 27, 1819. Antommarchi therefore did not give him the idea, as he says he did.
[18] Lowe Papers, 20-130.
[19] Blakeney, *Report*, August 2, 1818 (Lowe Papers, 20-123).

NAPOLEON'S GARDEN, LONGWOOD

THE POOL, LONGWOOD
See Page 420

Marchand's turn came too at the opposite end of the building: "Marchand! *Mamzelle* Marchand! It's daylight—get up!"

When Marchand appeared, Napoleon would look him over gaily: "Did you get enough sleep last night? Were your slumbers interrupted? You'll be sick all day from getting up so early in the morning!"

Then resuming his habitual tone of command:

"Come on now—this pick, this spade! Make a hole for me to plant this tree in."

A moment later he would call again:

"Marchand! A little water—here! Or rather—no! Go and get me my rule—the yard-stick!"

Or it might be someone else:

"Go and tell Archambault to bring some manure—and tell the Chinaman to cut some sod—there isn't any any more."

Passing Aly who was trundling a wheelbarrow: [20]

"What! Haven't you finished carrying that dirt away yet?"

"No, sire, and I haven't been wasting time either."

"By the way, you scamp! Have you done the chapter I gave you yesterday?"

"No, sire."

"You preferred to sleep, I suppose, eh?"

"But, sire, Your Majesty did not give it to me till last evening."

"Try to finish it today. I have another to give you."

The Emperor was now dictating but rarely. He was, however, having a good deal of copying done, especially by Aly.

Pierron would be placing sod along the earthen wall:

"What! Haven't you finished that wall yet? Have you enough sod to cover it?"

"Yes, sire."

Then going back to Aly:

"Is Montholon awake?"

"I do not know, sire."

"Go and see! But don't wake him up! Let him sleep!"

Noverraz would be digging on his own:

"Come, what's the matter, lazybones! What have you done all this forenoon?"

---

[20] Aly, p. 206. Aly has given the most vivid and doubtless the most accurate account of all this period of the Captivity.

"But, Your Majesty told me yesterday to have the bathtub tarred. As I couldn't find anyone who could do it, I did it myself." The tub here in question was to be used in the garden as a pool.

Napoleon would tweak the young man's ear. He was delighted with Noverraz. The fellow seemed to know everything about that sort of work. Napoleon called him his gardener-in-chief. At that moment a servant would announce:

"Sire, here is Monsieur de Montholon!"

"Ah, good-morning, Montholon!"

Montholon would bow double as though he were at the Tuileries:

"How is Your Majesty today?"

"Pretty well! Did they disturb you?"

"No, sire. I was already up when they came for me."

The Emperor would ask him mischievously:

"Has Your Excellency any news to report? They tell me there's a ship in sight."

"I do not know, sire. I have not seen anybody yet."

"Take a glass. Go and see if it's in sight."

Montholon would be back a minute later. Napoleon would walk up and down chatting with him. Towards eight o'clock Bertrand would arrive, stately as always. Sometimes the Emperor would hand him a spade—as he often did to Montholon. But they were not skilful at such work, so he would say:

"Gentlemen, you're not worth a shilling a day."

The Emperor even attempted to entice Mme. Bertrand, by arguing that there could be nothing better for her health than digging in the ground. She refused to believe any such thing, and neither cajoleries nor scowls could lure her into the gardening project.

"Why exchange one bore for another?" she asked.

On a number of occasions Napoleon tried to dig and rake himself, but his hands were soon covered with blisters and he gave it up. "The work is too rough," he said one day to Antommarchi, "I can't stand any more of it. It hurts my hands. So—till the next time!" And he would throw his spade aside.[21]

At ten o'clock the Emperor would ask for his breakfast and sit down with Montholon to wait for it in the shade of an orange tree or more often under "his oak." The servants who attended table would straightway drop their tools, run to wash their faces and hands,

[21] Antommarchi, Vol. I, p. 279.

and brush their coats. Bertrand would go back to his own house unless he had been specially invited. On rare occasions the Emperor would ask the priests or the doctor, but very often he kept the Bertrand children, who helped in the garden by carrying water in watering-cans. Noisy, undisciplined, spoiled, they were terribly ill-behaved, but Napoleon enjoyed their tom-fooleries. He would take little Arthur on his knees and tease him. A handsome child, with blonde hair and rosy cheeks, he must have reminded him of the King of Rome. Sometimes he would kiss him with a strange violence. "A cobbler is happier than I am!" Aly heard him say one day. "He at least has his wife and children with him."

Work would then be resumed until eleven or twelve o'clock.

"Go to your lunch now!" the Emperor finally ordered. "Enough for today! It's getting too hot."

And he would go to his own room to read or sit in his bath. He would reappear about four o'clock and start watering the flowers with a little pump that was pushed around on wheels. Aly or Noverraz would work the handle while the Emperor held the nozzle. He often got so wet that he would have to change his clothes.

Roused from the torpor of the previous months the whole household had changed in aspect. Napoleon seemed to have recovered strength and health. Once he had created a new world. Now he was applying himself to the lowliest and most ephemeral of all sorts of creation—a garden. But nothing could have been more alive—and he loved life. An imaginative soul, he nevertheless retained a profound sense of the real. He probably took keener delight in mapping out those flower-beds, those sunken paths, his little rose-garden, than he had taken of yore in working with his architects on the improvements at Compiègne or Fontainebleau.

On the west side, in front of the Emperor's own windows, stretched what he called "Marchand's Garden" or "The Flowerbed." It was a rhombus of lawn sketched out by narrow paths, which were in turn filled out into a square by clumps of rose-bushes bordered with box. Four orange trees were planted in front of the casement windows and he himself sowed gilly-flowers and immortelles of all colors between their trunks from seeds that Lady Holland had bought in France—for an added touch of thoughtfulness—and sent to him. The window nearest the corner formed by the wall of the drawingroom was changed into a glass door sheltered by a little trellised verandah which was decorated with climbing plants. A flight of two steps let Napoleon down into "The Flowerbed." There he could walk about without being seen, because an arched picket fence covered with passion flowers formed a compact wall all around. On the other side of the main building "Aly's Garden" or the "Grove" had been laid out, balancing "Marchand's Garden" symmetrically. In the centre was a grassy oval in which two large orange trees were planted. The whole place was soon so overgrown that the sun could not get to it.[22]

After that a more extensive garden was laid out to the east. Sheltered by the earthen wall and separated from the grove by a covered arbour where the Emperor liked to walk, it was filled with peach trees, acacias, willows, cane-apples. A carpet of strawberry plants covered part of the ground. In order to have shade immediately Napoleon had a number of grown oaks transplanted. Many of them died, and one by one they were replaced with peach trees. "The Emperor," writes Aly (p. 198), "was in such a hurry when he ordered anything done that it was impossible to do it very well." In the later months of 1820 Napoleon was to have a hillock about seven feet high thrown up at the far end of the grassed wall in Aly's garden. On it he set a summerhouse of sail-cloth, lighted by glass windows and lined inside with muslin. He intended to use it as an observatory whence he could watch the sea and the ships that half-circled the island on that side on their way in from the Cape. His illness prevented him from ever entering it.[23]

The garden to the east was christened "Noverraz's Garden." The Emperor was much interested in it. At the lower end a little grotto had been contrived which the Chinese covered with a panelling decorated with dragons and birds. It was furnished with a round table and a number of chairs. Napoleon often used it as a retreat. Two or three times he had luncheon there.

But the great affair was the irrigation of the grounds. Napoleon had a basin dug and lined with cement. It was shaped like a half-moon and fed by a tiny thread of water that came from springs under Diana's Peak. A number of carp were put into it, but they died, much to the Emperor's regret. This basin overflowed into a drain, and the

[22] The details supplied by Aly are confirmed in every point by Captain Lutyens' reports. Lutyens replaced Nicholls as orderly officer February 10, 1820 (Lowe Papers, 20-129).
[23] Aly, p. 193.

NAPOLÉON'S ARBOUR, LONGWOOD

drain led into a cistern [24] located in the middle of Noverraz's Garden, thence flowing off through the grotto to fill a third basin at a still lower level. Chandellier found a lead pipe and succeeded in making a little jet of water spout in the middle cistern. The Emperor was delighted. When he went out he would say to Aly or Marchand: "Come, let's start the water!"

They would run and turn on the spiggot in the reservoir and, standing between the grotto and the last pool, Napoleon would watch the water rush down and reach his feet. At such moments perhaps he may have thought of the great falls of Saint-Cloud, or the green smoothly idling river along which the swans of Malmaison swam in their straight lines. The noise of the rushing water would hold his attention for a time, then he would laugh at himself for being amused by so little. The game came to an end when water in the reservoir gave out. [25]

Up over the first basin the Emperor had the most skilful of the Chinese build a three-storied birdhouse made of carved wood, decorated with designs and topped by an eagle. [26] A pheasant and a few hens were placed in it, for lack of other birds—for the canaries bought at Jamestown had all died. A few pigeons were also added, but they escaped as soon as the door was opened. So "the bird-house was left without birds just as the pool was without fish." [27]

When Noverraz's garden was done Napoleon started on another just like it on the west side of the house—he was a stickler for symmetry. There too there were basins—one of them the old lead-lined bathtub that had served the Emperor during his first days at Longwood.

The old park was still in existence down towards Bertrand's house, in part made up of a lawn sprinkled with a few pines and willows,

[24] This tub, twelve feet in diameter, was made of lead. It had been constructed by Gordon, the one-eyed plumber and tinker at Jamestown. Napoleon was so tickled when Gordon brought it to Longwood that he served the plumber a glass of wine with his own hands (Lowe Papers, 20-129).

[25] Aly, p. 202. Longwood is a high plateau and has no springs. Water was scarce there. Lowe began laying extensive water conduits, which were completed towards the middle of 1820. From then on the water was better and there was plenty of it. The same conduits supply Longwood today. With M. Colin, the curator at Longwood, and with the *Souvenirs* of the mameluke as a guide, the author was enabled to find the exact positions of the Emperor's garden by carefully surveying the land. M. Colin afterwards drew up—and for the first time—a complete plan.

[26] The bird-house was taken back to France by the Grand Marshal in 1821. It is now visible at Châteauroux in the Bertrand Museum.

[27] Aly, p. 205.

and for the rest of a kitchen garden. Napoleon liked to see beans and peas growing there. Later on, when the Emperor was served with vegetables or a salad he would always ask whether "they came from his garden." If the answer was yes—and to humour him it was the usual answer—he would say:

"Well, after all, our pains were not all wasted. We are living off the land!"

One or another of the valets would smile at that, whereupon he would exclaim:

"What, you rascal! You laugh?"

And he would laugh himself.[28]

One morning he noticed some hens pecking about among his peas and beans. Furious, he snatched up a shotgun and killed three of them. The chickens belonged, not to the chef, Chandellier, as Marchand says, but to Noverraz, who flew into a rage and asked permission of Lowe to leave the Emperor's service. Lowe did not act upon the request.[29] The Emperor also shot a goat of Mme. Bertrand's that had ventured into his garden, then a suckling pig, and finally a bull from the farm. This latter execution stirred the Governor, and all the more since Montchenu tried to emphasize the possible diplomatic resonances of the murder. The French Commissioner told Lowe that Napoleon had probably had the garden gate left open in order to lure the Company's cattle and kill them at his ease.

"Do you really think so?" asked Lowe.

"I have no doubt of it," replied Montchenu. "He knows that you use those cattle. He wanted to deprive you of them and perhaps prove to you that he can still make trouble." [30] Lowe wrote to England to ask whether Napoleon could be tried, in case he should kill a man accidentally or otherwise, and what the punishment might be.

The Emperor sowed seeds of a great many vegetables, but in that claylike soil they did not do very well. Such as matured were tough and fibrous. Only cabbages grew at all vigorously and there were some good peaches and strawberries. But drought and pests came to ravage everything. The pleasure of creation passed and the Emperor gradually lost his interest. He still watered his plants with the help of the little Bertrands, but more frequently he was satisfied with just walking about the covered paths or around "The Flowerbed." He

[28] Aly, p. 210.                          [30] Ibid.
[29] Lowe Papers, 20-129.

would bend over, pick a passion flower or a pansy and hold it for a long time in his hand, dreaming. Sheltered now from prying eyes, he would sit down on a grassy mound and watch the fire-coloured cardinals, that had been imported from Brazil, pecking about the ground or flying among the branches, or those *avedevats* as long as bumblebees which swarm over the fields of St. Helena in clouds at harvest time and plunder the sheaves.

At any rate, from those occupations that had lasted over a period of more than six months, the Emperor gained a certain tranquillity of mind. Furthermore by appearing daily in his gardens he kept the Governor reassured, and the Governor underlined the lessening of the strain by repeated attentions. He made gifts of plants, seeds and garden furniture. He, of course, kept Bathurst informed of everything and the Minister wrote to Lowe, June 2, 1820, to assure General Bonaparte that "if there are any plants either at the Cape or at any other British settlement, or in this country, which he may wish to add to his present collection, no effort on my part shall be wanting to procure and forward them to St. Helena." [31] Lowe placed soldiers and workmen at the Emperor's disposal for the terracing, and horses and wagons for moving materials. He enriched the stable by importing four horses from the Cape. Finally—a tremendous concession as it seemed to him—in order to encourage Napoleon to resume his rides he enlarged the boundaries of the reserve and, more especially towards the west, gave the Frenchmen free privileges over about a quarter of the island.

The improvements at Longwood were the subject of much talk in Jamestown, but no one was being allowed to visit there any longer. The youngest of Lowe's step-daughters, Suzanne Johnson, did venture to make the trip one afternoon and she asked Montholon to show her the gardens. The General offered her his arm and escorted her all through the paths. Suddenly they came face to face with the Emperor who was sitting in his arbour. Montholon could not do otherwise than introduce the young girl. Petite, rather pretty, her blushes enhanced her charm. Napoleon spoke to her kindly, ordered a tray of sweets brought to her, led her himself to see his pools, apparently not realizing that she was so closely related to the Governor. When

[31] Lowe Papers, 20-233; Forsyth, Vol. III, p. 238.

she took her leave, he picked a rose and offered it to her "as a souvenir." [32]

This sense of greater well-being gave Napoleon a zest for working again. He resumed his dictation to Montholon and Marchand—fragments on his campaigns, notes on his foreign policies, reflections on suicide, an outline for a national constitution.

But now it was only at night or on rainy days that he spent his time in that way. When the weather was fine, as it were a secret warning from his physical organism kept him out of his close and dingy rooms. Often he would not return indoors again till sundown. [33]

[32] Seaton to the contrary, there is no doubt about this visit on the part of Lowe's step-daughter. It is mentioned not only by Montholon (Vol. II, p. 401) but also by Marchand. Masson is of our opinion too (*Revue des Deux Mondes*, May 15, 1921). Suzanne Johnson did not boast of her escapade to her step-father. Lowe seems never to have heard of it.

[33] Aly, p. 242.

# III

## *1820*

RECONCILED WITH LOWE AND ENGAGED TO MISS JOHNSON, COUNT BAL-
main nevertheless kept insisting that he be recalled. He did not care
to live any longer at the end of the world where his sovereign would
be forgetting him. On March 7, 1820, he received permission to leave
St. Helena. He married Charlotte in the great drawingroom at Plantation House, and on May 3 he and his wife set off for Europe.

On taking leave of his French colleague he said to him ironically:
"You are going to be a widower, *monsieur le Marquis.*"

For those four years Montchenu had been making out his reports
from such news only as Stürmer and Balmain saw fit to give him.
Now he was left in truth as the sole representative of the Powers.
He was not sorry. At last, he thought, he would have a chance to
deploy his talents. He was still seeing Montholon quite often and
the latter continued to flatter him shamelessly. In speaking of the
Emperor to Montchenu, Montholon always referred to him as "Napoleon," unless it were a question of events anterior to the abdication
of 1815. That was a little mark of deference towards the powers that
were.[1] When the news of the assassination of the Duc de Berry
reached the island, he dared to say that the Emperor had been crushed
by it and had shut himself up in his room repeatedly crying, "Poor
France!"

Writing to Bathurst on May 19, Lowe contradicts Montholon on
this point. The day Napoleon learned of that event he says, he read
the English papers which he [Lowe] had just sent him and afterwards
walked in the gardens.[2] Montholon was therefore lying, as he was
to lie, in his *Récits de la Captivité*, when he declared that the Emperor had sent him to offer his "official condolences" to the Marquis.
"M. de Montchenu," he declares (II, 402), "received my message
with demonstrations of deepest emotion, and assured me that he
would transmit it to the King, his master, and would hasten to repair

---

[1] Lowe Papers, 20-152.
[2] Lowe Papers, 20-130.

to Longwood to express the sentiments which he felt so deeply. He came the next day, in fact, but was not received by the Emperor."

All that is pure invention. Montholon ascribed the most extraordinary sentiments to Napoleon in order to stand well, himself, with the Marquis. He went so far as to make Napoleon say: "It is a misfortune for France that my son lives, because he has great rights." [3] And, in the name of Napoleon, he went to congratulate Montchenu on the birth of the Duc de Bordeaux!

Montchenu invited him to luncheon and Montholon took young Napoleon Bertrand along with him. The child was then twelve years old. As he sat looking at some engravings of the royal family, his attention was struck first of all by Louis XVIII.

"Who is that big fatty there?" he asked.

"That is the King," replied Montchenu.

"Oh! A big rascal, then!"

Next he spied a picture of the Duc de Berry.

"As for that one there," he said, "they killed him. That's one big scamp less." [4]

One may imagine that the lad was rebuked, but his naïve prattle must have given Montchenu an edifying glimpse of the mourning at Longwood over the fate of the Duc de Berry.

To test the man out farther, perhaps, Montholon confided to Montchenu that he hoped to be mentioned in Napoleon's will for a million pounds. He told the Marquis that the Emperor had two hundred million pounds on deposit in different banks in Europe! This information was at once passed on to Sir Hudson, but he was incredulous.[5] He was however alarmed when he learned that Montholon had offered Montchenu some green beans and some white beans born of the recent farming activities at Longwood and, the Marquis having accepted those compromising specimens, Lowe brought a matter of such capital importance to the attention of the British Cabinet. On

---

[3] Lowe to Bathurst, May 22, 1820 (Lowe Papers, 20-130).

[4] Lowe to the Hon. Sir Edward Thornton, English Minister to Brazil, July 1, 1820. Unpublished. This letter contains details that are not to be found either in Montchenu's reports or in Lowe's archives. I owe a copy of it to the kindness of Miss Thornton, granddaughter to the English diplomat, through the kindness of Mme. Ternaux-Compans.

[5] Lowe to Bathurst, May 19, 1820. But the Marquis insisted. When Montholon went to Montchenu's house, he was generally accompanied by Lt. Croads, adjutant to Nicholls, who knew French and could listen to the conversations and afterwards report on them to the Governor (Lowe Papers, 20-144).

May 14, 1821, he wrote to Bathurst: "Whether the '*haricots blancs*' and '*haricots verts*' bear any reference to the '*drapeau blanc*' of the Bourbons, and the '*habit vert*' of General Bonaparte himself, and the livery of his servants at Longwood, I am unable to say; but the Marquis de Montchenu, it appears to me, would have acted with more propriety if he had declined receiving either, or limited himself to a demand for the white alone." *

In the end Montholon succeeded in so wheedling Montchenu as to prompt him to rebel against the Governor and—after a sixteen months' delay—carry out his orders, which stipulated that he should see the French in order to get direct information about them. The Marquis informed Lowe that "on the first day of good weather" he intended to "repair to Longwood." "If, contrary to all rules of common decency, you order a sentinel to guard the door, you are aware that I do not know English and shall not understand what he says, but I shall go in, even if he fires at me a shot that will echo throughout Europe." [6]

Lowe immediately stiffened. He wrote to Montchenu in such a tone that the old émigré was induced to give up the idea of forcing an entrance at Longwood, but for three months he remained the Governor's implacable enemy. Addressing Montholon with letters that were all read at Plantation House he asked him for books "to help him endure a solitude that was very tedious, but which he nevertheless preferred to such society as was available at St. Helena." Another day he wrote: "I am reduced to envying your situation, which however you dislike. Console yourself, for if your eyes do not see much society, you at least are living with people who have French breeding and manners. I shall say no more on this point in order not to say too much."

He thought he could annoy and harass Lowe by such allusions, but the Governor paid no attention to them. That, the Governor said, was just the rage of impotence. He was certain that Montchenu, who had abstained from Lady Lowe's dinners deliberately, would not hold out very long when his pleasure was at stake. And in fact the Marquis eventually reappeared with lowered crest to tell him "that he set the greatest store on the Governor's esteem." He was surrendering! Lowe duly rewarded him by offering him hospitality at

* Forsyth, Vol. III, p. 223.
[6] Montchenu to Lowe, September 7, 1820 (Lowe Papers, 20-131).

Plantation House while he was recovering from an intestinal impaction. From that time on they were on the best of terms and Montchenu saw but little more of Montholon.

.    .    .    .    .    .    .

On May 26, 1820, the Emperor finally yielded to the urgings of his suite and consented to take a ride on horseback. Attended by Archambault, he rode from 6 to 8 o'clock in the morning in the gum-tree forest. He kept up the exercise for several days. Then he found that it tired him and gave it up. He suffered a number of new attacks from his liver. Drugs administered by Antommarchi, in line with O'Meara's earlier prescriptions, seemed to relieve him and no one considered his condition alarming. Napoleon himself paid no attention to it. He was, however, suffering from another fear, vague though it still was. On November 17, 1819, some weeks after his arrival at Longwood,[7] Antommarchi came upon him poring anxiously over a huge tome that the doctor had brought with him. It was Mascagni's *Introduction to General Anatomy*. As he turned the pages his face took on a very grave expression. Some time later he began talking to Antommarchi of his father's last illness and asked the physician whether he thought that he could himself have inherited his parent's pyloric cancer. Antommarchi tried to reassure him, but the next day Napoleon insisted on seeing Mascagni's plates again.

By that time he had formed the worst possible opinion of Antommarchi. He could have no confidence in an impudent cadaver-cutter who posed as a professor but persisted in seeing in the Emperor's hepatitis nothing but a diplomatic ailment.[8] Neither the family of the Grand Marshal nor Montholon would consent to be treated by Antommarchi. Dr. Verling continued to attend them. When Verling left the island, they called in Dr. Henry. Antommarchi, moreover, was taking no interest in his work. On pretext of doing botany or visiting hospitals he went to Jamestown every day to find amusement. Lowe's regulations interfering with his pleasure, he broke them whenever necessary and so provoked no end of unpleasant incidents. His conduct meantime was causing a scandal among the English. Bertrand and Montholon felt obliged to call him to order on numerous occasions. He would appear before the Emperor carelessly attired and address him in a shockingly familiar tone. On a comment by

7 Antommarchi, p. 763.
8 Lowe Papers, 20-128.

the Emperor, Bertrand "obliged him to dress more decently." Lowe wrote to Bathurst, May 29, 1820: "The following alteration has recently been observed in the etiquette which is still affected to be maintained at Longwood. Professor Antommarchi, who had been in the habit of paying his daily visits to General Bonaparte in a common morning dress, with pantaloons and boots, has during this month past changed this dress for that of black breeches, silk stockings, and shoes; he pays his visit to General Bonaparte thus attired at about ten o'clock every morning, remains with him from about five to ten minutes, returns to his own apartments, resumes his pantaloons and boots, and does not see the General during the remainder of the day." [9]

Antommarchi called the two generals "Bertrand," and "Montholon" as if they were old pals of his and, by way of compensation, treated Marchand, Aly and the other servants as the servants they were. He was soon reduced to the society of the two priests, who took their meals with him and so could not entirely avoid his company.

Since Mme. de Montholon's departure, life at Longwood had narrowed appreciably. The Emperor dined in his own apartments with Montholon or entirely alone, when he felt fatigued. He ceased shaving every morning and shaved at the most every two or three days. He dressed less and less frequently, often wearing his dressing gown all day long, or putting on his "farmer's clothes." There were still a few Sunday dinners with the Bertrands, but these parties of four were so melancholy, they so strongly emphasized the absence of the old faithfuls, that Napoleon gave them up.

Now that the former purveyors of news had vanished, very little of what was happening on the island came to be known at Longwood, and the island, for its part, seemed to forget the existence of the French. Travellers passing through were simply told that up there, on that high platform girt about by precipices, where the mists could be seen dancing between two shafts of sunlight, a prisoner was living behind his sod-covered walls and thickets of shrubbery, with his few remaining attendants. And sailors and officials returning from the Far East to ports in Europe could only manifest surprise that so many soldiers and ships and guns should be needed to guard such a hopeless Captive.

When strangers appeared near Longwood, Napoleon would hurriedly lock himself into his rooms. Nicholls noted for January 26,

[9] Lowe Papers, 20-130; Forsyth, Vol. III, p. 226.

1820: "Lord Charles Somerset, Governor at the Cape, and his two daughters, came today to see the new building and the grounds. At that moment General Bonaparte was at dinner in his garden under the oak-trees with Count Montholon. The Governor, Lord Charles Somerset, and the young ladies passed round the garden in the wood: however, as soon as they were perceived from the house, the General rose from his dinner and ran into the house. The dinner was carried after him into the house. . . . After Lord Charles's party had left Longwood, General Bonaparte immediately walked out." * Gorrequer had requested an audience for the Governor of the Cape. Montholon told Nicholls that Napoleon listened to him and made no answer.[10]

But if their prisoner had ceased thinking of escapes, Lowe, Bathurst, and the Cabinet at the Tuileries were still afraid of one. It is certain, as a matter of fact and regardless of whatever may have been said to the contrary, that a number of actual plans were made towards the end of the Captivity to carry off Napoleon by a surprise descent on St. Helena. Commodore Stephen Decatur, one of the most glorious sailors of the United States, working in concert with General Clauzel, submitted to the ex-king of Spain a plan which Lakanal was later to accuse Joseph of having rejected "out of weakness and greed." [11] The famous filibuster, Lafitte, the terror of the English in the Gulf of Mexico, fitted out another expedition; but a tornado destroyed six of his ships and he was obliged to give up. A later effort, which came nearest to realization, was to rescue from oblivion the name of a Frenchman, Nicolas Girod, who had settled in New Orleans and was Mayor there at the time of Jackson's victory over the English (1814). He was a rich man and energetic and cherished an abiding admiration for the Emperor. His house was filled with portraits, prints and statues of Napoleon. He opened a subscription among his French countrymen scattered over the South of the United States and he himself donated the bulk of the capital. A swift, well-armed clipper, the Séraphine, was built in great secrecy at Charleston. The captain chosen to command her was Dominique Yon, Lafitte's righthand man. Sailors and soldiers had been recruited among Lafitte's former comrades and the "soldier-labourers" of the Champs

---

* Forsyth, Vol. III, p. 209.
[10] Lowe Papers, 20-129.
[11] In a letter to Bignon, February 26, 1838. (See Masson, Napoléon et sa famille, Vol. XII, p. 249). Decatur was killed in 1820 in a duel with Commodore Barton.

d'Asile. Girod had so little doubt of success that he had a house built and richly furnished in which the Emperor might live the moment he should set foot in New Orleans.[12] Lakanal was mixed up in the affair, but it does not seem that Joseph, whose selfishness was now a matter of common knowledge, was invited to join or even informed of it. The *Séraphine* was about to sail when news of the Emperor's death arrived.

Too many men were involved in most of such plans and news of them leaked out. Bathurst kept Lowe informed and the Governor's fears were only too easily aroused. Bathurst wrote, September 30, 1820: "The reports which you have recently made of the conduct of General Buonaparte and of his followers make me suspect that he is beginning to entertain serious thoughts of escaping from St. Helena, and the accounts which he will have since received of what is passing in Europe will not fail to encourage him in this project. The overthrow of the Neapolitan Government, the revolutionary spirit which more or less prevails over all Italy, and the doubtful state of France itself, must excite his attention. . . . That his partisans are active cannot be doubted. . . . You will therefore exert all your attention in watching his proceedings, and call upon the Admiral to use his utmost vigilance, as upon the navy so much must ultimately depend." * So after the period of calm Lowe again began to suspect Longwood of the wildest of plots, though Longwood was not even dreaming of such things.

A whim on Napoleon's part greatly alarmed Lowe. While walking in his garden in a cotton jacket and a straw hat one morning in May, the Emperor suddenly thought of taking a ride. He mounted his horse without changing clothes and, followed by Archambault, took a little gallop in the direction of Deadwood. Every few seconds he would halt and survey the landscape through his glass. This strange behaviour disturbed Lowe. On being told of Lowe's reaction the Emperor was much amused. Father Vignali was about his height. He had him put on an exactly similar garb and then ordered him to ride across the plateau, accompanied by a groom, but fast enough to prevent anyone from recognizing him. Everyone, he thought, would take the Abbé for Napoleon, all the more if he were careful

[12] The house, known in New Orleans as the "Old Napoleon House," was still standing in 1905.
* Forsyth, Vol. III, pp. 250-51.

to study the landscape through his glass every now and then, as the Emperor was accustomed to do. Vignali followed his instructions exactly. Even Lutyens was deceived and did not discover [13] his error until afterwards. Plantation House trembled. Reade, Gorrequer and Lowe rushed to Longwood and dragged Lutyens roundly over the coals. That, thought Lowe, was a rehearsal for a flight! Napoleon had dressed up the Abbé to impersonate him out of doors while he himself remained at home making preparations to escape. What did that mean? Vignali would parade on horseback in full view of the English while meantime the prisoner could have reached some hidden spot and be waiting for his rescuers to make their landing. Napoleon attached no importance to the jest at all, but it cost Lowe many sleepless nights.

. . . . . . . .

Meantime the governments in Europe were keeping an open eye on St. Helena. Among other enemies of Napoleon Metternich never relaxed in his hatred. He feared that England might weary of carrying such a heavy burden of expense all by herself, and some day set him at liberty. He told Caraman, the French Ambassador, that in such a case the ex-Emperor could only expect to have a change of jailors. "If the opinions or the interests of the English Cabinet should induce them to abandon custody of the prisoner," Caraman wrote to Baron Pasquier (April 28, 1820), "the Allied Powers would claim him as *their property*, and if the English should decide to send him away from St. Helena, they would demand that he be put into the hands of the Powers to be disposed of according as their safety might require."

The public at large on the other hand had lost interest in Napoleon. Balmain wrote to his father-in-law on his arrival in Europe: "Your illustrious prisoner is entirely forgotten in London. No one is interested in him and the dandies do not dare so much as utter his name. It has gone altogether out of fashion. Your conduct towards him and all your measures have universal approval in England, as well as in the rest of Europe. . . . Baron Stürmer has assured me that in Germany and France also no one ever speaks of Bonaparte. He is forgotten everywhere." [14]

This growing indifference towards Napoleon was just what his

---

[13] Lutyens to Lowe, *Report*, July 22, 1820.
[14] Balmain to Lowe, London, July 20, 1820 (Lowe Papers, 20-132. Unpublished).

companions most feared. Exile, dragging on towards no visible end, was becoming intolerable to them. In each of his letters Montholon kept urging his wife to find a substitute for him. "I have some hopes," he wrote, August 11, 1819, "that before winter I shall be with you. I hope so so passionately that I cannot believe that my wishes will not be granted." And again October 31: "If you have not yet sent someone to replace me, do not lose a moment—*no matter whom*, provided it be one of his former officers, generals or friends." Learning that her husband had been seriously ill, the Countess wrote to him at first to hurry back to Europe and not wait to be relieved, since Fesch and Pauline, to whom she had appealed regarding a choice, had left her without a reply. To Montholon's honour be it said that he refused. Mme. de Montholon wrote to Las Cases and herself began to hunt for a volunteer. Long months were to pass before she found one. Planat de la Faye had been suggested at the very beginning, but Fesch would not consider him. From Trieste Planat wrote to the Cardinal and to Madame Mère, September 4, 1820, asking their permission to set out. Fesch replied on the 23rd with a disdainful refusal: "Every time they ask for somebody at St. Helena, they turn to me. . . . Furthermore we think that there are no grounds for sending any more people to St. Helena." Finally it came to the point where, in exasperation at such great delay, Napoleon decided that Mme. de Montholon should choose the substitute, or substitutes, herself without further consulting his relatives. "My family," he said, "send me nothing but animals. I prefer not to have them interfere in this matter. A worse choice than the five they sent me could not have been made." [15]

Bertrand was having countless scenes with his wife. Mme. Bertrand was cut off from all society and almost never went out any more. She spent whole days in bed writing pitiful letters to her family. Bertrand finally made up his mind to ask permission of the Emperor to take her back to England along with his children, as it was now becoming imperative for them to begin their schooling. The two eldest, ten and eleven respectively, could barely read and write. Bertrand's father was in charge of his affairs in France. In 1817 he asked him through official channels to send him the schoolbooks that his children ought to be using. The elder Bertrand had not been able to get them to him, nor clothes and other articles that he had asked for,

[15] Montholon to Mme. de Montholon, October 10 and November 6, 1820.

the Duke de Richelieu withholding the necessary authorization. Bertrand promised, in good faith, to return immediately afterwards—he would not be gone, he said, more than nine or ten months. But once in Europe, caught up again by family cares and interests, under the sole influence of his wife—would he come back again? The Emperor did not think so. He had a number of painful talks with the Grand Marshal. One day Marchand found a list written in pencil of people of consequence who, Napoleon thought, might possibly replace Bertrand. He could not accustom himself to the idea of not having near him, in the eyes of the English and of Europe, a well-known man who had played a conspicuous rôle in the army or government of the Empire. Caulaincourt, Savary, Ségur, Montesquiou, Turenne, Denon, Daru—those were the names he had written down. But would any one of them consent to leave everything in order to come and add lustre to his exile? It was so doubtful! The servants too were growing discouraged again. The chef, Chandellier, was having his fainting spells every other moment. Montholon wrote to his wife, April 30, 1820: "Chandellier is really not in a condition to continue his duties and we are sometimes reduced to the Chinese cook. The poor man realizes his condition and is begging to go away." The Elban, Gentilini, went to Plantation House on July 26th to ask whether he might take advantage of an early opportunity to go to the Cape.[16] "Poor Gentilini is weeping and groaning day and night for permission to leave and he gets nothing. He goes around like a madman and is a pitiable sight. I hope for his sake that I shall finally succeed in having the door opened for him." Montholon did succeed, for Gentilini left with his wife, Juliette, the October 4th following. On September 30th he deposited 16,900 francs that he had saved with the Grand Marshal, to be reimbursed to him in Rome by Madame Mère or Fesch. He received in addition a letter of credit of 15,000 francs.[17]

Once more Napoleon fenced for time. Whenever the Grand Marshal would bring up the question of his departure, he would raise some new difficulty:

"Doesn't he see," he said to Marchand, "that if I let him take his wife back to Europe he will not find me here on his return?"

16 Montholon to Mme. de Montholon, September 20.
17 *Ibid.*, October 10, 1820.

From that time on he exhibited a stony face to Bertrand, and relied more and more on Montholon's kindness and eagerness to please. His irritation turned especially on Mme. Bertrand. He stopped paying her visits and seized every pretext not to receive her when, at long intervals, she still crossed the hundred yards that separated her from the Emperor's house. After November, 1820, he was never to see her again till the very end.

Had Mme. Bertrand chosen to go away by herself Napoleon would have approved thoroughly. But the thought that she was to take her children with her cut him to the heart. The Bertrand children had become his chief distraction. Their withdrawal from him would have left a void that nothing could fill. He had been associating them with his life more and more of late. They came running to him when they caught sight of him in the garden. Vignali, a good fellow after his rustic fashion, was teaching them Italian. Going to him twice a day, they passed in front of the Emperor's windows and never failed, if the windows were open, to make a noise and attract his attention. Napoleon would then call them in, talk, laugh and play with them, giving them candy and oranges. In that way they often missed their lesson altogether. He took an interest in their games and sides in their quarrels. The freshness of their emotions delighted him.

"There is nothing devious about them," he kept remarking. "They say right out whatever comes into their heads." [18]

Because he had recited his multiplication table correctly Napoleon Bertrand received a gold watch.[19] The Emperor sent for coral earrings for Hortense and ordered Antommarchi to pierce her ears that she might wear them. When little Arthur saw the larding-needle that was to be used in the operation, for lack of a better instrument, he began to shriek in terror, jumped up and down, cursed the Emperor in his pidgin English, and flung himself at him with clenched fists.

"What are you saying?" asked Napoleon, amused. "Look, rascal, if you don't stop, I'll have your ears pierced too."

All this time Hortense, held by Montholon, was enduring her torture. When the earrings were in place, the Emperor congratulated her on her courage:

"Now go and show your ears to your Mamma. If she is not

[18] Aly, p. 242.
[19] Arthur Bertrand, p. 109.

pleased, if she finds them ugly, tell her that it was not I but this wicked *dottoraccio* who pierced them." [20]

One morning, as the little girl came into his bedroom with her brother, Napoleon noticed her dress. It was made of a yellow material that had been bought at Jamestown:

"You are badly dressed today, my poor Hortense!"

"Sire," the Grand Marshal replied, "the dress comes from St. Helena and there is not much choice."

"Wait, Hortense, I am going to give you something to make a pretty jacket of."

He asked Marchand to go and get the coat that he wore as First Consul—a cerise velvet trimmed with gold and silk. That magnificent piece of wreckage meant nothing to him now. He threw it over the child's frail shoulders.

"With that," he said, "you will at least be beautiful."

She ran out, radiant, dragging the glorious coat behind her, the tails brushing the greensward. [21]

Little Arthur was always the favourite. The boy saw a pretty Java pony one day and asked the Emperor to buy it for him. Napoleon smiled and replied:

"Come tomorrow at noon."

The next day Arthur appeared with the boom of the gun on High Knoll. The Emperor was asleep and the boy fought a pitched battle with Marchand to get in to him. Fearing that the child's cries would waken his master, Marchand finally allowed him to sit on a stool at the foot of the bed on a promise that he would be quiet. The little fellow waited, without stirring, his eyes fixed on the sleeping Emperor. After a while Napoleon opened his eyes.

Arthur rushed at him and began his jabber, clamouring for the pony that the Emperor had promised him. Napoleon thereupon ordered Marchand to give him twelve hundred francs, the sum the owners were asking. The child gathered the coins together in his apron and ran off to buy the pony. From then on he rode it every day, advancing gravely on horseback to greet the Emperor.

He also wanted a pair of gold spurs and tried to explain that state of mind to Napoleon.

[20] Antommarchi, Vol. I, p. 35; Arthur Bertrand, Vol. III.
[21] Arthur Bertrand, p. 113. The coat, which Bonaparte had worn when he signed the Concordat, was carefully kept by the Bertrand family and never cut up. Today it belongs to Prince Napoleon's collection.

"Ask me for them in French and I will give them to you."

That was too much for Arthur. When he left the island he was still unable to express himself in his own language. That surely had been the fault of Mme. Bertrand.

.     .     .     .     .     .     .

Threatened with total desertion the Emperor came to confide more and more in the one whose devotion he could feel sure of every hour of the day and night—the man of them all who never, never could desert him.

"Marchand, my son," he said, "you alone will be left to close my eyes."

What Marchand meant to the Emperor in those painful days has never been sufficiently told and he, modest as he was, never boasted of it. Always in a good humour that nothing could ruffle, he endured his master's whims and tried to distract his thoughts when he saw his grief showing. He watched over his restless nights. When the Emperor forgot to dismiss him, as often happened, he would watch till dawn. He stood witness to the dreams that plunged the hero back again into his imperishable past. One morning Napoleon told him that he had dreamed of Marie-Louise and of "his son whom she was holding by the hand."

"She was as fresh as when I saw her at Compiègne. I took her in my arms, but however much strength I used in trying to hold her, I felt that she was escaping, and when I tried to take her in my arms again, everything had disappeared and I woke up."

Marchand confessed to the Emperor that he had been frightened by the expression on his face and was about to waken him when the Emperor rang.

Napoleon leapt from his bed and seized the young man by the throat.

"So it is your fault, you wretch," he cried, "that I did not stay longer with my wife and child! What punishment does your crime not deserve!"

Marchand apologized as best he could. He would have liked nothing better, he said, than to be able to place the Empress and her son in the Emperor's arms and so atone for his mistake.

Napoleon released him and heaved a deep sigh:

"It is bad enough to be suffering without having them here as witnesses." [22]

The Emperor was now calling Marchand "my son" quite regularly. He was right. If ever he knew filial care it came from that faithful servant—and he was not to forget it.

A few boxes of books came in at long intervals. The unpacking of them was still a keen delight to Napoleon. When he received Fleury de Chaboulon's *Mémoires* [23] he expressed his anger that that writer could have spoken of Ney and Grouchy as traitors.[24] He was hurt too by the laboured pamphlet in which his brother Louis, throwing bouquets at himself, dared to criticize Napoleon for "despotism." [25]

"Ah!" he said, "Louis too!" Louis, for whom in days gone by, as a young officer, he had gone without food himself!

He scarcely read the few letters that came from his family, all months old and worn thin, as it were, by too many censoring eyes. What was the use? What could they have told him? He knew that his mother was "under Fesch's snuffer," that his brothers and sisters were forgetting him, that Hortense and Eugene were absorbed in their own interests. Pauline alone pitied him, loved him, would have rushed to his rescue. But what could that pretty head do, all given over as she was to pleasure, luxury and care for her shattered health? From his wife, from his son, never a word!

Was it not better so perhaps? Marie-Louise was reigning in her duchy, smiling for Neipperg. The child was growing up in Austrian palaces, being reared as a German by a family eager to erase any memory of his origin from his young mind. That must have been a terribly bitter thought for the Emperor. And yet he did not give up hope. He was convinced that the King of Rome would sooner or later free himself from the Austrian snare, be recalled to France, and restore his dynasty there. The torture of the father might crown the son!

"If I die here," he would say, "he will mount the throne!"

The thought made him resigned to expiring on his islet, the thought

---

[22] Marchand Papers (Thiers Library, Carton 22. Unpublished).

[23] *Mémoires pour servir à l'histoire de la vie privée, du retour et du règne de Napoléon en 1815*, published early in 1820 in London (Longman) with the following epigraph: "*Ingrata patria ne ossa quidem habes.*"

[24] Montchenu, *Report*, June 28, 1820.

[25] *Documents historiques et réflexions sur le gouvernment de la Hollande*. Paris, London, 1820.

that through his death he would be opening a future of infinite possibilities to the one being whom, in all his life, he had undoubtedly loved the most.

. . . . . . . .

Vexations and irritations affected him more seriously now that his physical organism was weakening, for he was conscious almost all the time of a dull, deep-seated pain. So in July, 1820, he had a return of his hepatitis. A note from Lowe to the Abbé Buonavita, accompanying a letter from Bathurst regarding Bertrand's probable departure, had upset him. He was ill for several days, but "the bilious attack" and the fever that went with it, soon passed. Gentilini testified to that on questioning by Gorrequer: "He said that for a fortnight the General had been complaining of swellings of the legs, and rubbed them with brandy or *eau de Cologne*. That was better now, but afterwards he had liver trouble, and also caught cold whenever he went out of doors, which made his malady worse." [26]

On July 18th Antommarchi wrote a letter to Colonna Leca. Since it had to pass under Lowe's eye it purposely exaggerated the seriousness of the Emperor's illness. It did, however, call attention to something new—that the Emperor had developed an inflammation, something like erysipelas, extending from the sole of the foot up the lower third of the. leg. The doctor attributed the symptoms to disorders in the digestive system and to the poor functioning of the biliary organs. "However," he added, "the patient's condition does not suggest any immediate danger." Nevertheless Napoleon's depression lingered for some time. He lay long hours in bed. He had grown yellow again—his face was like a tallow candle. At the least breath of air he had violent attacks of coughing and choking. He complained of pains in his right side. No one paid any attention.

"Oh, gentlemen," he would say, putting a hand to his side. "You think I am making believe? It's true nevertheless. I feel something out of the ordinary in here."

They did not believe him.[27]

In August he resumed his walks about the inner park at Longwood.

. . . . . . . .

Admiral Plampin, much decried and unregretted, had been replaced by Admiral Robert Lambert who had come in on July 14 on

[26] Gorrequer, *Minutes*, July 26, 1820 (Lowe Papers, 20-131).
[27] Aly, p. 184.

the *Vigo*. He left his card at Longwood but was not received by Napoleon. The French had long been hoping that Malcolm would return either as Governor or again as naval chief. Malcolm had actually tried in London to supplant Lowe. He had set his friends to work and brought pressure to bear upon the Prince Regent. Even from the English point of view his return to St. Helena would have solved a painful problem, and such a concession would have transformed the atmosphere of the whole Captivity. But Bathurst was not the man to see that. He had a punctilious and zealous executive in Lowe, and backed him against wind and tide, ready of course to desert him later when Lowe could be of no further use.

Shortly afterwards, August 23, 1820, Colonel John Pine-Coffin came to succeed Bingham in command of the land forces. He had the local rank of brigadier-general. His personality was as ridiculous as his name. His taste for business and his greed soon became the joke of the island. He took up residence near the Plantation in a tumble-down farmhouse situated in a big meadow. He had all the manure from the camp and the barracks brought there and soldiers of the 66th built stables, sheeppens, pigsties, henhouses—and it did not cost the General a penny. Then he bought cows and sheep at the Cape at a bargain and began to fatten them in his own well-fertilized pastures. Not being able to get on with the butcher, the General turned butcher himself, and still using man-power from the regiment, had his own animals slaughtered and cut up. He made presents of legs of mutton, sirloins and ribs of beef to the officers and even to natives, but at the end of the month sent in his bills. Indignation ran high at the camp where he was already hated by officers and rank-and-file alike for the useless manoeuvres and countless "fatigues" he ordered. Young Dr. Henry and several comrades decided to offer him a public affront. They placarded the gate at Plantation House, the guardroom at Deadwood and Jamestown Square with a handprinted advertisement that ran as follows:

"The public are respectfully informed that Brigadier General Coffin will kill a fat bullock at his house on Wednesday the 10th instant, and three fat sheep on the Friday after. Beef, from 11d. to 1s. per pound, according to the piece. Mutton—Hind Quarter, 1s. 1d.—Fore ditto, 11d. The General further gives notice that Tripe is to be had at a reasonable price, and Geese are grazed on his grounds at one penny a head per week—the Ganders to pay double." *

---

* Henry, *Trifles from My Portfolio*, Vol. II, p. 3.

A loud laugh went up from all over the island and orders rained in on Pine-Coffin. Lowe, however, took the situation in hand and the General was persuaded to drop his butcher's business.

. . . . . . .

The Emperor's old barouche was almost worn out. Lowe had offered to replace it as early as the fall of 1818. Nicholls mentioned the matter to Bertrand, who replied: "Let the carriage alone." [28] Reade now sent his own phaeton to Longwood. Every day and often twice a day Napoleon would go out in it with Montholon for a short drive in the gum-tree woods or along the road to the camp. The Emperor had taken himself in hand and was doing his best to bear up under his diminishing strength, but his spirits were still gloomy.

"This air," he would say, "is bad for me."

In a moment of despondency he dictated to Bertrand a letter to Lord Liverpool, asking for the last time for a transfer to another climate.[29]

"My Lord, I had the honour to write to you, June 25, 1819, to inform you of the state of health of the Emperor Napoleon, who had been suffering from chronic hepatitis since the month of October, 1817. Towards the end of September last, Dr. Antommarchi arrived and has attended him. At first he experienced some relief, but since then that physician has declared, as can be seen from his day-book and his bulletins, that the malady has developed to such a state that remedies can no longer avail against the deadliness of the climate, that he needs mineral waters, that all the time he remains in this locality will be naught but a painful agony, that he cannot expect any improvement unless he returns to Europe, his strength being so weakened by five years of residence in this frightful climate, deprived of everything, a prey to the worst sort of treatment.

"The Emperor Napoleon therefore orders me to ask you to be transferred to a European climate as the sole means of lessening the sufferings to which he is subject.

"I have the honour . . .
                                          "COUNT BERTRAND."

No reply was ever received.

On September 18th, just after dawn, the Emperor went out on horseback accompanied by Archambault and a groom. For the first time in four years he left the precincts of Longwood and made a tour of the new boundary line. The ride lasted two hours and a half. It

[28] Lowe Papers, 20-130.
[29] The letter (unpublished) is dated September 2, 1820 (Lowe Papers, 20-131).

exhausted him. He stayed in bed all the next day and kept to the phaeton the days following.

On October 4th, thinking that a "good fatigue," as he said, would deaden his discomfort, he decided to go for luncheon to Mount Pleasant, the residence of Sir William Doveton, on the slope of the wooded chain that dips towards the sea to form the vast and magnificent basin of Sandy Bay. He set out about seven o'clock in the morning with Bertrand, Montholon, Archambault, and three attendants, who carried provisions. Riding through Hutt's Gate he gained the highroad that skirts Diana's Peak between verdant dales. Slowly the little company climbed the grade, discovering a wider horizon at each turn in the road. Before them the whole southern portion of the island stretched out like a map in bold relief as far as the pallid sea.

As the riders passed, native children, with coffee-coloured faces, hands and arms, watched, open-eyed, from the mountain-sides where they were guarding their goats. Now and then they could be heard singing a tune. Their voices, sweet, earnest, mounted into the limpid sky like the puffs of smoke that rise at night from thatch-covered roofs to become one with the early stars. Some few of them greeted Napoleon, and he raised his hat.

The aged Mr. Doveton had not been forewarned of this visit of the Captive, but he caught sight of the little cavalcade from afar. In the account that he sent to Sir Hudson Lowe five days later, Doveton relates that he was walking in his garden when he saw some riders advancing in the direction of his estate. "On spying I concluded they were the state prisoners from Longwood. I went in to my daughter Mrs. Greentree's room who was in the act of dressing her youngest child, and told her I apprehended we were likely to have a visit from Buonaparte. . . ." [30] Montholon was riding in the lead. He dismounted and entered the avenue of great pink and white camelias that led to a terrace on which the bungalow was located. From there he could look out over one of the most wonderful landscapes in the world. Green mountains, red and black rocks, terraced pastures of short-napped velvet, here and there a cottage squatting under a mossy roof! Doveton came out to meet Montholon, who told him that the Emperor asked permission to rest for a while with him. The old man placed his house at Napoleon's service. He wel-

[30] Lowe Papers, 20-144. Retranslated.

comed the Emperor respectfully and begged him to mount the few steps of the verandah and take a seat in the drawingroom. The Emperor sank upon the divan and beckoned to Doveton's daughter, Mrs. Greentree, to take a seat beside him. He complimented her on the good appearance of her two little girls, Ann and Eliza.

"There you see some good healthy children," he said to Bertrand.

He gave them some liquorice which he took from a tortoiseshell bonbonnière.

Sir William invited the Emperor to breakfast, but the latter proposed rather that his host share the cold meal they had brought from Longwood. A table was set up on the lawn. Great cedars, magnificent cypresses lent their shade. Hibiscuses in four colours stood about here and there, arrayed like great bouquets. At their feet arum lilies lifted bronze lances around their white trumpets.

The planter sat at Napoleon's right. The Emperor poured him a glass of champagne and in return accepted a little orange liquor that had been distilled on the property. Everyone ate with good appetite. Mrs. Greentree was asked to pour coffee. Then they returned to the drawingroom, where the conversation continued in a familiar vein. The Emperor asked Doveton the question he asked of almost everyone in English—did he ever drink?

"I like a glass of wine sometimes," the good man replied.

The breakfast seemed very sumptuous to the Dovetons. It "consisted of a cold pie, potted meat, cold turkey, curried fowl, ham or pork, I could not tell which; coffee, dates, almonds, oranges, and a very fine salad."

Doveton thought "the General" was very pale, but his obesity deceived him as to the state of his health. "He looked," he wrote to the Governor in his report, "as fat and as round as a China pig." [31]

The pleasant animation caused by the repast suddenly lapsed. Napoleon said he felt very tired and wanted to get home to Longwood. He remounted his horse painfully and rode back along Bluff Road at a walk. He was glad to find the phaeton at Hutt's Gate, got into it, and at once dozed off to sleep. Bertrand and Montholon were obliged to help him climb the flight of five steps at Longwood, each holding him by an arm. His eyes were closed and his face was of an ashen colour.

[31] Lowe Papers, 20-144; Forsyth, Vol. III, p. 245.

# IV

## THE CANCER

That was napoleon's last drive outside the precincts of long-wood. From that time on he led the life of an invalid, with a few intermissions—rare intervals when his reserves of strength, as well as his fortitude, deceived even those who were nearest to him. "One day is like the next, or nearly so," Montholon wrote to his wife on November 6, 1820. "At half-past eight or nine the Emperor sends for me. I often lunch with him—if he takes luncheon. At half-past eleven or by noon he goes to bed again. At one o'clock he receives Bertrand, whom he detains for a greater or lesser length of time, rarely beyond two o'clock. Then Bertrand comes to see me. At three o'clock, if the Emperor goes out, I dress to accompany him on the drive. At five I dine with the Emperor alone and remain with him till eight, nine, ten. Three-quarters of the time he has dinner in bed. If I leave him before half-past nine I go for a cup of tea to Mme. Bertrand's, and come back at half-past ten to keep the Emperor company again. If I stay until ten o'clock, he usually sends for me during the night. He has not done any work for several months now. His health has become so bad that he seldom leaves his bed or his couch. I have the greatest difficulty in persuading him to take a drive in the phaeton or even to step out into his garden when the weather is very fine. The horse tires him so much that he has almost given up riding. Last week he was very ill and gave us two hours of great anxiety. Happily he is all right now, but exceedingly weak. He wishes to be remembered to you and asks you to send him some books. Books are his one consolation at present. He has someone read to him, for his eyes tire immediately."

On October 10, as he was getting out of a bath that had been too hot and too prolonged, Napoleon fainted and had to be carried to his bed. He complained of headaches almost continuously and felt a pain in his right side "like a gentle thrust from a sharp blade." He called that pain his "knifing." He was stubbornly constipated and daily

444

enemas weakened him still more. Antommarchi advised an application of vesicants to both arms. Napoleon refused.

"Don't you think Mr. Lowe is torturing me enough?" [1]

Bertrand and Montholon insisting, he at last consented.

But Antommarchi did not know how to apply the vesicants properly. The Emperor was annoyed and sent the servants to call him back. But he had gone to Jamestown on a holiday. When he returned and asked what effects the remedy had had, Napoleon replied:

"I do not know. Let me alone. . . . You put vesicants on me that have no shape. You do not shave the spot before applying them. A pauper in a poorhouse would be treated better than that. It seems to me you might have left me one arm free instead of undertaking both at once. That is not the way to treat a poor man."

As Antommarchi was about to answer:

"Come—you are an idiot, and I'm a greater one to submit to it." [2]

For that matter Napoleon did not submit readily to treatment. Montholon was to say to Lowe: "You have no idea what a bad patient he is. He is worse than a two-year-old child. You can't do anything with him." [3] He had no faith in remedies, save for the famous "chicken water" which Mme. Letizia had used in days of old for his childhood illnesses. He asked the cook to make some. His limbs were heavy. He was always cold. Light hurt his eyes, and he was now asking that his bedroom be tightly closed and the blinds and curtains drawn. Montholon and Marchand groped their way about in the dark. Even in the billiardroom the shutters were closed. He spent the greater part of his days in a doze. The slightest sound brought a groan of impatience from him.

Whatever he might say, the vesicants relieved him a little. His digestion was better and he began to have a touch of appetite. On October 16, Lutyens observes,[4] he walked for two hours in his garden. On the 22nd, feeling much better, he invited Bertrand to dinner.[5]

But soon he weakened again and his pulse was slow. He suffered

[1] Montholon, Vol. II, p. 430.
[2] Masson, *"La Mort de l'Empereur"* (*Revue des Deux Mondes,* May 13, 1921); Marchand Papers (Thiers Library).
[3] Lowe Papers, 20-131.
[4] *Diary,* Lowe Papers, 20-131.
[5] Lutyens, *Diary* (Lowe Papers, 20-131).

from nausea and so virtually stopped eating. His intimates saw nothing abnormal in that. The Emperor had always vomited easily. "A mere tickling cough," Las Cases wrote,[6] "was enough to make him give up his dinner." "He takes roast," says Marchand, "only when he is served the brown part, from which he sucks the juice, but is unable to swallow the meat. Bouillon is the only broth he can take, and it overheats him." [7]

Though he protested that his stomach was still good and willing, that he never had any pains there, the thought of his father's malady worried him and he asked Antommarchi, in case he should die, to open his body. He thought that in that way his son might be forewarned of the fatal inheritance and be better able to guard against it.

Montholon sent word to Lowe that Napoleon was seriously ill. The Governor shrugged his shoulders. That was in spite of a confirmation from Lutyens (November 1). The orderly officer said that the General seemed pretty bad, but that when Montholon had suggested calling Dr. Arnott (the surgeon of the 20th), for a consultation, he had replied: "I will be better in a few days. There's no danger."

On November 4th Napoleon took a salt-water bath and it seemed to do him good. He went down into the garden almost every day and sat beside one of the pools. On November 7th he began to use the carriage again. Lowe caught a glimpse of him the next day when he was taking one of his drives: "I was returning through the grounds of Longwood, towards Longwood House, when I observed a phaeton drawn by four horses with General Bonaparte and Count Montholon in it. As soon as they perceived me, the drivers were desired to turn off by another road, but this could not be done so soon as to prevent my having a good view of General Bonaparte's side face, at about thirty yards' distance. He wore a round hat, and green surtout buttoned close over his breast. He appeared much paler than when I had last seen him, but not fallen away. I should have inferred, however, a looseness of fibre and inability at the moment of any active exertion. A sallow, colourless look is characteristic of his appearance in general, and any degree of indisposition would naturally add to it." [8]

The Emperor's walks in the garden, or his drives in the phaeton,

6 Vol. I, p. 453.
7 Marchand Papers (Thiers Library).
8 November 8, 1820 (Lowe Papers, 20-131); Forsyth, Vol. III, p. 248.

the moment he felt better, as well as Antommarchi's careless attitude, all helped to deceive Lowe. "That General Bonaparte cannot be in any very alarming state of illness," he wrote to Bathurst, November 16, 1820, "is, however, sufficiently obvious, from his physician taking daily rides, at such distance as would create a delay of an hour and a half, before his assistance could be availed of." [9]

However, Napoleon sank farther and farther towards prostration. On the 17th, Lutyens informed Lowe: "Count Montholon further said that the General was so heavy and drowsy that he would scarcely speak to any person . . . and did not even think of reading." [10]

Coming out of one of his long silences, Napoleon told Antommarchi that he could not master his weakness:

"Bed has become a place of delight to me. I would not give it up for all the treasures in the world. What a change! How I have gone down! It takes an effort to raise my eyelids. My strength, my faculties are failing. . . . This is vegetation! It is not living."

Lutyens wrote to Gorrequer, December 4th: "Count Montholon informed me that General Bonaparte was getting weaker every day, and that now Doctor Antommarchi thought seriously of the General's state of health; that he fainted the last time when he returned from the carriage; that whatever he ate he immediately threw off his stomach; that he, Count Montholon, had the greatest trouble to get the General to move off his bed or sofa." Two days earlier, December 2, Lutyens had noted: "General Bonaparte and Count Montholon took an airing in the phaeton for a short time last evening. Count Montholon said the General was so weak that he was obliged to return. Sowerby [the English gardener in charge at Longwood, who served as a spy for all the orderly officers] was near General Bonaparte yesterday. He says the General looked very ill." [11]

Stage-play, diplomacy, Lowe still thought! And when he came to read a letter that Montholon wrote to his wife, the following day, the 5th, he was confirmed in that opinion, since, at the end of the letter, Montholon still asked to leave:

"The Emperor's illness has taken a bad turn. His chronic affection has been complicated by a definitely characterized prostration. His weakness has become such that he cannot perform the slightest vital function without experiencing extreme fatigue and often losing con-

[9] Ibid.; Young, Vol. II, p. 197.        [11] Ibid.; Knowles, Letters of Lutyens, p. 72.
[10] Ibid.; Young, Vol. II, p. 197.

sciousness. . . . His pulse can be felt now only with the greatest difficulty. His gums, his lips, his nails, are entirely colourless. His feet and legs are continually wrapped in flannels and hot cloths, but are nevertheless cold as ice. Sometimes the cold mounts to the middle of his thighs. His hands are just as cold. I do my best to induce him to go out into the open air every day, a thing that the doctor strongly recommends in order to restore his vitality. But often it seems not to agree with him. His heart and his liver seem not to be functioning properly, and what he says is, alas, only too true: 'There is no more oil in the lamp.' "

However Lowe insisted on having Dr. Arnott call at Longwood, assuring that "he would be allowed to attend 'the General' as an ordinary private patient, which had been originally the captive's own proposal."

Late in December (the 26th), newspapers from Europe reported the death of Elisa, Napoleon's eldest sister.[12] He appeared to be greatly distressed by it. "He sat in his armchair with his head bowed, motionless. . . . Deep sighs escaped him at intervals." [13] He said to Montholon:

"She was a capable woman, with noble qualities and a respectable intelligence. But there was never any intimacy between us—our temperaments were too different."

He went on to talk of divorce, of Hortense, of Eugene. A flood of memories had risen in him.

A little later he went out with Antommarchi into the arbour of the passion flowers, let himself fall into a folding chair and murmured:

"Well, doctor, you see? Elisa has just shown us the way! Death seemed to have overlooked my family. Now it is beginning to strike. My turn cannot be far off." [14]

He still received the Bertrand children. Their childish babbling was a joy to him. Little Hortense told him that she was going to

[12] Elisa died on August 7, 1820, on her estate, Villa Vicentina, near Aquilea. She was still young—forty-three. The official cause of her death was "putrescent and bilious fever." No autopsy was made. E. Rodocanachi, in his excellent *Elisa Napoléon en Italie* (p. 280), writes that she died of the same disease as Napoleon. She left two children: a son who was to be killed in 1833 by a fall from his horse, at a very young age, and a daughter, Napoléone, who married Count Camerata and was later to be known as the Princess Baciocchi.
[13] Antommarchi, Vol. I, p. 412.
[14] Antommarchi, Vol. I, p. 416.

marry Tristan de Montholon. The Emperor promised to give the latter a dowry of two millions.[15] That cheered poor Montholon a little, for once an aide-de-camp he had now turned nurse, and to tell the truth was doing his best to second Marchand. "My life," Montholon wrote to his wife, December 20, "is all with him, since his complete breakdown. He wants to have me always with him. He will not take any medicine that I do not give him or advise him to take. His physician is beside himself because of it. I am the only one who finds any favour with him."

Lowe sent word to Bertrand that the ship which was to take him back to Europe with his family was coming in from the Indies and that he could sail on it. We may imagine that the Grand Marshal's cottage must have shivered with the cries, tears and bitter reproaches of the indolent Fanny, who had turned into a veritable shrew during those last months. Bertrand held his ground. He thanked Lowe, but said that "he could not leave the Emperor in his present state of health."[16] As late as January 19, 1821, Montholon was to write to his wife: "*La belle Fanny* will not consent for anything in the world to seeing another of her springtimes lost on this wretched rock. She wants to spend the few good days she still has left amid the gaieties of Europe. Her husband will miss St. Helena. He foresees that and does not want to go away at all. But in this as in many other things he is completely overpowered by his wife. So far Bertrand's request has not gone beyond Longwood, but you may consider it certain that, aside from events which I cannot reasonably foresee, they will not be in St. Helena three months from now." However, that was just a postponement, whatever Masson says [17]—for Masson was prejudiced in Bertrand's favour.

.     .     .     .     .     .     .

New Year's Day, 1821, was lugubriously sad—it was the last that Napoleon was to see on earth. Marchand entered his room and opened the blinds, then gave the Emperor his best wishes.

"Well," said the Emperor, "what are you giving me for a present this time?"

"Sire," replied the faithful valet, "the wish of seeing Your Majesty soon well again and leaving a climate that is so bad for your health."

[15] Montholon to Mme. de Montholon, December 20, 1820.
[16] Lowe Papers, 20-132.
[17] *Napoléon à Sainte Hélène*, p. 443.

"That will not be so far away, my son. My end is near. I cannot go far."

Marchand protested, and he sighed:

"It will be as God wills." [18]

He received neither Mme. Bertrand nor the children and kept to his apartment all day.

During the month of January he felt better. He went out once in a while on Montholon's arm or with Marchand, and at times even took the phaeton for a round of the gum-tree woods, always at a walk, for too lively a pace nauseated him. The month was as follows in Lutyens' diary: [19]

January 4. "This morning about eight o'clock I saw General Bonaparte near the bird-cage. . . . I likewise saw St. Dennis come out of the diningroom door with something covered with a cloth. I therefore believe General Bonaparte took his coffee or breakfast in the Chinese summer-house, or at the end of the covered walk. . . . Count Montholon did not go to the house till four o'clock yesterday. Surby says he [the General] walked much as usual and he thinks he looks as if mending." *

"January 5. I saw the General sitting on a chair near the veranda of his bed chamber. He remained there near an hour. At eight he sent for Count Montholon."

On the 12th, 16th, 17th, drives in the phaeton with Montholon. Lutyens saluted Napoleon on his return on the 17th. The Emperor was very pale.

On the 18th, between six and seven in the morning, leaning on Marchand's arm, Napoleon took a walk in the direction of Bertrand's house, looked at New House, watched the workmen for a few minutes, then went back to his room.

On the 19th, at half past six in the morning, he took a walk of about a hundred yards along the drive that led to the woods, leaning on Marchand's arm. He then got into the phaeton, with the help of Marchand and Archambault. Marchand accompanied him on horseback.

On the 21st, Lutyens saw the Emperor walking on Montholon's arm in front of the stables. He entered the phaeton and got out again with difficulty, even though he was helped.

[18] Marchand Papers (Thiers Library).    * Knowles, *Letters of Lutyens*, p. 86.
[19] Lowe Papers, 20-132.

On the 26th, Lutyens was at Plantation House and reported Napoleon's condition in detail to the Governor: "His face has grown thin and very white—as white as a sheet of paper. He seems weak and staggers when he walks. His body is bent. He is as fat as ever. He goes muffled up in a great-coat and wears long pantaloons." (The officer therefore could not see whether his legs were swollen.) Finally he added: "General Bonaparte has been going downhill rapidly for some time. He is very much broken. However, Count Montholon told me that he was better." *

February 10. In the late afternoon, Napoleon went out in the phaeton with Montholon and Arthur Bertrand.

On the 11th, the Bertrand children spent the evening at Longwood.

On the 20th, they killed a turtle. A person came from Jamestown to cook it, since Chandellier did not know how.

On the 22nd, Napoleon went down into the garden with Montholon about five o'clock in the afternoon. He was wearing his dressing gown and his madras handkerchief.

Similar notes run along for about three weeks, down to March 15.

Antommarchi had been sharply rebuked for his conduct by Bertrand and Montholon and the Emperor did not like to see him. He called on Sir Thomas Reade without informing anyone at Longwood and announced his intention of returning to Europe. Lowe visited Montholon to discuss the matter and Montholon asked for orders of the Emperor. Napoleon gave Antommarchi his release in a harsh and only too well-deserved letter, forbidding him his bedroom from that time on. "For the fifteen months you have been in this place you have given His Majesty no cause to have confidence in your moral character. You could not be of the slightest use to him in his illness and there would be no object in your continuing your stay here for several months longer." [20] When these documents are compared with what Antommarchi had the courage to write in his *Last Moments*, about the care he gave the Emperor and the respect the latter had for him, one is astounded at the impudence of the man. The Emperor dictated an official note in which he requested a physician and at the same time suggested several well-known persons belonging to his old circle who might replace Bertrand. "He will be glad to receive as

* Retranslated.
[20] Montholon, Vol. II, p. 482.

a substitute for Count Bertrand anyone who has been attached to his person, especially the Duke of Vicenza or the Duke of Rovigo, the Count de Segur, the Count de Montesquiou, MM. Daru, Druout and de Turenne, or, among men of letters, Baron Denon and M. Arnault" (January 30, 1821). For the actual choice he preferred to rely on the King of France and his ministers.[21] "All that has to be done can be done only through the English or the French governments," Montholon said to Lowe, January 27th:[22] "The present ministry is made up of men who almost all served under him and know his habits—for example, Pasquier, for ten years a minister of his, with whom he talked every day. Mounier also knows him perfectly and so do Ségur, Siméon, Daru, and Latour-Maubourg, now Minister of War, who was his aide-de-camp, went with him to Egypt and owes his fortune to him. Decazes himself was formerly secretary to Madame Mère and knows all about him."

So Napoleon had reached that point! Worn down by a disease, the irremediable progress of which he alone suspected, and having plumbed the selfishness of all about him, he was relying on Louis XVIII to soften the last stage of his imprisonment! Even if proceedings were hastened, the relief proposed could not reach St. Helena under nine or ten months. That shows that in spite of everything Napoleon still cherished some hope as to his condition.

Father Buonavita was suffering from high-blood pressure and seemed to be in danger of total paralysis if he remained much longer on the island. It was decided that he should leave by the first vessel. Vignali was devout and pious enough, but too uneducated. The Emperor, therefore, asked for another priest. Montholon wrote to his wife, February 8, 1820: "Vignali told us the other day that Alexander was the greatest man who had come out of ancient Rome. To prevent him from making similar blunders in future, he was sentenced to read two hundred pages of Rollin every day and to make abstracts of it."

New Longwood had at last been carpeted and furnished. Lowe had been giving close attention to the matter, going to Longwood almost every day. He had taken the upholsterer, Darling, to Montholon's lodgings, to ask him to choose the wall-paper and furniture for the

[21] Montholon, Vol. II, p. 482.
[22] Gorrequer, *Minutes* (Lowe Papers, 20-132).

NEW HOUSE. BUILT FOR NAPOLEON BUT COMPLETED TOO LATE FOR HIS
OCCUPANCY

DR. ARNOTT

Emperor's apartment and his own. Montholon would give only "semi-official suggestions" which implied no acquiescence on Napoleon's part.[23] The furnishings, according to Aly (p. 256), were very commonplace. "The main rooms were decorated with tinted papers. The carpets were of an ordinary thick green cloth. The furniture was of mahogany, but had no ornaments. Small chandeliers, or antique lamps of bronze or alabaster, hung from the centre of each room. The shabbiness of the hangings and furniture strangely contrasted with the imposing grandeur of the apartments. On the beautiful mantelpieces there was not a clock nor a vase, and not a picture hung on the walls. Mirrors were very scarce. I saw two of them, I think. The curtains at the windows were of a flowered cotton material, of the kind that was in fashion a century ago." [24]

Since the place was ready for guests, Lowe insisted that Napoleon should take possession of it, and the Emperor had almost become reconciled to the idea of living there. He could not help saying, November 1, 1820, that he "would be much better off there than in old Longwood and that in fact to refuse to live there would be to act like children sulking in a corner." [25] But he still complained that it was too lacking in shade and too exposed to the eyes of the soldiers at the camp. It would be necessary, he thought, to transplant the largest trees from his present gardens. Moreover, he disliked intensely an iron fence that was too conspicuous and was placed too near the house. Lowe accordingly had the fence moved back and sunk deeper into the ground in such a way as to make it less obnoxious. A few changes could be made in the gardens along lines that Montholon might suggest and a part of old Longwood would still remain at the disposal of the French in case of a fire. That Napoleon had made up his mind to live at New House is evident. On March 7, Montholon was to write to his wife: "It is probable that I shall shortly be changing lodgings. The new house is finished, or nearly so."

. . . . . . .

The Grand Marshal and Montholon interceded for Antommarchi, trying to excuse him on grounds of his youth. Under their pressure the Emperor finally consented to receive him again. But he did

[23] Montholon, Vol. II, p. 478.
[24] Jamestown Archives, 1821. The inventory drawn up by Darling shortly after Napoleon's death confirms Aly's description.
[25] Montholon, Vol. II, p. 430.

not forgive him. Antommarchi resumed his duties on February 6.

The Emperor disliked going out more and more. The wind and the sunlight distressed him. He returned from his short walks exhausted. "He went into the drawingroom," writes Aly (p. 259), "and, stretching himself on a couch that had been rolled up in front of the table, lay there as though he were utterly fatigued, trying for several minutes to catch his breath and rest. Meanwhile the table was being made ready for luncheon. 'Let me get my breath,' he said to Pierron and me and, rolling his eyes back and forth alternatively between M. de Montholon and us, he added: 'I don't know what is the matter with my stomach. I feel as if someone had plunged a knife into it and were amusing himself by turning it round and round.' When he was a little rested, he had the table drawn up to him and sent for his meal. He had been hungry during his drive, and was still hungry when he spread out his napkin. But the moment the first spoonful of soup touched his lips his appetite vanished. He forced himself to eat, however, but with no pleasure. Nothing tasted good to him."

To take the place of the walks, and at the same time provide a little exercise, he had a see-saw made of a long piece of timber supported in the centre by a notched post. It was set up in the billiardroom. He hoped that the up and down movement would keep up his strength. The two ends of the beam were shaped like saddles, well padded, with an iron $T$ fixed in front for the rider to grasp. As the Emperor was fairly heavy, the end facing him was weighted with lead till it was properly balanced. Montholon was as a rule the one who rode opposite him. "Often," writes Arthur Bertrand (p. 115), "he had my sister or two of my brothers, or me, at the other end of the see-saw and thought it a great joke to give us such violent jerks that sometimes we were thrown off." The exercise seemed to agree with him, and he kept at it for about a fortnight. Then he gave it up. "Before he became seriously ill," writes Aly, "the machine was taken apart and the floor restored to its former condition." [26]

The spells of vomiting became more frequent. Napoleon could now take nothing but light nourishment, such as cold beef bouillon. Learning that what he could most easily digest was veal jelly, Hudson Lowe sent a supply on several occasions from Plantation House. He

---

[26] *Before he became seriously ill*—an unwitting confession that, as late as February, 1821, Napoleon's retinue did not consider him in danger. That helps one to understand the scepticism of the English.

also sent a cook who, according to Montholon, "made a very good soup." [27] The Emperor's pulse had long seemed sluggish. It now slowed down even more. The only way to stimulate it a little seemed to be by applications of flannel cloths so hot that the attendants could scarcely touch them, though the Emperor seemed not to feel them at all. He was having serious lapses in memory. At intervals he suffered severe chills. Down to the end of 1820 Napoleon audited and initialed Pierron's account book. He verified it again that December. Beginning with January, 1821, we find the signatures of Montholon, Bertrand and Marchand replacing his, and so it would be to the end. [28]

Allowing his head to fall upon his chest he would take a few steps in the arbour and then sit down as soon as he felt his legs weakening. He kept repeating over and over again:

"Ah, me; poor me!" [29]

He also repeated two verses from Voltaire's *Zaïre:*

"But I must not hope to see Paris again.
    You see, I am ready to go down to my grave."

Marchand and Aly would feel the tears come to their eyes.

He said one other time:

"The machine is worn out. It cannot run any more. It is over—I shall die here." [30]

Before he left Longwood, poor Buonavita, crippled in all his limbs and hardly ever leaving his room, received a visit from the Governor. Timidly he protested his respect for English authority and assured him that he had never had any thought of joining any intrigue. [31] Speaking of the Emperor he then said with all the strength left in his poor body:

"You know, Mr. Governor, the state of my relations with Longwood. I have tried to do as they wanted me to do. He cannot last long. If only you could see his face. I assure you, as an independent

---

[27] Lowe Papers, 20-132.
[28] Thiers Library, Carton 15. At the bottom of the page he wrote, in his own handwriting, in December:

| "Receipts | 13,000 |
| Expenses | 12,185 |
| Balance | 815 shillings." |

[29] Aly, p. 260.
[30] Conversation Montholon-Lowe, March 20 (Lowe Papers, 20-144).
[31] Gorrequer, *Minutes* (Lowe Papers, 20-144. Unpublished).

and honourable man, that he will not last. Remember what I am saying to you!"

Antommarchi gave the Abbé a letter for Fesch, saying that the liver trouble from which the Emperor was suffering was endemic at St. Helena and that if he were not quickly transported to some other climate, his death would not be far off. Antommarchi did not believe a word of what he wrote. "He keeps smiling," said Montholon to Bertrand, "when I tell him about the 'knifing,' and regards all those symptoms of internal disorders as the effect simply of lack of sufficient exercise." [32]

The morning of his departure, staggering, deeply moved, Buonavita entered the Emperor's room. The Emperor was in bed. In a weak voice he spoke to the old man of his family, whom the priest would be seeing in Rome, and gave him final instructions for them. He was calm. The Abbé wept. When he left, the Emperor waved him a last good-bye. He ordered Antommarchi to accompany the old man to Jamestown. Lowe sent a carriage to take him to town. Montholon entrusted Buonavita with a letter for Pauline Borghese, imploring her to move heaven and earth to obtain Napoleon's transfer to some other place. "The Emperor is counting on Your Highness to inform influential Englishmen of the true state of his malady. He is dying without help on this frightful rock. His agony is terrible." Montholon enclosed with it the note he had written on January 30 to the English government. Pauline was not to receive either the letter or the note till after Napoleon's death.

A little later, about nine o'clock, Montholon came to suggest a drive in the phaeton. Napoleon rebelled:

"I feel so badly when I come back, and I am so comfortable in my bed!"

Montholon had often been told by the Emperor that when he hesitated "he must use force." Montholon therefore insisted, and also Antommarchi, who had not yet gone.

"Well, since you wish it, Montholon! See if the carriage has come up."

The General went out and returned immediately saying that the carriage was ready and that there was almost no wind. Napoleon sighed and, after taking a little jelly, put on a pair of trousers, a coat,

[32] Montholon, Vol. II, p. 486.

and his slippers. He allowed Marchand to tie his cravat. Leaning on Montholon's arm he went down into the garden. But once at the carriage step he felt too weak to get in. A chill ran over him. He insisted on going back to his room. He got into bed, cold to the bone.

"I have no blood in my body," he said.

That too was a phrase he had been repeating for some time.[33]

They drew two woollen blankets over him and soon he began to sweat so heavily that they were obliged to change his flannels several times.

He then sent Montholon to luncheon and ordered Marchand to read to him from Dumouriez's *Campaigns*. The Grand Marshal came in in the afternoon as usual. They talked of the campaign of '93. The Emperor thought he would go out of doors while his bedroom was being aired. He went as far as his oak and sat down under it for a second. The next moment he all but fainted. Supported by Montholon and Noverraz he dragged himself back into the house. There he was seized with violent pains in the intestines and began to vomit. Montholon thought he detected a clot of blood in the basin.[34] They hunted everywhere for Antommarchi, who had lingered in town. When he finally returned Napoleon refused to see him.

That day at last the eyes of his companions were opened. Montholon wrote to his wife in the evening (March 17, 1821):

"In one way or another St. Helena is drawing to a close. It is impossible for HIM to live long. Our doctor claims that a change of climate would save him. My hope, however, is greater than my belief in that respect, for I have never seen anyone look the way he looks at this moment." However, the French still thought it a matter of being "run down." Aly wrote on the same date to his mother: "Our situation is still the same, with the exception, however, of our master who has been suffering from a sort of languour for a long time. It pulls him down more and more, exhausts him and changes his appearance to the greatest degree. . . . If he did not have such a strong constitution, there would be nothing left for us to do but bid him good-bye." [35]

The night was better than had been expected. In the morning the Emperor had no fever and his pulse was sixty-three—the normal as

[33] Marchand Papers (Thiers Library).     [35] Lowe Papers, 20-132. Unpublished.
[34] Montholon, Vol. II, p. 487.

observed by O'Meara and Antommarchi (in his youth Napoleon's pulse had been forty to fifty, at times). The Emperor thought he might go out. He drank a glass of port and ate a biscuit and then, supported by Montholon, climbed painfully into the phaeton. But soon they were obliged to return. He was seized with a new attack of pain and frightful nausea. He was given the same treatment as the night before, though he refused all the remedies suggested by Antommarchi. Towards evening his fever dropped and after the room had been cleared of flies he was able to sleep.

Against all that has hitherto been written, Napoleon did take another drive in the carriage on the 18th.[36]

On the 19th he seemed fairly well, but the fever returned at four o'clock as he was going down into the garden. Lutyens saw Noverraz running for Antommarchi.[37] The doctor was absent again. The night was broken by attacks of pain, but in the end the Emperor managed to get some sleep. In the morning his pulse was normal. March 20 seems to have been a day of quiet. On that day Lowe called on Montholon, having had news of the Emperor's illness. Montholon mentioned signs of mental collapse in Napoleon:

"The last time we went out he made such strange remarks that I called his attention to the fact. 'I do not understand what you are saying—perhaps I don't hear you.' "

"But what I said is clear enough," the Emperor replied.

Finally his talk became altogether irrational.

"He is a very sick man," Montholon concluded. "He could not be worse. His complexion is so yellow as to frighten one. He does not sleep any more—rather than sleep it is a form of coma. He cannot endure the slightest noise. If you waken him, he asks you to let him alone and declares that he does not need anyone near him, that it bothers him. But if he wakes up himself and you are not there, he blames you for neglecting him."

Lowe replied that in his opinion Napoleon was suffering from a slight anemia and would soon recover.

"Yes," said Montholon, "there is still a little hope, but in my judgment, apart from some radical change, he cannot live very long now."[38]

On the 21st he had another attack between four and five o'clock

---

[36] Lutyens, *Report* (Lowe Papers, 20-132).    [38] Lowe Papers, 20-132, 20-134.
[37] *Ibid.*

in the afternoon. Antommarchi, under arrest at Longwood by Montholon's order, examined the matter vomited by the Emperor and declared that he was suffering from a "remittent [intermittent] gastric fever." He prescribed an emetic. Sheerest folly! An emetic on a stomach which he knew was a wreck! With great good sense Napoleon refused to take it, but Bertrand and Montholon insisted. He finally yielded and promised to take a dose the next day. On the 22nd he took the medicine in two portions and immediately afterwards began to writhe with atrocious pains in his stomach. Montholon even saw him roll on the floor groaning aloud.[39] Antommarchi declared emphatically that in spite of everything the emetic was "the necessary remedy and that it should be continued at all costs." Later, as his pain lessened, the Emperor was able to take a glass of orange-blossom water and in the evening ate a little. Unable to sleep in his bed, where the mosquito-netting stifled him, he spent the night in an armchair, without any lamp, for fear of attracting the gnats. The adjoining room was dimly lighted by two candles. The 23rd brought a respite. The Emperor was able to shave and to brush his teeth.

Attributing the improvement to his drug, Antommarchi recommended a fresh dose. The patient this time submitted, but the strain of vomiting prostrated him anew. He declared that he would not take anything more that was ordered by that sawbones. In future, he said to Marchand, he would stick to a liquorice water flavoured with anise that he kept in a phial under his pillow or in his pocket.

"The best medicine," he murmured, pointing to the phial, "is that there."

Marchand was not leaving him once during the day.[40] Beginning with the 18th he watched for half the night, relieved by Aly and Noverraz. Montholon and Bertrand also volunteered, when Noverraz came down with a bad liver attack and was obliged to take to bed himself (March 24). The Emperor refused Bertrand's offer but accepted that of Montholon. Antommarchi did not even volunteer.

The next day, the 24th, Antommarchi urged him to take an emetic again.

"Take it yourself!" replied the Emperor.

The physician tried to persuade Marchand to slip an emetic into the liquorice. The valet protested, but an allusion of Bertrand's gave

[39] Montholon, Vol. II, p. 491.
[40] Lutyens, *Report*, March 21 (Lowe Papers, 20-132).

the sick man the impression that he had lent himself to the fraud.

"Well, Grand Marshal, how are you!" Napoleon said as Bertrand came in.

"Perfectly well, sire," Bertrand replied. "And I wish it were the same with Your Majesty. How do you feel after taking the emetic in your drink? Are you any better?" [41]

Napoleon gave Marchand a sharp rebuke and called for Antommarchi. But again the doctor was off to Jamestown. When he came back, he excused himself by saying that the Emperor "was endangering his life by refusing the aid of science."

"Well, sir," Napoleon retorted in rage, "do I have to justify myself to you? Don't you realize that for me death would be a blessing from Heaven? I am not afraid of it. I would not do anything to hasten its coming, but I would not draw lots on the chance that I might live."

That same day, March 24, Lowe wrote to Bathurst: "Count Montholon, in his account of General Bonaparte's illness, did not ascribe it either to climate or treatment here. The disease he evidently considered to lie in the languid circulation of the blood, in the weakness of the organs of digestion, and in the *mind*. What he said on the subject of the liver complaint was evidently introduced for no other purpose than to preserve a kind of consistency with what had been before so frequently advanced on this subject." [42]

For two days Napoleon refused to see Antommarchi. [43] Montholon pleaded with him to consult Dr. Arnott, who had come to Longwood several times at Lowe's bidding. Arnott, according to Montholon, would make up for Antommarchi's incompetence. Napoleon refused point blank.

The Emperor did not dislike Arnott. He had seen him at Montholon's one day when the latter was sick and had sent for the English doctor. Napoleon had thought that he had "the face and manners of a well-bred man." He even added: "In fact, if I felt very ill and it were absolutely necessary to dismiss this young fellow [Antommarchi], I would like no one better than Arnott." [44]

Montholon's anxiety became even greater when he learned, through a conversation with Lowe on March 30th, that the latter had been frightened by despatches from Bathurst. On the 29th Reade had

[41] Marchand Papers (Thiers Library).
[42] Lowe Papers, 20-132; Young, Vol. II, p. 209.
[43] Lutyens, *Report*, March 28 (Lowe Papers, 20-132).
[44] March 1, 1821. Montholon, Vol. II, p. 484.

already written to Lutyens: "If General Bonaparte is really so ill as Dr. Antommarchi and Count Montholon have represented him to be, it is an act of humanity on their part to insist upon calling in other medical advice. . . . It is your duty to insist, . . . upon having an opportunity afforded to you of seeing him, if an English medical person is not admitted to him." [45]

Bathurst informed Lowe that there was better reason than ever to fear an escape, insisting that he assure himself of Napoleon's presence at Longwood. For two weeks the orderly officer had not had a glimpse of him. If a British medical officer was not admitted, Lowe had made up his mind to force the door of the alleged patient. He would be sorry, he said, to use force, but he could not delay any longer. [46] "I shall not demand that General Bonaparte show himself to the orderly officer at Longwood provided he admit an English physician. There is nothing improper in my suggestion, I think. I am not asking him to consult the doctor in question, but simply to receive him in such a way that I can be assured of the General's presence in his house. At the present moment I have no proof of it. I cannot tolerate such a state of affairs any longer."

Montholon replied that he hoped the Governor would not go to such extremes at such a moment.

"I have made up my mind, I tell you," said Lowe, "and if necessary I shall resort to force."

"Then, monsieur, you will assume full responsibility for anything that may happen."

Lowe was so nervous that he came to Longwood twice during the course of the 30th, and Sir Thomas Reade [47] once. In the evening Montholon wrote to his wife: "All our efforts are concentrated on having Dr. Arnott called in, and you know me too well not to realize how worried I am. . . . My first letter will inform you what God has decided about the Emperor, for according to all the calculations of the doctor the disease cannot run a long course and we are now at the critical moment. I am so obsessed by this thought that every morning when I open my eyes I dread lest I am to be told that it is all over." [48]

Montholon judged the Governor so capable of resorting to that

[45] Lowe Papers, 20-132; Forsyth, Vol. III, p. 271.
[46] Conversation Lowe-Montholon, March 30 (Lowe Papers, 20-144). Retranslated.
[47] Montholon, Vol. II, p. 502.
[48] It should not be forgotten that these letters passed under the Governor's eye.

odious procedure, that he got Bertrand and returned to the charge with the Emperor, both of them begging him to receive Arnott but without giving their reasons. Napoleon did not yield. Meanwhile, to avoid any intrusion on Reade's, or even Lowe's, part, Montholon and Marchand agreed to let Lutyens get a glimpse of the Emperor when he sat on his closet. It was placed near a window where the curtain was a little raised. This pathetic device succeeded and on March 31 the orderly officer was able to convince himself of the presence of Napoleon without the latter's knowledge of it.[49]

Napoleon was kept in ignorance of Lowe's attitude. On March 30 he remarked:

"That Calabrian of a Governor is leaving us very much alone. What does it mean? He probably hears from the Chinese that I am ill."

During the night he must have thought the matter over, for on the morning of April 1st he said to Bertrand:

"Your English doctor would go and report to that hangman on my condition. It would really be giving him too much satisfaction to let him know the agony I am in. Besides, what will he not make me say if I consent to see him? Well, after all, it's more to satisfy the people about me than for myself. I expect nothing from his learning."

He decided that Antommarchi should meet his English colleague at Bertrand's house and give him the history of his case. Afterwards, at ten o'clock in the evening, he would receive Arnott.

.        .        .        .        .        .        .

The bedroom was dark. The covered lamp cast a feeble halo of light in the adjoining study. Arnott entered, Antommarchi leading the way. He was a tall man, about fifty years old, clad in a long blue riding coat.[50] Marchand drew the mosquito-netting back from the bed. Arnott stepped forward. Though unable to see anything he felt the Emperor's pulse, palpated his body and his limbs. He murmured a few comforting words and asked permission to return the next morning. The scepticism of the English was such that Arnott said to Lowe that same night: "I felt him, or someone else. . . . I perceived there was considerable debility, but nothing that indicated immediate danger."

---

[49] Aly, p. 267; Lutyens, *Report*, March 31 (Lowe Papers, 20-132).
[50] Aly, p. 268. Archibald Arnott had served in Egypt, at Walcheren, and in Spain. He came to St. Helena in 1819 with the 20th.

And he reappeared in fact at nine the next morning, Bertrand serving as interpreter. Napoleon received him courteously.

It was because of the esteem in which Arnott was held in his regiment, Napoleon said, "that he had consented to see him, and on his promise not to report on his condition to the Governor." What Arnott had promised Montholon was to treat Napoleon "like any other patient." Lowe had approved and declared that he would not demand any "report" unless there were actual need, in which case Arnott should inform him.[51] However, Arnott did report to the Governor on each of his visits. He could scarcely have done otherwise.

Napoleon complained of his fever and of his sweats. Then he spoke of his stomach:

"I have a sharp piercing pain that seems to cut into me like a razor. My father died of that disease at the age of thirty-five. Might it not be hereditary?"

Arnott proceeded to a detailed examination. He declared that there could be no question of anything more than an inflammation of the stomach, that the pylorus was in good condition, the liver normal. The intestinal pains were due to an accumulation of gas and to the patient's chronic constipation. The Emperor objected that his digestion, apart from a little vomiting, had always been regular.

Arnott listened absentmindedly. It was evident that he considered the disease of a benign type. Napoleon sighed and began talking to the doctor about the campaign in Egypt which Arnott had fought under Abercromby. Finally he dismissed him with the notice that he would receive him every afternoon at four. Actually Arnott saw the Emperor twice daily, in the forenoon, and around four or five o'clock in the afternoon, during virtually the whole course of the Emperor's illness. His notes prove that. They were not communicated to Lowe till after Napoleon's death.[52]

Arnott came back during the days that followed, accompanied by Bertrand and Antommarchi. The Emperor detained them a moment, then remained alone with Bertrand until evening. Montholon had his dinner and then relieved the Grand Marshal, keeping watch until two in the morning. Marchand finished out the night.

Short on knowledge despite his years, Arnott continued optimistic. It was useless for Antommarchi to declare in his morning reports to

[51] Lowe Papers, 20-133.
[52] Lowe Papers, 20-157.

the English doctor that the Emperor was racked with fever, sweating and vomiting. Arnott thought those symptoms were being deliberately exaggerated and said as much to the Governor.

On April 5 he wrote to Gorrequer: "I did not find him labouring under any of the symptoms there detailed." [53] Reade had a long talk with Arnott. On the 6th he wrote to the Governor: "Dr. Arnott informed me that he had never found him, during any of his visits, in the state in which he had been described by Dr. Antommarchi. . . . He appears to think that General Bonaparte is not affected with any serious complaint, probably more mental than any other. . . . He told [Count Bertrand] that he saw no danger whatever. During his visit this morning he recommended General Bonaparte to rise and get shaved. He replied he was too weak at present, that he would shave when he was a little stronger. . . . His beard is very long, and Dr. Arnott describes his looks in consequence as horrible. I inquired if he appeared much emaciated? His reply was in these words: 'No; I feel his pulse frequently, and he has as stout a wrist, with as much flesh upon his arm, as I have, neither does his face appear to have fallen away much. I see nothing very peculiar in his appearance except his colour, which is very pallid—cadaverous. I saw him vomit this morning, which is the only extraordinary thing I have observed; he did not, however, vomit much." [54]

Marchand wrote under date of April 3: "On leaving His Majesty's apartment Dr. Arnott examined his vomitings. It was a blackish substance which by its nature made him say that there was an ulceration in the stomach. He informed the Grand Marshal and Count de Montholon and left various prescriptions, but the Emperor was just as rebellious to them as to Dr. Antommarchi's." [55]

Napoleon passed the day in a half stupor.[56] The person on watch kept a cloth waving to drive flies and mosquitoes away. About noon, on days when the weather was fine, Marchand and Montholon would help him into his winged chair near the glass door that opened on "The Flowerbed." They would read a few pages from a book aloud

[53] Lowe Papers, 20-133; N. Young, Vol. II, p. 212.
[54] Ibid.
[55] Marchand is mistaken as to the date. The reports of Arnott and Antommarchi place this significant vomiting on the 25th or 26th of April. As Masson suggests, Marchand must have made an error in writing at a time when his recollections were not quite so fresh.
[56] Aly, p. 270.

to him, or he might glance at a paper. But soon he would tire and go back to bed with a sigh of relief. He was taking nothing now but meat jelly, sometimes a bit of bread, some milk, more often barley water or currant syrup, and his favourite liquorice.

Convinced that it was all a matter of hypochondria, Arnott kept bidding his patient to "cheer up." The doctor should at least have been worried at the fact that he was finding Napoleon's pulse between 72 and 90, whereas his normal, as Antommarchi, irresponsible as he was, must have warned him, scarcely ever went above 60. In the state of medical science then prevailing such a symptom was of capital importance. The Emperor asked him one day whether he would get well:

"Don't be afraid to tell me, doctor. You are dealing with an old soldier who likes frankness. Tell me—what do you think?"

Arnott assured him that he had every chance in the world to recover, and very soon. On several occasions he urged him to move to New House where he would have better air and more room. Everything was in readiness to receive him there. Napoleon shook his head:

"Doctor, it's too late. I told your Governor when he submitted plans for that house that it would take five years to build it and that by that time I would need a grave. You see—they are offering me the keys and it is all over with me."

For that matter Antommarchi was opposed to such a drastic change in habits. In that he was not wrong. If the Emperor did not have enough air in his room, he said, he could be carried into the drawing-room. Arnott kept prescribing drugs and pills. Napoleon would answer "that he saw no great objection to them," but then changed the subject and always managed not to take any.[57]

Once as the doctor was feeling his pulse and asked him how he was, Napoleon answered:

"Not well, doctor. I am about to restore to the earth a remnant of life that the kings are so anxious to get."

Arnott insisted upon his "taking some remedies."

"All right, doctor, we'll take some! What disease is most prevalent in your hospitals?"

On April 8th he decided to shave himself. To give him more light his bed was pulled out into the middle of the room. Aly then noticed (p. 271) how greatly his appearance had altered. His arms and legs

[57] Marchand Papers.

had grown very thin, "his thighs had fallen off a third, his hands were less plump, his fingers more tapering." Since he had previously been very fat, Arnott could not have been aware of the degree of his emaciation, having seen him only once. That was why he could say to Lowe on April 11 that he found "his chest, shoulders and abdomen full and round. His calves may have been very big at one time. In that case they may have fallen away." [58]

"The Devil has eaten my calves away," the Emperor said to Montholon, laughing.

On the 9th he seemed better. "This is the twenty-third day of his illness," Montholon wrote to his wife. "The fever began to go down day before yesterday and the physicians are inclined to think that he is out of danger and that in a little while he will be convalescent."

If this respite revived hopes in the Emperor's companions, it also increased the confidence which he had gradually acquired in his physician. Arnott had travelled a good deal, he conversed delight- fully, and his manners were deferential. Napoleon talked Italian with him. He even got to the point of taking some of Arnott's drugs. [59] On the other hand, he was treating Antommarchi with the severity and disdain which that doctor's conduct deserved. "Antommarchi's be- haviour is unexplainable," Montholon wrote (April 9). "He could not be less attentive, more irresponsible. He never learns anything from anything and the sight of a petticoat so attracts him that he lets everything else go. Not once, I do believe, has he been found at home when wanted." His vanity hurt, Antommarchi had the impudence to approach Lowe again and ask permission to leave on the next ship. Lowe seemed much surprised and urged the doctor to be patient. The Corsican declared that he had not the slightest animosity against Dr. Arnott, but that General Bonaparte's disposition was making his situation too painful for him. He was treated more as a valet than as a physician.

"Professor," replied Lowe, "you must take the temperament of the patient into consideration and the circumstances."

Antommarchi insisted. The Governor then replied, rather dryly, that his request required thought and that he must refer it to Eng- land. The Professor went back to Longwood much discomfited. [60]

[58] Lowe Papers, 20-157. Retranslated.
[59] Montholon to Mme. de Montholon, April 9.
[60] Lowe Papers, 20-133 and 20-146.

On a plea by Arnott, Napoleon saw Antommarchi again on the evening of the 11th.

On April 10th, during the afternoon, while out of bed, the Emperor was seized with vomiting again. His fever had gone, as he said, but he felt very weak and complained of his liver. He had a burning sensation in that region. He asked Arnott to examine him again. The doctor palpated his abdomen. Napoleon gave a start, yet Arnott found "neither hardening nor swelling." The organ was simply sluggish, he said.

From then on the nights became wretched again. Arnott was called at six in the morning on April 11th. Napoleon had vomited four times since three o'clock.

The night of the 11-12th was better, the Emperor having taken a sedative. But on the 13th, at two o'clock in the morning, he began vomiting again and had a violent sweat. "I changed the Emperor seven times," Montholon notes,[61] "and each time his flannels and linen were soaked, even to the madras handkerchief around his head. The changes in linen are very hard to make without rousing his impatience. He will not have any light in his room and can stand only a candle in the next room. In that feeble light I am obliged not to give him, but to put on him, everything he needs, even tying the handkerchief on his head."[62]

During the daytime the Emperor suffered less, but his strength was failing. Now he could not stand on his feet without help, he told Arnott. He asked the doctor "whether one could die of just weakness and how long one could live when one ate as little as he did." The physician replied evasively "that there was nothing to be worried about." However, he found the patient "very downcast, very depressed."[63]

His eyes, however, were clear and his mind alert. He would lie for hours without saying a word, but every now and then his lips would move. It was as though he were mobilizing the little energy he had left in order to perform a very solemn duty.

[61] Vol. II, p. 508.
[62] Lowe Papers, 20-137.

[63] Lowe Papers, 20-137.

# V

## THE TESTAMENT

As early as April 10th Napoleon had discussed the matter of his final directions with Montholon. He asked him, in Marchand's presence, "whether two millions would be sufficient to buy back his family's property in Burgundy." "I tried," writes Montholon, "to give him hope that that would be a useless precaution, but he persisted and said to me: 'I shall write it tomorrow if my improvement continues.'"[1]

On the 12th, at his dictation, Montholon jotted down the main lines of his will.[2] At that time the people about him had more hope, but he knew that his life was drawing to a close. For a long time, even when he kept repeating that his end was near to his attendants, his physicians, his friends, in order to calm their homesickness or revive their interest, he had doubted it in his own heart. But now he was sure. The Visitor was there, still indistinct to the others, but for him unveiled. He waited His approach with no tremor of soul, no shrinking of the flesh. His hand pressed to his ruptured side, he was counting footsteps that were inaudible to everyone else. He who had taken so much from Life did not turn his face away in the presence of Death. Death was his only friend. Death would bring to a close at last the struggle of a colossal energy against empty days and a miserable audience. When all had failed, all betrayed, Death would save! Through Death he would escape at last from his wretched prison, from his jailors, from himself. Death would restore to him peace, freedom and an unassailable glory.

On the 13th at noon he had Montholon push the bolt in his bedroom door and, propped up on his pillows, he began calmly to dictate:

"I die in the Catholic, apostolic and Roman faith in which I was born more than fifty years ago."

[1] Marchand Papers; Montholon, Vol. II, p. 507.
[2] There is no reference to this subject on the 12th in Montholon. Marchand, however, is very positive.

468

A formal admission: He may have fought the Church—he had never been hostile to her spirit. Dying, he accepted her law, which in the light of death he deemed beneficent and necessary to the social order.

"I desire that my ashes repose on the banks of the Seine, in the midst of the French people whom I have loved so dearly."

A diplomatic prayer which he guessed would not be immediately satisfied! However, the future was a long time. That greeting to France from an exiled Frenchman would cause a thrill in numberless hearts.

"I have always had occasion to be proud of my very dear wife, Marie-Louise, and I hold the tenderest feelings for her to the end."

Such his remembrance for Marie-Louise, the adultress, who had deserted him! It must have taken courage to put it into words. But for the sake of his son, to smooth the way for an eventual reversal of fortunes, he did not hesitate—he would forget! The mother would perhaps have pity at last when he should be no more, and redeem her sins as a wife by protecting their child. He implored her to do so:

"I beg her to be ever on the watch to save my son from the traps that still are laid about his childhood."

To the little schoolboy, whom they were trying to recast in the mould of the princes of Austria, he addressed a basic injunction which was to serve as the pivot of the child's life:

"I urge my son never to forget that he was born a French prince and never to lend himself to being an instrument in the hands of the triumvirs who are oppressing the peoples of Europe. He must never fight against France nor harm her in any other manner. He must adopt my motto: 'All for the French people.'"

That, he thought, would be the sesame that would open France to the Duke of Reichstadt and give the Empire back to him.

Then he turned towards the authors of his torture, making one last appeal to the honour of a nation that he had never condemned, against its rulers:

"I die prematurely, murdered by the English oligarchy and its hired assassin. The English people will not be slow in avenging me."

He forgave those who had betrayed him—Marmont, Augereau, Talleyrand. To his mother, to his family, he sent a touching remembrance and then disavowed the pamphlets that had been attributed to him, and in particular the *Manuscript of St. Helena.*

Then came the question of bequests. What first of all should he give his son? Not money, evidently! What could Napoleon's heir do with a fortune? His name alone was enough!

But for love of him and also to surround him with everything that could speak to him of his father's glory, combat ideas that might have been sown in him, envelop him, from beyond the grave, with his father's spirit, will, breath, he bequeathed to him all the objects that had served for his personal use and touched his person, further designating them in the greatest detail in an "Appendix A" to be attached to the testament—the cloak of Marengo, his uniforms, boots, linen, camp beds, weapons, the sword of Austerlitz, Sobieski's sabre, his pistols, guns, saddles, orders, decorations, seals, the urns from his chapel, his gold dressing case, his army glasses, his little clock, the alarm clock of Frederick II, his watches, medals and silver, his wash-basin, the Sèvres service, his most beautiful books. Bertrand, Montholon, Vignali, Marchand, Aly, and Noverraz, were each to keep a specified group of such objects and hand them over to his son "when he should be sixteen years old." And he finished with tender pride:

"I desire that this slender legacy may be dear to him as retracing for him the memory of a father of whom the whole world will speak to him."

To the members of his family he left intimate souvenirs: to Madame Mère his silver alarm clock, to Fesch a dressing case, to Caroline and Hortense rugs, to Pauline his little medal cabinet, to Jerome a sword-hilt, to Eugene a silver and gold candlestick. Louis was the only one he overlooked. Marie-Louise herself was to receive his laces. With all such gifts would go a ringlet made of his hair. In gratitude for Lady Holland's active kindnesses he left to her the antique cameo that Pius VI had given him at Tolentino.

Napoleon estimated the amounts he had on deposit at Laffitte's at 6,000,000 francs. That deposit, as we know, amounted to only 3,800,000 francs, which were increased by the 400,000 francs paid in by Lavalette and by interest, but were reduced by payments made during the Captivity to the Emperor's order. The result was a total of 3,129,000 francs for which Lafitte acknowledged indebtedness.[3]

Montholon would get the largest share—two millions, "as a token

[3] *Constitutionnel*, February 28, 1822.

of my satisfaction for the filial care that he has bestowed on me for
six years and to reimburse him for the losses which his sojourn in
St. Helena has occasioned him."

Bertrand got only 500,000 and no word of affection. In spite of
the Grand Marshal's plans for departure, Napoleon was too forgetful
of the six hard years in which, torn between his family and his duty,
Bertrand had shown the Emperor a resigned devotion.

Marchand almost reached the same level with 400,000 francs, but
he received in addition the thanks which his tact, his care, his un-
flagging devotion, deserved: "The services he has rendered me have
been those that a friend would render."

Vignali, Aly, Noverraz, Pierron got 100,000. Archambault 50,000,
Coursot and Chandellier 25,000. Father Vignali must have confided
to the Emperor his intention of retiring to Corsica, for Napoleon
added, with his usual interest in detail: "I desire that he build a house
near Ponte Nuovo di Rostino."

The remainder of the supposed 6,000,000 went in bequests of
100,000 to those who had helped him in his youth—Costa di Bas-
telica, Poggi de Talavo, or those who had remained loyal to him in
his day of disaster—Las Cases, Lavalette, Larrey, Brayer, Lefèbvre-
Desnouettes, Druout, Cambronne, Lallemand the elder, Réal, Clauzel,
Ménéval, Arnault, Marbot, Bignon, Émery; and finally to children of
faithful friends who had died for him—Mouton-Duvernet, Labédoyère, Gerard, Chartran, Travot. To certain persons he sent greetings or special tributes: "Surgeon Larrey, the most virtuous man I
have known"; Colonel Marbot—"I urge him to continue writing in
defence of the glory of French arms and to confound slanderers and
apostates"; Baron Bignon: "I urge him to write the history of French
diplomacy from 1792 to 1815."

If there was a residue it was to be given to the wounded of
Waterloo and to soldiers from the Isle of Elba.

He dictated in that way for two hours and then asked Montholon
to read it aloud:

"Would you like to have me give you more?" he asked.

Montholon, deeply moved, made no answer.

"Come," the Emperor resumed, "go and recopy what I have dictated to you. Then we'll read it over. I shall write it in my own hand.
Send Marchand to me—no! Have the Grand Marshal come in."

·   ·   ·   ·   ·   ·   ·   ·

He had a fairly good night and slept a little.[4] In the morning he took a little food without vomiting. Shutting himself in again with Montholon, he resumed his dictation. They were hiding from Bertrand. Napoleon was to inform him of what they were doing on the 12th, thus confronting him with a *fait accompli*. The Emperor had been thinking of his private fortune—money he had saved on his army salaries, furnishings from his palaces, silver services, jewellry, stables. He valued the whole at "more than 200 millions." Did he imagine that the Bourbons would restore those vast possessions? No law, he said, had deprived him of them. Once more his imagination ran away with him. But who could foretell what the morrow was to bring? The legacies he was about to make might perhaps be executed later on, in spite of governments then existing. So he dictated:

"I bequeath my private domain, half to the officers and soldiers of the French army that fought between 1792 and 1815 for the glory and independence of the nation, the division to be made proportionately to salaries paid on active service; half to the towns and villages of Alsace, Lorraine, Franche-Comté, Burgundy, Île-de-France, Champagne, Forez, Dauphiné, that may have suffered by the first or the second invasion. One million of this sum shall be set aside for the town of Brienne and another million for the town of Méry."

In the former he had been a student. The latter had been sacked in 1814. This uncertain but magnificent gift would, he thought, touch the imagination of the French and help to keep his memory alive.

Coming back to realities, he named "Counts Montholon, Bertrand, and Marchand" his testamentary executors.[5] Montholon knew what Marchand had done for their master and undoubtedly recognized the nobility of that act of signal gratitude. In any event, he did not bat an eyelash.

Napoleon had the papers put away and locked up in order to receive Arnott. The doctor examined him. Montholon having asked whether the liver were not affected, Arnott repeated that he could "find no hardness or swelling." The General's eyes, he said, "appeared

---

[4] Arnott's bulletin, April 14 (Lowe Papers, 20-157).

[5] Marchand was not made a count by the Emperor's will. On the original autograph between Bertrand's name and that of Marchand, a comma is plainly visible. Marchand, however, was to benefit for forty years by a doubt of courtesy, and finally receive the title of Count by letters patent of Napoleon III, dated April 7, 1869. The title was to pass to his son-in-law, E. Desmazières, and to his grandsons.

quite clear, he could observe no yellow suffusion either in them or in the skin." [6]

In very direct language Arnott urged the patient to take a purgative. Napoleon refused, remarking goodnaturedly that the doctor should not treat him altogether as if he were a soldier in his regiment. He went on to speak of the English army, praising a number of their generals, among others Marlborough, on whose campaigns he would have liked to write a commentary. He asked the doctor whether the 20th Infantry had a biography of Marlborough. Arnott doubted it. The Emperor thereupon sent Marchand to get Coxe's two volumes that had been presented to him a few months previous by Robert Spencer, a grand-nephew of Marlborough.[7] Mme. Bertrand had translated some passages from it into French for Napoleon's benefit.

"See here, doctor," he said to the physician, "I like brave men of whatever country. Add these books to your regiment's library."

A moment later he said:

"I am going to write to the Prince Regent and to your ministers. They have wanted me to die. They are about to be satisfied. I want my body to rest in France. Your government will object, but I predict that the monument it will raise to me will be its shame and that John Bull will crawl out from underneath my ashes to crush the English oligarchy. Posterity will avenge me on the hangman they sent to be my guard, and your ministers will all die violent deaths."

It is curious to note that the most spiteful of his enemies, Castlereagh, did die by his own hand a year later.

Did that apostrophe amuse Antommarchi? He began to snicker. The Emperor glared at him severely, and the next day he gave him a thoroughgoing reprimand. Antommarchi excused himself rather feebly by saying that a memory of *Malbrouk* had crossed his mind. On Napoleon's order, Montholon made Antommarchi write a letter on April 17, in which he swore on oath not to reveal anything he

[6] Lowe, *Notes*, April 14 (Lowe Papers, 20-157); Forsyth, Vol. III, p. 497; Young, Vol. II, p. 217.

[7] The Honourable Robert Spencer belonged to the Opposition. He had touched at St. Helena in October on the way home from India and had requested an audience with Napoleon. Already too ill, the Emperor had not been willing to see him. Spencer thereupon called on Bertrand and Montholon and left in their hands for the Emperor the two volumes by William Coxe, well bound. On the fly-leaf of the first, Spencer had written: *Hunc de Proavi rebus gestis librum Napoleoni mittit Ducis Marlburiensis Pronepos Robertus Spencer.*

As in all the volumes at Longwood Aly wrote "The Emperor Napoleon" on the right-hand page of the half-title, affixing the seal with the Imperial arms.

might see or hear in the Emperor's house. Napoleon had, in fact, been angered at learning (through gossip of the servants, says Montholon) that Antommarchi had permitted himself "some indiscretions or pleasantries on the care the Emperor took of his toilet, sick though he was." [8] From a note that the Emperor dictated on the subject, we also learn that Antommarchi "had reported to Mme. Bertrand something that Napoleon had said to him." The Emperor added: "I expressed my disapproval to him, and I have not sent for him since." [9]

By an oversight, perhaps, Arnott failed to take the Marlborough volumes with him. The Emperor then had them left at the house of the orderly officer to be sent to Major Jackson, acting commander of the 20th. The Governor ordered Jackson to return the volumes to Lutyens with a reprimand, because they bore "the imperial title." Lutyens did not accept the rebuke and resigned as orderly officer. Napoleon was never to know the wretched reception that was given to his little gift, nor the motives that were to be ascribed to his act by the Governor. A few days later he asked Arnott if the officers of the 20th had been satisfied with the remembrance. The doctor replied evasively and changed the subject.[10] After the Emperor's death, the officers who had criticized the conduct of Lowe and of their commander claimed the volumes. The Duke of York, the British General-in-chief, authorized Sir Wm. Houston, Colonel of the 20th Infantry, to accept them from the hands of Montholon.

The courtesy and the tact of Captain Lutyens had been appreciated by the French. When he left, Montholon paid him a visit and said to him: "Napoleon has ordered me to express to you his satisfaction for your attentiveness during your residence at Longwood." After the Emperor's death, Mme. Bertrand sent him a lock of Napoleon's hair with a coral trinket. Lutyens was replaced at Longwood by Captain Crokat.[11]

The night of the 14th-15th was a hard one. The Emperor vomited

[8] Montholon, Vol. II, p. 516.

[9] Masson, *Papers* (Thiers Library, Carton 14. Unpublished). The note, written in pencil and dated April 17, was on the back of the "Advice" which the Emperor dictated for his son on the same date.

[10] Lowe Papers, 20-133.

[11] William Crokat (1789-1879) had served in the Spanish war. He was a Scotchman, six feet tall. Promoted Lieutenant-General in 1861, he was to be the last survivor of all those who saw Napoleon on his death-bed.

three times, his pulse was low, and he was bathed in a viscous sweat.[12]
Montholon and Marchand kept his linen changed and warmed him
with hot-water bottles. In the morning, after a few hours of restless
sleep, he felt better and took a little bouillon, which, however, gave
him trouble. He ordered Marchand to make an inventory of his silver,
his porcelain and all his personal effects. Then he began to copy his
will from Montholon's dictation. Sitting up in bed, he used a sheet
of cardboard as a desk, striving diligently to make his writing more
legible. That very touching effort is visible throughout the twenty
pages of the will. Never since the days of his youth had Napoleon
written so clearly and so steadily (the document is preserved in the
French National Archives in the "Iron Case"). Montholon stood at
the head of the bed and held the inkwell. Twice he was obliged to
call on Marchand to help the Emperor through attacks of vomiting.
To nerve himself before resuming his task Napoleon decided to drink
a little of the wine that Las Cases had sent on from the Cape. Montholon and Marchand protested in vain. He took a glass and dipped
a biscuit in it. Montholon urged him to take a rest:

"Sire, there is no hurry."

He shook his head:

"My son, I must get it done—I feel it!"

He had always found it hard to write, and had always dictated,
using a pencil on rare occasions for a note. That day, instead, he
insisted on continuing his task until three o'clock in the afternoon,
breaking off at times when the strength of his hand failed.

Arnott found him depressed and restless. He recommended not
taking any more wine.

"It is oil on the fire," he said.

Napoleon threw a sudden question at him:

"What are my chances?"

Arnott hesitated. Finally he replied that his condition was serious
but that he, Arnott, was still very hopeful.

"You are not telling me the truth, doctor. You are wrong in trying
to hide my situation from me. I know what it is."

He spoke feelingly of Larrey, the chief surgeon of the Grand
Army, and of his devotion:

[12] Arnott, April 15. In Masson, who follows Marchand, we find a number of errors of date—the gift of the Marlborough being ascribed to the 15th and Napoleon's
copying of his will to the 16th. We rectify these errors to fit Arnott's reports and
Lowe's notes, which are detailed and persuasive.

"If the army ever erects a column of gratitude, it should be to Larrey."

In the late afternoon, he seemed weaker, but his night was fairly good.[13] In the morning he refused to take any medicine. A vesicant was dressed in the presence of Arnott.

Montholon asked the orderly officer to hurry repairs to the drawingroom floor, which had rotted through in places. "The physicians were advising General Bonaparte to move into a room where he would have more air." [14] Lutyens asked why he did not move to New House where he would have been much more comfortable. Montholon replied "that they had already made every effort in the world to induce him to accept the drawingroom." The carpenters went to work that very day. Beginning with that night Napoleon slept in the drawingroom, but during the daytime he went back to his bedroom where one of the two field cots had been left. He felt "more at home there," he said. Aly (p. 272) notes specifically that he "wrote the last codicils of his will" there.[15]

Napoleon again wrote with Montholon until three o'clock. He was to finish the first copy of his will [16] that day, and likewise dictate the two first codicils. They were dated April 16. The codicils are to be regarded in the main as a precaution on the Emperor's part against possible seizure by the English of his property at St. Helena. They were to be opened immediately after his death, whereas the will was not to be opened till the executors arrived in Europe.

The first codicil was so framed as to be communicated to the Governor. It specified:

"I bequeath to the Counts Bertrand, Montholon and to Marchand, my money, jewellry, silverware, crockery, furniture, books, arms, and in general everything that belongs to me at St. Helena."

The second was a sort of summary of the will, and could serve temporarily to replace it. It further provided for the division between his companions of the little treasure that had been brought on from France and which, patiently nourished, had come to amount to nearly

[13] Lowe, *Notes*, April 16 (Lowe Papers, 20-137).

[14] Lowe, *Notes*, April 16 (Lowe Papers, 20-157). Lutyens was still at Longwood. Crokat did not take over his functions until April 26 (Lowe to Montholon, April 26. Thiers Library, Carton 8. Unpublished).

[15] *Ibid.*

[16] The Emperor's testament was written on quarto-sized sheets bearing the watermark "J. Whatman, 1819—Balston & Co.," and a shield containing the letters *V.E.C.L.* intertwined.

300,000 francs: "30,000 will be deducted to pay the advance wages of domestics. The remainder will be distributed: 50,000 to Bertrand, 50,000 to Montholon, 50,000 to Marchand, 15,000 to Vignali, 10,000 to Archambault, 10,000 to Coursot, 5,000 to Chandellier. The remainder will be given in gratuities to the English physicians, servants, Chinese, and the choir leader of this parish."

The night of the 16th-17th passed indifferently with vomitings and sweats. Napoleon drank a concoction of quinine. Arnott found him drowsy on his first visit. The doctor saw Lowe that afternoon and asserted that he was "more and more confirmed in the opinion that the disease was hypochondriasis." There were "no symptoms of immediate danger about him," he repeated. But, the doctor thought, if an improvement did not occur, the ordinary outcome of that sort of illness was to be expected. Napoleon's mind seemed to Arnott to be particularly affected: "This morning he was sitting in an armchair. He began whistling, when, suddenly stopping, he opened his mouth quite wide, projected it forward and for a moment looked at me with a kind of vacant stare." The patient, Arnott added, was still complaining of his liver, putting his hand to his side. "That I show no symptoms of imminent death," he kept repeating, "I am well aware. But I feel in such a condition that the whistle of a bullet would be enough to carry me off." [17]

This report of Arnott's upheld Lowe in his misapprehension—and also the other English officers. On April 22, Major Harrison was to write to Sir George Bingham: "I don't know what to think of the invalid, but I now begin to believe that it is all humbug. He still continues confined to his bed, but from what I can collect is considerably better. His new doctor, Arnott, attends him twice a day regularly, and he tells me that he is the most extraordinary man he has ever had to deal with in his life, and the conviction on his mind is, that if he were told there was a 74 arrived to take him back to France, he would make use of both his mental and bodily faculties." [18] The idiot Montchenu, on information from the Governor, was to write to Damas and Metternich: "Since it is an old finesse that he has long been using whenever he has wanted to make himself interesting, or was brewing some scheme, *we take no stock in this illness.*"

.    .    .    .    .    .    .    .    .

[17] Lowe Papers, 20-167; Young, Vol. II, p. 218.
[18] *Cornhill Magazine*, February, 1901.

About three o'clock that same day (April 17), says Montholon, the Emperor sent for him. He was sitting up in bed, his eyes bright with fever:

"I don't feel any worse, but talking with Bertrand I began to wonder what my executors are to say to my son when they see him. Bertrand does not understand me. He is an Orleanist. The man I made Grand Marshal of my Empire! I had better make a summary of the advice I am bequeathing to my son. Write:

"My son must not think of avenging my death. He must take advantage of it.

"When he comes to the throne, he should not try to imitate his father. Let him be a man of his own times!

"It would be a monkey's imitation for him to try my wars again. The same thing is never done twice in one age. I saved the Revolution when it was dying, I cleansed it of its crimes, I revealed it to the world as a thing resplendent with glory, I implanted new ideas in France and in Europe. They must never be allowed to languish."

It was the task of Napoleon's son to bring all those seeds to fruitage:

"If he does that, he can still be a great ruler."

He was obliged to lie back on his pillows for a moment and rest. His eyelids closed, his cheeks were bathed in perspiration. Then in a low voice, but with extraordinary clarity of mind, he continued his message to the future:

"The Bourbons will not last." They had recaptured France but they would not be able to hold her. She was no longer adapted to them, to their principles, to their methods of governing. Whatever they might do, another exile was in store for them. As soon as Napoleon was dead, the world would recognize how great a contribution in terms of justice and utility he had made to mankind. When that time came his son's hour would not be far from striking. But he must not accept power from Europe. The Bonapartes were patriots above all else. They could owe nothing to the foreigner.

The Orleanists alone were to be feared. His son should scorn all parties and see only the masses. Let him rally round him all Frenchmen of merit, excepting those only who had betrayed their country.

Napoleon's family had cost him dearly. However, at that last hour he still clung to the Corsican concept of the clan. His son must come into closer touch with his relatives.

"My mother is an old-fashioned woman. Joseph and Eugene can give him good advice. Hortense and Catherine are superior women. If he remains in exile, he should marry one of my nieces. If France calls him back, he should look for a Russian princess—that is the only Court where family ties control public policy."

Those who had attended the Emperor during his last days would have the honour of publishing his writings. His son would draw inspiration from them. They would tell him to favour and reward those who had served his father.

"And," he sighed, "they are goodly in number!"

A poignant cry, straight from the heart, escaped him:

"My poor soldiers! So noble! So loyal! They are perhaps without bread!"

After a moment he added:

"Let my son often read history and ponder it. It is the only true philosophy. Let him read and consider the wars of the great captains. That is the only way to learn war.

"But everything you tell him, everything he learns, will be of little use to him if at the bottom of his heart he has not that sacred fire, that love of the good, which alone accomplishes great things. . . .

"But I choose to think that he will be worthy of his destiny. . . .

"If you are not allowed to go to Vienna. . . ."

His voice faded. His strength was gone. He fainted. Montholon had him take a spoonful of medicine.[19]

The next day, the 18th, Montholon said to Lutyens (and it seems to corroborate the fact of the interview of the 17th): "All his strength seems to have passed from his body into his brain. He is now thinking only of things of the past. His dulness is gone. His memory has returned and he talks continually of what will happen on his death."[20]

.    .    .    .    .    .    .    .

[19] Montholon, Vol. II, pp. 517, 526.
[20] Lowe Papers, 20-157. It has long been thought that this last advice of Napoleon to his son was a fabrication of Montholon's. Writing from the fortress of Ham, after the failure of the raid on Boulogne, Montholon was supposed to have assembled around the Emperor's genuine remarks a text inspired by the ideas of the Pretender, the future Napoleon III: rapprochement with England, the need of democratic institutions, and especially of a free press, the creation of a sort of European federation, satisfaction of national aspirations in Europe, co-operation with the Church, and so on. I myself believed that at one time. But I found in some as yet uncatalogued papers in the Masson materials (Thiers Library, Carton 14) the rough draft of Napoleon's document—seven pages of large-sized paper of English make

During those last days Bertrand and Montholon scarcely spoke to each other. The Grand Marshal held Montholon responsible for the coldness that Napoleon was showing him and thought that he was doing his best to capture the inheritance. Mme. Bertrand came almost every day to enquire for the Emperor. She asked to be admitted to his presence, but he refused, not harshly, however:

"I am not a good thing to look at. I shall receive Mme. Bertrand when I feel better. Tell her that I thank her for the devotion that has kept her here in this desert for six years." [21]

During the night of the 17th-18th Napoleon vomited almost continuously. That evening at six o'clock, with Arnott's consent, he took a little scraped meat and drank a few spoonfuls of Bordeaux cut with water. At eight o'clock he took a tonic. He blamed it for his bad night. Antommarchi had finally moved out of his bedroom and was sleeping in the Emperor's apartment. He was constantly in attendance, with Marchand. In the morning the Emperor took a little broth with vermicelli, but his stomach rejected it immediately. Antommarchi tried to make him accept some medicine.

"No," said the Emperor, pushing his hand away, "England wants my corpse. I shall not keep her waiting. I can die just as well without drugs." [22]

Arnott examined him and was satisfied with continuing the same treatment. That afternoon Lowe sent Dr. Shortt and Dr. Mitchell

with the watermark "S. and C. Wise, 1818." That was one of the papers most in use at St. Helena. It was used for the authentic *Report* on the autopsy and for the official accounts of May 7 and 8 (Thiers Library, Carton 14). The hastily pencilled writing has been partially erased and is difficult to read. However, with a little patience it can be deciphered. On the eighth page, as we saw, is the note regarding Antommarchi dictated by the Emperor under date of April 17. To argue that Montholon wrote the document in question around 1840, one must therefore assume that he had not only kept this rough draught, which could have had no significance to him, but that he also kept for twenty years a blank double sheet of the same identical paper of the same shape and size with the same watermark, and that he finally used those relics to give a semblance of genuineness to his forgery. Now all that is not impossible, but we are inclined to adopt a simpler solution—that the document is not by Montholon but is genuine. The manuscript bears manifest traces of haste. Everything fits in. There is no paragraphing as in ordinary writing. The seven pages were written under dictation, very rapidly, and all on the same day. For that matter, as they are attentively read, one is struck by their spirit and by their workmanship. They can belong only to Napoleon. Alongside of his will he set forth in a few pages the political and social ideas to which his experience in power and his meditations during the Captivity had led him.

[21] Thiers, *Consulat et Empire*, Vol. XX, p. 700. Thiers got this remark from Bertrand. It is confirmed by Marchand (Thiers Library, Carton 22).

[22] Antommarchi, Vol. II, p. 103.

to Longwood.[23] They held a consultation with Arnott and Antommarchi in Montholon's room. They did not dare arrive at any conclusion.

It was a beautiful day. The Emperor asked Marchand to open the door into the garden:

"Open it, my son, and let me get a breath of the air God made."

A familiar phrase with him! Then he added:

"How sweet a thing air is! Bertrand, go pick me a rose!"

When the Grand Marshal brought the flower, he took it and inhaled its perfume with a sort of voluptuous delight.

Then, for a long time, he looked in silence at the sky where pearl-grey clouds were drifting as the brief twilight drew near. It seemed to quiet him.[24]

The relief continued during the evening. At midnight Napoleon asked for some fried potatoes and kept them down. In the morning, the 19th, he told Arnott that he felt much stronger. His pulse was regular. He was in a cheerful frame of mind, but complained of a pain in his lower right side. He was relieved by an injection.[25]

He talked with Montholon about the return of his companions to Europe after his death, going over the stocks of provisions that would be on hand and might be carried aboard for use during the voyage. He did not forget the sheep that were kept in the stable.[26]

That afternoon he asked Bertrand to re-read Hannibal's campaigns to him. He had no illusions left, but no bitterness either. He said, smiling:

"They won't know what ails me till they cut me open."

Arnott protested. He was suffering, he assured him, merely from lack of amusement and exercise. As Montholon called his attention to the improvement in his condition, Napoleon broke him off.

"Don't fool yourself. I am better today, but my end is not far off."[27]

[23] Dr. Thomas Shortt (1789-1843) succeeded Baxter as surgeon-in-chief at St. Helena. He reached the island in December, 1820. Dr. Charles Mitchell (1785-1856) was surgeon on the *Vigo*, the Admiral's flagship that was stationed at St. Helena during the two years '20 and '21.

[24] Marchand Papers, and Aly, p. 165.

[25] Arnott, April 19 (Lowe Papers, 20-157).

[26] Marchand Papers.

[27] Antommarchi, Vol. II, p. 112. Antommarchi says that he added: "When I am dead, each of you will have the sweet consolation of returning to Europe. You will see, some your relatives, others your friends, and I–I shall be meeting my brave soldiers again in the Elysian Fields. Yes, Kléber, Desaix, Bessières, Duroc, Ney,

That evening he had Marchand continue reading from the wars of Hannibal.

About three o'clock in the morning he seemed to grow feverish. He had gas on his stomach, with a burning sensation. Though he had a raging thirst he could take only a few drops of water. By keeping absolutely still he managed to hold them down.[28] Finally he got to sleep. During the forenoon of the 20th he was very restless. When Bertrand came in the Emperor sent Aly to get the *Iliad* and he asked the Grand Marshal to read him a canto:

"Homer so well describes the councils I have often held on the eve of a battle that I always listen to him with pleasure."

Montholon having left the room, he informed Marchand, who was alone with him, that he had named him executor of his will.

The young man was completely overcome and kissed his hands. Then Napoleon said to him:

"I have a will at the Grand Marshal's. Ask him to give it to you and bring it to me."

Marchand went to Bertrand's at once. The Grand Marshal seemed surprised, but went and found the envelop in his desk.

Napoleon broke the seals, glanced through the paper, tore it up, and ordered Marchand to throw it into the fire. He got up and managed to reach his armchair. The physicians had come, accompanied by Bertrand. In a firm, almost formal tone he complained to Arnott of the treatment he had received during his captivity. Bertrand translated the little speech sentence by sentence. The English doctor listened, standing, to the cutting rebuke:

"That is the hospitality of your government. . . . I have been murdered piecemeal and with premeditation. Hudson Lowe has made himself the executioner of the capital sentence of your ministers. You will end like the proud republic of Venice, and as for me, dying on this ghastly rock, I bequeath the disgrace of my death to the Royal Family of England."

Murat, Masséna, Berthier—all will come to meet me. They will talk of the things we did together, and I will tell them of the last events of my life. At sight of me they will all go mad again with enthusiasm and glory. We will talk over our wars with the Scipios, the Hannibals, the Caesars, the Fredericks. They will like that! Unless the people get nervous down there at seeing so many dangerous fighters together!"

The passage is famous. Napoleon may well have talked that way. But as neither Montholon nor Marchand mention it and as Antommarchi is all too open to suspicion, it is safer to reserve judgment.

[28] Arnott (Lowe Papers, 20-157).

Arnott made no reply. In that wretched room, about that arm-chair in which Napoleon sat erect with shining eyes, there was an air of grandeur that abashed him. On a nod of the Emperor's head he withdrew. That evening (April 20) Montholon wrote to his wife and forewarned her (with what unexpressed relief?) of the Emperor's death. "The vomitings," he wrote, "have somewhat abated, but no words can express the change in him. Death seems to have been stamped on all his features. I am passing my days and nights as a sick-nurse, yet I am not tired by it. I go to bed at five in the morning. Marchand is leading the same sort of life. Bertrand comes in sometimes during the day and acts as interpreter for Dr. Arnott. As for that poor Mme. Bertrand, she is in despair because the Emperor will not permit her to see him.

"Noverraz is still quite seriously ill with his liver complaint. Mme. Saint-Denis [Aly's wife] is also ill. You see our Longwood has become a sort of hospital.

"I suppose that by the time this letter reaches you, you will be at some watering-place and it is very probable, unfortunately, that I shall be rejoining you on your return. I say unfortunately, for I shall pay very dearly for a reunion that I have so longed for, if I have to owe it to the death of a man whose friendship for me has long since known no limits and who, in his last moments, is giving me greater proofs of it than ever."

The French were now convinced that Napoleon might pass away from one day to the other. They were already making preparations for their departure and made no great secret of it. Lutyens wrote to Lowe on the 20th: "Henly, Count Montholon's servant, informed me that his master had been speaking to him about his going to Europe with him, and had desired him to enquire at the shop in camp if they had any large trunks. Countess Bertrand said, when I read to her Doctor Short's note, 'I am sorry the woman is a bad character, for I want a person who will go to England with me. I must have some woman-servant.' " [29]

. . . . . . .

The night of the 20th-21st was tolerable. In the morning Napoleon shaved. He had asked for Vignali. When the priest arrived, he said to him in dialect:

"Father, do you know what a mortuary chapel is?"

[29] Lowe Papers, 20-157; Knowles, *Letters of Lutyens*, p. 116.

"Yes, sire."

"Have you ever kept one?"

"No, sire!"

"Well, you will keep mine."

And he went into minute details at once:

"You will say Mass every day in the chapel that will be set up in the next room. You will expose the Blessed Sacrament and you will say the prayers of the Forty Hours. When I am dead, you will place this altar at my head [He pointed to the wall behind him.] and you will continue to celebrate Mass before it with all the customary ceremonies. You will not cease until I am in the ground."

Antommarchi was standing at the foot of the bed. Napoleon saw him make a grimace. The sawbones was trying to be facetious. The Emperor blasted him:

"Your idiocies bore me, sir. I can overlook your irresponsibility and your lack of manners, but your lack of heart—never. Please withdraw!" [30]

He detained the Abbé for a moment to chat with him about Corsica. When he had gone he spoke to Marchand appreciatively of that uncouth but kindly priest.

"As for that idiot," he added, referring to Antommarchi, "he really is not worth my bothering about. Did anyone ever receive poorer care than I have had from him?"

The next day, the 22nd, he refused to receive him. Arnott was admitted alone. The Grand Marshal then interceded for Antommarchi. "What do you expect?" said the Emperor. "If he has not a bad heart, at least he is a fool." Montholon insisting, Napoleon allowed Antommarchi to return on the 23rd.

He spent the forenoon of the 22nd completing matters connected with his will. He dictated to Montholon four new codicils in which he bequeathed to his friends and attendants sums to be collected from Marie-Louise, from Eugene, and from the Crown of France. He was so poor as compared with what he would have liked to give! He was obsessed with the desire not to forget any one of the many who had

[30] Antommarchi, Vol. II, p. 118, pretends that Napoleon said to him: "You are above such weaknesses? What do you expect. I am neither a philosopher nor a physician. I believe in God. I belong to my father's religion. One cannot be an atheist by just wanting to be." Marchand (Thiers Library, Carton 22) declares that those words were never uttered.

served him, and to aid and rescue them at the end of lives that they had devoted to him.

The codicils were dated as of April 24. The first codicil appraised at five or six hundred thousand francs the diamonds belonging to him which had been mixed in with those belonging to the Crown. He put at 200 or 300 thousand francs certain stocks that he had left with the banker Torlonia. Napoleon bequeathed them to the Duca d'Istria, to Duroc's daughter and to former comrades-at-arms. In case those sums could not be recovered, the legacies mentioned were to be paid out of the Laffitte funds.

The second remedied a number of oversights. He remembered the children of Baron du Theil who had directed the school at Auxonne, of General Dugommier who commanded at Toulon, of the Conventionalist Gasparin, of his aide-de-camp Muiron. There again the bequests, in default of the collections presumed, were to be paid out of the Laffitte funds. In this codicil Napoleon bequeathed 10,000 francs to non-commissioned officer Cantillon, who was tried and acquitted for attempting to assassinate the Duke of Wellington. "Cantillon had as much right to assassinate that oligarch as the latter had to send me to perish on the rock of St. Helena."

Napoleon has been greatly criticized for this bequest by the English. It shows what a deep grudge he cherished against Wellington who, for that matter—and he knew it—had odiously jeered at him in his exile.

The third codicil disposed of two millions which Napoleon had delivered to Marie-Louise at Orleans in 1814. He redivided this sum between Bertrand (300,000) and Montholon (200,000), Las Cases (200,000), Marchand, (100,000) and numerous other heirs—the servants at St. Helena, the Mayor of Ajaccio, Duroc's daughter, the sons of Bessières, Druout, Lavalette and Planat, the inhabitants of Brienne, the officers and soldiers of his guard at Elba.

The fourth claimed two millions from Eugene on the liquidation of back pay claims on Italy. They were redivided in similar bequests: Bertrand received another 300,000 francs, Montholon, 200,000, Marchand 200,000, and so on. The legatees were requested, however, to pay a part of these legacies into a reserve fund to meet certain bequests involving matters of conscience.

Montholon wearying, he continued the dictation to Marchand, giving full and precise directions to his executors. They comprised thirty-seven articles, which show a prodigious memory as well as an astonishing grasp of detail. Again he was thinking of his son. He adjured his executors "to rectify his ideas as to facts and things and set him on the right road." He begged his mother, his brothers, his sisters, his attendants, to be ever near the boy. They were to encourage him to assume the name of Napoleon again. With Denon, d'Albe, Fain, Méneval, Bourrienne, Appiani, they would find many objects that would make him understand, and bring truly home to him, all that his father had been: "My memory must be the glory of his life. Collect for him, purchase for him, or help him to purchase, everything that can create an environment for him in that sense." He gave another thought to Marie-Louise, commending to her their child who would have "no resources that did not come from her." His anxious love still trembled in those supreme lines.

He signed the articles that Marchand had written out, and then asked for his casket of valuables. Once more he went over his medals, his miniatures, the crosses that Marchand was to take to Vienna. In the little box ornamented with the cameo of Pius VI he placed a card on which he had written in his own hand: "Napoleon to Lady Holland, in testimony of his esteem and affection." Among the objects that he had spread out on his bed, he chose a gold snuff box to give to Dr. Arnott. The lid was decorated with grapes surrounding an empty shield. With the point of his scissors the Emperor scratched an awkward $N$ upon it. He ordered Montholon to put twelve thousand francs in gold inside it.

In the casket was the diamond necklace that Hortense had forced upon him that last day at Malmaison.

"Look," he said to Marchand, "I don't know how my affairs in Europe will stand. Take this necklace. The good Hortense gave it to me, thinking that I might need it. I think it is worth two hundred thousand francs. Hide it on your person. Once in France it will enable you to await the lot I am providing for you in my will." [31]

He dangled the gleaming stones for a moment in his hands and then held them out to the man who had been his greatest comfort in his suffering:

"Make an honourable marriage. Choose a wife from among the

[31] Hortense's necklace was not worth 200,000 francs. It was valued on official appraisal at 80,000 francs and returned to the Queen, Marchand receiving its value in money (Hortense, *Mémoires*, Vol. III, p. 37).

daughters of the officers or soldiers of my Old Guard. Many of those good fellows are having a hard time. Better luck would have been in store for them had it not been for the reversals of fortune that came upon France. Posterity will credit me with what I would have done for them had circumstances been very different."

He wished himself to lock the three mahogany caskets that contained his snuff boxes. He tied them with green silk ribbons, sealed the knots and handed them back to Marchand. To revive his strength he drank a glass of constantia. Almost immediately he was seized with atrocious pains, but he clung to his task though his face was reeking with sweat.

He was urged to stop.

"I am very tired," he replied, "but I have so little time left—I must get through with it."

That evening he finally informed Bertrand of his last arrangements.[32] He wanted to die a Catholic. Father Vignali would give him "communion, extreme unction, and everything that is customary in such a case." Antommarchi, either alone or with Arnott, would perform the autopsy. He spoke of his interment. What he desired, he said, was to be buried in the cemetery of Père la Chaise. They could put him between Masséna and Lefébvre, and in the centre erect a little monument to him—a column. If the Bourbons wanted to do themselves honour, they could put him at Saint-Denis, but they probably would never feel that inclination. If the Bourbons would not permit the return of his remains to Paris he would like to be buried on an island at the confluence of the Rhone and the Saône near Lyons, or else in the cathedral at Ajaccio.

"Corsica," he said, "is still France. But the English government has probably foreseen my death. In case orders have been given for my body to remain on this island, which I do not think, have me

[32] This conversation with Bertrand and the ones that followed, on the 24th, 25th and 26th of April, were written down by the Grand Marshal. His manuscript was bequeathed by his daughter to Prince Napoleon and is now in the archives at Prangins. M. Ernest d'Hauterive published the substance of it in an important article in the *Revue des Deux Mondes*, December 15, 1928. It is an historic document of the first order. In those notes Bertrand declares that Napoleon told him that he did not believe in anything. Marchand, the man who stood closest to Napoleon's heart at St. Helena, declares that "the Emperor was a religious soul." It is possible, for an hypothesis that would reconcile everything, that, out of human considerateness, Napoleon may have concealed his real bent of mind from Bertrand, who was an unbeliever, and have represented his request for the sacraments as an act of policy.

buried in the shade of the willows where I used to rest on my way to see you at Hutt's Gate, near the spring where they go to draw my water every day." He was thinking of 1816, for he had not gone back there since. He had named that little glade "the Valley of the Geranium," because of a big geranium he had seen standing there against Dr. Kay's cottage. It had grown to the size of a tree and was covered with flowers. Two Chinamen went there every day to get water for the Emperor. He had drunk some of it from his hands and found it excellent.[33]

He informed Bertrand that he had appointed him executor conjointly with Montholon and Marchand since "he owed that much to them." He wanted "to raise Marchand" and hoped that "the King would make a baron of him some day." He expressed with emotion a wish that Bertrand might "keep close to Montholon."

He left nothing to Antommarchi, less because he did not believe in his skill than because the doctor had shown no attachment to him.[34]

He spoke of his servants with gratitude and friendship and asked Bertrand to look after his two natural children, Alexandre Walewski and little Léon. He then gave some affectionate advice to the Grand Marshal as to his return to France and the life he was to lead there.

He searched his memory at length lest he might have overlooked someone to whom he owed gratitude and whom he could assist by a legacy.

At eight o'clock he was exhausted and motioned to Bertrand, who withdrew.

.    .    .    .    .    .    .    .    .

The next day, the 23rd, he appeared better. He ate some minced pheasant and offered Dr. Arnott a taste—Lowe had been sending pheasants from Longwood from time to time.[35] He consented to take a medicine that he had been refusing for several days. He dictated one

[33] The spring still exists in the same condition as when Napoleon saw it.

[34] He was supposed to have added "that Antommarchi was still in time to have his share in his benefits—that he could make a codicil." Such a codicil, in spite of confirmations by Montholon and Marchand, was undoubtedly never written. Five different versions of it have been given, says Masson, who has examined "the case of Surgeon Antommarchi" in detail. Article 2 of the codicil was supposed to have run as follows: "I beg Marie-Louise to take Antommarchi into her service. To him I bequeath a pension for the duration of his life of 6,000 francs, which she will pay him." That was not at all in Napoleon's style. The executors, however, recognized it as valid, as a result of negotiations of which little is known. After some arbitration a pension of 3,000 francs was finally paid to Antommarchi.

[35] Lowe Papers, 20-157.

last codicil—the seventh. It was to be dated the 26th, the day when Napoleon seems to have copied it. This codicil was to remain secret. It bequeathed to the Emperor's mother, uncle, brothers, sisters, nephews and nieces, and to Hortense and Eugene, "a soup plate, a plate, a knife, fork and spoon, a serving knife, and a silver goblet with the Imperial arms." Louis was not excepted this time. He gave 300,000 francs "to the ward of Ménéval's father-in-law, named Léon. The sum shall be used by him to buy land in the neighbourhood of property belonging to Montholon or Bertrand." If he should die the said property should go to Alexandre Walewski. 100,000 francs were bequeathed "to Grand-vicar Arrighi, who was on the island of Elba; 20,000 to Father Recco, who taught me to read; 10,000 to the son or grandson of my shepherd, Nicolas de Bocognano; 10,000 to the shepherd Bogaglino, the one who came to the Island of Elba; 20,000 to the good citizen of Bocognano who, in 1792 or 1793, opened the door of a house in which some bandits had locked me up." This extreme solicitude to leave a mark of gratitude to his first and humbler friends is one of the most beautiful traits in the dying Napoleon. "He went about it," said Bertrand, "in an anxious sort of way."

The Emperor did not leave his bed while dictating and fell asleep at intervals. Arnott thought he noticed that he had grown "hard of hearing." He frequently asked Bertrand and Montholon to repeat what they had said. The English doctor was still optimistic: "The cure would be probably tedious . . . but there was no symptom of danger." He told the Governor that he could not give the sick man "that which would set him right." Lowe asked what that was. "Liberty," replied Arnott. He gave the Governor the following details: "The patient does not wear a nightshirt. He has only a flannel vest and when he gets out of the bedclothes his legs are wrapped in a big bag, likewise of flannel. He often shows impatience at the attentions his servants lavish on him and gives way to shrill exclamations." * Lowe, however, was more worried than the doctor. He suggested a consultation. Arnott replied that he saw no need of one.[36]

On the 24th there was no change. The Emperor had a slight recurrence of fever. He again did some writing alone with Montholon and Marchand and afterwards chatted with Bertrand. He told the Grand Marshal that he wished the Bonapartes could establish con-

* Retranslated.
[36] Lowe Papers, 20-157; Young, Vol. II, p. 221.

nections with families in Rome. Some of his relatives might live in America and Switzerland, and even become members of the government there. In that way the Bonapartes could make sure of having influence in the Catholic world, in the United States, and in Berne.[37]

He did not succeed in keeping down his dinner that evening, and vomitings recurred during the night. He did not sleep and talked in a low voice, deliriously, uttering disjointed sentences that could not be understood. Between three and seven on the morning of the 25th, he managed to get some rest. He then expressed a wish to sign the instructions to his executors. Marchand brought them, all copied. Bertrand came and read them aloud to him, and also translated an article from an English newspaper which severely criticized the rôles of Caulaincourt and Savary in the affair of the Duc d'Enghien. Napoleon sat up straight in his bed.

"That's disgraceful!" he exclaimed.

He sent for Montholon and asked him to bring him his will. He opened it and wrote without a halt at the end of Article 8:

"I had the Duc d'Enghien arrested and tried because it was necessary for the safety, the interest, and the honour of the French people at a time when the Count d'Artois was, by his own admission, supporting sixty assassins in Paris. Under similar circumstances I would again do the same."

So on the threshold of death he was formally endorsing the act for which he had been most criticized, which, doubtless, he had never willed, but which he never disavowed. He had the shoulders of a leader and considered himself responsible even for crimes committed by his agents. It is also noteworthy that he did not use the word "executed." At that solemn moment, as his whole testament bears witness, he weighed every word.

He put down his pen, handed the will back to Montholon, and dismissed him.[38]

During the evening the Emperor talked of his son again, to Bertrand. Madame Mère, Pauline and Fesch ought to leave the boy the bulk of their fortunes. He was afraid they might try to make a cardinal of him. Above all else he must not be allowed to become

[37] Bertrand to Joseph, October 6, 1821.
[38] Montholon, Vol. II, p. 538.

a priest. One could not tell what his destiny might be, but he should do nothing that might alienate him from the French or turn them against him. "Let him learn Latin, mathematics, geography, history." [39]

Bertrand asked what line of conduct the Emperor's friends were to follow and what goal he thought they should aim at. He replied forcefully:

"The interest of France and the glory of the country. I see no other."

His night was broken by bad dreams. When day dawned on the 26th he wanted to affix his seal to his will and codicils. Then, growing very weak, he dozed off. In Arnott's presence, and for the first time, it seems, he threw up "something black like coffee-grounds." [40] Arnott at last became alarmed. He sent word to Lowe who hurried to Longwood and insisted upon having a consultation. "I have been detained here since eleven o'clock," wrote Arnott. "General Bonaparte is sicker than I have seen him so far. He cannot keep anything on his stomach." Shortly afterwards he sent another note: "I do not fear any serious developments for the moment, but the vomiting is disquieting." [41]

The nausea stopped at half-past three and Napoleon fell asleep. In the evening he rose and, in his dressing gown, supported by Marchand and Aly, seated himself in his armchair. The nine testamentary folders —the will, his instructions to his executors, and the seven codicils—tied in red or green ribbons, were laid on his stand near him. He sent for Bertrand and Father Vignali. Together with Montholon and Marchand they affixed their signatures and their seals to each of the nine folders, while Bertrand drew up a descriptive report in the light of the covered candle. The paper was dated 9 P.M., April 27th, 1821. When they had finished, the Emperor was left alone with Vignali. He entrusted to him under confessional secrecy a duplicate of the will and two of the codicils.[42] Marchand returned and helped him back

---

[39] Bertrand to King Joseph, October 6, 1821; E. d'Hauterive, *Op. cit.*

[40] Lowe Papers, 20-157. April 26th. Arnott's report is precise, as is Lowe's note dated the 27th.

[41] Lowe Papers, 20-157. Retranslated.

[42] Masson (*Op. cit.*, 472) states that the Emperor handed to Father Vignali "a duplicate of the testament and the codicils which he had copied himself, so that they might be as valid as the originals." That is a mistake. M. Ernest d'Hauterive is marvellously conversant with the Prangins archives. He has kindly supplied the following definite information: The Emperor's will and the two codicils were merely *signed* by him "and placed under a white paper band which was closed

into bed. Napoleon entrusted to him the originals of the will, of the codicils and of Laffitte's receipt acknowledging the deposit of his funds. On his death these documents were to be handed over to Montholon. Meantime he had his manuscripts and his caskets taken to Montholon's room, his weapons to Bertrand's. Marchand himself took charge of the dressing case and the mahogany boxes. Though wearied by these great efforts Napoleon seemed to be happier in his mind. When Montholon came in to spend the night, he said:

"Well, my son, wouldn't it be a pity not to die after putting my affairs in such good order?"

Black vomitings occurred again during the night. They were extremely distressing.[43] He talked incoherently, in a faint voice, and refused any medical treatment. Lowe hastened to New House and conferred with Arnott. The doctor now considered the situation desperate. He warned Bertrand and Montholon that an early end was to be expected. He wanted a consultation at last. The two Frenchmen were obliged to reply evasively. How induce the Emperor to accept any other English physicians? During the forenoon (the 28th), Napoleon's mind became perfectly lucid again. Everybody insisting, he finally gave up his little room and allowed his bed to be moved into the drawingroom. It would be easier to care for him there. One of his camp beds had been placed between the two windows, opposite the fireplace. The other stood in the corner to the right, near the billiardroom door. The Emperor could go from one to the other, if he wished, as he had done all through those years. Tottering, leaning on Montholon and Marchand, he left the narrow room where he had passed so many painful hours. His legs swayed under him.

"I have no strength left," he said. "Here I am—on the ground."

They tried to carry him, but he refused:

"No—when I am dead! Just now it will be enough if you support me."

with a seal of red wax, showing the Eagle." On the band the following lines in Napoleon's handwriting can be read:

"The enclosed are papers entrusted under seal of the confession to Father Vignali. He is authorized to open them and make a copy of them one year and one month after my death. He will send a copy of everything to Madame Mère; if she is dead, to the Cardinal; if he is dead, to the one of my brothers who shall be living. He will keep the [an illegible word—remembrances (?)], which he will take to my son when he is sixteen years old."

[43] "The matter rejected by his stomach is black in colour, clotted and sprinkled with little spots of blood" (Arnott, April 28, Lowe Papers, 20-157). Retranslated.

When he was in bed again he sighed with relief. He said to Antommarchi:

"You will attend to the opening of my body.[44] I insist on your promising that no English physician shall lay hand to me. If you need help, Dr. Arnott is the only one you can employ. I hope you will take my heart and put it in spirits of wine and carry it to Parma to my dear Marie-Louise. You will tell her that I have loved her tenderly, that I have never ceased loving her. You will tell her everything touching my situation and my death. I recommend especially that you examine my stomach carefully and draw up a detailed and accurate report which you will deliver to my son. I am not far from thinking that it is affected by the lesion that brought my father to the grave—I mean by a growth at the pylorus. I suspected as much from the time my vomitings became frequent and stubborn."

Antommarchi promised. No one tried to express any hope. The Emperor dictated a letter to Montholon which the latter was to deliver to Lowe on the Emperor's death:

"Your Excellency: The Emperor Napoleon died on . . . as a result of a long and painful illness. I have the honour to inform you of that fact." [45]

Shortly after that speech failed him. He could not keep any food on his stomach. Several times he dozed off. In the darkened room, Bertrand, Montholon, the two physicians stood waiting.

.        .        .        .        .        .        .

During the night of the 28th-29th, while in a raging fever, the Emperor dictated to Montholon a plan for the ultimate disposal of Versailles. He entitled it *First Revery*. Marchand relieved Montholon and the Emperor then dictated a *Second Revery* on the defence of national territory by a national guard.[46] He had moments of complete delirium. During one of them he pulled off a cautery. During another he cried:

"I feel so strong that I could ride fifteen leagues on a horse." [47]

At the approach of dawn the fever abated and he got three hours of sleep. He allowed a vesicant to be applied to his stomach and

[44] Antommarchi, Vol. II, p. 130.
[45] Montholon, Vol. II, p. 544.
[46] Montholon, Vol. II, p. 545. Montholon claims that he gave these two *Reveries* to the Duc de Bassano, who mislaid them. Nothing is less certain. In any case they seem to be lost.
[47] Marchand, *Précis des guerres de Jules César*, Preface, p. 14.

Antommarchi adjusted two others on the inner sides of the thighs.[48] The day passed quietly. His mind being clear, he had Montholon write two letters relating to the settlement of his inheritance. The first accredited the Emperor's testamentary executors at Laffitte's bank. The second, addressed to Baron de la Bouillerie, former treasurer of his private estate, gave power of attorney to Montholon.[49] Marchand recopied them and the Emperor signed them.

In the evening the fever and the delirium reappeared. He spoke of his son in barely distinguishable words—the last fragments of his thought drifted to his child who was also a prisoner. Had he done enough for him? In the unlighted bedroom he wished to dictate some new clauses to Marchand.

"Have you any paper?"

"Yes, sire."

The young man took up his pencil and pretended to write on the back of a playing card:

"I bequeath to my son my dwelling house at Ajaccio near the Salt Works, with the gardens, all my possessions in the district of Ajaccio, sufficing to bring him an income of fifty thousand francs."

Property altogether imaginary! He tried to go on, but could not pronounce the words.

"I bequeath . . ." He stopped and his head fell back on the pillow. His eyes closed.[50]

Towards morning he hiccoughed for two hours. After that he breathed more easily. Arnott declared his condition stationary. However, speaking of the hiccoughs, Arnott said: "I consider the symptoms very serious, *if the thing is true*." [51] So, five days before the end, he was still suspecting the French of misrepresenting facts!

Napoleon passed the 30th in a sort of stupor, though at certain moments he spoke very distinctly. He even manhandled Bertrand as the latter suggested replacing Montholon, who was worn out, for the night.

"I have already told you—Montholon is enough for me. It is your

[48] Lowe Papers, 20-157; Antommarchi, Vol. II, p. 136.

[49] These two letters are dated as of the 25th, but according to Marchand's testimony, they must have been dictated on the morning of the 29th.

[50] In his preface to the *Précis des guerres de Jules César*, Marchand gives this scene under the date of May 2, in the evening. In his more accurate *Souvenirs*, Marchand places it on the evening of the 29th.

[51] Arnott, April 30 (Lowe Papers, 20-157).

fault if I have grown accustomed to his attentions. He will be the one to receive my last gasp. That will be the reward for his services. Don't mention it to me again." [52]

How hard his resentment died! Though he still respected Bertrand, he had withdrawn his friendship from him. To be sure Montholon had also wanted to leave, but he had been more careful in expressing his desire, flattering Napoleon with pleasanter lies. To the conquered hero the falsehood was beyond any doubt the greater charity.

However, a little later he repented. Poor Bertrand, too, would have stayed to the very end! After all, he too had sacrificed himself, and his wife and children! . . .

That same day after the physicians had visited the Emperor, Bertrand, who was in the drawingroom, came and stood motionless at the foot of the bed. The Emperor seemed to be asleep. Bertrand suddenly saw him raise his eyelids, and Napoleon said to him in a gentle tone:

"You are sad, Bertrand? What is the matter?"

He could see plainly that if his death was to free his first officer, it was also to tear his heart.

Bertrand lowered his head without replying.

Then Napoleon spoke to him of his wife. How was she? She must come tomorrow with the children!

After six months of constant refusal he was at last consenting to see the ungrateful, jealous, but kindhearted and unhappy Fanny again. It was an act of forgiveness that undoubtedly came hard.

During the evening he asked Pierron if he had brought back any oranges from town. What were they saying of him in Jamestown? The march of life was still interesting him.

Often his eyes went up towards the portrait of his son that hung between the two windows over his bed. "It was considered advisable to take the picture down," says Aly (p. 276), "and put it in another place where he could not see it. For some time his eyes wandered about the room looking everywhere for it and, gazing turn by turn at those who came near his bedside, he seemed to ask: 'Where is my son? What have you done with my son?' "

About eleven o'clock he was seized with chills and turned deathly

[52] Montholon, Vol. II, p. 546. Those painful words were certainly uttered. Marchand also reports them. In spite of the respect he had for Bertrand, the valet does not hide Napoleon's harshness towards the Grand Marshal during his last days.

cold. His pulse was imperceptible at intervals, his respiration halted. Antommarchi sent for Arnott. The attack, however, passed and the pulse resumed its beating. Napoleon slept a little.

On the forenoon of the 1st, the hiccoughs reappeared. This time Arnott himself was able to certify to the fact.[53] The patient refused nourishment and medicine. His mind wandered. He asked to go out into the garden. He had forgotten that Dr. Baxter had left the island and that Dr. Shortt, who had been suggested to him as a physician, had replaced him:

"Strange I never knew anything about it. Why wasn't I told before?"

The name Antommarchi surprised him:

"What is that—Antommarchi?"

He took him for O'Meara and called Arnott Stokoe. Sometimes he said:

"Am I in danger? Am I dying?"

Bertrand's presence surprised him:

"What do you want? What brings you here at this hour?"

At last his mind cleared. Montholon showed the Emperor the letter in which Lowe offered the services of new physicians. Napoleon replied:

"No, I know that I am dying. I have confidence in the people around me and do not wish any others to be called." [54]

At eleven o'clock Mme. Bertrand entered the drawingroom.

"Ah, Madame Bertrand!" the Emperor murmured.

"How does Your Majesty feel?"

"Ouch! Be careful!" [55]

He motioned to her to sit down at the head of his bed.

"So now you are quite well!" he said, recalling that she had been ill. "They know your trouble. Mine they don't, and I am dying of it."

He spoke of the children. Why had she not brought Hortense? She must come and see him again.

Mme. Bertrand replied in broken words. She was choking with sobs. She rose and curtseyed. The door once closed behind her, she burst out weeping:

"What a change in the Emperor! He has been very cruel in refus-

[53] Lowe Papers, 20-157. May 1st.
[54] Reade, *Note*, May 1st (Lowe Papers, 20-157).
[55] Aly, p. 275.

ing to receive me for so long a time. I am happy at being called back again, but I should be even more so had he allowed me to nurse him!"

From then on she came back every day to spend a few moments at the bedside.

. . . . . . . .

On the night of the 1st the two physicians slept in the library. For the first time Bertrand watched with Marchand. Montholon and Aly relieved them.

The day of May 2nd was fairly calm. Napoleon continued to shake his head, saying, "No, no," wearily when they offered him a drink, or food.[56]

Beginning with May 2 Lowe communicated Arnott's reports daily to Admiral Lambert and Montchenu. The Marquis replied on May 2 with this indecent note: "That sudden relapse and the hiccoughs which accompanied it seem to me a very bad sign, especially in view of the stubbornness with which he continues to refuse all treatment. If he is positively determined to die, I cannot conceive why he chooses such a painful manner of death, unless it be through an excess of religious zeal and in order to do greater penance in this world." [57]

Arnott and Antommarchi were in open conflict. The former wished to administer an enema against the patient's will. Antommarchi refused to force it, maintaining that "the slightest movement would bring on the hiccoughs again and that the irritation would aggravate the patient's weakness." Arnott was obliged to give in.

The evening and the first part of the night passed without any crisis. At three o'clock the hiccoughs began again. The abdomen was swollen and sensitive. Spots of sloughing were noticed on the small of the patient's back. On the morning of the 3rd Arnott reverted again to the idea of freeing the distended bowels at all costs and he suggested a dose of calomel. Antommarchi was against it. Tormented by thirst, the dying man drank some sweetened water with every now and then a little wine.

"It's good! It is very good!" he said to Marchand, looking at him with a tender expression.

Noverraz, who was recovering, asked to see his master. Napoleon had him come in.

[56] Conversation Lowe-Montholon, May 3 (Lowe Papers, 20-144).
[57] Lowe Papers, 20-133.

"You are much changed, my boy. Are you better?"

"Yes, sire."

"I am very glad to know that you are out of danger. Don't tire yourself by standing on your legs. Go and rest."

The young Swiss, trembling, was barely able to reach the diningroom. There he fainted.

Towards two o'clock in the afternoon, the fever abated somewhat. Following an order he had received from the Emperor, Montholon sent for Vignali. The Abbé appeared in civilian dress, carrying an object that he tried to hide. Marchand showed him in, left him alone with Napoleon, and stood guard in front of the door.[58] A half hour later Vignali came out of the room and said to Marchand:

"The Emperor has just taken the last rites. The condition of his stomach does not allow any further sacraments."

Why the mystery? Why did Napoleon hide from his companions at such a solemn moment? Because, to the very end, he remained a man of the Revolution. In his final hour he wished to return to the altar of his fathers and bow before it. But for too many years he had ridiculed the priests too much, he had professed his scepticism too loudly not to court secrecy, when, still in company for the most part with unbelievers, he wished to resort to the supreme rites of the faith. There can be no doubt about it—his act was sincere. Helpless, despoiled of everything, he turned towards God as towards a prop that could not fail. He would find it a little less bitter to close his exile with his hands clasped, if only for a moment. When Madame heard of it in Rome, she would be a little comforted, and the thought of his mother too made him feel less alone in death.

Marchand went back into the drawingroom. Prostrated, his eyes closed, his arms lying limp on the bed, the Emperor seemed already dead. The young man cautiously approached and kissed the hand that hung over the side. He went for Aly and he, in his turn, touched his lips to the pale fingers.[59]

[58] Marchand Papers (Thiers Library).

[59] Aly, p. 276. Antommarchi (Vol. II, p. 145) fixes at this moment what amounts to a speech by the Emperor to his executors: "I am about to die and you to return to Europe. I owe you a few words of counsel as to the conduct you are to follow. You have shared my exile. You will be loyal to my memory. You will do nothing to blemish it. I have sanctioned all [moral] principles. I have infused them into my laws, my acts. There is not one that I have not hallowed. Unfortunately circumstances were harsh: I found myself obliged to be severe, to temporize. Reverses came. I was not able to unbend the bow, and France was deprived of the liberal

Lowe was at that moment at Longwood whither he had hurried on information from Reade as to the disagreement between the doctors. He had offered some cows' milk for the Emperor—milk was lacking at Longwood. Arnott wanted to try it. Antommarchi objected, the milk, he said, being too heavy and indigestible. Arnott yielded.[60] Convinced at last that his prisoner was in danger, Lowe was sincerely anxious to give him all the aid in his power. Stationing himself with Gorrequer and Arnott at Montholon's, he did his utmost to have Shortt and Mitchell, the two best physicians on the island, called at last to the dying man's side. Montholon still objected. Though often unconscious, the Emperor, he said, was still having too sudden awakenings for them to dare to admit any other doctors to his bedside without his permission. "Their unexpected presence might produce a shock that would be fatal." It was finally agreed that "when the General had entirely lost consciousness" the English physicians would be allowed to enter the room.

"In short, M. le Comte," said Lowe in taking his leave, "I am strongly desirous that English medical science should at all events have the chance of saving his life." [61]

Gorrequer settled at New House to be ready for anything that might happen. Shortly after Lowe's departure Antommarchi ran to Gorrequer's and told him that since Napoleon "might die during the day he wished Doctors Shortt and Mitchell to be present at a consultation that would be held at his house. The two physicians were summoned by signalling and before long they gathered in conference with Arnott and Antommarchi, in the presence of Montholon and Bertrand.

Antommarchi was worried now at the responsibility he had assumed by disagreeing with Arnott's advice. When Shortt and Mitchell declared in their turn that if the patient was to be relieved a dose of calomel had to be administered without his suspecting it, Antommarchi deferred to their judgment. The English consultants also ad-

institutions that I had intended for her. She judges me indulgently. She takes account of my intentions, she cherishes my name, my victories. Follow her example, be faithful to the opinions we have defended, to the glory we have won. Beyond that there is nothing but shame and confusion."

It is evident that on May 3 Napoleon was not in a condition to utter any such words. Neither Montholon, nor Marchand, nor Bertrand refer to them. The apostrophe has a ring of nobility, but it is an invention of Antommarchi.

[60] Antommarchi, Vol. II, p. 143.
[61] Gorrequer, *Minutes*, May 3 (Lowe Papers, 20-144); Forsyth, Vol. III, p. 285.

vised rubbing the patient's back with eau de Cologne and giving him a sedative. Antommarchi, however, was certainly right. The dose ordered by Arnott (ten grains) was much too strong for a weakened organism, even taking no account of the cancer of which he knew nothing. It certainly hastened the Emperor's death.

"All right, we'll see," Napoleon murmured, when the recommendations of the physicians were imparted to him.

But when Bertrand had left the room, he exclaimed to Marchand, contemptuously:

"What a result from science! A fine consultation! Wash my back with eau de Cologne! Well, all right! As for the rest, I won't have any of it!"

Bertrand ordered Marchand to administer the calomel without the Emperor's knowledge. The valet was unwilling, whereupon the Grand Marshal asserted himself in a tone of authority: [62]

"It is one last resource to try. The Emperor is lost. We must not have to reproach ourselves for not doing everything that was humanly possible in order to save him."

Marchand mixed the powder in some sweetened water and held out the glass to the Emperor.

Napoleon managed to swallow it but with difficulty. At the bottom of the glass he tasted the drug.

"Oh," he said to Marchand reproachfully, "so you too are deceiving me!"

Cut to the heart Marchand could scarcely hold back his tears. But half an hour later Napoleon again asked him for a drink, and reached for the glass confidently.

"It is good! It's very good," he repeated.

During the evening he had trouble with his tongue. He sent for Pierron and tried to tell him how to prepare the orangeade. "He repeated the word *orange* over and over again but could not finish his sentence." [63]

·    ·    ·    ·    ·    ·    ·

The night of the 3rd-4th was quiet. None of the attendants went to bed. The calomel had a violent effect—six evacuations, says Arnott,[64] nine, says Antommarchi,[65] and he added some painful and

62 Marchand Papers (Thiers Library, Carton 22).
63 Montholon, Vol. II, p. 458.
64 Lowe Papers, 20-157.
65 Antommarchi, Vol. II, p. 149.

doubtless accurate details. The last time they changed the Emperor's linen, as Aly was straining to lift him so that Marchand could slip the fresh sheet under him, Napoleon struck him on the side with his fist and exclaimed: "Ah, rascal, you're hurting me!" [66] After that they did not try to change his linen again.[67] The patient was now hic-coughing incessantly, his weakness increasing if anything. But that morning, the blind Arnott reported to Reade: "Things are no worse. There is even some improvement. All in all I have more hope today than I did yesterday, or the day before." * He ordered soups and a little wine. Shortt and Mitchell were now there on permanent duty, but Montholon dared not admit them to the sick-room. The Emperor accepted a little soup and drank a great deal of sweetened water, most of which he lost again. He seemed less depressed, however, and talked more easily. But there was almost no intermission in the hic-coughing. To overcome it Arnott ordered a potion based on opium and ether.

For several days the weather had been bad. It rained almost con-stantly and the winds were high. The freshly planted fields were ruined. Aly reports (p. 273), specifying however that he did not see it himself, that "along towards the middle of the last fortnight a little comet, barely perceptible to the eye, was seen in the evening towards the West." When the Emperor learned of the portent he said: "It has come to mark the time of my career." The Jamestown archives carefully noted the most insignificant meteorological details. They make no mention of such a comet.

From time to time Napoleon groaned. His fever, which had dropped at first, went up again. In the afternoon he tried to rise, but Antommarchi put him back to bed. The Emperor seemed an-noyed. Then gradually his consciousness faded. "He was peaceful and drowsy," says Aly (p. 279). "From time to time he spat, and what he coughed up looked like coffee-grounds of a rather reddish tinge, like chocolate. His flannel vest and the part of the sheet that covered his chest were soiled with it." At ten in the evening he made a violent effort to vomit, got up a black substance, and then sank back on his pillows.

The night seemed endless. The two screened candles gave out a dim light. Bertrand, Montholon, Antommarchi, Marchand, Aly, half

[66] Aly, p. 279.                           * Retranslated.
[67] Lowe Papers, 15-729.

dead from fatigue, dozed on chairs in the drawingroom itself or in the room adjoining. One or the other would awaken, run to the bed, lift the mosquito-netting, try to catch the almost imperceptible breathing of the Emperor and slip a spoonful of sweetened water into his mouth. His cheeks twitched with nervous chills.[68] About two o'clock in the morning of the 5th, a few incomprehensible words escaped his lips. Montholon was later to claim that he had understood them:

"France—army—army head—Josephine."

According to a letter written by an English officer and published in the *Evening Star* of July 10, the Emperor's last words were said to have been the following: "In a moment of delirium he muttered: 'My son'; then he pronounced distinctly 'the head of the army,' shortly afterwards he stammered 'France,' and from then on he did not utter a word."

Whatever the words were and whatever their order, they were his last. He lapsed again into unconsciousness.[69] A little after five o'clock, he vomited. His arms and legs were bathed in sweat. They saw him slowly raise his trembling hands and cross them. Then he let them fall back to either side of his body. After that he did not move again. His open eyes were glassy, his lower jaw fell. His pulse was now imperceptible. A faint beat could be detected at his throat.[70]

Arnott came at six o'clock. He ordered mustard plasters for the soles of the feet and vesicants on the legs and chest. They had no effect.

Day dawned. The blinds were opened. Mme. Bertrand came and sat at the foot of the bed. At eight o'clock all the French attached to Longwood entered the drawingroom on tiptoe and stood in line against the walls to see the Emperor die.

[68] Aly, p. 279.

[69] Montholon embellishes the night of the 4th-5th with a dramatic incident: "The Emperor flung himself out of bed with a convulsive movement that I struggled in vain to resist. His strength was so great that he dragged me with him to the carpet. He pressed me so violently in his arms that I could not call for help. Fortunately Archambault was on duty in the next room. He heard the noise and ran to help me lift the Emperor back upon his bed. A few seconds later the Grand Marshal and M. Antommarchi, who had thrown themselves down on a sofa in the library, also came. But the Emperor was already in bed and calm" (Vol. II, p. 548). Marchand explicitly denies that there was any such incident: "Pure imagination!" he comments. Archambault did not enter the Emperor's room before the morning of May 5th. Antommarchi and Aly report a somewhat similar episode for the night of the 2nd-3rd. Montholon was mistaken by two days and, as usual, embroidered copiously.

[70] Arnott, May 5 (Lowe Papers, 20-157); Antommarchi, Vol. II, p. 150.

# PART SIX

## *NAPOLEON'S DEATH AND TRIUMPH*

# I

### *DEATH*

CAPTAIN CROKAT ORDERED RAISED THE SIGNAL THAT HAD BEEN AR-
ranged for long in advance to announce to Plantation House that
"General Buonaparte was in imminent danger." Lowe at once
mounted a horse and dashed for Longwood with Reade and Gorrequer. Just before they arrived they were met by a dragoon who
bore a piece of paper on which Arnott had pencilled:

"He is dying. Montholon prays I will not leave the bedside. He
wishes I should see him breathe his last." [1]

Lowe settled at New House at nine o'clock in the morning to
await the event. He immediately despatched a note to Admiral Lambert. A postscript read: "Have the goodness to apprize the Marquis
I shall make an immediate signal if he dies. The signal will be number
three." [2]

The curtains on the Emperor's bed were raised, and the bed was
moved away from the wall and set facing the fire-place, that it might
be easier to move about it. For the first time in many days the windows were left open and the room was flooded with light. Napoleon
had shunned the light all through his illness. He did not seem to feel
it now as it streamed across his ivory face. He lay on his back, his
thighs spread and his heels together, his left hand lying against his side,
his right hand hanging limp. Save for a faint hiccough he was perfectly still. [3] Antommarchi kept moistening his lips with a sponge,

[1] Arnott to Crokat (F. G. di Giuseppe Collection). The note is undated. It must
have been sent to the orderly officer about seven o'clock in the morning. Forsyth,
Vol. III, p. 286.
[2] Lowe Papers, 20-133. Retranslated.
[3] Aly, p. 281.

and trying to feel the pulse, now at the wrist, now at the throat. His feet and legs were cold.

The forenoon was foggy, but about eleven the sun cleared the mists away. The green slopes of the Diana Range came into view, the sharp profile of High Knoll, and the sea glistening in the distance.[4]

Around the bed were Mme. Bertrand, biting her handkerchief, her equine profile bent forward; Bertrand in uniform, white breeches, high boots, the Grand Cordon and cross; Montholon, his face drawn with fatigue; Marchand, dressed in black, modest, silent, useful, as heartbroken as a son. Arnott, in a long blue coat, stood behind Antommarchi at the head of the bed. Aly, Coursot, Chandellier, Archambault, Noverraz, Mme. Saint-Denis, and Mme. Noverraz were grouped to either side of the fire-place. The Abbé was praying in the diningroom-chapel, the door being open. So deep was the silence that one could hear the priest's murmuring voice and the ticking of the little gilded clock on the night-table at the Emperor's right.

Each in turn the spectators withdrew to the kitchen for a bit of luncheon and then returned hastily to the drawingroom. In the afternoon the four Bertrand children were led in. They began to weep. The emotion was too great for young Napoleon. He fainted and was carried out into the garden.

The day dragged on without visible change.[5] Just after three o'clock Arnott sent a note to New House:

[4] In spite of all that has been said and repeated so far. For example, Forsyth, Vol. II, p. 287: "A violent hurricane was sweeping the island. . . . While the tempest raged and howled it seemed that the spirit of storms rode abroad on the squalls to announce to the world that a formidable power was sinking into the obscure abyss of nature." And Frémeaux (p. 337): "A relentless rain had been falling since the night before. . . . As if to accentuate the horror of the moment with its voice, a wind from the Southwest was blowing a gale, howling over the high bare plateau where amid the gum trees with their bony arms the house of tragedy rose." All that is in keeping with the romantic literature that has gradually accumulated around the Captivity. Actually, if the days just preceding had been almost constantly rainy, May 5 was a beautiful day, bright with sunshine, as is shown by the *Annual Register* of St. Helena for 1821 and also by the unanimous oral tradition of the inhabitants of the island. As a matter of fact, hurricanes are a great rarity at St. Helena. That is one of the peculiarities of the place. A certain William Carrol who was living on the island in Napoleon's day wrote on the margin of a copy of Forsyth: "This is all false. W. C." (Communication from Mr. Kitching, secretary to the Government of St. Helena.)

[5] Aly, pp. 280-81. Aly's account is the most trustworthy that we have of the Emperor's end. Antommarchi has once again altered the truth by noting: "Spasmodic arched twitchings of the epigastrum and of the stomach, deep sighs, lamentable cries, convulsive movements which ended in a loud and sinister sob." Napoleon's life burned out little by little, without movement and, it would seem, without pain. Arnott, Aly and Marchand testify to that in categorical terms.

THE PASSING OF NAPOLEON
From an Engraving by Steuben

"The pulse cannot be felt at the wrist now, and the heat is departing from the surface, but he may hold out some hours yet." At a quarter to four Lowe transmitted the bulletin to Admiral Lambert.[6] At five o'clock the latter, at whose house Montchenu was waiting, wrote to the Governor: "The Marquis wishes to see the body as soon as he could after the demise. I suggested waiting until after the morning, but as it is probable all may be over before our arrival we propose setting off immediately in preference to going up in the dark. We shall wait at the guard-house to hear the event." [7]

Some little doves of the species peculiar to St. Helena—silver plumage, pink, bare claws, came and alighted on one of the window frames and sat there cooing. An attendant tried to drive them away. They came back again. Two of them stayed till evening. The fortress on High Knoll grew dark in the distance. The sun was sinking. The sea looked like a sheet of metal under its slanting rays. The brilliant sky stood reflected in the mirror above the fireplace. All eyes were fixed on the little bed of Austerlitz. The Emperor's hiccoughing was not so frequent now. His breath was coming with more difficulty. At times it seemed to have stopped. His eyes were rolled up under his upper lids until only an opaque oval was left showing. Antommarchi put a finger to the artery in his throat and made a sign. Arnott scribbled a third bulletin in pencil.

"5.30. He is worse, the respiration has become more hurried and difficult."

The flames of the sunset reddened the mirror. Who would be the first to die—the sun or Napoleon? It was the sun. Suddenly daylight was gone. Everything paled. The sun had dipped into the ocean.[8] The sunset gun boomed from Alarm Signal. No one stirred in the bedroom, where faces had grown indistinct. The only things that now seemed white, with an unbroken, terrifying whiteness, were the Emperor's bedclothes, his forehead, his hands. Ten very long moments passed in that agony. The swift tropical night fell. Someone made a move to go into the diningroom to get a lamp. Just then Antommarchi leaned over Napoleon. He straightened up and bowed his head. Without a tremor, without a murmur, the Emperor had died. A slight foam wet his lips. It was nine minutes to six.

[6] Lowe Papers, 20-133; Young, Vol. II, p. 225.
[7] Lowe Papers, 20-123. Retranslated.
[8] On May 5, the sun set at 5.40 exactly (*Annual Register*, St. Helena, 1821).

Someone—Mme. Bertrand perhaps—stopped the clock, while Arnott sent Crokat to Lowe with a last little square of paper on which he had scrawled these words:

"He has this moment expired." [9]

There was an outburst of sobbing among Napoleon's friends and domestics. All of them, even those who were least attached to him, who had seen him least often and had most longed to get away, felt strangely alone and helpless when confronted with that simple stopping of a heart. All faces were wet with tears and even Arnott wiped his eyes. Bertrand was the first to step up to the bed. Falling to his knees, he kissed the hero's hand. Montholon did likewise; then in turn and in the order of their rank, the domestics; finally the women and the Bertrand children, whom their mother had called back.

Antommarchi closed the Emperor's eyes. He lay there, calm, his face without a wrinkle and with something like a faint smile on his colourless lips. His beard had grown during those last days. It suffused his chin and cheeks with an ashen cast.

Lowe came hastening from New House. Montholon received him and expressed the wish that he wait a few hours that the death chamber might be put in presentable order, the body washed and the linen changed. The Governor replied that it was indispensable that Dr. Shortt and Dr. Mitchell be admitted at once to certify to the decease. Montholon consented. It was agreed that Arnott would not leave the body during the first night. Crokat, the orderly officer, had already been led to the death-bed and had saluted the corpse solemnly. [10]

Lowe sent Gorrequer to inform the Admiral and Montchenu. The Marquis insisted upon seeing the body at once, insinuating "that the persons who surrounded General Buonaparte might place poison in his throat and render him unrecognizable." He was assured that the presence of Dr. Arnott in the death-chamber would be sufficient guarantee against any attempt of that nature. He finally allowed himself to be persuaded that he had better wait till the next day. He went to Plantation House and spent the night there. [11]

[9] The Governor noted on the bottom: "Received at six o'clock."
[10] Lowe Papers, 20-133.
[11] Ibid.

Meanwhile Bertrand, Montholon, Marchand and Vignali proceeded to the billiardroom to draw up a report certifying to the decease of the Emperor, to the delivery of the will and codicils to Montholon and to the integrity of the seals. "Marchand handed over the package containing the will and the codicils to M. de Montholon," writes Aly (p. 282). "The seals having been recognized as intact, Father Vignali went into the drawingroom alone and the three others opened the various envelopes." The death certificate was drawn up by Bertrand in his capacity as Grand Officer of the Emperor's Household. Montholon sealed the letter which the Emperor had dictated to him to announce his demise and sent it to the Governor. Then the three executors returned to the drawingroom to receive the English physicians. The chandelier had been lighted. All the French were present, standing in line to right and left of the bed.

Shortt and Mitchell entered, accompanied by Crokat. They raised the cover, felt the body lightly, then withdrew, correct, cold.[12] Marchand, Aly, and the latter's wife remained alone with Arnott at the Emperor's bedside. Antommarchi had adjusted a chin-bandage to the corpse. The others went back to their own homes. In the adjoining room the Abbé kept praying. The sentries had been withdrawn. The night was black and silent.[13] The only sounds were a rustling of leaves and, almost incessant, the piercing, strident cry of a cricket. Seated on a couch, the three attendants talked in low tones, glancing frequently at the outstretched form. Mme. Saint-Denis sat rocking her little girl, who was a year old. Suddenly Marchand took the child in his arms, stepped over to the bed, and made her touch her lips to the inert hand.[14]

When midnight struck Bertrand and Montholon were roused from their beds, and in their presence, Marchand, Aly, Pierron, and Noverraz proceeded to dress the Emperor for the last time. "We began the sad and painful operation of washing him," writes Aly (p. 284). "We hardly dared touch our hands to the body. It seemed to us to possess a sort of electric property. Our hands trembled and touched him only with respect mingled with fear." Antommarchi and Arnott had ordered them to wait till midnight for this first attention to the corpse. The Emperor's face was shaved and the body, bathed in eau

[12] Aly, p. 283; Montholon, Vol. II, p. 550.
[13] "May 6th, new moon" (Annual Register, St. Helena).
[14] Aly, p. 284.

de Cologne, transferred to the second camp bed which was set between the two windows in the drawingroom, in the same place as the death-bed. The shroud that was drawn over it left the face uncovered. Antommarchi changed the chin-bandage. On the breast Vignali laid the silver crucifix that Madame Mère had sent and to which, doubtless, in thinking of her son she had pressed her aged melancholy lips. Most of the furniture was removed. On either side of the bed, at the head, little tables were placed and on them candles from the chapel in their holders, lighted.

Death seemed to have restored Napoleon's youth. As he lay there at that moment he had the face of the First Consul. All the witnesses agree on that—Marchand, Aly, the English officers. Not a grey hair, not a wrinkle! His complexion was of a flat, warm colour, clearer than in life. He did not look more than thirty. The spot of candle-light cast a serene radiance over his face. A little colour had crept back into his cheeks. "His mouth," says Marchand, "had contracted slightly and lent his face an expression of satisfaction."

The Abbé, Arnott and Pierron finished out the night.

.    .    .    .    .    .    .

Word came at dawn that the Governor had left Plantation House on his way to Longwood. Walking up and down the evening before in front of his residence with Gorrequer and Henry, the young physician, Lowe said to them, as they were speaking of Napoleon:

"Well, gentlemen, he was England's greatest enemy, and mine too, but I forgive him everything. On the death of a great man like him we should only feel deep concern and regret." [15]

Words that painted him to the full, in his lack of tact, his fatuous vanity, and even the unwilling respect which he had never quite succeeded in banishing from the depths of his hesitant soul!

Lowe arrived about seven o'clock on Sunday, the 6th, escorted by Admiral Lambert, General Coffin, Montchenu, Gors, five physicians (Doctors Shortt, Mitchell, Burton, Livingstone and Henry), a number of officers (Captains Browne, Hendry and Marryat, and Ensign Vidal), two members of the Council of St. Helena (Brooke and Greentree), and Commissary Denzil Ibbetson, the chief purveyor. They were received by Bertrand and Montholon. All the French

[15] Henry, *Events of a Military Life*, Vol. II, p. 80 (*Trifles from My Portfolio*, Vol. II, p. 7).

were present. Lowe advanced slowly towards the bed, followed by
Montchenu. He fixed his eyes on the majestic face, then said to the
Marquis in a half tone, not daring this time to utter the words: "Gen-
eral" or "Bonaparte":

"Do you recognize him?"

The Commissioner of France and Austria bowed his head:

"Yes, I recognize him."

They stood silent a few seconds. Behind them the English officers—
indifferent or hostile as they might hitherto have been—were struck
by the nobility of the dead man and stood erect, motionless, filled
with admiration. "A finer face I never saw," Brooke was to write.[*]
And Vidal, secretary to the Admiral: "The head was beautiful, the
expression of the face calm and mild, and not the slightest indication
of suffering." [†] And Shortt: "His face was in death the most beautiful I ever beheld, exhibiting softness and every good expression in
the highest degree, and really seemed formed to conquer." [‡] And
Henry: "Everyone exclaimed when the face was exposed, 'How very
beautiful!' for all present acknowledged they had never seen a finer
or more regular and placid countenance." [||] Even Montchenu in
writing to Damas, May 6th, said: "I have never seen a corpse so little
disfigured. All his features were perfectly preserved and had it not
been for his pallor one would have said that he was sleeping." And
the Marquis added (that was before the autopsy): "The strange thing
is that among five physicians there is not one who knows what he
died of."

Hudson Lowe brought his heels together and saluted. The others
followed suit. Then one by one they filed past the bed and left the
room behind the Governor.

Assuming authority from the fact that the Emperor had named
him first among the executors, Montholon had taken precedence over
Bertrand since the Emperor's death. Bertrand went into a sulk and
kept out of the way. It was Montholon who attended to everything.
It was he who informed Lowe in the billiardroom of the codicil in
which Napoleon expressed a wish to be buried in France. The Governor replied that that question had been settled in advance by Lord

[*] Young, Vol. II, p. 227.
[†] *Ibid.*
[‡] *Ibid.*
[||] Henry, *Trifles from My Portfolio*, Vol. II, p. 9.

Bathurst away back in 1817 and that the interment would have to take place on the island "with the military honours due to an English General." [16]

Montholon then informed him that the Emperor had requested that an autopsy be made. Lowe had no orders to the contrary.[17] According to Antommarchi (Vol. II, p. 156), who is followed by Montholon, Lowe at first requested an immediate autopsy. They say that the French protested, Montholon even appealing to Montchenu in the matter. Lowe yielded. But towards noon Antommarchi warned that the first signs of decomposition had set in. Montholon therefore informed the Governor that the autopsy could not be delayed any longer. No difficulty was raised on the point. In that damp climate the examination of a body even ten hours after death could not raise any reasonable objection and Montholon and Antommarchi were too eager to conciliate the Governor, in view of their approaching departure, to hold out very energetically against his wishes. Lowe therefore decided that the operation would take place at two in the afternoon of the 6th.

Before leaving Longwood the Governor suggested to Antommarchi that Dr. Burton help him "make a cast of the dead man's face." [18] Antommarchi declined the assistance, saying that all he needed was plaster. Burton rode off on his horse to procure some in Jamestown. Arnott, Crokat, Ensign Ward, and Captain Marryat were authorized by Montholon to make sketches of the Emperor. Marryat, who was later to become a celebrated novelist, made several copies of his sketch which left for England on the evening of the 6th.[19] The Commissary, Denzil Ibbetson, even made a rapid painting in oil.

A large table was set up on trestles in the billiardroom and covered with a cloth. The body was placed on it. Soon Sir Thomas Reade appeared. He had been sent by Lowe to witness the autopsy. Montholon, Reade was to write [20] the same day in his report to Lowe,

[16] Bathurst to Lowe, September 16, 1817. The order had been reaffirmed in 1820.
[17] Lowe Papers, 20-133; Antommarchi, Vol. II, p. 156; Montholon, Vol. II, p. 157.
[18] Antommarchi, Vol. II, p. 156.
[19] The Statesman, July 8, 1821.
[20] Reade's Report is preserved in the British Museum (Lowe Papers, 20-133). It is the most valuable record we have of the autopsy. It may be usefully compared with the official statement signed by the English physicians, with Antommarchi's description—both technical, and the notes left by Henry.

raised no objection. On the contrary he said that he thought it extremely useful and appropriate that an officer should have come in the name of the Governor. Consequently, accompanied by Major Harrison and the guard officer, Reade entered the room where the body lay. Present at that moment were Count Bertrand, Count Montholon, Father Vignali, Marchand, Pierron and Aly, Doctors Shortt, Mitchell, Arnott, Burton, Henry, Rutledge and (during a part of the meeting only) Livingstone, surgeon in the service of the East India Company. Professor Antommarchi was the operator. All present followed Antommarchi's motions with the greatest attention. He was a skilful dissector. Assistant-Surgeon Rutledge, from the 20th, helped him to detach the organs from the body. Assistant-Surgeon Henry, at the request of Shortt, who presided at the meeting, took notes for the official report. The examination was over at four o'clock.[21]

During the first part of the operation, says Reade, nothing seemed to attract the attention of the physicians except the extraordinary quantity of fat that covered almost all the inner parts below the chest, but particularly in the region of the heart, which was literally enveloped. So much fat greatly astonished the physicians. Henry was to write: [22] "As during his eventful career there was much of the mysterious and inscrutable about him, so, even after death, Bonaparte's inanimate remains continued a puzzle and a mystery; for notwithstanding his great sufferings and the usual emaciating effects of the malady that destroyed him, the body was found enormously fat."

On opening the lower part of the body where the liver lay, they discovered that the stomach had adhered to the left side of the liver, the former organ being greatly diseased. The physicians at once and as one man expressed the conviction that "the diseased state of the stomach was the sole cause of death." The stomach was taken out and shown to Reade. Two-thirds of it seemed to be in horrible condition. It was covered with cancerous substances and a short distance from the pylorus there was a perforation large enough to pass the little finger through.

The liver was next examined. When the operator removed it, Dr. Shortt observed that "it was enlarged." All the other practitioners were of a different opinion, notably Dr. Burton, who combated Dr. Shortt's opinion heatedly. Dr. Henry agreed with Burton. Dr. Arnott said that there was nothing abnormal in the appearance of the liver.

[21] Lowe Papers, 20-133.
[22] *Events of a Military Life*, Vol. II, p. 82.

It might be large, but certainly was not larger than the liver of anybody of General Bonaparte's age. Dr. Mitchell saw nothing extraordinary about it and Rutledge remarked that it certainly was not enlarged. In spite of those observations Dr. Shortt persisted in saying:
"It is enlarged." That so impressed Reade that he went forward and
remarked to the physicians that it seemed to him very important that
they should come to an agreement in order to render a prompt and
definite opinion on the true condition of the liver, and he recommended a new and careful examination. Dr. Shortt said nothing
further, but all the others confirmed their first judgment. At that
moment the liver was in the operator's hands and, at Reade's apparent
desire to see it more closely, Antommarchi immediately took out his
knife and opened it from one end to the other, saying: "It is good,
perfectly sound, and has nothing extraordinary in it." He remarked
at the same time that it was a large liver. He did not seem to mean
by that what Dr. Shortt had meant when he said that the liver was
enlarged. "There is a great difference between a 'large liver' and a
'liver being enlarged,'" said Reade. Drs. Burton and Arnott nodded
in agreement.

.      .      .      .      .      .      .      .

That brutal autopsy, where opinions clashed in the presence of the
yawning cadaver, and where a sawbones vaunted the quality of
Napoleon's viscera like a butcher calling his wares from a stall, proved
one thing: that the Emperor died of the same disease as his father—
of an ulcer, probably malignant, of the stomach, the growth of which,
long unsuspected, was hastened towards the end.

Caroline was to die of the same disease, as the following unpublished letter proves. The letter was addressed by her secretary, Cavel,
to Mercey, and dated from Florence, May 12, 1839. It affords a
number of comparisons with Napoleon's symptoms:

"My dear Mr. Mercey: In reply to your letter of May 3, I have very
bad news to give you of the Queen. For two months she has been confined to her bed, prey to a malady which so far has shown no respite.
She began to feel indisposed after the death of Princess Charlotte. She
went daily to see Queen Julie, and the spectacle of sorrow for one thing,
and the chilliness of the house for another, increased her indisposition.
Add to that personal troubles, and an accumulation of little annoyances
over several months' time, and you have the explanation of the jaundice
which has lasted for two months and which, after a period of appreciable
improvement, has become much worse again during this past week. In

the beginning the jaundice was accompanied by fever and Mr. Playfair, who was treating the Queen alone at the time, did not notice the fever. For three weeks he did nothing to dissipate the jaundice which unfortunately seems to have taken a good hold. His remedies were confined to giving the Queen two attacks of pain a day by making her eat meat. The vomitings she used to suffer from long ago returned with the beginning of her illness. The Queen vomits as many as five times a day. As a result her stomach is unable to bear either food or medicine, she is getting weaker and weaker, and the disease, which cannot be treated with any remedy, merely gains and gains.

"I have not told you yet of the cause of these vomitings which have been continuing now for forty months with ever-increasing severity. The Queen has two lesions in the digestive canal, one high up and more recent, the other in the large colon. The nature of these lesions and their degree of advancement the physicians cannot determine, so that if they were to cure her of the jaundice it would still be uncertain whether the stomach could ever be serviceable after the attacks through which it has been passing. The lesions in the digestive canal can be of two kinds, either cancerous, or formed by thickenings of the tissue. In either case a more or less early and painful death lies at the end. You know now the condition of the patient. Helpless in the face of her disease the doctors cannot foresee the outcome. The executioner who was unfortunately dismissed too late was Playfair." [23]

Caroline died a few weeks later.

Madame Mère succumbed in 1836 to a lung congestion. Louis died of an attack of apoplexy, Jerome of pneumonia. Joseph died at the age of 76. Of what is not known. It has been said, but without proof, that Lucien died of a cancer of the stomach. Pauline's health seems to have been undermined both by tuberculosis and by an internal cancer. No autopsy was performed on any of them.

As Reade testifies,[24] neither Bertrand nor Montholon had any doubt as to the Emperor's malady nor as to its hereditary character. Bertrand wrote to Fesch that same day, May 6th, an altogether commonplace letter in which he said, informing him of the Emperor's death: "He seems to have died of the same disease as his father, an ulcer of the pylorus. Towards the last of his long illness he had suspected the cause of it." He wrote the same day to Napoleon's brother Louis in identical terms.

At the same time Montholon wrote to his wife much more explicitly: "All is over, my good Albine. The Emperor breathed his

[23] Masson *Papers* (Thiers Library, Carton 58).
[24] Lowe Papers, 20-133.

last yesterday at ten minutes to six. . . . The opening of his body has proved that he died of the same disease as his father, of an ulcerous growth in the stomach near the pylorus. Seven-eighths of the surface of the stomach were ulcerated. The ulcer probably started four or five years ago. In our misfortune it is a great consolation for us to have obtained proof that his death is not and could not have been in any manner the result of his captivity nor of the lack of all those attentions that Europe might have been able to offer him. We are working busily at all the necessary preparations for his interment."

The stomach was shown to Mme. Bertrand, Rutledge relates. "She introduced the point of her own little finger through the cancerated hole, and said that 'Cancer was what the Emperor had always said to be the matter with him, and of which he anticipated his death.' " *

However the honest Shortt was not wrong. There *was* a swelling of the liver. In spite of Antommarchi's scepticism and Lowe's angry and self-interested denial, Napoleon certainly suffered from a chronic hepatitis, as first O'Meara, and then Stokoe, diagnosed. Shortt had always thought so and he even said so with no little courage before the Emperor died, to the infinite disgust of the Governor who denounced him to Bathurst: "Dr. Shortt thought that the disease proceeded from the liver even without his *having seen the patient*, but he feels a little ashamed, I believe, of the opinion he has offered." [25]

After the autopsy, to be sure, Shortt, like the others, was of the opinion that death could have been due only to cancer. The liver affection was something merely accessory, which had not influenced the duration of Napoleon's life. A private letter that he wrote to his brother-in-law, May 7, 1821,[26] makes a definite assertion: "His disease was cancer in the stomach, that must have lasted some years, and been in a state of ulceration some months. . . . During the whole of his illness he never complained, and kept his character to the last. The disease being hereditary, his father having died of it, and his sister, the Princess Borghese, being supposed to have it, proves to the world that climate and mode of life had no hand in it."

In a note addressed to the Governor on May 8, Shortt further declared that "had the edges of the ulcer which penetrated the coats of

* Young, Vol. II, p. 237.
[25] May 10, 1821 (Lowe Papers, 20-133; Young, Vol. II, p. 233).
[26] Published in the *North British Advertiser*, August 2, 1873; Young, Vol. II, pp. 233-34.

the stomach near the pylorus not firmly adhered to the liver, death would have taken place much sooner, as part of the contents of the stomach would have escaped into the abdomen." The liver therefore played the rôle of a stopper.[27]

For years, with long intervals of quiet, to be sure, Napoleon had suffered from liver troubles as well as from malarial fevers. He had not died of them. He died of the ulcer only. As Shortt said in the same letter, he would have succumbed to it "on the throne of France as well as at St. Helena." [28] But undeniably its progress was hastened by the damp climate of the island, and also by the mental depression from which the Emperor suffered from 1819 on. In addition, Napoleon had been treated in an absurd, almost criminal fashion. The wretched medicos who attended him, from O'Meara down to Antommarchi and Arnott, simply corroded his stomach and intestines away by an abuse of mercurial drugs.

The autopsy ended about four o'clock. Antommarchi was in fine fettle and was bridled by no reverence whatever. He was inclined to attack the brain. "The state of that organ in a man like the Emperor would have been," he said, "of the highest interest. I was rudely halted, however, and had to yield." [29] The interference came from Bertrand and Montholon. Sick at heart they could see in it only a useless profanation. The "professor" therefore sewed up the body with a needle, in the presence of Reade and several of the physicians. According to Aly (p. 286), "before closing the body, Antommarchi seized a moment when English eyes were not fixed on it and ex-

[27] Lowe Papers, 20-133; Forsyth, Vol. III, p. 293.

[28] In Shortt's letter of May 7th, 1821, already quoted. Antommarchi's *Remarks*, published in his memoirs, describe the upper lobe of the left lung as "sprinkled with tubercles, with a few small tuberculous excavations." It is hard to lend any credence to that statement. Antommarchi's report, dated Longwood, May 8, 1821, the original of which appears among Montholon's papers (Thiers Library, Carton 20), declares that "the lungs were in a normal state." That report, drawn up immediately after the autopsy, seems more trustworthy than the *Remarks* which were written later on with an exaggerated bias. It agrees besides with the official statement: "The lungs were quite sound." The whole argument of Dr. Cabanès therefore falls. As is well known Cabanès declared emphatically that "Napoleon was tubercular."

[29] A number of physicians have recently put forth an interesting hypothesis. According to them Napoleon must have been suffering from an hypertrophy of the pituitary gland, the main symptoms of which are increasing obesity, the loss of hair, atrophy of the genital organs, extreme smoothness of the skin, and so on. These symptoms were in truth present in the Emperor. An affection of the pituitary gland would further explain his marked tendency to feel cold during his later years. In the absence of any autopsy of the brain, however, any conclusion would be hazardous.

tracted two little fragments of bone from a rib, which he gave, one to
Father Vignali, and the other to Coursot." The relic preserved by
Coursot is today in the possession of his grand-niece, Mme. Michault-
Bize.[30]

Montholon and Marchand insist that Lowe objected to the em-
balming of the body.[31] There was never any question of an embalm-
ing.[32] The inside of the body was sprayed with eau de Cologne. When
the cadaver was bathed, Antommarchi took down all the necessary
measurements and dictated them to Father Vignali. "The sheet,"
writes Aly, p. 286, "on which the autopsy was peformed, was stained
with blood in a number of places. Pieces were cut from the sheet by
the majority of those present and all of them had curios from it—
the English taking the larger share." Finally Marchand and Aly
dressed the body: drawers, a flannel shirt, silk stockings, cashmere
breeches, a white vest, a muslin cravat fitting a black collar that was
fastened by a pin, a coat from Napoleon's uniform as a Colonel of

[30] Two fragments of pitted intestine were likewise supposed to have been stolen
by Antommarchi, who gave them to O'Meara in London. They are today in the
museum of the Royal College of Surgeons. Professors Sir Ashley Cooper and Sir
James Paget thought they found cancerous nodules and patches in them. On the
other hand histological examinations conducted first by Sir Frederick Even and later
by Dr. Shallock, in 1910, did not reveal any trace of neoplasms. Professor Keith
himself concluded that the fragments present a "lymphoid hyperplasia" due to attacks of malaria. Such technical discussions are fatuous so long as there is no convincing proof that the fragments preserved in London are genuine.

Dr. de Mets has tried to prove that Napoleon died not of a cancer but of a gastric ulcer. That is also the conclusion of Dr. Takino Kalema of Helsingfors. Dr.
Héreau had suggested that as early as 1829 (Dr. Héreau was surgeon to Madame
Mère and Marie-Louise, at the Tuileries). Héreau diagnosed the case as an acute
and chronic gastritis, occasioned by the climate of St. Helena and made fatal by
the irritating, corrosive, "incendiary" remedies that had been forced on him, especially by Antommarchi. (Dr. Héreau, Napoléon à Sainte-Hélène, pp. 125-28.)

S. Abbatucci, surgeon-in-chief for the French Colonies, positively eliminates
cancer. According to him Napoleon succumbed to a suppurative hepatitis: "After
inducing an encysted peritonitis by establishing adherences with the wall of the
stomach, the abscess opened into the gastric and peritonic cavities to induce a fatal
infection."

[31] Masson, Op. cit., p. 486, follows them. Frémeaux says (Op. cit., p. 341): "After
the autopsy, the body was embalmed." In that, as in other details, Frémeaux did
not go back to the sources.

[32] Dr. Héreau declared that Antommarchi was inexcusable for not trying, at least,
to embalm Napoleon's body: "The island," he wrote, "was abundantly provided with
gun-powder, sulphur, coal-tar, slaked lime, common salt, deuto-chlorure of mercury
and other chemicals still, which were very suitable substances for inducing mummi-
fication." It is probable that the English authorities were not anxious for an em-
balming. They would not have objected to one. Antommarchi's negligence merely
seconded their preferences.

the Chasseurs of the Imperial Guard, gold epaulettes, boots, spurs, a sword, a tricorn hat with the tricolour cockade, the star and ribbon of the Legion of Honour, and two crosses, the one of the Legion, the other of the Order of the Iron Crown. "Fearing," says Aly (p. 286), "that the Governor might try to get possession of the Emperor's sword, the Grand Marshal's was substituted for it."

These attentions completed, the Emperor was borne to his little bedroom that was hung in black and lighted with all the resources available in the house. The altar was set up. Clad in surplice and stole, the Abbé knelt before it. The attendants laid Napoleon to rest on his little bed and over him was thrown the blue cloak of Marengo. His head sank deep into a pillow. The crucifix again lay on his breast. His face still retained the faint smile. His hands, soft, white, seemed to be living. At the head of the bed stood Bertrand, at the foot Montholon and Marchand. Antommarchi, Arnott, Rutledge and the domestics dressed in black coats stood in line along the windows, so leaving a narrow passage free to accommodate the throngs of visitors.

They came from all over the island as had been the case six years before at Plymouth. Montholon wrote to his wife, May 6th: "An immense crowd of people came to file past the bed." And the next day (the 7th) an English officer was to write: "An enormous crowd flocked to see him yesterday and today. It is one of the most extraordinary sights I have ever witnessed in my life." [33] The road to Longwood was one long file of soldiers, sailors, farmers, natives, women and children, who were all shocked and deeply moved at the news that the great captive had at last escaped from his prison. Many of the visitors were in their working clothes. Some, who had come from long distances, were foul with dust and sweat, for the weather during all those days was fair and hot. [34] Captain Crokat was in charge of the procession which did not halt till nightfall. "They entered through the valet's hallway, passed on into the bathroom, then the dressing-room, and finally the bedroom, or mortuary chapel, where they stood for a few seconds. They left by the diningroom, the drawingroom and the billiardroom." [35] The officers of the 20th and the 66th came first, then the non-commissioned officers, then the privates and the crews from the ships, finally the civilian population. The crowd moved in deepest silence. Several brought flowers which they laid on the floor

[33] *The Statesman*, July 8, 1821.     [35] Aly, p. 288.
[34] Aly, p. 287.

in front of the bed: white arums, moon-flowers, hibiscuses. A soldier said to his little boy, whom he held by the hand:

"Take a good look at Napoleon. He is the greatest man in the world."

Some few knelt and made a sign of the cross over the Emperor's forehead.

That evening Crokat took his leave of the French. They presented him with a snuff box and a silver plate from the Emperor's service. Lowe was hurrying him off on the *Heron* to carry the news of Napoleon's death and the autopsy report to Lord Bathurst.[36]

The report was drawn up by Shortt and it angered the Governor. All the afternoon of the 6th, in fact, Plantation House was in feverish agitation on account of it. It declared that "the liver was perhaps a little larger than usual." That would be an argument for those who would see fit to claim that Napoleon had died of an affection of the liver caused by the climate. The Governor brought every pressure to bear on Shortt to make him modify the wording. Finally, at the end of his patience, the doctor recopied his report and suppressed the incriminating words. The first official statement had been signed by Shortt, Burton, Mitchell and Arnott. The second was signed by Livingstone also. That was the report that Lowe sent to Lord Bathurst. Antommarchi refused to sign it,[37] not that he disapproved of it in its spirit or wording, but because the text had not been submitted to him first.[38] It seems that Bertrand persuaded Antommarchi not to sign because the Emperor was designated as "Napoleon Bonaparte." [39]

"Two or three attendants" watched at the bier with Assistant-Surgeon Rutledge. The next morning (the 7th), Father Vignali said Mass, then the procession of inhabitants began again and lasted several hours. It was interrupted for the taking of the death mask which, owing to the condition of the body, could no longer be deferred.

Dr. Burton had not been able to procure any plaster-of-Paris in

[36] Crokat reached England on July 4. He was at once promoted to the rank of Major and given a reward of 300 pounds.

[37] The first draught has been re-discovered among Shortt's papers, the phrase relating to the liver being scratched out, with this note: "The words obliterated were suppressed by the order of Sir Hudson Lowe. Thomas Shortt." (N. Young, *Op. cit.*, p. 235.)

[38] Antommarchi, Vol. II, p. 170 (Lowe Papers, 20-133).

[39] Burton to Goulburn, August 13, 1821.

Jamestown on the 6th. That was the only substance suitable for the operation in question. An ensign told him, however, that gypsum crystals could be found on George Island, a rock situated to the south-east of St. Helena. That night, Burton manned a longboat with a few sailors and ran out to the reef in a dangerous sea. He collected as much gypsum as he could by torchlight and hurried back again to town, roasted it and crushed it very skilfully, so that he had a grey clay-like plaster in sufficient quantity to serve, better than nothing, for the moulding required. He lost no time in carrying it to Longwood.

Actually some attempts had already been made to take a likeness of the Emperor. Arnott made a first effort, using candle wax. That, it seems, was during the night of the 5th-6th while he was guarding the body with Vignali and Pierron.[40] Antommarchi seems then to have tried, at Mme. Bertrand's request, with a poor plaster that he managed to scrape together at Longwood. The material was too porous, however, and he gave it up. Finally, on the night of the 6th-7th, the attendants guarding the body must have used their ingenuity secretly to obtain an imprint with some silk paper soaked in whitewash.[41] This mask was, he said, "in Italy, at Count Pasolini's." Marchand does not speak of these various attempts. He confines himself to repeating the official version—untrue—of the cast taken by Antommarchi on the 7th with the help of Burton. We attach no importance at all to the "Sankey mask," so-called, brought back from St. Helena in 1830 by the Reverend Boys. That seems to be merely a retouched replica of the so-called Antommarchi mask.

By the time Burton arrived, the Emperor had been dead forty hours and decomposition had set in. The facial muscles had sagged, bringing the bones of the face into prominence. The protruding cheekbones, the pinched nose, the lips half opened over the white teeth, the fallen chin, lent him a distant, tragic aspect.

At sight of the powder Burton had obtained, Antommarchi expostulated. It was useless, he declared, to attempt a new cast. Mme. Bertrand urging, Burton replied that he would try nevertheless.[42]

[40] That, we believe, is the mask which, after a series of romantic adventures, is today in the possession of Mr. and Mrs. Alfred Day Pardee.

[41] And not papier-mâché, as Masson writes, *Autour de Sainte Hélène*, p. 141.

[42] Burton to Mme. Bertrand, May 22, 1821; another letter from the same, published in the *Courier*, September 10, 1821; Lowe to Bathurst, June 13, 1821 (Lowe Papers, 20-140).

The Emperor's collar was opened at the throat. Noverraz shaved him again—for his beard had grown in the two days—and cut his hair on the forehead and at the sides. Burton first covered the face with plaster. The experiment proved successful. After taking off the first mould, Burton cast the back of the head, while Archambault held it up. This time Antommarchi aided his English colleague. Lt. Duncan Darroch, of the 20th, entered the mortuary chapel at that moment. He wrote his mother a letter [43] in which he said: "I went in once again when they were taking the cast of the head, but the stench was so horrible that I could not remain. Dr. Burton was taking it with the French doctors."

The skin was peeling off in places and it was found impossible to renew the operation.

It is curious that no one thought of taking a cast of the beautiful hands, which would have been so much easier.

The Emperor's clothing was readjusted. The weather was very warm. To protect the body from the flies that gathered in swarms about it, the face was covered with mosquito netting.

The body now had to be placed in its coffin without further delay. "The second day," writes Aly (p. 290), "the body was so far gone that in the afternoon it was in a state of complete putrefaction." Three coffins arrived in the course of the evening, the first of tin, the second of mahogany, the third of lead. The first coffin was built by the sergeant-armourer, A. Mellington, the second by Metcalfe, a cabinet-maker who had often worked at Longwood.

Napoleon's body was lowered by the domestics into the first coffin under the supervision of Assistant-Surgeon Rutledge. Rutledge and Arnott, working in relays, had not left the body at any time. Rutledge especially guarded the heart and the stomach, which Lowe was afraid might be carried off.

"I was directed by Sir Thomas Reade . . . ," he wrote, "not to lose sight of either the body or the vase, *to take care and not to admit of the cavities being opened a second time for the purpose of removal of any part of the body*." Those precautions were due to Mme. Bertrand's tireless solicitations. In deference to the Emperor's express desire she wanted to take them back to Europe. Antommarchi likewise insisted upon keeping the stomach, "in order," he said, "to be able to prove to Napoleon's relatives and friends that his death was

[43] It was published in 1904 in the *Lancashire Fusiliers' Annual* (12).

the result of an incurable malady and that no blame could be attached to him for the failure of his treatment." [44]

The bottom and sides of the coffin were lined with white satin. The head rested on a pillow of the same material.[45] The coffin proved to be too short, so the hat had to be removed. It was placed in the coffin on the thighs. In spite of all urging, Lowe refused to allow Napoleon's viscera to be carried to Europe as he desired. Rutledge therefore enclosed the heart in a round silver sponge box, borrowed from the Emperor's smaller dressing case. He filled it with brandy and sealed it by soldering a shilling to the lid. The stomach was placed in a silver pepper-box "without any means of preventing the putrefactive process." [46] The two "urns" were deposited in the coffin with a sauce-boat, a plate, a silver knife, fork and spoon engraved with the Imperial coat-of-arms, six double napoleons, four napoleons, a French silver coin and two Italian double napoleons.[47] Rutledge also slipped in a plate on which he had scratched his name "as being the last British officer who had ever seen" the deceased.

The French gathered around the coffin. Just as the plumber started to fasten on the lid, Bertrand grasped the Emperor's left hand and pressed it in his own.

The coffin was slid into the mahogany box, and then both into the lead casket. The whole was then set on trestles, inside the bed, from which the mattress and webbing had been removed. Over the triple bier, twice soldered—Lowe could be very sure that Napoleon would never escape from it—they spread the cloak of Marengo. During the night of the 7th, the Emperor was watched by his domestics only. They passed half the time, says Aly (p. 292), "walking up and down along the little path that ran under the bedroom windows and along the study, and half the time seated indoors, giving themselves over to all sorts of reflections." Arnott and Rutledge returned to their quarters at Deadwood.

[44] Lowe Papers, 20-133.

[45] It has been said that Napoleon was buried, by oversight, in a sheet bearing the crest of Louis XVIII. There may well have been sheets at Longwood that belonged to the King—such articles were gathered together hastily at the time of the departure from the Tuileries. But the Emperor did not wear a shroud. The burial report testifies to that.

[46] Rutledge, *Report* (Lowe Papers, 20-133). Antommarchi claims that he took these precautions (Vol. II, p. 170). His statement cannot stand. The English did not trust him and would not have permitted it. Rutledge's report is conclusive.

[47] Official burial report; and see Montholon, Vol. II, p. 56; Aly, p. 291; and Rutledge's *Report*.

The following day, May 8th, Vignali celebrated the requiem. It was attended by the French and by a few English Catholics. A fourth coffin of mahogany, which had not been finished the evening before, had now come. The three others were encased in it and the lid fastened down with silver screws. Visitors were once more admitted and all who had been unable to see the Emperor on his deathbed approached and—whatever their faith—sprinkled the coffin with Holy Water.

.      .      .      .      .

The mould of the mask, in two pieces, was left to dry on the mantelpiece in the drawingroom. Burton went back to the camp at Deadwood to be gone until the 9th, the day of the obsequies. He did not find the mask of the face again. With the complicity of Antommarchi, Mme. Bertrand had whisked it away and, in spite of Burton's vehement demands for it, he was left with the imprint of the skull and the back of the neck.[48] Lowe wrote to Bathurst, June 13, 1821: "Dr. Burton has not been very well used by Count and Countess Bertrand. They wished to have a cast of General Bonaparte's head in plaster-of-Paris. Professor Antommarchi undertook to have it done, but could not succeed. Dr. Burton by a happy combination of skill and patience succeeded, though with very indifferent materials, in obtaining an almost perfect cast. The Bertrands have kept the face. Dr. Burton has preserved the back of the skull or craniological part." [49] *

[48] Burton to Mme. Bertrand, May 22, 1821.
* Young, Vol. II, p. 247.
[49] The cast was carried away by Mme. Bertrand in her luggage and was never to be returned to Burton despite his protests and even the legal action that he brought on his return to England. Two or three copies were made from it under Antommarchi's direction. The first was given to Mme. Bertrand. Her daughter, Hortense, inherited it and bequeathed it to Prince Napoleon. It appears today in the collection at Brussels. Antommarchi kept one, doubtless the better. Burton died of a pleurisy in 1828. That safeguarded Antommarchi against any claim. In 1833 he used Burton's model for casting the various copies of the mask that have since been made, and notably the plaster and bronze editions that were sold to the public by subscription. The Antommarchi copy was bought in 1841 by Prince Demidoff, husband of the Princess Mathilda, and enclosed by him in a perfect miniature of the coffin of the "Return of the Ashes." It passed after his death into Lord Rosebery's collection and is at present in the possession of the author, who intends to present it to the Invalides.
What became of Burton's original mask? That is not known. Was it broken up after the drawing of the first copies? That is Masson's opinion. Did Antommarchi take it to America? In any case all trace of it seems to be lost. As for the cast of the neck, it should still be in England in the possession of Burton's heirs.

THE DEATH-MASK OF NAPOLEON

Formerly owned by Prince Demidoff and Lord Rosebery. Now in the possession of the
Author who intends to present it to the Invalides

THE BARN. PRESENTING THE DEATH-MASK OF NAPOLEON

Cynical wranglings! Burton had acquired no rights in the cast just because he had taken it. Napoleon's mask could belong only to his family or to France. But Antommarchi and Mme. Bertrand behaved very badly towards the English doctor. Later on they failed to give him so much as a copy of the precious souvenir which, without him, would not have existed.

Astonishment has sometimes been expressed at the relative small-ness of the Emperor's death mask, and to discredit its genuineness capital has been made of the fact that its dimensions do not corre-spond to the measurements that Antommarchi took on the corpse. That discrepancy is due merely to the fact of the double shrinkage that has reduced proportions by about a sixth—first the shrinkage of the plaster used in making the original—a twelfth, about; then the shrinkage of the plaster which was run into that mould to make a copy—another twelfth. The Emperor's head was larger than normal and, as the English physicians remarked, "almost disproportioned to the rest of the body."

That imprint, obtained so tardily by a nondescript Englishman with such inadequate materials, may nevertheless satisfy our wish to greet the features of the Exile with our eyes. But for the traveller there is another mask much more worthy of Napoleon, and by a strange miracle it is St. Helena itself that offers it—it was St. Helena that secreted it. Were the imaginations of the French in those days struck by the shape of the Barn, the bronze-coloured mountain that bounds the plateau of Deadwood to the east? We do not know. Their memoirs make no mention of it. The first Frenchman to note the resemblance was Emmanuel de Las Cases in his *Diary Aboard the "Belle-Poule"* written in 1840. But that mountain enlarges Na-poleon's effigy on a measureless scale. So exact, so terrible is the re-semblance that it stops the beating of one's heart. A gigantic figure-head, the face turned towards the southern sea, the eyes closed, the mouth half opened in a faint smile. Above the forehead the cocked hat bulges! The immense neck—nothing is so long as the neck of a dead man—plunges into the ocean that decks it eternally with bands of foam. Just as the Emperor looked on his little bed, the evening of May 5th, so he is there, forever, sculptured at the dawn of the world through the volcano's action, the inexorable wind, and the rain. Even the driest soul might tremble at the thought that from his first days at Longwood he may have recognized himself in it and seen on that massive pillow of rock the face he was to wear in death!

.     .     .     .     .     .     .     .

Work had been begun on a tomb on May 6th and it was completed in the course of that day. At Montholon's request, Lowe had the grave dug in the Vale of the Geranium, which Napoleon had designated, in the worst case, for his interment.[50]

A sort of huge basin was dug in the clay near the two willows that mingled their long fronds, and not far from the spring that had supplied the Emperor with water for five years. It was heavily lined inside with masonry, the sides to a thickness of two feet, while the bottom took eight stones a foot thick—a veritable funeral prison that would defy any attempt at a rescue! It was twelve feet deep, eight long and five wide. On the lining was built a sort of sarcophagus of Portland cement—"a trough," says Aly (p. 296), which was to hold the coffin. A huge stone was to close it. The mound of earth that was to be thrown over it was to be covered again by three other slabs eight feet long by four feet wide and five inches thick. They were taken from the kitchen floor at New Longwood. The work was done by soldiers of the Corps of Engineers, under the direction of Major Emmet.[51] The *Courier* of July 9th was to write: "All precautions have been taken so that the body cannot be carried off. We are assured that these precautions are the result of a common agreement that was arrived at between the French Commissioner and the English authorities on the island."

Like the coffin, the tomb was not to receive a name. Montholon requested that the following be inscribed on it in French:

NAPOLEON

Born at Ajaccio, August 15, 1769,
Died at St. Helena, May 5, 1821

Lowe insisted that "Bonaparte" be added. That he should have quarrelled with his prisoner's last friends at such a moment for the right to draw up an epitaph shows the character of the man and

---

[50] The land belonged to Mr. Torbett, who received 650 pounds from the colony "for the damage caused to his property," and 50 pounds a year so long as Napoleon's body should remain there. In 1826 the damages were liquidated at a sum of 1,200 pounds *in toto* (Jamestown Archives, 1824-26).

[51] Lowe Papers, 20-133.

NAPOLEON'S TOMB IN THE VALE OF THE GERANIUM

condemns him. Farsighted as Bathurst had been, he had not foreseen that question. The French decided therefore to leave the stone bare. It was better so. Napoleon had no need of a few letters on a slab for the world to remember him.

On the 8th, Bertrand, Montholon and Marchand took an inventory of the furniture, the wardrobe, the library and the ready cash found in the Emperor's boxes. The cash reached a total of 327,833.20 [52] francs.

On the same day Lowe sent the following invitation to Montchenu: "Sir, I do myself the honour to inform you that the remains of Napoleon Bonaparte will be interred with the honours due to a General officer of the highest rank at 12 o'clock tomorrow, at a particular spot in the valley, between the Alarm House and Longwood, where I have been made acquainted it was his desire to be buried, if his body should be interred in this island." [53]

.        .        .        .        .        .

The morning of May 9th, Father Vignali officiated for the last time before the Emperor's bier. The Governor and the Admiral accompanied by their staffs, Montchenu, Gors and the notables of the island, all clad in mourning, waited on the lawn in front of the verandah till it was over. All the troops in St. Helena had been under arms since break of day.

At noon twelve grenadiers from the 20th entered the mortuary chapel. They lifted the heavy coffin with great difficulty to their shoulders and then proceeded through the billiardroom, descended, with unsteady tread, the short flight of steps to the crêped hearse drawn by four horses which was standing in the broad drive. The hearse was the chassis of the Emperor's old barouche. The seats had been taken out and a flat roof built on top.[54] The soldiers deposited their burden on it. The multiple caskets were covered with a cloth of violet-coloured velvet and the military cloak of Marengo on which Bertrand placed his sword.

The cortège began to move, with Father Vignali in front in his vestments, attended by Henri Bertrand, who carried the holy-water basin and the aspersory. Just as the cortège was forming a "lively dispute," says Aly (p. 292), took place between Montholon and Vignali

[52] Montholon, Vol. II, p. 563.
[53] Lowe Papers, 20-133. Unpublished.
[54] The hearse thus improvised was presented to France by Queen Victoria and is now in the Church of the Invalides.

who, according to usage, had put on only his stole. Montholon insisted that he also put on the chasuble. After protesting Vignali finally complied. Next after them came Antommarchi and Arnott. Then came the hearse, the horses driven at a walk by soldiers riding as postillons. Six grenadiers marched on either side. The corners of the funeral-pall were held in front by Marchand and Napoleon Bertrand, and behind by the Grand Marshal and Montholon, both in full dress uniform. After them came the Emperor's favourite horse, Sheick, led by Archambault, then the personnel of Longwood and, in the phaeton driven by her servants, Mme. Bertrand with Hortense and Arthur. Then came a double file of midshipmen from the fleet, then the Governor, the Admiral, the General, the Commissioner from France and Austria, and a large number of officers on horseback.[55] The entire garrison of the island, about three thousand strong, with arms reversed and their bands at intervals playing a solemn music formed a hedge on the left side of the route in the direction of Hutt's Gate. The music had been composed specially for the occasion by Lieutenant MacCarthy of the 66th Infantry.[56] The regimental flags flapped in the wind, but they bore, in letters of gold, ill-omened names: Minden, Talavera, Albufera, Orthez.[57] When the hearse and all the notables had passed the soldiers fell in, two by two, behind. A gun on the *Vigo*, that lay at anchor in the harbour, boomed every two minutes. A battery of fifteen guns, stationed at Hutt's Gate above the road, replied.

In a beautiful sunlight, slowly, the cortège followed the winding path around the black Punch Bowl that Napoleon had so often trod in the first months of the Captivity on his way to see Bertrand. In those days he had still been filled with illusions and hopes. He did not believe that St. Helena would hold him long. In the distance the almost perfect ring of the sea closed the horizon. On all the slopes, on the edges of the raised precipices, on the tops of the rocks, between the aloes and the cactuses, at times even up in the trees, Chinamen in blue jackets, half-naked negroes, Hindus in turbans, half-breeds in their cotton clothes, the entire population of the island, watched

[55] The order of the procession has been faithfully described by Marryat in an etching that has often been reproduced. He made but one mistake—placing Bertrand and Montholon behind the Emperor's horse, whereas they carried the corners of the pall (Aly, p. 293).

[56] Lowe Papers, 20-133.

[57] Henry, *Events of a Military Life*, Vol. II, p. 85.

the funeral procession of the mysterious and formidable man of whom all of them had talked so much but whom the majority of them had never seen.[58] All that pomp, the most sumptuous that could be found on the little Atlantic isle, was poor indeed for Napoleon. It was not, at least, insulting. He went to his last rest amid a martial clanguor and a universal respect. Many hearts were heavy, many a face was wet with tears. Enemies, indifferent people, poor men in black or yellow skins, were all very certain that someone immensely "big" had just died.

At the turn at Hutt's Gate, Lady Lowe and Miss Johnson, dressed in mourning, were waiting in a barouche. They joined the cortège. "The deepest emotion was evident on their features," writes Aly, p. 295. "Their cheeks were wet with tears." A quarter of a mile farther along there came a halt. The troops drew up in battle line above the highway. Twenty-four grenadiers, selected from all the regiments in St. Helena, took turns in relays, eight by eight, in carrying the coffin down the steep path which the engineers had improvised in the ravine during those three days. The mourners had all left their carriages or dismounted from their horses. Officers, women, natives, children, followed in no particular order. Arriving at the tomb, which was draped in black, they massed in silence in the little dale.

The coffin was set down near the open grave. Bertrand took the sword and Montholon the velvet pall. Three volleys of musketry rang out, the sound re-echoing among the hills. Guns on the fleet and at the harbour forts boomed as Father Vignali recited the last prayers. Lowe asked the Grand Marshal and Montholon whether they wished to say a few words. They declined. Then a tripod derrick lifted the enormous coffin and let it down into the vault. A great slab was then lowered upon the opening and carefully cemented.[59] Up on the road the companies of soldiers had re-formed and were already marching back to their quarters. The music from their fifes faded in the distance. That melancholy music, born on the heaths of the North, had reached the Emperor's ears in his little bedroom to his dying day, piping retreat from the camp at Deadwood.

The French gathered a few willow branches and turned back towards Longwood. Thereupon the crowds of spectators flung themselves on the trees and stripped them bare. Everyone wanted a branch.

[58] *The Courier,* July 9.
[59] Aly, p. 297; Montholon, Vol. II, p. 564.

Lowe did not like that. He at once gave orders that a fence be put up to cut off access to the dale and that a guard of twelve men, commanded by an officer, should be stationed there permanently. Sheltered in a sentry-box, a soldier mounted guard over the Emperor as if he had been alive.[60]

The Emperor's end left but feeble traces in the Jamestown Archives. *Register*, 1821:

"Saturday, the 5th, General Napoleon Buonaparte died."

On the line above one reads:

"Thursday, the 3rd, the *Waterloo* arrived from England."

On the line after:

"Monday, the 7th, the *Heron* set sail for England." *

On the other hand the Reverend Boys actually inscribed Napoleon's title on the burial record of his parish. On the sheet for May, 1821, one finds:

"7th. Edmond Howes, resident.

"9th. Napoleon Buonaparte, former Emperor of France. He died the 5th current in the old Longwood house and has been buried on the property of Mr. Richard Torbett.

"Same day. Maria Mills, widow of Major Mills, of the Artillery of St. Helena." *

Intolerant, but punctilious and a passionate lover of justice, Boys disapproved of Lowe's conduct towards Napoleon. It was not so much that he pitied the Captive. He condemned the jailor. Shortly afterwards, addressing Lowe and the authorities of the island in a sermon, he hurled at them from the pulpit:

"Verily, I say unto you, publicans and whores shall enter before you into the Kingdom of Heaven!"

. . . . . . .

Back again at Longwood, the French found themselves completely at sea. In spite of their sincere grief, at the bottom of their hearts they had experienced a first moment of relief. The death of the Emperor was opening France to them again. They could at last think of themselves. They could see their families once more. They were free. But they had lived too long by their master, in his atmosphere, in the thought of him. For too many years they had been absorbed in his

---

[60] Lowe to Bathurst, May 14, 1821 (Lowe Papers, 20-133).
* Retranslated.

person. Their minds, their hearts, had gravitated around Napoleon. Now that he was gone, they felt useless, deserted, empty. His death had made them orphans. They wandered about through rooms that were still filled with his presence, or through the gardens that he had loved. "They stopped at the spots that he had most frequented, the places where he was wont to rest, as if they thought they could actually see him." [61] Accustomed to speaking in low tones so as not to disturb his sleep, his work, or his meditations, they had forgotten how to raise their voices.

With the house set in order again, Montholon busied himself with drawing up the burial certificate, which Bertrand and Marchand signed. The next day Lowe sent word that he had orders to take an inventory of Napoleon's effects. The French were expecting that. He came accompanied by Lady Lowe, who courteously asked that she be permitted to see the apartments in which the Emperor had lived. All his things—his clothing, linen, arms, silver, table-services— had been laid out in the drawingroom. Attended by Reade and Gorrequer, the Governor examined them. The mahogany boxes which the Emperor had sealed were opened and he inspected the contents. He admired the Sèvres service, the dressing cases and, among the snuff boxes, the one that the Emperor had bequeathed to Lady Holland. Bertrand and Montholon showed whatever papers of the Emperor's they chose: notes on his campaigns, memoranda in his own hand, pieces of paper on which he had pencilled notes as to books he should read for his work.[62] Finally they disclosed the contents of the first codicil and the pertinent inventories. That was the codicil that divided everything the Emperor had at St. Helena between his three executors. Lowe authorized them to proceed with the provisory execution of the Emperor's arrangements subject to ratification by his government.[63]

Meanwhile Lady Lowe was visiting the rooms where the Emperor had lived. She was astonished at their wretchedness. As long as Napoleon had been alive, his presence had somehow distracted attention from the narrow walls and the cheap furniture. Now the poverty of Longwood came out to meet the eye.

Whatever may have been written on the subject, Lowe at that time

[61] Aly, pp. 297-298.
[62] Aly, p. 299; Lowe Papers, 20-133.
[63] Official statement of May 12, 1821; Montholon, Vol. II, p. 515.

was conciliatory. He was well aware that he was being shown merely a façade and that many things were escaping his auditing. He shut his eyes to the fact and did not ask to see the will. Moreover he himself was among the first to be affected by Napoleon's death. With his prisoner he had lost his crushing responsibility, it is true, but he had also lost his post, his fat and pleasant vice-royalty, that had flattered his pride and his love of authority and which, for five years, had enabled him to lead a princely existence. He would be going away like the French. What position would he find at home? What command would be offered him! He too was all at sea.

Perhaps, also—though he was perfectly sure he had done his duty to his country—his conscience felt a vague but painful twinge, something akin to remorse. He had always refused to believe in Napoleon's illness and Napoleon had died after a long and harrowing agony. He did not believe that the climate or the confinement had contributed in any respect to his death—the autopsy, he thought, had proved that. But Napoleon had died too young, he had died too soon. One of these days Lowe would assuredly be blamed for that untimely demise. Napoleon's partisans would call his severity a crime. That certainly was not the moment to add to the indictment by a useless inquisition, by too offensive an attitude towards people who, in a few days now, would be escaping his surveillance and thereafter be free to talk and write against him.

Softened, on his own side, he was even more inclined towards complaisance by the new attitude of the French—their considerateness, their effusiveness, their manifest desire to defer to him. Mme. Bertrand told Admiral Lambert that Napoleon had advised the Grand Marshal to make peace with the Governor.[64] Was that true?[65] Were not the Bertrands, as well as Montholon, eager above all else to hasten their departure from St. Helena and make their residence in England, once they had landed there, easier by coming to terms with Lowe? In any case he hastened to correspond to their outstretched hands. He sent Reade to tell Mme. Bertrand, "that he was very sensible

[64] Lambert to Sir Hudson Lowe, no date, but probably May 10. (Lowe Papers, 20-133; Young, Vol. II, p. 256.) Lowe informed Bathurst on May 15 of this conciliatory attitude.
[65] In the notes he left on his final interviews with the Emperor, Bertrand does not make the slightest allusion to any such thing. Napoleon's legacy to Cantillon did not betray any particularly forgiving attitude in him.

of the disposition shown by Count Bertrand to forget the past, and that his inclination was precisely the same." [66] The next day Bertrand and Montholon appeared at Plantation House for an official visit. Lowe returned their politeness without delay. After that there were luncheons and dinners at the Governor's, in company with persons of prominence in the colony. There were two evening parties, even, that were very gay. It is hard to imagine that only a few days after the Emperor's death his last companions could be showing such thoughtless levity. [67]

Of the Commissioner from the King of France, they hoped for even greater services and behaved towards him in the very same manner. Montholon did not stop at lathering Montchenu with flatteries in his usual way. He made confidences to him that were a compound of falsehood and conceit—his joy at being Napoleon's chief heir, his dislike of the Bertrands, his eagerness to find favour with Louis XVIII, in view of his return to France. It was one scaffolding of cajoleries. He invented a tale that two or three days before his death Napoleon had had him burn no end of papers concerning France. The Emperor was represented as saying at that time: "You have written it all out, so you must remember everything that was in them. You and I are too French to be willing to have foreigners sticking their noses into our affairs. What I have confided to you can be told only to the King, or to my son."

Napoleon never talked like that. It is pure Montholon. He was putting himself at the King's disposal! But Montchenu was blinded by attentions that were being showered upon him—he had been invited to luncheon at Longwood. [68] He believed it all, and in his report to the Tuileries he pleaded earnestly for the companions of the Usurper. "I see nothing to prevent Mme. Bertrand's return to France," he wrote. "She is not an intriguer. She is more interested in fashion and coquetry than in politics. She is in bad health, moreover, and like myself is so greatly changed that one would hardly recognize her. She is not a person to be feared. As for her husband, that is another matter. He is a very hot-headed person who might have been dangerous during the lifetime of Buonaparte. But he has been so much

[66] Lowe to Reade, May 11 (Lowe Papers, 20-133. Retranslated). "He added, nevertheless, that he could not take the first step, being Governor of the island."
[67] Henry, *Events of a Military Life*, Vol. II, p. 86.
[68] May 22 (Lowe Papers, 20-133).

abused, and, especially during these last three months, he has swallowed so many humiliations, that he is sore all over from it. I think besides that he is very much disappointed and especially very ill-satisfied. He is at no pains to hide it."

Montchenu pleaded in particular for Montholon. "He is a man of great intelligence," he wrote. "He has important materials in his possession, and I could not swear that he might not make very bad use of them. As he says he has a huge fortune, I think he is a man to be nursed. It would, moreover, be easier to watch him (him and his wife—she is a very different sort of person) in France than abroad." And he added:

"At any rate, they are all delighted at what has happened. It frees them from a great slavery and they will be able to say, moreover, that they stuck to him to the very last."

There is the same remark in Lowe's letter to Bathurst, under date of May 15: "They [Bertrand and Montholon] appear not greatly depressed at the event which has taken place and have some motive for consolation at it, in the very large fortunes, as it is supposed, to which they will succeed by it." [69]

That was true. The first shock over, life caught them up again in its whirl. They could think of nothing except preparations for their departure. On the 14th the executors divided the Emperor's effects, manuscripts, books, and money. Montholon drew up the statement and it was signed by Bertrand and Marchand. [70] The manuscripts that were to be published in Europe were divided between the two generals—Bertrand took Egypt, Montholon Italy and the Consulat. Back in France Montholon was to give the Consulat to Gourgaud, and Marchand was to receive from Bertrand, but later on, the *Abstract of Caesar's Campaigns*. Everyone was wrapping, packing, nailing, with an enthusiasm born of physical exuberance. Everything was to be taken away—even the muslin curtains in the Emperor's rooms—even his funeral draperies. All of which prompted Montchenu to write with his usual wit: "They are carrying off the Imperial cloak, all his old uniforms and worn shoes—probably to work as many miracles with them as Deacon Paris [a celebrated "convulsionist" and miracle worker of the Jansenist cult, d. 1727]." Al-

[69] Lowe Papers, 20-133. Retranslated.
[70] Montholon, Vol. II, p. 566.

most every day some of them visited the Tomb [71] and Mme. Bertrand planted it with geraniums, pansies and tuberoses. But they were all in a hurry to get away and they besieged Lowe to put a ship at their disposal. Mme. Bertrand began to worry about the boat she was going to take even before Napoleon was buried.[72]

A freighter, the *Camel*, touched at Jamestown on the 10th, on its way home from the Cape. It was to sail two weeks later for Europe. The Governor arranged that they should sail on her.

Longwood had already taken on the aspect of a deserted house. The books were gone from the shelves, the papers from the tables, the picture-frames from the walls. Lowe had ordered that all books that he had himself supplied should be restored to him.[73] The rooms echoed cruelly under one's footstep. They were bare of everything except the furniture. That was the property of the English government—Darling, the upholsterer, made a detailed inventory of it. That inventory was taken on May 12, 15, and 25, 1821. It now reposes in the Jamestown Archives. It comprises the furnishings of Old Longwood, of New House, and of the cottage occupied by the Bertrands. The Emperor's companions were authorized to take with them only those articles that had come from France—except for the piano, which Napoleon had given to Mme. Bertrand and which she claimed.[74]

While awaiting a public auction the furniture remained *in situ*, except articles that Lowe selected for his own use and which were appraised by Darling at a value of 352 pounds 15 shillings.[75] They were sent to Plantation House. The Governor acquired enough furniture and other things in this way to fill eleven huge cases. On leaving the island he was unable to carry everything with him, and ordered

[71] Aly, p. 302.

[72] Croads to Lowe, May 9, 1821 (Lowe Papers, 20, 209).

[73] According to an inventory drawn up by Aly (Thiers Library, 21. Unpublished) the library at Longwood stood as follows on May 5, 1821:

"Books brought from France, 588 volumes; books sent from London for the Emperor by Wm. Holmes, 284; books sent by Lady Holland, 475; books brought by Father Buonavita, 108. Total: 1,465. Books belonging to the English government, first shipment, 1,663; second shipment, 252. Total, 1,915 volumes. Grand total, 3,370 volumes."

[74] Lowe Papers, 20-133.

[75] The auction was held at Jamestown the year following. It lasted nine days, scattered between April 1 and June 3. It grossed nearly 3,000 pounds (Lowe Papers, 20-229). The highest prices were brought by the billiard table (21 pounds), the Emperor's mahogany wardrobe (18 pounds), a dressing-table (25 pounds), and a group of mahogany stands (31 pounds). Mme. de Montholon's piano brought 33 pounds.

them to be sent on later to England. However the newly appointed Governor, General Walker, confiscated them to his own profit for the price indicated, and with the approval of two members of the Council of St. Helena, Brooke and Greentree, sent them to his own home in Scotland.

When Lowe learned of that operation, Lord Curzon relates,[76] he mobilized all his resources in the Colonial Office. After two years the question was settled by a letter from the India Company to the Colonial Office in favour of Lowe, but criticizing both Governors. Lowe then gave up his claims, save for a mahogany table and two bookcases, of which he intended to make a gift to his friend, General Coffin. Lord Curzon concludes that Hudson Lowe was within his rights. "But," he remarks, "he had a knack of doing the right thing in a very clumsy and irritating way."

．　　．　　．　　．　　．　　．　　．

On May 26th, the Bertrands, Montholon, Father Vignali, and all the servants—a "black little group"—left Longwood. With them they had Sambo, the Emperor's dog. Silently they reached the drive that led to the Guardhouse, now unoccupied, then the Hutt's Gate road that their feet had so often trod. At each turn they looked back for one more view of the unpretentious building on the plateau in front of the gum-tree forest, with its water-stained, wind-beaten roof. The window-panes glittered in the sunlight.

Rounding the Punch Bowl they went down for one last visit to the Emperor's tomb. Lowe had had an iron fence put around it—those same grilles that had been intended for New House and had annoyed the Emperor so much. Not having served for his prison, the fence was now serving at his grave! Around it they arranged bouquets of the flowers he had liked best: immortelles from Marchand's garden, passion flowers from the arbour, pansies, violets. There the air was calm and clear. A few pines, some yellowing oaks, the willows, made it look like some dell in France. A picket of soldiers presented arms. But the real sentinel there, the one that struck the eye, was the sea. The eternal companion of the Islander, it lifted a wall of cobalt and silver to the level of vision, between hills that were the colour of faded rose. One seemed to be at the bottom of a bowl, or a crater crowned by waves—one had to look upward to recover the freedom

76 *Note Book*, p. 399.

of the sky. Father Vignali blessed the slabs once more. Mme. Bertrand and her children knelt in prayer, their faces pale. The Grand Marshal then put on his hat and took to the path again, followed by the others.

Beyond Alarm House they looked back again at Longwood across the chasm that now lay between it and them. Descending the hill in zigzags they passed the happy terraces of The Briars. There too they halted. The pavilion where Napoleon had lived was open, and from it came sounds of children's voices. The cascade was swollen by recent rains and was falling in a roar from its heart-shaped rock. Marchand and Aly sighed. They had been the closest to the Emperor's life in those first months at The Briars.

The French had expected to leave that same day. But they had too much luggage, and it was too heavy. It could not all be stowed away.[77] The domestics were put aboard the *Camel* that first night, but Lowe invited the Bertrands, Montholon, the Abbé, and Antommarchi to Plantation House. The dinner was brilliant, "magnificent." The Governor and Lady Lowe could not have been more gracious or more attentive. Lowe pushed his obligingness to the point of lending Montholon a thousand pounds to settle debts he had contracted at Jamestown. His creditors were unwilling to let him leave until they had been paid.[78]

The next day the Lowes drove their guests to the dock. Montchenu too was waiting there with Gors. He asked permission to kiss Mme. Bertrand. Though his mission was over he was not sailing with his countrymen. The *Camel*, for one thing, struck him as too uncomfortable, but then too he was not eager to seem to be on too intimate terms with Napoleon's suite in the eyes of his Court at the moment when he expected to claim his reward of it. All the notables of the island, from the Reverend Boys down to the good Miss Mason, who had ridden into town from her cottage, waved farewell to the French as they entered the tenders and pushed off. To the island, their departure, with the diminution of the garrison that it implied, was a catastrophe. They had never won any love, but they were carrying away many regrets.

The *Camel* was a horrible vessel, unsteady, too narrow of beam, and filthy beyond words. She served ordinarily as a cattle boat. The

[77] Antommarchi, Vol. II, p. 180.
[78] Henry, Vol. II, p. 87.

exiles were disappointed when they went aboard, but the joy of returning home inclined them to overlook everything. At three o'clock, the wind rose and the captain made sail.[79] Until twilight the French leaned over the rail, watching the black cliffs that had shut in six of their years recede and fade in the distance. Jamestown, the Castle, the houses, the church, were first lost to view. But for a long time, to the right they could see the forbidding outline of High Knoll and in front of them the white dot of Alarm House overlooking the ravine where they were leaving Napoleon. Probably, they thought, they would never come back again, never again see the green dell where the greatest of warriors, after such a din of glory, had crept into the shelter of a boundless peace. Sated with injustice, weary of the fear and the admiration of men, there he would turn to dust, guarded by the ocean, by solitude, by silence, fit attendants for his greatness. About his heavily sealed tomb, in the hollow of that gentle valley, there would be no more hatred, just as there was no more wind. The faint trickle of the spring, the babble of the brook that ran from it behind a bronze shield of arum leaves, the songs of the birds—those great black and white thrushes that came from India and perched on the horns of the oxen as they swayed along, and those Javanese sparrows with their ash-coloured plumage and their white collar that looked like little Grey Sisters—those would be the only sounds to soothe the slumbers of the victor of Arcole, and the vanquished of Waterloo.

They could not tear their eyes from the huge pile of rocks that was sinking little by little into the waves. But night came on. St. Helena was now nothing but a shadow among shadows. The eye had to strain to pick it out. Then suddenly night, a black, starless, tropical night, swallowed it up.

[79] Aly, p. 303.

# II

## *THE GOSPEL OF ST. HELENA*

IT WAS SLOW SAILING. THE "CAMEL" WAS CLUTTERED WITH SOLDIERS whom Lowe was sending back to Europe. She rolled along the African coast under scorching winds that parched her sails. Mme. Bertrand almost never left her cabin, where she was suffering not only from seasickness, but from dysentery.

By a heart-breaking irony, while the Emperor's companions were making their way home, the people whom Mme. de Montholon had persuaded, after many efforts, to share the Emperor's exile, were preparing to set out for St. Helena. She, first of all, had resolved to return there with her children. She feared lest Montholon, too unhappy in his loneliness, might impulsively come to rejoin her, so losing the royalties on his devotion. Besides, she had found in France, it seems, social disappointments, and money difficulties which she had not been expecting. The death of her little daughter saddened her. At a distance St. Helena seemed less hateful. But also, as a woman of good sense, she saw the infinite moral advantage it would be for her and her husband to be present at Napoleon's death-bed, if, as she thought, his illness was beyond help.

Planat had finally triumphed over Fesch's ill-will and was to accompany her. Dr. Pelletan, the younger, family physician to the king, would replace Antommarchi. Pelletan had been designated by Desgenettes with the consent of the French ministry, which now, by a very marked change of front, was thinking of surrounding Napoleon's captivity with a decorative society. When Monsignor de Quelen, Bishop-coadjutor of Paris, was consulted by the Minister of Foreign Affairs on the choice of a priest, he had replied generously:

"I shall go myself. I should gladly offer my services in order to win that soul for God."

The Minister having reminded him of the advanced age of the Archbishop, whom he would undoubtedly soon be called upon to succeed, Monsignor de Quelen designated Father Deguerry, a young priest of great merit, who was to make a name for himself. Finally Mme. de Montholon had found a teacher at the Juilly School to act as instructor to her children.

They were about to set sail when news of the Emperor's death reached France. After that there was nothing left for Mme. de Montholon to do but to await the return of her husband.

.        .        .        .        .        .        .

On July 25th the captain announced that the *Camel* was entering European waters. In deference to the Emperor's wish Montholon opened the will and the codicils. Bertrand was stupefied. His last conversations with Napoleon had led him, in spite of everything, to hope for a better share in the inheritance. The accounts were checked by the three executors. First came the funeral expenses (draperies, lights, mourning livery for the English servants, gratuities to the soldiers who carried the coffin, and so on), all of which were paid out of the Emperor's privy purse (England supplied nothing but the coffins). A sum of 18,060 francs was paid to Antommarchi, nominally as a gratuity, though some months of arrears in his salary may have figured in it.[1] When other bills were disposed of, including the amounts due the domestics, a sum of 145,000 francs remained to be divided in equal parts among the executors.

.        .        .        .        .        .        .

On August 2, 1821, the *Camel* dropped anchor before Spithead. The people from St. Helena were welcomed with curiosity and respect. George IV happened to be in those waters. He sent one of his officers aboard to enquire after Mme. Bertrand's health. Calls immediately poured in upon the vessel, where the French remained for three days. The same kind attentions continued in London, where the exiles were obliged to wait until all obstacles to their return to France were removed. In London the Bertrands settled first in Leicester Square, at Brunet's, then in a house on Edward Road. They were much sought after. On the other hand, Montholon, "with his officious airs," writes Lady Jermingham," was not liked by the English."

The sensation caused in England by the Captive's death had been profound. The newspapers had announced the event with unexceptionable good taste—the *Statesman* and *Courier* on July 4; the *Times*

---

[1] *Statement*, August 18, 1821.

on July 5; the *Gazette* on July 7. The *Sun* on July 5 reported, with disapproval, an incident that occurred just before the general meeting of the India Company. A certain Lowndes had dared to voice his satisfaction with the news. "The strongest marks of disapproval," wrote the reporter of the *Sun*, "were at once heard from all sides." On July 7th notices posted on the streets invited "all who admired talent and courage in adversity" to wear mourning for Napoleon— a point for English honour. Meantime government bonds went up, which goes to show how deeply the fear of "Boney" was rooted in English opinion.

In France, on the other hand, the news was received without any great emotion. If loyal supporters of the Emperor were struck with consternation, if young men wearing bands of crêpe on their arms assaulted a news-vender who was crying the death of Napoleon,[2] if old veterans, men of the people, shopkeepers, approached one another on the streets and shook hands with tears in their eyes, the public in the mass, sincerely supporting the monarchy, glad that peace and prosperity had returned, remained unmoved. The *Foudre* of July 20 said: "His death could now be nothing more than a piece of news like any other. People discussed it for two or three days the way one discusses the rain or the good weather. Today it has been quite forgotten." "I remember," the Countess de Boigne was to write, "how greatly the few of us who think a little were surprised at that strange indifference." The *Journal des Débats*, July 11, 1821, relates an anecdote which indicates the tone the ministerial newspapers were to take in regard to the event:

"General Rapp, being on duty with the King at Saint-Cloud, learned of the death of Bonaparte just as he was about to go to luncheon with His Majesty. The General could not at first believe what he had heard, but on being assured that the King had been apprised of it during the night, he could not restrain his tears and confessed aloud that the death of his old general, whom he had served as aide-de-camp for fifteen years, was a great blow to him. 'I am not an ingrate,' he said, and he withdrew at once to his own house. On being told of the General's loyal conduct the King sent for him after Mass and addressed him feelingly in the following terms: 'Rapp, I know that you are deeply grieved by the news I have

[2] *Gazette de France*, July 9.

received. That does honour to your heart. I like and respect you all the more for it.' General Rapp replied with great emotion: 'Sire, I owe everything to Napoleon, in particular the esteem and the kindnesses of Your Majesty and your august family.' Touched by the General's reply the King deigned to repeat it that same day to his family and his ministers."

Lamartine relates that he was at dinner with Marmont when he saw the latter push back his plate and rise, very pale, on learning the news.

The Emperor's death was made known to the country at large by a sort of official circular that gave without comment an extract from the *Courier* of July 4th: "Bonaparte is no more. He died Saturday, May 5, at six o'clock in the evening, of a lingering illness that had kept him in bed more than forty days.

"He asked that after his death his body be opened that it might be determined whether his illness were not the same as that which had ended his father's life, namely, a cancer in the stomach. The opening of the body proved that he was not mistaken in his conjecture. He preserved consciousness to the last and died without pain."[3]

The press of the ultra-Right was bitter on the whole. The *Drapeau Blanc* blamed "Buonaparte for failing to die a good death." *L'Ami de la Religion et du Roi* branded "the ravager of kingdoms, the curse of God, the man who all by himself consumed more lives than the Convention, the massacres and the scaffolds of the Revolution." The *France Chrétienne* wrote: "The man dies forgotten. Fame does not lift a single voice that is in his service."

Among the moderate papers the *Journal des Débats*, which, however, had had complaints to make of Napoleon, evinced the most propriety: "We did not trust ourselves and thought it our duty to avoid any expression of personal sentiments in regard to that extraordinary man, through fear of seeming to betray truth either through hatred or through a generosity we did not really feel."

The liberal papers recalled that Napoleon "had rendered eminent services to the social order," and they pointed to his military renown.[4] The *Constitutionnel*, July 11, added: "We do not hesitate to say that the prisoner of St. Helena will be counted among the great men." The *Journal du Commerce* concluded: "The tomb of St. Helena

[3] A document kindly supplied by Mme. Léouzon Le Duc.
[4] *Le Courrier Français*, July 11.

will stand there in the midst of the seas to give this eternal lesson to the rulers of the earth: that one may have received all the gifts of genius from nature, one may have flown flags of victory from the Tagus to the Dnieper, one may have made the laws of twenty nations and ruled over twenty kings, but in spite of that one must succumb when one is not defended by the love of the peoples and by institutions of their choice. Europe, conspiring against Napoleon and despotism, was able to overthrow both. Europe would have retreated before Napoleon and liberty." [5]

The news reached Rome on July 16, but Madame Mère, for reasons unknown, did not hear of it until the 22nd.[6] On the 9th or the 10th, old Buonavita, who had not as yet heard anything himself, appeared at her house, bringing Montholon's letter to Pauline. The Emperor's mother and uncle were still buried in their mysticism. Fesch had even intercepted letters from O'Meara to Madame informing her of Napoleon's condition, which O'Meara knew was desperate, having heard from Buonavita and Gentilini, who arrived in England early in May. The part played by Fesch during those last years was as inept as it was contemptible.[7] Neither Fesch nor Madame saw fit to believe the Abbé. "Father Buonavita was not well treated," Pauline was to write to Planat, July 11, "for Mamma asked him if he had really seen the Emperor. The poor man, so devoted, was deeply pained. I am taking him to Frascati with me, for they do not intend to give him a sou." In a terrible scene Pauline implored and threatened. The Emperor was going to die—she was sure of it! Montholon's letter said so, and it was telling the truth! Her indignation, her despair, angered Fesch. "The scene was terribly violent. I started such a quarrel that I shall never be able to see the Cardinal again." Pauline decided to set out for St. Helena at once. She communicated her wish to Lord Liverpool—she wanted Napoleon to have some one of his family beside him to close his eyes. That was on July 11. She wrote to Montholon on the 15th: "I have consulted only my heart in taking this step, for I am far from being as well as I might wish. But I hope that my strength will sustain me in order to prove to the Emperor that no one loves him as much as I do."

Pauline did influence Madame Mère. With her eyes at last open,

[5] *Courier*, July 14, 1821.
[6] Baron Larrey, *Madame Mère*, Vol. II, p. 262.
[7] Masson, *Napoléon et sa famille*, Vol. XIII, p. 192.

the mother acted with a sort of violent impulsiveness. On the one day of July 14, she wrote to Lucien, Jerome, Lord Holland, O'Meara, Liverpool, the English Parliament and even—a painful step which, however, she considered necessary—to Marie-Louise, to implore her to intercede with the Powers to have the Emperor transferred to another climate. This document is a touching one and not very well known:

"In spite of my uncertainty as to whether this letter, like so many others, will reach you, I owe it to myself and to you to inform you of your husband's condition. . . . Use every means in your power. The almoner who has just arrived left him on the 17th of March, last, stretched on a sofa, speaking of you and of his son, and, in spite of his great character, saying that if they did not make haste to get him away from there, it would not be long before they learned of the end of his days. . . .

"I pray God to keep you and, if you still have any memory of me, of the mother of Napoleon, pray accept the assurance of my devotion.

"MADAME MÈRE.

"Rome, July 14, 1821."

A week later the Cardinal confessed to her that her son was dead. The poor woman, usually so courageous, was prostrated. Her mourning was doubled by an immense remorse. She had been unwilling to believe in Napoleon's torture. His death was a supreme rebuke to her. In her sorrow she shut herself up, refused to see her brother or any member of the family, passed several days without speaking a word and almost without moving, weeping, praying, and, in moments of calm, thinking of the past and doubtless seeing again under the now motionless features of the martyred Emperor the small, impulsive, mobile face, the sparkling eyes and the laughter of her baby son.

Buonavita, it will be remembered, had been sent home from St. Helena to die, yet he was to survive Napoleon by twelve years. He could not settle down either in Rome or in Corsica, so strong a spell had travelling cast over him. He went to the Île de France, South East Africa, to become vicar of the parish of St. Louis, and died at Pamplemousses, November 2, 1833, at the age of 81. His gravestone with its epitaph may still be seen in the Pamplemousses cemetery.[8]

The shock of the Emperor's death played havoc with Pauline's nervous nature. She took to her bed again, passing from an extreme depression to a painful exhilaration. Napoleon's other brothers and

[8] I owe this information to M. Olivier Taigny.

sisters received the news with distress, but their families, their affairs, their cares, were enough to distract them. While the Emperor's death robbed them of a hope it also, perhaps, relieved them of a remorse.

On August 15th, Napoleon's birthday, his mother asked England for his body. Her letter, addressed to Lord Castlereagh, still preserves a stirring quality:

"The mother of the Emperor Napoleon comes to claim her son's ashes of his enemies. . . . Among the most barbarous nations, hatred has never reached beyond the grave. My son has no further need of honours—his name is sufficient for his glory, but I need to embrace his inanimate remains. My hands have prepared a tomb for him in a humble chapel far removed from the clamours and noise of the world. In the name of justice and humanity I implore you not to refuse my prayer. To obtain my son's remains I have a right to make my prayer to the Ministry, to make my prayer to His Britannic Majesty. I gave Napoleon to France and to the world. In the name of God, in the name of all mothers, I come to implore you, Milord, not to refuse me the ashes of my son!"

Not knowing what answer to make Castlereagh made no answer at all.

On September 21, the Emperor's executors wrote to Lord Liverpool to claim Napoleon's body. They received a verbal answer from the British Ambassador in Paris that the British Government considered themselves only as guardians of the ashes of Napoleon Bonaparte and would restore them to France "if a formal application were made by the French Government." In May, 1822, the executors appealed to Louis XVIII, requesting interment for Napoleon at Ajaccio. That step too was vain.

Marie-Louise learned of her widowhood through the *Gazette du Piémont*. She was at the opera in Parma at the time, with Neipperg, listening to the *Barbier de Séville*. The Court of Vienna had not considered it important to inform her. She experienced the sort of sadness—and it has been a mistake to doubt it—the half-tender melancholy, that her passive and shallow nature allowed of. She was then about to give birth to another child, having already given one bastard to Neipperg. She was happy in her unhonoured life. The Emperor's death could only remind her that she had once feared him and then loved him, and that she had not waited very long to be false to him. To her intimate friend, Mme. de Crenneville, she wrote:

"They separated me from the father of my child to no purpose. Death makes one forget everything that has been unpleasant. It grips at one's heart, especially when one thinks of the horrible agony he went through for years. I would, therefore, be utterly heartless, had I not been deeply moved." To the Duchess de Montebello, she confided, in the same tone: "I have been greatly shocked and affected, for I should have to be lacking in feeling indeed not to remember that the deceased was never anything but good to me in the short time I spent with him" (October 20, 1821).[9]

The Court of Parma went into mourning for three months. A thousand masses were ordered at Parma, a thousand at Vienna. Marie-Louise, in widow's weeds, attended a service that was celebrated in the chapel of her castle at Sala for the repose of Napoleon's soul. By order of Neipperg Napoleon's name was not pronounced in the ritual. The clergy designated him by the formula, "husband of our Duchess." "On the sarcophagus," Neipperg wrote to Metternich, "there was no sort of emblem or ornament that could have recalled the past" (July 31, 1821).[10]

One evening towards the end of July, in the castle at Schönbrunn, a little lad of ten with blue eyes and golden hair saw his assistant tutor, Captain de Foresti, approach him with unusual gentleness. For the first time he heard him pronounce the name of St. Helena. Respectfully he said: "The Emperor Napoleon." The child looked at him in amazement. For years now those about him had avoided any mention of his father. They had met his questions with silence and sought to efface any vestige of his life in France that might have remained in his mind. Carefully, tenderly, Foresti announced that the child's father was dead. He added that he had passed away without suffering and in a most Christian frame of mind.

The child sat down near a window and wept a long time. In spite of all their efforts he had never forgotten his father. Often, in his little bed, sheltered from eyes and voices, he had pictured his face to himself, trying to recall the pale man with the beautiful hands who used to toss him in his arms. To that frail memory of childhood, which so much hostility had assailed, he had remained secretly, earnestly faithful. He was proud to be the son of Napoleon. He did not tell anyone so. For years now he had kept silent. He would con-

[9] Marie-Louise, *Correspondance*, p. 228.
[10] See Octave Aubry, *La trahison de Marie-Louise*, p. 73.

tinue silent. But he was in a hurry to grow up, to become a man! Time alone could give him his freedom. At a still younger age he had often said that "he wanted to be a man to go and rescue his papa." Now that Napoleon was dead, he had no one but himself to rescue. He would be patient! He would wait!

.     .     .     .     .     .     .     .

Sir Hudson Lowe left St. Helena on July 25th accompanied by his family and all his staff, with the exception of Gorrequer. Sailing likewise on the *Lady Melville* were Montchenu and Gors. On his arrival in London Lowe was coldly received. Lord Bathurst gave him an official *satisfecit*. George IV honoured him with a handshake. But he received no rank, cross or pension—the contrary to what he had hoped for. Falling from the local rank of lieutenant-general to the lower order, he was appointed to the command of a regiment. His chiefs had no fault to find with him—he had merely been the executor of their orders. A good administrator he had managed his little colony perfectly and he left it prosperous. But around him there already floated a sinister aura that was to thicken and thicken until—as we shall see—the wretched man was to perish in it. He began receiving rebuffs and affronts at the very start. Lady Holland refused to see him in order not to be obliged to talk to him of Napoleon. "It would be distressing to me," she wrote, "to be under any constraint in talking of the treatment he received from the English Government and the consequences of it to his health and life; and it would be equally so to you to hear any warm expressions I might use." [11]

The Marquis de Montchenu, proud of having so well played his rôle, asked Louis XVIII for the red ribbon and the rank of lieutenant-general. He received nothing. Vainly did he besiege the ministry— all he got was retirement on a pension. He died poor and forgotten in 1831, without ever understanding how the legitimate monarchy (ungrateful by nature, since it owes nothing to anybody) could fail to reward him for having made a laughing-stock of France for five years and for the sole achievement of following the coffin of the Usurper to its grave.

On October 19, 1821, Bertrand and Montholon landed at Calais and went on to Paris. Montholon was authorized to do so by the amnesty law of June 25, 1821. Bertrand was still under a capital

[11] Lowe Papers, 20-133; Young, Vol. II, p. 351.

sentence, pronounced *in absentia*, and was obliged to write to the King asking permission to return to France. Louis XVIII replied that he was disposed to grant him a pardon, but that Bertrand would first have to surrender to the Minister of Justice. The Grand Marshal had only to re-enter the service again at his pleasure, since the Restoration at once gave him back his army rank. But in part out of a sense of loyalty, in part owing to his gloomy disposition, he preferred, to the great regret of Mme. Bertrand, to remain in retirement in his house at Châteauroux. He sometimes spent a few days in Paris in the house which had been given him by Napoleon long before, rue Chantereine, 52. Watched by the police he would receive no one but his comrades of the Captivity and avoided all luxury, all ostentation.

Montholon lived sumptuously in Paris and in his château at Périgny. Unfortunately he became involved in unsuccessful manufacturing enterprises in which Napoleon's generous legacy was swallowed up. He was declared bankrupt in 1829. Rehabilitated in 1838, but still pursued by his creditors, he went to England to live, and there he became an intimate of Prince Louis-Napoleon. He was to follow the latter in his raid on Boulogne. He had meantime separated from his wife, who retired to Montpelier and died there suddenly in 1847. She was buried in the crypt of the Pénitents Bleus, and may still be seen in her glass coffin, wearing her black headdress and her flounced frock.

Marchand bought a little estate near Auxerre according to his master's wishes, and married the daughter of General Brayer, who had returned to France after his South American adventures. He kept up his relations with all his fellow companions at Longwood and waited like a good respectable bourgeois for the Royal Police to cease regarding him as a plotter of sedition.

Father Vignali was refused by Marie-Louise as her almoner. He returned to Corsica and, as the Emperor had advised him to do, built a house at Ponte Nuovo di Rostino. He was to be murdered there a few years later, the victim of some obscure vendetta.

Antommarchi left for Parma, where he tried in vain to obtain an audience with Marie-Louise. Neipperg showed him the door, giving him a ring of little value and some vague promises. At Rome he saw Fesch, whom he found indifferent, then Pauline and Madame Mère, who questioned him with tearful eyes as to the Emperor's last moments. There again Antommarchi tried to turn his loyalty into money.

Mistrustful or perhaps forewarned, Napoleon's mother stopped at the gift of a diamond. In 1825 he published his memoirs in which, plagiarizing Las Cases and O'Meara, he magniloquently recounted imaginary conversations with the Emperor and portrayed himself in a touching rôle. Noverraz said of his book: "The doctor's memoirs are absurd. He claims to have had a great influence over the Emperor. He had none at all. The Emperor could not endure him." [12] His memoirs caught the fancy of the public, however, and netted him handsome royalties. At the same time he resumed his exploitation of Mascagni's Anatomy, but in that he met a disappointment. He was to be more fortunate in selling the Emperor's mask by subscription in 1833. He went to America and died of yellow fever at Santiago de Cuba in 1838, apparently surrounded by great public respect.[13]

Aly retired to Sens, his native town, with his wife and daughter. Pierron settled at Fontainebleau, Archambault at Sannois, Chandellier at Menilmontant, Noverraz and Josephine in Switzerland. The legacies they received from the master assured them all an independent living. Those humble souls kept him ever reverently in mind and lived in his memory.

. . . . . . .

The settlement of the Emperor's estate gave rise to bitter quarrels and complicated transactions. The will was deposited in the Prerogative Court of the Archbishop of Canterbury, December 10, 1821. It was not probated till August 5, 1824.

A copy of it was produced in April, 1822, before the civil court of Paris, which declared the testament null and void, since Napoleon was civilly dead at the time it was made. The executors then negotiated directly with Laffitte. The Government of Louis XVIII, through fear of scandal, wisely abstained from making any demands.[14] Napoleon had relied on Prince Eugene's gratitude and on a sense of decency in Marie-Louise to increase by four millions the amounts on deposit at Laffitte. That would have enabled his executors to meet all the legacies in full. In spite of his vast fortune Eugene turned a deaf ear to his benefactor's appeal. He acted as a strict accountant, showed that he had paid out more than the deposit with which he

[12] A. Cahuet, *Après la mort de l'Empereur*, p. 275.

[13] According to oral testimony gathered at Santiago by an American army surgeon, H. Thomason (Thiers Library, Carton 343).

[14] Chateaubriand to Baron de Vincent, April 31, 1824.

had been entrusted,[15] and then settled back into his fat existence as a German prince.[16] Steered by Neipperg and Metternich, Marie-Louise not only refused to admit that she was a debtor for the two millions that Napoleon had entrusted to her in 1814, but, in the name of her son, she contested the Emperor's bequests and claimed her dower right. Her claims, which were urged through diplomatic channels, did not cease till June, 1833, at which time she renounced all interests in Napoleon's inheritance. That renunciation she renewed May 18, 1837.[17]

Laffitte was not very certain that the executors had sufficient authority to give him a valid release. He was in no hurry, further-more, to hand over money that his bank was putting to good use. The case had to go to court. Montholon liked litigation and directed the whole affair. After many incidents Laffitte transferred the fund to the Receiver's Office. There it remained until 1826. At that time the claims of Marie-Louise were finally denied by the French Gov-ernment, and the executors were allowed to proceed to a division of the money according to the will. An arbitration board, composed of Maret, Caulaincourt and Daru, decided that the three millions and a half on deposit at Laffitte's, being insufficient to meet the legacies, should be allotted proportionately to the sums bequeathed. The exact amount was 3,418,785 francs which, with interest accrued, came to 3,786,121 francs. Montholon got 1,351,298 francs, Bertrand 285,514, Marchand 248,572. The Longwood staff of servants were paid almost in full (94 percent). No account was taken of the bequests made in the codicils. Nearly thirty years later, in 1853, Napoleon III ap-pointed a Commission to examine the situation resulting from the division of 1826, and the Assembly appropriated eight millions, four of which were devoted to the individual bequests, and four to the collective bequests. Under this arrangement the heirs of Montholon received another 667,282 francs. He had died in 1853. Bertrand had died in 1844. His heirs received 522,967. Marchand, still living, drew 213,980. The 4,000,000 appointed to paying the collective legacies went to the survivors of the Elba battalion, the wounded of Ligny

[15] He had received 800,000 francs. Counting the endowment which he established to pay Gourgaud's pension, he had disbursed 812,768 francs.
[16] The Executors to Eugene, July 3, 1822; The Prince's Reply, August 30, De-cember 7, 1822.
[17] Archives, Foreign Affairs, Vienna, Vol. 404. See *Archiv für Oesterreichische Geschichte*, H. Schlitter, Tome LXXX.

and Waterloo, and surviving veterans of the wars between 1792 and 1815. 400,000 francs were given to the town of Brienne and 300,000 to the town of Méry.

The King of Rome, or rather the Duke of Reichstadt, did not receive the bequests which his father had made to him with such painstaking affection. The executors—and Marchand in particular—made repeated efforts to reach him through Marie-Louise and Apponyi, the Austrian Ambassador in Paris. They were not permitted to go to Vienna. Finally they delivered the Coronation laces, a bracelet, and a watch chain woven from the Emperor's hair, to the Ambassador. All the other mementos were to remain in the hands of the executors until the prince should reach his sixteenth year. When that time came they made a fresh effort. It also failed. On March 18, 1832, Marchand wrote directly to the young man asking permission to visit him. Metternich objected, and a few months later the Eaglet was dead. He was to disappear too soon to witness the apotheosis of his father, but he had lived long enough at least to see Europe reconquered by Napoleon's ideas and Napoleon's soul.

His death occurred July 22, 1832. Thereupon the executors placed the majority of the objects that the Emperor had entrusted to them for his son in the hands of General Arrighi, Duke of Padua, who held power of attorney for Madame Mère. When Madame Mère's will came to be probated, they were divided among her children. The wash-basin from the Élysée and one of the camp beds from St. Helena fell to Caroline. That was the bed on which Napoleon had died. Today it forms part of the collection of Prince Murat. The other bed, the one on which the Emperor's body was laid after death, was bought in 1911 by Mr. Edward Tuck and donated by him to Malmaison. The Emperor's large dressing case and the silver night-lamp belong to Princess Moskowa, née Bonaparte. The vases and ornaments of the chapel, with numerous other relics of the Captivity, are at Brussels in the possession of Prince Napoleon .

.     .     .     .     .     .     .     .

O'Meara was of an Irish blood that never forgave. In July, 1822, he published *Napoleon in Exile or A Voice from St. Helena*. Twisting facts, conversations and dates to suit the purposes of his hatred, with a rather gross but still vivid style and a curious gift for dialogue, he gave the public a picture of the first three years of the Captivity.

He sketched by cumulative touches an atrocious portrait of Lowe, declaring flatly that the Governor had driven him, O'Meara, away only because he had called attention to the pernicious influence of the climate at St. Helena on Napoleon's health. Then reaching over Lowe's head he accused the British ministry.

The work met with an instantaneous and tremendous success. Editions and translations followed one on the other. O'Meara became famous throughout all Europe and throughout all Europe Sir Hudson Lowe appeared as a criminal and a torturer. O'Meara took advantage of his renown to marry a rich widow thirty years his senior. He died in London June 10, 1836, and was buried in St. Mary's church at Paddington Green.

In the month of October, 1822, Emmanuel de Las Cases, at that time twenty-two years old, challenged Lowe to a duel. Ever since his departure from St. Helena he had been brooding over an act of revenge. He stalked the General in front of his house in Paddington, in the suburbs of London, and, when he appeared, struck him twice full in the face with a whip.[18] A crowd gathered, ready to manhandle the aggressor. But Emmanuel shouted to them: "That man insulted my father!" And then it was Lowe's turn to be in danger. He did not accept the challenge, however, but ran to a justice of the peace, while young Las Cases made for Brighton and got safely across to France.

Attacked by all the Opposition press, covered with a flood of contemptuous abuse, meeting nothing but insulting rebuffs in society, in the clubs, in the army, Lowe faced the music, for he was not a coward. He brought suit against O'Meara for defamation of character and marshalled against him the testimony of former subordinates at Plantation House—Bingham, Reade, Wynyard, Gorrequer, Harrison, Verling, Henry, Baxter, Balcombe, Burton. O'Meara called on Reardon, Poppleton, Younghusband, Montholon, Las Cases, Antommarchi and Marchand. A legal technicality threw Lowe out of court. He had waited too long before bringing his action. He appealed to Bathurst, but Bathurst deserted him. He and Lord Liverpool were not loath to see public opinion cast the responsibility for the treatment they had inflicted on Napoleon on their agent. They were

[18] Emm. de Las Cases, *Diary Written on Board the "Belle-Poule,"* Vol. VII (Lowe Papers, 20-230).

eager, however, to get their scapegoat out of the way. They offered him a ridiculous post at Antigua. Lowe refused. In the end, to get rid of him, they appointed him to a subordinate position in Ceylon.

There he spent sad years, so much an outcast from society that many pitied him. He was retired in 1831. Poor and lonely, he settled in Chelsea where he died of paralysis in 1844, a completely unhappy man. He was buried in the crypt of St. Mark's, North Audley Street, where his wife had been awaiting him for thirteen years.

When he left St. Helena Lowe was a rich man as a result of the considerable savings he had made from his salary. He had invested 20,000 pounds sterling in government bonds. He had a very fine library. Ruined by unlucky speculations he was obliged to sell the greater part of the books in 1829. He had had one daughter and two sons. One son died at an early age. The survivor, Edward William de Lancy Lowe, born at St. Helena, February 8, 1820, served in India and died in 1880. It was he who sold to the British Museum the immense mass of papers that his father had collected and which filled 240 volumes in all. Lowe's daughter was left almost without resources and received a small pension from Queen Victoria.

In 1853 William Forsyth tried to rehabilitate Sir Hudson Lowe by publishing a *History of the Captivity of Napoleon*. This laborious compilation of the former Governor's papers was made in a spirit systematically unfavourable to the French. To Forsyth the martyr of St. Helena was not Napoleon, but Lowe. That opinion seemed untenable to the majority of the English, and Forsyth's heavy volumes went to gather dust on the shelves of the over-stock bookshops.

. . . . . . .

Towards the end of 1821 Las Cases came into possession again of those of his papers that Lowe had confiscated as he was leaving St. Helena. With the help of Emmanuel, he resumed his editing, amplified the work, adorned it with novelistic embellishments, even stuffed it with forged or apocryphal documents,[19] and in the autumn of 1823,

[19] Examples: Napoleon's letter to Murat, dated March 29, 1808, which was forged in order to hold Murat responsible for continuing the war in Spain; his letter to Bernadotte, August 8, 1811; his letter to his brother, Louis, April 3, 1808; his instructions to an unnamed plenipotentiary, which represents the reconstitution of Poland as the purpose of the invasion of Russia; finally the letter which the Duc d'Enghien is alleged to have written to the First Consul on the night of his trial and which Talleyrand is alleged to have intercepted. Those five documents, all equally false, were designed to exculpate the Emperor of the main charges that could be levelled against his policy. Las Cases does not seem to have been the

published it in nine volumes as a *Mémorial de Sainte-Hélène*. It is really astonishing that Louis XVIII's police should have allowed not that bonfire, but that conflagration, to be lighted. But the politicians of the Bourbonist régime, from the most fatuous down to the shrewdest, thought that with Napoleon dead, everything that he represented—ideas, memories, hopes—went with him to the tomb. His son was just a bastard Archduke, his brothers despicable adventurers, the last of his loyal comrades a handful of trouble-lovers, who dispersed of their own accord before anyone attacked them now that they had no flag and no leader. It was owing to that blindness, which masqueraded under the colours of a contemptuous liberalism, that the *Mémorial* was able to appear. It caused an immediate and widespread sensation. In spite of his rhetorical hotchpotch, his deliberate errors, Las Cases made Napoleon live again, during those six terrible years, with an entrancing vividness. He painted him in the daily routine of exile as at once imposing and gentle, always concerned about France, glorifying her past, prophesying her future, a true Messiah of an era of bliss which a coalition of the kings had prevented from opening to the nations. Reporting with the greatest emotion no end of confidences that the Emperor had made to him, Las Cases showed Napoleon in the beginnings of his career, during his rise to power, in his affections, his habits, his ideas while on the throne, at once soldier and prince, legislator and diplomat, man and hero. The voice of the martyr escaped from the abyss into which the Holy Alliance thought it had cast him forever, re-echoing as if it were alive, with a masterful accent and an incredible volume. Never has an historical figure encountered such wizardry. Leaving the captive corpse under its drooping willows, the Emperor returned again among his faithful followers—there he was near them, breathing, moving his hands, looking at them! Some refused to believe that he was dead.

What could the dependents and the pensioned henchmen of the Restoration do against such a spell? Victor Hugo had written lines which later on he was to atone for by a music more worthy of him:

> *Il mourut. Quand ce bruit éclata dans nos villes,*
> *Le monde respira dans ses fureurs civiles,*
> *Délivré de son prisonnier! . . .*

forger—the first four had already appeared in 1819, in the *Bibliothèque historique*. But he eagerly made use of them since they corroborated his views (See Ph. Gonnard, *Les origines de la légende napoléonienne*, p. 110).

*Retombé dans son coeur comme dans un abîme,*
*Il passa par la gloire, il passa par le crime,*
*Il n'est arrivé qu'au malheur.*[20]

And Lamartine:

*Son cercueil est fermé; Dieu l'a jugé. Silence!*
*Son crime et ses exploits pèsent dans la balance.*
*Que des faibles mortels la main n'y touche plus,*
*Qui peut sonder, Seigneur, ta clémence infinie?*
*Et vous, fléaux de Dieu, qui sait si le génie*
*N'est pas une de vos vertus?* [21]

Auguste Barbier was to curse "the Corsican with the flat hair." Chateaubriand was silent. Such judgments were pleasing to the powers that were, but they had echoes only in the closed circles of the Restoration. The masses did not hear them. They listened to the refrains of Béranger and repeated *The Old Flag:*

*Parlez-nous de lui, grand'mère,*
*Parlez-nous de lui;* [22]

or *The Fifth of May:*

*Il fatiguait la Victoire à le suivre;*
*Elle était lasse, il ne l'attendit pas;* [23]

or *The Old Sergeant:*

*De quel éclat brillaient dans la bataille*
*Ces habits bleus par la victoire usés! . . .* [24]

Even Vigny and Musset, for all of their royalism, were to thrill with involuntary enthusiasm every time they wrote his name. Casimir Delavigne dedicated his *Eleventh Messénienne* to the man who had

[20] *Odes,* 1822. "He died! When that report burst upon our cities, The world caught its breath in its civil rages, Delivered from its prisoner. . . . Plunged down into his own heart as into an abyss, He went through glory, he went through crime, To reach disaster only."

[21] "The Death of the Duc d'Enghien" (*"Bonaparte," Seventh Poetic Revery,* 1821): "His coffin has closed upon him. God has judged him. Silence, therefore! His crime and his exploits are on the scales. Let no weak mortal hand try to tip them for or against. Who, O Lord, can fathom Thine infinite clemency? And you, O Scourges of God, who can say that genius is not one of your virtues?"

[22] "A tale of him, Grandma!
Tell us a tale of him!" (*Memories of the People.*)

[23] "He outstripped Victory in her pursuit of him. She wearied. He could not wait for her."

[24] "With that splendour shone in battle That old blue coat worn thin by victory!"

died at St. Helena. Later Victor Hugo used the same theme in his *Expiation*.

In other countries, meantime, justice was beginning to be done and by the foremost writers.

In his "Age of Bronze" Byron celebrated the "great modern," the "new Sesostris," blasted the English Cabinet and saluted O'Meara:

> The stiff surgeon who maintained his cause
> Hath lost his place and gained the world's applause.

In Russia, in the full midst of Alexander's reign, the most beautiful verses of Lermontov and of Pushkin were inspired by Napoleon. Fearless of Metternich, Manzoni intoned the funeral hymn of the man who united Italy—*The Fifth of May*, and Goethe read Manzoni's ode with enthusiasm and translated it into German. All Germany was rocked. Chamisso composed a drama: "The Death of Napoleon," and a Prussian, Stägemann, wrote: "No stone was raised to him? Not one? Better so. A flight of eagles passes, and invisible the flags of Austerlitz, Marengo and Jena dip over the hill of Longwood." An Austrian, Zedlitz, published a *Nocturnal Review*, the one thing that would keep Zedlitz's name alive for posterity: "At midnight the drum-beat sounds and he issues from his tomb." Heinrich Heine, finally, had as a child seen Napoleon ride through the park in Düsseldorf on a little white horse. He had sung the *Marseillaise* on the knees of Le Grand, the soldier. His *Two Grenadiers*, set to music by Schumann, was being sung by all the young people of Germany. Heine now, in his *Travel Pictures*, hurled his famous curse at England:

"To you belongs the sea, but the sea has not water enough to wash away the shame that that illustrious dead has bequeathed to you in dying. . . . To the remotest ages the children of France will tell tales of the grim hospitality of the *Bellerophon*, and whenever those tearful and ironical chants resound on the other side of the Channel, the cheeks of all honest Englishmen will blush for shame. But a day will come when that song will be heard and then there will be no more England. That proud nation will grovel in the dust. And St. Helena will be the Holy Sepulchre where the peoples of East and West will come in pilgrimage in ships gay with flags."

The poet was far ahead of the future. But wise heads were already measuring how dearly it was to cost the politicians for not having the future in mind. By deporting Napoleon to that islet, refusing him his title, multiplying vexatious precautions around him, refusing to believe in the disease that was gnawing at his vitals, the London Ministry had made the conquered hero a martyr and, in nailing Napoleon to the Southern Cross, they had set him up on the pinnacle of the world as a new Messiah, harbinger of a human Gospel of peace, order and liberty.

Had he ended his days as an American colonist or as a country squire in the neighbourhood of London, he would have meant nothing more to his age or to posterity. He would have been just a Cromwell growing fat and old as a tyrant dismissed from his job. The men of 1815 rendered to his career and his memory the marvellous service of rescuing it from the commonplace. St. Helena made his downfall unprecedented and holy. It laid him to sleep in an indelible purple that neither Time nor man could rob him of again. His dreary end was his finest victory; the purest, since it was altogether due to the prestige of a spirit, the most complete, since it defied any reversal of fortune, and the noblest since it had not been paid for with the blood of soldiers, but with the tragedy of the Chief himself. His agony washed everything away—his abuse of power, his mistakes, nay, his crimes, if crimes they were. Napoleon was nothing now except a glorious idea, in the sole light of which the kings would soon be falling.

He was sleeping so quietly down there, with his beautiful hands outspread along his uniform! But his ideas were sown to the four winds and were to swarm over all the earth. His companions in captivity, the last of his attendants, his former soldiers, were there to seize upon them again. Just as he had desired, just as he had foreseen, a whole political system was to be born of them, aspiring to nothing less than a remodeling of Europe by an achievement that was not granted to Caesar living, but which was promised to Caesar dead. The continent that Metternich and his aids had dismembered and re-sewn together as best served their interests, the continent that they had bound in the worm-eaten bandages of "before '89," was to awaken suddenly and with an irresistible shudder cast off her nervous monarchs. Oppressed nationalities were to break their chains. Germany, Italy, Poland were to spring forth from that dawning day. No more slave countries—freedom for peoples as well as for individuals! The Holy Alliance of Kings was to be superseded by the

Holy Alliance of men, leagued together at last by the same principles of equality, fraternity, justice. France, mother of the Revolution,
was to march at their head as the bulwark of the new social order,
the protectress of new-born peoples. Ideas those, big words, generous,
perhaps unhealthy, dreams! [25] But the time was to come when they
would march out in column to meet the European masses advancing
towards better destinies with their eyes fixed on St. Helena as on
the Holy Mount.

.　　　　.　　　　.　　　　.　　　　.　　　　.　　　　.

While the half-witted Charles X, in the last years of his reign, was
trying to bring the monarchy back in the direction of a divine right
that had become impossible, the legend of the Emperor slowly,
powerfully, laid hold on France. Once again Napoleon was coming
back! But this time he had no need to fear a Waterloo—he was
invincible because he was dead. Plates, knives, forks, spoons, bottles, andirons, tobacco-pipes, handkerchiefs, jewellry—everything was
adorned with his image. Vainly did the police try to run down the
pedlars who were selling to peasants in the remotest countrysides of
France wretched lithographs depicting "The Farewell to Fontainebleau," or "The Prisoner of St. Helena." Vainly did the civil and
military courts serve prison sentences to retired army officers and
Carbonari, now for a pamphlet, now for a plot at times real, more
often imaginary.[26] Napoleon had become the "Little Shaver," the
"Little Corporal," for the soldiers who spoke of him among themselves with intimate affection. An Imperial shadow was creeping over
the monarchy. Not a lip that did not tremble at the name of Austerlitz! The dead were dead and mourning was over. The world forgot
Napoleon's despotism. It saw only his glory.

That great magazine of pent-up ideas exploded in July, 1830. During the few days when Paris stood hesitating to offer the crown to
Louis-Philippe, it looked as though it might re-establish the Empire.
Pictures of Napoleon and his son crowded the shop-windows. In the
groups that gathered on the streets, St. Helena was the sole subject
of conversation. Street-singers foretold the avenging return of Napoleon II. The theatres gave plays on the "Great Epic" before enthu-

[25] See Jacques Bainville, *Histoire de trois générations. L'Évangile de Sainte-Hélène.*
[26] Examples: the prosecutions of Béranger, Paul-Louis Courier, Barthélemy and
Méry, the Fabvier, Caron and Berton cases, and the case of "the four sergeants of
La Rochelle." Note also the Bidassoa affair.

siastic audiences. The army was preparing eagles to place on top of the reconquered tricolour. Had the youth of Schönbrunn appeared on the bridge at Strasbourg, all France would have risen. He would have ridden to Paris between two rows of veterans, workmen and women, who would have kissed his hands with tears streaming down their faces.

But Metternich did not slacken his net. The Eaglet remained in his cage. From that moment, as the Emperor had foreseen on his death-bed, the Orleanist intrigue was to become stronger than a wave of adoration that had lost any visible goal. Louis-Philippe quickly snatched up the crown. In fear of worse the Holy Alliance recognized him, but without troubling to conceal its contempt.

The new monarchy strove to be patriotic—it had to be in view of its origin and the dangers that girded it about. It claimed kinship with the popular rights of '89 and of Napoleon. One of the first decrees of the Government set the statue of the Emperor back on the Vendôme Column, the memorial to the Grand Army. When the ex-king Jerome gave the news to Madame Mère, now blind and helpless, she clasped her hands and burst into tears and for several days went about murmuring: "The Emperor is coming back to Paris!" Louis-Philippe and his ministers, however, did not intend to go so far. Surrounded by pitfalls, balancing between revolution and war, they carefully watched their every step. They ordered the rejection of petitions of October 7, 1830, and September 13, 1831, pleading that Napoleon's ashes be reclaimed by France. Victor Hugo dated his poem "To the Column" October 9, 1830. It was in an entirely new strain:

> . . . Oh va, nous te ferons de belles funerailles. . . .
> Nous y convierons tout, Europe, Afrique, Asie.
> Et nous amènerons la jeune poésie,
>     Chantant la jeune liberté.[27]

In August, 1832, a few weeks after the death of the King of Rome, he was to write *Napoleon II*. Finally in 1837 he published: *À l'Arc de Triomphe de l'Étoile*, the noblest poem that he owed to a Napoleonic inspiration.

However, the King received Queen Hortense privately. The Arc

[27] "Oh, come! We will give you a wondrous funeral. And we shall invite them all—Europe, Africa, Asia. And we shall bring a youthful poetry, singing a youthful liberty."

de Triomphe was completed. Officials and generals of the Empire resumed, in serried ranks, honours, posts and dignities. Bertrand was recalled to active service and appointed head of the École Polytechnique, before being elected a Member of the Assembly, as Las Cases also was. Montholon was re-instated in the Army. Gourgaud became a lieutenant-general and aide-de-camp to the King. He had married Mlle. Roederer in 1822. Continuing his relationship with the Bertrands and the Montholons, and becoming one of the heads of the Bonapartist party, he published, in collaboration with Montholon, an eight volume work entitled: *Mémoires pour servir à l'Histoire de France sous Napoléon* (1823). He replied to Philippe de Ségur's *Histoire de la Grande Armée* by an *Examen critique* so harsh that it provoked a duel in which Ségur was wounded. In 1827 he undertook to refute Walter Scott's *Life of Napoleon*.

So the years went by. While Napoleon slept there on his volcano, visited only by a few voyagers of the Oriental seas, the renown of his name filled the land and grew so vast that everything else became dim and silent as compared with it.

After many difficulties Louis-Philippe at last was settled securely on his throne. The Republicans were checkmated. The Bonapartists were well looked after and rallied to the bourgeois monarchy. The King of Rome had disappeared. The Emperor's brothers were allowing themselves to be forgotten. Joseph was living like an epicurian in London. Lucien had walled himself up in his Italian villas. Louis was nursing his gout in Florence. Jerome was scraping and bowing at the Tuileries in order to get back to France on a pension. One and all they were so intent on a comfortable living that they *disavowed*, and almost violently, a scatter-brained nephew of theirs, Hortense's son, whose uprising they had seen miscarry at Strasbourg in '36.

A bustling little lawyer, Adolphe Thiers, had become imbued with a sincere admiration for Napoleon while preparing a *Histoire du Consulat et de l'Empire*. In 1840 he became Louis-Philippe's Prime Minister. He was afraid that the French public, disappointed by reverses in the Far East, might become bored—the stumbling-block of all prosperous régimes. He dreamed of gilding the dynasty of July with beams reflected from the sun of Austerlitz, and enhancing its prestige in the eyes of France and Europe by identifying it with the tradition of glory. He suggested to Louis-Philippe that Napoleon's remains should be brought home to his native land. The King hesitated a long time. He was afraid of the idea. Would not such a reminder of past glories arouse too many sleeping passions in an emotional people? Each year on the 5th of May and the 15th of August one could see files of aged veterans trudging along the streets of Paris on their way to lay flowers at the foot of the Vendôme Column. Thiers insisted. Louis-Philippe finally yielded. On May 1, 1840, when his ministers came to congratulate him on his birthday, he said to their chief:

"Monsieur Thiers, you have been wanting to have Napoleon's remains brought back to France. I give my consent. Come to an agreement on the matter with the British Cabinet. We will send Joinville to St. Helena."

The next day Thiers asked Guizot, the French Ambassador in London, to present the request of the French Government to Lord Palmerston.[28] Guizot made a face. His cold heart had never warmed to Napoleon. Deferring to an order that he found absurd, he went to call on Palmerston.

Palmerston was not at all a sentimental person. "That," he wrote ironically to his brother, "is a typically French request." But he made haste to accede to it, all the more since he was just then playing a trick on France in the Far East. He wrote a letter to his ambassador in Paris notifying Thiers that England assented. In it he voiced the hope that the promptness of his reply would be considered as testifying to the eagerness of the British Government to extinguish any surviving remnants of the national animosities that had kept the two countries in arms during the life of the Emperor.[29] No more "General Buonaparte!" The Emperor! Just that! Nineteen years had changed the manners, if not the aims, of the English oligarchy.

The French Government had entered upon this serious undertaking very lightly under the drive of public opinion. Louis-Philippe was to say to Apponyi: "Sooner or later it would have been forced upon me by petitions. I prefer to bestow it as a gift. There is no danger. The family is of no importance."[30]

Forthwith, on May 12th, the Minister of the Interior, M. de

[28] Thiers to Guizot, May 7, 1840.
[29] Palmerston to Granville, May 9, 1840; Young, Vol. II, p. 301.
[30] Princess de Lieven to Guizot, May 21.

Rémusat, took the floor in the Assembly and moved an appropriation bill.

"The King," he said to the astonishment of the Members—for the secret had been well kept, "has ordered His Royal Highness, the Prince de Joinville, to sail on a frigate to the Island of St. Helena to recover the mortal remains of the Emperor Napoleon. We come to ask you for means to receive it worthily on French soil and to raise a tomb to Napoleon."

An almost unanimous applause greeted his words. In spite of all his ministerial precautions, M. de Rémusat, a good soul squeezed into a black afternoon coat, had roused the sleeping chords of French grandeur by pronouncing a single name!

The Commission appointed to examine the proposal thought it shabbily conceived and brushed it aside. They proposed sending a fleet to St. Helena! They asked to have Napoleon buried under the dome of the Invalides, with the understanding that never should any other man, however glorious, be laid to rest there in his turn.

When the debate opened before the Assembly, Lamartine arose. The poet saw more clearly than professional politicians:

"This deification of a man—does it not involve a risk of leading France into war or tyranny? Or of throwing her into the arms of Pretenders, of men ambitious for power?"

And he exclaimed:

"Do not forget to carve on his monument the one inscription that will bespeak both your prudence and your enthusiasm, the only one that is suitable both to that unique man and to the age in which you live:

"'To NAPOLEON, *alone!*'"

He succeeded in having the conclusions of the Commission rejected and the more modest plan of the ministry was adopted.

From the outset Louis-Philippe had designated his third son, Joinville, to lead the expedition. That jolly bewhiskered sailor did not seem to be particularly pleased. It cost him something to go and bring back the enemy of the Bourbons on his frigate. Associated with him as the Government's Commissioner was the young Count de Rohan-Chabot, secretary to the Embassy in London. Since they had gone with the Emperor in the day of his disaster, his surviving companions were invited to accompany their ruler on his triumphal return. All save Montholon! An exile in London in the circle of Louis-Napoleon, he was brewing another adventure that would lead him to the madcap raid of Boulogne and to prison at Ham. With the exception also of Las Cases, now blind, infirm, and nearing his end—he was to die two years later. His son Emmanuel, who had become a deputy in Parliament and a councillor of State, would replace him. Bertrand was now sixty-seven years old. Fanny had died in 1836. Pale, broken, despondent, tired of living, Bertrand was in retirement at Châteauroux, worrying over the escapades of his children. He asked permission to take Arthur, his youngest son, along, and before setting sail, handed over to the King the sword of Austerlitz. Joseph Bonaparte protested in the press against the bestowal, without his permission, of a relic that Bertrand had unlawfully kept.

Gourgaud had aged—his side whiskers showed a touch of grey— but he still carried his chin high. He was the same impulsive, straightforward and jealous soul. This home-coming of the Emperor quite turned his head. He promptly raised questions of precedence and refused to yield to anyone but Bertrand.

Marchand joined them at Toulon where the two ships selected for the expedition, the frigate *Belle Poule* and the corvette *La Favorite*, were being fitted out. Napoleon's former valet was now nearing fifty. In order not to cut too poor a figure beside the two generals, he had put on his uniform as a staff officer of the National Guard. He was the one to give the Commission that Thiers appointed to oversee preparations for the voyage the most valuable information. And it was he, with his old time devotion, who looked after the coffins and the funeral ornaments that were to be taken with the expedition. Antommarchi, O'Meara, Buonavita, Vignali were dead. Dr. Guillard and Father Coquereau were chosen to replace them. In the party also went Aly, Pierron, Archambault, Noverraz, and Coursot.

A mortuary chapel had been built below the orlop deck on the *Belle Poule*, between the officers' messroom and the hatch that led into the hold. It was covered in black velvet studded with silver. Monsignor Michel, the old bishop of Fréjus, came and consecrated it on June 22. He also blessed the two ships and the crews. On July 6th the Prince de Joinville attended a dinner given at the Navy Building to the members of the Mission. The whole town was lighted. The next day, towards evening, the vessels set sail.

# III

## *RETURN*

THE VOYAGE LASTED THREE MONTHS. AFTER TOUCHING AT MADEIRA as in 1815, the expedition took the usual route that Cockburn had avoided and sailed for Brazil. On August 26th, they dropped anchor at Bahia and, from too much celebration, did not leave for three weeks. At the end of September they were becalmed for six days. Then the wind whistled again in the riggings and the two ships made a straight run to St. Helena.

During the voyage on the *Belle Poule* the witnesses of the Captivity related to the newcomers and to the officers of the ship the episodes of the struggle against Hudson Lowe of whom nothing had been heard for four years now. Emmanuel de Las Cases read the *Mémorial* aloud. Arthur Bertrand recalled childhood memories. Not very sympathetic towards anything Napoleonic at first, Joinville little by little fell under the spell of the environment. His was a sensitive and very French temperament. By the end of the voyage he was admiring the Emperor almost without reserve.[1] He had been piqued by the fact that Thiers had vested full powers in Philippe de Rohan, therefore making him the responsible commander of the Mission in precedence over Joinville. That created a certain atmosphere of constraint. Other differences arose to disturb harmony among the members. Gourgaud and Emmanuel de Las Cases renewed ancient rancours and had several altercations. Gourgaud exchanged heated words with Commander Hernoux, Joinville's aide-de-camp and the expedition's chief of staff.

Marchand and the others among the Emperor's old servants remained indifferent to these disputes. The thoughts of those Robinson Crusoes of glory were wholly with the dead Emperor. They could see in their mind's eye the little man in green staggering on the slippery deck of the *Northumberland* as the English vessel rolled on the swells. One by one, each evening, those strange stars that whitened his tomb rose before their eyes. How would they find him? Would

[1] Cahuet, *Le Retour de Sainte-Hélène*, p. 135.

they at least recognize that the corpse had been he? It seemed to be their naïve thought that the reparation of France towards Napoleon would not be complete unless they brought him back exactly as they had laid him to rest in the Vale of the Geranium.

On October 7th, at three o'clock, in a rough sea, a sailor posted in the mizzen crows'-nest sighted land. A grey spot began to rise on the ocean. On the morning of the 8th the *Belle Poule* was to the southward of the island, off Sandy Bay. She circled the frowning cliffs and proceeded on her way to Jamestown. As they passed the Barn the passengers made out the gigantic profile of Napoleon. "We learned afterwards," the younger Las Cases adds (p. 158), "that that circumstance was very well known on the island." Then they sighted the gum-trees in the park and the buildings of Longwood. Behind, the peak of Diana was wrapped in clouds. They drew near the coast. A ship appeared flying the French flag. It was the brig *Oreste*, commanded by Captain Doret, who, as a young ensign at Rochefort in 1815, had suggested carrying off Napoleon on a lugger. Struck off the navy lists by the Restoration, Doret had been re-admitted to the service in 1830.

Standing on the quarter-deck the Emperor's companions gazed at the procession of lava hills behind which their master had lain for twenty years. France in their persons was coming back to get him! Nearly all of them were weeping and the sailors of the frigate's crew gathered about them in silence. From the son of the King, scion of the old monarchy, to the lowliest cabin-boy, all the French felt chilled by the aura of a sepulchre and a shiver of glory. At last the little harbour appeared—alive with some fifteen ships, and the straggling yellow village, poured in among its rocks. The church tower was gone—it had been torn down. But one could recognize the barracks on Ladder Hill, the Company garden, the old Castle, the wharf. . . . A crowd had gathered on the quay. On the ridge-pole of Solomon's shop a tri-coloured flag was waving; for the Jewish shopkeeper had become consular agent for France. An English brig, the *Dolphin*, and the harbour batteries, fired a salute. At three o'clock, after difficult manoeuvring in the trade-wind, the ships dropped anchor.

Major-General Middlemore, now Governor of the island, was old and sick. He sent his son and a number of officers to welcome the Prince. In their wake came several boats that drew alongside the

*Belle Poule*. They carried residents of St. Helena whom Bertrand, Gourgaud, and Marchand were delighted to recognize. Arthur Bertrand was highly excited at seeing his native land again. He "kept smiling," he writes, "at those time-blackened rocks." He thought them "beautiful and majestic." [2] Marchand received sad news. Poor Esther, whom the Emperor had forbidden him to marry, was dead. His natural son, the only child remaining of the two she had borne him, had turned out badly and had been deported to the Cape a month before.

The next day, the ninth, at eleven o'clock, with Joinville in the lead, the Mission went ashore on the green-covered stones of the sea-steps which the Emperor had climbed in 1815. Colonel Trelawney, representing the Governor, came forward to welcome the Prince and conduct him to the Castle. Three hundred men of the 91st Infantry formed a double hedge. The population of the island, their hats in their hands, crowded close behind them. After Trelawney had introduced the island authorities to the Prince, the French found horses waiting for them in the little square and rode up Ladder Hill to Plantation House where General Middlemore welcomed them. The Governor, Joinville and Rohan conferred in the grove outside as to the best way to effect the disinterment. The conference lasted an hour. Then the Governor returned to the drawingroom where the other members of the Mission were waiting impatiently and announced solemnly:

"Gentlemen, on Thursday the 15th, the mortal remains of the Emperor Napoleon will be placed in your hands." [3]

The French immediately repaired to the Tomb, accompanied by Captain Alexander, Mr. Wales, chief justice on the island, and two army officers. Following the curves of the road, the former companions of the Captivity gazed eagerly at the landscape that had shut in the longest hours of their lives. It was difficult for them to recognize it. In many ways it had changed, thanks to Hudson Lowe's forestation in pine, hemlock and olive trees that now decorated the

[2] Arthur Bertrand, p. 74.
[3] We are here following the account of Father Coquereau, checked however by the Jamestown Archives, 1840, and the narratives of E. de Las Cases, Gourgaud, Marchand, Dr. Guillard, Arthur Bertrand and Ensign Pujol. Joinville's brief account, which will be found in his *Vieux Souvenirs* (pp. 207-25), is insignificant and rather antagonistic in tone. Written long after the event it bears the mark of the stubborn resentment aroused in the son of Louis-Philippe by the events of '48.

crests of Alarm Hill, the approaches to Diana Range, and the deep basin of Sandy Bay. The improved water supply had extended the meadow and pasture lands. Flocks of fine cattle were grazing on them. The swamps and the mosquitoes were gone. The roads had been paved and made fit for vehicles. On the whole, however, the island had remained the same, with its burned chasms, its steep rocks, its many suggestions of European character that seemed so strange under that tropical sky. The Emperor's friends had first seen it through the smoked glasses of exile. Now they discovered in it a charm, a variety, a brilliancy that astonished them. Approaching Hutt's Gate, they went down into the dip of the Punch Bowl. There from afar off they could see a pale stone among some cypresses.

They dismounted and advancing down hill crossed a barrier that was painted black. In front of a sentry-box that was also painted black, an old sergeant saluted. The Prince removed his hat and walked towards the Tomb. Before the iron fence, the Abbé fell to his knees. Napoleon's servants did likewise. Bertrand and Gourgaud remained standing, but they trembled with emotion. Young Arthur almost fainted.

Crowned by dark trees and bathed in their bitter perfume, the Emperor's tomb looked like a rectangle of brightness. It had been kept with great care. Between the slabs and the iron fence posts the geraniums and pansies planted by Mme. Bertrand were still growing. Arthur gathered a few of them. The Prince picked some forget-me-nots. Of the two willows that shaded the grave at the time it was dug, one was still standing, but it was cracked and of scanty foliage. The other had fallen from old age and was lying on the grass, where it had been left as a tribute of respect. Other willows, still young, had been planted near by by Lady Dallas, wife of Middlemore's predecessor.[4]

The little spring was still trickling into its trough of stone, which was overgrown with moon-lilies and wake-robins. On it an iron goblet was hanging from a hook. Every visitor drank a little of the water that Napoleon had loved. The French went back towards Hutt's Gate, carrying the dead willow with them in a cart. The wood was to be divided among the sailors of the expedition. Before leaving, the Prince had Commander Hernoux give the English veteran a handful of gold. The Mission then wound its way towards Long-

4 A. Bertrand, pp. 82-83.

wood. The wind had risen. It was raining. All of them were struck by the desolate aspect of the plateau.

The long drive was overgrown with grass. Many of the gum-trees that had formerly lined it had disappeared. In front of the Emperor's house there was no lawn now, but an area of close-cropped pasture land where a few sheep were browsing. The pilgrims went through the unkempt hedge and drew near the buildings. Longwood was nothing now but a ruined farm! They entered the lattice-work verandah over broken-down steps. The glass of former days was gone. The old billiardroom was empty except for a pine table that was shoved against the wall—on it lay a book for visitors to write their names in. The walls were covered with other names that had been carved with jackknives.

The drawingroom had lost its mantelpiece and its doors. The windows were three yawning holes. The wall-paper had been torn off, the floor had rotted. A winnowing mill occupied half the room and to install it the ceiling had been staved in. Fearing that he could not control his feelings, Emmanuel de Las Cases went out. Gourgaud's face was red with anger. Bertrand lowered his head sadly. The English seemed ashamed.

Marchand pointed out the spot where the Emperor had died. "He was lying there, his head turned this way. . . ."

They passed into the diningroom and the library. Those rooms were now cluttered with farming implements. Napoleon's two little rooms that he had called his "interior," and which had witnessed his sufferings and his dreams, had been turned into a stable. On the spot where he dictated his campaigns stood a feeding-trough and a hay-rack. A mule's halter was hooked to the nail on which he had hung his sword. The casement windows had been boarded up. The floor was covered with stable-litter.

The French went out, choking with sorrow and indignation. What? There was no housing problem at St. Helena! How then had the Emperor's house, next to Plantation House the most considerable on the island, been allowed to fall into that condition? London—and Governor Walker, Lowe's successor, had doubtless followed the lead of London—must have been eager to wipe out all traces of Napoleon's Captivity! The best way, it seemed, to obliterate that memory, was to sully and disfigure the house in which he had lived! On June 5, 1823, at the suggestion of Governor Walker, the

Council of the island had decided to add the buildings of Old Long-wood to the Longwood farm. In his report Walker wrote "that they could not be applied to a more profitable and necessary utilization." [5] The Council attached but slight importance to the place as a land-mark. They found it easy and economical to place those buildings at the disposal of the farmer of Longwood. Besides, in everything touch-ing St. Helena, one must always take the easy-going ways of the Colonial into account. If the Emperor's bedroom had become a stable, later on it was to become a sheep-cot. The author met a very old lady at St. Helena, a Mrs. Alexander, who well remembered having seen "sheep jumping through the Emperor's windows."

The pilgrims were now walking over the empty grounds where Napoleon had tried, with so much effort, to make himself a garden. There was nothing left of it save a section of the grassed mound and the largest of the basins that was now serving as a watering-trough. But the immortelles that the Emperor had sown in 1819 in "The Flower Bed" had spread everywhere. The white, red and violet ones had died—leaving only the golden—the colour of glory, as a sort of unconscious homage on the part of the earth. [6]

The paths, the arbour, had disappeared. The Emperor's oak, his "beautiful oak," under which he had so often lunched, was still standing. It had not grown at all. The forest of gum-trees, consid-erably thinned out, still covered the plateau to the north-east. The lodgings of Las Cases, of the Montholons, of Gourgaud, and of the orderly officer, had become barns or haymows. Bertrand did not have the courage that day to revisit the house where he had lived often in such discouragement, where his wife had spent so many discon-solate days, where their children had grown up, and where Arthur had been born.

It was still raining. The French re-mounted their horses and rode down towards the town. The sadness of that dishonoured spot had overwhelmed them. Just before they reached Hutt's Gate the riders saw coming towards them at a rapid trot a lady on horseback who suddenly pulled rein and came and flung her arms around Gourgaud's neck. It was Miss Mason, still the most daring horsewoman on the

[5] Jamestown Archives, 1823. Retranslated.
[6] Today the immortelles have overspread the whole plateau of Longwood. In the spring it is as resplendent with them as Brittany is with broom in the blossoming season.

island. In twenty years' time she had not changed a bit. She was over-joyed to see her old friends again, in particular Gourgaud, who had been her favourite.

At Hutt's Gate Arthur found his old nurse, Mrs. Dickson. With tears running down her cheeks she clasped him in her arms. A widow, burdened with eight children, she was keeping an inn and wine-shop at that turn in the road. Gourgaud had the Dickson family come aboard the *Belle Poule* and gave them little gifts.

At The Briars the sun was shining. They found the Balcombe cottage unchanged and the charming pavilion where Napoleon had occasionally forgotten the fact of his exile in the society of little friends. It was now occupied by Colonel Trelawney, an amateur genealogist, who gravely claimed cousinship to the Prince de Join-ville and "on the side of the distaff" relationship to the Sultan Mah-moud. Old Toby was no more, but his gardens and terraces were bursting with flowers and fruits, as in his day.

In the evening General Middlemore gave a large banquet at Plan-tation House and another was arranged at the Castle the following day by the army officers resident at St. Helena. Toasts were offered by Trelawney and Gourgaud to the indissoluble friendship of France and England. In the days following Joinville gave three dinners on board his frigate. Waiting for the date the Governor had set for the disinterment, the French visited all the island, almost always in rain and fog, calling on all the old inhabitants they had known, and chief among them Miss Mason at Orange Grove, where the Emperor had sometimes rested in the early days of his stay, Colonel Hodgson at Maldivia House, old Sir William Doveton at Sandy Bay, whither Napoleon had taken his last ride. Most of those trips yielded relics. Darling the upholsterer gave them remnants of the furniture from Longwood that had not been sold at the sale—the bathtub, the Em-peror's sofa, the Chinese bird-cage, a table, a case of drafting instru-ments, and a footstool. The sailors from the vessels had despoiled the funeral willows and otherwise increased the devastation at Long-wood by their thefts. As a result shore-leaves were withdrawn.

. . . . . . .

On the 14th, at eight o'clock in the evening, with a cold drizzle falling, the members of the Mission entered the enclosure of the Tomb. They were escorted by Sheriff Wilde, Messrs. Trelawney, Hodgson, Alexander and Darling, and a number of other Englishmen. Joinville had remained on his vessel, in a pique because in compliance with orders from London the work of exhumation had not been entrusted to his sailors.

Two tents had been set up: the first to serve as a chapel, the second to shelter the spectators and the military. At intervals a pale moonlight, sifting through rifts in the clouds, whitened the fog. Red-coated soldiers from the 91st Infantry held lanterns and torches aloft to provide light for their comrades who were to do the work. Three sides of the iron fence were torn down. The last plants that bordered the flagstones were carefully gathered. Then the heavy slabs were loosened from their cement and moved to one side. Picks and shovels began digging into the earth, the shovelfulls falling with muffled thuds. Motionless, chilled to the bone despite their coats, the French stood huddled together in a small dark group.

It was four o'clock when the picks began to return a new sound. They had reached the bed of cement. The Commissioners, Philippe de Rohan and Alexander, went down into the grave and made certain that the masonry was intact. It took three hours to break it out with chisels and remove it. Meantime Father Coquereau was preparing Holy Water at the spring. It was dawn when the long slab that covered the vault finally appeared. Several voices were heard. Captain Alexander answered, reproachfully:

"Gentlemen, hardly six inches separates us at this moment from Napoleon's coffin."

It was now broad daylight, but the fog had not gone and it was still raining heavily. Work was begun at setting up a tripod derrick over the tomb. The members of the French Mission and the English officers went under the tent to put on their uniforms. A double hedge of soldiers was drawn up on the slopes of the dale to keep back the curious.

At half-past nine the stone was lifted. Heads were bared. The mahogany coffin could now be seen lying free in its vault. It seemed damp, but had not suffered otherwise. The heads of the silvered screws glittered brilliantly. Father Coquereau, in a surplice, sprinkled Holy Water, and sang the *De Profundis*. Then ropes were fastened to the coffin. It was raised and carried by foot-soldiers under the tent. There the priest completed the religious rites.

In a silence so profound that every man could hear the beating of his own heart, Dr. Guillard began to open the coffin. The screws had to be cut away and two sides of the mahogany had to be sawed through in order to free the lead coffin from its outer covering. The lead coffin was then placed in the ebony casket, ornamented with rings, with an *N*, and with chiseled corners, that had been brought from France.

Just then General Middlemore and Lieutenant Touchard, representing Joinville, arrived at a gallop. The lead coffin was opened, then the mahogany coffin which it contained. This last was so little altered that the screws still turned. The last coffin now remained. The same plumber who had soldered it twenty years before opened it with a chisel. The waiting had become almost intolerable.

The top lid of tin was lifted and a vague form came into view. It was covered with the wadded satin that had loosened from the walls and dropped over it to form a shroud. With the greatest care Dr. Guillard rolled the satin up, beginning at the feet. The air seeping in between the material and the body made the cloth move so plainly that it seemed as though the body were stirring. The spectators, nervous, exhausted from their long vigil, leaned forward in terror.

A froth of cotton clung to the corpse so that the latter was seen, as it were, through a mist. It was amazingly intact. Napoleon seemed to be sleeping. The French had been afraid that they would find nothing but a skeleton or shapeless dust. The Emperor was returning to the light of the world as though he had been placed in his tomb the day before. His head seemed very large. The face had retained its serene expression. The Emperor's complexion had been very yellow at death. The yellow had deepened somewhat. Guillard touched the eyelids with a finger. They had hardened. Some of the lashes were still there. The cheeks were a little puffed. The nose had broken down at the nostrils. The lips had parted a little to show three very white teeth. The chin was bluish from the beard that had grown since the burial. The body, firm under the pressure of the hand, seemed to have mummified. The hands had remained flexible and held their colour as if alive. The left hand still rested on the thigh where Bertrand had placed it, after clasping it in his own, as the coffin was being closed. The clothes had withstood time and the damp. The red bordering and facings seemed to be as good as new, and so did the cordon of the Legion of Honour on the vest. The gold epaulettes and the crosses had blackened as had the silver vases containing the internal organs. The seams of the high boots had given way and the tips of the toes had come through. They were a dull white.

The Emperor seemed strangely young as he had on the day after his death. How old Bertrand looked beside him—though he was the younger man! And Gourgaud and Marchand, young as they had been in the days of the Captivity! They had gone on living—they! Their hair had whitened. Wrinkles furrowed their faces. Their bodies had wearied, their hearts relaxed. Whereas he, protected by his tomb, had kept a youthful placid face, an unlined forehead, his smooth hands! That France might recognize him the better he was re-appearing before her in his historic form, with an immortal countenance.

All filled their eyes with the resurrection. Emmanuel de Las Cases, Arthur Bertrand, Philippe de Rohan, the servants, were unable to restrain their tears. Gourgaud sobbed aloud. Bertrand swayed with fatigue and emotion. In a low tone Dr. Guillard suggested lifting the body that the examination might be completed. He also wanted to open the vases. Gourgaud protested violently. There could be no doubt as to the identity of the corpse. A longer research would be a profanation. To prevent disintegration he asked that the coffin be closed again at once. Philippe de Rohan ordered the doctor to replace the satin. It was then soaked with creosote. "The tin coffin could not be re-soldered," writes E. de Las Cases (p. 238). "The workmen declared that it had been too deeply oxidized, that it would take several hours, and that there was not time for that." But the mahogany coffin was screwed tight again and the old lead coffin was soldered. This was lowered into the ebony casket that had come from France. When the French coffin had been closed Captain Alexander handed the key to the King's Commissioner.

The rain fell relentlessly. It took forty-three men to carry that crushing weight—a ton and a half—to the hearse. There it was covered with the magnificent pall that had been brought from France—a violet velvet sprinkled with gold bees and edged with ermine. The corners, embroidered with crowned N's, were held by Bertrand and Gourgaud, Las Cases and Marchand.

The steep road up the valley wall was a mass of oozing mud. The horses slipped and stumbled. They were helped by twenty gunners who pushed from behind and pulled at the spokes of the wheels. But at last the procession reached the Alarm Hill Road and moved slowly on towards Jamestown, between two files of soldiers and militia and followed by the entire population of St. Helena clad in mourning. By an oversight for which the French were as much to be blamed as the English, the grave was not filled in again. For nineteen years it was to remain a sort of rubbish heap.

In the straggling village the shops were closed and the street deserted. The inhabitants were all at their windows or under the verandahs, saluting. The guns of the fort on High Knoll, in the port batteries, and on the French and English vessels boomed incessantly. The rain had ceased meanwhile. It was half-past five when the long procession arrived at the wharf. The Prince de Joinville, surrounded by his staff, was waiting there. He took the aspersory from Father Coquereau's hands and sprinkled the sarcophagus with Holy Water. The French vessels had been painted black. Their riggings were draped in mourning. All their flags were flying. With a few courteous words General Middlemore transferred the body of Napoleon to the son of Louis-Philippe.

A French longboat with a mast came alongside the stone stairway. The Emperor's coffin was lowered into it. The gunwales sank low under the weight. A broad tricolour flag was flying at the mast of the barge. It was the gift of the young girls of Jamestown who had cut and sewn it.[7]

At six o'clock, with night falling fast, the French sailors, at a command from Joinville, dipped their oars. Napoleon left St. Helena at the very hour when he had arrived there twenty-five years before on the *Northumberland*. A shaft of sunlight, the only one that had shone on that diluvian day spread out horizontally across the sea. The cannon were rumbling incessantly like a terrific thunderstorm.

On the *Belle Poule* the crew were in the yards. The staffs of the three French ships were drawn up in parade formation, with bared swords. The coffin was hoisted on deck. The drums beat a general roulade. The bands played a funeral march. It was now black night. By torchlight Father Coquereau recited the service of absolution. Then the body of Napoleon, with his Imperial cloak spread over the sarcophagus, was left on deck under guard of four sentinels and of the officers of the watch.

It was lowered into the candle-lighted chapel the next morning.

[7] Notably Miss Mary Gedeon and Miss Seale. The Prince de Joinville presented a gold bracelet to Miss Gedeon, with whom the idea had originated.

THE REMOVAL OF NAPOLEON'S BODY FROM ST. HELENA

From a Drawing of 1840

In the course of that day the stones that had closed the grave in the Vale of the Geranium were put aboard. For a long time they were to be left, forgotten, in a storage vault in the arsenal at Cherbourg. There M. Maurice d'Ocagne was eventually to find them. Today they repose in the Invalides.

The morning after that, October 18, the *Belle Poule* set sail for France.

.     .     .     .     .     .     .

She made port at Cherbourg on November 29, 1840. The sarcophagus was put aboard a river boat, the *Normandie*, which followed the coast to the Havre and there entered the Seine, proceeding slowly up the river. Towns and villages saw it come to them with its flags stiff with ice, but in spite of the cold the river banks were lined with peasants and workingmen, women and children. No ceremony had ever before had that dreary grandeur. Under colourless clouds, in a din of cheering that must have reached the dead Emperor as a faint murmur, the black-hulled boat bore the recovered hero into the valley of La Haye below Rouen. There the catafalque was removed from the *Normandie* and put aboard the *Dorade*. When the *Dorade* passed under the bridge at Rouen the Archbishop blessed the body, and a nation, chanting the *De Profundis*, flung laurel leaves on the bier. On the 14th of December, it arrived at Courbevoie. There a great eagle, driven from the forests by the winter, circled about in the sky.[8]

The journey was in charge of Guizot who had succeeded Thiers. It was so mismanaged that, in freezing weather, the members of the Mission and Joinville himself had to sleep on benches and tables using their overcoats for bedclothing. And the voyage lasted eight days!

Guizot had also done his best to dampen the pomp of the Return, fearing its consequences. In his love for subtile finesses he had decided that the ceremonies should be strictly military and that none of the principal departments of State should participate in it officially. In a meeting at the English Ambassador's, the diplomats accredited to

---

[8] Abbé Coquereau, *Relation*. Of the return to Paris there are any number of contemporary records: Chateaubriand, *Mémoires d'Outre-Tombe*, Vol. IV, p. 123; Victor Hugo, *Choses vues*, First series; Duchess de Dino, Comtesse de Boigne, Premier Pasquier, *Mémoires;* Princess de Lieven, Liszt and the Countess d'Agoult, *Letters.* In his *Retour de Sainte-Hélène*, M. Albéric Cahuet has given the most complete account of the Return of the Ashes.

Paris, decided not to attend the funeral ceremonies in order to play a trick on Louis-Philippe.

All Paris was at Courbevoie to welcome Napoleon. Both banks of the river were covered with people, more helpless from emotion than stiff from the cold. Old Soult, the major-general of Waterloo, and now President of the Council, came to prostrate himself before the coffin in which lay the man who had made his fortune and whom, to please Louis XVIII, he had called an adventurer. That night aged "moustaches" of Spain, Russia, and the Campaign in France, stood gun on shoulder, stolid, frozen, to watch over "the Old One." On December 15, at dawn, Napoleon was carried under the Arc de Triomphe, a gateway befitting his own stature that he had given to Paris.

"Sire, you will come back to your capital!" [9] Hugo had sung. He was returning in fact in a snowstorm that was pierced at times by a pale shaft of sunlight. He was greeted along the whole length of the Champs-Élysées with all the magnificence that cardboard, false marble, stucco and painted canvas could lend to such an occasion. But for an age of such wretched taste the hearse was handsome—sixteen horses in gold trappings dragging a circle of Victories which, in turn, bore a shield that supported the sarcophagus. A large drapery in violet crêpe was drawn around it and floated behind like a cloud. Very handsome too were the thundering guns, the bells pealing from every church, an army of eighty thousand men reaching from the Arc de Triomphe to the Invalides, while the man in the street felt that Napoleon's return had at last avenged France for Waterloo and restored to her a right that the Holy Alliance had denied her, the right to lift her head on high again. But best of all, in fact as grand as the Epic itself and a thing that reduced gaping idiots, who at first had been shouting and singing, to silence, was the parade of the Old Guard, the ghosts of the Grand Army. Poor fellows reduced to the meagre occupations of the aged, they had in honour of the day brushed and patched their old uniforms, which the younger generation in Paris had never seen. They came from all parts of the land, often from far away. Some of them had done a hundred, a hundred and fifty, miles on foot, and they had bivouacked at Courbevoie before open fires, as at Wagram, refusing beds that were offered them. They were all there,

[9] *Le Retour de l'Empereur*, November, 1840.

grenadiers wearing their caps of Russian bearskin, sailors in worn-out Brandenburgs, the light infantry, the Mamelukes, the Hussars, the Lancers, the Dragoons, in faded coats, leaning on canes, magnificent in their loyalty and in their poverty. They had all devoted their lives to the Emperor. They were the ones to whom his thoughts had turned in his last moments. They straightened up, with set jaws and fixed eyes, with no thought but for their god. Several of them were to fall that evening to their poor straw mattresses and never get warm again. But they died happy! The crowds were stirred, and saluted them with wild hurrahs. The friends of the Duchess Dino, the guests of the Embassies, sitting on the balconies, might make fun of them, but an awakened France bowed before the purest remains of her glory, and a tremendous shout rent the air, a hoarse, brutal shout, loud enough to rouse the Corsican who was sleeping on his shield: *"Vive l'Empereur! Vive Napoléon!"* Old Letizia had been walled up for the past five years in her Roman tomb, but she must have trembled at those cheers. They drowned out the church bells, the cannon, the sound of the horses' hoofs, the rattle of arms. The name of Napoleon filled the city. Once again, after a long denial, Paris was reconsecrating herself to him.

In the gloomiest days at St. Helena, he had predicted as much to his companions:

"You will hear Paris shouting again: *'Vive l'Empereur!'* "

He had not been mistaken. A million people acclaimed him with a sad and frantic love as he went by on his shield, held up by his Victories, high above the beating of hearts and the terrible dipping of the flags. Passing with him was the greatest epoch, perhaps, in History—the age of the Revolution and the Empire. How much bloodshed, how many tears—but how much greatness! For twenty years France had been mistress of the earth in a tumult of pride that not even Rome had known. That is what the people, shaken to the marrow of their bones, were thinking of. "Down with the traitors of 1815!" [10] they were grumbling now. And when they caught sight of Bertrand who was marching beside the hearse, with bowed head, bewildered, overwhelmed by his memories, their shout repaid him in one flash for his years at St. Helena: "Long live fidelity!" There was not a cry of "Long live the King!" [11] On the other hand the forbid-

[10] *Constitutionnel*, December 16, 1840.
[11] *National*, December 16, 1840.

den strains of the *Marseillaise* could be heard all about town sung by young people.

The procession entered the Court of the Invalides, which had been decorated in hideous style and was choked by the grandstands which were packed with impatient throngs. The coffin was to have been carried by veterans, but they proved not to be strong enough and had to be replaced by soldiers and sailors in active service. Louis-Philippe came forward to meet it. Joinville, with drawn sword, presented the relic to him. The King uttered a few words which the *Moniteur* was to elaborate and embellish.

"It seems," Joinville relates,[12] "that a short speech had been prepared in Council which I was to recite on meeting my father, and also the reply that he was to make. Only nobody thought of letting me know! Accordingly, on our arrival, I merely saluted with my sword and disappeared. My father, after a moment's hesitation, improvised an appropriate sentence or two. The thing was afterwards fixed up for the *Moniteur*." [13]

" 'Sire,' said the Prince, lowering his sword to the ground, 'I offer you the body of the Emperor Napoleon.'

" 'I receive it in the name of France,' the King replied in a loud voice."

Soult produced the sword of Austerlitz.

"General Bertrand," said the King, "I command you to place the Emperor's sword on his coffin."

The Grand Marshal was too affected. Gourgaud obeyed in his stead.

"General Gourgaud, place the Emperor's hat on his coffin."

Then the funeral service began. It lasted two hours. The *De Profundis*, the *Dies Irae*, and Mozart's *Requiem* were chanted. No one paid any attention. The Peers and the Members conversed in loud voices, the ladies toyed with their fans. Finally came the Mass for the Martyrs, and the Archbishop gave absolution. The Governor of the Invalides, Marshal Moncey, was sick and in fact dying, but he had had himself carried to the foot of the catafalque in an armchair. He was eighty-seven years old. For a week he had been saying to his physician:

[12] *Vieux souvenirs*, p. 228.
[13] *Moniteur*, December 16.

"Doctor, keep me alive a little longer. I want to receive the Emperor!"

When the ceremony was over he murmured:

"Now let's go home and die."

.    .    .    .    .    .    .    .

That evening, convinced that they had stuffed the monarchy of July into the lion's skin, Louis-Philippe and Guizot must have congratulated themselves in good faith. There, they thought, we have reconciled mediocrity with grandeur! But that was the fatuousness of well-meaning souls! Napoleon had not come back to the banks of the Seine alone. That corpse, lying outstretched in the uniform of the Chasseurs of the Guard, with the white toes pushing through the boots, was not all there was in the quadruple coffin. With it came prospects, ideas, a bounding hope. From that clay which was to crumble day by day under the dome of the Great King, invisible radiations were to dart, travel underground from heart to heart and in the end prepare the country for a resurrection. Prince Louis-Napoleon, with Montholon, may well have been locked up in the fort at Ham after his pitiable effort at Boulogne on the very day [14] that the *Belle Poule* was anchoring at St. Helena. But the Empire was destined to lay hold on France again. It was to take time, to be sure. A fortnight was enough to carry the Eagle from the Gulf of Juan to the towers of Notre-Dame. Eight years were to pass before the Monarchy of July would die from having tried to drape itself in Napoleon's shroud.

On February 6, the Emperor's coffin was borne to the chapel of St. Jerome. There it lay until 1861. Then one day in April, in the great crypt that Visconti had sunk, Napoleon III, the Empress Eugénie, and their son, saw it enclosed in the porphyry sarcophagus that had been brought from Russia. And over it his Victories resumed their eternal watch.[15]

Some four years earlier, Napoleon III had come to understand that it would be a disgrace for France and for himself to allow the

[14] October 7, 1840.

[15] It was not a gift of Czar Nicholas to France, as has been supposed. The Czar merely allowed it to be cut from the quarry at Karelie which belonged to him. It cost the government of Napoleon III a pretty sum—about 200,000 francs (L. Léouzon Le Duc, *Études sur la Russie*, p. 12). Léouzon Le Duc was the Emperor's commissioner on that errand, and brought it to a happy conclusion in the face of many difficulties.

house where the Emperor had dragged out his last years, and the tomb where he had slept so long, to disappear. He therefore asked the British Cabinet to cede Longwood and the Vale of the Geranium to France. That was not an easy thing to arrange. The difficulties were surmounted only through the personal intervention of Queen Victoria. The farmer at Longwood and the owner of the Vale were reimbursed to amounts totalling 178,565 francs, which were covered by an appropriation voted by the Legislative Body. On May 7, 1858, the two properties became a French domain. Captain Masselin of the French Engineering Corps went to St. Helena and set to work on a restoration. With painstaking care and boundless patience Masselin reconstructed the exterior and the interior of Longwood proper, as it had been in 1815. He set up the grille around the Tomb again and covered the spot where the grave had been with a cemented slabbing. Today twelve cypresses, three araucarias, and a willow, are grouped about it. Another willow was planted there on May 5, 1921, in the name of Marshal Foch. In August, 1925, a little olive tree was set out there by the Prince of Wales.

The year 1934 saw the completion of the restoration, which the too niggardly Second Empire had not carried to the end. With funds supplied by the late M. François Coty, the French Association of Friends of St. Helena had the buildings that Montholon and Gourgaud had occupied rebuilt as a lodge for the curator of the French domain. Free at last, the six rooms that had formed the Emperor's apartment were converted into a museum where, thanks to the generous gifts of the Governor of St. Helena—Sir Spencer Davis, and of many French and English donors, the setting of the Captivity has been restored in a very impressive way.

.          .          .          .          .          .

The sepulchre that France, a belated Antigone, raised to Napoleon in Paris dazzles the eye with the blaze of its gilded glass. But is it as satisfying to the spirit as the nameless stone at St. Helena over which a willow tree still trembles? So from his rock, lost in the emptiest of oceans, that great man spoke the loudest, not only to the French, but to all mankind! The Dome of the Invalides never makes one forget the Vale of the Geranium. On that spot, in that vale, which a meteor scooped out at the end of its fall on some primordial night, he dug his real grave, the grave that beckons to us with its secret and which the passing ages will never refill.

# BIBLIOGRAPHY OF REFERENCES

Abell, Lucia Elizabeth (Betsy Balcombe), *Recollections*. London, 1844.

Alison, Sir Archibald, *History of Europe*. Edinburgh, 1849-50. 14 Vols.

Aly the Mameluke, see St. Denis.

Antommarchi, Dr. Francesco, *Mémoires: Les derniers moments de Napoléon*. Paris, 1825. 2 Vols.

Arago, François, *Biographie de Gaspard Monge* (*Mémoires de l'Academie des Sciences*, Vol. XXIV). Paris, 1854.

Aubry, Octave, *La trahison de Marie-Louise*. Paris, 1933.

Bainville, Jacques de, *Histoire de trois générations: L'Évangile de Ste. Hélène, 1815-1918*. Paris, 1918.

Bajert-Beker, Comte de Mons, General Léonard Nicolas, *Relation de ma mission près de Napoléon*. Paris, 1841.

Bausset, Louis-François-Joseph, *Mémoires anecdotiques*. Paris, 1827-29. 4 Vols.

Beauharnais, Hortense (Queen of Holland), *Mémoires*. Paris, 1927. 3 Vols.

Beker. See Bajert-Beker.

Bertrand, Arthur, *Lettres sur l'expédition de Ste. Hélène en 1840*. Paris, 1841.

Bibesco, Marthe Lucie, Princess, *Une fille de Napoléon: Mémoires d'Emilie de Pellapra*. Paris, 1921.

Blücher, Gebhard, *Blücher in Briefen*. Stuttgart, 1876.

Bonaparte, Louis, *Documents historiques*. Paris-London, 1820.

Bonaparte, Lucien, *Mémoires secrets*. Paris, 1819. 2 Vols. in 1.
—— *La verité sur les Cent Jours*. Paris, 1835.

Boulay de la Meurthe, Antoine, *Bourrienne et ses erreurs*. Paris, 1830.

Bourguignon, Jean, *Les Adieux de Malmaison* (*Collections et souvenirs de Malmaison*). Paris, [1924].

Cahuet, Albéric, *Après la mort de l'Empereur*. Paris, 1913.
—— *Le retour de Ste. Hélène (1821-1840)*. Paris, 1932.

Callwell, J. M. (Mrs.), *Old Irish Life*. Edinburgh, 1912.

Campbell, Sir Neill, *Napoleon at Fontainebleau and Elba*. London, 1869.

Carnot, Comte Lazare Nicolas, *Mémoires historiques et militaires sur Carnot*. Paris, 1824.

Castlereagh, Lord (Robert Stewart Londonderry), *Memoirs and Correspondence*. London, 1848-53. 12 Vols. (*Letters and Despatches*, Vols. 9-12).

Caulaincourt, General Armand, *Mémoires*. Hanoteau ed. Paris, 1933. 3 Vols.

Chaplin, Arnold, *A St. Helena's Who's Who*. London, 1919.

Cockburn, Admiral Sir George, *Bonaparte's Voyage to St. Helena* (*Diary*). Boston, 1833.

Constant, Benjamin, *Mémoires sur les Cent Jours*. Paris, 1829.

Coquereau, Abbé Félix, *Souvenirs du voyage à Ste. Hélène*. Paris, 1841.

Curzon, Lord (George Nathaniel, Baron Curzon of Kedleston), *Leaves from a Viceroy's Notebook*. London, 1926.

Davoust, Marshal Louis Nicolas, *Correspondance*. Paris, 1885. 4 Vols.

Ellis, Sir Henry, *Journal of the Proceedings of the Late Embassy to China*. London, 1817. 3 Vols.

Fleury de Chaboulon, Baron Pierre Antoine Edouard, *Mémoires*. London, 1819. 2 Vols.

Forsyth, William, *History of the Captivity of Napoleon at St. Helena*. London, 1853. 3 Vols.

Frémeaux, Paul, *Souvenirs d'une petite amie de Napoléon* [Betsy Balcombe]. Paris, 1912.

Gonnard, Ph., *Les origines de la légende napoléonienne*. Paris, 1906.

Gourgaud, General Gaspard, *Sainte-Hélène: Journal inédit de 1815 à 1818*. Paris, 1903. 2 Vols.

Hall, Basil, *Narrative of a Voyage to Java, China and the Great Loo Choo Island . . . with an interview with Napoleon Bonaparte at St. Helena*. London, 1840.

Harrison, Major, *More Light on St. Helena*. (Letter, Harrison to Sir George Bingham). *Cornhill Magazine*, February, 1901.

Hauterive, Ernest, *Les objets de l'Empereur à Ste. Hélène*, in *Revue des études napoléoniennes*, February, 1933.

Henry, Dr. Walter, *Events of a Military Life*. London, 1843. 2 Vols. American ed.: *Trifles from My Portfolio*. Quebec, 1839. 2 Vols. in 1.

Héreau, Dr. Joachim, *Napoléon à Ste. Hélène*. Paris, 1829.

Home, George, *Recollections of a Midshipman*, see Shorter.

Hortense, Queen, see Beauharnais.

Houssaye, Henry, *1815 (Waterloo)*. Paris, 1902.

Joinville, François Ferdinand Philippe Louis d'Orléans, Prince de, *Vieux Souvenirs*. Paris, 1834.

Knowles, Sir Lees, *Letters of Capt. Engelbert Lutyens*. London, [1915].

Laffitte, Jacques, *Mémoires* in *Revue des Deux Mondes*, 1930.

Larrey, Baron Félix Hippolyte, *Madame Mère*. Paris, 1892. 2 Vols.

Las Cases, Comte Emmanuel de, *Mémorial de Sainte-Hélène*. Paris, 1823-24. 8 Vols.

Las Cases, Emmanuel de, the younger, *Journal écrit à bord de la frégate la "Belle Poule."* Paris, 1841.

Lavalette, General Antoine, Comte de, *Mémoires et souvenirs*. Paris, 1831. 2 Vols.

Lenôtre, G. (Théodore Gosselin), *Napoléon: Croquis de l'épopée*. Paris, [1932].

Lieven, Princess Dorothea (Benckendorff), *Correspondence of Princess Lieven and Earl Grey (1824-41)*. London, 1890. 3 Vols.

Lyttleton, Lord William Henry, *A Few Notes on the Arrival of Napoleon Bonaparte on Board the "Northumberland."* London, 1836.

Madelin, Louis, *Le Consulat et l'Empire*. Paris, 1932-33. 2 Vols.
—— *Fouché, 1759-1820*. Paris, 1901. 2 Vols.

Maitland, Capt. Frederick Lewis, *Narrative of the Surrender of Napoleon*. London, 1826.

Malcolm, Lady Clementina (Elphinstone), *Diary*. London, 1929.

Marchand, Louis, *Précis des guerres de Jules César*. Paris, 1836.

Marie-Louise, Empress, *Correspondance*. Vienna, 1887.

Masson, Frédéric, *Autour de Ste. Hélène*. Paris, 1909-12. 3 Vols.
—— "*La Mort de l'Empereur*" in *Revue des Deux Mondes*, 1921.
—— *Napoléon et sa famille*. Paris, 1911-20. 13 Vols.
—— *Napoléon à Ste. Hélène, 1815-1821*. Paris, 1913.

Melliss, John Charles, *St. Helena*. London, 1875.

Montholon, Albine Hélène, Comtesse de, *Souvenirs de Ste. Hélène, 1815-16*. Paris, 1901.

Montholon, Charles Tristan, Comte de, *Mémoires*. London, 1823-24. 6 Vols.
—— *Récits de la Captivité*, Paris, 1847. 2 Vols.

Napoleon I, *Campagne de 1815*. Paris-London, 1818.
—— *Correspondance*. Paris, 1858-70. 32 Vols.

O'Meara, Barry, *An Exposition of the Transactions that Have Taken Place at St. Helena*. London-Paris, 1819.
—— *Napoleon in Exile, or A Voice from St. Helena*. London, 1822. 5 Vols.

Pasquier, Étienne, Duc de, *Mémoires*. Paris, 1893-95. 6 Vols.

Planat de la Faye, Nicolas Louis, *Vie de Planat de la Faye*, Paris, 1895.

Pontécoulant, Louis Gustave Doulcet, Comte de, *Souvenirs historiques et parlémentaires, 1764-1848*. Paris, 1861-65. 4 Vols.

Rovigo, Anne Jean Marie René Savary, Duc de (General Savary), *Memoires*. Paris, 1828. 8 Vols.

Rosebery, Lord Archibald Philip Primrose, *Napoleon: The Last Phase*. London-New York, 1901.

Santini, Noel, *Souvenirs* (Chautard ed.). Paris, 1855.

Schlitter, Hanns, *Kaiser Franz und die Napoleoniden*, in *Archiv für Oesterreichische Geschichte*, 1898.

Seaton, Richard Cooper, *Notes and Reminiscences of a Staff Officer*. New York, 1903.

Shorter, Clement King, *Napoleon and His Fellow Travellers*. London, 1908.

Silvestre, Jules, *De Waterloo à Ste. Hélène*. Paris, 1904.

Stanhope, Philip Henry, Earl of, *Notes of Conversations with the Duke of Wellington*. London, 1888.

St. Denis, Louis Étienne, *Souvenirs du mameluk Ali*. Paris, 1926.

Talleyrand-Périgord, Charles Maurice de (Prince de Bénévent), *Correspondances inédites*. Paris, 1881-91. 6 Vols.

Thibaudeau, Comte Antoine Claire, *Le Consulat et l'Empire*. Paris, 1834-35. 10 Vols.

Villemain, Abel François, *Souvenirs contemporains*. Paris, 1854. 8 Vols.

Verling, Dr. James Roche, *Diary*, see Forsyth.

Warden, William, *Letters Written on Board the* "Northumberland." Philadelphia, 1817.

Young, Norwood, *Napoleon in Exile: St. Helena*. Philadelphia, 1915. 2 Vols.

# INDEX

## A

Abell, Mrs. Lucia Elizabeth, see Balcombe, Betsy.

*Adamant*, the, 175, 178

Addington, Henry (Viscount Sidmouth), 204 note

Agreement of Allies, August 2, 1815, 87 note, 175, 189

Aix, Isle of, Napoleon at, 52, 54-56, 61-70

Aix la Chapelle, Conference of, 338 note, 371-72, 378, 381, 386-87, 394

Ajaccio, 77, 262 note, 357, 485, 487, 494, 543

Alarm Hill, 153, 571; — House, 149, 293, 535, 536; — Signal, 222, 505

Albani, Francesco, 308

Albe, Baron d', 194, 486

Albine, see Montholon, Mme. de.

Alexander I of Russia, 33, 112, 185, 189, 192, 267, 337 and note, 350, 351 and note, 354-55, 359, 370-71, 371 note, 376-79, 386, 394, 554

Alexander, Capt., 564, 568, 571

Alexander the Great, 306, 452

Aly the Mameluke (Louis Étienne Saint-Denis), sketch, 48 and note, 145-46; his *Souvenirs*, 9-10, 141, 417 note, 420 note; as N.'s amanuensis, 151, 213, 417; reports on N.'s memoirs, 234; marriage, 413; as librarian, 194-95; entrusted with relics for King of Rome, 470; on Mme. de Montholon's intrigues, 398; tries to leave St. H., 388; his garden, 420; gardening with N., 416-17, 419-20; then: 50, 72 note, 102-03, 119, 132, 142, 146, 153, 155-56, 158, 231, 290, 302-03, 312, 333, 381, 402-03, 410, 411 note, 412, 415, 421, 429, 450, 453-55, 457, 459, 465, 471, 473 note, 476, 482, 491, 495, 497-98, 501, 502 note, 504, 507-08, 511, 515-17, 520-21, 524-25, 535, 547, 561

America, see United States.

Amherst, William Pitt, first Lord, 263-65, 316

Amiens, Peace of, 204 note

Andrews, Street & Parker, bankers, 297

Angèly, see Regnault.

*Anse des Anglais* (Isle of Aix), 55

Antioch, Gut of, 73

Antommarchi, Dr. Francesco, sketch, 405-06, 408-09; embraces theory of N.'s diplomatic illness, 408, 456, 514; neglect of duty, 445-46, 451, 457, 459-60; scandalous conduct at St. H., 428; relations with N., 409, 428-29, 445, 451, 453-54, 457-60, 466-67, 473, 484, 488; requested by N. to perform autopsy, 446; rebuked for indiscretions, 474; attempts to resign, 451, 466; performs autopsy, 493, 510-12; his death masks of N., 519-20, 522-23; his rights under N.'s will, 488 and note; his *Last Moments*, 10, 451, 481 note, 504 note, 547; then: 361 note, 416-18, 428-29, 435, 439, 441, 446, 448, 458-59, 462-65, 473, 480-81, 480 note, 484 and note, 487-88, 488 note, 494, 496-97, 499-501, 502 note, 503-07, 515-18, 515 note, 520, 521 note, 526, 535, 537, 546-47, 550, 561

*Appeal to the English Nation* (Santini's), 256, 368

Appiani, Andrea, 486

Apponyi, Count George, 549, 559

Arago, François, 42 note

*Arc de Triomphe de l'Étoile*, 35, 557-58, 574

Archambault brothers, N.'s coachmen, 144, 152, 190, 213; the younger, banished, 220-21, 248; the elder, his marriage, 413; at Deadwood fair, 302; N.'s legacy, 471; then: 320, 324, 374, 417, 428, 431, 442, 450, 462, 502 note, 504, 520, 526, 547, 561

Arenenberg, 376

Arnault, Antoine Vincent, 374 note, 452, 471

Arnna, J., 111, 336 note

Arnott, Dr. Archibald, sketch, 462 note; accepted by N., 460-63; first visit, 462; N.'s illness, 462-67, 477, 489, 494; his snuff box, 486; abounds in his sense, 512; reports N.'s death, 506; then: 401, 446, 448, 467, 472-77, 480-83, 486-89, 491-93, 496-97, 499-508, 510-11, 515, 517-20, 526

Arrighi, Father, 549

Arrighi di Casanova, General Giovanni (Duke of Parma), 549

Artois, Comte d', see Charles X.